Praise for Best Places® Guidebooks

"Best Places *are the best regional restaurant and guide books in America.*"
—THE SEATTLE TIMES

"Best Places *covers must-see portions of the West Coast with style and authority. In-the-know locals offer thorough info on restaurants, lodgings, and the sights.*"
—NATIONAL GEOGRAPHIC TRAVELER

". . . *travelers swear by the recommendations in the* Best Places *guidebooks . . .*"
—SUNSET MAGAZINE

"*For travel collections covering the Northwest, the* Best Places *series takes precedence over all similar guides.*"
—BOOKLIST

"Best Places Northwest *is the bible of discriminating travellers to BC, Washington and Oregon. It promises, and delivers, the best of everything in the region.*"
—THE VANCOUVER SUN

"*Not only the best travel guide in the region, but maybe one of the most definitive guides in the country, which many look forward to with the anticipation usually sparked by a best-selling novel. A browser's delight,* Best Places Northwest *should be chained to dashboards throughout the Northwest.*"
—THE OREGONIAN

"*Still the region's undisputed heavyweight champ of guidebooks.*"
—SEATTLE POST-INTELLIGENCER

"*Trusting the natives is usually good advice, so visitors to Washington, Oregon, and British Columbia would do well to pick up* Best Places Northwest *for an exhaustive review of food and lodging in the region. . . . An indispensable glove-compartment companion.*"
—TRAVEL AND LEISURE

"Best Places Southern California *is just about all the inspiration you need to start planning your next road trip or summer vacation with the kids.*"
—THE FRESNO BEE

"Best Places Alaska *is the one guide to recommend to anyone visiting Alaska for the first or one-hundredth time.*"
—KETCHIKAN DAILY NEWS

"Best Places Northern California *is great fun to read even if you're not going anywhere.*"
—SAN FRANCISCO CHRONICLE

TRUST THE LOCALS

The original insider's guides, written by local experts

COMPLETELY INDEPENDENT

- No advertisers
- No sponsors
- No favors

EVERY PLACE STAR-RATED & RECOMMENDED

★★★★ The very best in the region

★★★ Distinguished; many outstanding features

★★ Excellent; some wonderful qualities

★ A good place

NO STARS Worth knowing about, if nearby

MONEY-BACK GUARANTEE

We're so sure you'll be satisfied, we guarantee it!

HELPFUL ICONS

Watch for these quick-reference symbols throughout the book:

 FAMILY FUN

 GOOD VALUE

 ROMANTIC

 EDITORS' CHOICE

BEST PLACES®

NORTHWEST

The Best Restaurants and Lodgings
in Washington, Oregon, and British Columbia

Edited by
GISELLE SMITH

EDITION

SASQUATCH BOOKS
SEATTLE

Printed in the United States of America
Published by Sasquatch Books
Distributed by Publishers Group West

Fourteenth edition
09 08 07 06 05 04 03   6 5 4 3 2

ISBN: 1-57061-356-7
ISSN: 1041-2484

Series editor: Kate Rogers
Cover and interior design: Nancy Gellos
Maps: GreenEye Design

SPECIAL SALES

Best Places® guidebooks are available at special discounts on bulk purchases for corporate, club, or organization sales promotions, premiums, and gifts. Special editions, including personalized covers, excerpts of existing guides, and corporate imprints, can be created in large quantities for specific needs. For more information, contact your local bookseller or Special Sales, Best Places Guidebooks, 119 South Main Street, Suite 400, Seattle, Washington 98104, 800/775-0817.

SASQUATCH BOOKS
119 South Main Street, Suite 400
Seattle, Washington 98104
206/467-4300
books@sasquatchbooks.com
www.sasquatchbooks.com

CONTENTS

Oregon

British Columbia

Contributors and Acknowledgments

JOEL BELL was working as a record producer when his wife, Julia Kuskin, began to take him on photo shoots as her assistant. He started writing accounts of their adventures on the Olympic Pennisula. A long-time columnist for *Strobe* and *Coffee Project,* he is now working on an original radio drama.

Bellingham resident **LES CAMPBELL** has written for the Vancouver, Washington, *Columbian* newspaper and frequently spends vacations exploring southwest Washington. In the process of researching this book, he left his heart—and much of the original front end of his car—in the region.

A longtime fan of Best Places, **KIM CARLSON** wishes the series would include guides to all of North America. The editor of *Best Places Portland,* she is also a freelance wordsmith and stay-home parent.

NOVELLA CARPENTER, a regular contributor to Seattle's *The Stranger,* is a full-time chow hound and freelance writer who enjoyed commenting on Washington's wine country (Southeast Washington) and cowboy country (North Cascades). She still struggles to get through the terrible Seattle winters despite co-authoring *Don't Jump! The Northwest Winter Blues Survival Guide.*

Author-broadcaster **JACK CHRISTIE** is the outdoors columnist with the *Georgia Straight* newspaper in Vancouver, British Columbia. In addition to his Best Places contributions, he is the author of five regional travel guides, including *Inside Out British Columbia.*

Frequent Best Places contributor **RICHARD FENCSAK** is a food, fitness, and travel writer and bike store owner in Astoria, Oregon. His "Mouth of the Columbia" restaurant column appears weekly in the *Daily Astorian* newspaper, and he's a regular contributor to Portland's *Oregonian* and other Northwest newspapers.

ANDREW HEMPSTEAD, who updated the Southern Interior and the Kootenays chapter for this edition, has written four guidebooks about Canada, including guides to British Columbia.

Eugene writer and editor **BONNIE HENDERSON** knows her Willamette Valley territory well. An editor and travel writer for *Sunset* magazine since 1984, she is also the author of Oregon hiking guidebooks.

JUDY JEWELL will use almost any excuse to drive to the far corners of Oregon. She has written and contributed to several books about the Pacific Northwest, including *Camping! Oregon.*

LESLIE KELLY grew up in the Seattle area, but almost feels settled after living in Spokane for 20 years. She loves being the *Spokesman-Review*'s restaurant critic and wine columnist nearly as much as she enjoys traveling the region and world with her husband and daughter.

Freelancer **SUE KERNAGHAN** has written about the Pacific Northwest for publications including *Alaska Airlines Magazine, Western Living,* and Vancouver's *Georgia Straight.*

Washington native and Northwest explorer **JENA MCPHERSON** is a former staff editor and regular contributor to *Sunset* magazine. She also writes for *Journey,* has contributed to several guidebooks, and is the author of a travel book on the Northwest.

Northwest native **MEGAN MONSON** was delighted at the chance to revisit her favorite places on the planet as she covered Southern Oregon and the Oregon Cascades. An Oregon newpaper editor for a dozen years, she is now a full-time freelance writer and editor.

SHANNON O'LEARY didn't have to stray far to write the Seattle chapter, and that's just the way she likes it. The lifelong Northwest resident has been writing about the Puget Sound area for more than a dozen years. She is the editor of *Washington Law & Politics* magazine and edited *Best Places Seattle.*

KASEY WILSON is a freelance food and travel writer, editor of *Best Places Vancouver,* and author of several cookbooks. A contributor to CNN, PBS, and NBC, she also co-hosts a weekly radio show called "The Best of Food and Wine" on Vancouver's CFUN 1410 AM.

Special thanks are owed to series editor Kate Rogers, project editor Laura Gronewold, copy editor Julie Van Pelt, and proofreader Amy Smith Bell.

Editor **GISELLE SMITH** is a Northwest native and lifetime Seattleite who spends her vacations exploring the roads, mountains, and waterways of this region. She is a past editor of *Best Places Seattle, Seattle Magazine,* and *Alaska Airlines Magazine,* and a contributor to several print and online publications.

About Best Places® Guidebooks

People trust us. Best Places® guidebooks, which have been published continuously since 1975, represent one of the most respected regional travel series in the country. Each guide is written completely independently: no advertisers, no sponsors, no favors. Our reviewers know their territory, work incognito, and seek out the very best a city or region has to offer. Because we accept no free meals, accommodations, or other complimentary services, we are able to provide tough, candid reports about places that have rested too long on their laurels, and to delight in new places that deserve recognition. We describe the true strengths, foibles, and unique characteristics of each establishment listed.

Best Places Northwest is written by and for locals, and is therefore coveted by travelers. It's written for people who live here and who enjoy exploring the region's bounty and its out-of-the-way places of high character and individualism. It is these very characteristics that make *Best Places Northwest* ideal for tourists, too. The best places in and around the region are the ones that denizens favor: independently owned establishments of good value, touched with local history, run by lively individuals, and graced with natural beauty. With this fourteenth edition of *Best Places Northwest*, travelers will find the information they need: where to go and when, what to order, which rooms to request (and which to avoid), where the best music, art, nightlife, shopping, and other attractions are, and how to find the region's hidden secrets.

We're so sure you'll be satisfied with our guide, we guarantee it.

NOTE: *The reviews in this edition are based on information available at press time and are subject to change. Readers are advised that places listed may have closed or changed management, and, thus, may no longer be recommended by this series. The editors welcome information conveyed by users of this book. A report form is provided at the end of the book, and feedback is also welcome via email: bestplaces@ SasquatchBooks.com.*

How to Use This Book

This book is divided into twenty major regions, encompassing Washington, Oregon, and British Columbia. All evaluations are based on numerous reports from local and traveling inspectors. Best Places reporters do not identify themselves when they review an establishment, and they accept no free meals, accommodations, or any other services. Final judgments are made by the editors. **EVERY PLACE FEATURED IN THIS BOOK IS RECOMMENDED.**

STAR RATINGS Restaurants and lodgings are rated on a scale of zero to four stars (with half stars in between), based on uniqueness, loyalty of local clientele, performance measured against the establishment's goals, excellence of cooking, cleanliness, value, and professionalism of service. Reviews are listed alphabetically, and every place is recommended.

★★★★	The very best in the region
★★★	Distinguished; many outstanding features
★★	Excellent; some wonderful qualities
★	A good place
NO STARS	Worth knowing about, if nearby
UNRATED	New or undergoing major changes

(For more on how we rate places, see the Best Places Star Ratings box below.)

PRICE RANGE Prices for restaurants are based primarily on dinner for two, including dessert, tax, and tip (no alcohol). Prices for lodgings are based on peak season rates for one night's lodging for two people (i.e., double occupancy). Peak season is typically Memorial Day to Labor Day; off-season rates vary but can sometimes be significantly less. Call ahead to verify, as all prices are subject to change.

$$$$	Very expensive (more than $100 for dinner for two; more than $200 for one night's lodging for two)
$$$	Expensive (between $65 and $100 for dinner for two; between $120 and $200 for one night's lodging for two)
$$	Moderate (between $35 and $65 for dinner for two; between $80 and $120 for one night's lodging for two)
$	Inexpensive (less than $35 for dinner for two; less than $80 for one night's lodging for two)

RESERVATIONS (for Restaurants only)
We used one of the following terms for our reservations policy: reservations required, reservations recommended, reservations not accepted, reservations not necessary.

ACCESS AND INFORMATION At the beginning of each chapter, you'll find general guidelines about how to get to a particular region and what types of transportation are available, as well as basic sources for any additional tourist information you might need. Also check individual town listings for specifics about visiting those places.

BEST PLACES® STAR RATINGS

Any travel guide that rates establishments is inherently subjective—and Best Places is no exception. We rely on our professional experience, yes, but also on a gut feeling. And, occasionally, we even give in to a soft spot for a favorite neighborhood hangout. Our star-rating system is not simply a AAA-checklist; it's judgmental, critical, sometimes fickle, and highly personal. And unlike most other travel guides, we pay our own way and accept no freebies: no free meals or accommodations, no advertisers, no sponsors, no favors.

For each new edition, we send local food and travel experts out to review restaurants and lodgings anonymously, and then to rate them on a scale of zero to four. That doesn't mean a one-star establishment isn't worth dining or sleeping at—far from it. When we say that *all* the places listed in our books are recommended, we mean it. That one-star pizza joint may be just the ticket for the end of a whirlwind day of shopping with the kids. But if you're planning something more special, the star ratings can help you choose an eatery or hotel that will wow your new clients or be a stunning, romantic place to celebrate an anniversary or impress a first date.

We award four-star ratings sparingly, reserving them for what we consider truly the best. And once an establishment has earned our highest rating, everyone's expectations seem to rise. Readers often write us letters specifically to point out the faults in four-star establishments. With changes in chefs, management, styles, and trends, it's always easier to get knocked off the pedestal than to ascend it. Three-star establishments, on the other hand, seem to generate healthy praise. They exhibit outstanding qualities, and we get lots of love letters about them. The difference between two and three stars can sometimes be a very fine line. Two-star establishments are doing a good, solid job and gaining attention, while one-star places are often dependable spots that have been around forever.

The restaurants and lodgings described in *Best Places Northwest* have earned their stars from hard work and good service (and good food). They're proud to be included in this book—look for our Best Places sticker in their windows. And we're proud to honor them in this, the fourteenth edition of *Best Places Northwest*.

THREE-DAY TOURS In every chapter, we've included a quick-reference, three-day itinerary designed for travelers with a short amount of time. Perfect for weekend getaways, these tours outline the highlights of a region or town; each of the establishments or attractions that appear in boldface within the tour are discussed in greater detail elsewhere in the chapter.

ADDRESSES AND PHONE NUMBERS Every attempt has been made to provide accurate information on an establishment's location and phone number, but it's always a good idea to call ahead and confirm. If an establishment has two area locations, we list both at the top of the review. If there are three or more locations, we list only the main address and indicate "other branches."

CHECKS AND CREDIT CARDS Many establishments that accept checks also require a major credit card for identification. Note that some places accept only local checks. Credit cards are abbreviated in this book as follows: American Express (AE); Carte Blanche (CB); Diners Club (DC); Discover (DIS); Japanese credit card (JCB); MasterCard (MC); Visa (V).

EMAIL AND WEB SITE ADDRESSES Email and web site addresses for establishments have been included where available. Please note that the web is a fluid and evolving medium, and that web pages are often "under construction" or, as with all time-sensitive information, may no longer be valid.

MAPS AND DIRECTIONS Each chapter in the book begins with a regional map that shows the general area being covered. Throughout the book, basic directions are provided with each entry. Whenever possible, call ahead to confirm hours and location.

HELPFUL ICONS Watch for these quick-reference symbols throughout the book:

FAMILY FUN Family-oriented places that are great for kids—fun, easy, not too expensive, and accustomed to dealing with young ones.

GOOD VALUE While not necessarily cheap, these places offer you the best value for your dollars—a good deal within the context of the region.

ROMANTIC These spots offer candlelight, atmosphere, intimacy, or other romantic qualities—kisses and proposals are encouraged!

EDITORS' CHOICE These are places that are unique and special to the Northwest and beyond, such as a restaurant owned by a beloved local chef or a tourist attraction recognized around the globe.

    Appears after listings for establishments that have wheelchair-accessible facilities.

INDEXES All restaurants, lodgings, town names, and major tourist attractions are listed alphabetically in the back of the book.

MONEY-BACK GUARANTEE Please see "We Stand by Our Reviews" at the end of this book.

READER REPORTS At the end of the book is a report form. We receive hundreds of reports from readers suggesting new places or agreeing or disagreeing with our assessments. They greatly help in our evaluations, and we encourage you to respond.

PORTLAND
AND ENVIRONS

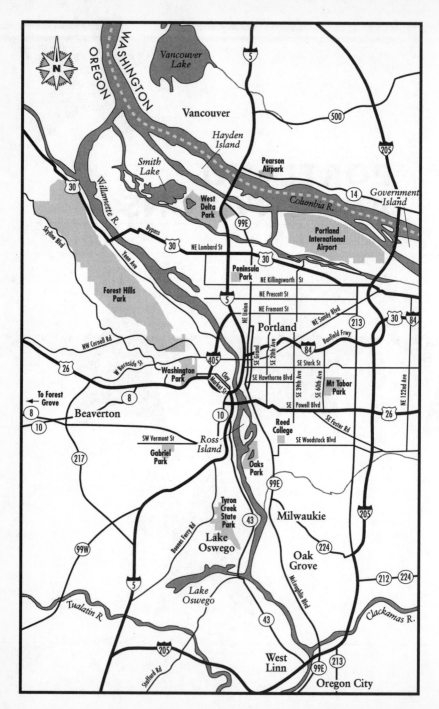

PORTLAND AND ENVIRONS

Although Portland has had a stellar reputation among American cities, it has recently come into its own as a destination. In 2002 *Gourmet* magazine called it "the next Napa." "The city itself," said editor Ruth Reichl, "[is] a marvel."

Why the sudden buzz? The local bounty is huge, and foodies in the rest of the country are catching on to what Portlanders have always known. Napa or not, Portland is a place to take seriously—but not just for its food and wine.

We think the best thing Portland has going for it is its location: it is a city with a river running through it; a pair of dramatic, volcanic mountains watching over it; and the lush and beautiful Willamette Valley spreading away from it to the south.

Portland is a nice size—not so big that it's an expedition to get downtown from the suburban or residential areas (each of which has its own personality); not so small that there's nothing going on once you get there. Downtown bustles with commerce and culture, and is an easy place to spend a few days—or a few years.

Then there are the people, a mix of lifelong Oregonians with strong opinions about such issues as salmon recovery, educational reform, and radical-minded newcomers; and newcomers, with their own strong opinions about salmon and schools—and about conservative old-timers. But what's heartening here is the way everyone comes together for classic events such as the Portland Rose Festival and the Mount Hood Festival of Jazz; nobody's a newcomer for long. Portlanders know how to throw a party when the occasion calls for one (there's a killer blues festival every Fourth of July), and they take seriously their civic responsibilities, as evidenced by the urban planning that's become a model for the country, a burgeoning arts scene, and an ever-expanding library and parks system.

Of course, the City of Roses has detractors, and many of them resent the rain—buckets of it every year. True Oregonians don't mind, though; they just get out in the rain and play as hard as ever—or they curl up indoors with a book. Still, if you want good weather, come in late summer and early fall. The best-kept secret here is the Indian summer; September and October are usually glorious, but a few showers are needed to keep the place green all year.

ACCESS AND INFORMATION

PORTLAND INTERNATIONAL AIRPORT, or PDX (7000 NE Airport Wy; 503/460-4234; www.portlandairportpdx.com), is served by most major airlines, with excellent connections from points around the Pacific Northwest and beyond. Allow plenty of time, especially during rush hours, to get from airport to town—30 minutes at least—and the same on your return. All major **CAR RENTAL** companies operate from the airport. Taxis and shuttles are readily available; expect to pay at least $25 for the trip downtown. The most economical ride ($1.55) is via the shiny new airport **METROPOLITAN AREA EXPRESS (MAX)** train. Catch MAX just outside baggage claim; the ride to Pioneer Courthouse Square takes 38 minutes. Another mode of transportation is the **GRAYLINE OF PORTLAND AIRPORT EXPRESS** (503/285-9845); buses leave every 45 minutes.

Most drivers reach Portland via either **INTERSTATE 5,** which runs north-south, or **INTERSTATE 84** (east-west). **US HIGHWAY 26** goes to Beaverton; **INTERSTATE**

205 loops off Interstate 5 and passes near Lake Oswego, West Linn, Oregon City, and Milwaukie, among other towns. Rush hours in Portland can mean standstill traffic, but if you arrive midday (after 9am, but before 3pm) or after 7pm, you should have clear sailing into town.

AMTRAK (503/273-4866 locally or 800/USA-RAIL; www.amtrak.com) operates out of lovely Union Station (800 NW 6th Ave) just north of downtown. This romantic structure memorializes the bygone era of the great railways. Trains come and go from points north, east, and south daily. The nearby GREYHOUND station (550 NW 6th Ave; 503/243-2357 or 800/231-2222) has a complete daily schedule of buses. Both stations are within walking distance (about 12 blocks) of downtown.

Portland

Portland has much to offer, and its increasing number of citizens make the most of it. The nationally noted light-rail service goes east to Gresham, west to Beaverton, and now to the airport. A cultural district downtown is home to a jewel of a performing arts center, a first-class art museum, and a historical center, all located along a greenbelt called the SOUTH PARK BLOCKS, which run from PORTLAND STATE UNIVERSITY north to Salmon Street. In the lively downtown core, lunchtime concerts entertain summer weekday crowds at PIONEER COURTHOUSE SQUARE, at SW Broadway and SW Yamhill Streets, and a shopping complex stars Saks Fifth Avenue. Also in town are a major convention center, pleasant strolling neighborhoods, an attractively remodeled minor-league ballpark, and stunning digs for one of the city's favorite all-age hangouts: the OREGON MUSEUM OF SCIENCE AND INDUSTRY (see Major Attractions, below).

ACCESS AND INFORMATION

TRI-MET (503/238-7433; www.trimet.org) operates the city bus system and the sleek MAX light-rail trains; tickets for the two are interchangeable. Almost all bus lines run through the PORTLAND TRANSIT MALL (SW 5th and 6th Aves); MAX lines also pass through downtown. You can ride free downtown in "Fareless Square," which also extends across the river to the Convention Center; from downtown to most outlying neighborhoods, you'll need a two-zone ticket ($1.25), which you can purchase on the bus (exact change only) or at MAX stops. Another popular transportation option that travels from the South Park Blocks to NW 23rd Avenue through the Pearl District is the new PORTLAND STREETCAR (www.portlandstreet car.org), which costs the same as Tri-Met.

MAJOR ATTRACTIONS

Outfit yourself with information at the new visitor center in PIONEER COURT-HOUSE SQUARE at SW Broadway and SW Yamhill Streets (503/275-8355; www.travelportland.com). Here you can make hotel or dinner reservations, buy tickets to events, and talk to someone who's eager to give you the lay of the city.

OMSI, the OREGON MUSEUM OF SCIENCE AND INDUSTRY (1945 SE Water Ave; 503/797-4000), is an engaging place to take the whole family. There's a submarine moored in the Willamette to board, an IMAX theater, fascinating exhibits, even a toddler room. The OREGON HISTORY CENTER (1200 SW Park Ave; 503/222-1741) pays tribute to our ancestors—Native Americans, white settlers, sea-

PORTLAND THREE-DAY TOUR

DAY ONE: Spend this first day exploring downtown Portland. King salmon hash at the **HEATHMAN RESTAURANT AND BAR** is a tasteful—and tasty—way to begin your day, or if coffee and a pastry are all you need, head around the block to the **FLYING ELEPHANT DELI** (812 SW Park St; 503/546-3166). After breakfast, stretch your legs along the elm-lined **SOUTH PARK BLOCKS.** Art lovers then go to the **PORTLAND ART MUSEUM,** history buffs to the **OREGON HISTORY CENTER,** and shoppers to **PIONEER PLACE.** For lunch, stop for a sandwich at **RED STAR TAVERN & ROAST HOUSE.** In the afternoon, catch an art film at the **KOIN CINEMAS** (SW 3rd Ave and SW Clay St; 503/225-5555, ext. 4608 for recorded film schedules) or explore **OLD TOWN,** but save time for **POWELL'S CITY OF BOOKS.** Make a dinner reservation at either **HIGGINS**—where local ingredients receive reverential treatment—or, if you're in the mood for top-drawer Mexican cuisine, **CAFE AZUL.** Check into the elegant **HEATHMAN HOTEL,** or the **5TH AVENUE SUITES.**

DAY TWO: Excellent breakfasts are the norm at **ZELL'S: AN AMERICAN CAFE,** or for lighter fare have a cuppa joe and pastry at the **PEARL BAKERY** (102 NW 9th Ave; 503/827-0910). After breakfast, explore some of the parks in the city's pastoral West Hills: the views are dramatic from the **WASHINGTON PARK INTERNATIONAL ROSE TEST GARDEN** or the **JAPANESE GARDEN.** For a bit more of a workout, hike through **HOYT ARBORETUM** on the Wildwood Trail (start near the **OREGON ZOO**—itself an intriguing place to walk). Later, browse the boutiques and shops along NW 23rd and 21st Avenues. Outstanding Thai food at lunchtime can be had at **TYPHOON!** or make your way down NW 23rd Avenue for a salad and voluptuous dessert at **PAPA HAYDN.** Spend the afternoon restraining yourself in **THE PEARL DISTRICT'S** art galleries and shops. Reserve ahead for dinner at **PALEY'S PLACE** or **WILDWOOD.**

DAY THREE: Jump in the car; this is a day to see the outlying parts of the city. A late breakfast at the **ORIGINAL PANCAKE HOUSE** is popular with everybody and will keep you going through the afternoon (expect to wait for a table, though service is snappy once you're seated). Then head to historic Oregon City, where you can catch the multimedia presentation at the **END OF THE OREGON TRAIL INTERPRETIVE CENTER.** For dinner it's back to Portland to board a river cruise on the **PORTLAND SPIRIT** from Tom McCall Waterfront Park. Late night, check out the eclectic music offerings at **BERBATI'S PAN** or the **ALADDIN THEATRE.**

farers, and others. Its gift shop is first-rate. Not exactly a museum, but having an impressive (living) collection nonetheless, is the **OREGON ZOO** (4001 SW Canyon Rd; 503/226-1561), where myriad exhibits include many species common to the Pacific Northwest; ride MAX for an easy trip from downtown. CM2, aka the new **CHILDREN'S MUSEUM,** is located across the parking lot (503/223-6500).

During the month of June, the city's roses—and its **ROSE FESTIVAL**—are in full bloom. Highlights of this monthlong extravaganza include three parades, the largest of which is the Grand Floral Parade; an air show; a carnival in Tom McCall Waterfront Park; the Festival of Flowers, for which Pioneer Courthouse Square is transformed with some 25,000 potted plants; and, of course, a world-class rose show.

The Willamette River flows right through the middle of town, and Portlanders flock to one of their city's two major waterways—the other, of course, being the mighty Columbia River just to the north. **TOM MCCALL WATERFRONT PARK,** on the west side of the Willamette, is the perfect place for a run or stroll. The **PORTLAND SPIRIT** riverboat (503/226-2517) docks here. The new Eastbank Esplanade, a floating walkway that extends from the Steel Bridge to the Hawthorne Bridge on the east side of the river, makes it possible to enjoy a three-mile loop along both banks.

Just north of downtown, on a city block surrounded by parking lots and highrises, is the **CLASSICAL CHINESE GARDEN, THE GARDEN OF THE AWAKENING ORCHID** (corner of NW Everett St and NW Third Ave; 503/228-8131). Completed in 2000, this garden has quickly become a favorite stop for visitors who appreciate its authenticity (it was designed and built by garden experts from Portland's sister city, Suzhou). Be sure to stop for tea in the tea house.

The old warehouse district just west of the Chinese garden (between NW 9th and NW 15th Aves, and NW Burnside and NW Lovejoy Sts) known as the **PEARL DISTRICT** is the gentrified home of art galleries, restaurants, and shops—as well as **POWELL'S CITY OF BOOKS,** the country's largest bookstore (see "City of Books" in this chapter).

GALLERIES AND MUSEUMS

Gallery walks once a month (on "First Thursdays") encourage visitors to expose themselves to art; galleries, clustered in the Pearl District or downtown, showcase both local and national work. The **PORTLAND ART MUSEUM** (1219 SW Park Ave; 503/226-2811; www.portlandartmuseum.org) is the big name for exhibits of international acclaim; PAM has hosted many "blockbuster" shows, some of which require no small amount of political effort to bring to Portland—such as an exhibit on the tombs of China; work by Dale Chihuly; and Empire of the Sultans, Ottoman art from the Khalili Collection. Check out the smaller **CONTEMPORARY CRAFTS GALLERY** (3934 SW Corbett Ave; 503/223-2654), a good place to purchase a unique art gift, perhaps chess sets by various artists, contemporary basketry, quilts, and affordable ceramics, as well as more costly sculpture.

The city is popping with public art, too; pick up the "Public Art: Walking Tour" booklet, free at the **REGIONAL ARTS AND CULTURE COUNCIL** (620 SW Main St, Ste 420; 503/823-5111) to hunt down these treasures. Pioneer Courthouse Square, at SW Broadway and SW Yamhill Streets, is a good place to begin, and the stunningly renovated **CENTRAL LIBRARY** (801 SW 10th Ave; 503/988-5123) is a great place to end.

PARKS AND GARDENS

Besides the sprawling and primitive **FOREST PARK** (see Sports and Recreation, below), the city has nearly 150 other parks, and **WASHINGTON PARK** (West Hills; 503/823-3636) is home to several of them: The **HOYT ARBORETUM** (503/228-8733), close to the Oregon Zoo (see Major Attractions, above), has an impressive collection of native and exotic flora and well-kept trails. More formal grounds are the **INTERNATIONAL ROSE TEST GARDEN** (503/823-3636), the **JAPANESE GARDEN** (503/223-1321), and, across town, the **CRYSTAL SPRINGS RHODO-DENDRON GARDEN** (503/823-3640). Also in Washington Park is the largest memorial of its kind in the nation, the **VIETNAM VETERANS' LIVING MEMORIAL,** an inspiring outdoor cathedral commemorating the Oregon victims of that conflict. It's possible for a person to walk from one of these parks to another without really realizing it, so continuous is their reach of trails through Portland's West Hills. Although parts of Washington Park have a wild, overgrown feeling, much of it is well tended. Forest Park, on the other hand, is not a manicured park at all, but is rather a "wilderness" for the city.

SHOPPING

A few uniquely Portland shops not to miss: **POWELL'S CITY OF BOOKS** (1005 W Burnside St; 503/228-4651), which is legendary for its number of volumes, both new and used; **TWIST** (30 NW 23rd Pl; 503/224-0334), where jewelry and folk art rise to new heights of function and form; **MADE IN OREGON** (10 NW 1st Ave; 503/273-8354; and branches), where such names as Jantzen and Pendleton get top billing; and **IN GOOD TASTE** (231 NW 11th Ave; 503/248-2015), one of the city's many stores for cooks, complete with its own class schedule and top-drawer lunch counter.

Crafts—and a carnival atmosphere—can be found weekends at **SATURDAY MARKET** under the Burnside Bridge (closed Jan–Feb). Upscale specialty shops and eateries are found downtown, many in the area around Pioneer Courthouse Square, including the expansive **PIONEER PLACE** (between SW Morrison and Yamhill Sts, and SW 3rd and 5th Aves). Across the river near the Convention Center is **LLOYD CENTER MALL** (between NE Halsey and Multnomah Sts, and NE 9th and 15th Aves), with its beloved ice-skating rink. Posh and happy **NW 23RD AVENUE,** the arty **PEARL DISTRICT** (north of Burnside St between 9th and 15th Aves), and countercultural **SE HAWTHORNE BOULEVARD** (between 20th and 45th Aves) are must-visits for shoppers. You may also want to check out **SELLWOOD,** southeast of downtown, across the Sellwood Bridge; it's an entire neighborhood of antique stores.

PERFORMING ARTS

Portlanders pack the **ARLENE SCHNITZER CONCERT HALL** (1000 SW Broadway) 52 weeks a year for concerts and lectures; contact the box office in the **PORTLAND CENTER FOR THE PERFORMING ARTS** (PCPA; 1111 SW Broadway; 503/796-9293) for tickets. One show that plays regularly at "the Schnitz" is the **OREGON SYMPHONY ORCHESTRA** (503/228-1353; www.orsymphony.org), under conductor James DePreist. Classical music fans should also know about **CHAMBER**

MUSIC NORTHWEST (522 SW 5th Ave, Ste 725; 503/294-6400; www.cmnw.org), which presents a summer festival spanning four centuries of music, and events throughout the season in various venues.

The PCPA's resident theater company, PORTLAND CENTER STAGE (1111 SW Broadway; 503/274-6588; www.pcs.org), offers excellent production values, whatever the play. You can always be assured of work by Shakespeare with productions by TYGRES HEART (503/288-8400; www.tygresheart.org), housed in the same facility. Plays by ARTISTS REPERTORY THEATRE, staged at the Reiersgaard Theatre (1516 SW Alder St; 503/241-1278; www.art.org), often garner lavish critical praise.

The OREGON BALLET THEATER (Keller Auditorium, 222 SW Clay St; 503/222-5538; www.obt.org) enlists youth and daring to serve the needs of Portland's ballet fans. Also watch for performances presented by WHITE BIRD, an organization that exists solely to promote dance (at various venues; call 503/245-1600 for information). And finally, contemporary art fans are energetically served by the performances and exhibitions of PICA (Portland Institute for Contemporary Art; www.pica.org; 503/242-1519).

NIGHTLIFE

Check local newspapers' calendar listings for what's happening in the popular music world (*Willamette Week* is out each Wednesday; the *Oregonian*'s Friday A&E section is also a good source). Rock fans get their licks at BERBATI'S PAN (10 SW 3rd Ave; 503/248-4579) or LALUNA (215 SE 9th Ave; 503/241-5862), while folkies hang at the ALADDIN THEATRE (3017 SE Milwaukie Ave; 503/233-1994). If you feel like dancing, head to the CRYSTAL BALLROOM (1332 W Burnside St; 503/225-5555, ext 8811), where the music—anything from reggae to ballroom—starts at 9pm. Check out the BRAZEN BEAN (2075 NW Glisan St; 503/294-0636), where the posh ambience lends itself to something icy cold served up in an elegant glass; or JAKE'S FAMOUS CRAWFISH (401 SW 12th Ave; 503/226-1419), where people have been bellying up to the bar for more than a century.

Some cities overflow with sports bars, but Portlanders love brewpubs. One longtime favorite is the BRIDGEPORT BREW PUB (1313 NW Marshall; 503/241-3612); you can eat renowned pizza and hoist a classic Portland microbrew in a casual, noisy atmosphere.

SPORTS AND RECREATION

The town's big-league action can be found at the ROSE GARDEN ARENA (1 Center Ct), a huge dome easily visible from Interstate 5, home of the NBA's PORTLAND TRAIL BLAZERS (Ticketmaster: 503/224-4400). The Blazers may have a reputation as the NBA's bad boys, but they often make the playoffs (although they haven't won the championship since 1977). The PORTLAND WINTER HAWKS (Ticketmaster: 503/224-4400), of the Western Hockey League, play at Memorial Coliseum (1401 N Wheeler Ave) or Rose Garden Arena, and hit the ice 36 times a season at home. Baseball fans are still waiting for the major league, but content themselves with the PORTLAND BEAVERS—who play to loyal crowds at refurbished PGE PARK (SW 20th Ave and SW Morrison St). The PORTLAND TIMBERS soccer team also plays the park. (For PGE Park tickets, call 503/553-5555.)

Individual sports thrive in the region: runners, hikers, and mountain bikers have access to more than 50 miles of trails in primitive 5,000-acre **FOREST PARK** (503/823-7529), easily accessed at points throughout the West Hills. A good map of Forest Park is a must; the Audubon Society of Portland's **NATURE STORE** (5151 NW Cornell Rd; 503/292-9453) is a great resource for maps and information. Rowers are guaranteed miles of flat water on the Willamette; and cyclists use hundreds of miles of off- and on-street paved bike paths in the greater Portland area, including the new Eastbank Esplanade along the Willamette River.

RESTAURANTS

Al-Amir / ★★

223 SW STARK ST, PORTLAND; 503/274-0010 In Portland's most elaborate and satisfying Lebanese restaurant, the smoky, intense baba ghanouj and the creamy hummus are outstanding. The kitchen also does a particularly savory job on meats. The shish kebab, lamb vibrant with spices and juices, highlights a menu that stretches to *kharouf muammar,* a huge pile of moist, faintly sweet lamb chunks, and *dujaj musahab,* a charcoal-grilled chicken breast in lemon and olive oil. Don't depart without trying the grape leaves. A little Lebanese beer makes the light through the Bishop's House's stained-glass windows shine even more brightly. *$$; AE, MC, V; no checks; lunch Mon–Fri, dinner every day; full bar; reservations recommended; between NW 3rd and 4th Aves.* &

Alexis / ★★

215 W BURNSIDE ST, PORTLAND; 503/224-8577 This boisterous institution of a Greek restaurant opened more than two decades ago and is still owned and operated by the same family. Here every diner feels like a cousin: the welcome is warmer than the flaming *saganaki* (Greek cheese ignited with ouzo). On their journey toward substantial, fork-tender lamb dishes and other entrees, diners are slowed by plump grape-leaf packets, terrific calamari (one of the restaurant's most popular dishes), and the little pillows of phyllo and feta known as *tiropetes.* Be entertained by the appetizers, but save room for moussaka and lamb souvlaki. The food could even distract you from the belly dancers on weekends. *$$; AE, DC, MC, V; no checks; lunch Mon–Fri, dinner Mon–Sat; full bar; reservations necessary for groups of 10 or more; between NW 2nd and 3rd Aves.* &

Bluehour / ★★★

250 NW 13TH AVE, PORTLAND; 503/226-3394 Don't leave Portland without a dinner at Bluehour, and if it's summer, make a reservation for late in the day, so the light from the street illuminates the tables and the shimmery curtainlike walls—you'll appreciate the poetic name all the more. This is an astonishing space, with high ceilings, huge windows, and dramatic furnishings, a place to see as well as a place in which to be seen. Food is sometimes upstaged by the ambiance, but you will probably not be disappointed when it's time to eat. Chef Kenny Giambalvo's menu is an intriguing swath of Mediterranean classics with unusual and lavish flourishes—risotto, insalata caprese, seared tuna served with fresh lemon taglioni—and the restaurant is experimenting with small plates that are good for sharing. Don't miss drinks or one of the toothsome desserts. Expect service to be top-notch; Bruce Carey, one of the troica who put Portland on the culinary map in the '90s with Zefiro, is the man behind the magic here. Even a trip to the restroom is unusual—each is unique. Valet parking is on the house. *$$$–$$$$; AE, DC, MC, V; no checks; dinner every day; full bar; reservations recommended; bluehour@teleport.com; corner of NW Everett St.*

Bread and Ink Cafe / ★★

3610 SE HAWTHORNE BLVD, PORTLAND; 503/239-4756 If a restaurant could survive just on the strength of its blintzes, the beloved Bread and Ink would do it. But lots of other dishes in this homey, neighborhood bistro in the heart of the funky Hawthorne district are striking: sizable sandwiches, impressive baked desserts including a legendary cassata, and a serious hamburger, with homemade condiments that do it justice. With intriguing framed line drawings on the walls, crayons on the table, and huge windows onto Hawthorne, the place has become a landmark for good reason. But the blintzes, delicately crisped squares of dough enfolding cheese, are hallowed—especially with Bread and Ink's raspberry jam. Even after changes in the kitchen and ownership, the restaurant has a powerful identity, especially at breakfast and lunch. Dinners such as an arugula salad with grilled figs and warm goat cheese, dressed with a black currant vinaigrette and accompanied by fennel black pepper flat bread, also have fans. *$$; AE, MC, V; checks OK; breakfast, lunch, dinner Mon–Sat, brunch and dinner Sun; beer and wine; reservations recommended; at SE 36th Ave.* &

Cafe Azul / ★★★

112 NW 9TH AVE, PORTLAND; 503/525-4422 First, erase the image of sombreros and beans you conjure when someone says, "Mexican restaurant." This place serves Mexican cuisine, sure, but the comparisons stop there. The warm, high-ceilinged room draws a stream of diners eager for thick, rich moles; prawns rubbed with achiote and garlic paste; and corn-husk-wrapped tamales filled with wild mushrooms, or chicken and plantain. Choose from a range of different, carefully described tequilas, and accompany it with a handmade corn tortilla taco filled with Yucatán-style pork. Flavors are vivid and unexpected, with punchy chiles and unusual salsas. The creativity spreads buoyantly into dessert, with options such as a red banana ice cream sundae with chocolate crust, caramel, and candied peanuts. This is more than you're accustomed to spending for Mexican food, but you've probably never had Mexican food like this. If you can't get a reservation, consider the diminutive bar, where the company is usually good. *$$$; DIS, MC, V; checks OK; dinner Tues–Sat; full bar; reservations recommended; between NW Couch and Davis Sts.* &

Cafe des Amis / ★★★

1987 NW KEARNEY ST, PORTLAND; 503/295-6487 For years, people have come to Dennis Baker's polished little restaurant knowing what they'll order before they sit down. Specialties at this cozy, intimate cafe tucked onto a Northwest Portland residential street are legendary: Dungeness crab cakes; fillet of beef in port garlic sauce; salmon in a sorrel sauce; duck in blackberry sauce. Diners are more likely to have a hunger for a favorite than to wonder what's new. They're also drawn by cobblers and fruit tarts that look like they've just been glazed in a Boulevard St. Germain patisserie. Specials might include a melting lamb shank. *$$–$$$; AE, MC, V; checks OK; dinner Mon–Sat; full bar; reservations recommended; at NW 20th Ave.* &

Caffe Mingo / ★★

807 NW 21ST AVE, PORTLAND; 503/226-4646 You might pass this tiny restaurant row hot spot, see the queue out the door, and wonder, "Is it worth the fuss?" After all, plenty of places to eat are within a five-minute walk. But stick around to discover Mingo's charm. Diners eagerly wait—or head down the street for a drink; the cheerful Mingo staff will call when the table is ready—for the handmade ravioli (it changes daily) or the *penne al sugo di carne,* beef braised in chianti and espresso, tossed with perfectly cooked tubes of pasta. The place has endured some minor changes over the years but remains a solid, inviting Italian cafe, with knowledgeable servers and a homey feeling. A seat in back gets you a close-up view of the kitchen preparing your dinner. *$$; AE, MC, V; local checks only; dinner every day; beer and wine; reservations recommended for 6 or more; between NW Johnson and Kearney Sts.* &

Caprial's Bistro / ★★★

7015 SE MILWAUKIE AVE, PORTLAND; 503/236-6457 People love Caprial the TV chef, and many also love Caprial's Bistro. The original storefront is a large, warm, colorful space, with big soft chairs and walls as flashy as the cuisine, and now there's a new place for the cooking school around the corner. A night's offerings might include wok-steamed fish with a persimmon compound butter, or a pan-seared duck breast with a pomegranate glaze. There's still the Hot as Hell Chicken at lunch (grilled chicken with chile sauce over pungent peanut-sauced pasta) and creative sandwiches and salads. Mark Dowers has brought additional skills to the kitchen, and Melissa Carey is an impressive dessert chef; try the raspberry/blackberry linzertorte with caramel sauce. The menus shift but never stray far from the Northwest. *$$–$$$; MC, V; checks OK; lunch, dinner Tues–Sat; beer and wine; reservations recommended; www.caprial.com; in Westmoreland.* &

Castagna / ★★★

1752 SE HAWTHORNE BLVD, PORTLAND; 503/231-7373 Amidst the Hawthorne district's swirl of tie-dye and crystals, Castagna stands apart—like a little black dress and pearls. Owners Monique Siu and Kevin Gibson have combined an artful, sparsely decorated space with a straightforward, deftly executed menu. The offerings change frequently, but you're likely always to find subtle, clean flavors, highlighting what the current season and local purveyors have to offer, and drawing from classic French and Italian dishes. Prime Angus NY steak with a heap of shoestring potatoes is an enduring favorite. Castagna maintains the drama of the hottest new places but less of the overpowering noise level—unless you go next door to the bustling Cafe Castagna. The cafe features a less pricey, simpler menu—a locally famous Caesar for instance, along with roast chicken, and a standout burger. *$$$ (restaurant), $$ (cafe); AE, DIS, MC, V; no checks; dinner Tues–Sat; full bar; reservations recommended (restaurant); at SE 17th Ave.* &

AN EMPIRE BUILT ON BEER

Most cities in the world have McDonald's; for that matter, Portland has McDonald's. But Portland also has **MCMENAMIN'S,** and when it comes to choosing between a Big Mac, fries, and a Coke at the Golden Arches or choosing a Communication Breakdown Burger, fries, and a glass of Terminator Ale at the **HILLSDALE BREWERY AND PUB** (1505 SW Sunset Blvd; 503/246-3938), there's no contest. McMenamin pubs—and there are dozens in the greater Portland area—are old-fashioned, art-filled hangouts, where you meet friends and linger long into the evening to the strains of the Grateful Dead, for instance, or grab a quick dinner with the family.

Brothers Brian and Mike McMenamin have been making handmade ales for a couple of decades now, but you won't find their brews in your grocer's cooler; they are sold only in the McMenamin pubs—and McMenamin hotels, movie theaters, and dance halls. The McMenamins' diverse establishments are tied together by a comfortable, quirky, slightly mystic decorating scheme, including paintings created by artists who are members of the McMenamin's staff.

One of the special things these guys do, besides provide appealing, mostly non-smoking spots for Portlanders to get out of the rain, is refurbish old, dilapidated buildings. Several sites are on the National Register of Historic Places and have interesting histories. **EDGEFIELD** (2126 SW Halsey St, Troutdale; 503/669-8610), for example, a "destination resort" (20 minutes from downtown Portland), was a former poor farm; the **KENNEDY SCHOOL** (5736 NE 33rd Ave, Portland; 503/249-3983) in northeast Portland was a grade school; and the **GRAND LODGE** (3505 Pacific Ave, Forest Grove; 503/992-9533) was the former Masonic and Eastern Star Home.

You may not appreciate the ambience of every McMenamin establishment, but chances are great that if you're in Portland long enough, you'll find one you like well enough to visit again. Check out www.mcmenamins.com for more information, including menus, current movie offerings, and room rates.　　　　　*—Kim Carlson*

Couvron / ★★★

1126 SW 18TH AVE, PORTLAND; 503/225-1844 This 32-seat, award-winning upper-upper-scale restaurant gets more and more elaborate, but Tony Demes's skills can keep up with it. Couvron now offers three seasonally changing, prix-fixe menus: vegetarian at $65, seven-course at $75, and the nine-course Chef's Grand Menu at $95. Presentation is as elaborate as the menu—each dish is highly architectural—and the descriptions equally so. Diners might choose between "pan-roasted Maine diver scallops served with crème fraîche, melted leeks, hand-pressed herb pasta, and lobster glaze" or "cherrywood-smoked Oregon quail served with a salad of assorted autumn garden vegetables with summer truffles,

Italian white truffle oil, and port sauce." Demes is particular about ingredients, flying in seafood from Maine and selecting local organic vegetables. He makes it all work; a several-hour meal here is lovely and inviting, right down to the closing chocolate afterthoughts. It's also heartening to see a place with a cheese course. The dining rooms may feel a bit small and crowded, but the location is striking—Couvron is directly on the new west-side light-rail line, and really deserves its own station. *$$$$; AE, MC, V; no checks; dinner Tues–Sat; beer and wine; reservations required; www.couvron.com; between SW Salmon and Madison Sts.* &

Daily Cafe in the Pearl / ★★

902 NW 13TH AVE, PORTLAND; 503/242-1916 What neighborhood couldn't use a place like this? This Pearl District diner is a bit Scandinavian, a bit Pacific Rim, with wood-paneled walls and paper-lantern lights, accented with citrus-colored plastic chairs. You can get a singularly special weekend brunch here (three courses: a basket of sweet and savory breads, an "appetizer"—try the broiled grapefruit—and an entree—maybe butternut ravioli), a delicious panini at lunch (order at the counter), or a full-fledged dinner. The dinner menu is short, but almost everything is carefully prepared and big on flavor: pan-seared mahi mahi arrives on a bed of smashed yams, topped with avocado salsa. A small plate of perfectly prepared potato gnocchi with chard, roasted garlic, red grapes, and marscapone is easy to share. Food in Bloom, the folks behind the Daily, have been catering Portland events for years; now they've brought their good ideas to the table for everyone to enjoy. *$$; MC, V; no checks; breakfast, lunch every day, dinner Wed–Sat, brunch Sun; beer and wine; no reservations; corner of NW 13th Ave and Kearney St.* &

El Gaucho / ★★★

319 SW BROADWAY (BENSON HOTEL), PORTLAND; 503/227-8794 Steak is not as coveted in Portland as some places, but you can find it, and it can be excellent. Ensconced in the classic Benson Hotel, El Gaucho is a branch of the serious Seattle steakhouse, serving up some of the city's finest beef. It's all dark shadows and leaping flames—from the open kitchen grills at the back to the flaming shish kebabs tableside. In fact, everything served tableside is performance art; El Gaucho may hold the record for most ingredients in a Caesar salad, all lovingly assembled at your table. Come for the whole picture: service, steak, setting. *$$$–$$$$; AE, DC, MC, V; no checks; dinner every night; full bar; reservations recommended; www.elgaucho.com; corner of SW Washington St.* &

Esparza's Tex-Mex Café / ★★★

2725 SE ANKENY ST, PORTLAND; 503/234-7909 People may wonder how a Tex-Mex restaurant has become a landmark in Portland—but the question doesn't survive the first visit, or the first smoked beef brisket taco. By then, new visitors have been educated by a restaurant resembling a San Antonio garage sale, with a stunning jukebox and a sweeping array of tequila bottles. It's a challenge deciding which tequila goes with the Cowboy Tacos, filled with thick slabs of smoked sirloin, barbecue sauce, guacamole, and pico de gallo, or the *uvalde,* a smoked lamb enchilada, or some *nopalitos,* the best cactus appetizer around. Watch the blackboard—and the faces of other diners—to catch the latest inspiration of Joe

Esparza. Esparza's is so much fun, you might not appreciate how good it is—and so good, you might not realize how much fun you're having. *$$; AE, DC, DIS, MC, V; no checks; lunch, dinner Tues–Sat; full bar; reservations recommended for large parties; at SE 28th Ave.*

Fong Chong / ★★

301 NW 4TH AVE, PORTLAND; 503/228-6868 In a three-block stretch of Portland's Chinatown, near the Classical Chinese Garden, there are enough dim sum places to cause serving-cart gridlock, but it's not just Fong Chong's historical reputation as the local dim sum star that should make you maneuver to this one. Along with vibrant humbao buns and addictive sticky rice in a lotus leaf, you might find something surprising, such as shallot dumplings and implausible but heartwarming pork cookies. Fong Chong has a Chinese grocery next door, is crowded and loud, and the staff maneuvers the carts through the tables like race cars. It's fun, inexpensive, and impressively tasty. At night, Fong Chong is transformed into a quiet Cantonese eatery. *$; AE, MC, V; no checks; lunch, dinner every day; full bar; reservations not necessary; at NW Everett St.* &

Genoa / ★★★★

2832 SE BELMONT ST, PORTLAND; 503/238-1464 Genoa continues its supreme reign as many Portlanders' favorite destination for a special occasion. Menus for the elaborate, seven-course meals (with a fewer-course option available at the early evening seatings) change every two weeks, and for more than 30 years fans have been returning to see what's next. The atmosphere of the dining room has not changed much over the decades—it's still heavily curtained and open, with the same dark chocolate walls—and somehow that is a comfort: all the innovation and much of the effort goes into amazing food and unparalleled, unpretentious service. You choose the entree—maybe a partridge stuffed with thyme and figs, wrapped in pancetta, roasted, flamed with grappa, and finished with a sauce of shallots, red wine, and fig preserves. At Genoa, that will be the fifth course; antipasto, soup, pasta—maybe ravioli filled with beets and caramelized onions—and fish come first, and dessert and fruit follow. At least once or twice in the meal, Genoa will stun you; the overall effect is bliss. *$$$$; AE, DC, MC, V; checks OK; dinner Mon–Sat; beer, wine, and apéritifs; reservations required; www.genoarestaurant.com; at SE 29th Ave.* &

The Heathman Restaurant and Bar / ★★★

1009 SW BROADWAY, PORTLAND; 503/790-7752 In 2001 the James Beard Foundation selected Heathman chef Philippe Boulot as Pacific Northwest Chef of the Year. This, just after the Heathman Hotel was sold and McCormick & Schmick's took over the restaurant. Although some old-timers have groused about the service falling off—suggesting the once-great restaurant is resting on its laurels—the Heathman seems largely to have weathered the changes and the hype of the past couple of years. Most agree that the dining room remains the center of Portland power breakfasts and lunches. On the extensive and nightly changing menu are dishes that highlight the best of the region's ingredients, prepared with a nod to the chef's native Normandy. King salmon hash prevails at breakfast, and lunch produces rich soups, pungent salads, and heartening stews. Evenings bring live jazz and brandy in the bar. Don't miss the Andy Warhol prints. *$$$–$$$$; AE, DC, MC, V; checks OK; breakfast, lunch, dinner every day; full bar; reservations recommended; www.heathmanhotel.com/heathmanrestaurant/; at SW Salmon St.* &

Higgins / ★★★

1239 SW BROADWAY, PORTLAND; 503/222-9070 Greg Higgins cooks with skill and principle, distilling dazzling dishes from the Northwest soil and seas. Dedicated to local producers and the idea of sustainability, he sets out deft, creative cuisine such as medallions of pork loin and foie gras, or crab and shrimp cakes with chipotle crème fraîche, or perhaps a saffron bourride of regional shellfish. Part of Higgins's policy is to maintain a vegetarian component on the menu, which can mean a forest mushroom tamale with hazelnut mole and tangerine salsa, or a black- and white-truffled risotto. In the bar—which is often jammed—is an inviting bistro menu, with offerings ranging from an excellent burger to smoked goose to Higgins's signature sandwich: house-cured pastrami with white cheddar. Spectacular presentation endures, especially in desserts, which might be a roasted pear in phyllo or a chocolate-almond-apricot tart. *$$–$$$; AE, DC, DIS, JCB, MC, V; checks OK; lunch Mon–Fri, dinner every day; full bar; reservations recommended; higgins.citysearch.com; corner of SW Jefferson St.* &

Jake's Famous Crawfish / ★★

SW 12TH AVE, PORTLAND; 503/226-1419 This is the place that spawned an empire; owners Bill McCormick and Doug Schmick have almost as many restaurants as items on their fresh list. The menu lists seafood from Fiji to Maine to New Zealand. The catch might appear in a shiitake soy ginger glaze, or blackened with corn-pepper relish, or in a bouillabaisse. Jake's is strong on tradition, from the polished wooden fixtures to the waiters' white jackets, but the menu features constant experimentation. The combination of old tradition and new ideas applied to very fresh seafood could keep Jake's going for another 100 years. Those without reservations might wait an hour, knowing their patience will be rewarded with some of the better seafood in the city, and some of the best service anywhere. Lots of folks in the bar are in no hurry at all. Jake's was an early fan of Oregon wines, and it also has a powerful dessert tray: the three-berry cobbler endures, as does the legendary chocolate truffle cake. *$$; AE, DC, DIS, MC, V; no checks; lunch Mon–Fri, dinner every day; full bar; reservations recommended; at SW Stark St.* &

Le Bouchon / ★★

517 NW 14TH AVE, PORTLAND; 503/248-2193 Portland has welcomed other "authentic" French bistros in recent years, but this tiny, loud storefront in the Pearl District sets the standard. The menu is studded with French specialties— onion soup, escargot, pâté, and pommes frites. The authenticity continues through entrees and desserts, from entrecote in red wine sauce through—*naturellement*—a potent chocolate mousse. The decibel level and closely packed tables may discourage some diners, but that's part of the atmosphere. Servers could not be more delightful; these folks know what they're doing. *$$; AE, DIS, MC, V; no checks; lunch*

Tues–Fri, dinner Tues–Sat; beer and wine; reservations recommended; between NW Glisan and Hoyt Sts.

Legin / ★★

8001 SE DIVISION ST, PORTLAND; 503/777-2828 At first glance, this huge, garish building among the fast-food architecture of SE 82nd Avenue looks like the chop suey palace of all time. It's only when you get inside, and see the huge Chinese menu and the multiple live seafood tanks, that you discover what may be the best Chinese restaurant in town. You'll find items here you just won't find anyplace else around—bamboo marrow? six kinds of shark fin soup?—and you can accompany them with live geoduck or a whole tilapia. Look for anything that's alive when you order it; try to find a place for the pepper and salt lobster; and take a shot at something you don't recognize—Cantonese ham, maybe. On Sundays, a giant, bustling dim sum scene seems to be dispensing all the chicken feet and shiu mai in the world. *$$; MC, V; no checks; lunch, dinner every day; full bar; reservations not necessary; at SE 82nd Ave.* &

Lemongrass / ★★★

1705 NE COUCH ST, PORTLAND; 503/231-5780 Shelley Siripatrapa's exquisite Thai restaurant in an elegant old Portland Victorian house is an enduring favorite among Thai food aficionados—especially those who appreciate heat. Tastes here are bright and sharp, sweet and hot and tangy, from emerald pools of green curry to snap-your-eyes-open shrimp with garlic and basil. Siripatrapa has a magical touch with seafood, such as shrimp snuggled into pad thai noodles or just floating in a clear-your-sinuses broth of lemongrass, Kaffir lime, and chile. She also produces a stunning peanut sauce, and in her inspiration of prawn satay, the two specialties come together dramatically. There's a choice of heat intensity, but getting much past mild takes you into a place of pain. Reservations are not taken, and nothing is cooked in advance; you'll wait for a table, and then wait again at your table. But then you'll come back and wait again. *$$; no credit cards; checks OK; lunch Tues–Fri, dinner Tues–Sat; beer and wine; reservations not accepted; at NE 17th Ave.*

McCormick & Schmick's Seafood Restaurant / ★★★

235 SW 1ST AVE, PORTLAND; 503/224-7522 This place is the template of the McCormick & Schmick's chain dotting the country. But you have to admire a restaurant where the fresh fish offerings include salmon stuffed with Dungeness crab and Brie, one of the most popular dishes. McCormick & Schmick's has a vast range of both seafood and imagination, from blackened escolar from Fiji to pecan catfish with fried green tomatoes. The menu changes daily, but the place has its specialties, notably grilled alder-smoked salmon, crab cakes, and bouillabaisse. M&S is frequently jammed, offering a lively bar scene complete with a pianist and an extraordinary selection of single-malt Scotches; cigar nights are a thing of the past. *$$; AE, DC, MC, V; no checks; lunch Mon–Fri, dinner every day; full bar; reservations recommended; at SW Oak St.* &

mint / ★★½

816 N RUSSELL ST, PORTLAND; 503/284-5518 Owner Lucy Brennan and chef Dan Spitz joined forces after stints at Zefiro and Saucebox to create this sleek, slip-of-a-place in the increasingly trendy North Portland neighborhood. The ultra-cool mint gets its heat from the kitchen, which offers Latin-inspired dishes such as moist and flavorful plantain-crusted halibut with a black bean–tomatillo salsa and avocado coulis or rich, smoky Negra Modelo pork stew. Seasonal greens get a stimulating lift from a clementine-mint vinaigrette, while traditional ceviche gains substance by adding chayote squash and orange. Start with a round of exotic drinks to share—the avocado daiquiri is a real surprise, deliciously smooth and refreshing. *$$; AE, DIS, MC, V; checks OK; dinner every day; full bar; reservations recommended; near N Interstate Ave, at N Albina Ave (call for directions).* &

Oba / ★★

555 NW 12TH AVE, PORTLAND; 503/228-6161 "Oba" must mean "sizzle" in some language, for this place rarely fails to impress those seeking a little heat (so it's not the best place to take your mother-in-law, and leave the kids at home). With its flashy red walls and star-hung ceiling, and its dizzying bar scene, it's won awards for design. Diners have also given thumping approval to its cuisine, but nothing could be as hot as the ambience. Chef Scott Newman's style is called Nuevo Latino, and the menu extends across everything Latin, from Brazilian feijoada to Cuban flank steak to fish Veracruz-style, and from sangria to Brazilian sugarcane liquor. The ribs with guava-habanero barbecue sauce have big fans, though many people prefer putting together arrays of openers such as crispy shrimp tostadas and shiitake mushroom rellenos. The bartenders are talented. Private dining is newly available, by reservation, for groups of 10 to 90 in the Havana Room. *$$; AE, DC, MC, V; checks OK; dinner every day; full bar; reservations recommended; at NW Hoyt St.* &

The Original Pancake House / ★★

8600 SW BARBUR BLVD, PORTLAND; 503/246-9007 In 1999 the Original Pancake House was designated by the James Beard Foundation as a regional landmark restaurant, a thick-battered legend, but Portlanders didn't need New Yorkers telling them where to go for pancakes: since this place opened in 1955, the lines have been long. The place hums from the time it opens at 7am until it closes in midafternoon. Sourdough flapjacks—from wine-spiked cherry to wheat germ to a behemoth apple pancake with a sticky cinnamon glaze—are made from scratch. A good bet is the egg-rich Dutch baby, which arrives looking like a huge, sunken birthday cake, dusted with powdered sugar and served with fresh lemon. Omelets big enough for two (made from a half-dozen eggs) arrive with a short stack. The name may mention only pancakes, but this is a place that knows how to handle eggs. Service is cheerful and efficient; after all, people are waiting for your table. *$; no credit cards; checks OK; breakfast, lunch Wed–Sun; no alcohol; reservations not accepted; www.originalpancakehouse.com; at SW 24th Ave.*

Paley's Place / ★★★

1204 NW 21ST AVE, PORTLAND; 503/243-2403 Paley's Place rarely disappoints. Vitaly and Kimberly Paley (he oversees the kitchen, she the front) opened their restaurant in 1995, and it's only improved with time. Diners appreciate the combination of small, humming dining room and sharp, attentive service—plus the reassuring but elegant dishes coming from the kitchen (think perfect french fries or tuna tartare). In winter the seasonal menu might offer crispy veal sweetbreads with herbed spaetzle and chestnuts, or a mixed grill of bacon-wrapped pork tenderloin, venison sausage, and duck confit. You might warm up with escargot, or with the Belgian mussels with mustard aioli that have become a local addiction. Other seasons might bring a bisque of spring asparagus and broccoli, or steelhead set off by a smoked seafood sausage. Menus change with the harvests, but the dessert tray is consistently impressive. *$$$; AE, MC, V; local checks only; dinner every day; beer and wine; reservations recommended; paleysplace.city search.com; at NW Northrup St.*

Papa Haydn / ★★★

701 NW 23RD AVE, PORTLAND; 503/228-7317 / 5829 SE MILWAUKIE AVE, PORTLAND; 503/232-9440 Portland's dessert headquarters trails waiting diners out of its doors the way it trails chocolate sauce across its cakes; fortunately there's good people-watching along NW 23rd Avenue for those in line. Dozens of choices include huge architectural cakes such as Autumn Meringue (layers of chocolate mousse and meringue, festooned with chocolate slabs), *boccone dolce* (a mountain of whipped cream, chocolate, meringue, and fresh berries), cookies, house-made sorbets, and ice creams. Before dessert, Papa Haydn offers salads and sandwiches at lunch (try the chicken club with avocado and sun-dried tomato mayonnaise), and dinner choices that change monthly to reflect the seasons, such as pasta with scallops and Gorgonzola cream, and filet mignon bresaola. The Sellwood location is more low-key with a less ambitious menu, but don't think that's a way to avoid the lines—it has most of the same desserts, and regulars know it. *$$; AE, MC, V; no checks; lunch, dinner Tues–Sat, brunch Sun; full bar (NW 23rd Ave), beer and wine (SE Milwaukie Ave); reservations not accepted Fri–Sat nights; at NW Irving St (NW 23rd) and between SE Bybee and Holgate (SE Milwaukie).* &

Pazzo Ristorante / ★★

627 SW WASHINGTON ST, PORTLAND; 503/228-1515 Off the lobby of the Hotel Vintage Plaza, Pazzo has something for everyone: bring your family, friends, or colleagues for consistently good regional Italian dishes in the high-energy dining room; bring your date for a romantic dinner in the wine cellar. Pazzo prominently displays a wood-burning pizza oven, and the kitchen where chef Nathan Logan and his assistants prepare your meal is center stage. You might start with the burrata cheese, served with Italian black truffles, then move on to a pasta or risotto. Save room for the tiramisu. For breakfast and lunch, Pazzoria Cafe next door sets out pastries, panini, and pasta, but you can also eat in the dining room. *$$–$$$; AE, DC, MC, V; checks OK; breakfast every day, lunch Mon–Sat, dinner every day; full bar; reservations recommended; pazzoristorante.citysearch.com; at SW Broadway.* &

Red Star Tavern & Roast House / ★★

503 SW ALDER ST, PORTLAND; 503/222-0005 In this towering-ceilinged restaurant of the 5th Avenue Suites Hotel, Rob Pando describes his cooking as regional American cuisine, from seared Nantucket scallops to Texas-grilled baby back ribs. He covers the continent impressively, using the huge wood-burning grill and rotisserie at the center of the restaurant, as well as the kind of sauté skill that produces splendid crab and smoked-salmon cakes. Pastas also garner rave reviews, including butternut squash and spinach lasagna. Longtime favorites include a moist skillet of corn bread and a tangy barbecued pork sloppy joe sandwich with wild mushrooms at lunch. The range is considerable, portions are sizable, the atmosphere is entertaining—the tone reflects giant workingman murals of the restaurant's bounty—and you couldn't be closer to the middle of downtown. A great place for breakfasts too. *$$; AE, DC, MC, V; no checks; breakfast, lunch, dinner every day; full bar; reservations recommended; at SW 5th Ave.* &

Restaurant Murata / ★★★

200 SW MARKET ST, PORTLAND; 503/227-0080 One can reserve a tatami room, and if you prize elbow room, that may be the way to go. But for an authentic Tokyo-style experience, sit at the tiny sushi bar, where specials are listed in Japanese, with a "translation" underneath: Japanese names spelled out in English. But once someone has translated the specials, they're often worth the culinary gamble: crisp grilled sardines, mackerel necks, layers of deep purple tuna. Murata has a particular affinity for fish, displayed in terrific sushi, great grilled fish, and the *nabe*—huge bowls of stewlike soups, thick with seafood. The elaborate, prearranged Japanese multicourse banquet, *kaiseki*, runs as high as your wallet allows. *$$–$$$; AE, DC, MC, V; no checks; lunch Mon–Fri, dinner Mon–Sat; beer and wine; reservations recommended (except at sushi bar); between SW 2nd and 3rd Aves.*

Southpark / ★★

🌲 **901 SW SALMON ST, PORTLAND; 503/326-1300** The spot to fortify yourself before or after a tour of the art museum up the street, Southpark is lively, convivial, and pretty to look at, with dramatic, high ceilings and an enormous mural in the bar. The food is good too: ravioli stuffed with butternut squash and ricotta, topped with toasted hazelnuts and marsala is a favorite; so is the grilled pork tenderloin with dried cherries and balsamic vinegar. The extensive wine list is helpfully organized by characteristics rather than region. Take a second to check out the salmon sculpture above the corner entrance. *$$; AE, DC, MC, V; no checks; lunch Mon–Sat, dinner every day, brunch Sun; full bar; reservations recommended; on SW Park Ave.* &

Sungari / ★★

735 SW IST AVE, PORTLAND; 503/224-0800 You might be seated next to the kids' end of a large family celebration dinner—everybody likes Sungari—but this place still has an elegant feel, with white papered tabletops set with votives and orchids and huge arched windows. The Szechwan fare is the best in town, and the service is efficient (though not effusive). Here the old favorite, General Tso's chicken, is succulent but not too heavy and expertly spiced. Dry sautéed string beans come pared into bite-sized pieces that pack the perfect amount of bite themselves. Spicy sesame beef, served on crunchy rice noodles, has a crackly texture on the outside but is deliciously tender. This is not the Chinese restaurant of your youth, where takeout was the preferred mode of dining; at Sungari, you'll want to linger. *$$; AE, MC, V; checks OK; lunch Mon–Fri, dinner every day; full bar; reservations recommended; www.sungarirestaurant.com; downtown between SW Yamhill and Morrison Sts.* &

Swagat / ★

2074 NW LOVEJOY AVE, PORTLAND; 503/227-4300 / 4325 SW 109TH AVE, BEAVERTON; 503/626-3000 Neither of the two locations of this fragrant, accomplished Indian restaurant—the suburban house-and-garage in Beaverton, nor the expansive restaurant-bar space in Northwest Portland—are big on atmosphere. But if you close your eyes and breathe deeply, you can get closer to the spicy tandoori dishes and vindaloo stews that make Swagat so inviting. The range here is substantial, from curries and samosas to South Indian specialties such as the oversized rice pancake dosas. Nothing will cost much, especially the mandatory Indian restaurant lunch buffet. Swagat is also a fine place for vegetarians. *$; AE, DIS, MC, V; no checks; lunch, dinner every day; full bar (in Portland), beer and wine (in Beaverton); reservations not necessary; at NW 21st (in Portland), a few blocks off Beaverton-Hillsdale Hwy (in Beaverton).* &

Tapeo / ★★

2764 NW THURMAN ST, PORTLAND; 503/226-0409 To a deceptively modest storefront on a quiet Northwest Portland street, Ricardo Segura has brought the flavors of his native Spain—notably the flavors of serrano ham, salmon cured with manzanilla sherry, and boneless quail with bittersweet chocolate sauce. Thirty different tapas—small plates designed for casual munching—and a list of 20 sherries have captivated Portlanders accustomed to big entrees and pinot noir. In a place of powerful relaxation and an almost Iberian lack of hurry, diners might start by combining a few cold tapas—some marinated trout, or ham and cheese on thick toasted bread—with some hot items, such as a white bean stew or a zarzuelita, seafood in brandy, almonds, and cinnamon. Then, after some sipping and some conversation, and some wiping off the empty plates with crusty bread, retrieve the menu and explore a bit further. As in a sushi bar, the bill can mount up, but it will record some striking flavors. Come summer, tables outside make NW Thurman seem even more Southwest European. *$$; MC, V; no checks; dinner Tues–Sat; beer and wine; reservations not accepted; between NW 27th and 28th Aves.* &

Typhoon! / ★★

2310 NW EVERETT ST, PORTLAND; 503/243-7557 / 400 SW BROADWAY (THE IMPERIAL HOTEL), PORTLAND; 503/224-8285 Bo Kline is a gifted chef, and her two Portland restaurants, with their hip interiors, rarely disappoint. From openers of *miang kum* (spinach leaves to be filled with a half-dozen ingredients) and mouth-filling soups, the menu moves into a kaleidoscope of curries, inspired seafood dishes, and multiple pungent Thai noodle dishes. Try the King's Noodles, and know why it's good to be king. Scored into a checkerboard grid, a fried fish blossoms into a pinecone, and dishes with names such as Fish on Fire and Super-wild Shrimp turn out to be named right. Typhoon! also offers 145 different teas—including one that goes for $65 a pot. *$–$$; AE, DC, DIS, MC, V; no checks; lunch Mon–Sat, dinner every day; beer and wine; reservations recommended; typhoon. citysearch.com; at NW 23rd Ave (in NW Portland), between SW Stark and Washington Sts (downtown).* &

Wildwood / ★★★

1221 NW 21ST AVE, PORTLAND; 503/248-9663 Emanating from the busy, modern restaurant at the north end of NW 21st Avenue's restaurant row, the fragrance from Cory Schreiber's wood oven has become the signature aroma of Portland's new Northwest cuisine. Among the standards on a changing menu are skillet-roasted mussels in tomato, garlic, and saffron, and crispy pizzas that might hold bacon, Bosc pear, and sweet onion. Schreiber does steadily interesting things with salmon, such as give it a mushroom and thyme crust, and with Muscovy duck breast. You also might see a mesquite-roasted pork loin chop with corn bread and bacon stuffing. The bar is rousing—the noise level hums all around the restaurant—and offers some more casual menu choices. Try the highly hospitable brunch, and don't miss the basket of breads. In its open, boisterous style, Wildwood feels a bit like San Francisco, but tastes like the best of Oregon. *$$$; AE, MC, V; checks OK; lunch, dinner every day, brunch Sun; full bar; reservations recommended; wildwoodrestaurant.citysearch.com; at NW Overton St.* &

Zell's: An American Café / ★★

1300 SE MORRISON ST, PORTLAND; 503/239-0196 Zell's serves one of the best breakfasts in this time zone: a range of waffles and pancakes (try ginger if they're available) and inspired eggs—the Hangtown frittata, eggs Benedict, and even a salmon Benedict. The trademark chorizo-and-peppers omelet has been joined by a Brie-and-tomato effort and, if you're lucky, scrambled eggs with smoked salmon, Gruyère, and green onions. Lunch means a whole other set of specialties, from meatloaf and vegetarian sandwiches to clam cakes and homemade soups. The catch, especially on weekend mornings, is the wait for a table. *$; AE, DIS, MC, V; checks OK; breakfast, lunch every day; full bar; reservations not accepted; at SE 13th Ave.* &

LODGINGS

Avalon Hotel and Spa / ★★★

0455 SW HAMILTON CT, PORTLAND; 503/802-5800 OR 888/556-4402 The new Avalon Hotel lives up to its reputation as a sophisticated, boutique hotel. It's located just south of downtown Portland on the Willamette River, and many of the 99 rooms have balconies and river or mountain views. Ask for a room on the upper floors to avoid having trees block your view. The staff is professional and attentive; the rooms comfortable and well appointed. Heating and air-conditioning controls that can be reached without getting out of bed, fluffy feather pillows, cordless phones, plush robes, and fabulous marble-clad bathrooms all reflect the hotel design's attention to detail. Less pleasing are the apparently uninsulated walls separating the rooms. Prepare to be pampered at the Avalon Hotel, but bring your earplugs in case you have noisy neighbors. The spa portion of the facility includes an on-site fitness club and salon. Rivers American Grill, adjacent to the hotel, offers room service. *$$$$; AE, DC, DIS, MC, V; checks OK; info@avalonhotelandspa.com; www.avalonhotelandspa.com; south of downtown Portland, exit 299A off I-5.* &

The Benson Hotel / ★★★

🌲 **309 SW BROADWAY, PORTLAND; 503/228-2000 OR 888/523-6766** The Benson is the grand dame of Portland hotels; since the early part of the past century, it has been a frequent host of significant goings-on. Many locals who want to spend the night downtown opt for the Benson—as at many luxury hotels, special rates abound—and it is still the first choice for politicos and film stars; with 287 rooms, there's space for everyone. The palatial lobby—a fine place to linger over a drink—features a stamped-tin ceiling, mammoth chandeliers, stately columns, and a generous fireplace, surrounded by panels of carved Circassian walnut imported from Russia. The guest rooms, though comfortable, lack the grandeur of the public areas, with modern furnishings in shades of black and beige. With completely competent though sometimes impersonal service, the Benson is, literally and figuratively, quite corporate (it's run by WestCoast Hotels), but the place is well loved. Attached to the Benson, El Gaucho (see review) has become a popular place for steak; downstairs, the London Grill caters to an old-fashioned dining crowd. *$$$$; AE, DC, DIS, JCB, MC, V; checks OK; www.bensonhotel.com; between SW Oak and Stark Sts.* &

Embassy Suites Downtown Portland / ★★

319 SW PINE ST, PORTLAND; 503/279-9000 OR 800/EMBASSY The most interesting thing about this hotel on the edge of the downtown center is its pedigree: it's in the former Multnomah Hotel building, a lavish hostelry that hosted royalty and U.S. presidents, plus practically any Hollywood star who passed through town, until its closure in 1965. For the next 30 years, the place led a sort of Orwellian existence as home to a large number of boxy federal offices until the Embassy Suites chain bought and remodeled it in an effort to restore its original grandeur. The spacious lobby is probably the finest room, with its gilt-touched columns and player grand piano (pounding out carols during December), but the Arcadian Gardens, where both a complimentary happy hour and a complimentary full breakfast are served, is less charming. Guest rooms are large with average furnishings but lots of nice touches— ample glassware, basic kitchen facilities, his-and-her television sets, and a coffee-table book describing the building's history. The hourglass-shaped pool, sunk beneath the ground in what was for years a parking lot, is a plus in this pool-shy town; there's an exercise room and sauna as well as a pair of spa pools. *$$$; AE, DC, DIS, MC, V; no checks; www.embassy-suites.com; between 2nd and 3rd Aves.* &

5th Avenue Suites Hotel / ★★★

👫 🐷 **506 SW WASHINGTON ST, PORTLAND; 503/222-0001 OR 800/711-2971** A truly pleasant stay in the city—for business travelers, yes, but excellent for families too. Most of the 221 rooms are spacious suites, but even those that are not have a sense of grandeur (and plenty of room for a crib, if requested). Yellow-and-white striped wallpaper makes the rooms look like well-wrapped presents; sliding French doors divide sleeping quarters from sitting areas. Each suite has three phones (with personalized voice mail and data ports), a couple TVs, and its own fax machine, plus traveler details such as pull-down ironing boards and irons, plush cotton robes, and hair dryers. The staff is gracious and bellhops are extremely attentive—and like its sister inn, the Hotel Vintage Plaza, 5th Avenue Suites welcomes the occasional dog or lizard. The Kimpton Group has covered its bases: everything from indoor parking with an unloading area to protect you from the rain to the stunning but welcoming lobby with its large corner fireplace, where you'll find complimentary coffee and newspapers in the morning, and wine tastings come evening. The Red Star Tavern & Roast House (see review) and an Aveda spa are on the ground floor. *$$$; AE, DC, DIS, JCB, MC, V; checks OK; www.5th avenuesuites.com; at 5th Ave.* &

The Governor Hotel / ★★★

611 SW 10TH AVE, PORTLAND; 503/224-3400 OR 800/554-3456 On the northwestern edge of the downtown core—and an easy walk from Powell's City of Books and the rest of the Pearl District—sits the handsome Governor. The hotel's lobby makes a good first impression: a dramatic mural depicting scenes from the Lewis and Clark Expedition spans one wall, and Arts and Crafts–style furnishings, yards of mahogany, and a true wood-burning fireplace give the place a clubby feel. Alas, the rooms are less dramatic: done in Northwest earth-tone pastels, they feature standard hotel furnishings; some have whirlpool tubs, and suites feature gas-burning fireplaces, wet bars, and balconies. Most rooms have big windows, but the upper-floor rooms on the northeast corner of the adjacent Princeton Building sport the best city views (guest rooms 5013 and 6013 are the only standard rooms with private balconies). The list of amenities is long, and includes 24-hour maid service, access to the business center, and use of the adults-only Nelson's Nautilus Plus ($8 fee)—or call Studio Adrienne for an invigorating Pilates workout (it's under the same roof). The restaurant downstairs, Jake's Grill, also provides better-than-average room-service fare. *$$$–$$$$; AE, DC, DIS, JCB, MC, V; checks OK; www.govhotel.com; at SW Alder St.* &

The Heathman Hotel / ★★★★

1001 SW BROADWAY, PORTLAND; 503/241-4100 OR 800/551-0011 The intimate, elegant Heathman continues to keep pace with the competition. While its appeal is broad—excellent business services, a central downtown location, and fine artistic details—guests especially appreciate the meticulously courteous staff, who provide exceptional but low-key service from check-in to check-out. (Those not accustomed to the rain will appreciate the umbrella service.) Common rooms are handsomely appointed with Burmese teak paneling, and the elegant lobby lounge is a great place to enjoy afternoon tea or evening jazz. The Symphony Suites guest rooms, with a sofa and king bed, are our favorite. Depending on your interests, you might be impressed by the video collection, the library (with author-signed volumes), or the fitness suite (personal trainer available). A strong supporter of the arts, the hotel itself features an impressive display of original artwork, from Andy Warhol prints to the fanciful Henk Pander mural on the east wall of the Arlene

CITY OF BOOKS

Other cities might have bragging rights to majestic cathedrals or towering monuments, but Portland has Powell's. Since 1971, **POWELL'S CITY OF BOOKS** (1005 W Burnside St; 503/228-4651) has wielded a huge influence on the intellectual life of this city—not only in terms of its inventory, but also with readings, a cafe (aka the Anne Hughes Coffee Room), and its sponsorship of literary events. The shelves in its half-dozen outlets cater to a reader's every whim. If you're the bookish type—or even if you're not, but want to be impressed—check out the downtown store with its full city block of new and used books, or visit the **TRAVEL STORE** (SW 6th Ave and SW Yamhill St; 503/228-1108) in Pioneer Courthouse Square or **POWELL'S BOOKS FOR COOKS AND GARDENERS** (3747 SE Hawthorne Blvd; 503/235-3802). While you're shopping, here's a list of titles you might look for that will get you just a little closer to Portland's essence.

Ramona the Pest lives in northeast Portland, like her author, Beverly Cleary, once did. Any of the Ramona books are almost sure hits with children (and their grown-ups); check out the Ramona statues in **GRANT PARK** (corner of NE 33rd Ave and U.S. Grant Pl, Irvington).

Local publisher Timber Press can take credit for William Hawkins and William Winnigham's *Classic Houses of Portland, Oregon: 1850–1950* (1999). Complete with black-and-white photos, this book tells stories of many local residences. *An Architectural Guidebook to Portland,* by Bart King (Gibbs Smith, 2001), goes into greater detail on the

Schnitzer Concert Hall. And, finally, you're just steps (or room service) away from one of the city's finer restaurants (Heathman Restaurant and Bar; see review). *$$$–$$$$; AE, DC, DIS, JCB, MC, V; checks OK; www.heathmanhotel.com; at SW Salmon St.* &

Heron Haus Bed and Breakfast Inn / ★★

2545 NW WESTOVER RD, PORTLAND; 503/274-1846 Although Heron Haus is just blocks from NW 23rd Avenue, with some of Portland's best-known restaurants and hippest boutiques, its location at the base of the West Hills has a residential feel. The common areas in this 10,000-square-foot English Tudor home include a bright living room with a cushy sectional sofa, a mahogany-paneled library punctuated by an inviting window seat, and a cozy sunroom. Six guest rooms, each with a fireplace and private bath (one bathroom has a seven-nozzle shower), are comfortably furnished in pastels, with massive wooden beds, sitting areas, telephones, and TVs. The extraordinary bath in the Kulia Room features an elevated spa tub with a city view and deluxe bathing accoutrements—from his-and-her robes to a rubber ducky. Innkeeper Julie Keppeler caters to the business crowd, with a reduced corporate rate, phone hookups, and no-frills continental breakfast served at individual tables in the dining room. *$$$; MC, V; checks OK; www.heronhaus.com; near NW 25th Ave and Johnson St.*

more public buildings in the city. *Wild in the City: A Guide to Portland Natural Areas* (Oregon Historical Society Press, 2000), edited by Mike Houck and M. J. Cody, is organized by watershed and is full of maps and illustrations.

Author and cooking teacher extraordinaire James Beard grew up in Portland during the early part of the 20th century. His book *Delights and Prejudices* contains lavish passages about Portland markets, the city's social life, the summer trip to the Oregon Coast on the train—and other aspects of life in Portland 100 years ago. *The Solace of Food: A Life of James Beard,* by Robert Clark, affords a broader view of Beard's world than Beard himself would offer.

With its adoring and detailed descriptions of Portland's many varied bridges, a new edition of *The Portland Bridge Book* (Oregon Historical Society Press, 2001), by Sharon Wood, is a good walking companion.

Oregon's beloved poet William Stafford taught for years at Portland's Lewis and Clark College, and contributed much to the literary life of his adopted city until his death in 1993. *The Way It Is: New and Selected Poems* (Graywolf Press, 1998) is an invaluable collection of Stafford's work.

Finally, *Best Places Portland* (Sasquatch Books, 2001) is *Best Places Northwest's* city companion. With some 200 restaurant reviews, plus the city's best shopping, arts, recreation, and top attractions, it lays Portland bare.

—Kim Carlson

Hotel Vintage Plaza / ★★★

422 SW BROADWAY, PORTLAND; 503/228-1212 OR 800/243-0555 In a city that's becoming crowded with luxury hotels, the Vintage still shines, mostly because of what it offers for what you pay. Weekend rates are competitive, making this an ideal destination for out-of-town shoppers who want to stay somewhere special in the city center. Just blocks from Nordstrom and Pioneer Courthouse Square, Vintage Plaza is run by the Kimpton Group, and like other Kimpton hotels, its decor is elegant but not opulent. We appreciate the intimate scale (107 rooms), the inviting lobby, and the gracious staff. In the early evening, complimentary Northwest wines are served in the lobby. Even pets get royal treatment here; just inquire well in advance. Best rooms are the top-floor starlight rooms with greenhouse-style windows (ask for one of the larger corner rooms) or the spacious bi-level suites. All rooms come with two phone lines, complimentary shoe shine, nightly turndown service, morning coffee in the lobby, and the newspaper delivered to your door. Pazzo Ristorante and Pazzoria Cafe are on the main floor (see review). *$$–$$$; AE, DC, DIS, JCB, MC, V; no checks; www.vintageplaza.com; at SW Washington.* &

The Lion and the Rose / ★★★

1810 NE 15TH AVE, PORTLAND; 503/287-9245 OR 800/955-1647 Housed in a 1906 Queen Anne mansion in the Irvington District (not far from Lloyd Center), the Lion and the Rose maintains its status as one of Portland's more elegant B&Bs. The hosts let few details go unchecked—from candles in the baths, to beverages in the refrigerator, to extra pillows and blankets in each room. The best rooms are Joseph's (rich colors contrast with ample natural light) and Lavonna (done in lavender and white, it boasts a spacious bay window reading nook); the place is well decorated, with rich drapery, fine rugs, and antiques. Breakfast is lavish (in the formal dining room or your room), and tea is offered to guests from 4pm until 6pm. Those set on relaxing appreciate the porch swing—roofed to guard against rain—but businesspeople find plenty of phone lines and other amenities. *$$; AE, DIS, MC, V; checks OK; www.lionrose.com; north of NE Broadway.*

Mallory Hotel / ★

729 SW 15TH AVE, PORTLAND; 503/223-6311 OR 800/228-8657 Some things never change; look no farther than the Mallory for evidence. Located just west of downtown, a 15-minute stroll from Pioneer Courthouse Square, the beloved Mallory remains the favorite lodging of many regular visitors to the City of Roses—and has been since they were kids. It's an older establishment in every sense, from the massive hunks of ornate wooden lobby furniture to the senior staff. It's also one of the best bargains in town, starting at $90 for a spotless double and topping out at $160 for a suite—so it's a good idea to reserve a room far in advance. The Mallory sits in a quiet area of town where its new four-story garage makes parking a breeze (and it's free). Have breakfast in the restaurant—simple, charming touches and almost motherly service—and dinner downtown. The quirky cocktail lounge draws denizens from both the older and retro crowds for the reasonably priced well drinks and bowls of cheesy popcorn. *$$; AE, DC, DIS, JCB, MC, V; checks OK; www.malloryhotel.com; at SW Yamhill St.* &

Marriott Residence Inn/Lloyd Center / ★

1710 NE MULTNOMAH ST, PORTLAND; 503/288-1400 OR 800/331-3131 This hotel near Lloyd Center has 168 rooms that you might mistake, from the outside at least, for apartments. It's geared toward longer stays (four to seven days) and rates drop accordingly. Each suite has a full kitchen, as well as a sitting area with a couch and a desk, and most have wood-burning fireplaces. Extra conveniences include weekday dry cleaning and complimentary grocery-shopping services. The hotel doesn't have much of a view or a restaurant, but a continental breakfast and afternoon hors d'oeuvres are served in the lobby. Three Jacuzzis and a heated outdoor pool are on premises for guest use. An extra $5 a day gains you access to the Lloyd Center Athletic Club seven blocks away. *$$; AE, DC, DIS, JCB, MC, V; no checks; www.marriott.com; 2 blocks east of Lloyd Center.* &

Portland's White House / ★★★

1914 NE 22ND AVE, PORTLAND; 503/287-7131 The feeling here is classic Portland: understated elegance combined with a studied informality. Owners Lanning Blanks and Steve Holden hired a historian to help with the restoration of this stately old home, built in 1911 of solid Honduras mahogany by local timber baron Robert F. Lytle. On the outside, Portland's White House looks a bit like its Washington, D.C., namesake, complete with fountains, a circular driveway, and a carriage house with newly converted guest rooms and baths. In the house are more guest rooms, also with private baths. The Chauffer's Quarters is romantic, with Jacuzzi tub and double-headed shower. The Garden Room's private veranda is nice in summer, and if you like, you can have your breakfast here. Evenings, take yourself down to the formal parlor for a game of chess. Book early for your summer stays; the White House has become a favorite for weddings. *$$; AE, DIS, MC, V; no checks; www.portlandswhitehouse.com; 2 blocks north of NE Broadway.*

RiverPlace Hotel / ★★★

1510 SW HARBOR WY, PORTLAND; 503/228-3233 OR 800/227-1333 If you're looking for a room with a view, look no further than RiverPlace. This downtown luxury hotel fronts the busy Willamette River and the boat show that comes with it. The European-style RiverPlace (run by the same hoteliers who run the Benson) is lovely to look at and glorious to look out from. The better rooms among the 84—doubles, suites, and condominiums—face the water or look north across park lawns to the downtown cityscape. Inside are plush furnishings, TVs concealed in armoires, and generously sized bathrooms. Complimentary continental breakfast can be brought to your room, along with your requested newspaper; massage and spa treatments are available by appointment. Use of the adjacent River-Place Athletic Club is complimentary, but on nice days there's plenty of opportunity for exercise outside: wide, paved paths lead from the hotel through the fountains and monuments of Tom McCall Waterfront Park. Downstairs, the Esplanade restaurant makes a stunning location for a meal. *$$$; AE, DC, MC, V; checks OK; www.riverplacehotel.com; south end of waterfront park.* &

Sheraton Portland Airport Hotel / ★★

8235 NE AIRPORT WY, PORTLAND; 503/281-2500 OR 800/325-3535 For the traveling businessperson, the airport's Sheraton tops the list. For one thing, it's located—literally—on the airport grounds (FedEx planes load up next door, and some arrival and departure times are broadcast at the hotel's main entrance). Inside, amenities abound: everything from meeting rooms and a small but complete complimentary business center (with a computer, printer, fax machine, and secretarial service) to an indoor swimming pool, sauna, and workout room. The minisuites consider the personal needs of the businessperson, providing two phones, sitting areas, jacks for computer hookup, and pullout makeup mirrors in the bathrooms. Mount Hood stands tall to the east, but you'd never know it from the airport-facing rooms. *$$; AE, DC, JCB, MC, V; corporate checks OK; www.sheratonportland.com; on right as you approach terminal.* &

BRIDGES OF PORTLAND

Engineer and writer Henry Petroski describes Portland as an open-air bridge museum: in total 12 bridges (plus two railroad bridges) span the Willamette River, from the cathedral-like **ST. JOHNS BRIDGE** on the north to the **OREGON CITY BRIDGE** on the south. The city features all three bridge types, all three movable span types, bridges that are close to one another (most within 3/10 of a mile), and midtown bridges with short and safe approaches for pedestrians.

While all are interesting, some are unique. The **STEEL BRIDGE** is the only vertical-lift bridge in the world with twin decks capable of independent movement. The lower railroad deck, normally kept in the raised position, moves independently of the upper deck, which carries cars, pedestrians, bicycles, and the city's light rail trains. The **HAWTHORNE BRIDGE** is the world's oldest vertical-lift bridge still in full operation, and the **FREMONT BRIDGE** is America's longest tied-arch bridge, with no in-water pier supports. Its 902-foot tied-arch midspan was built off-site and assembled on Swan Island, a mile downstream from the bridge site. Engineers from around the world came to watch as its 6,000 tons were raised 175 feet above the river at a rate of 7 feet per hour.

For an insider's look at Portland's bridges, go on one of Sharon Wood-Wortman's bridge tours. Call her office at 503/222-5535 or see Waterfront Bridge Walks in the Walking Tours section of this chapter.

—*Sarah Thomas*

The Westin Portland / ★★★

750 SW ALDER ST, PORTLAND; 503/294-9000 OR 800/937-8461 Among the newer of downtown Portland's luxury hotels, the Westin is also one of the better. The ground-floor lobby and desk have an intimate feel; a sitting room with a fireplace is comfortably separate from the bustle of guests checking in and out. The knowledgeable and professional staff are pleasant and helpful. And it's a handsome place; the architectural style suggests both modern and traditional (with lots of tile, even on elevator floors). Rooms house tasteful modern furniture, big televisions, fax machines (some rooms), phones with data ports and voice mail, clock/radio/CD players, and uncommonly luxurious beds with down comforters and tons of pillows. But the bathroom is worth the price of admission: a separate, spacious glass shower stall, nice deep tub, tile floor, and a big slab of marble for the counter. No pool, but the workout room has an array of weight and aerobic machines. *$$$; AE, DC, DIS, JCB, MC, V; checks OK; www.westin.com; at SW Park Ave.* &

Forest Grove

Pacific University is why most people come here, and the towering firs on the small campus do justice to the town's name. But there's also quite a collection of local wineries, making the area worth exploring, perhaps on your way to the ocean. South of town on Highway 47 is the huge **MONTINORE VINEYARDS** (3663 SW Dilley Rd, Forest Grove; 503/359-5012), with a fancy tasting room and wines that improve with each vintage. In nearby Gaston, **ELK COVE VINEYARDS** (27751 NW Olson Rd, Gaston; 503/985-7760) has a spectacular site for a tasting room perched on a forested ridge, and **KRAMER VINEYARDS** (26830 NW Olson Rd, Gaston; 503/662-4545) is a tiny place in the woods with tasty pinot noir and excellent raspberry wine. West of Forest Grove on Highway 8, on the site of a historic Oregon winery, **LAUREL RIDGE WINERY** (46350 NW David Hill Rd, Forest Grove; 503/852-7050) specializes in sparkling wines and makes good sauvignon blanc. **SHAFER VINEYARDS** (6200 NW Gales Creek Rd, Forest Grove; 503/357-6604) has produced some fine, ageable chardonnays, and **TUALATIN ESTATE VINEYARDS** (10850 NW Seavey Rd, Forest Grove; 503/357-5005) produces exquisite chardonnay, as well as an excellent Müller Thurgau. Finally, just outside of town you can sample sake from **MOMOKAWA SAKE** (820 Elm St, Forest Grove; 503/357-7056), where quality rice wines are brewed on-site.

RESTAURANTS

El Torero / ★

2009 MAIN ST, FOREST GROVE; 503/359-8471 You may have a tough time getting past the terrific light, crisp chips, but if you do, you'll probably end up devouring all your excellent *frijoles refritos*. For the main course, stick with specialty beef items—the massive serving of *carnitas de res* is super. Fajitas are a favorite of regulars, and the *camarones a la diabla* are devilishly good. The decor is college hangout, but service is friendly and English (authentically) limited. *$; DIS, MC, V; checks OK; lunch, dinner every day; full bar; reservations recommended for large groups; just off Hwy 8.* &

Lake Oswego, West Linn, and Oregon City

South of Portland, these three towns have differing characters and qualities but taken together make a nice excursion. You might start with a walk in Lake Oswego's 645-acre **TRYON CREEK STATE PARK** (11321 SW Terwilliger Blvd, Lake Oswego; 503/636-9886), where—in early spring—you'll see the trillium light up the hiking trails. The scenic campus of **LEWIS AND CLARK COLLEGE** (0615 SW Palatine Hill Rd; 503/768-7000) is nearby, as is the lake itself, though swimming and boating access is private.

Next, drive south on Highway 43 to Interstate 205 and go east to historic Oregon City. Visit the **END OF THE OREGON TRAIL INTERPRETIVE CENTER** (1726 Washington St, Oregon City; 503/657-9336), with its easy-to-spot covered-wagon architecture. See what it was like coming to Oregon 150 years ago—but call ahead for show times. You won't be allowed into the multimedia presentation unless you're on the tour, except to see a few exhibits and the well-stocked museum store.

RESTAURANTS

Bugatti's Ristorante / ★★

18740 WILLAMETTE DR, WEST LINN; 503/636-9555 Lydia Bugatti and John Cress's endearing Italian neighborhood restaurant features seasonal foods and nightly specials. Keep watch for rigatoni carbonara, the salmon saltimbocca, or the veal scaloppine with chanterelle mushrooms in a rosemary-Dijon sauce. Other menu favorites are *vongole* (Manilla clams in a garlicky white wine sauce served over linguine) and cioppino d'oro—shellfish, shrimp and salmon in a saffron white wine sauce. There's a nice olive oil spiked with garlic for bread dipping, but save room for dazzling desserts such as the cloudlike tiramisu. The atmosphere is comfortably elegant—but not fussy. *$$; MC, V; local checks only; dinner every day; beer and wine; reservations recommended; south of Lake Oswego on Hwy 43.*

COLUMBIA RIVER GORGE AND MOUNT HOOD

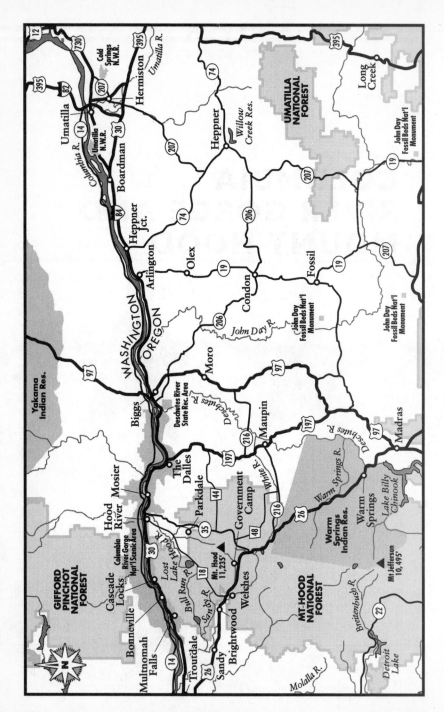

COLUMBIA RIVER GORGE AND MOUNT HOOD

Cataclysmic Ice-Age floods carved the Columbia Gorge about 15,000 years ago, leaving cliffs as high as 4,000 feet. Streams plunged into the newly created canyon, becoming the waterfalls that still grace the gorge's steep, craggy walls. Until the Columbia River Highway opened in 1915, views of the gorge were enjoyed mainly by Native Americans, who for centuries netted salmon from the Columbia River, and by Oregon Trail pioneers, who reached the Willamette Valley either via the river or across the flanks of Mount Hood. The highway, built to display the gorge rather than to blemish it, was an engineering marvel of its day, featuring intricate stonework, arched bridges, viaducts, tunnels, and lookout points. For a memorable excursion, drive a stretch of the old highway from Troutdale to Multnomah Falls.

On the western edge of The Dalles, the beautifully designed Columbia Gorge Discovery Center offers a look at the gorge from prehistory to the present. Hood River, the gorge's only other real city, is the sailboard capital of the Pacific Northwest, and has been long renowned for its fruit trees. A drive on Highway 35 takes you past acres of apple, pear, peach, and cherry orchards, and eventually to the snowy slopes of Mount Hood.

The mountain's crown jewel, Timberline Lodge, is worth a visit in any season. President Franklin D. Roosevelt dedicated it in 1937, praising the masons, craftsmen, and artists who made this mountain lodge an enduring classic. High above the lodge, lifts ferry skiers and snowboarders to Palmer Snowfield nearly year-round. In 1845 Joel Palmer stood here to scout what would become the last leg of the Oregon Trail, Barlow Road. At several places westward along US Highway 26, you can still see wagon ruts cut into the ground, indelible traces of the first white settlers.

ACCESS AND INFORMATION

The Columbia River Gorge and Mount Hood are most commonly approached from Portland, via **INTERSTATE 84** east; follow the freeway through the gorge to Hood River and The Dalles. Another option is exiting at Troutdale to follow the **HISTORIC COLUMBIA RIVER HIGHWAY,** or cutting over to **HIGHWAY 26** and heading southeast to Mount Hood.

In winter, usually after mid-November, traction devices are required on Mount Hood. Call the **OREGON DEPARTMENT OF TRANSPORTATION** (503/588-2941 outside of Oregon or 800/977-6368; www.odot.state.or.us/travel/) to see if roads are snowy or icy on Mount Hood. The online Travel Advisor (www.tripcheck.com) has excellent, up-to-date information on road conditions. Also, an Oregon Department of Transportation **WINTER SNO-PARK PERMIT** is required if you plan to stop. Permits are sold at Timberline Lodge (see review), as well as service stations, Department of Motor Vehicle offices, and sporting goods stores in the gorge and on the mountain: $3 for one day; $7 for two days; $15 for the season.

GREYHOUND (503/243-2357 or 800/231-2222) has daily bus service up the Columbia River Gorge from Portland, stopping at Hood River and The Dalles, as well as service from Portland to Government Camp on Mount Hood.

The **COLUMBIA RIVER GORGE VISITORS ASSOCIATION** (2149 W Cascade Ave #106A, Hood River; 800/984-6743; www.gorge.net/crgva) and **MOUNT HOOD INFORMATION CENTER** (65000 E Hwy 26, Welches; 503/622-4822 or 888/622-4822; www.mthood.org) provide tourist information.

Columbia River Gorge National Scenic Area

The Columbia River Gorge National Scenic Area was created by an act of Congress in 1986 to shield the river corridor from rapacious development, while also fostering and guiding industry in designated urban areas. It begins near the mouth of the Sandy River, near Troutdale, and ends at the Deschutes River, east of The Dalles. It encompasses 292,500 acres in Oregon and Washington.

Troutdale

Named for the town founder's trout ponds, Troutdale was a welcome sight to Oregon Trail pioneers who rafted their covered wagons here from about 40 miles up the Columbia River. From the freeway, Troutdale looks like a jarring assortment of truck stops, factory outlets, and fast-food joints. But behind all the neon you'll find the town's heart, a quaint street of antique shops, galleries, and cafes that marks the beginning of the **HISTORIC COLUMBIA RIVER HIGHWAY,** built in 1913–15. Until it merges with Interstate 84, 5 miles east of Multnomah Falls, the highway winds along 22 miles of breathtaking views and awesome waterfalls. **THE VISTA HOUSE** (40700 E Historic Columbia River Hwy; 503/695-2230) at Crown Point, constructed in 1916–18 as a rest stop, sits atop a 733-foot-high cliff. Built of stone, its interior features a marble floor, stairs, wainscoting, ornate carvings, stained glass, and other decorative elements. It's open May 1 through October 15, and has historic displays, a gift shop, and rest rooms. For more information contact the **TROUTDALE CHAMBER OF COMMERCE** (338 E Historic Columbia River Hwy; 503/669-7473).

RESTAURANTS

Multnomah Falls Lodge

53000 HISTORIC COLUMBIA RIVER HWY 30 E, BRIDAL VEIL; 503/695-2376 Designed by Portland architect A. E. Doyle, this rustic lodge was built in 1925 with every type of stone found in the gorge. For a great view of the falls, sit in the restaurant's back room. The food is basic but satisfying (sandwiches at lunch; prime rib and salmon at dinner), especially when it follows a vigorous hike. A bigleaf maple forms the backdrop to the cozy bar; try to nab a seat on the Mission-style couch by the fireplace. *$$; AE, DIS, MC, V; no checks; breakfast, lunch, dinner every day, brunch Sun; full bar; reservations not necessary; www.multnomahfallslodge.com; exit 31 from I-84.* &

Tad's Chicken 'n' Dumplins

1325 E HISTORIC COLUMBIA RIVER HWY, TROUTDALE; 503/666-5337 Tired of trendy Northwest cuisine? Then plan a dinner at Tad's, where comfort food is served up without a hint of fake sophisticated irony. Though stewed chicken is the signature dish, Tad's is also a good place for seafood. Come prepared to wait, especially

COLUMBIA RIVER GORGE THREE-DAY TOUR

DAY ONE: Begin in Troutdale after spending the night at **MCMENAMIN'S EDGEFIELD;** enjoy your complimentary breakfast, then head east on a 22-mile stretch of the **HISTORIC COLUMBIA RIVER HIGHWAY,** across the Sandy River and into the hills above the Columbia River Gorge. Follow the highway to Multnomah Falls and stop for a hike and lunch at **MULTNOMAH FALLS LODGE.** (It's a steep 1-mile hike on a mostly paved trail to the head of the falls.) Get on Interstate 84 and drive to the **BONNEVILLE DAM** visitor center. Watch fish swim up the fish ladder, then check out the giant sturgeon at the **BONNEVILLE FISH HATCHERY.** For the rest of the afternoon, either stop in Cascade Locks and ride the **STERN-WHEELER** *Columbia Gorge* or continue east to Hood River and ride the rails on the **MOUNT HOOD RAILROAD** past apple, pear, apricot, and cherry orchards. No matter how you spend the afternoon, enjoy dinner at the **NORTH OAK BRASSERIE** in Hood River and bed down at the elegant **COLUMBIA GORGE HOTEL** or, for budget travelers, next door at the **VAGABOND LODGE.**

DAY TWO: Eat the bountiful farmhouse breakfast at the Columbia Gorge Hotel and head east. At Mosier, exit the freeway and take a walk along the hiker/biker stretch of the **HISTORIC COLUMBIA RIVER HIGHWAY STATE TRAIL.** Back in your car, head east along another 9-mile stretch of the historic highway to **ROWENA CREST** viewpoint and the **TOM MCCALL PRESERVE.** Stop at the crest to take in a spectacular view and acres of wildflowers and native plants. Continue east along the historic highway to The Dalles, and lunch at the **BALDWIN SALOON.** Spend a couple of hours going through the **COLUMBIA GORGE DISCOVERY CENTER** and adjoining **WASCO COUNTY HISTORICAL MUSEUM.** Return west to Hood River for dinner at **ABRUZZO,** then head 15 miles south on Highway 35 to the **MOUNT HOOD HAMLET BED & BREAKFAST** for the night.

DAY THREE: When you open your eyes and look out your bedroom window, you'll think Mount Hood is close enough to touch. Take your time; you're almost there. After a leisurely breakfast, have a soak in the outdoor spa with its heated deck. Drive south and then west over Bennett and Barlow Passes to Government Camp. Have a late lunch here, perhaps a gourmet personal pizza, at **THE BREW PUB AT MOUNT HOOD BREWING CO.** Spend the afternoon hiking and exploring the mountain. You'll work up an appetite for dinner at the **CASCADE DINING ROOM** at **TIMBERLINE LODGE,** and be ready to sink into bed while the snowy peak of Mount Hood shimmers in moonlight.

on weekends. But even the wait can be pleasant—Tad's is right on the Sandy River. *$; AE, MC, V; checks OK; dinner every day; full bar; reservations not accepted; just south of the east end of Sandy River bridge.* &

LODGINGS

McMenamin's Edgefield / ★

🌲 **2126 SW HALSEY ST, TROUTDALE; 503/669-8610 OR 800/669-8610** Built in 1911 as the county poor farm, Edgefield was transformed by local microbrew barons Mike and Brian McMenamin into a sprawling complex of lodging, libations, eateries, golf, and a cinema. About 100 rooms, most with shared bathrooms, all free of telephones and TVs, are furnished with 1930s-era furniture and brightened by whimsical paintings. The murals and paintings on doors and walls are a virtual gallery of ex-hippie artistry, and there's plenty to do, from golfing on the 18-hole par-3 course to catching a recent release at the Power Station Movie Theater to strolling the gardens on the 38-acre estate. Choose from several bars—with much of the beer, wine, and spirits produced on-site—for lunches and dinners. Guests are served a complimentary breakfast in the Black Rabbit Restaurant. *$$; AE, MC, V; checks OK; edge@mcmenaminspubs.com; www.mcmenamins.com; Wood Village exit off I-84, south to Halsey St, turn left, drive ½ mile to Edgefield sign on right.* &

Cascade Locks

The cascades (rapids) here were once so treacherous that boats had to be portaged. Navigational locks built in 1896 solved the problem, but when Bonneville Dam was built in 1937 and the river behind it rose 60 feet, the locks, for which this town was named, were submerged. Now the former home of the lock tender is a museum, next door to the ticket office for the **STERN-WHEELER COLUMBIA GORGE** (Cascade Locks Marina Park, 355 Wa-Na-Pa St; 541/374-8427; www.sternwheeler.com). This 600-passenger replica of turn-of-the-century paddle-wheel riverboats that used to churn their way east from Portland makes three two-hour narrated excursions daily, as well as brunch and dinner cruises. Between Thanksgiving and New Year's, the stern-wheeler sails out of Portland; call for scheduling details.

Just west of town is **BONNEVILLE DAM** (exit 40 from I-84 or Hwy 14; 541/374-8820), built in 1937, and the 1909 **BONNEVILLE FISH HATCHERY** (541/374-8393). No matter what you may think of hatchery programs, it's worth stopping to visit the giant green sturgeon at the nicely landscaped hatchery. One dam visitor center is on Bradford Island and another is on the Washington shore, at the second powerhouse, built in 1981. At the navigational locks, built in 1993, watch barges and boats moving up- or downriver.

A perfect spot for watching river traffic is **CHARBURGER** (714 SW Wa-Na-Pa St; 541/374-8477), a cafeteria-style restaurant with great burgers and homemade pie. From a booth next to the large windows, you can admire the river and the graceful **BRIDGE OF THE GODS,** a cantilever toll bridge built in 1926 to link Oregon and Washington. The bridge is also part of the 2,000-mile Pacific Crest National Scenic Trail, which runs from Mexico to Canada.

For more information contact the **CASCADE LOCKS VISITOR CENTER** (Cascade Locks Marina Park; 541/374-8619).

Hood River

Once known simply for the glorious fruit orchards in the neighboring hills, Hood River has broadened its appeal. The vibrant town owes its renaissance to the adventurers who come from all points of the globe to launch sailboards on the Columbia River. The closest of Mount Hood's five ski areas is just 27 miles away; a multitude of hiking and biking trails are similarly close. What better location for July's annual **GORGE GAMES** (541/386-7774), with windsurfing, mountain biking, paragliding, kayaking, and other sports. Rent gear or sign up for lessons at the **GORGE SURF SHOP** (13 Oak St; 541/386-1699; www.gorgesurfshop.com).

The Hood River valley's rich volcanic soil continues to support thousands of fruit trees, particularly pears, which make up 75 percent of the fruit grown here. Pick your own fruit, or buy from roadside stands along Highway 35 south of town. For more information, contact the **HOOD RIVER COUNTY CHAMBER OF COMMERCE** (405 Portway Ave; 541/386-2000 or 800/366-3530; www.gorge.net/fruitloop). Trees are beautiful in spring, when they blossom, kicking off a months-long series of festivals, highlighted by the **HOOD RIVER VALLEY BLOSSOM FESTIVAL** in April and October's **HOOD RIVER VALLEY HARVEST FESTIVAL**.

The Fruit Blossom Special, a spring rail excursion through the orchards, is one of many special-occasion trips on the **MOUNT HOOD RAILROAD** (110 Railroad Ave; 541/386-3556 or 800/872-4661; www.mthoodrr.com). The restored trains depart from the historic 1911 depot and follow their original route through the valley, past packing plants, lumber mills, and orchards. Excursion trains and brunch or dinner trains run regularly from March through mid-December.

Old and new mix comfortably in Hood River. **FRANZ HARDWARE** (116 Oak St; 541/386-1141) has been owned and operated by the same family since 1909, and still sells nails and bolts individually. Just up the street, at **ANNZPANZ** (315 Oak St; 541/387-2654), you'll find stylish cookware alongside a gourmet's lunch counter. Across the street at **WAUCOMA BOOKS** (212 Oak St; 541/386-5353) are books for every taste and age and local pottery. Visit elaborately carved carousel animals at the **INTERNATIONAL MUSEUM OF CAROUSEL ART** (304 Oak St; 541/387-4622), then stop by **FULL SAIL BREWERY AND PUB** (506 Columbia St; 541/386-2247) for a tour and a taste of some of Oregon's best microbrews.

RESTAURANTS

Abruzzo / ★★

1810 W CASCADE ST, HOOD RIVER; 541/386-7779 This small, unpretentious olive-green building on the busy commercial strip just west of downtown is easy to miss. Originally a minimart and ice-cream store, then a Mexican restaurant, it's been transformed into a warm, cheerful Italian restaurant. The cement floors and wood tabletops lend an informal note, enhanced by the friendly staff. Locals gather here to eat huge plates of pasta topped with rich sauces, many featuring pancetta or tasty Italian sausage. *$; MC, V; local checks OK; dinner Tues–Sat; full bar; reservations not accepted; west of downtown on north side of Cascade St.* &

The Big Easy Cajun Barbeque / ★

1302 "B" ST, HOOD RIVER; 541/386-1970 Fun without being goofy or forced, and sophisticated without a hint of stuffiness—some would say that's the New Orleans way. Oregonians can pull it off too, as Big Easy proves. The newest of Mike and Shawna Caldwell's three outstanding Hood River restaurants, it has a Cajun theme, and the menu includes such standards as po'boy sandwiches, crawfish étouffée, and jambalaya (veggie and seafood versions are available). Don't skip the fresh, briney oyster shooters or the velvety corn, shrimp, and sweet potato bisque. The food is not highly spiced but is served with a variety of hot sauces on the side. In summer, there's outside seating, but tables inside this converted house are also pleasant. *$$; AE, DIS, MC, V; checks OK; dinner every day; full bar; reservations not accepted; www.hood riverrestaurants.com; corner of 13th St and "B" St.*

North Oak Brasserie / ★★

113 3RD ST, HOOD RIVER; 541/387-2310 The adventure begins when you descend a stairway from the sidewalk to the basement level. Inside, you enter a place apart from the sporty sunny bluster of Hood River, a place that's at once a cozy locals' lunch spot and a sophisticated wine lovers' bistro. Owners Mike and Shawna Caldwell make a great team; Mike, the former cellarmaster at Flerchinger Vineyards, selected about 150 wines for a list that complements the food. Shawna, a former art teacher, gave the basement a warm Mediterranean glow and added her touch to the menu. A shiitake mushroom ravioli whets your appetite for entrees such as a pork chop stuffed with Italian sausage and mushrooms, served with Calvados sauce, Hood River pears, and garlic potatoes. Kids are welcome. *$$; AE, DIS, MC, V; checks OK; lunch, dinner every day; full bar; reservations recommended; northoak@gorge.net; www.hoodriverrestaurants.com; downtown, at Oak St.*

Sixth Street Bistro & Loft / ★

509 CASCADE AVE, HOOD RIVER; 541/386-5737 Upstairs are a pool table, nine microbrews on tap, a tandem bike hanging from the ceiling, and clever art reproductions painted right on the walls. Pastas and sandwiches satisfy the lunch crowd. Downstairs, tables are set with white linen. That's where dinner—perhaps T-bone steak with garlic mashed potatoes and sautéed kale; salmon; seared halibut with couscous and vegetables; or linguine with scallops and shrimp—is served, along with the restaurant's popular herb bread, baked fresh daily. On summer nights, sit under the maple tree on the patio. *$$; MC, V; local checks only; breakfast, lunch, dinner every day; full bar; reservations recommended in summer; at 6th St.* &

Stonehedge Gardens / ★★

3405 CASCADE DR, HOOD RIVER; 541/386-3940 The approach is the same as ever: drive up a winding gravel road to the historic house built in 1908 as a summer residence for a prominent Portland family. But much has changed at the Stonehedge since Hood River über-restaurateurs Mike and Shawna Caldwell took over in 2000. The biggest updates are a huge five-level, landscaped garden area that houses dozens of tables, making this the best outdoor dining in the gorge. Inside, the old house is charming but a little shabby. In or out, the food is delicious, and portions generous. "Light dinners," including polenta or seared ahi tuna, are reasonably priced. The Caldwells and their engaging staff have changed the Stonehedge from a place that was a tad inapproachable into a comfortable spot that doesn't scream "special occasions only." *$$; AE, DIS, MC, V; checks OK; dinner every day; full bar; reservations recommended; exit 62 off I-84, look for sign on south side of Cascade Dr, follow gravel road for ⅓ mile.* &

LODGINGS

Columbia Gorge Hotel / ★★☆

4000 WESTCLIFF DR, HOOD RIVER; 541/386-5566 OR 800/345-1921
Timber baron Simon Benson built his luxury hotel in 1921 to accommodate motorists on the new Columbia River Highway; it's now on the National Register of Historic Places. This Spanish-style, golden stucco beauty with green shutters and a red-tile roof has elegant, spacious common areas, but many rooms are a tad cozy. Some larger suites have fireplaces; a few rooms have polished brass or canopy beds. Enjoy acres of beautiful gardens, stone bridges, and a 208-foot waterfall cascading to the Columbia. The hotel features nightly entertainment, and evening turndown service includes a rose and chocolate. Included in the room rate is the five-course "World Famous Farm Breakfast," with eggs, pancakes, fresh fruit, and oatmeal. *$$$; AE, DIS, MC, V; checks OK; cghotel@gorge.net; www.columbiagorgehotel.com; 1 mile west of Hood River, exit 62 off I-84.* &

Hood River Hotel / ★

102 OAK AVE, HOOD RIVER; 541/386-1900 OR 800/386-1859 This sweet old downtown hotel was built in 1912 as the annex to the long-gone Mount Hood Hotel. The lobby, with inviting chairs and a fireplace, is a pleasant place to relax; the rooms themselves are small and, though tastefully decorated with antique reproductions, not overly fancy. As with all gorge hotels, there's a bit of noise from night trains and highway traffic. The river view rooms aren't really worth the extra fee (the parking lot and the Mount Hood Railroad depot are much more prominent than the river) and the "rooftop garden" also houses the hotel's HVAC equipment. All that said, it's still a charming hotel in a prime downtown location. *$$; AE, DIS, MC, V; checks OK; hrhotel@gorge.net; www.hoodriverhotel.com; at 1st Ave.* &

Pheasant Valley Orchards Bed and Breakfast / ★★

3890 ACREE DR, HOOD RIVER; 541/386-2803 Nestled in the foothills of Mount Hood, this delightful farmhouse overlooks 40 acres of organic pear and apple orchards. Working farmers Scott and Gail Hagee opened their home as a B&B in spring 2001, but continue to grow, pack, and ship eight varieties of pears and apples. Comfortably off the beaten path, the cheerfully decorated house welcomes travelers with two large living rooms and a wide view porch. Upstairs rooms feature private baths and a lovely view of the orchards, mountains, and surrounding Hood River valley. The main floor suite has a shared bath and looks out into the orchard. The slightly more expensive Comice Suite is considerably larger than the other guest rooms and includes a king-sized bed, Jacuzzi tub, and long private deck. Any jealousies over room size and bath jets are forgotten, however, when you sit down to breakfast (which always features fresh fruits from the orchard), sip hot coffee, and look out the large windows at towering Mount Hood. The Hagees are also full of ideas for activities in Hood River or day trips. *$$; MC, V; checks OK; innkeeper@ pheasantvalleyorchards.com; www.pheasantvalleyorchards.com; about 5 miles south of downtown Hood River, ½ mile east of Tucker Rd on Acree Dr.*

Vagabond Lodge

4070 WESTCLIFF DR, HOOD RIVER; 541/386-2992 Turn in just past the cement buffalo to find one of Hood River's best lodging values. The motel itself wins no beauty prizes, but if you ask for a riverfront room you'll get an outstanding view at a good price. Several suites are available, including some with kitchens. The Vagabond, on 4 acres in a parklike setting with a playground, is right next door to the Columbia Gorge Hotel (see review), where folks pay about $100 more for the same views. For an evening stroll, cut across the parking lot to the fancier hotel's gardens. *$; AE, DC, DIS, MC, V; no checks; jcranmer@gorge. net; www.vagabondlodge.com; go west on Westcliff Dr past Columbia Gorge Hotel.*

Mosier

This quiet town of 365 was livelier when orchards, lumber mills, and sawmills were operating, and motorists taking their Model Ts out on the highway stopped for refreshment. It's still a good place to take a spin on the Historic Columbia River Highway. Follow a 9-mile stretch of the old highway east to The Dalles, ascending to **ROWENA CREST,** a high bluff overlooking the gorge, and the **TOM MCCALL PRESERVE,** a 230-acre Nature Conservancy refuge for native plants, including rare and endangered wildflowers. Trailhead parking is just beyond mile 6 on Historic Highway 30. A 1-mile trail leads along the plateau, and a 3-mile trail gains 1,000 feet in elevation and is open only May through November.

About a half mile west of town, along Rock Creek Road, is the **HISTORIC COLUMBIA RIVER HIGHWAY STATE TRAIL,** a 4½-mile hiking, biking, and wheelchair-accessible trail along the old highway to Hood River, passing through the **MOSIER TWIN TUNNELS.** The tunnels, which took highway engineers two years to complete in 1921, proved too narrow for modern cars, but are perfect for cyclists.

LODGINGS

Mosier House Bed & Breakfast / ★

704 3RD AVE, MOSIER; 541/478-3640 This beautiful 1904 Queen Anne home was built by Jefferson Newton Mosier, son of the town's founder and a civic leader in his own right. Sitting on a knoll with a great view of the river (and some rumble from Interstate 84), his lovingly restored home is on the National Register of Historic Places. Up the wooden staircase are four rooms with shared baths; the master guest room has a private bath (with a claw-footed tub and shower) and a private entrance and porch. An abundant breakfast is served in the dining room, which overlooks nicely tended gardens. *$$; MC, V; checks OK; innkeeper@mosier house.com; www.mosierhouse.com; turn up Washington St and go left on 3rd St.*

WATERFALL TOUR

More than 70 waterfalls line the Oregon shore of the Columbia River Gorge. Driving Interstate 84, you can look up and see many falls cascading (or trickling) down towering, moss-covered cliffs. For more information, contact the **TROUTDALE CHAMBER OF COMMERCE** (338 E Historic Columbia River Hwy, Troutdale; 503/669-7473).

For a better view, start at the **VISTA HOUSE AT CROWN POINT** (40700 E Historic Columbia River Hwy, Corbett; 503/695-2230). From that breathtaking viewpoint, 733 feet above the river, wind down the scenic Historic Columbia River Highway until it parallels the freeway. Hugging the hillside, the old road comes so close to a series of dramatic waterfalls that you may even have to switch on your windshield wipers to clear away the mist. Most roadside falls have parking lots, picnic tables, and hiking trails; some have restrooms.

You'll see **LATOURELL FALLS** as you cross a lovely bridge that arches over the water rushing to the Columbia. A short distance away is **SHEPPERD'S DELL,** named for the family that once owned the property.

Like a blushing bride, **BRIDAL VEIL FALLS** hides from motorists. It can be seen by taking a ⅔-mile round-trip hike from the parking lot.

WAHKEENA FALLS is part of the property that lumber baron Simon Benson donated to the city of Portland, along with its famous neighbor to the east, Multnomah Falls. A ¼-mile trail leads to a bridge over the 242-foot falls' lower tier. *Wahkeena*, a Yakama Indian word meaning "most beautiful," is just a warmup for what's to come: 642-foot **MULTNOMAH FALLS,** the nation's second-largest year-round waterfall. A trail leads to the bridge overlooking the lower falls.

ONEONTA GORGE, just beyond Multnomah Falls, is for the truly adventurous. The falls at the end can be reached only by hiking the riverbed upstream. The wildflowers and rare plants growing along the narrow gorge make drenching your sneakers worthwhile.

Finally, before the old highway joins Interstate 84 at Ainsworth State Park, **HORSE-TAIL FALLS** is so close to the road, it practically swishes you in the face. Hiking trails lead to various points along the 176-foot falls, as well as to an upper cascade called Pony Tail Falls.

—*Susan Hauser*

The Dalles

French traders and voyageurs dubbed this point on the river Le Dalle, meaning "the trough," after fierce rapids that flowed through a narrow channel, now covered by the reservoir behind The Dalles Dam. Lewis and Clark shot those rapids in large canoes, then camped at Rock Fort, just west of what is now downtown The Dalles. About 40 years later, The Dalles became the decision point for Oregon Trail pioneers. From here they either hired rafts to float their wagons downriver, or continued on a land route southwest across Mount Hood's foothills. Samuel Barlow blazed the trail in 1845, then charged a toll for wagons and livestock. Although travelers on the Barlow Road avoided an arduous river journey, their trip was just as difficult and dangerous.

Be sure to spend several hours at the **COLUMBIA GORGE DISCOVERY CENTER** and the adjoining **WASCO COUNTY HISTORICAL MUSEUM** (5000 Discovery Dr; 541/296-8600), which overlooks the river 3 miles west of town. You'll learn about the origins of the Columbia River Gorge and the history of the area, including Native Americans, Lewis and Clark, and the Oregon Trail. Interactive exhibits bring you up to date, even offering a simulated ride on a sailboard. **FORT DALLES MUSEUM** (15th and Garrison Sts; 541/296-4547), housed in the fort's 1857 surgeon's quarters, has its own collection of memorabilia from pioneer days. **ST. PETER'S LANDMARK** (3rd and Lincoln Sts; 541/296-5686), an 1898 Gothic Revival church, was built of local red brick and adorned with stained-glass windows made by Portland's famed Povey Brothers. The spire is adorned with a 6-foot rooster.

At **THE DALLES DAM** (2 miles east of The Dalles, off I-84; 541/296-9778), a free train tour departs from the visitor center and makes stops at the dam, powerhouse, fish ladders, and a picnic area.

Seventeen miles east of The Dalles is **DESCHUTES STATE PARK** (just off I-84) on the Deschutes River, renowned for steelhead and trout fishing, and white-water rafting. The park has a campground with RV hookups, hiking and biking trails, fishing, and swimming.

RESTAURANTS

Bailey's Place / ★

515 LIBERTY ST, THE DALLES; 541/296-6708 This is a reincarnation of the beloved Ole's Supper Club, which literally fell down around itself in 1998. Ross and Laura Bailey, who also owned Ole's, subsequently opened Bailey's in an 1865 Victorian home that's on the National Register of Historic Places. The high Italianate windows with lace curtains, the quiet tables dressed in white linen, and the soft jazz playing in the background set the mood. Prime rib is the most requested menu item; seafood is also well represented and very popular. The extensive, reasonably priced wine list has a reputation all its own and reflects the Baileys' expertise. A full bar—and a view—are in the upstairs lounge. *$$; AE, MC, V; checks OK; dinner Tues–Sat; full bar; reservations recommended; at 4th St.* &

Baldwin Saloon / ★

205 COURT ST, THE DALLES; 541/296-5666 After stints as a steamboat office, a warehouse, a coffin storage site, an employment office, and a saddlery, the 1876 Baldwin Saloon has returned to its roots, right down to the original brick walls and fir floor. Gracing those walls and flanking the antique mahogany bar is an impressive collection of turn-of-the-century Northwest landscape oil paintings. Seafood's a specialty here—try Salmon Rockefeller with parmesan sauce, one of the chef's favorites (he also serves the Rockefeller sauce, made with spinach and licorice liqueur, on oysters). The long list of homemade desserts includes a Snickers-like mousse. *$; MC, V; checks OK; lunch, dinner Mon–Sat; full bar; reservations recommended for 6 or more; at 1st St.* &

Mount Hood

Topping out at 11,245 feet, Mount Hood is Oregon's highest point. Dotted with lakes, campgrounds, and hiking and biking trails, the mountain has abundant recreation year-round. Its five ski areas attract skiers and snowboarders of all levels.

From the east via Hood River, drive 27 miles south on Highway 35 and you'll first encounter **COOPER SPUR** (11000 Cloud Cap Rd; 541/352-7803; www.cooper spur.com), elevation 4,500 feet, on the north side of the mountain. It's an inexpensive day- and night-ski area popular with beginners, with a T-bar and rope tow. Next you'll come to **MOUNT HOOD MEADOWS** (2 miles north of Hwy 35 on Forest Rd 3555; 503/337-2222; www.skihood.com). At 7,300 feet elevation, it's the largest area on the mountain, with 87 runs, four high-speed quads, six double chairlifts, and a Nordic center with groomed tracks, instructors, and rentals. Many of the lodgings in the Hood River–Mount Hood area offer bargain-priced Meadows lift tickets to their guests.

From Portland, drive 53 miles east on Highway 26 to the town of **GOVERNMENT CAMP**, so named because a contingent of U.S. Army Rifles (mounted riflemen) wintered here in 1849. Here you'll find **MOUNT HOOD SKIBOWL** (87000 E Hwy 26; 503/272-3206 or 503/222-2695, recorded information; www.skibowl.com), at 5,026 feet, America's largest night-ski area with 34 lighted runs, four double chairlifts, and a tubing hill. At 4,306 feet, **SUMMIT** (54 miles east of Portland on Hwy 26, near rest area at east end of Government Camp; 503/272-0256) is good for beginners, or families who want to slide on inner tubes; ski and tube rentals are available. At 6,000 feet, **TIMBERLINE** (4 miles north of Hwy 26, just east of Government Camp; 503/622-7979; www.timberlinelodge.com) has six lifts; four—including Palmer Lift, which takes skiers up to Palmer Snowfield for year-round skiing—are high-speed quads.

Timberline is popular with people who never want to put their skis away, including the U.S. Ski Team, which trains here in summer. Summer also offers plenty of hiking, biking, horseback riding, golf, and other sports. The **MOUNT HOOD SKI-BOWL SUMMER ACTION PARK** (87000 E Hwy 26; 503/272-3206 or 503/222-2695, recorded information; www.skibowl.com; open 11am–6pm weekdays and 10am–7pm weekends) boasts more than 25 summertime activities, including a ½-mile dual alpine slide, Indy Karts, miniature golf, croquet, bungee jumping, a mountain-bike park with 40 miles of trails, horseback and pony rides, batting cages, volleyball, horseshoes, and other attractions. Get an all-day pass or pay for individual activities.

Climbers who want to scale the mountain's 11,235 feet must register and obtain a free mandatory wilderness permit in the 24-hour climbing room of Timberline's Wy'east Day Lodge. Guided climbs are available through **TIMBERLINE MOUNTAIN GUIDES** (541/312-9242). Recreation on the south side of Mount Hood (the easiest climbing route) is managed by the **ZIGZAG RANGER DISTRICT** (503/622-3191).

TIMBERLINE LODGE (see review) is another popular stop for summer visitors. From here, the Palmer Snowfield is accessible even to nonskiers. It takes just 6 minutes to travel the **MAGIC MILE SUPER EXPRESS** chairlift 1,000 vertical feet to Palmer Junction. The Magic Mile Interpretive Trail leads back to Timberline Lodge.

RESTAURANTS

The Brew Pub at Mount Hood Brewing Co. / ★

87304 E GOVERNMENT CAMP LOOP HWY, GOVERNMENT CAMP; 503/272-3724 Tuck into an armchair and look out onto the snow from this warm, inviting pub. If you're not driving back down the mountain, sample such bold brews as a strong Scottish ale, a porter, a barleywine, and an oatmeal stout. Spring visitors should try Illumination Ale, a unique herbal ale flavored with tea, elderberries and elder flowers, ginger, and a host of other flowers and herbs. Fill up on Tuscan-style white pizza, topped with garlic dressing, spinach, red onion, zucchini, asparagus, red pepper, oregano, and a three-cheese blend. The extensive kids' menu includes quesadillas, burgers, and grilled cheese sandwiches. *$; AE, DIS, MC, V; checks OK; lunch, dinner every day; beer and wine; reservations not necessary; pubinfo@mthoodbrewing.com; www.mthoodbrewing.com; west end of Government Camp, next to Mount Hood Inn.* &

Cascade Dining Room / ★★★

TIMBERLINE LODGE, TIMBERLINE; 503/622-0700 Beyond the hand-forged iron gate on the lodge's second level is the Cascade Dining Room, renowned for 20 years for the award-winning cuisine of executive chef Leif Eric Benson. Don't let the rustic setting fool you; the food here is very sophisticated, with a wine list to match. Although Benson is Swiss, he loves to showcase foods of the Northwest, such as skewers of quail with a pomegranate molasses glaze, Tazo tea–roasted salmon fillet, or apple wood–smoked prime rib. The fine food and service are two reasons many Portlanders make the drive here for special occasions. *$$$; AE, MC, V; checks OK; breakfast, lunch, dinner every day; full bar; reservations recommended; food@timberlinelodge.com; www.timberlinelodge.com; 60 miles east of Portland off Hwy 26.* &

LODGINGS

Falcon's Crest Inn / ★★

87287 GOVERNMENT CAMP LOOP HWY, GOVERNMENT CAMP; 541/272-3403 OR 800/624-7384 This Government Camp B&B is a good base for groups of friends or extended families. On both the second and third floors, a central lounge area is dominated by floor-to-ceiling windows and flanked by bedrooms, including the exuberantly decorated Safari Room and the more subdued Mexicalli Suite, complete with a Jacuzzi for two. With advance notice, hosts Bob and Melody Johnson will prepare an elaborate six-course dinner (you don't need to stay at the inn to eat dinner here, but reservations are a must). *$$$; AE, DIS, MC, V; checks OK; info@falconscrest. com; www.falconscrest.com; just off Loop Rd, on north side.*

Mount Hood Hamlet Bed & Breakfast / ★★

6741 HWY 35, MOUNT HOOD; 541/352-3574 OR 800/407-0570 The newly built 18th-century-style New England colonial sits on a hill overlooking the farm where owner Paul Romans was raised. After careers as schoolteachers, he and his wife, Diane, returned and built this gorgeous house, inspired by the family's ancestral home in Rhode Island. Three second-floor guest rooms have pri-

NATIVE AMERICAN FISHING

For centuries the shores of the Columbia River were a meeting ground for Native Americans who came from hundreds—even thousands—of miles away to trade. The commodity that local tribes traded was like gold—red gold. It was the flavorful and nourishing meat, either fresh or dried, of the wild salmon. You can still see Native Americans from the Umatilla, Nez Perce, Warm Springs, or Yakama tribes fishing with dip nets from the river's shore, often from wooden platforms.

CELILO FALLS, flooded and filled when The Dalles Dam was built in 1957, was a vital fishing area for about 10,000 years. Petroglyphs and pictographs preserved near The Dalles attest to the native peoples' ancient presence. The touring train at the dam (see The Dalles) takes you to **PETROGLYPH WALL,** where pictures of faces, animals, figures, spirals, spirits, and symbols are displayed. The famous petroglyph, Tsagaglalal—"She Who Watches"—is on the Washington shore at Horsethief State Park. It and other petroglyphs there may be seen only on ranger-guided tours (509/767-1159; 10am Fri–Sat, Apr–Oct); reservations are required.

To get an idea of Celilo Falls's power and magnificence, visit the **COLUMBIA GORGE DISCOVERY CENTER** in The Dalles (5000 Discovery Dr; 541/296-8600) and watch documentary film clips dating from 1910 to 1950, when the roar of the falls was deafening. Also at the museum is a 33-foot-long model of the Columbia River that shows its before- and after-dam appearance. As the water recedes, the extraordinary rock formations and falls appear, as well as Memaloose Island, which was the largest Native American burial island on the river and now is only partially above water.

Local Native Americans still mourn the loss of the falls but continue to celebrate the arrival of the first spring chinook salmon at Celilo Village. The village longhouses are open to the public for the **CELILO SALMON FEED** on the second weekend of April; contact The Dalles Convention & Visitors Bureau (404 2nd St; 541/296-6616 or 800/255-3385). —*Susan Hauser*

vate baths and TVs, one with a fireplace and Jacuzzi; all have views. Ample common areas include a warm, inviting library, which shares a fireplace with the great room, where guests can read or enjoy the view of Mount Hood. Full breakfasts are served family style in the dining room or on the 44-foot-long patio, and feature fruits of the valley or berries from the Romans' own garden and homemade jams and jellies. Breakfast offerings may be a Belgian waffle with fruit topping or an omelet soufflé. The outdoor spa can be used year-round and has a heated deck and an extraordinary view of Mounts Hood and Adams. *$$$; AE, DIS, MC, V; checks OK; hoodhamlet@gorge.net; www.mthoodhamlet.com; 20 miles north of Mount Hood Meadows on Hwy 35.* &

Old Parkdale Inn / ★★

4932 BASELINE RD, PARKDALE; 541/352-5551 Colorful gardens surround the 1911 Craftsman house, and the three themed rooms reflect owner Heidi Shuford's passion for art. Named Monet, Gauguin, and Georgia O'Keeffe, each of the rooms has a distinctive decor, art, and quotes from the artist written on the door. "I perhaps owe having become a painter to flowers" is attributed to Monet. Two of the rooms are actually suites with complete kitchens and can sleep up to four. Shuford delivers award-winning breakfasts (perhaps baked apples and coffee cake) to your room. She's also a master gardener, and the grounds are lovely for a stroll. *$$$; MC, V; checks OK; parkdale@hoodriverlodging.com; www.hood riverlodging.com; Hwy 35 north from Mount Hood, turn off to Parkdale, and look for sign on right.*

Summit Meadow Cabins

JUST OFF FOREST RD 2560, GOVERNMENT CAMP; 503/272-3494 A visit to one of these Trillium Basin cabins is plenty of fun in summer, when hiking and mountain biking outings may lead to swims in nearby Trillium Lake. But staying here is truly special in winter, when it takes a 1½-mile cross-country ski or snowshoe journey to reach the cabins. The trek is long enough to gain you bragging rights, but—and only you need to know this—it's not particularly arduous. Groomed cross-country ski trails abound; in fact, the Summit Meadows crew manicures trails all over the Trillium Basin. All the cabins—from the cozy Mineral Creek Cabin to the large chalets that sleep up to 12—are furnished in a way that's more functional than elegant, and are equipped with cookware, bedding, and towels. Good dogs are welcome. Two-night minimum. *$$$; no credit cards; checks OK; info@summitmeadow.com; www.summitmeadow.com; north of Still Creek Campground off Hwy 26 (and about a mile south of Government Camp).*

Timberline Lodge / ★★★

TIMBERLINE SKI AREA, TIMBERLINE; 503/622-7979 OR 800/547-1406 Built at the 6,000-foot level on Mount Hood as a Civilian Conservation Corps project during the Depression, this rustic stone-and-timber lodge was dedicated by President Roosevelt in 1937 and is now a National Historic Landmark. A huge central stone fireplace, the focal point of both levels, is surrounded by hand-made furnishings and artwork, including wonderful examples of wood- and iron-working, rug weaving, mosaics, and painting. The 70 rooms range from dorm rooms with bunkbeds and shared bath to the Timberline Fireplace Room. Many of the upholsteries, draperies, rugs, and bedspreads in the public and guest rooms have been re-created in their original patterns—in some cases with the help of the original craftspeople. A wintertime dip in the outdoor heated pool is a bracing experience, best followed by a sauna. In summer, Timberline is a great base for hikers, can't-quit skiers, and poolside loungers. The lodge's Cascade Dining Room (see review), the Blue Ox Bar, and the Ram's Head Bar are all fun places to eat. *$$$; AE, MC, V; checks OK; reservations@timberlinelodge.com; www.timberlinelodge.com; 60 miles east of Portland off Hwy 26.* &

Welches

Coming west off Mount Hood, you reach Welches, which takes its name from Samuel Welch, who welcomed travelers at the hotel (now the Old Welches Inn) he built in 1890. Stop by the **FLYING FROG** (67211 E Hwy 26, in the Arrah Wanna Rendezvous Center; 503/622-7638) for the best cup of tea on the mountain and a delicious pastry. (Full breakfasts and lunches are also served in the bright, cheery cafe.)

RESTAURANTS

The Rendezvous Grill and Tap Room / ★★★

67149 E HWY 26, WELCHES; 503/622-6837 Since it opened in 1995, this has grown into one of Mount Hood's best restaurants. Although her emphasis is on seasonal, local products, including chanterelle mushrooms and huckleberries, chef/co-owner Kathryn Bliss is quick to try something new, such as hosting a harvest moon tribal bellydance festival with a fine spread of vegetarian noshes. On a more normal night, expect to choose from rigatoni with alder-smoked chicken in a champagne cream sauce with toasted hazelnuts, dried cranberries, and fresh spinach; Oregon white truffle and wild mushroom risotto; or fried Willapa Bay oysters with rémoulade sauce. Choosing a bottle of wine is easy with succinct but conversational reviews written by co-owner Tom Anderson. *$$; AE, DIS, MC, V; checks OK; lunch, dinner every day; full bar; reservations recommended; rndzvgrill@aol.com; www.rendez vousgrill.com; north side of Hwy 26, just west of traffic light.*

LODGINGS

Old Welches Inn / ★

26401 E WELCHES RD, WELCHES; 503/622-3754 You'd never guess this rambling blue-roofed white house behind a picket fence was more than a century old. Built in 1890, it was the first hotel and summer resort on Mount Hood; the Welch family converted it into their private home in the 1930s. The four cozy guest rooms in the main house are named after wildflowers. Three of the rooms are on the second floor, while the Forget-Me-Not Room is tucked away atop two flights of stairs. Whole families, and their pets, are welcome at the cottage next door. It's a bit more modern—built in 1901—with two bedrooms, bath, kitchen, and a fireplace in the living room. The lush lawn extends all the way to the shore of the Salmon River. *$$; AE, MC, V; checks OK; oldwelchesinn@lodging-mthood.com; www. lodging-mthood.com; 1 mile south of Hwy 26.*

The Resort at the Mountain / ★★

68010 E FAIRWAY AVE, WELCHES; 503/622-3101 OR 800/669-7666 Clan crests decorate the lobby walls, the Scottish Shoppe sells all manner of Scottish collectibles, and the Highlands Dining Room and Tartans Inn are your sources for food and drink. And, just as in Scotland, golf is a big deal here. Though many come for the 27-hole golf course, you'll also find tennis, croquet, lawn bowling, volleyball, badminton, swimming, hiking, biking, fishing, and, of course, skiing just up the road. Many of the 160 spacious, modern guest rooms have fireplaces, and the grounds, not unlike the surrounding forests, seem to go on forever. Condos and suites face the fairway; other rooms face the wooded courtyard and pool area. *$$$; AE, MC, V; checks OK; www.theresort.com; 1 mile south of Hwy 26.*

Sandy

Sandy fairly hops in the winter, when carloads of skiers and snowboarders clog the highway on their way to and from Mount Hood. En route, folks may stop here for cross-country ski rentals, advice, and gear at **OTTO'S** (38716 Hwy 26; 503/668-5947) or for cheap gas at the local filling station.

On a clear day, turn off Highway 26 at Bluff Road and go 1 mile north to **JON-SRUD VIEWPOINT,** where interpretive signs help you find where the last leg of the Oregon Trail came down the mountainside. It's a spectacular lookout over the Sandy River and the forested foothills of Mount Hood.

About 5 miles east of Sandy, stop at the **OREGON CANDY FARM** (48620 SE Hwy 26; 503/668-5066) and watch caramels, marshmallows, and chocolates—including Bavarian truffles—being made the old-fashioned way. Plenty to taste and buy here, too.

RESTAURANTS

The Elusive Trout Pub

39333 PROCTOR BLVD, SANDY; 503/668-7884 The row of decorative German beer steins gives a clue as to what is prized here: 19 Northwest microbrews are on tap. An upside-down canoe, wagon-wheel chandeliers, and no-smoking policy complete the Northwest touch. Owners Jim and Kim Simonek specialize in burgers, as well as Mexican and vegetarian fare. *$; AE, MC, V; local checks only; lunch, dinner Tues–Sun; beer and wine; reservations not necessary; on westbound Hwy 26 at Hoffman Ave.* &

WILLAMETTE VALLEY

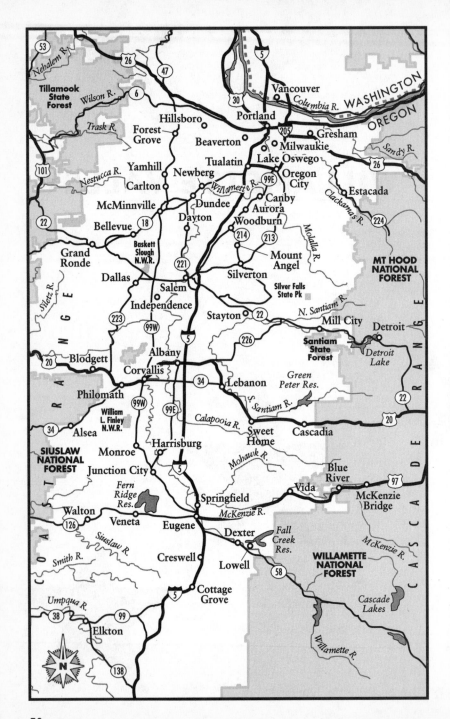

WILLAMETTE VALLEY

A lush, temperate river valley edged by mountains and dotted with farms and small towns, often rainy in winter but rarely snowy. Sound quintessentially like Oregon? In fact, most of the state is in mountains or high desert. But it's the Willamette Valley that most people picture when they think of this state. And it's here that nine out of ten Oregonians live. In that sense, the Willamette Valley *is* Oregon.

The Willamette River defines the valley. Its forks wind their way out of the Central Cascade mountains to merge southeast of Eugene; from there the river heads north to meet the Columbia at Portland. The valley, barely 10 miles wide near Eugene but broadening to more than 30 miles near Salem, is also defined by mountains: the Coast Range to the west, the Cascades to the east, and—south of Eugene—the Siskiyous. That broad, flat valley and the uncrowded rural roads that traverse it are inviting to cyclists, as are extensive networks of paved bicycle paths, especially in Eugene and Corvallis. Venture into the foothills of those ranges for some memorable hiking—past waterfalls, through wild bird refuges, to the summits of modest peaks.

When the pioneers pushed west with covered wagons in the mid-1800s, they were lured by promises of an agricultural paradise. What they found, and what you'll find today, isn't too far off the mark. Wherever you live in the United States, there's a good chance your Christmas tree, dahlias, and irises, the berries in your pie, the hazelnuts in your biscotti—even your front lawn—was grown in the Willamette Valley. Driving from Portland to Eugene along Highway 99W west of the Willamette River, and along lesser routes, you'll still find roadside stands with fresh produce, flowers, honey, and jams, spring through fall; some are open year-round. On weekends, farmers markets bloom in many town centers.

The wine at your table may also have come from here, especially if you favor fine reds; pinot noir has emerged as the Willamette Valley's star varietal. First came the vines, some 30 years ago, and then came the wineries. Happily for travelers, fine dining was the next step.

So what about that rain? There's plenty, but not more than in a lot of places: around 45 inches a year. Locals don't necessarily wait for the sun to shine to get out hiking, nursery browsing, or touring wine country. Less well-known is the valley's summer surprise: sunny and hot, with low humidity, from about July 5 into September and sometimes through October.

ACCESS AND INFORMATION

Commuter airlines America West, Horizon Air, United, and United Express serve the **EUGENE AIRPORT** (north of town, off Hwy 99; 541/682-5544). The greatest choice of flights is to and from Portland, Seattle, San Francisco, and Denver. **CAR RENTALS** are available at the airport and in town.

Most travelers arrive by car via **INTERSTATE 5**, its four lanes (at Eugene) widening to six around Salem. This is the express route; figure less than two hours from Eugene to Portland. More leisurely north-south travelers prefer scenic old **US HIGHWAY 99W**, parallel to Interstate 5 west of the Willamette. At the north end it's known as the "wine road," where it passes through the wine-country hubs of Newberg, Dundee, and McMinnville; unobtrusive blue signs point the way to wineries.

For road conditions, contact the **OREGON DEPARTMENT OF TRANSPORTATION** (503/588-2941 or 800/977-6368 outside of Oregon; www.odot.state.or.us/travel/); the online Travel Advisor (www.tripcheck.com) also has helpful, up-to-date information on road conditions.

AMTRAK (800/USA-RAIL; www.amtrak.com) from Seattle and Portland stops at Salem, Albany, and Eugene; the Coast Starlight continues south to Los Angeles. Service and schedule improvements have made the train more attractive for getting into and out of the Willamette Valley; Spanish-made Talgo trains have a little less leg room and no white-linen dinner service, but they're faster, with contemporary amenities such as plug-ins for laptops (and a snack bar). If you want to go by train, make sure that's what you're getting when you make reservations; Amtrak uses motor coaches on some links.

The **ALBANY VISITORS CENTER** (541/928-091 or 800/526-2256; www.albany visitors.com) is a good source for information on the Willamette Valley.

Wine Country

Wine is a growth industry in Oregon: acres of grapes and numbers of wineries have more than doubled in the past decade. The greatest concentration of the now 175-plus wineries is in Yamhill County, mostly between Newberg and McMinnville. Here among rolling oak-covered hills are increasing numbers of vineyards and enough wineries (more than 50 in the North Willamette Valley appellation) to keep touring wine lovers tipsy for a week. The wine country stretches south past Salem and Eugene, west of the Willamette; wineries down this way are more widely scattered but well worth visiting.

So many of Oregon's pinot noirs have achieved international renown that many of the better-known bottlings are quite pricey. But ardent wine explorers can still find up-and-coming producers cheerfully selling fabulous wine at reasonable prices out of the winery's front door. Summer weekends, as well as Memorial Day and Thanksgiving weekends, can be busy but are good times to visit, because some wineries are only open then. Most are open year-round, at least on weekends (though a few are not open to visitors at all). Many are small family operations well off the beaten track, and visitors are rare enough that you'll receive a hearty welcome. Tasting is free most places; some charge a small fee to try a sampling of wines, or just for "premium pours"—worth paying, since visitors are fewer at these spots and you tend to get more time to converse with your host. (The fee may be applied toward any wine you purchase.) Or stop at an independent tasting room where, for a small fee, you can sample the best of the lesser-known labels.

The best advice is to arm yourself with a map (it's easy to get lost on the backroads) and the winery guide from the **OREGON WINE ADVISORY BOARD** (1200 NW Naito Pkwy, Ste 400, Portland, OR 97209; 800/242-2363; www.oregonwine. org) or from any member winery. Use it to seek out your favorites: a particular varietal, sparkling wines, or boutique wineries. When you come across a wine you especially like, ask the vintner (or whoever's pouring) to suggest other wineries in that vein to visit. In fine weather, take along a picnic; many wineries have tables outside, and some sell chilled wine and lunch supplies.

WILLAMETTE VALLEY THREE-DAY TOUR

DAY ONE: Start at the valley's north end, epicenter of the wine country. Spend the day touring wineries, stopping for lunch at **DUNDEE BISTRO.** Take a break from tasting with antiques-prowling in Lafayette and Yamhill or a little browsing in downtown McMinnville. You might stop for a microbrew at **HOTEL OREGON**—try the Terminator Stout. Then drive out to **YOUNGBERG HILL VINEYARDS & INN,** where your room awaits. Take a walk on one of the old roads in the vicinity, but don't be late for your dinner reservations at **JOEL PALMER HOUSE** in Dayton.

DAY TWO: Enjoy the view as you breakfast in the dining room at Youngberg Hill, then mosey southwest on Highway 18, stopping at another winery or two, before reaching the **LAWRENCE GALLERY** and **FIRE'S EYE** in Bellevue. By now it's lunchtime, or at least brunchtime; take yours at the **FRESH PALATE CAFÉ.** Fortified, hop back in the car and, with help from your detailed state map, follow farm roads east, crossing the Willamette River on the tiny **WHEATLAND FERRY** (503/588-7979). Continue east to hook up with Highway 214, taking you to **SILVER FALLS STATE PARK,** where you ogle the eye-popping waterfalls as you hike as far as your energy and interest carry you. Allow 1½ hours to take Highway 214 west and Interstate 5 south to Eugene and the **CAMPBELL HOUSE,** where a short soak in the Jacuzzi revives you for dinner at **CHANTERELLE,** 2 blocks away. If you forgot to make reservations, never mind; **ZENON CAFÉ** is just a few blocks farther, and the food's grand.

DAY THREE: What's your pleasure? The **BEACH** is just an hour west, and fishing and rafting on the **MCKENZIE RIVER** is even closer. Alternately, wander down to **FIFTH STREET PUBLIC MARKET** for local color and fun shopping, following your nose west down Fifth for more shops and cafes, or over to Eighth and Oak Streets if the **SATURDAY MARKET**'s in swing; food booths at either spot can provide lunch. Spend the afternoon driving the rolling farmland southwest of Eugene, stopping at some secluded wineries, and wind up at **MOUNT PISGAH,** south of Springfield, for a late-afternoon hike along the river or up to the summit to take in the valley from on high. Try to arrive at **MCKENZIE VIEW BED & BREAKFAST** while you can still enjoy the view in the daylight, and make your dinner reservations: perhaps fireside at **ADAM'S PLACE.**

Newberg

LODGINGS

Springbrook Hazelnut Farm / ★★

30295 N HWY 99W, NEWBERG; 503/538-4606 OR 800/793-8528 Informal Oregonians are surprised by the colorful elegance of this landmark farmhouse. Owner Ellen McClure, an artist by training, has created an exquisitely decorated B&B filled with original art. The large paneled dining room makes you feel as if you're in some Italian palazzo. Two upstairs wicker-furnished guest rooms share a sitting room and a bathroom; downstairs, two more guest rooms are furnished with antiques and have half-baths, sharing a full bath down the hall. The Rose Cottage and Carriage House are behind the main house; each is a perfect little private suite with a kitchen well-stocked with breakfast fixings. They're near the old barn, which now houses a one-man winery. Guests may explore the 60-acre filbert orchard, take a swim in the pool, or play tennis on the private court. *$$–$$$; no credit cards; checks OK; info@nutfarm.com; www.nutfarm.com; just off Hwy 99W north of Newberg.*

Dundee

Not much more than a wide spot in the road a generation ago, Dundee has become the culinary capital of Northern Oregon's wine country. Highway 99W—the wine road—runs right through town, and crossing it on foot is a challenge on weekends. But it's one worth taking, to hop from Dundee Bistro (see review) to the sparkling wines awaiting your palate at **ARGYLE WINERY** (691 Hwy 99W; 503/538-8520). A handful of stellar restaurants now lines the highway's west side; any one is worth a visit. Some say Dundee is a bit like Napa 20 years ago—a farming town still rough around the edges, with touches of refinement. Visit now so you can say you knew it when.

RESTAURANTS

Dundee Bistro / ★★★

 100-A SW 7TH ST, DUNDEE; 503/554-1650 This smart, bustling bistro-pizzeria-bar on Dundee's restaurant row was built by the Ponzi family, respected local wine makers. The courtyard arrangement and large windows, walls, and floor in tones of sage and pumpkin lend it a Tuscan air, but the food is inventively, seasonally Northwestern. A fall dinner might start with garnet yam flan with smoked salmon, or roasted butternut squash soup with comice pear. The half-dozen entree choices could include mesquite-roasted chicken with apples and fig vinaigrette, or locally grown pork loin with hedgehog mushrooms and applesauce. Pizza appears as an appetizer at dinner or an entree at lunch, topped with unusual combinations such as air-dried sausage, crimini mushrooms, roasted onion, and Gorgonzola. The same care is evidenced in the handful of desserts and eclectic wine list: not long, but well chosen, with a dozen available by the glass. Next door is the Ponzi Wine Bar, where you can taste Ponzi and other premium Oregon wines. *$$; AE, MC, V; local checks only; lunch, dinner every day; full bar; reservations recommended; www.ponziwines.com/touring/bistro.html; on Hwy 99W at 7th St.* &

Red Hills Provincial Dining / ★★

276 HWY 99W, DUNDEE; 503/538-8224 You'll be warmly received in this 1912 Craftsman-style house-turned-restaurant. The simple European-country dinner menu changes often, and the choices are all intriguing: veal osso buco with creamy polenta, perhaps, or fricassee of game hen with chanterelles and black trumpet mushrooms, or a classic coquilles St.-Jacques. All the details are just right, whether it's bread dusted with fresh rosemary or a crisp mesclun salad, or poached pears with caramel sauce and chocolate ganache. Add to this an award-winning wine list with a huge selection from all over the world. A private dining room seats up to 12. *$$; MC, V; checks OK; lunch Tues–Fri (mid-April–mid-Oct), dinner Tues–Sun year-round; full bar; reservations recommended; info@redhillsdining.com; www.red-hillsdining.com; north edge of town.*

Tina's / ★★★

760 HWY 99W, DUNDEE; 503/538-8880 This jewel box of a restaurant—something of a gathering place for the local wine crowd—resides in a small, unassuming house on the side of the highway. Inside, it's stylish and pretty, bright with white walls and warmed by a fireplace. Chef-proprietors Tina and David Bergen seem to be taking their culinary cues from contemporary French cuisine, with a bias toward fresh, local ingredients cooked perfectly: the sea scallops and thyme-infused sauce, for example, or purée of corn soup, creamy without cream. Surprises include salmon spring rolls served with a hazelnut sauce. The green salad is perfectly fresh; the herbs flavoring your entree are likely homegrown. The list of house-made desserts is short and the wine list long: the right proportion in these parts. *$$; AE, DIS, MC, V; checks OK; dinner every day; full bar; reservations recommended; center of town, across from fire station.* ঌ

Dayton

RESTAURANTS

Joel Palmer House / ★★★★

600 FERRY ST, DAYTON; 503/864-2995 A trip to Oregon's wine country is no longer complete without a pilgrimage to the Joel Palmer House. Chef Jack Czarnecki is a renowned authority on cooking with mushrooms, and rare is the dish that emerges from his kitchen without some variety of fungus in either a starring or supporting role. Appetizers might include a three-mushroom tart, escargot with black chanterelles, or a silky corn chowder with dried *cèpes*. The rack of lamb comes with a rich pinot noir–hazelnut sauce, while wild mushroom duxelles and a Creole–pinot gris sauce accompany tender sautéed scallops. Or, consider Jack's Mushroom Madness, a prix-fixe multicourse dinner emphasizing—what else?—wild mushrooms. Service is attentive if somewhat haphazard, but the chef's presence and the setting—a white Southern Revival home built in the 1850s by town co-founder Gen. Joel Palmer—give a sense of romance and formality. The extensive wine list is a gushing ode to Oregon pinot noir. *$$–$$$; AE, DIS, MC, V; local checks only; lunch Tues–Fri, dinner Tues–Sat; full bar; reservations required; joel-palmerhouse@onlinemac.com; www.joelpalmerhouse.com; downtown.* ঌ

LODGINGS

Wine Country Farm / ★

6855 BREYMAN ORCHARDS RD, DAYTON; 503/864-3446 OR 800/261-3446 In the "red hills of Dundee" (the soil really is red), surrounded by vineyards, you'll find the Wine Country Farm. From the hilltop, watch clouds drift across the valley; the setting and view are the draws here. All seven guest rooms in the white stucco 1910 house have private baths and down comforters, and two have fireplaces. Guests can enjoy a hot tub and sauna, and massage is available. The farm also has a commercial winery, Wine Country Farm Cellars, with a public tasting room next door to the inn; a spacious two-room suite occupies the second floor and is also available to guests. In warm weather, enjoy the hearty farm breakfast on the sun-washed deck. Owners of the 13-acre farm also raise Arabian horses; guided trail rides to nearby wineries and horse-drawn buggy rides are available. *$$–$$$; MC, V; checks OK; www.winecountryfarm.com; right onto McDougal just past Sokol Blosser Winery, then right to Breyman Orchards Rd.*

Carlton-Yamhill

At the western edge of the Yamhill wine country and just a few miles apart, these two towns are worthwhile destinations in a driving tour of the valley's north end. Carlton's 19th-century brick and stone storefronts, its old-fashioned feed store, and its gentle pace are a tonic. Enjoy the shops (quilting, garden arts) arrayed along Main Street, check out **CUNEO CELLARS** (750 W Lincoln St; 503/852-0002) at the north end of town, and stop to taste (small fee) and chat with the knowledgeable owner at **THE TASTING ROOM** (105 W Main St; 503/852-6733), which offers wines from nearby wineries that are generally closed to the public. Yamhill is worth a stop if only to browse the antiques at **RD STEEVES IMPORTS** (140 W Main St; 503/662-3999). The **FLYING M RANCH** (23029 NW Flying M Rd; 503/662-3222), 10 miles west of town, is great for families and offers horseback riding, spartan overnighting, an airstrip for private pilots, and meat-and-potatoes fare in a big log lodge.

RESTAURANTS

Caffe Bisbo / ★

214 MAIN ST, CARLTON; 503/852-7248 When Claudio and Joanne Bisbocci opened their trattoria in little Carlton, fourth-generation restaurateur Claudio could barely speak English. But communication has never been a problem; this Italian speaks volumes with his food and his infectious enthusiasm. The food is straight-ahead, traditional northern Italian, the likes of rice torta redolent with extra-virgin olive oil and basil, Genoa shrimp with garlic and marsala, and fresh cannelloni. Minestrone is thick and basily, salad dressed simply in the Italian manner—much as you would expect somewhere along the Cinque Terre, Claudio's home turf. The tiramisu is the real thing, and wines (by the glass or bottle) are mostly modestly priced Italian and Northwest. Some dishes disappoint a bit (are those canned mushrooms?); come to enjoy the food and a small-town Italian welcome. *$$; MC, V; local checks only; lunch and dinner Thurs–Sun; beer and wine; reservations required for dinner; downtown.* &

McMinnville

McMinnville is growing up; the feed stores are still here, now cheek by jowl with stores supplying the burgeoning wine industry. Driving through town, turn off the highway onto Third Street to reach the gracious old tree-shaded city center sporting a growing collection of wine shops, cafes, and boutiques. Its central location makes this town a good headquarters for wine touring; pick up information at the **MCMIN-NVILLE CHAMBER OF COMMERCE** (417 N Adams St; 503/472-6196; www.mcminnville.org). Serious wine lovers can OD on great wine and food while hobnobbing with wine celebrities (including some of France's hot young wine makers) at the three-day **INTERNATIONAL PINOT NOIR CELEBRATION** (503/472-8964 or 800/775-4762), held in late July or early August on the campus of Linfield College; tickets tend to sell out well in advance. Need a break from vino? Try a pint at **GOLDEN VALLEY BREWPUB AND RESTAURANT** (984 E 4th St; 503/472-2739), housed in a recycled bottling plant.

RESTAURANTS

Coty's Restaurant / ★

729 E 3RD ST, MCMINNVILLE; 503/474-1888 The sign outside—"Steak & Seafood"—doesn't quite do justice to this newcomer, but the acronym in the name—for chef-owner Anthony J. Danna's 2000 Chef of the Year award for Oregon—may raise expectations a bit too high. The setting is the first floor of a vintage home—calm, carpeted, with a huge bookcase stuffed with cookbooks. Appetizers include a classic preparation of escargot and a passable French onion soup. Entrees all come with soup or salad and include several cuts of steak plus prime rib and creative preparations of lamb, chicken, duck, and seafood, from salmon with pear chutney sauce, to Asian duck and pork Calvados. Sauces are just right, and nothing's over-cooked. Not as much care is given to the side vegetables, the desserts (homemade) are a little uninspiring, and service only so-so; count on a good meal with possible moments of brilliance. *$$; AE, DC, MC, V; checks OK; lunch Mon–Fri, dinner Mon–Sat; full bar; reservations recommended; downtown at N Galloway St.* &

Nick's Italian Cafe / ★★

521 E 3RD ST, MCMINNVILLE; 503/434-4471 Long before Dundee's restaurant row emerged, Nick's in McMinnville was the culinary headquarters of Oregon's wine country, with owner Nick Peirano turning out the northern Italian cooking he learned at his mother's knee. It's still a winner, though it's been eclipsed by more dazzling restaurants in nearby Dundee, and its funky charm—mismatched plates, the location a former luncheonette—is wearing thin. Still, there's plenty to enjoy in the prix-fixe, five-course meal, including the second-course tureen of heavenly, garlicky minestrone and the simply dressed green salad. The seasonal antipasto might include shellfish in winter, or melon with prosciutto in summer. The fourth course is always delicious pasta. Entrees could include perfectly grilled swordfish steak, or top sirloin marinated in garlic and rosemary. Dessert choices include crème brûlée, truffles, and tiramisu. Guests are welcome to order à la carte. *$$$; AE, MC, V; checks OK; dinner*

Tues–Sun; beer and wine; reservations recommended; www.nicksitaliancafe.com; next door to Hotel Oregon. ♿

LODGINGS

Hotel Oregon / ★★

310 NE EVANS ST, MCMINNVILLE; 503/472-8427 OR 888/472-8427 Oregon's ubiquitous microbrew meisters, the McMenamin brothers, have revitalized a 1905 hotel in the center of McMinnville, contributing to its downtown renaissance and giving adventurous wine-country tourers a rather spartan but lively new lodging option. Ceilings are high, beds firm, furnishings predominately antique, and decor a bit brooding (including original artwork). Only a handful of the 42 rooms have private baths; the rest either share a bath with an adjoining room or utilize one down the hall (terry-cloth robes provided). All have phones, but no TVs. Late-night street noise can be a bit much, due in part to the hotel's own pub downstairs. As at other McMenamin accommodations, a featured activity is drinking, with a large main-floor pub as well as diminutive basement and rooftop bars starring the brothers' formidable brews and wines from their Edgefield winery. Breakfast, lunch, and dinner—tasty tavern fare—are served in the pub. Breakfast vouchers provided to overnighters cover most options, from steel-cut oats with all the trimmings to creative variations on eggs Benedict. *$$; AE, DIS, MC, V; checks OK; reserve@hotel oregon.mcmenamins.com; www.mcmenamins.com; at 3rd St.* ♿

Steiger Haus Inn / ★

360 WILSON ST, MCMINNVILLE; 503/472-0821 Tucked in a neighborhood of older homes on the edge of the Linfield College campus, Steiger Haus is a peaceful oasis. The contemporary cedar-shingled house has a comfortable Northwest feel, with lots of light. Predecessors of current hosts Susan and Dale DuRette designed the inn as a B&B, so downstairs rooms have private decks, offering guests the opportunity to sip coffee outside and enjoy the large, woodsy backyard. All five rooms and suites (three downstairs, two up) have private baths; one downstairs has a fireplace; and the upstairs suite has a soaking tub and bay window. A conference room is available. Full breakfast might include fresh poached pears, raisin muffins, and German pancakes; the DuRettes provide a specially roasted coffee. *$$; DIS, MC, V; checks OK; steigerhaus@onlinemac.com; www.steigerhaus.com; ¼ mile east of Linfield College entrance.*

Youngberg Hill Vineyards & Inn / ★★★

10660 YOUNGBERG HILL RD, MCMINNVILLE; 503/472-2727 OR 888/657-8668 The setting of this gracious inn can't be beat: from the crest of a 700-foot hill you have views that stretch 180 degrees across the Willamette Valley, including the inn's own 12-acre vineyard. Even in winter, guests may want to take their coffee on the wraparound porch. The inn's vineyard skirts the house, and hosts Ken and Tasha Byrd offer tastings of their stellar pinot noir as well as other local wines. Seven spacious rooms and suites (three with fireplaces) in the rambling contemporary house have private baths, fabulous views, and comfortable furnishings. Common areas, including a cozy music room and gracious living room, double as gallery space for local artists. The three-course breakfast in the bright dining room includes fresh, local ingredients: a fruit course, homemade bread or muffins, perhaps apple French toast with an herbed poached egg, or eggs and crab in pastry. The quiet is deeply refreshing, and guests can walk for miles on old logging roads. *$$$; MC, V; checks OK; youngberg@netscape.net; www.youngberghill.com; 12 miles southwest of McMinnville off Youngberg Hill Rd, call for directions.* &

Bellevue

A crossroads 8 miles southwest of McMinnville on Highway 18, this wide spot in the road from Portland to the beach at Lincoln City is a destination in itself, mainly for the **LAWRENCE GALLERY** (19706 SW Hwy 18; 503/843-3633), Oregon's largest—and some say finest—art gallery; don't miss the water-and-sculpture garden outside. The attached **OREGON WINE TASTING ROOM** (19700 SW Hwy 18; 503/843-3787) lets you sample offerings from some two dozen Oregon wineries. Across the street, a second gallery—**FIRE'S EYE** (19915 SW Muddy Valley Rd; 503/843-9797)—features clay artists.

RESTAURANTS

Fresh Palate Café / ★

19708 SW HWY 18, BELLEVUE; 503/843-4400 Break up a drive to the beach with breakfast or lunch at this pleasant atelier cafe. The informal, airy space feels like an extension of the Lawrence Gallery it overlooks, with original art on the walls; to the west, windows look toward forest and farmland, and the door opens onto a broad deck (for summer supping). Everything is freshly made, from salad dressings to bread and desserts. The lunch menu includes sandwiches plus entrees such as pasta dishes and acclaimed crab cakes. At dinner choose from a half-dozen entrees, from grilled honey mustard filet mignon to a Northwest cioppino. On the 60-bottle list of local wines, at least 15 are always available by the glass. *$$; AE, MC, V; checks OK; lunch every day, dinner Fri–Sat; full bar; reservations recommended; www.fresh palatecafe.com; 7 miles southwest of McMinnville.*

Grande Ronde

This small valley community serves as hub for the Confederated Tribes of Grande Ronde, flourishing largely thanks to the success of **SPIRIT MOUNTAIN CASINO** (27100 SW Salmon River Hwy, Willamina; 800/760-7977). The public is also welcome at the tribes' annual powwow in August, and at the **SPIRIT MOUNTAIN STAMPEDE** rodeo in June.

LODGINGS

Spirit Mountain Lodge / ★

27100 SW SALMON RIVER HWY, GRANDE RONDE; 888/668-7366 Oregon's number 1 tourist attraction? Spirit Mountain Casino, the state's largest gaming facility. Surprisingly, the attached five-story, 100-room lodge completed in 1998 is understated, stylish, and comfy—a refreshing contrast to the casino's glare and glitz. Pendleton blankets drape every bed; quiet touches of Native American art adorn the walls.

Colors are muted and earthy, and solid soundproofing keeps the slots out of earshot. It's everything you'd expect of a modern resort hotel in a remote location—except there's not much to do but gamble: no pool, no spa, no stationary bicycles, not even a walking trail. There is a play area for kids and a video arcade for teens. And food—nothing surprising, but well prepared and reasonably priced—in the Legends Restaurant and Coyote Buffet, as well as in two 24-hour cafes, Rock Creek (light meals and snack foods) and Spirit Mountain Cafe (espresso and pastries). *$$; AE, DIS, MC, V; no checks; www.spirit-mountain.com; ¼ mile west of Valley Junction.* &

Salem and Vicinity

What was once a staid state capitol surrounded by sleepy farmland is now growing like crazy, as Portlanders' notion of an acceptable commute broadens. Look beyond the interstate and its malls, though; you'll still find the upper valley's rural heart in small towns and fields of tulips and irises, brilliant in spring.

Aurora

Antique hunters find a fertile field in this well-preserved historic village. In 1856 Dr. William Keil brought a group of Pennsylvania Germans called the Harmonites to establish a communal settlement. After the death of its founder, the commune faded away; today most visitors are drawn to the town, on the National Register of Historic Places, to comb through antique stores occupying the many clapboard and Victorian houses along US Highway 99E. A former ox barn is now the **OLD AURORA COLONY MUSEUM** (212 2nd St NE; 503/678-5754), with unusual and well-displayed artifacts.

History-minded visitors also enjoy nearby **CHAMPOEG STATE PARK** (off Hwy 99W, 7 miles east of Newberg; 503/678-1251), site of a historic meeting in 1843 to create the first provisional government by Americans on the Pacific; it's now a fine place to picnic, hike, browse the heirloom garden, or camp in cabins, yurts, or one's own tent or RV. Rose lovers wander a few miles farther up the river (west on Champoeg Rd and across Hwy 219) to **HEIRLOOM OLD GARDEN ROSES** (503/538-1576), one of the country's premier commercial growers of old garden roses.

LODGINGS

Willamette Gables Riverside Estate / ★★

10323 SCHULER RD, AURORA; 503/678-2195 It could be an old mansion, well restored, but in fact it's a new mansion, built as a B&B in Southern Plantation style and perched on a bluff overlooking the Willamette. Open since Spring 1999, it's already a favorite for weddings, with beautifully landscaped grounds and an elegantly appointed interior. Follow the spiral staircase upstairs to five guest rooms, each with private bath and individually decorated with antiques and convincing reproductions. The Captain's Room features a king-sized sleigh bed, fireplace, and claw-footed tub; the Music Room has a four-poster double bed with wedding ring quilt. The Monet Room also has its own wood-burning fireplace. Downstairs, settle into the lower parlor with its fireplace and baby grand piano, or enjoy a full breakfast with a view of the river. *$$$; MC, V; checks OK; w.gables@juno.com; www.willamettegables.com; 5 miles west of I-5 at exit 282B, call for directions.* &

Mount Angel

Visit **MOUNT ANGEL ABBEY** (1 Abbey Dr, St. Benedict; 503/845-3030), a century-old Benedictine seminary, on a foggy morning when its celestial setting atop a butte sacred to local Native Americans makes it seem as if it's floating in the clouds. The seminary's library (503/845-3303) is a gem by the internationally celebrated Finnish architect Alvar Aalto. The town is best known for its pull-out-the-stops **OKTOBER-FEST** (503/845-9440) in mid-September; the rest of the year, try the home brew and hearty fare at cavernous **MOUNT ANGEL BREWING COMPANY** (210 Monroe St; 503/845-9624).

Silverton

The historic downtown is pretty in summer, with hanging baskets overflowing with flowers and interesting shops to browse; take tea or enjoy lunch at the **OREGON TEA GARDEN** (305 Oak St; 503/873-1230). It's named after the **OREGON GARDEN** (503/874-8100), about 2 miles southwest of town off Highway 213, which opened in May 2000; its 240 landscaped acres should make this a world-class attraction as plantings mature. Southeast of town is lush, dramatic **SILVER FALLS STATE PARK** (off Hwy 214, 26 miles east of Salem; 503/873-8681), with its concentration of waterfalls, plus camping and hiking, biking, and horse trails. Iris farmers cultivate acres of fields around the town, creating a brilliant palette in late May; that's also the time to wander **COOLEY'S IRIS DISPLAY GARDENS** (11553 Silverton Rd NE; 503/873-5463).

RESTAURANTS

Silver Grille Café & Wines / ★★★

206 E MAIN ST, SILVERTON; 503/873-4035 In March 2000 chef Jeff Nizlek took the reigns at this contemporary bistro and wine shop in Silverton's historic down-town and has since made it his own. Inside, it's as elegant as a lacquered Chinese box, dimly lit with dark wood wainscoting below dark red grass-paper walls. The menu changes seasonally, with specials chalked on a blackboard, and it is the sea-sons, and the bounty of Willamette Valley farms and fields, that set direction. Fall finds three locally foraged wild mushrooms merged with white Oregon truffles in a faultless risotto, and a perfectly seared ahi fillet on a bed of black rice, wrapped in a truffle wine sauce. Start with a salad of local organic greens or a terrine of smoked salmon and bay shrimp, and wind up with, say, a dense chocolate cake graced with essence of marionberries; desserts are as seasonal and sensational as entrees. The wine selection is displayed just inside the front door, convenient for retail customers; diners choose here, too, then add a modest corkage fee. *$$; AE, MC, V; checks OK; dinner Wed–Sun; full bar; reservations recommended; jeff@silvergrille.com; www.silvergrille.com; at 1st St.* &

Salem

Handsome parks flank Oregon's 1938 **CAPITOL BUILDING** (900 Court St NE; 503/986-1388), topped by a pioneer sheathed in gold; take in the Depression-era murals in the rotunda, on your own or on a free tour, offered daily in summer. Just behind is **WILLAMETTE UNIVERSITY** (900 State St; 503/370-6300), the oldest university in the West. The campus is a happy blend of old and new brick buildings, with Mill Creek nicely incorporated into the landscape. It's a pleasant place to stroll, and plant lovers should visit the small but well-tended botanical gardens. The university's **HALLIE FORD MUSEUM OF ART** (700 State St; 503/370-6855) is the second largest in the state, with some 3,000 pieces of art from around the globe.

Across the road from Willamette University is **HISTORIC MISSION MILL VIL-LAGE** (1313 Mill St SE; 503/585-7012; tours 10am–4:30pm, Tues–Sat). The impressive 42-acre cluster of restored buildings from the 1800s includes a woolen mill, a parsonage, a Presbyterian church, and several homes. The mill, which drew its power from Mill Creek, now houses a museum that literally makes the sounds of the factory come alive. **JASON LEE HOUSE,** dating from 1841, is the Northwest's oldest remaining frame house; picnic along the stream and feed the ducks. The **SALEM VISITOR INFORMATION CENTER** (503/581-4325 or 800/874-7012) is part of the complex.

BUSH HOUSE (600 Mission St SE; 503/363-4714) is a Victorian home built in 1877 by pioneer newspaper publisher Aashal Bush. It sits in a large park complete with conservatory, rose gardens, hiking paths, and barn turned art gallery. Tours are available.

GILBERT HOUSE CHILDREN'S MUSEUM (116 Marion St NE; 503/371-3631) on the downtown riverfront between the bridges is a delightful hands-on learning and play center for young children. Kids also appreciate **ENCHANTED FOREST** (8462 Enchanted Wy SE, Turner; 503/371-4242), a nicely wooded storybook park with picnic space.

WILLAMETTE VALLEY VINEYARDS (8800 Enchanted Wy SE, Turner; 503/588-9463), a big investor-owned winery offering a broad range of wines, commands a spectacular view just south of town. Follow Highway 221 northwest of town to visit several smaller noteworthy wineries, including Stangeland, Witness Tree, Cristom, and Bethel Heights.

If you visit during the 10 days of the **OREGON STATE FAIR** (503/378-3247), held around Labor Day, don't miss it—it's one of the Northwest's biggest.

RESTAURANTS

Alessandro's 120 / ★★

120 COMMERCIAL ST, SALEM; 503/370-9951 Simple, elegant pasta and seafood dishes are the strong suit at this longtime downtown favorite. The menu isn't particularly original, but the classics are mostly done well, starting with fresh ingredients: perfectly cooked veal piccata, rich meat-stuffed tortellini in light cream sauce. In addition to the regular menu, a multicourse dinner is offered; the staff asks only if there's a particular dish you don't like, and they surprise you with the rest. The wine menu is strong on Italy. Service is quiet and professional, and jazz is live Friday and Saturday nights. *$$; AE, DIS, MC, V; no checks; lunch Mon–Fri, dinner every day; full bar; reservations recommended; info@alessandros120; www.alessandros120.com; near Court St.* &

The Arbor Café / ★★

380 HIGH ST NE, SALEM; 503/588-2353 The Arbor Café feels a bit out of place— an informal, airy garden cafe camped in a steel-and-concrete "plaza" at the foot of a downtown office tower. It's not the most elegant spot, but it's the locals' eatery of choice. Stop for continental breakfast—house-made pastries and espresso. Midday, try a muffaletta panini, some homemade soup, maybe honey-mustard chicken salad. At dinner, you can go simple with soup and a sandwich, but entrees are compelling: Sichuan stir-fry is lightly spicy and comes with beef or prawns, and cashew chicken is sauced with ginger, lime, and chile. Provençal meatloaf dresses up this old chestnut with a savory roasted-shallot brown gravy. A number of microbrews are joined by a small selection of Oregon and Italian wines. Desserts perform solidly, particularly dense, flavorful cakes. *$$; MC, V; local checks only; breakfast, lunch Mon–Sat, dinner Tues–Sat; beer and wine; reservations recommended; between Center and Chemeketa Sts.* &

Fleur de Sel / ★★

1210 STATE ST, SALEM; 503/363-3822 Chef-owner Bernard Malherbe has created a genuine French bistro in a former deli near the center of Salem, naming it for the coveted sea salt of Brittany. Don't expect fine dining; it's hearty provincial fare. From such appetizers as *tartiflette* (sautéed potatoes, bacon, and melted roblochon cheese) and a charcuterie plate with pâté and homemade pork rillettes to the entrees— monkfish with mushrooms, steak *au poivre vert*—it's what you'd expect in a Paris neighborhood dive, but with American-sized portions. The menu shifts seasonally. Cheeses, wines (listed by region), the dessert menu of sorbet, crème au caramel, and mousse au chocolate—it's all French. *$$; MC, V; local checks only; lunch Tues–Fri, dinner Tues–Sat; beer and wine; reservations accepted for 6 or more; fleurdesel@ attbi.com; across from Willamette University at 12th St.* &

j. james restaurant / ★★

325 HIGH ST, SALEM; 503/362-0888 Chef-owner Jeff James's eponymous restaurant is a bright light in the Salem dining scene. An Oregon native, James uses the region's ingredients in simple but creative dishes, including starters such as Oregon shrimp, whole kernel corn, and fresh dill risotto or Bandon white cheddar and goat cheese tart with spicy onion jam and citrus reduction. There are entrees to please all tastes, like grilled pork loin marinated in molasses or salmon poached in a lightly spiced broth. The kitchen occasionally missteps—overdone fish in one daily special and a mustard vinaigrette that overwhelmed a salad—but the chef's experience more than often prevails. The large, awkward space by a parking garage is softened by white linens, floor-to-ceiling windows, and bold paint. The service is crisp and professional, the wine list moderately priced. *$$; AE, MC, V; no checks; lunch Mon–Fri, dinner Mon–Sat; full bar; reservations recommended; www.jjamesrestaurant.com; downtown, in Pringle Park Plaza.* &

Morton's Bistro Northwest / ★★★

🌲 **1128 EDGEWATER ST, SALEM; 503/585-1113** A clever design puts the diner below roadway level, looking out on an attractive courtyard backed by an ivy-covered wall that screens a busy highway. The interior is intimate, with dark wood beams, soft lighting, and a convivial feel from the ricocheting conversations. The menu is solidly Northwestern with hints of international influences, and everything on the plate works together brilliantly. A salmon fillet might be accompanied by a potato-pumpkin mash with basil and balsamic braised tomatoes; vegetarian lasagne combines roasted red peppers, mushrooms, goat cheese, and spinach. Give serious consideration to the mixed grill or the cioppino. Service is expert and pleasant, and the selection of reasonably priced Northwest wines is good. *$$; MC, V; checks OK; dinner Tues–Sat; full bar; reservations recommended; steve@mortons bistronw.com; www.mortonsbistronw.com; between Gerth and McNary Aves in West Salem.* ♿

LODGINGS

Mill Creek Inn

3125 RYAN DR SE, SALEM; 503/585-3332 OR 800/346-9659 In a town dominated by chain lodgings, this well-kept motel is the nicest of the lot. The 109 spacious guest rooms all have microwaves, minifridges, data ports, even irons and ironing boards. Amenities include an indoor pool, Jacuzzi, and fitness room. It's just off Interstate 5, but close enough to the city center to be convenient for business or pleasure travelers. *$; AE, DC, DIS, MC, V; no checks; bwmci@open.org; www.bestwestern. com/millcreekinn; exit 253 off I-5.* ♿

Independence

This riverside town looks pretty untouched by modern times. If you want to remind yourself (or learn) what an old-fashioned fountain was like, visit **TAYLOR'S FOUNTAIN AND GIFT** (296 S Main St; 503/838-1124), at Monmouth St. The **RIVER GALLERY** (184 S Main St; 503/838-6171) exhibits the work of local artists, who also take turns staffing the place; in September the gallery organizes an annual "Fish Run," in which foam-core salmon embellished by area artists are displayed outdoors and auctioned off to fund an art scholarship. Just northeast of the town center is Independence State Airport, where you can grab a basic breakfast at **ANNIE'S AT THE AIRPORT** (4705 Airport Rd; 503/838-5632) and hobnob with pilots of the small and often homebuilt planes that frequent the place. Southeast of town the four-car **BUENA VISTA FERRY** still shuttles cars across the Willamette the old-fashioned way; it operates Wednesday through Sunday, April through October.

RESTAURANTS

Buena Vista House Café and Lodging / ★★

11265 RIVERVIEW ST, INDEPENDENCE; 503/838-6364 "Sort of a wayward house for people who like good food, good music, and quiet places" is how innkeeper Claudia Prevost describes the welcoming hostelry she's created out of a 110-year-old house 2 blocks from the Buena Vista Ferry. Stop for a stellar scone and an excellent cup of coffee or espresso, or stay for lunch, choosing from a small menu that might include salmon croquettes one day or wild mushroom quiche another. In sunny weather, sit under the ancient apple trees in the garden out back. Dinner is served Friday nights by reservation only (Wednesdays, too, in summer); entrees are fresh, original, and well prepared, and local musicians usually gather to jam, with Claudia on guitar and vocals. The outdoor wood-fired pizza oven should be cooking by summer 2002. Three guest rooms upstairs are appointed with antiques in a refreshingly spare country style; all share one large bath *$; no credit cards; checks OK; breakfast and lunch Wed–Sun, dinner Fri (Wed in summer); no alcohol; reservations required for dinner; www.buenavistahouse.com; south of Independence on the ferry access road.*

Albany and Corvallis

Time and the interstate have bypassed Albany, which is probably a blessing. Once you get off the freeway (ignore the smell of the nearby pulp mill), you'll discover a fine representative of the small-town Oregon of an earlier era, with broad, quiet streets, neat houses, and a slow pace. Corvallis is a pleasant mix of old river town and funky university burg. In 1998 Corvallis was the first city in Oregon to ban all smoking in restaurants, bars, and taverns, and it's ideal for biking and running; most streets include wide bike lanes, and routes follow both the Willamette and Marys Rivers.

Albany

Once an important transportation hub in the Willamette Valley, Albany has an unequaled selection of historic homes and buildings in a wide variety of styles; many of them have been lovingly restored. You can see 13 distinct architectural styles in the 50-block, 368-building Monteith Historic District. Then there are the Hackleman (28 blocks, 210 buildings) and Downtown (9½ blocks, 80 buildings) Historic Districts. Many buildings are open for inspection on annual tours—the last Saturday in July and the Sunday evening before Christmas Eve. A handy, free guide, "Seems Like Old Times," is available from the **ALBANY CONVENTION AND VISITORS CENTER** (300 SW 2nd; 800/526-2256; www.albanyvisitors.com).

Wander First Avenue, where it all began: have a cup at **BOCCHERINI'S COFFEE AND TEA HOUSE** (208 1st Ave SW; 541/926-6703) or a pint at **WYATT'S EATERY & BREWHOUSE** (211 1st Ave NW; 541/917-3727). In summer, enjoy an outdoor concert at **MONTEITH RIVERPARK** (Water Ave and Washington St; 541/917-7772).

The **COVERED BRIDGES** that were so characteristic of this area in the mid-1900s are disappearing; from 300 throughout Oregon, their number has dwindled to fewer than 50. But that's still more than in any state west of the Mississippi. Most remaining bridges are in the Willamette Valley counties of Lane and Linn and, to the west, Lincoln. Best starting points for easy-to-follow circuits of the bridges are Albany, Eugene, and Cottage Grove. Six bridges lie within an 8-mile radius of Scio, northeast of Albany; for a map, contact the Albany Convention and Visitors Center. For other tours, send an SASE with two first-class stamps to the **COVERED BRIDGE SOCIETY OF OREGON** (PO Box 1804, Newport, OR 97365; 541/265-2934).

LATINO WOODBURN

When the highway bypassed historic Woodburn's city center, the town's fate seemed sealed, finished off by construction of a huge outlet mall along Interstate 5 in 1999. But a transformation has since taken place here, as local Latinos have reclaimed the 100-year-old brick-and-stone buildings for cafes, shops, and tortillerias reminiscent of their roots in Mexico and Central America.

Take the Woodburn exit (exit 271) from Interstate 5, head east 1 ½ miles, then follow signs right (Settlemeier Ave) and left (Garfield St) to the city center, minutes from the freeway. Most Latino-owned businesses are clustered within a block or two of First and Hayes Streets.

Your first stop should be **SALVADOR'S BAKERY** (405 N 1st St; 503/982-4513) for fresh-baked sugar cookies or *bolillos*, or traditional Mexican deli items such as *carnitas* or *queso cotija*. Stop in at **LA MORENITA TORTILLERIA** (270 Grant St; 503/982-8221) for tortillas fresh off the griddle or for masa to make your own.

You'll find several fast and inexpensive taquerias, with flavors more familiar in Michoacán than middle America. These aren't the fish tacos they serve at the upscale restaurants back home; **TAQUERIA EL REY** (966 N Pacific Hwy; 503/982-1303), for instance, lists *cabeza* (head), *tripa* (tripe), and *lengua* (tongue) on its taco menu, but no *pescado* (fish).

LUPITA'S RESTAURANT (311 N Front St; 503/982-0483) is a good choice for a sit-down meal; the English-Spanish menu includes offerings from several regional cuisines. **MEXICO LINDO** (430 N 1st St; 503/982-1832) is one of the oldest Latino restaurants in Woodburn and has an attached import shop. There and at **SU CASA IMPORTS** (297 S Front St; 503/981-7361), you can find piñatas, religious statuary, and other staples of Latin American culture.   —*Bonnie Henderson*

Corvallis

The Willamette River lines small, lively downtown Corvallis, with the 19th-century **BENTON COUNTY COURTHOUSE** (120 NW 4th St) lending a nostalgic charm. Get touring information downtown at the **CONVENTION AND VISITORS BUREAU** (420 NW 2nd St; 541/757-1544 or 800/334-8118; www.visitcorvallis.com). Poke around interesting shops, and stop for pastry and coffee at **NEW MORNING BAKERY** (219 SW 2nd St; 541/754-0181) or **THE BEANERY** (500 SW 2nd St; 541/753-7442).

The **OREGON STATE UNIVERSITY** (15th and Jefferson Sts; 541/737-0123) campus is typical of big Northwest universities, with a gracious core of old buildings, magnificent trees, and open space. Corvallis has a thriving art scene; visit the **CORVALLIS ART CENTER** (700 SW Madison Ave; 541/754-1551) in a renovated 1889 Episcopal church off Central Park.

Tree lovers will enjoy **MCDONALD STATE FOREST** (off Hwy 99W, 6 miles north of Corvallis), with its 10 miles of biking, horseback riding, and hiking trails, including one among the native and exotic plants of **PEAVY ARBORETUM**. For a bigger outing, head west on Highway 34 to **MARYS PEAK**, the tallest point in the Coast Range at 4,097 feet; stroll the last mile to the summit, or try any of several interconnecting forest paths. Waldport Ranger District (541/563-3211) has details. Look for dusky Canada geese from trails in **FINLEY NATIONAL WILDLIFE REFUGE** (541/757-7236), 10 miles south of town on Highway 99W.

RESTAURANTS

Big River / ★★★

101 NW JACKSON ST, CORVALLIS; 541/757-0694 Arty, jazzy, noisy—Big River brought big flavors to Corvallis and became a big hit. Against an industrial-strength background (high ceilings with exposed beams and ductwork), Big River has added lots of bold original art, color, and whimsy. Food is bold as well, and solidly, eclecticly Northwest, with a taste of Sichuan here, a bit of curry there, and lots of fresh (often organic) local produce. Appetizers range from grilled homemade bread with kalamata olive tapenade to garlicky steamed Manila clams. You'll find at least a dozen entrees, half of them vegetarian, on the menu, which changes weekly; consider the rolled polenta with spinach, provolone, and portobellos, or the duck with orange and dried black cherry sauce. Interesting pizzas are baked in a wood-fired oven, and desserts are equally original and good. Order off the menu in the Bow Truss Bar too; perch at a high table or burrow into an upholstered chair to enjoy live jazz and a glass of wine or a shot from a long menu of Kentucky bourbons and single-malt Scotches. A private dining room seats up to 100. *$$; AE, DC, MC, V; checks OK; lunch Mon–Fri, dinner Mon–Sat; full bar; reservations accepted for 9 or more; www.bigriverrest.com; at 1st St.* &

Bombs Away Cafe / ★

2527 NW MONROE AVE, CORVALLIS; 541/757-7221 This is a taqueria with an attitude. You'll find several Tex-Mex favorites—with a wholesome twist: heaps of herb-flavored brown rice and black beans and hardly any fat. Among the favorites are flautas stuffed with duck confit, top sirloin steak with tasty tomatillo chipotle sauce, and a smoked tofu, shiitake, peppers, and zucchini chimichanga. The menu is loaded with vegetarian options, and has a short list of simple, inexpensive kids' meals. Order at the counter in the front room. The ambience is basic college campus casual, the help is friendly, and the service speedy. The bar in back offers an impressive variety of tequilas. *$; MC, V; checks OK; lunch Mon–Fri, dinner every day; full bar; reservations recommended for 6 or more; at NW 25th St.* &

Le Bistro / ★★

150 SW MADISON AVE, CORVALLIS; 541/754-6680 The name is misleading: this is a fine French restaurant, a modest chef d'oeuvre of French chef Robert Merlet, who arrived in Corvallis via Paris, Bordeaux, and the Bay Area. The atmosphere is quiet and intimate, the food lovingly prepared in the classic French manner: no fireworks but ingredients are fresh, and everything is cooked just right. Roast duckling might come with fresh rhubarb and a French sweet-and-sour demi-glace; grilled fish choices are lightly sauced; cheese tortellini comes with diced vegetables and roasted-garlic pesto. Not all restaurants get risotto right, but Le Bistro does. You know it's French when the menu includes not only escargots and sweetbreads but the sim-plicity of sliced tomatoes with a bit of anchovy and feta, and dessert choices include profiteroles, a fresh fruit tartlet, and melt-in-your-mouth mousse. *$$; MC, V; local checks only; dinner Tues–Sat; full bar; reservations recommended; www.lebistro. com; downtown near NW 1st St.*

Iovino's / ★★★

126 SW 1ST ST, CORVALLIS; 541/738-9015 From concrete floors to high ceil-ings in this former garage, Iovino's has the industrial feel of a converted New York loft—and a stylish sophistication you don't expect in Corvallis. Nothing on the nouvelle Italian menu is quite what you expect, and the surprises are all pleasant. Consider starting with bruschetta swathed in piquant caramelized onions, tomatoes, capers, and Gorgonzola (you'll need a fork for this finger food), or insalata de noce—chopped greens and a cache of minced hazelnuts. The sweet marsala sauce on the turkey scallops melds brilliantly with mashed ricotta potatoes, and a basil dressing happily marries the plate of tiger prawns to the herb-breaded eggplant underneath. Many entrees come in either small or full-sized portions. The tiramisu is terrific, as is chocolate mousse served in a lemonade glass. The short wine list is matched by an inventive martini menu. *$$; AE, MC, V; checks OK; dinner every day; full bar; reservations accepted for 6 or more; at Monroe Ave.* &

Magenta / ★★

1425 NW MONROE AVE, STE A, CORVALLIS; 541/758-3494 "European style with Asian flair" is how chef-owner Kim Hoang describes her elegant little bistro just off campus. Inside she's created the feel of a genteel establishment in French colonial Vietnam—antiques and tropical plants—and her eclectic menu of well-prepared dishes follows suit. You'll find seafood and fowl on the menu, but Hoang special-izes in unusual meats, from buffalo steak to cabernet-glazed emu. Appetizers might include green papaya salad or fresh spring rolls. A menu of small dishes is available in the bar all evening and in the dining room after 8:30pm. *$$; AE, DIS, MC, V; lunch Mon–Fri, dinner every day; full bar; reservations recommended; next to Oregon State University.* &

LODGINGS

Hanson Country Inn / ★★

795 SW HANSON ST, CORVALLIS; 541/752-2919 The inn is just a few minutes from town, but you'll feel you're in the country when you reach this wood-and-brick 1928 farmhouse. Formerly a prosperous poultry ranch, it's now a registered historic home, thanks to extensive renovation by former San Franciscan Patricia Covey. The gleaming living room (with piano and fireplace), sunroom, and library are often used for weddings. Step outside to a formal lawn and garden. Two large guest suites upstairs are luxuriously wallpapered and linened, each with its own sitting room, deck, and private bath. After breakfasting on crepes with blackberries, or a fresh frittata, explore the grounds and the original egg house. If you're traveling with kids, take the two-bedroom cottage behind the main house with fully equipped kitchen, private bath, and living area. *$$–$$$; AE, DIS, MC, V; checks OK; hcibb@aol.com; 5 minutes west of town.*

Harrison House Bed and Breakfast / ★

2310 NW HARRISON BLVD, CORVALLIS; 541/752-6248 OR 800/233-6248 Three blocks from the Oregon State University campus, Harrison House makes a homey base camp for a Corvallis stay—nothing innovative in the way of decor, but nicely appointed and immaculate. The restored 1939 Dutch Colonial is in a neighborhood of older homes, and owners Maria and Charlie Tomlinson are gracious and accommodating. Four large rooms are furnished with a mix of antiques and reproductions, and all have private baths. The English Garden Cottage comes with kitchenette and sitting area; it's available when the hosts' sons are out of town. Enjoy a microbrew or a glass of wine when you arrive, and let Maria know your breakfast preferences for the next morning: just fruit with scones or muffins, or a full meal with the likes of eggs Benedict or stuffed crepes. *$$; AE, DC, DIS, JCB, MC, V; checks OK; stay@corvallis-lodging.com; www.corvallis-lodging.com; at 23rd St.*

Eugene

Portland's laid-back sister to the south may be the state's second-largest urban area, but it's still something of an overgrown small town, with enough local color—from tree-hugging hippies to pro-growth developers—to keep life interesting. There's no skyline here—unless you count the grain elevator and 12-story Hilton—and a Eugenean's idea of a traffic jam is when it takes more than five minutes to traverse downtown.

Still there's a sophisticated cultural scene, with respected symphony, ballet, opera, and theater companies. The **UNIVERSITY OF OREGON** (13th Ave and University St; 541/346-3111)—the state's flagship institution—provides more speakers and events than one could possibly attend. The university also features natural history and art museums, several historic landmark buildings, and a good bookstore (541/346-4331). There are other good bookstores in town—don't miss **SMITH FAMILY BOOKSTORE** (768 E 13th Ave; 541/345-1651 or 541/343-4714)—as well as the requisite number of coffeehouses, fabulous bakeries, and trendy brewpubs. Try **STEELHEAD** (188 E 5th Ave; 541/686-2739), in the Fifth Avenue historic district, or the **WILD DUCK** (169 W 6th Ave; 541/485-3825). Two serious chocolatiers set up shop here: **EUPHORIA** (6 W 17th Ave; 541/345-1990) and **FENTON & LEE** (35 E 8th Ave; 541/343-7629), and there's an elegant French tea shop—**SAVOURE** (201 W Broadway; 541/242-1010) in the new Broadway Place development. Breathe deep; every restaurant and bar in town is smoke-free by law.

The **WILLAMETTE AND MCKENZIE RIVERS** run through or near town and provide opportunities for canoeists and rafters. Hikers find miles of forest trails just outside the city limits. Runners love the city's several groomed, packed running trails. Run along the banks of the Willamette through **ALTON BAKER PARK** (off Centennial Blvd) on the groomed **PREFONTAINE TRAIL**. Solo runners may feel safer on the sloughside circuit that borders **AMAZON PARK** (off Amazon Pkwy). **HENDRICKS PARK** (follow signs from Fairmont Blvd), the city's oldest, features an outstanding 10-acre rhododendron garden; best blooms are in May and early June.

Whatever else you do in Eugene, hike the 1½-mile trail up **SPENCER'S BUTTE** (off S Willamette St), the landmark just south of town, for a spectacular view of the city, valley, and its two rivers. Spend a morning at **SATURDAY MARKET** (Oak St at Broadway; 541/686-8885; April through fall), the state's oldest outdoor crafts fair; shop and eat your way through the **FIFTH AVENUE PUBLIC MARKET** (5th Ave and High St) one afternoon; and attend the **HULT CENTER FOR THE PERFORMING ARTS** (7th Ave and Willamette St; 541/342-5746), the city's world-class concert facility, with two architecturally striking halls. In early July, don't miss the area's oldest and wildest countercultural celebration, the **OREGON COUNTRY FAIR** (541/484-1314).

RESTAURANTS

Adam's Place / ★★★

30 E BROADWAY, EUGENE; 541/344-6948 Adam Bernstein, a third-generation restaurateur who trained at the Culinary Institute of America, has tastefully decorated this intimate downtown spot by adding mahogany wainscoting, arches, pillars, sconces, and a lovely fireplace. The result is quietly sophisticated, unpretentious yet classy—think San Francisco. Service is attentive, presentation exquisite, and the cuisine inventive, with a menu that changes seasonally. Catch the salmon and dill potato pancake with dill crème frâiche and salsa appetizer; or the grilled eggplant, tomato, and warm duck salad. For an entree, consider salmon—perfectly undercooked—topped with a sweet, tangy, chutneylike orange glaze; or seared Hawaiian ahi over marinated cucumber in soy-ginger sauce. Vegetarian options are always interesting, and desserts are stunning. An award-winning wine list, with many by the glass, adds to the experience. Attached to the restaurant, Luna is the spot to hear live jazz; it has lighter pub fare with tapas and oyster shots. *$$–$$$; AE, MC, V; checks OK; dinner every day; full bar; reservations recommended; on the downtown mall.* &

Ambrosia / ★

174 E BROADWAY, EUGENE; 541/342-4141 Pizzas are wonderful here: small, crisp pies topped with rich plum tomato sauce and trendy ingredients (sundried tomatoes, artichoke hearts, roasted eggplant), baked in a huge woodburning oven. But Ambrosia is much more than a designer pizzeria: take the ravioli San Remo, homemade and stuffed with veal, chicken, and ricotta; or the dill-sauced crepes filled with smoked salmon, spinach, and ricotta. Low lighting creates a warm, intimate atmosphere in this cavernous restaurant, where tables are tucked into "rooms" on the ground floor or scattered on an airy mezzanine; sit at the gorgeous wooden bar to take in the chefs' oven action. End the evening with a cool bowl of homemade gelato. *$$; MC, V; checks OK; lunch Mon–Sat, dinner every day; full bar; reservations recommended for 6 or more; at Pearl St.* &

Beppe and Gianni's Trattoria / ★★★

1646 E 19TH AVE, EUGENE; 541/683-6661 Italian native Beppe Macchi teamed up with John Barofsky in 1998 to create a neighborhood trattoria with the spirit and flavor of Beppe's homeland—with great success. The old house it occupies retained most of its interior walls, creating nice nooks for intimate dining, though there's a family feel to the place, with Beppe shouting greetings to friends and customers, and tables jammed with a town-and-gown crowd. Antipasto choices include bruschetta, and melon with prosciutto di Parma. Salads include a lovely fresh orange-and-grapefruit arrangement with a light Sicilian vinaigrette. Primi dishes—mostly imported or homemade pasta with lovely, light sauces and accompaniments—are generous enough to serve as the main course, including melt-in-your-mouth ravioli of the day, and excellent risottos. Secondi entrees are classical presentations of, for example, grilled fish, sautéed chicken breast (with wild mushrooms in a marsala sauce), or rosemary-perfumed lamb chops. Choose a glass or bottle from a short, modestly priced wine list. Bambini have several inexpensive menu choices. Desserts don't disappoint. *$$; MC, V; dinner every day; beer and wine; reservations accepted for 8 or more Sun–Thurs; east of Agate St.* &

Cafe Soriah / ★★

384 W 13TH AVE, EUGENE; 541/342-4410 In this jewel box of a neighborhood restaurant, chef-owner Ibrahim Hamide has wrapped an adventurous Mediterranean and Middle Eastern menu in an elegant little package, comfortable enough for everyday dining but deserving of special occasions. Squeeze past the tiny bar—a work of art in wood—to reach the pretty, well-appointed dining room, airy and smart with original art and fine woodworking; the atmosphere is intimate but not claustrophobic. In good weather, dine outdoors in the leafy, stylish walled terrace. Hamide's roots are revealed in the menu, starting with a stellar appetizer plate of hummus, baba ghanouj, and stuffed grape leaves sized for two or more. The menu changes monthly and might include roasted salmon with a coconut-curry sauce, or marlin Gaza-style (spicy); count on favorites such as lamb tagine and moussaka. Memorable desserts range from wonderful amalgams of sponge cake and buttercream to a subtly exotic cardamom-scented flan. *$$; AE, MC, V; checks OK; lunch Mon–Fri, dinner every day; full bar; reservations recommended; www.soriah.com; at Lawrence St.* &

Chanterelle / ★★

207 E 5TH ST, EUGENE; 541/484-4065 Chef Ralf Schmidt's intimate restaurant is sophisticated and understated, with a small menu that reflects Schmidt's classical French culinary sensibilities and hints at his Austrian roots. You'll find *escargots bourguignon* and oysters Rockefeller among a handful of appetizers; the traditional baked French onion soup is deeply satisfying. A dozen entree choices—from delicate coquilles St.-Jacques to richly sauced tournedos of beef and a classic *zwiebelsteak*—are supplemented by a wide selection of specials, from spring lamb to chinook salmon. All come with salad and choice of potatoes or spaetzle. You'll find a respectable wine list and extraordinary desserts. *$$$; AE, DC, MC, V; checks*

OK; dinner Tues–Sat; full bar; reservations recommended; www.clickoregon.com/ chanterelle; across from public market. ♿

Excelsior Inn Ristorante Italiano / ★★★

754 E 13TH AVE, EUGENE; 541/342-6963 OR 800/321-6963 When it opened some 30 years ago, the Excelsior was the first restaurant to bring European sophistication to Eugene; it's since met with serious competition, but the Ex remains one of Eugene's better restaurants. Current owner–executive chef Maurizio Paparo has brought his Italian background to bear in the menu and the interior. Look for medallions of elk sauced with a fig-molasses demi-glace, or fresh fettucini with chicken in a garlic-rosemary-sherry sauce. The filet mignon, topped with a brandy mushroom demi-glace, may be the best in town. Desserts by pastry chef Milka Babich are themselves worth a visit, ranging from the simplicity of crème caramel to the Grand Marnier–infused Maurizio's cake topped with white and dark chocolate curls. The wine list is well chosen and extensive. Sit by the fireplace in the formal dining room, in the airy European-style bar, on the skylit terrace, or in the walled courtyard out front. *$$–$$$; AE, DC, DIS, MC, V; checks OK; breakfast and dinner every day, lunch Mon–Fri, brunch Sun; full bar; reservations recommended; info@excelsiorinn. com; www.excelsiorinn.com; across from Sacred Heart Medical Center.* ♿

The LocoMotive Restaurant / ★★

291 E 5TH AVE, EUGENE; 541/465-4754 Owners Lee and Eitan Zucker came to Eugene via Israel, the Caribbean, and Manhattan, and they bring sophistication and subtlety to vegetarian cooking in their friendly restaurant backed against the railroad tracks in the lively Fifth Street Public Market district. The menu is 100 percent vegetarian (vegan on request), ingredients nearly 100 percent organic, and results 100 percent delicious. The Zuckers know the world's variety of legumes and grains and enjoy playing with them. With your bread, you're served an "appetizer mix" of nicely seasoned beans. The menu changes weekly but always includes wonderful soups; try the south Indian rasam. Musts include portobello mushrooms in reduced red wine sauce with garlicky mashed potatoes, and curried eggs with house-made chutney. Don't miss the Oregon Snow—creamy white sorbet with flavors of lime and coconut. *$$; MC, V; checks OK; dinner Wed–Sat (closed 2–3 weeks in Jan and July); beer and wine; reservations recommended; www.thelocomotive.com; across from public market.* ♿

Marché / ★★★

🌲 **296 E 5TH AVE, EUGENE; 541/342-3612** The name of this elegant restaurant, on the ground floor of the Fifth Street Public Market, says it all: Marché's menu is an ode to the seasonal Northwest bounty, prepared with French sensibility. Each day's menu lists well-crafted combinations of fresh and often organically grown local foodstuffs. In fall, locally raised pork chops may come with an autumn fruit-and-onion confit, and the sage-infused roasted leg of venison is accompanied by sweet potato purée, baked apple, and huckleberry sauce. Lunch is lighter, with the addition of a few pizzettas (picture pancetta, delicata squash, sage, and romano cheese) and sandwiches (consider portobello mushroom with sundried tomato relish and smoked mozzarella on homemade flatbread). The wine list and dessert menu reflect the same regional leanings and attention to detail. The interior is elegantly hip with dark gleaming wood and wry artwork. In a hurry? Try Café Marché upstairs. *$$–$$$; AE, DC, DIS, MC, V; checks OK; lunch and dinner every day, brunch Sun; full bar; reservations recommended; www.marcherestaurant.com; in public market.* &

Ring of Fire / ★★

1099 CHAMBERS ST, EUGENE; 541/344-6475 Pull open the heavy entry door, inhale the exotic fragrances from the kitchen, and allow Ring of Fire's elegant, tranquil ambience to transport you far from busy, strip-malled W 11th Street. The menu claims inspiration from many Pacific Rim cuisines, mainly Thai and Indonesian. Start with a Korean-style vegetable tempura served with Japanese tagaragi spice, or a taste of beef satay with black bean–ginger sauce. Curries are coconut-based, Thai style, and noodle dishes include the reliable phad thai as well as *phad se yu,* with sweet wheat noodles and broccoli. Crispy ginger red snapper comes with roasted garlic and vegetables. Many dishes offer meat, tofu, or tempeh options. Portions are generous. Takeout is available until midnight. Try a "My Thai" or other original tropical drink from the stylish little Lava Lounge. *$$; MC, V; no checks; lunch, dinner every day; full bar; reservations recommended; rof@ringoffire restaurant.com; www.ringoffirerestaurant.com; off W 11th Ave.* &

Zenon Café / ★★★

898 PEARL ST, EUGENE; 541/343-3005 A compelling combination of culinary imagination and consistency has made Zenon one of Eugene's best restaurants. Urbane, noisy, crowded, and invariably interesting, Zenon offers an ever-changing international menu featuring, on any given night, Italian, Greek, Middle Eastern, Cajun, Caribbean, Thai, and Northwest cuisines. Nothing disappoints, from Chinese "Hot as Hell" skewered pork tenderloin with cucumber relish and daikon-carrot salad, to sautéed duck breast with raspberry demi-glace, sautéed shiitake mushrooms, and wild rice. Vegetarian dishes range from a lovely eggplant-based dish named "The Priest Fainted" to Southwest-inspired black bean-and-posole chili. For a light meal, have a bowl of the day's soup and a basket of fresh breads. A good selection of regional wines by the glass (and bottle) is available, as is Zenon's complex summer sangria, juicy with fresh seasonal fruits. Zenon's dessert list is the city's largest and one of the best. In the spirit of lively European restaurants, this is a good place for kids; it's already loud, and the chef is happy to provide plates of plain fettucine with cheese. *$$; MC, V; checks OK; breakfast, lunch, dinner every day; beer and wine; reservations not accepted; corner of E Broadway.* &

LODGINGS

Campbell House / ★★★

252 PEARL ST, EUGENE; 541/343-1119 OR 800/264-2519 Built in 1892 and restored as a grand bed-and-breakfast inn, Campbell House has everything: a location that's quiet (an acre of beautifully landscaped grounds) yet convenient (2 blocks from Fifth Street Public Market); elegant, light-filled rooms with old-world charm (four-poster beds, high ceilings, dormer windows) and modern amenities (TVs and VCRs tastefully hidden, phones with data ports, stocked minifridges); and smart, attentive service. Each of the 18 rooms has a private bath, several have gas fireplaces, and one—the Dr. Eva Johnson Room—has a luxurious bathroom alcove with jetted tub. The inn is designated nonsmoking, but the Cogswell Room offers a private entrance that opens onto a pretty patio for those who must. If you like the personalized service of a B&B but don't like to feel hovered over, if you love country-cottage decor but lament the day Laura Ashley was born, this is your kind of place. Full breakfast features waffles, homemade granola, and a special egg dish. *$$–$$$$; AE, DC, DIS, MC, V; no checks; campbellhouse@ campbellhouse.com; www.campbellhouse.com; 2 blocks north of public market.* &

Eugene Hilton / ★

66 E 6TH AVE, EUGENE; 541/342-2000 OR 800/937-6660 For convenience to downtown, the Hilton fills the bill, and extensive renovations completed in 1999 nicely spiffed up common areas and guest rooms. It's attached to the Eugene Conference Center, across a brick courtyard from the Hult Center for the Performing Arts, a block from the downtown mall, and within easy strolling distance of most of Eugene's best restaurants. Rooms are predictable, but have nice city views from south-facing rooms and quiet views of Skinner Butte from north-facing rooms. Amenities include a (very small) indoor pool along with sauna, Jacuzzi, and fitness room. *$$–$$$; AE, DC, DIS, MC, V; checks OK; www.eugene.hilton.com; exit 194B off I-5.* &

Excelsior Inn / ★★

754 E 13TH AVE, EUGENE; 541/342-6963 OR 800/321-6963 This European-style inn sits atop the Excelsior restaurant, 2 blocks from the University of Oregon. Each of the 14 rooms is named for a composer and is charmingly decorated, featuring hardwood floors, arched windows, vaulted ceilings, and marble-and-tile baths with fluffy towels. All rooms have TVs, VCRs, and computer hookups; two have Jacuzzi tubs. The Bach Room, with its king-sized sleigh bed, pretty sitting area, and Jacuzzi, is a favorite. The downside: Most rooms are small, some with a view of a blank wall, and we've found the reception at the inn's alley entrance to be uncertain; you may have to chase down an innkeeper at the attached restaurant. The upside: Old-world ambience, good soundproofing, and amenities that cover the bases. An excellent complimentary breakfast is served in the restaurant, where guests order from the regular menu. *$–$$$; AE, DC, DIS, MC, V; checks OK; info@excelsiorinn.com; www.excelsiorinn.com; across from Sacred Heart Medical Center.* &

Secret Garden / ★★

1910 UNIVERSITY ST, EUGENE; 541/484-6755 OR 888/484-6755 Originally a 1910 farmhouse, this is now an airy, enchanting 10-room inn on a hilltop just south of the University of Oregon campus. Thoughtfully chosen art and antiques give the inn a refined feeling reminiscent of the Edwardian era from which the novel of the same name sprung. Each room is individually decorated, taking cues from the garden, from the rusticity of the Barn Owl to the refinement of the Scented Garden. All rooms have private baths as well as TV/VCRs, minifridges, and phones. Fix yourself a cup of tea in the second-story sitting room, or lounge in the great room downstairs, where you may meet Angus (the house dog) or a guest playing the baby grand piano. Breakfasts are inventive and generous. Depending upon the season, the street noise in this university neighborhood can be a bit much. *$$–$$$$; AE, DIS, MC, V; checks OK; gardenbb@att.net; www.secretgardenbbinn.com; 1 block south of campus.* &

Valley River Inn / ★★

1000 VALLEY RIVER WY, EUGENE; 541/687-0123 OR 800/543-8266 This elegant, low-profile hotel is neighbor to a regional shopping mall with acres of parking, but the hotel itself looks toward the Willamette River for its ambience. With pretty inner courtyards, lovely plantings, and an inviting pool, this sprawling complex effectively creates a world of its own. The 257 rooms are oversized and well decorated, with the best ones facing the river. Guests can use a workout room, sauna, Jacuzzi, and outdoor pool, or rent bicycles for a spin on the paved riverside path just out the door. The inn's Sweetwaters restaurant has an outdoor dining area overlooking the river that is wonderful for drinks and hors d'oeuvres. *$$$–$$$$; AE, DC, DIS, MC, V; checks OK; reserve@valleyriverinn.com; www.valleyriverinn. com; exit 194B off I-5.* &

Springfield

"Gateway" is the catchword for Springfield, Eugene's smaller neighbor to the east. The town promotes itself as the gateway to the **MCKENZIE RIVER,** wild with white water upstream but placid and sweet where it flows by town. And the Gateway district along Interstate 5 is fast becoming the de facto town center. Here you'll find chain motels, fast food, and large **GATEWAY MALL** (300 Gateway St; 541/747-3123).

The old downtown isn't much to look at these days, but second-hand and collectibles shops sometimes yield a gem. Lively **PARK SWIM CENTER** (6100 Thurston Rd; 541/736-4244), the state's first wave pool, is a kid magnet at the east end of town. Down by the river, wander the old orchards and riverside paths of **DORRIS RANCH LIVING HISTORY FARM** (2nd St S and Dorris St; 541/747-5552), birthplace of the state's hazelnut industry (they're still called filberts here).

RESTAURANTS

Crossroads Grill / ★★

737 MAIN ST, SPRINGFIELD; 541/741-3366 A welcome surprise in Springfield's dilapidated downtown, Crossroads Grill features three classic and flavorful American cuisines: the Creole, Cajun, and country-style French fare of New Orleans, the traditional and modern fare served in Santa Fe, and old-fashioned, slow-smoked barbecue. Whatever you order—the bouillabaisse or jambalaya, the grilled ahi with mango cactus salsa, the pulled pork, or baby back ribs—comes cooked just right, with just the right accompaniments. Desserts, mostly house-made, range from sangria sorbet to pear bread pudding with whiskey cream sauce. A fireplace in the middle of the dining room is welcoming in winter, as is the courtyard in summer; call for the schedule of live jazz and blues. Sunday's brunch features a good selection of New Orleans–style entrees. *$$; AE, MC, V; checks OK; lunch and dinner every day; full bar; reservations recommended; www.crossroadsgrill.com; between 7th and 8th Sts.* &

Kuraya's

1410 MOHAWK BLVD, SPRINGFIELD; 541/746-2951 Its location is off the beaten path, but Kuraya's remains a popular spot with local Thai-food fanciers. The casual atmosphere, friendly service, and large, inventive menu keep people coming back. So do the seafood basket—shrimp and scallops in a hot, coconutty sauce—and the Bangkok prawns, charcoal broiled and served with a crabmeat-and-peanut dipping sauce. *$; MC, V; no checks; lunch Mon–Sat, dinner every day; beer and wine; reservations recommended for 7 or more; at Market St.* &

Mookie's Place / ★

1507 CENTENNIAL BLVD, SPRINGFIELD; 541/746-8298 Housed in a former drive-in, Mookie's is a local favorite for come-as-you-are, sit-down dinners or ready-to-eat takeout. It's not nouvelle cuisine, but chef Randy Hollister's menu is playful and surprising, like spicy Cajun chicken Alfredo, honey-marinated grilled salmon, and hot artichoke dip with garbanzo beans. Slow-roasted prime rib is offered Friday and Saturday nights. Eat in, ensconced in plush orange banquettes at teal-and-pink-tiled tables, or order to go, from an entire meal to just your favorite sauce or salad dressing. Expect to take something home in either case: portions are generous. There's a decent selection of microbrews, several West Coast wines, and an extensive children's menu. *$–$$; AE, MC, V; checks OK; lunch Mon–Fri, dinner Tues–Sat; beer and wine; reservations not accepted; pam@mookiesplace.com; www.mookies place.com; at Mohawk Blvd.* &

LODGINGS

McKenzie View Bed & Breakfast / ★★★

34922 MCKENZIE VIEW DR, SPRINGFIELD; 541/726-3887 OR 888/625-8439 Roberta and Scott Bolling's large, contemporary country home is 15 minutes—and a world away—from downtown Eugene. There's nothing between your room and the wide, placid lower McKenzie River but a broad back porch, immaculate gardens, lawns dotted with hammocks, and a maple-shaded deck hanging over the river's edge. The four rooms have private baths and range from good-sized to spacious; three overlook the river through large picture windows, and two have gas fireplaces. Rooms have no TVs or VCRs, phones, or data ports, but guests can get their fix in the common areas. Roberta's full breakfasts are inventive and satisfying, and you are welcome to raid a well-stocked minifridge and cookie jar. The recently (1996) transplanted Midwesterners have furnished the house with antiques and quality reproductions, giving it a conservative feel by Oregon standards, but one freshened by the Bollings' enthusiasm for innkeeping and for their adopted home. *$–$$$$; AE, DC, MC, V; checks OK; mckenzieview@worldnet.att.net; www.mckenzie-view.com; exit 199 off I-5.* &

NORTHERN OREGON COAST

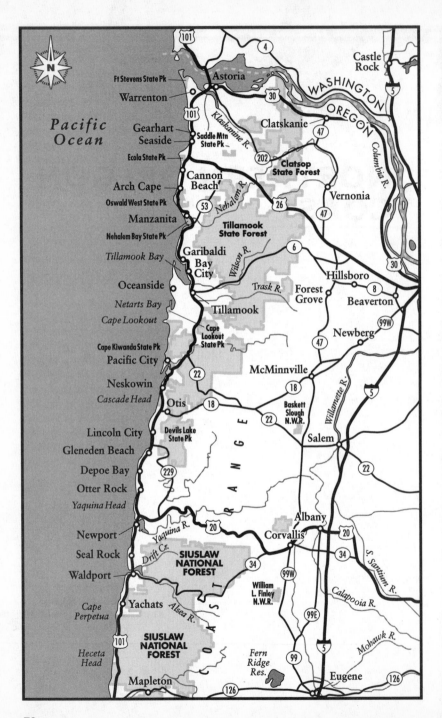

NORTHERN OREGON COAST

Living comes easy along Oregon's north coast. Folks are friendly, the climate's mild, and the scenic splendor is second to none.

But the place is changing. Even though everyone comes to escape the big city, aspects of urban life such as fast-food franchises, big-box retailers, and even outlet malls are already part of the landscape. And summer traffic through Seaside, or between Lincoln City and Newport, can be stifling.

Fortunately, commercial progress hasn't undermined the area's breathtaking geography. From Astoria to Yachats—the mouth of the Columbia River to Cape Perpetua—this rugged coastline is embossed with a series of spectacular headlands holding out against Neptune's fury, separated intermittently by broad expanses of sand. Stark sandstone cliffs sculpted by weather and waves distinguish other headlands, such as Cape Kiwanda, purportedly the coast's most photographed landmark. Many stretches of coastline remain pristine, preserved as state parks, and Oregon's "beach bill" (unique in the United States) guarantees public access to the state's beaches.

The Oregon Coast Trail begins at the South Jetty of the Columbia River (within Warrenton's Fort Stevens State Park), then traverses beaches and headlands to the California border. Surfers will tell you The Point in Seaside boasts the best waves north of Santa Cruz, and that the north coast's windsurfing conditions are second only to the Columbia River Gorge. Thousands of cyclists pedal US Highway 101 every summer, and kayakers paddle the region's numerous rivers, lakes, and backwaters.

It's no surprise that tourism now surpasses commercial fishing and logging as the north coast's foremost economic activity. Tiny hamlets of a few hundred people—Manzanita, in Tillamook County, for example—showcase upscale lodgings and galleries. Once a culinary wasteland, this area is now loaded with top-drawer restaurants. Even those quintessential Northwest urban establishments, brewpubs, are thriving in Astoria, Cannon Beach, Pacific City, Lincoln City, and Newport.

Certainly it rains—55 to 80 inches a year; that's why the landscape is forever green. Winter storms that carry much of the moisture—sou'westers, they call them—afford one of nature's greatest spectacles: rain falls in horizontal sheets, beach sands swirl, and the Pacific becomes a frothing cauldron. What the locals keep to themselves is that come summer, days are mostly sunny, temperatures rarely dip below 55°F or crest 80°F, and a refreshing breeze blows daily.

ACCESS AND INFORMATION

Driving is your best bet to and from the Northern Oregon Coast. From Seattle, take Interstate 5 to Longview, Washington, cross the interstate bridge, and follow US Highway 30 west to Astoria. From downtown Portland, take US Highway 26 west (the road traverses the Coast Range mountains and can be dangerous in winter) to its intersection with US Highway 101 at the Cannon Beach Junction. **HIGHWAY 101** (also known as the Coast Highway) is the only route along Oregon's coast. The **STATE WELCOME CENTER** (111 W Marine Dr, Astoria; 503/325-6311 or 800/875-6807) or the **SEASIDE VISITORS BUREAU** (7 N Roosevelt Dr, Seaside; 503/738-3097 or 888/306-2326) are good starting points.

Limited alternatives include bus and air transportation. **COACHWAYS OF OREGON** (800/442-4106) offers one bus daily from Portland to Astoria, and then south to Cannon Beach. Local transport is through **SUNSET EMPIRE TRANSPORTATION** (866/811-1001). **CARAVAN** (888/743-3847) has shuttle service to Lincoln City, while **GREYHOUND** (541/265-2253) offers bus service to Newport and Astoria (though this changes frequently; call ahead to verify).

Weather on the north coast is rainy in winter and dry—but almost never hot—in summer (generally July 4 through September). After Labor Day, crowds thin and days are gorgeous.

Astoria

The oldest American city west of the Rockies features a bustling waterfront (with a river walkway and a year-round trolley), neighborhoods dotted with Victorian homes, and numerous historic attractions. The recently renovated **COLUMBIA RIVER MARITIME MUSEUM** (1792 Marine Dr; 503/325-2323) features a Great Hall with restored fishing and lifesaving vessels and visitor-friendly galleries with interactive exhibits depicting different aspects of the region's maritime history. The lightship *Columbia,* the last of its kind on the Pacific coast, is moored outside and open to visitors. Named for a prominent 19th-century businessman and one of the first Columbia River bar pilots, **CAPTAIN GEORGE FLAVEL HOUSE** (8th and Duane Sts; 503/325-2563) is the city's best example of ornate Queen Anne architecture. Both the Flavel House and the restored **HERITAGE MUSEUM** (1618 Exchange St; 503/325-2203), 8 blocks away, feature local history. Six miles southwest of Astoria, off Highway 101, the Lewis and Clark Expedition's 1805–06 winter encampment is re-created at **FORT CLATSOP NATIONAL MEMORIAL** (92343 Fort Clatsop Rd; 503/861-2471). You can watch videos and view period artifacts in the visitor center and, during summer, enjoy living-history demonstrations, such as musket firing and candle making, inside the reconstructed fort.

For a breathtaking panorama of the Columbia River estuary, the Pacific Ocean, and more, climb the 166 steps of the **ASTORIA COLUMN** (drive to the top of 16th St and follow the signs), which sits atop Coxcomb Hill, Astoria's highest point.

FORT STEVENS STATE PARK (off Ridge Rd, Hammond; 503/861-1671), 20 minutes northwest of Astoria off Highway 101, is a 3,500-acre outdoor wonderland of forest trails, paved bike paths, a freshwater lake, and uncrowded beaches—including the permanent resting place of the *Peter Iredale,* a sailing vessel wrecked in 1906. The **SOUTH JETTY** lookout tower, perched at Oregon's northwesternmost point, is a supreme storm-watching spot and a good place to spy whales in calmer weather. It also marks the start of the **OREGON COAST TRAIL,** which traverses sandy beaches and forested headlands all the way to the California border. With 536 campsites, 15 yurts, and 4 group camps, Fort Stevens is Oregon's largest publicly owned campground.

NORTHERN OREGON COAST THREE-DAY TOUR

DAY ONE: Drive up to the **ASTORIA COLUMN** and soak in the superb view. Meander back down the hill along Franklin and Grand Avenues (between 16th and 17th Sts) for a look at some of the restored Victorian homes. At the foot of 17th, tour the **COLUMBIA RIVER MARITIME MUSEUM** (and the lightship *Columbia*), then stroll west along the riverfront walkway. Retire to the **HOME SPIRIT BAKERY CAFE** for lunch; save room for Key lime pie and buy some raisin-nut scones or a baguette for later. Check in at the **ROSE RIVER INN BED & BREAKFAST,** and schedule an evening massage with proprietor Kati Tuominen. Next, drive south to **FORT STEVENS STATE PARK,** where you can frolic on the beach, inspect the remains of the *Peter Iredale,* and climb the South Jetty viewing tower. Detour back to Astoria via **FORT CLATSOP NATIONAL MEMORIAL.** Have dinner at the funky but fun **COLUMBIAN CAFE,** then take a riverfront walk to the 6th Street viewing tower, where you can watch seals, sea lions, and river traffic.

DAY TWO: Following a sumptuous breakfast at the Rose River Inn, head south to Cannon Beach and browse the shops and galleries along **HEMLOCK STREET** (public parking lots are in downtown and midtown, with free bus service between the two), then walk to the beach and majestic **HAYSTACK ROCK.** Or drive north into **ECOLA STATE PARK,** where a cliffside trail affords wondrous vistas. Enjoy a slice at **PIZZA 'A FETTA** or a more ambitious lunch (and a craft brew) at **BILL'S TAVERN & BREW-HOUSE,** then drive south to Manzanita and check in at **THE INN AT MANZANITA.** Drop off your bags and drive north again to the **NEAHKAHNIE MOUNTAIN** trailhead (look for a green sign on the highway's east side). The trail to the summit is steep, but you'll be rewarded with the north coast's finest panorama. Return to Manzanita, take a quick spa, and dine at the fusion-food–oriented **BLUE SKY CAFE.** The beach is a couple of blocks away and ideal for an evening stroll, especially at low tide.

DAY THREE: Take a bracing morning walk or jog on the beach, enjoy a hearty breakfast at Manzanita's **BIG WAVE CAFE** (822 Hwy 101; 503/368-9283), and head south on Highway 101. North of Tillamook, visit the **TILLAMOOK CHEESE** plant, enjoy an ice-cream cone, then detour to **THREE CAPES SCENIC DRIVE,** a route that rejoins Highway 101 just south of Pacific City. Continue on to Lincoln City and savor lunch at the **BLACKFISH CAFE.** Afternoon entertainment comes courtesy of the finny, feathery, and furry critters at Newport's **OREGON COAST AQUARIUM.** Check in to the literary-inclined **SYLVIA BEACH HOTEL** for a restful night of reading and stimulating dinner conversation at the hotel's **TABLES OF CONTENT** restaurant. Or venture across the street to **APRIL'S,** for some Mediterranean-inspired cuisine.

RESTAURANTS

Cannery Cafe / ★

I 6TH ST, ASTORIA; 503/325-8642 The setting couldn't be better at this aptly named eatery, housed in a century-old former cannery building perched on pilings over the Columbia River. Every table offers a superb view of ship traffic and the finned and feathered critters cavorting outside. Clam chowder is credible, and the panini du jour is built around thick focaccia slices. More substantial fare includes seafood cakes concocted with crab and shrimp, grilled halibut garnished with seasonal fruit chutney, and a superb bouillabaisse. Carnivores can savor a blackened rib eye or a teriyaki-glazed flank steak. After your meal, stroll to the end of the 6th Street pier (or to the top of an adjacent viewing tower) for an even better Columbia River panorama. *$$; DIS, MC, V; checks OK; lunch Mon–Sat, dinner Tues–Sat; full bar; reservations recommended; on 6th St pier.* &

Columbian Cafe / ★★

1114 MARINE DR, ASTORIA; 503/325-2233 Earning raves from as far afield as the *New York Times,* this trendy, diminutive and usually crowded cafe woos customers with veggie-oriented lunches (broccoli and cheese crepes or a wilted spinach salad redolent of walnuts and blue cheese) and fabulous seafood-pasta preparations. Look for fresh Columbia River salmon paired with asparagus, sturgeon piccatta or halibut cheeks slathered with mole verde, all of them tossed with fettuccine. From borscht to vegetable bisque, soups are satisfying and arrive with hearty slabs of grilled garlic bread. From his small grill in the open kitchen, chef Uriah Hulsey presides over the place like a prince in his palace, bantering with counter and booth customers. If you're feeling frisky, order his Chef's Mercy, a surprise potpourri of the day's best fixings. The adjacent Voodoo Lounge offers pizza and other light fare, plus occasional live music. *$$; no credit cards; checks OK; breakfast, lunch, dinner Mon–Sat; beer and wine; reservations not accepted; at 11th St.* &

Home Spirit Bakery Cafe / ★★★

1585 EXCHANGE ST, ASTORIA; 503/325-6846 For about the same price as supermarket bread, you can savor myriad artisan loaves baked daily (don't miss the Columbia sourdough) at this gorgeously restored 1892 Victorian home. Other treats include delicately flaky yeast-dough croissants, fruit and raisin scones, and sweet mounds of puffy perfection called Gateway cinnamon rolls. Noontime fare might include pasta carbonara, chanterelle-and-shrimp quiche, or a croissant sandwich stuffed with Black Forest ham. Comforting soups—butternut bisque, seafood chowder, and a hearty cheddar ale—are Astoria's finest. Prix-fixe dinner menus change bimonthly and feature what chef Michael Henderson calls "world cuisine"—say, gnocchi with four cheeses, a vegetarian tapas platter, *boeuf bourguignon,* and shrimp Creole. Not-to-be-missed desserts are as varied as crème brûlée and Key lime pie. *$$; no credit cards; checks OK; breakfast, lunch Tues–Sat, dinner Wed–Sat, Fri–Sat in winter; beer and wine; reservations recommended (dinner); corner of 16th St.* &

Rio Cafe / ★

125 9TH ST, ASTORIA; 503/325-2409 Instead of the usual taco-and-burrito Tex-Mex fare, authentic south-of-the-border chow is purveyed by this gaily decorated cantina. Begin with a plate of greens tossed with a creamy, piquant jalapeño dressing or an order of chalupitas, deep-fried corn masa "boats" topped with zesty black beans and cheeses. The *puerco en salsa verde* features pork stewed tender with onions, chiles, and tomatillos, while the grilled beef slices in the carne asada are flavored with green peppers, tomatoes, and jalapeños. Heat-craving diners opt for the *pescado rojo*, lightly breaded sole grilled with a fiery red chile and garlic sauce. A trio of salsas is prepared fresh daily. *$; MC, V; checks OK; lunch Mon–Sat, dinner Thurs–Sat; beer and wine; reservations not necessary; 1 block south of the Columbia.* &

LODGINGS

Benjamin Young Inn / ★

3652 DUANE ST, ASTORIA; 503/325-6172 OR 800/201-1286 Painted in antique gold and bedecked with scalloped shingles, this 20-room mansion was built in 1888 on Astoria's east side for Benjamin Young, a Swedish immigrant and pioneer salmon packer. Wrought-iron gates lead to a roomy front porch outfitted with wicker furniture. Stained-glass panels adorn inner doors leading to a living room with gold wallpaper, elegant drapes, red-velvet settees, and a huge white-brick fireplace. Five guest rooms (one downstairs, four on the second floor) are lavishly decorated; all have river views. The Honeymoon Suite has antique Eastlake furnishings and a turret with a sitting room overlooking the garden and the river. *$$–$$$; AE, DIS, MC, V; checks OK; benjamin@benjaminyounginn.com; www. benjaminyounginn.com; 1 block above Marine Dr.*

Clementine's Bed and Breakfast / ★★

847 EXCHANGE ST, ASTORIA; 503/325-2005 OR 800/521-6801 This stylish Italianate Victorian built in 1888 is across the street from the Flavel House (the town's most recognized Victorian) and on the edge of downtown. Innkeepers Judith and Cliff Taylor possess a wealth of local knowledge, and their B&B has a lived-in look, with a baby grand piano and a crystal chandelier in the living room and a bevy of antiques throughout, including a collection of vintage glassware and bowls. Upstairs rooms feature private balconies and captivating river vistas. Next door are two suites equipped with kitchens, fireplaces, and two bedrooms apiece (ideal for families and pets). Judith also serves one of Astoria's finest breakfasts: wild mushroom omelets and baked French toast stuffed with cream, cottage cheese, and peaches, for example, plus a stunning array of sweet treats. *$$; AE, DIS, MC, V; checks OK; jtaylor@clementines-bb.com; www.clementines-bb.com; across 8th St from Flavel House.* &

Rosebriar Hotel / ★★

636 14TH ST, ASTORIA; 503/325-7427 OR 800/487-0224 Small, intimate hotels are popular on the Oregon Coast, and the 11-unit Rosebriar, situated in a residential area 3 blocks above the waterfront, is a top-notch example. Inside, a homey lobby is furnished with comfy chairs and a fire-place. Guest quarters (all with private baths) range from cozy rooms trimmed with richly stained fir to more spacious view units featuring fireplaces and spas. A sepa-rate carriage house—built in 1885, it predates the main building by 17 years—has all that, plus a kitchen. The included full breakfast might feature blueberry cobbler and baked omelets. Outside, a porch (supported by stately columns) and front-yard benches afford river views. A man-made "brook" flows through the lush side yard, while a shrine made of stones and seashells is a reminder that the Rosebriar was for-merly a convent. *$$; AE, DIS, MC, V; checks OK; rosebriar@oregoncoastlodgings. com; www.astoria-usa.com/rosebriar/; corner of Franklin Ave.* &

Rose River Inn Bed & Breakfast / ★★

1510 FRANKLIN AVE, ASTORIA; 503/325-7175 OR 888-876-0028 With a blush-pink exterior and lush gardens teeming with flowering shrubs, ever-greens, and climbing rosebushes, the Rose River Inn is easy to spot. From Finland, proprietors Kati and Jaakko Tuominen lend European flair to their circa-1912 lodging (four guest rooms; no children or pets), which exemplifies American four-square architecture. He's a former Finnish Olympic hurdler; Kati is a licensed therapist who offers massages ($45 an hour). Reserve the River Suite and sweat away your worries in a Finnish sauna paneled in Alaskan yellow cedar, soak in the claw-footed tub, or gaze at the Columbia River from a private sunporch. Afterward, relax with a warm beverage in the glow of the parlor fireplace. *$$; DIS, MC, V; checks OK; jaska@pacifier.com; 3 blocks up from waterfront.*

Gearhart and Seaside

Isolated from Highway 101, Gearhart is a bedroom community backed by grassy dunes and a wide, uncrowded beach. Seaside, conversely, is the Oregon Coast's oldest resort town and sprawls north and south along Highway 101. Visitors stroll Broadway, eyeing the entertainment parlors, bumper cars, and sweet-treat conces-sions, and then emerge at **THE PROM**, the 2-mile cement walkway that parallels the beach. Throughout town are the coast's most delightful streetside theme gardens, planted with a collage of flowers, shrubs and plants. Duck into **PACIFIC BENTO** (111 Broadway, Ste 12; 503/738-2079) for espresso or nutritious fast food—try charbroiled chicken over yakisoba noodles. Surf fishing is popular in the Cove area (along Sunset Boulevard). Steelhead and salmon can be taken (in season) from the **NECANICUM RIVER**, which flows through town. **QUATAT MARINE PARK** (down-town Seaside, along Necanicum River) is a relaxing picnic spot and the setting for summer concerts. Sunset Empire Park and Recreation District, headquartered at **SUNSET POOL** (1140 E Broadway; 503/738-3311), has water slides, lap swims, and a covered skateboard park. On Seaside's south end, a 7-mile trail begins at the end of Sunset Boulevard, winds over Tillamook Head—a rock promontory that's part of **ECOLA STATE PARK** (primitive camping only)—and ends at Indian Beach.

RESTAURANTS

Ambrosia / ★

210 S HOLLADAY DR, SEASIDE; 503/738-7199 This chi-chi hangout housed in a former bank showcases its location as much as its cuisine. The restaurant's innards are splashed with orange, yellow, shades of red, and other bold colors. Massive paintings of flowers decorate the walls, and bunches of bouquets adorn floor pots fronting the bustling open kitchen. Food flavors, on the other hand, are more subtle than assertive. A stout pork chop arranged atop a mound of mashed potatoes is certified comfort fare, while linguini tossed with a mellow marinara, mussels, clams, and scallops oozes deep-sea tang. Fancier are the seared and skewered beef medallions bathed in Gorgonzola pesto and a crusted rack of lamb ringed with cannellini beans. Before or after your meal, tour the former bank vault, a spacious, tomblike enclosure with seaside scenes adorning the walls and a rippled carpet underfoot. *$$; AE, DIS, MC,V; no checks; dinner Tues–Sat; full bar; reservations recommended; www.ambrosiaseaside.com; corner of Holladay Dr and Ave A.* &

Corpeny's / ★

2281 BEACH DR, SEASIDE; 503/738-7353 Not everyone likes omelets. So for breakfast, Suzanne Ziegler, the baker-owner of this delightful corner cafe with a rock fireplace and porcelain tile floors, also serves plates of eggs scrambled with sausage, salami, or veggies. Ziegler's omelets are fine choices, too, especially a Torres version bursting with jalapeños, roasted garlic, mushrooms, zucchini, and pork sausage. Everyday pastries include French apple tarts, Marionberry scones, Seaside's yummiest coffee cake, and a muffin du jour. Noontime selections feature sumptuous soups and extraordinary sandwiches, such as chicken salad spiked with toasted almonds, dried cranberries, and pineapple; or a meat-and-cheese extravaganza called a Deli Blue. Adventurous eaters can opt for a tamale pie built with sausage and veggies tucked inside a moist polenta-style crust swathed in melted cheeses. The massive, ground-chuck burgers are the best around. *$; no credit cards; checks OK; breakfast, lunch Thurs–Sun; no alcohol; reservations not necessary; corpenys@ pacifier.com; at Ave U, 1 block from beach.* &

Pacific Way Bakery & Cafe / ★★

601 PACIFIC WY, GEARHART; 503/738-0245 The concept of an Oregon coastal cafe goes back maybe a decade and a half, and this welcoming 14-year-old, chic and airy establishment decorated with walls of historic photographs was one of the first. Lisa Allen's baked goods—breads, croissants, cinnamon rolls, and cheesecakes, among others—are stellar. So is a broiled Island Ham sandwich garnished with dilled cream cheese and a zippy, cilantro-pineapple-jalapeño relish, or a halibut taco flavored with chipotle sour cream. Seafood stew, a snappy broth brimming with shellfish, salmon, and other ocean bounty, is a superior catch, while parmesan-crusted and pan-fried chicken breast finished with an apple-brandy sauce is a fine way to prepare fowl. Pizzas push the borders of what pizza might be (Thai chicken slathered with a sassy peanut sauce?). For dessert, try the homemade ice creams and sorbets. *$$; MC, V; checks OK; lunch, dinner Thurs–Mon; beer and wine; reservations recommended (dinner); corner of Cottage Ave.*

LODGINGS

Gilbert Inn / ★★

341 BEACH DR, SEASIDE; 503/738-9770 OR 800/410-9770 Sure, Seaside is crowded and ofttimes noisy. But this Queen Anne–style Victorian, built in 1892, is the city's finest lodging and an oasis of comfort just a block off the Prom and on the edge of downtown. All 10 guest rooms within the light-yellow structure are appointed with period furnishings and include private baths. Richly finished tongue-and-groove fir covers walls and ceilings throughout, and a large fireplace dominates the downstairs parlor, decorated with lush green carpeting and cushy couches. What remains of the original Gilbert cottage has been incorporated into the house and serves as a main-floor suite with sitting room. Upstairs, the Turret Room has a four-poster bed and an ocean view. The Garret, a third-floor suite with three hand-hewn fir beds, is ideal for families. Breakfasts, served in summer on the side porch, are superior. *$$; AE, DIS, MC, V; checks OK; closed Jan; gilbertinn@theoregonshore.com; www.gilbert inn.com; at Ave G.*

Cannon Beach

Often called the Carmel of the Northwest, Cannon Beach is a hip, artsy community showcasing aesthetically pleasing structures constructed with cedar and weathered wood (no neon signs are allowed). Come summer (and most winter weekends as well), the town explodes with tourists, who come to browse the galleries, craft shops, and boutiques along bustling Hemlock Street.

Still, the main draw is the wide-open white-sand beach, dominated by **HAYSTACK ROCK,** one of the world's largest coastal monoliths and approachable at low tide. In summer, interpreters with the **HAYSTACK ROCK AWARENESS PRO-GRAM** (on the beach; 503/436-1581) explain the geology and marine life.

Cannon Beach counts some of the coast's best galleries; most are clustered along Hemlock Street. Not to be missed are the **WHITE BIRD** (251 N Hemlock St; 503/436-2681), with an eclectic collection on two levels; the **BRONZE COAST GALLERY** (224 N Hemlock St, Ste 2; 503/436-1055 or 800/430-1055), with dramatic bronze sculptures of wildlife and landscapes; and the **PACIFIC RIM GALLERY** (131 W 2nd; 503/436-1253), displaying wood and copper sculptures, ceramics, and jewelry. Watch two glass blowers working in tandem at **ICEFIRE GLASSWORKS** (116 Gower St; 503/436-2359). Quick eats and picnic fixings can be found at **OSBURN'S ICE CREAMERY & DELI** (240 N Hemlock St; 503/436-2234) and **ECOLA SEAFOOD MARKET** (208 N Spruce St; 503/436-9130). **PIZZA `A FETTA** (231 N Hemlock St; 503/436-0333) offers slices, or quaff a handcrafted beer at **BILL'S TAVERN & BREWHOUSE** (188 N Hemlock St; 503/436-2202). A natural gas–powered free shuttle travels the length of town (along Hemlock St) year-round.

ECOLA STATE PARK (on the town's north end) offers fabulous vistas, quiet picnic areas, and fantastic hiking trails (but no camping). A mile offshore is the former **TILLAMOOK ROCK LIGHTHOUSE,** built more than a century ago and decommissioned in 1957 (today it's a columbarium, a repository for cremated remains).

TOLOVANA PARK, as the locals call the south side of Cannon Beach, has a laid-back, residential feel. Leave your vehicle at the **TOLOVANA BEACH WAYSIDE** (at

Hemlock St and Warren Wy), with parking and rest rooms, and stroll a quiet beach, especially in the off-season. At low tide you can walk all the way to **ARCH CAPE,** some 5 miles south (check your tide book, so the ocean doesn't block your return).

RESTAURANTS

The Bistro / ★★

263 N HEMLOCK ST, CANNON BEACH; 503/436-2661 After graduating from the California Culinary Institute in San Francisco, homeboy Matt Dueber returned to his roots and opened The Bistro 16 years ago, when Cannon Beach was lacking quality restaurants. Since then, this charming establishment has won a following for its unpretentious seafood dinners and its pint-sized bar, an ideal locale to enjoy grilled crab cakes (with a lemon-sake sauce) or a steak sandwich, a glass of wine, and Swedish creme capped with raspberry compote. Top-drawer entrees served in the diminutive dining area include broiled salmon finished with lemon chutney, grilled halibut coated with avocado salsa, and seafood stew that's a cross between cioppino and bouillabaisse. Beef eaters opt for tenderloin bathed in port and slathered with portobellos. *$$; MC, V; local checks only; dinner every day (Wed–Mon in winter; closed most of Jan); full bar; reservations recommended; opposite Spruce St downtown.*

Kalypso / ★★★

140 N HEMLOCK ST, CANNON BEACH; 503/436-1585 Saltwater bounty reigns supreme at this elegant but understated dinner house named after the seductive siren who tempted Greek king Odysseus on his return from the Trojan War. Grilled calamari stuffed with prosciutto and mushrooms, crab cakes concocted with sweet corn and cilantro, petrale sole finished with a Scandinavian shrimp sauce and Northwest clam fritters are some of the offerings. Land-based preparations are tempting too: rack of lamb rolled in a Dijon crust, tea-cured duck breast, and flank steak marinated in herbs and molasses, among others. Captivating desserts include Swedish cream covered in a mixed-berry purée and sweet ricotta pie. A back deck affords seasonal alfresco dining. *$$; MC, V; checks OK; dinner Thurs–Tues; beer and wine; reservations recommended; downtown, at W 2nd St.* &

LODGINGS

The Argonauta Inn / ★

188 W 2ND, CANNON BEACH; 503/436-2601 OR 800/822-2468 Visitors, particularly first timers, are ofttimes flustered by the numerous lodging choices in and around downtown Cannon Beach. The Argonauta, not really an inn but a cluster of cottagelike lodgings, is fewer than 150 feet from the beach and within easy walking distance of galleries, restaurants, and the Coaster Theater. The Light House has two suites, both with fireplaces and a sundeck or private courtyard. Built in 1906 and one of Cannon Beach's oldest residences, the two-story Town House (with two bedrooms and bathrooms, kitchen, oceanview deck, and stone fireplace) accommodates five. Families should consider the cozy Chartroom, with one large bedroom, a living room (with fireplace), and kitchen (but no ocean view). Most expensive is the Beach House, an impressive oceanfront home (three bedrooms, two baths) that sleeps nine. If the Argonauta is full, inquire about The Waves or the White Heron Lodge nearby, under the same management. *$$$; DIS, MC, V; checks OK; 3-night min in summer; thewaves@ seasurf.com; www.thewavesmotel.com; corner of Larch Rd.*

Cannon Beach Hotel / ★

1116 S HEMLOCK ST, CANNON BEACH; 503/436-1392 OR 800/238-4107 In view of sprawling resort motels, this century-old former boardinghouse a block from the beach feels like a tidy European inn. A comfy-cozy lobby is appointed with a fireplace, flowers, and a huge bowl of fresh fruit. Nine guest rooms (eight upstairs, one at ground level) vary from a nicely appointed one-bedroom to a suite with gas fireplace, spa, and ocean views. A light breakfast (juice, baked goods, fruit, hot beverages, and a newspaper) is brought to your door in a French market basket. (If the hotel is full, ask about The Courtyard or The Hearthstone, both nearby and under the same management.) Bistro-casual JP's serves superb seafood fettuccine, a Black Forest salad garnished with garlicky chicken and lamb, and blackened filet mignon stuffed with crab and mushrooms. *$$; AE, DC, DIS, MC, V; checks OK; info@ cannonbeachhotel.com; www.cannonbeachhotel.com; corner of Gower St.*

Sea Sprite Guest Lodgings / ★

280 NEBESNA ST, TOLOVANA PARK; 503/436-2266 This cute and clean oceanfront motel is a good choice for families (but no pets) and for couples who want to sleep a few steps from the broad Tolovana beach. All six units have kitchens, color TV/VCRs, decks, and ocean views. Many enjoy glass-front woodstoves. Cozy, oceanfront Studio 1B is best for couples. A two-bedroom cottage sleeps eight; the living room features a stellar vista. Guests can use the washer and dryer and an outdoor grill. Beach towels and blankets are provided on request. Also available is Hemlock House, a fully furnished home a block from the beach (with backyard deck and hot tub) that accommodates 12 and has minimum-stay requirements year-round. *$$; MC, V; checks OK; www.seasprite.com; on the oceanfront.*

Stephanie Inn / ★★★

2740 S PACIFIC ST, TOLOVANA PARK; 503/436-2221 OR 800/633-3466 Perhaps the most attractive lodging on the north coast, this gorgeous oceanfront getaway radiates the elegance of a large New England country inn: 50 spacious rooms are luxuriously appointed with gas fireplaces, spas, wet bars, and exquisite furnishings. Most rooms (some are two-bedroom suites) have outdoor balconies or patio decks with ocean or mountain scenes. The third-floor oceanfront Dormer Rooms offer the most privacy; the separate Carriage House has four suites. Every afternoon, Northwest wines are served in the chart room, with a wall of windows overlooking the ocean. Grab a book and sink into an overstuffed chair, tickle the piano keys, or eye migrating whales through a tripod-mounted spotting scope. A masseuse is on call, and a shuttle transports you downtown. A complimentary breakfast buffet is served in the second-floor dining room, decorated with scores of fresh flowers. Dinners are elegant, four-course prix-fixe affairs (reservations required). Look for gingered seafood cakes, herb-marinated lamb chops, Northwest salmon smothered with shiitakes, maybe even passion fruit cheesecake for two.

SEE THE WHALES

Those darn **GRAY WHALES.** They migrate past Oregon's coastline (they winter in Baja California, Mexico, and spend the summer in Arctic waters) during some of the worst weather of the year. Not to worry; the north coast affords a few sheltered spots to spy these magnificent creatures, sometimes close enough to eye the barnacles attached to their backsides. Spotting them usually isn't difficult: adults measure 45 feet and weigh 35 tons, and more than 22,000 whales of all sizes take part in the two annual migrations—typically late December and late March. Here's a specialized, north-to-south guide for intrepid whale-watchers hoping to sight a spout or witness a breach. During **WHALE WATCH WEEK** (last weeks of Dec and Mar; call 541/563-2002 for information), volunteers are on hand at the following sites (and numerous others) to answer questions.

ECOLA STATE PARK (2 miles north of Cannon Beach, off Hwy 101): A short walk from the parking area is a spacious, covered picnic shelter with cliffside vistas of—one hopes—spouting whales. Lincoln City's **INN AT SPANISH HEAD** (4009 SW Hwy 101; 541/996-2161 or 800/452-8127): The inn's 10th-floor viewing lounge is open for whale-watchers. The **CAPE PERPETUA INTERPRETIVE CENTER** (south of Yachats on Hwy 101): Good looks can be had from inside the center, or outside on a covered deck.

Want a closer look? Get eye to eye with gray whales from the safety of a chartered boat. The leviathans travel less than 5mph during their migrations, and sometimes surface almost alongside the boat. Weather permitting, many **CHARTER OPERATORS** throughout the Northern Oregon Coast offer tours. In **GARIBALDI,** try Linda Sue III Charters (304 Moving Basin Rd; 503/322-3666 or 800/232-4849) or Garibaldi/D&D Ocean Charters (607 Garibaldi Ave; 503/322-0007 or 800/900-4665). **DEPOE BAY**'s offerings include Tradewinds (Hwy 101 at north end of bridge; 541/765-2345 or 800/445-8730; www.tradewindscharters.com) and Dockside Charters (270 Coast Guard Pl; 541/765-2545 or 800/733-8915). In the **NEWPORT** area, Bayfront Charters (1000 SE Bay Blvd, Newport; 541/265-7558 or 800/828-8777) and Marine Discovery Tours (345 SW Bay Blvd, Newport; 541/265-6200 or 800/903-2628) are two reputable operations. —*Richard Fencsak*

$$$$; AE, DC, DIS, MC, V; checks OK; 2-night min weekends and Aug; info@stephanie-inn.com; www.stephanie-inn.com; oceanfront at Matanuska. ⅍

Arch Cape

Stretching from Hug Point south to Arch Cape (a rock formation you can walk through at extreme low tides), this is a quiet community of shoreside residences. The **OREGON COAST TRAIL** winds up and over Arch Cape (beginning at east end of Hwy 101, just north of tunnel; ask for directions at the post office, 79330 Hwy 101) and into **OSWALD WEST STATE PARK** (4 miles south of Arch Cape along Hwy 101; 800/551-6949), where you walk ½ mile from a parking lot to tent sites (wheelbarrows are available to carry your gear) among old-growth trees. The ocean, with a protected cove and tide pools, is just beyond. Surfing and kayaking are favorite year-round activities. No reservations are taken, and the place gets packed in summer.

LODGINGS

St. Bernards / ★★

3 E OCEAN RD, ARCH CAPE; 503/436-2800 OR 800/436-2848 This palatial-looking wooden lodging is perched at forest's edge on a 1½-acre estate on the east side of Highway 101. The interior is no less impressive, decorated with tiled floors, elegant tapestries, French Provincial furnishings, and winding castlelike stairways. All seven rooms have spacious private baths, gas fireplaces, TV/VCRs, and refrigerators. Least expensive is the main-floor Parisian, graced with hand-painted wallpaper and a carved armoire, while the Provence suite features a spa and French doors leading to a private patio. Best views are from the top-floor Tower, a multilevel abode equipped with a soaking tub. A multicourse breakfast—salmon soufflé, maple-glazed pears, sour-cream coffee cake, for example—is served in the Conservatory overlooking the gardens. Guests can enjoy a sauna and workout room. Outside is a sizable deck and a windless courtyard. No children under 12. *$$$; AE, MC, V; checks OK; bernards@pacifier.com; www.st-bernards.com; across from post office.* &

Manzanita

This growing community (lots of Willamette Valleyites retire here) rests mostly on a sandy peninsula covered with beach grass, Scotch broom, and shore pine. Still uncrowded, the town is a popular destination for Portland day trippers and wind-surfers, who flock to the always-breezy oceanfront and nearby Nehalem Bay. Over-looking town is **NEAHKAHNIE MOUNTAIN** (1 mile north of Manzanita, along Hwy 101), with a steep, switchbacked trail leading to its 1,600-foot summit, the best panorama on the Northern Oregon Coast.

Three miles south of Manzanita, **NEHALEM BAY STATE PARK** (off Hwy 101; 503/368-5154) offers hiking and paved biking trails as well as miles of little-used beaches. At the mouth of the Nehalem River (on the park's south end), resident Steller's sea lions bask in the sand.

For sweet treats and espresso, visit **MANZANITA NEWS AND ESPRESSO** (500 Laneda Ave; 503/368-7450). Take-out burritos are the specialty at **LEFT COAST SIESTA** (288 Laneda Ave; 503/368-7997). Boats and tackle to explore or fish Nehalem Bay can be rented at **WHEELER MARINA** (278 Marine Dr, Wheeler; 503/368-5780); rent kayaks at **WHEELER ON THE BAY LODGE** (580 Marine Dr, Wheeler; 503/368-5858).

RESTAURANTS

Blue Sky Cafe / ★★★

154 LANEDA AVE, MANZANITA; 503/368-5712 Enter a world of unexpected gastronomic pleasures, where recipes are as wild as winter sou'westers. Blue Sky's chef, Julie Barker, believes in mixing and matching. Witness her crab and coconut soup garnished with lemongrass and crispy noodles, Thai peanut chicken graced with gingered fruit salad, and oven-roasted pork chops paired with pumpkin-sage bread pudding. Surf 'n' turf here means baked salmon sided with butternut squash polenta, and grilled filet mignon accompanied by mascarpone mashed potatoes. Even desserts, such as chocolate bread pudding slathered with raspberry sauce and a dollop of orange whipped cream, enter unfamiliar, but tasty, territory. Avant-garde decor—every table sports a conversation-starting pair of salt 'n' pepper shakers, and the walls showcase provocative artwork—keeps the hip clientele occupied between courses. Service is relaxed but efficient. *$$; no credit cards; checks OK; dinner every day (Fri–Sat in winter); full bar; reservations recommended; at 2nd.* &

Nehalem River Inn / ★★

 34910 OREGON HWY 53, MOHLER; 503/368-7708 OR 800/368-6499 Nestled against the verdant green Nehalem River shoreline, this reconverted tavern is a culinary oasis in the heart of cow country. First-time patrons are surprised at the scope of chef Stephen Tinkham's menu: selections range from a cognac-flamed filet mignon to a vegetarian Fantasia Platter. Salmon might arrive brushed with a dill and lemon tapenade, while roast duckling enhanced with herbs, gooseberries, and kumquats is sweet protein at its finest. Sides could include scalloped buttermilk potatoes, a Brie-stuffed baked tater, or pan-fried eggplant battered with bread crumbs. Meals are presented in a modestly decorated ledgelike dining area with an open-beamed ceiling and a handful of tables. A covered outdoor porch overlooking some massive old-growth spruce trees affords additional seating. Service is efficient but casual; expect dinner to last 90 minutes or more. *$$$; AE, DIS, MC, V; checks OK; dinner Thurs–Mon; full bar; reservations recommended;* info@river-inn.com; www.river-inn.com; *on Hwy 53 in Mohler.* &

LODGINGS

The Inn at Manzanita / ★★

67 LANEDA AVE, MANZANITA; 503/368-6754 A block from soul-soothing sand and surf, this tranquil retreat occupies a multilevel, woodsy setting similar to a Japanese garden. Each of 13 spacious, nonsmoking units is finished in pine or cedar and decorated with stained glass. Every room has a gas fireplace, a good-sized spa, TV/VCR, and some enjoy treetop ocean views. The larger Cottage and Laneda units are equipped with full kitchens and separate bedrooms. Extra touches include terry-cloth robes, fresh flowers daily, and the morning paper delivered. *$$$; MC, V; checks OK; 2-night min in summer;* dromano@nehalemtel.net; www.neahkahnie.net; *1 block from beach.*

Ocean Inn / ★★

32 LANEDA AVE, MANZANITA; 503/368-7701 OR 866/368-7701 You're so close to the beach here, the tide practically laps at your bedpost. Four cottagelike units (1 is the nicest, with beachfront living room, woodstove, and sheltered deck) are nestled on a grassy bluff a seagull's flight from the surf. All have knotty pine interiors and good-sized kitchens (with microwaves and dishwashers). Six newer units (9 is our favorite) boast vaulted ceilings with stained-glass chandeliers and gorgeous fir woodwork. Most have full kitchens and wood heaters set in brick alcoves. Number 10 is equipped for persons with disabilities, and 2 and 4 allow pets. Covered parking is provided. *$$$; MC, V; checks OK; 1-week min July–Aug (except units 5 and 10); oceaninn@nehalemtel.net; www.oceaninn@manzanita.com; at the beach.* &

Garibaldi, Bay City, and Tillamook

TILLAMOOK BAY is a mecca for salmon fishermen, and these burgs along Highway 101 are good places for fresh seafood. Drive out on the pier at Bay City's **PACIFIC OYSTER COMPANY** (5150 Oyster Dr, Bay City; 503/377-2323) for 'sters and a view. In Garibaldi, ask what's fresh at **MILLER'S SEAFOOD MARKET AND RESTAURANT** (1007 Hwy 101, Garibaldi; 503/322-0355). Out back is a viewing deck with interpretive signs, and a walkway along the bay and marina. Numerous charter boats operate from here and are good for whale-watching as well as fishing (see "See the Whales" in this chapter for more information). Anglers routinely haul in 30-pound chinook from the Ghost's Hole section of Tillamook Bay, and area rivers are well-regarded salmon and steelhead streams.

Best known as dairy country, the town of Tillamook is in a broad, flat expanse of bottomland formed by the confluence of three rivers: the Tillamook, Trask, and Wilson. On the north end of town sits the home of world-renowned Tillamook Cheese, the **TILLAMOOK COUNTY CREAMERY ASSOCIATION** plant, and the always-crowded visitor center (4175 Hwy 101 N, Tillamook; 503/842-4481 or 800/542-7290). The tour is self-guided but interesting, especially for children. Afterward, buy a scoop of Tillamook ice cream—31 flavors range from Brown Cow to vanilla bean. **MUNSON CREEK FALLS NATURAL SITE,** Oregon's newest state park, is 7 miles south of Tillamook (turn off Hwy 101 to Munson Creek Rd) and features a 319-foot waterfall—Oregon's second tallest.

Oceanside

A quaint seaside hamlet, Oceanside lies 8 miles west of Tillamook along the 22-mile **THREE CAPES SCENIC DRIVE.** Tracing one of Oregon's most magnificent stretches of coastline, the narrow, winding road skirts the outline of Tillamook Bay and climbs over Cape Meares. At **CAPE MEARES STATE PARK** (just north of Oceanside), you can walk up to and inside **CAPE MEARES LIGHTHOUSE** (503/842-2244) and inspect an oddly shaped Sitka spruce known as the Octopus Tree. The Three Capes route winds along Netarts Bay before reaching **CAPE LOOKOUT STATE PARK** (1300 Whiskey Creek Rd; 503/842-3182), with 250 campsites (and yurts), as well as headland-hugging trails and a huge expanse of beach. After scaling Cape

Lookout, the westernmost headland on the Northern Oregon Coast, the scenic drive traverses a desertlike landscape of sandy dunes. The road to Pacific City and the route's third cape, Kiwanda, runs though lush, green dairy country.

RESTAURANTS

Roseanna's Oceanside Cafe / ★★

1490 PACIFIC ST, OCEANSIDE; 503/842-7351 The town's lone fine-dining experience, this converted grocery store is fronted by wooden walkways and a weathered facade. Inside, Roseanna's has evolved from a funky fern bar to an elegantly understated dining room. Views of the ocean and offshore Three Arch Rocks make meals memorable and, best of all, the food is sublime. Seafood, especially, is afforded reverential treatment. Smoked salmon is baked in puff pastry, then finished with a chive vinaigrette. Halibut might arrive bathed in a Dijon-citrus sauce or an apricot-ginger glaze. Petite oysters can be panfried or poached (in wine and herbs), then baked with a Parmesan coating. Try the penne in a spicy ginger sauce, or umpteen other pasta preparations. Light eaters can order a bowl of excellent clam chowder, followed by a warm slice of Toll House pie topped with Tillamook ice cream, a Roseanna's favorite. *$$; MC, V; checks OK; breakfast Sun, lunch, dinner every day; full bar; reservations not accepted; on main drag.* &

Pacific City

A tidy river and ocean community, Pacific City is home to the **DORY FLEET,** Oregon's classic fishing boats. The vessels are launched from the beach in the lee of **CAPE KIWANDA** (a brilliantly colored sandstone headland), sometimes competing with sea lions, surfers, and kayakers for water space. If the wind is right, hang gliders swoop off the sandy slopes of the cape and land on the beach below. Just south of the cape, **PELICAN PUB & BREWERY** (33180 Cape Kiwanda Dr; 503/965-7007) has garnered awards for its Kiwanda Cream Ale and Tsunami Stout. The region's second **HAYSTACK ROCK** sits ½ mile offshore (Cannon Beach has the other). **ROBERT STRAUB STATE PARK** (at south end of town; 800/551-6949) occupies most of the Nestucca beach sand spit. The Nestucca and Little Nestucca Rivers are top-notch salmon and steelhead streams.

RESTAURANTS

Grateful Bread Bakery / ★

34805 BROOTEN RD, PACIFIC CITY; 503/965-7337 Transplanted New Yorkers Gary and Laura Seide found their way to tiny Pacific City and opened a bakery with a catchy name, a cheery interior, robust breads (don't miss the spinach-garlic loaf), and a scrumptious array of cakes, buns, and muffins. Gingerbread pancakes, a black bean chili omelet, garlic-potato soup, and a Hangtown Fry bursting with oysters highlight the extensive breakfast and lunch menus. Other options include dilled shrimp salad and New York–style pizza, or vegetarian plates including a cheese-and-nut loaf sandwich. A spacious deck allows alfresco dining. Purchase picnic goodies here for forays to Cape Kiwanda. *$; MC,*

*V; checks OK; breakfast, lunch Thurs–Tues (closed Jan and Wed–Thurs in winter);
no alcohol; reservations not necessary; on Pacific City loop road.* &

LODGINGS

Eagle's View Bed & Breakfast / ★★

37975 BROOTEN RD, PACIFIC CITY; 503/965-7600 OR 888/846-3292 Perched on a
steep hill backdropped by forest, this secluded B&B enjoys a bird's-eye view of Nes-
tucca Bay and adjacent dairy lands. Built in 1995, this attractive two-story country
cottage set on 4 acres (with walking trails and a fish pond) features a covered porch,
wraparound deck (with six-person hot tub), vaulted pine ceilings, rocking chairs,
and comfy country decor throughout. Five guest rooms, all with private baths, have
TV/VCRs, CD players (there's a video and CD library), and cheery quilts and dolls
crafted by innkeeper Kathy Lewis (who runs the B&B with her husband, Mike).
Three rooms feature spas, and one is wheelchair-accessible. Enjoy a full breakfast in
the privacy of your room, or dine with other guests in the downstairs great room or
out on the deck. *$$; DC, DIS, MC, V; checks OK; eagle@wcn.net; www.eagles
viewbb.com; ½ mile east of Hwy 101.* &

Neskowin

A mostly residential hamlet lying in the lee of Cascade Head—a steeply sloped and
forested promontory—Neskowin is the final port of refuge before the touristy "20
miracle miles" (as the stretch from Lincoln City south to Newport used to be called).
The beach here is narrower but less crowded than other locales. Just south, **CAS-
CADE HEAD** has miles of little-used hiking trails that traverse rain forests and
meadows; begin your hike at a marked trailhead about 2 miles south of Neskowin
(visible from Hwy 101). The **OLD NESKOWIN ROAD** (turn east off Hwy 101, 1 mile
south of Neskowin), a narrow route that winds through horse farms and past old-
growth groves, is an enchanting side trip.

   HAWK CREEK GALLERY (48460 Hwy 101; 503/392-3879; closed in winter)
offers an interesting browse, and **HAWK CREEK CAFE** (4505 Salem Ave; 503/392-
3838) is a good bet for breakfast, baked goods, sandwiches, and pizza.

LODGINGS

The Chelan / ★

48750 BREAKERS BLVD, NESKOWIN; 503/392-3270 You could get tem-
porarily lost looking for this place nestled in the trees in narrow-laned
Neskowin. Of course, that's part of the charm; even though it's near private
homes, the Chelan feels like a getaway retreat. A manicured front lawn and lush gar-
dens add to the seclusion. Eight condominium units each have two bedrooms, (a
ninth unit has three), well-equipped kitchens, and large living rooms with picture
windows and fireplaces. Ground-floor units each have a private entrance to a tiny
backyard, with the ocean just beyond. Upstairs accommodations (off-limits to chil-
dren) enjoy private balconies. *$$; MC, V; checks OK; just off Salem Blvd.*

Lincoln City

Welcome to coastal congestion. Every weekend (every day in summer), traffic creeps from one end of town to the other, past miles of strip development, including a gaming casino complex and a slew of factory outlet stores. Still, Lincoln City's restaurant scene is vibrant, and 7 miles of broad, sandy beaches stretch from Road's End (north end of town) to the peaceful shores of Siletz Bay. Kite festivals (see "Coastal Celebrations" in this chapter) are held throughout the year at **D RIVER BEACH WAYSIDE** (milepost 115, halfway through town).

Amid the chaos on Lincoln City's north end, retire to **LIGHTHOUSE BREWPUB** (4157 N Hwy 101; 541/994-7238) for handcrafted ales and good grub. **BARNACLE BILL'S SEAFOOD MARKET** (2174 NE Hwy 101; 541/994-3022) has fresh and smoked seafood galore. Walk among rhododendrons, azaleas, irises, and other flowers and plants that thrive in a coastal climate at the **CONNIE HANSEN GARDEN** (1931 NW 33rd St; 541/994-6338).

The arts flourish here ("keeper" glass floats created by local artists are distributed along Lincoln City beaches every winter; 800/452-2151). North of town, the quarter-century-old **RYAN GALLERY** (4270 N Hwy 101; 541/994-5391) has 3,000 square feet filled with the work of Northwest artists. On the south side of Lincoln City, the **FREED GALLERY** (6119 SW Hwy 101; 541/994-5600) exhibits functional and decorative glass, furniture, and sculptures, as well as paintings. A little farther south, **MOSSY CREEK POTTERY** in Kernville (½ mile up Immonen Rd; 541/996-2415) sells finely crafted high-fired stoneware and porcelain.

RESTAURANTS

Bay House / ★★★★

5911 SW HWY 101, LINCOLN CITY; 541/996-3222 We won't argue with loyal patrons who claim the spectacularly situated Bay House—with Siletz Bay out the back window and the ocean just beyond—is the Oregon Coast's finest eatery. Richly finished wood and brass, crisp tablecloths, and seasoned service personnel garbed in black and white lend a traditional ambience, and the wine list is exemplary. Chef Anthony Reeves's seasonal menu showcases an array of stellar standbys (herb-crusted lamb in a port demi-glace, grilled beef tenderloin swathed in Oregon mushrooms) and imaginative seafood dishes. Coconut-rum prawns are sided with purple sticky rice and pickled carrots, Dungeness crab and Asian vegetables fill delicately crafted wontons, while oysters are breaded and fried crisp, then bathed in an Asian broth redolent of lemongrass and ginger. Salmon might come poached in a tomato-herb vinaigrette or pan-seared and coated with a hazelnut crust (and a curried pear sauce). Creamy onion soup garnished with bay shrimp is renowned as the coast's finest rendition, while desserts such as lemon-almond cheesecake and ginger crème brûlée are as luminous as the Siletz Bay sunsets. *$$$; AE, DIS, MC, V; checks OK; dinner every day (Wed–Sun in winter); full bar; reservations recommended; south end of town.* &

COASTAL CELEBRATIONS

Want variety? Oregon coastal festivals highlight everything from berries and craft beers to kites and quilts. Some of the best center around food. Eat, drink, and be merry with thousands of revelers at February's **SEAFOOD & WINE FESTIVAL** (800/262-7844) in Newport, the coast's original (and, many say, still the best) seafood bash. Not to be outdone, the Astoria-Warrenton area hosts a **DUNGENESS CRAB AND SEAFOOD FESTIVAL** (800/875-6807) in April, featuring 140 vendors. Seaside (visitors bureau: 888/306-2326) holds a **COFFEE & CHOCOLATE LOVERS FESTIVAL** in February, and a **CHOWDER COOK-OFF** in March, an event geared to clam (both New England– and Manhattan-style) and fish chowder aficionados. Another well-regarded gathering is September's **CHOWDER, BREWS & BLUES** gala in Florence (Chamber of Commerce: 800/524-4864), where visitors taste myriad chowders, sip handcrafted ales, and listen to live music.

Some of the world's finest kite flyers gravitate to Lincoln City—situated on the 45th parallel, halfway between the equator and the North Pole, and considered one of America's premier kite-flying venues—for May's **SPRING KITE FESTIVAL** (541/994-3070) and the even more grandiose **FALL INTERNATIONAL KITE FESTIVAL** (800/452-2151) held in October. Probably the coast's best-known festival is Cannon Beach's annual **SANDCASTLE DAY** (800/546-6100), a contest that attracts national attention until the tide comes in and washes away the magnificent sculptures.

Other possibilities include Newport's classically oriented July **ERNEST BLOCH MUSIC FESTIVAL** (541/265-2787) and August's **TILLAMOOK COUNTY FAIR** (503/842-2272)—don't miss the pig 'n' Ford races, where drivers share vintage Model Ts with squealing porkers. The **BANDON CRANBERRY FESTIVAL** (541/347-9619), in September, has been going on for more than a half-century; Depoe Bay's **INDIAN SALMON BAKE** (800/452-2151) is a sumptuous September feast. Cannon Beach's appropriately named November **STORMY WEATHER ARTS FESTIVAL** (800/546-6100) features music, theater, and gallery hopping, while the **HOLIDAY LIGHTS & OPEN HOUSE AT SHORE ACRES** (541/269-0215), west of Coos Bay, showcases a dazzling display of more than 200,000 holiday lights between Thanksgiving and New Year's.

—Richard Fencsak

Blackfish Cafe / ★★★

2733 NW HWY 101, LINCOLN CITY; 541/996-1007 From the get-go (the cafe opened in 1999), this attractive cafe exuding an industrial-chic look—with exposed pipes, dark gray walls and ceilings, and a bustling open kitchen—has won raves for its unpretentious coast-inspired grub. Rob Pounding, past head honcho in Salishan's kitchen, is owner and chef, and he's fanatical about local ingredients. The frequently changing menu showcases offerings such as a white-cheddar (Tillamook, naturally) flatbread spiked with coastal chanterelles, Parmesan-crusted sea bass (harvested off Pacific City) and seared ahi atop yakisoba noodles bathed in a Vietnamese-cilantro vinaigrette (the cilantro comes from Neskowin). Grilled New York steak kissed with blue cheese butter, and Willamette Valley pork medallions roasted in an apple-cider jus and finished with blackberry compote are other stalwart preparations. Lighter fare includes fried cornmeal-breaded oysters, beer-battered rockfish-and-chips, and an exemplary clam chowder. Chocolate fanciers save room for the Blackfish ding dong, an ultrarich fudge cake oozing creamy innards. *$$; AE, DIS, MC, V; checks OK; lunch, dinner Wed–Mon (Thurs–Mon in winter); beer and wine; reservations recommended; www.blackfishcafe.com; west side of Hwy 101.* &

LODGINGS

Brey House Oceanview Bed & Breakfast Inn / ★

3725 NW KEEL AVE, LINCOLN CITY; 541/994-7123 Most Lincoln City overnighters are content with high-rise motels propped somewhere on the west side of Highway 101, so B&Bs have never thrived here. The Brey House (named for owners Milt and Shirley Brey) is a modest but roomy, 60-year-old Cape Cod–style home a block from the beach on the north side of town. Four guest rooms (with private baths and entrances) occupy three floors. Three rooms have ocean views (the first-floor Cascade Room does not). On the top level, the knotty-pine Admiral's Room enjoys the choicest vistas, along with a fireplace and a skylight above the bed. In usually frantic Lincoln City, staying here is like sleeping over at a friend's. A full breakfast adds to the feeling. *$$; DIS, MC, V; checks OK; breysinn@webtv.net; www.moriah.com/breyhouse; off Hwy 101.*

O'dysius Hotel / ★

120 NW INLET CT, LINCOLN CITY; 541/994-4121 OR 800/869-8069 Nondescript oceanfront motels rule Lincoln City's shoreline, backed by still more uninspiring lodgings along Highway 101. Fortunately, the O'dysius offers an alternative. This upscale, oceanfront hotel contains 30 sizable units outfitted with attractive furnishings, fireplaces, whirlpool baths, down comforters, and TV/VCRs (and a selection of videos). All units enjoy private decks or balconies looking seaward; suites have full kitchens. Slippers and terry-cloth robes are provided for lounging. Wine is served afternoons in the lobby sitting room, which also houses a well-stocked library. Continental breakfast and the newspaper arrive at your doorstep in the morning. *$$$; AE, DIS, MC, V; checks OK; odysius@harborside.com; www.odysius.com; just north of D River Beach Wayside.* &

Gleneden Beach

Across the highway from the famous Salishan resort, a cluster of shops includes the **GALLERY AT SALISHAN** (7760 N Hwy 101; 541/764-2318), which sells wood carvings, wool tapestry, pottery, paintings, even furniture. **EDEN HALL** (6675 Gleneden Beach Loop Rd; 541/764-3825) stages local and regional music and theater.

RESTAURANTS

Chez Jeannette / ★★

7150 OLD HWY 101, GLENEDEN BEACH; 541/764-3434 Windows with flower boxes, whitewashed brick walls, and an intimate woodsy setting away from the main highway lend the appearance of a French country inn. The food and prices, however, are decidedly uptown. You might find salmon stuffed with Dungeness crab, finished in a wine-and-dill beurre blanc, or the Northwest's signature fish might arrive pan-seared and awash in a blackberry-brandy reduction. Unlike most other coastal fine-dining enclaves, carnivores can rejoice in the favorable meat-to-seafood ratio: oven-roasted rack of lamb, duck breast served in a pool of raspberry demi-glace, chicken with mushrooms, apple wood–smoked pork loin, and filet mignon finished with Armagnac and Gorgonzola. Venison tenderloin is often a possibility. The coast's finest escargots are a mainstay, desserts are sinfully excessive, and the wine list is topped only by Salishan. *$$$; AE, DIS, MC, V; checks OK; dinner every day; full bar; reservations recommended; ¼ mile south of Salishan.* &

Side Door Cafe / ★★

6675 GLENEDEN BEACH LOOP RD, GLENEDEN BEACH; 541/764-3825 Unique on the Oregon Coast, this establishment combines an open, airy eatery exuding a bistro feel with a cozy entertainment venue named Eden Hall. The cafe occupies a large, stylized room with an exquisite wood-and-marble fireplace, colorful backdrops from theatrical presentations, and a high ceiling. The creatively cooked and plated food draws as many raves as the shows next door. Grilled and pesto-coated rack of lamb accompanied by spinach-Parmesan risotto, for example. Or, for seafood aficionados, sesame-encrusted seared sturgeon sided with coconut-lemongrass rice and a prawn-scallop combo deftly tossed with kalamata olives, sun-dried tomatoes, a multitude of veggies, then dusted with feta. Vegetarian meals, such as chanterelle-hazelnut lasagna graced with champagne-béchamel sauce, are fabulous. Carrot cake and caramel-hazelnut cheesecake are two dessert-tray stars. *$$; MC, V; local checks only; lunch, dinner Wed–Mon; full bar; reservations recommended; info@sidedoorcafe.com; www.sidedoorcafe.com; on old highway.* &

LODGINGS

The Westin Salishan / ★★★

7760 N HWY 101, GLENEDEN BEACH; 541/764-2371 OR 888/SALISHAN Hard to believe, but Salishan has been around since 1965. We're happy to report that the resort's many amenities remain intact, and a spirit of excellence permeates the place. Dispersed over a lush, 350-acre landscape, Salishan includes 205 guest units, arranged in eightplexes on a hillside rising from the main entrance. Golfers like the 18-hole course (par 72), driving range, 18-hole putting course, pro shop, and resident PGA professional. You can swim in a covered pool, play indoor or outdoor tennis, exercise in the sizable fitness center, sweat in a sauna, soak in a hot tub, or jog and hike the forested trails. Kids have their own game room and can partake in "Camp Salishan," an on-site activity center, three days a week. All guest accommodations have gas fireplaces and decks or balconies. The best deals are standard rooms—about the size of a typical motel room, only nicer. Premier accommodations (such as Estuary House) enjoy Jacuzzis, vaulted ceilings, and Siletz Bay vistas; suites can easily accommodate four. The massive wooden lodge houses two restaurants, a nightclub, a library, meeting rooms, and a gift shop. In the main dining room, a gorgeous venue with lovely views, prices continue to rise, while quality fluctuates. Wine lovers appreciate Salishan's 10,000-bottle cellar. Service personnel throughout the resort are well informed and eager to please. *$$$–$$$$; AE, DC, DIS, MC, V; checks OK; salishan@salishan.com; www. salishan.com; east side of Hwy 101.* &

Depoe Bay

Sprawl has intensified between Lincoln City and Newport, and Depoe Bay sits squarely in the middle of the commercial blitz. Fortunately, parts of this still-charming community remain intact, including its picturesque and tiny harbor (billed as the smallest anywhere). **WHALE-WATCHING** is big here, and during the gray whale migratory season (Dec–Apr), the leviathans may cruise within hailing distance of headlands, sometimes rubbing against offshore rock formations to rid themselves of troublesome barnacles (see "See the Whales" in this chapter). **CHANNEL BOOK-STORE** (243 S Hwy 101; 541/765-2352) is a used book–browsers' paradise. Metal art, ceramics, and unusual indoor fountains can be seen at **DANCING COYOTE GALLERY** (34 NE Hwy 101; 541/765-3366).

RESTAURANTS

Tidal Raves / ★

279 NW HWY 101, DEPOE BAY; 541/765-2995 Diners are drawn to this classy, cliffside eatery for the fabulous views (from every table) of swirling surf crashing on shoreside rocks and partially submerged reefs (plus a spouting whale or two during migrating season). But they return for the food, an enticing and extensive array of surf 'n' turf preparations. Appetizers include pungent black bean and snapper soup, smoked-salmon chowder, and Dungeness crab cakes. A lemon and rosemary–infused charbroiled chicken breast is freshened with cranberry relish; Pacific snapper is crusted in cornmeal. Thai barbecue prawns, a pan-fried New York pepper steak in a brandy-onion sauce, and an unusual crab casserole baked with white cheddar in a white wine sauce are other stalwart entrees. *$$; DIS, MC, V; checks OK; lunch, dinner every day; beer and wine; reservations recommended; west side of Hwy 101.*

LODGINGS

Channel House / ★★

35 ELLINGSON ST, DEPOE BAY; 541/765-2140 OR 800/447-2140 Spectacularly situated on a cliff above the Depoe Bay channel and the Pacific, this attractive inn has 12 units, all with private baths and ocean views. A rocky shoreline—not beach—lies below, so surf crashes right outside your room. Ten units are truly special, outfitted with private decks, gas fireplaces, and spas (the seven roomier, and spendier, suites feature oceanfront spas on private decks). Two additional (and similarly appointed) units are located in the owner's house a few doors away. Come morning, guests enjoy a continental buffet breakfast in an oceanside dining area that sports a nautical motif. Don't forget binoculars, especially during whale-watching season. No children. *$$$–$$$$; AE, DIS, MC, V; checks OK; cfin-seth@channelhouse.com; www.channelhouse.com; end of Ellingson St.*

Newport

The coast's busiest destination, Newport offers a potpourri of activities and attractions. Steer away from Highway 101's commercial chaos (turn east on Canyon Wy) and head for the **YAQUINA BAY** front, a working harbor going full tilt, where all types of fishing boats berth year-round. Many charter boat companies offer fishing trips, whale-watching excursions, and eco trips. Quaff a native beer (Shakespeare Stout or Mocha Porter, for instance) at **ROGUE ALES PUBLIC HOUSE** (748 SW Bay Blvd; 541/265-3188), with upstairs "bed & beer" rooms; or head for the brewpub **BREWERS ON THE BAY** (2320 OSU Dr; 541/867-3664), located directly underneath the Yaquina Bay Bridge. **SHARK'S SEAFOOD BAR & STEAMER CO.** (852 SW Bay Blvd; 541/574-0590) serves fresh fish and fine chowder. Just up the hill, the supposedly haunted **YAQUINA BAY LIGHTHOUSE** (536 Bay Front St; 541/265-5679) is open for tours.

Art reigns at numerous Newport galleries. **OCEANIC ARTS CENTER** (444 SW Bay Blvd; 541/265-5963) displays jewelry, paintings, pottery, and sculpture. The **WOOD GALLERY** (818 SW Bay Blvd; 541/265-6843) exhibits woodwork, pottery, and weaving. Watch glass blowing at **PYROMANIA GLASS STUDIO** (3101 Ferry Slip Rd; 541/867-4650 or 888/743-4116).

The **NYE BEACH AREA,** on the ocean side of the highway, has a funky arts-community feel and an easily accessible beach. Here the **NEWPORT PERFORMING ARTS CENTER** (777 S Olive St; 541/265-ARTS) hosts music, theater, and other events, some of national caliber. For a bird's-eye perspective of boats, bay, and ocean, take a drive through **YAQUINA BAY STATE PARK** (under Yaquina Bay Bridge), which wraps around the south end of town.

On the southeast side of the Yaquina Bay Bridge, Oregon State University's **HATFIELD MARINE SCIENCE CENTER** (2030 S Marine Science Dr; 541/867-0100) has an octopus tank (and a touch tank with other marine animals), interactive video displays and computer games, ecology classes, and nature walks. Nearby, the **OREGON COAST AQUARIUM** (2820 SE Ferry Slip Rd; 541/867-3474) features furry, finny, and feathery critters cavorting in re-created tide pools, cliffs, and caves. The blockbuster Passages of the Deep exhibit lets visitors stroll through an underwater acrylic tunnel surrounded by marine life. A couple of miles farther south is the area's best and most extensive camping site (including yurts), **SOUTH BEACH STATE PARK** (off Hwy 101; 541/867-4715).

North of town, above Agate Beach, **YAQUINA HEAD OUTSTANDING NATURAL AREA** (off Hwy 101; 541/574-3100) includes the restored Yaquina Head Lighthouse (circa 1873; open to the public), an interpretive center, hiking trails, and an intertidal area (for viewing marine organisms from seaweeds to shore crabs) that's accessible for people with disabilities and safe for kids.

RESTAURANTS

April's / ★★

749 NW 3RD ST, NEWPORT; 541/265-6855 Imaginative Mediterranean-inspired cuisine shines as brightly as a dazzling summer sunset at this smallish cafe (just a dozen tables) with a warm and charming interior pressed up against the Nye Beach sidewalk. Seafood is particularly noteworthy: pan-seared salmon receives a zinfandel and rosemary treatment and arrives sided by toasted-barley risotto; halibut comes coated with a Romesco sauce; and a half-dozen fish and shellfish are rolled into cannelloni tubes redolent of lemon, dill, and tarragon. Marinated Tuscan grilled chicken features a smear of mustard-herb butter and is paired with crispy polenta oozing melted Gorgonzola, while linguica sausage sees duty in fettuccine tossed with three peppers, wine, and a splash of cream. The wine list includes 70 bottles, with upwards of 15 wines sold by the glass at reasonable prices. *$$; AE, DIS, MC, V; checks OK; dinner Wed–Sun (closed Jan); beer and wine; reservations recommended; aprils@newportnet.com; across from Sylvia Beach Hotel.* &

Canyon Way Restaurant and Bookstore / ★

1216 SW CANYON WY, NEWPORT; 541/265-8319 This combination bookstore, gift shop, deli, and restaurant feels as much like an emporium as an eatery, and you could easily get sidetracked. Do find the restaurant, however, where a pleasingly diverse menu awaits. King Neptune's cocktail, built with poached prawns, sea scallops, shrimp, and a crab claw—all in an orange-dill aioli—is a primer on coastal bounty. Pacific Rim gumbo affords a fusion of chicken, andouille sausage, an array of seafood, Thai chiles, and Chinese okra served over jasmine rice. Oysters range from a batch of panfried Yaquina Bay beauties to Southwestern-style oysters Rockefeller baked with spinach, ham, and ancho chiles. Or choose Dungeness crab cakes, swordfish tacos, sassy seafood pasta, or prime rib (Friday only) sided with garlic mashed potatoes. Lower-priced "early entrees" are served before 6pm, and the deli (everything from massive subs to pb&j sandwiches) is a good bet for picnic grub. *$$; AE, DIS, MC, V; checks OK; lunch, dinner Tues–Sat (bookstore and deli open every day); full bar; reservations recommended; between Hurbert and Bay Sts.* &

Whale's Tale / ★

452 SW BAY BLVD, NEWPORT; 541/265-8660 It's been around for more than a quarter century, but this whale isn't stale. Open the wooden door and step into a cavelike interior decorated with whale paraphernalia and frequented by a diverse clientele (who long ago realized this place was superior to better-known Mo's down the block). The person at the next table might be a commercial fisherperson, a suit from "uptown" Newport, or an adventurous tourist. Huevos rancheros, a stack of poppy-seed pancakes, and plates piled with fried red potatoes, onions, and chiles smothered in cheese are morning favorites. At noon, the shrimp Louis sandwich and a lusty fisherman's stew draw raves. Panfried tiger prawns, grilled Yaquina oysters, and sausage lasagne are top evening choices. Service is kicked-back and friendly. *$$; AE, DC, DIS, MC, V; checks OK; breakfast, lunch, dinner every day; beer and wine; reservations not necessary; bayfront at Hurbert St.*

LODGINGS

Nye Beach Hotel & Cafe / ★

219 NW CLIFF ST, NEWPORT; 541/265-3334 Historic Nye Beach has been welcoming vacationers for more than a century, and some of the weathered beach cottages look like they've been around that long. Built in 1992, the Nye Beach Hotel & Cafe is a relative newcomer, but this '50s-looking oceanfront lodging fits in fine. Green metal railings lead to second and third floors with narrow carpeted hallways sporting wildly shaped mirrors and myriad greenery. All 18 tidy guest rooms have private baths, fireplaces, willow love seats, balconies, and ocean views (a half-dozen units have spas). A piano and a tiny bar grace the hotel's lobby. Steps lead down to a bistrolike area where meals (ranging from cioppino to seafood étouffée) are available. Outside is an expansive heated deck for oceanfront dining. *$$; AE, DIS, MC, V; checks OK; nyebeach@teleport.com; www.nyebeach.com; just south of Sylvia Beach Hotel.* &

Sylvia Beach Hotel / ★★★

267 NW CLIFF ST, NEWPORT; 541/265-5428 OR 888/795-8422 What a concept: a B&B tailored to book lovers. Owners Goody Cable and Sally Ford have dedicated each of the 20 guest rooms in their rambling, pleasantly funky bluff-top hotel to a renowned author. The spendiest rooms are "classics," such as the Agatha Christie Suite, decorated in lush green chintz, with tiled fireplace, large deck overlooking the ocean, and numerous "clues" (shoes poking out from beneath a curtain, bottles labeled "poison" in the medicine cabinet). "Best sellers" (views) and "novels" (no views) are smaller and not as impressive, but are equally imaginative (a mechanized pendulum swings over the Edgar Allan Poe bed, for example). Books are everywhere, especially in the oceanfront upstairs reading room (with the lodging's best view and a warming fireplace), where complimentary hot wine is served at 10pm. Breakfast is included and is served family style in the downstairs Tables of Content restaurant, where interaction among diners is encouraged. The emphasis is on local seafoods at the prix-fixe, reservation-only dinners. As at breakfast, the food is noteworthy, but meals take a back seat to the conversation. No phones, TVs, or radios. *$$–$$$; AE, MC, V; checks OK; www.sylviabeachhotel.com; on the oceanfront.* &

Waldport

Sleepy Waldport has much to offer. On the town's north end, the **ALSEA BAY BRIDGE**, built in 1937 and rebuilt in 1991 (on Hwy 101), is the coast's most picturesque span, and protected walkways stretch its length. At the south end, an interpretive center has photos and historical transportation displays.

Waldport's city center is unspoiled by tourism. Buy and fly a kite from **PACIFIC MOTION** (205 SW Hwy 101; 541/563-5575). Nearby, **GRAND CENTRAL PIZZA** (235 Hwy 101; 541/563-3232) offers massive "grinder" sandwiches, pizza, and second-deck dining overlooking Alsea Bay. In the Old Town section, **DOCK OF THE BAY MARINA** (1245 Mill; 541/563-2003) sells angling equipment and rents boats and crab rings. Buy some bait, then try your luck from the Port of Alsea pier (Port St and the bayfront).

Two miles north of town, the distinctive-looking **TRIAD GALLERY** (5667 Hwy 101; 541/563-5442) exhibits watercolors, jewelry, wearable art, and provocative metal figures (including an outdoor neon horse).

LODGINGS

Cliff House Bed and Breakfast / ★★

1450 ADAHI RD, WALDPORT; 541/563-2506 Waldport's finest views can be enjoyed from Cliff House, a romantic retreat geared to cuddling couples. Perched above the Alsea River's mouth, home to frolicking seals and sea lions, this bright blue B&B has garnered rants and raves over the years. Fortunately, new owners Sharon and Keith Robinson have restored the understated elegance and just plain wonderfulness that formerly made it great. Four rooms, all with ocean views, are appointed with antiques, TV/VCRs, and refrigerators (and satiny robes for guests); three have balconies. The opulent Suite includes a king four-poster bed, a century-old parlor stove, and a mirrored bath with spa. In the ocean-facing Great Room, guests can munch Sharon's cookies and sip afternoon lemonade, warm to a wood-stove fire, and savor memorable sunsets. Out back, a spacious, ocean-view deck is surrounded by glass and outfitted with a hot tub. Massages ($50 per hour) are administered in the gazebo, painted blue hues with fluffy white clouds on the ceiling. Full breakfasts might include Dungeness crab quiche, cheese blintzes, sugar-plum scones, and raspberry-hazelnut muffins. $$$-$$$$; MC, V; checks OK; innkeeper@cliffhouse oregon.com; www.cliffhouseoregon.com; 1 block west of Hwy 101.

Edgewater Cottages / ★

3978 SW PACIFIC COAST HWY, WALDPORT; 541/563-2240 The owners live on the premises, contributing to the homey atmosphere at these shaked, shingled, and very popular (full all summer) lodgings situated on a bluff above the beach. All eight units have ocean views, fireplaces, well-equipped kitchens, and sundecks, but no phones (guests can use the office phone). The pint-sized Wheel House (with a queen bed and skylights) is strictly a two-person affair, while the commodious Beachcomber can accommodate as many as 15. Children are welcome; even pets can stay with prior approval. Out back, a short trail leads to an uncrowded stretch of sand. $$; no credit cards; checks OK; min stay requirements; 2½ miles south of Waldport.

Yachats

Called the "gem of the Oregon Coast," this resort village of 600-plus residents hosts a mix of aging countercultural types, yuppies, and tourists, and exudes a hip, artsy ambience. Yachats (pronounced "YA-hots") also counts numerous galleries, such as **EARTHWORKS GALLERY** (2222 N Hwy 101; 541/547-4300), a remodeled myrtle-wood factory specializing in ceramics, handblown glass, and metal-and-wood sculptures. **BACKPORCH GALLERY** (4th St and Hwy 101; 541/547-4500) sells basketry, jewelry, handcrafted dolls, and soft-hued seascapes.

Beachcombers flock to the Yachats River, which intersects downtown and empties into the Pacific, providing a playground for seabirds, seals, and sea lions. **SMELT SANDS STATE RECREATION AREA** (off Hwy 101), a small day-use area on the north side of town, is the beginning of Yachats 804 Oceanfront Trail, a wheelchair-accessible, paved path that meanders north almost a mile above driftwood-strewn coves.

A 2,700-acre rain forest boasting twice the botanical mass, per square acre, of the Amazon jungle, the **CAPE PERPETUA SCENIC AREA** is just south of town. To get oriented, head for the **CAPE PERPETUA INTERPRETIVE CENTER** (2400 Hwy 101, 3 miles south of Yachats; 541/547-3289), which features please-touch exhibits and family environmental programs, such as tide-pool explorations, on spring and summer weekends. On a clear day, the West Shelter (above the Interpretive Center; accessible by road or trail) affords the coast's finest view, a 150-mile, north-to-south panorama from Cape Foulweather to Cape Blanco and 40 miles out to sea.

RESTAURANTS

La Serre / ★

160 W 2ND ST, YACHATS; 541/547-3420 The sole fine-dining option between Seal Rock and Florence, La Serre ("the greenhouse") houses the largest plant collection this side of Cafe Perpetua's rain forest. An expansive dining area with overhead skylights and a beamed ceiling is sided by a cozy lounge with comfy couches and a fireplace. Though the kitchen offers French-inspired dishes such as clams baked in puff pastry and an elaborate filet mignon wrapped in bacon, topped with prawns, and bathed in a cream sauce, simply prepared seafood is best: shrimp or crab cocktails, fishermen's stew, lightly breaded Umpqua oysters, Dungeness crab cakes, and grilled salmon. The seafood extravaganza is a cornucopia of saltwater bounty. Daily vegetarian specials are offered too. *$$; AE, MC, V; local checks only; dinner Wed–Mon (closed Jan); full bar; reservations recommended; at Beach Rd, downtown.*

LODGINGS

Sea Quest Bed & Breakfast / ★★

95354 HWY 101, YACHATS; 541/547-3782 OR 800/341-4878 At Sea Quest, you spend the night in a luxurious, estatelike cedar structure perched on a sandy knoll right above the Pacific. Four of five guest rooms have bathtub spas, private entrances, and ocean views. In the inviting living room, guests can scan the horizon with a spyglass, or plunk down with a good book in one of the plush chairs. Outside is a wraparound deck for seaward gazing. Elaine Ireland, who runs the place with her husband, George Rozsa, is renowned for her breakfast buffet: fresh pastries, blintzes topped with Oregon blueberries, Sea Quest puffs sided with bananas Foster, and a Chilean casserole blending eggs, black beans, and assorted chiles. *$$$; DIS, MC, V; checks OK; seaquest@newportnet.com; www. seaq.com; 6½ miles south of Yachats.*

Ziggurat Bed & Breakfast / ★★

 95330 HWY 101, YACHATS; 541/547-3925 A four-story, glass-and-wood structure that takes its name from the ancient Sumerian word for "terraced pyramid," this is surely the coast's most visually stunning B&B. The location is equally dramatic, on a sandy knoll just back from the ocean and beside the gurgling waters of Tenmile Creek. Inside, views from all 40 windows (including glass-enclosed decks) enthrall guests, especially during storms. Two 800-square-foot, first-floor suites are available: the Southeast Suite faces the Coast Range mountains and boasts a sauna and an additional bed; the West Suite enjoys a round, glass-block shower and stellar ocean views enhanced by a 27-foot wall of glass. A woodstove and a baby grand piano highlight the expansive living quarters. No children younger than 14. *$$$; no credit cards; checks OK; www.newportnet.com/ziggurat; 6½ miles south of Yachats.*

SOUTHERN
OREGON COAST

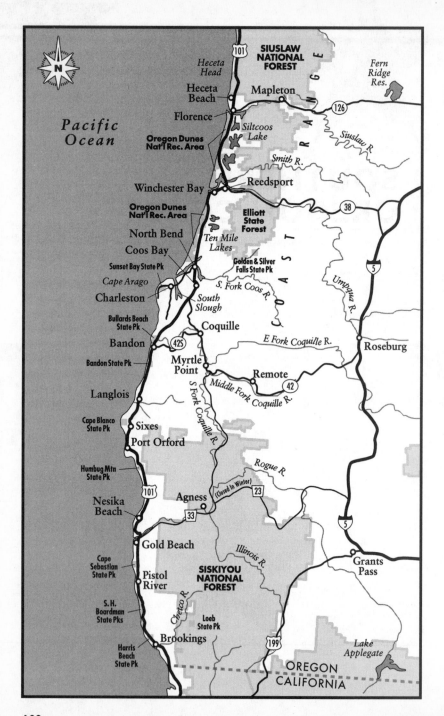

SOUTHERN OREGON COAST

Out of reach of any urban center, much of Oregon's south coast is isolated and undeveloped. Only a few cities of any size break up this 150-mile stretch of mostly wild seashore. The major towns are ports situated near the mouths of rivers: Florence, on the Siuslaw; Reedsport and Winchester Bay, on the Umpqua; Coos Bay and North Bend, on the Coos; Bandon, on the Coquille; Gold Beach, on the Rogue; and Brookings, on the Chetco, with a location almost equidistant from Portland and San Francisco and an eight-hour drive from either.

The south coast geography is world-class. Sahara-sized dunes within the Oregon Dunes National Recreation Area extend from Florence almost 50 miles to North Bend. Farther along, a series of state parks encompass rocky headlands forested with myrtlewood trees, wild azaleas, rhododendrons, and various conifers, including aromatic Port Orford cedars and, near Brookings, magnificent towering redwoods.

Coos Bay is the largest natural bay north of San Francisco, and for years was the Southern Oregon Coast's center for resource extraction—everything from gold and coal to oysters and forest products. There's far less maritime traffic these days, but the city (and neighboring North Bend) retain an unscrubbed, rough 'n' tumble look. Still, natural beauty abounds. A virtually untouched estuary here is habitat for thousands of migrating waterfowl. From lookouts on the rugged cliffs of Cape Arago, you can view offshore rocks populated with seabirds, seals, and barking sea lions.

Florence, Bandon, Gold Beach, Brookings, and even tiny Port Orford are seeing surges of tourism. Two developments promise increased visitation on a larger scale: the Coquille Indian Tribe has transformed a huge plywood mill on the Coos Bay waterfront into a thriving casino/hotel resort complex, which anchors a waterfront development plan; and near Bandon, sand dunes have been reconfigured into two well-regarded golf courses, reminiscent of Scotland's St. Andrews and California's Pebble Beach. Because the region is relatively undeveloped, recreational opportunities such as hiking, kayaking, surfing, mountain biking, windsurfing, and beachcombing are virtually unlimited. Locals are fiercely independent and almost universally friendly.

ACCESS AND INFORMATION
US HIGHWAY 101 follows the Pacific coastline from Washington to Southern California and links most of the towns along the Southern Oregon Coast. From Interstate 5, four two-lane paved roads follow rivers west to the south coast: from Eugene, **HIGHWAY 126** follows the Siuslaw River to Florence; from Drain, **HIGHWAY 38** follows the Umpqua River to Reedsport; from Roseburg, **HIGHWAY 42** follows the Coquille River to Bandon and Coos Bay; and from Grants Pass, **US HIGHWAY 199** follows the Smith River, then cuts through the redwoods and dips into Northern California near the Oregon border and Brookings. All are scenic routes.

Air service between Portland and North Bend is offered daily on **HORIZON AIR** (800/547-9308; www.horizonair.com); **GREYHOUND** (800/231-2222) has daily bus service.

SOUTHERN OREGON COAST THREE-DAY TOUR

DAY ONE: Breakfast in Florence's Old Town at the **BRIDGEWATER** (1297 Bay St; 541/997-9405), then head north to Heceta Head and the **SEA LION CAVES,** take in the scintillating vistas and ride the elevator from the top of the cliff into a natural ocean cave. Back in Florence, stop for coffee and check out the waterfront shops in **OLD TOWN.** Then take the one-hour lunch cruise aboard the *Westward Ho!* stern-wheeler on the Siuslaw River, or pack a picnic and hike through the sand dunes at **JESSIE M. HONEYMAN STATE PARK** south of town. Return to Florence for high tea at **LOVEJOY'S ENGLISH TEA ROOM** or have a beer in **LOVEJOY'S PUB;** both overlook the river. Drive south to Reedsport and check out the **UMPQUA DISCOVERY CENTER MUSEUM,** then watch elk grazing in fenced wetlands at the **DEAN CREEK ELK RESERVE.** Have dinner at **CAFE FRANCAIS** in Winchester Bay, and watch the sunset from the overlook at the **UMPQUA LIGHTHOUSE.** Drive south about 20 miles to Coos Bay and check in to **THE OLD TOWER HOUSE.** Relax and watch the passing ships outside your window, or try your luck at the **MILL RESORT & CASINO.**

DAY TWO: Following a full breakfast at The Old Tower House, follow the signs to Charleston and the ocean and spend a half day exploring the trails, gardens, and overlooks at **SHORE ACRES STATE PARK.** Return to the **CHARLESTON BOAT BASIN** and **CHUCK'S SEAFOOD** for fresh fried oysters or fish-and-chips (in summer get them to go, then sit on the jetty and watch brown pelicans scoop up fish). Stop by

Florence

Intersected by the deep, green Siuslaw River, Florence is surrounded by the beauty of the **OREGON DUNES NATIONAL RECREATION AREA.** The geography here—and for 50 miles south—is devoid of the trademark rugged Oregon Coast headlands. Instead, expansive, wind-sculpted sand dunes, some of them hundreds of feet high, dominate the landscape. Orient yourself to this intriguing ecosystem by exploring **SOUTH JETTY ROAD,** just south of the bridge across the Siuslaw River, or the **OREGON DUNES OVERLOOK,** 11 miles south on Highway 101. The dunes, some of which reach 600 feet high, hide excellent swimming lakes. Just east of the dunes, several large freshwater lakes and many lily-pad-studded ponds are circled by pines and, in spring and summer, bright pink and red rhododendrons.

Florence has transformed itself from a sleepy fishing village to a tourist mecca, but the local catch can still be had at **WEBER'S FISH MARKET** (802 Hwy 101; 541/997-8886). The revitalized **OLD TOWN,** a continually upgraded few blocks of 60 shops, restaurants, bed-and-breakfasts, and some of the town's oldest structures, has become visitor-oriented without selling out to schlock. The best coffee is at **SIUSLAW RIVER COFFEE ROASTERS** (1240 Bay St; 541/997-3443), with a river view from the deck and a paperback book library. A small stern-wheeler, **WEST-WARD HO!** (Maple and Bay Sts; 541/997-9691), offers half-hour and dinner river the interpretive center at **SOUTH SLOUGH NATIONAL ESTUARINE RESEARCH CENTER RESERVE,** then continue south on the side road that reconnects with Highway 101 north of Bandon. If you've arranged a tee-time for **BANDON DUNES** or **PACIFIC DUNES GOLF COURSE,** play 18 holes; if you haven't, check out the lodge (a sunny lounge with a full-service bar—and espresso—overlooks the first course). Nongolfers can go directly to **BANDON CHEESE FACTORY** for samples of cheddars (try the smoked) and a huge Umpqua ice-cream cone; then cross the street to **OLD TOWN** for cranberry fudge. Follow the Coquille River to the jetty at its mouth and hike the spectacular beach past enormous haystack rocks. Grab dinner at **HARP'S,** overlooking the river and the historic lighthouse. Reserve a cliff-front suite at Bandon's **SUNSET MOTEL,** and watch the sun and moon set from your room; all units have coffeemakers and microwaves, so stock up for an early breakfast.

DAY THREE: Rise at the crack of dawn, thermos of something hot in hand, and drive 40 scenic miles to **GOLD BEACH;** try to resist the charms of Cape Blanco and Humbug Mountain State Parks (near Port Orford) so you can go on a daylong **JET-BOAT TRIP** up the Rogue River (make arrangements in advance)—a stop is made for lunch on the way upriver. Stay overnight at **TU TU'TUN LODGE** overlooking the Rogue, and have dinner in the lodge's majestic dining room. Request a room with a hot tub on your deck, then have a soak and, perhaps, spy an eagle or an osprey soaring overhead in the fading light. Spend the evening wrapped up in a robe in front of your private fireplace.

cruises from Old Town. If you want a closer view, launch a kayak from **CENTRAL COAST WATERSPORTS** (1560 2nd St; 541/997-1812).

DARLINGTONIA BOTANICAL WAYSIDE (5 miles north of Florence on the east side of Hwy 101) is a bog featuring cobra lilies. The unusual burgundy flowers of these insect-eating plants bloom in May. Another 6 miles north, on the breathtaking cliffs of **HECETA HEAD,** are the **SEA LION CAVES** (91560 Hwy 101; 541/547-3111; www.sealioncaves.com)—far less kitschy than the advance hype might suggest. You descend 21 stories to a peephole in a natural, surf-swept cavern, where hundreds of golden brown Steller's sea lions frolic or doze on the rocks. During spring, peer over the cliffs with binoculars to watch cormorants' ritual mating displays. **HECETA HEAD LIGHTHOUSE** is the Oregon Coast's most powerful beacon and perhaps the most photographed lighthouse on the coast. Perched on the 1,000-foot headland, just off Highway 101, the 56-foot-high lighthouse isn't open to the public, but the grounds, with a trail to Heceta Head Lighthouse State Viewpoint, are yours for a $3 day-use fee.

RESTAURANTS

Lovejoy's / ★

85625 HWY 101, FLORENCE; 541/902-0502 Popular with Canadians, drawn by British flags whipping in the wind and the 1963 Austin taxicab out front, Lovejoy's is co-owned by London-born Martin Spicknell and his Dutch-Indonesian wife, Marianne. The Tea Room serves an array of teas and traditional English sandwiches: crustless white-bread triangles layered with smoked salmon, honey-roasted ham, cheeses, and cucumber. Rack of New Zealand lamb, cod 'n' chips, veal chops—maybe even wild boar—and bread pudding slathered with rum sauce are some dining room possibilities. We prefer the pub and its meat pies, Scottish kippers, and bangers, as well as the scores of brews from Great Britain and Australia. All areas showcase lovely views of the deep, green Siuslaw River and, on the far bank, Old Town Florence. Travelers who stop for a meal often stay overnight at the Pier Point Inn (riverfront rooms, two Jacuzzi spas, sauna, and indoor pool), which shares the building. *$$; AE, DIS, MC, V; checks OK; lunch, dinner every day, brunch Sun; full bar; reservations recommended; martin@restaurants-5560.com; south side of Siuslaw River bridge.* &

LODGINGS

Coast House / ★★

10 MILES NORTH OF FLORENCE; 541/997-7888 It's unlikely you'll see another soul during your stay at this secluded, one-of-a-kind lodging, although you might spot an eagle soaring overhead. Situated on a forested oceanfront cliff just south of Sea Lion Caves, this 1,000-square-foot, four-level getaway is owned by Florence residents Ron Hogeland and Nancy Archer. Dual sleeping lofts with skylights, a full kitchen, and commodious living quarters outfitted with an antique wood-burning stove (ample wood is provided) are some of the features, and fabulous seaward vistas can be enjoyed from many of the rooms. There's no phone or TV, but all necessities (except food, so pick up groceries beforehand) are provided, even a bottle of wine. Only one group (one or two couples) can rent this cozy retreat at a time. *$$$; no credit cards; checks OK; 2-night min, discounts for longer stays; call for directions.*

Edwin K Bed & Breakfast / ★

1155 BAY ST, FLORENCE; 541/997-8360 OR 800/8ED-WINK Ensconced in a quiet residential neighborhood just beyond the bustle of Old Town, this roomy, Craftsman-style home was built in 1914 by one of Florence's founders. Inside, the place looks formal but feels warm and homey. Ivory wall-to-wall carpeting contrasts nicely with aged and swarthy Douglas fir woodwork. There are six spacious guest rooms and one attached suite, all fitted with ultra-plush baths and adorned with antiques. Innkeepers Victor and Inez West serve multicourse breakfasts in the exquisitely appointed dining room. Out back are a private courtyard and waterfall. *$$–$$$; DIS, MC, V; checks OK; edwink@presys.com; www.edwink.com; west edge of Old Town.*

Reedsport and Winchester Bay

Reedsport is a port town on the Umpqua River a few miles inland, and Winchester Bay sits at the river's mouth. The former Antarctic research vessel *Hero* is moored on the Reedsport riverfront and is open to the public in summer. On an adjacent wharf is the **UMPQUA DISCOVERY CENTER MUSEUM** (409 Riverfront Wy, Reedsport; 541/271-4816), which features a weather station and exhibits on Native American tribal history and culture, marine life, ocean beaches, and logging. Observe wild elk grazing on the protected salt marsh and meadow, and watch for new calves in June, at the **DEAN CREEK ELK RESERVE**, 4 miles east on Highway 38.

Tours of the **UMPQUA LIGHTHOUSE** (1020 Lighthouse Wy, Winchester Bay; 541/271-4631) are available Wednesday through Sunday in summer; an adjacent museum in the former Coast Guard administration building displays photographs and pioneer history.

RESTAURANTS

Cafe Francais / ★★

HWY 101, WINCHESTER BAY; 541/271-9270 You may do a double take passing Cafe Francais on Highway 101; finding a French restaurant in the salmon-fishing harbor of Winchester Bay seems as likely as spotting a palm tree in the nearby Oregon Dunes. Nonetheless, this unpretentious former seafood market is a dining oasis amid burger joints, RV resorts, and charter-boat operations. The dining room is charming, and chef Francois Pere's menu is highlighted by salmon finished in a caper-cream sauce; duck l'orange; garlic, rosemary, and thyme–infused rack of lamb; and quail paired with seasonal mushrooms. Starters such as escargot, Cajun prawns, and luscious French onion soup served with house-baked bread are superb. True to his Gaelic roots, Pere is finicky about freshness; the catch of the day may not be announced until the fishing fleet docks. French selections dominate the well-chosen wine list, and desserts (crème brûlée, strawberry crepes) are not to be overlooked. *$$; MC, V; checks OK; dinner every day; beer and wine; reservations recommended; on Hwy 101.*

North Bend and Coos Bay

Side by side on the finest natural harbor between San Francisco and Seattle, the twin port cities of North Bend and Coos Bay, formerly the world's foremost wood-products exporters, have been undercut by a sagging timber industry and the political struggle to control Northwest forests. The cities are making a slow transition to a service-oriented economy.

The Coquille Indian Tribe transformed a former Weyerhaeuser plywood mill into the **MILL RESORT & CASINO** (3201 Tremont Ave, North Bend; 541/756-8800), with a restaurant overlooking the waterfront. The three-story hotel opened in spring 2000 and is furnished like a rustic lodge. Most rooms have sunrise views of the bay, river, and Coast Range mountains.

Fishing boats, tugs, and historical photographs can be seen on the **COOS BAY WATERFRONT**. The local arts scene includes the **COOS ART MUSEUM** (235 Anderson Ave, Coos Bay; 541/267-3901), with many big city–quality exhibits;

MYRTLEWOOD

Oregon's myrtlewood tree, a symmetrical beauty with shiny green leaves, related to the California bay, grows only within 90 square miles on the Southern Oregon Coast—between Coos Bay and the California border.

The **HOUSE OF MYRTLEWOOD** (1125 S 1st St, Coos Bay; 541-267-7804; www. oregonconnection.com or www.houseofmyrtlewood.com) has been churning out bowls, plates, salt shakers, and clocks (among other doodads) since 1929. Thousands of visitors, many of them on bus trips, tour the factory annually, and bowls are their favorite purchase. Trees used in production are usually about 100 years old, about 4 feet in diameter, and grow as tall as 150 feet. Cut trees regrow from undisturbed roots.

Unlike other hardwoods that have characteristic blond or dark wood, myrtlewood is blond, red, gold, and a deep chocolate brown—stressed trees produce the prettiest "fiddleback" grain. The aromatic leaves can be used in soups and stews; nuts are dried and drilled for jewelry. Coastal Native Americans knew all about myrtlewood—they husked newly fallen nuts and roasted them slowly in earth ovens. If harvested correctly, the nuts are slightly sweet, like chestnuts. If not, they're as bitter as bile. The native peoples also used the dried nut for adornment.   —Jan Halliday

SOUTHWESTERN OREGON COMMUNITY COLLEGE (1988 Newmark Ave, Coos Bay; 541/888-2525), which schedules art shows and musical performances; and July's two-week **OREGON COAST MUSIC FESTIVAL** (541/267-0938), which features classical, jazz, and world music.

Score newspapers, magazines, coffee drinks, and fresh-baked pastries at **BOOKS BY THE BAY'S GROUNDS CAFE** (1875 Sherman Ave, North Bend; 541/751-1114), and get Oregon wines and Bandon cheese from **OREGON WINE CELLARS ETC.** (155 S Broadway, Coos Bay; 541/267-0300).

RESTAURANTS

Blue Heron Bistro / ★

100 W COMMERCIAL AVE, COOS BAY; 541/267-3933 It looks a bit tired inside and out (as do a lot of structures in town), but this bistro still packs a culinary wallop. The innovative, reasonably priced menu lists a plethora of options: choose from among omelets and breakfast parfaits (yogurt, fruit, and muesli), assorted salads, and myriad sandwiches, such as a Reuben fashioned with pastrami, smoked gouda, and apple-infused sauerkraut. Continent-hopping evening fare runs the gamut from blackened snapper Southern style (with rice, black beans, and corn relish), to a fine veggie lasagna with spinach and three cheeses, to Tex-Mex entrees and a German sausage plate. The dessert lineup showcases a fine apple pie and variations on a chocolate theme. More than 40 kinds of bottled beer can be had.

$$; MC, V; local checks only; breakfast, lunch, dinner every day; beer and wine; reservations recommended for parties of 6 or more; at Hwy 101. &

Cedar Grill / ★

201 CENTRAL AVE, COOS BAY; 541/267-7100 Restaurant location isn't everything, but it's darn important. The Cedar Grill moved into the Coos Bay area's most popular watering hole, the former Bank Brewing Restaurant and Brew Pub, and almost instantly became the town's trendiest dining-out venue. The stately bank building still lends a chummy atmosphere, but food is the main attraction. Lunch brings downtown business types and tourists, who feast on pesto primavera, open-faced steak sandwiches sided with humongous onion rings, tuna burgers, and pork ribs slathered with mango barbecue sauce. Everyone from the cool and hip to Coos Bay's hard-core blue-collar crowd hangs here for dinner. Lightly breaded local oysters, almond-crusted halibut, prodigious cuts of prime rib, and sambuca-prawn linguine are evening favorites. *$$; AE, MC, V; local checks only; lunch, dinner Tues–Sat; full bar; reservations recommended; corner of 2nd.* &

Kum-Yon's / ★

835 S BROADWAY, COOS BAY; 541/269-2662 Kum-Yon's is a showcase of Asian cuisine, and what makes the place special is unknown territory for many diners. Try spicy *chap chae* (transparent noodles panfried with veggies and beef), *bul ko ki* (thinly sliced sirloin marinated in honey and spices), or yakitori (Japanese-style shish kebab). Other possibilities include shrimp tempura, moo-shu pork served with Chinese pancakes, and fiery Szechuan chicken. Kum-Yon's is also the south coast's sole sushi joint, serving sashimi, cucumber-and-rice wraps, spicy tuna rolls and such, as well as *tako* (octopus), *anago* (eel), *tobiko* (flying-fish eggs), and other exotica. *$; AE, MC, V; local checks only; lunch, dinner every day; beer and wine; reservations not necessary; south end of main drag.* &

LODGINGS

Coos Bay Manor Bed & Breakfast / ★

955 S 5TH ST, COOS BAY; 541/269-1224 OR 800/269-1224 A grand Colonial-style structure with large rooms and high ceilings, this B&B sits on a beautifully landscaped residential street overlooking the waterfront, but up the hill from Highway 101's commercial glitz. Five guest rooms (three with private baths) are distinctively decorated—the Baron's Room has a four-poster canopy bed in brocade and tapestry; the Victorian features lots of lace and ruffles. On mellow summer mornings, Patricia Williams serves breakfast on the upstairs open-air balcony patio. Mannerly children over 4, and dogs who tolerate cats, are welcome. *$$; DIS, MC, V; checks OK; 4 blocks above waterfront.*

The Old Tower House / ★★

476 NEWMARK AVE, COOS BAY; 541/888-6058 One of the few historic houses remaining in the former bustling Empire district of Coos Bay, this lovely Victorian built by Dr. C. W. Tower in 1872 overlooks in- and outbound ships. Owners Don and Julia Spangler have restored the historic home and filled it with a bevy of antiques. The main structure contains three guest rooms, which share two spacious baths. Our choice, the Rose Room, has a 150-year-old, four-poster bed with a handmade fishnet canopy. Outside, a private garden includes the original apple orchard, dozens of whimsical birdhouses, and two separate quarters (both with private baths): the Ivy Cottage, done in green and white; and the Carriage House, a ship-themed suite with its own kitchen. Full breakfast is served on white linen, china, and vintage crystal in the cozy sunroom. *$$; DIS, MC, V; checks OK; donspanl@gte.net; www.virtualcities.com; take Charleston exit from downtown.*

Charleston

Charleston's docks moor Coos Bay's commercial fishing fleet. Fresh fish is inexpensive here, the pace is slow, and there's lots to do, even if it's just watching brown pelicans or seals.

Visit **CHUCK'S SEAFOOD** (5055 Boat Basin Dr; 541/888-5525) for fish, and **QUALMAN OYSTER FARMS** (4898 Crown Point Rd; 541/888-3145) for oysters. Hikers, canoeists, and kayakers (no motor boats) explore the **SOUTH SLOUGH NATIONAL ESTUARINE RESEARCH CENTER RESERVE** (61907 Seven Devils Rd; 541/888-5558), 4 miles south of Charleston.

Southwest of town on the Cape Arago Highway, **SUNSET BAY STATE PARK** (12 miles southwest of Coos Bay; 541/888-3778), with year-round camping (including yurts), has a bowl-shaped cove with 50-foot cliffs on either side—good for a swim, because the water is perpetually calm, though cold. Farther down the road at **SHORE ACRES STATE PARK** (13 miles southwest of Coos Bay; 541/888-3732), a cliffside botanical garden contains a restored caretaker's house (impressively lit at Christmas) and an impeccably maintained display of native and exotic plants. Watch winter storms—or whales—from an enclosed shelter here. Farther south, **CAPE ARAGO STATE PARK** (541/888-3778) overlooks the **OREGON ISLANDS NATIONAL WILDLIFE REFUGE** (541/867-4550), home to seabirds, seals, and sea lions. The **OREGON COAST TRAIL** winds through all three parks. For more information, contact the Oregon Parks and Recreation Department (503/378-6305); for camping reservations, call 800/452-5687.

Bandon

Some locals believe Bandon sits on a "ley line," an underground crystalline structure reputed to be the focus of powerful cosmic energies; others know it lies close to the point where the Juan de Fuca plate is diving under the North American continent. Or maybe it's the grandeur of the scenery—huge haystack and monolithic offshore rocks—that inspires.

Begin in **OLD TOWN** on the Coquille River waterfront, where galleries include the **SECOND STREET GALLERY** (210 2nd St; 541/347-4133), the **CLOCK TOWER GALLERY** (198 2nd St; 541/347-4721), and **BANDON GLASS ART STUDIO** (240 Hwy 101; 541/347-4723). Buy fish-and-chips at **BANDON FISHERIES** (250 1st St SW; 541/347-4282) and nosh at the public pier. For another treat, try the *New York Times*-touted candies (and generous free samples) at **CRANBERRY SWEETS** (1st St and Chicago; 541/347-9475). Sample the famous cheddar cheeses (especially squeaky cheese curds) at **BANDON CHEESE** (680 2nd St; 541/347-2456).

The best beach access is from the south jetty in town or from Face Rock Viewpoint on **BEACH LOOP ROAD**. This route parallels the ocean in view of weather-sculpted rock formations, and is a good alternative (especially by bicycle) to Highway 101. Two miles north of Bandon, **BULLARDS BEACH STATE PARK** (541/347-2209) occupies an expansive area crisscrossed with hiking and biking trails leading to uncrowded, driftwood and kelp–cluttered beaches. The campground, with yurts near the entrance, is nestled in the pines. Built in 1896, the **COQUILLE RIVER LIGHTHOUSE** (open to the public) is at the end of the park's main road. Good windsurfing is on the river side of the park's spit. Tour the gently flowing Coquille River before the afternoon winds kick up, and poke around the edges of **BANDON MARSH NATIONAL WILDLIFE REFUGE** (look for osprey, harriers, and egrets) in a kayak from **ADVENTURE KAYAK** (315 1st St; 541/347-3480; www.adventurekayak.com).

Bandon's cranberry bogs make it one of the nation's largest producers and are the reason for the **BANDON CRANBERRY FESTIVAL** (541/347-9619) in September. Call **FABER FARMS** (541/347-1166) for directions to its tasting room (harvest tours begin in October). Seven miles south of Bandon on Highway 101, you can view lions, tigers, elk, and more at the **WEST COAST GAME PARK SAFARI** (541/347-3106).

RESTAURANTS

Harp's / ★★

 480 1ST ST SW, BANDON; 541/347-9057 Harp's is nicely situated on the Coquille River shoreline across from Bandon's lighthouse. Built in 1911, the structure has housed everything from a Coast Guard station to a concrete company and is now in its finest incarnation. Harp's extensive menu features myriad surf and turf choices—say, grilled halibut with a hot pistachio sauce or filet mignon marinated in a garlic and teriyaki mixture, then charbroiled to order. Other standouts include pasta primavera tossed in a sambuca-cream sauce, charbroiled oysters, veal scaloppine browned in a marsala sauce, and a seafood extravaganza stocked with lobster, scallops, salmon, two types of clams and, seemingly, every delectable marine critter this side of Hawaii. The wine list is superior, and the third-floor lounge enjoys fabulous river and ocean vistas. *$$; AE, DC, MC, V; checks OK; dinner every day (Tues–Sat in winter); full bar; reservations recommended; across from lighthouse.* &

Lord Bennett's / ★★

1695 BEACH LOOP DR, BANDON; 541/347-3663 Named for Bandon's founder, doubly-damned for bringing invasive Scotch broom and prickly gorse with him from Scotland, this upscale eatery is directly across Beach Loop Drive from oceanside cliffs and towering offshore rock formations, so views are scintillating. The cuisine is fancy, fussy, and filling. Skewered prawns are coated with an apricot-curry glaze; oysters are lavishly baked with spinach, bacon, and Pernod; and grilled hazelnut-encrusted lamb chops arrive on a mound of caramelized onions. Fowl is fantastic: chicken receives an herb marinade and port-cranberry-pomegranate treatment, or is stuffed with spinach and pancetta, baked, and finished with ginger-lime butter. The wine list is extensive; many Oregon quaffs are available by the glass. Weekend brunches include crab cakes, crab enchiladas, shrimp-topped eggs Benedict, and lemon soufflé pancakes. *$$; AE, DIS, MC, V; checks OK; lunch Mon–Fri, dinner every day, brunch Sat, Sun; full bar; reservations recommended; www.bandon bythesea.com; next to Sunset Motel.*

LODGINGS

Bandon Dunes Golf Resort / ★★★

ROUND LAKE DR, BANDON; 541/347-4380 OR 888/345-6008 This is golfers' heaven—a walking, Scottish links course, designed by Scot architect David McLay Kidd. It has garnered worldwide kudos from the golf press and been named one of the top 10 courses in the United States. In 2001, another celebrated 18-hole course—named Pacific Dunes and designed by Tom Doak—was added. Both courses are beloved by scratch players and duffers alike, in part because the prevailing attitude is fun and relaxed. The light and airy timber-and-shake clubhouse, with four monolithic spires of columnar basalt in the lobby and subtle Celtic symbols, is on the cutting edge of design. It's also a favored place to stay, offering 21 guest accommodations on the second floor. Four "cottages" surrounding a lily pad–covered pond have 48 additional rooms and suites (60 more rooms are planned for late 2002). All units are tastefully furnished, and some have ocean views. Hiking trails meander through dunes and forest (one reaches the beach), and salmon and steelhead fishing trips to the nearby Sixes and Elk Rivers can be arranged. Excellent repasts—chicken-provolone ravioli, Thai cioppino in a spicy coconut broth, duck with cranberry barbecue sauce—are served in the Gallery Restaurant (with full bar) every day. The Tufted Puffin and The Bunker offer lighter fare. Bring the kids. *$$–$$$$; AE, DC, DIS, MC, V; no checks; reservations@bandondunesgolf.com; www.bandondunesgolf.com; north end of Coquille River bridge.* &

Beach Street Bed and Breakfast / ★★

200 BEACH ST, BANDON; 541/347-5124 OR 888/335-1076 A homey, romantic place (floral bedspreads on king-sized beds, dried flowers, and a huge vaulted-ceiling living room with comfy chairs, skylights, and a massive fireplace), Beach Street is perfect for small wedding parties and honeymooners. Some of the six guest rooms have gas fireplaces and private balconies, all have unobstructed westerly ocean views; five have two-person spa tubs (our favorites are the Windsor and Oak Rooms). Breakfasts—perhaps blueberry and cran-orange muffins, fruit salad and Mediterranean quiche—are served buffet style in the living/dining room; guests can request a favorite Benedict or crepe, and co-owner Sharon McLean will add it to the morning repast. No children (unless you rent all the rooms) or pets. *$$$; AE, DIS, MC, V; checks OK; sharon@beach-street.com; www.beach-street.com; across from riding stable.*

Lighthouse Bed and Breakfast / ★★

650 JETTY RD, BANDON; 541/347-9316 Spacious and appealing, this contemporary home has windows opening toward the mouth of the Coquille River, its lighthouse, and the ocean, a short walk away. Guests can watch fishing boats, windsurfers, seals, and seabirds, and maybe spy the spout of a

OREGON DUNES NATIONAL RECREATION AREA

Between Florence and North Bend is an area of coast like no other. This 50-mile swath encompasses the Oregon Dunes National Recreation Area, a paradoxical land of desert-like panoramas. But water is, literally, everywhere. These 32,000 acres of desolate sand are dotted with multisized lakes, intersected by streams and backed by the Pacific. Islands of greenery—trees trapped by shifting sand—are remnants of earlier, more expansive coastal forest, and reminders that the sand here will bury anything in its way.

Even though the dunes are federally managed, a good access point is within **JESSIE M. HONEYMAN STATE PARK** south of Florence. Hundred-foot-high dunes and a surrealistic terrain loom just beyond the **CLEAWOX LAKE** day-use area. Eleven miles south is the **OREGON DUNES OVERLOOK,** another day-use area and a good orientation site with interpretive displays. Farther south, the **SILTCOOS RIVER** area features an estuary, a lagoon, beaches, wetland ponds, numerous trails, and a variety of wildlife. There are dune buggy concessions along Highway 101, and overnighters can stay in any of 13 campgrounds. Bring your hiking shoes, binoculars, even your pail and shovel. Most of all, bring your curiosity and sense of wonder to this varied ecosystem of stark, bare dunes interspersed by blue water and green foliage. The **OREGON DUNES VISITOR CENTER** (855 Hwy 101, Reedsport; 541/271-3611) has more information.

—Richard Fencsak

migrating gray whale. Five guest rooms (all enjoy ocean or river vistas) are roomy and wonderfully appointed. The top-of-the-inn Gray Whale Room is a stunner, with a king-sized bed, wood-burning stove, TV, and whirlpool tub for two in a view alcove. Breakfasts are top-notch. No children or pets. *$$; MC, V; checks OK; lighthouse@lighthouselodging.com; www.lighthouselodging.com; at 1st St.*

Sunset Motel / ★

1755 BEACH LOOP DR, BANDON; 541/347-2453 OR 800/842-2407 This complex of oceanfront motel rooms, cabins, and triplex houses gets our rave for spectacular views of Bandon's haystack rocks, especially Face Rock (it looks like a woman, head back, mouth open in reverie). For the most romantic view, ask for a room with a corner fireplace in the Vern Brown unit—a great spot for cuddling to watch storms and sunsets. All units have balconies and are equipped with coffeemakers and microwaves; several rooms have kitchens and fireplaces. Guests have use of the spa, pool, and laundry facilities. Stairs lead to the beach. *$$–$$$; AE, DIS, MC, V; no checks; sunset@sunsetmotel.com; www.sunsetmotel.com; across from Lord Bennett's.* &

Port Orford

Port Orford is the south coast's oldest town, dating to the mid-19th century, when settlers and Native Americans fought at **BATTLE ROCK** (in town, on beach on Hwy

101), where interpretive signs now tell the story. These days, locals are sheep ranchers, cranberry farmers, sea urchin divers, retirees, and fishermen (who use a five-story hoist to launch their boats into the ocean). Check out the **PORT ORFORD HEADS LIFESAVING STATION** (edge of town, on 9th St; 541/332-2352; open summer only), built in 1934 and one of the best remaining examples of period architecture. A gem of a grocery store, **PORT ORFORD BREADWORKS** (1160 Idaho St; 541/332-4022) purveys artisan loaves (country French, herb and cheese, kalamata olive), imported cheeses and meats (real French Roquefort, mascarpone, finocchiona salami, slabs of prosciutto), and black truffle oil, among other goodies.

About 10 miles north of town is **BOICE-COPE COUNTY PARK** (south of Langlois off Hwy 101; 541/247-7011), site of freshwater Floras Lake, popular with boaters and windsurfers. A trail system that skirts oceanfront cliffs and wanders through dense forests is suitable for hiking, running, horseback riding, and mountain biking (careful: some of the trails are in disrepair). You can pick seasonal flowers and organic produce—as well as bunk in an 1886 farmhouse—at **MARSH HAVEN FARM** (47815 Floras Lake Loop; 541/348-2564). **FISHER FOLK** visit the Elk and Sixes Rivers for salmon and steelhead.

CAPE BLANCO LIGHTHOUSE (541/332-2207) in **CAPE BLANCO STATE PARK** (5 miles north of Port Orford and 6 miles west of Hwy 101; 541/332-6774) is the oldest (1870) and most westerly lighthouse in the Lower 48 states—and the windiest station on the coast. The lighthouse, 245 feet above the ocean, and small interpretive center are open seasonally to the public. West of the light station, a path leads to the end of the cape. On the way to Cape Blanco, check out the restored **HUGHES HOUSE** (open Thurs–Mon, Apr–Oct), built by the English-born Hughes family, the area's first non-native settlers.

HUMBUG MOUNTAIN STATE PARK (5 miles south of Port Orford off Hwy 101; 541/332-6774) features a steep switchbacked trail to a top-of-the-world panorama at the summit.

LODGINGS

Home by the Sea Bed and Breakfast / ★

444 JACKSON ST, PORT ORFORD; 541/332-2855 You can see the south-facing ocean view from the two guest rooms (both on the second floor) in this modest, homey B&B atop a bluff near Battle Rock. Beach access is easy, and guests have the run of a large, pleasantly cluttered dining/living room with a view (plus laundry privileges). Quiche, waffles, omelets, and fresh strawberries are morning mainstays. Surf the Internet with chatty Alan Mitchell, a friendly whirlwind of information and a Mac enthusiast. *$$; MC, V; checks OK; alan@homebythesea.com; www.homebythe sea.com; 1 block west of Hwy 101.*

Gold Beach

Named for the gold found here in the 19th century, Gold Beach is famous as the town at the ocean end of the **ROGUE RIVER,** a favorite with white-water enthusiasts. It's also a supply town for hikers heading up the Rogue into the remote **KALMIOPSIS WILDERNESS AREA,** or for anglers hoping to hook a salmon or steelhead. Catch angling tips or rent clam shovels and fishing gear at the **ROGUE OUT-DOOR STORE** (29865 Ellensburg Ave; 541/247-7142). Pick up maps and hiking or rafting information from the **U.S. FOREST SERVICE** (1225 S Ellensburg Ave; 541/247-3600).

JET-BOAT TRIPS are a popular way to explore the backcountry. Guides discuss the area's natural history and stop to observe wildlife (otter, beaver, blue herons, bald eagles, and deer) on these thrilling forays (64–104 miles) up the Rogue. Boats dock at lodges along the way for lunch and sometimes dinner. (Prepare for sun exposure; most boats are open.) Outfits include **JERRY'S ROGUE RIVER JET BOAT TRIPS** (541/247-4571 or 800/451-3645) and **MAIL BOAT HYDRO-JETS** (541/247-7033 or 800/458-3511). Call **ROGUE RIVER RESERVATIONS** (541/247-6504 or 800/525-2161) for information on Rogue River outings, jet-boat trips, or overnight stays in the wilderness (including backcountry lodges).

The little-used **OREGON COAST TRAIL** (800/525-2334) traverses headlands and skirts untraveled beaches between Gold Beach and Brookings. A portion of trail winds up and over **CAPE SEBASTIAN,** 3 miles south of town off Highway 101. Take the steep drive to the top of the cape for breathtaking vistas. Gold Beach also is part of Oregon's coastal "banana belt," which stretches to the California border and means warmer winter temperatures, an earlier spring, and more sunshine.

RESTAURANTS

Chives / ★★★

 21292 US HWY 101, GOLD BEACH; 541/247-4121 At press time, Chives was relocating from Brookings north to Gold Beach, but we're confident this establishment will continue as the southern coast's premier eatery. For one thing, the restaurant moved from a nondescript strip-mall location to 3.5 oceanfront acres; inside, every table enjoys an ocean vista. Plus, Richard Jackson, chef and co-owner (with wife Carla) and formerly with San Francisco's Sheraton Palace Hotel and Four Seasons, will continue to offer a splendid menu with impressive breadth. Openers might include asparagus soup, shrimp bisque, crispy salmon cakes, or rock shrimp risotto. Jackson's dazzling entrees include a classic osso buco, and chicken stuffed fat with Brie and hazelnuts. Seared ahi sided with hot-pepper noodles, spicy cioppino, and halibut and prawns tossed with garlic fettuccine, bacon, Romano, and chives are also excellent catches. For dessert, try freshberry Napoleon, zabaglione, or warm bread pudding spiked with Jack Daniels. *$$; MC, V; checks OK; dinner Wed–Sun (closed Jan); full bar; reservations recommended; on west side of Hwy 101.*

Spinner's Seafood, Steak & Chop House / ★

29430 ELLENSBURG AVE, GOLD BEACH; 541/247-5160 As the name suggests, the menu here is extensive. You might begin with a wild mushroom Napoleon bathed in a cognac-herb sauce, then move on to, say, a charbroiled whiskey steak, cedar-planked salmon garnished with a pinot noir reduction, or a slew of chicken preparations (grilled lime-ginger breast) and pasta plates (seafood fettuccine tossed in an asiago sauce). Mandarin salad graced with candied walnuts and grilled prawns, lamb chops marinated in garlic and herbs, and pan-roasted halibut smeared with citrus sauce are other can't-miss selections. Burgers—massive half-pounders served with shoestring fries—are the south coast's finest. Every table enjoys an ocean view, and the sunset panoramas are impressive. *$$; AE, MC, V; checks OK; lunch, dinner every day (lunch Mon–Fri in winter); full bar; reservations recommended; on Hwy 101.*

LODGINGS

Gold Beach Resort

29232 ELLENSBURG AVE, GOLD BEACH; 541/247-7066 OR 800/541-0947 Motel life is fine at this sprawling in-town beachfront complex situated close enough to the ocean that roaring surf drowns out highway noise. All 39 rooms have private decks and ocean views. Five roomy oceanfront condos are equipped with kitchens and fireplaces. Guests can enjoy an indoor pool and spa; a private trail leads through the dunes to the ocean. *$$–$$$; AE, DC, MC, V; no checks; gbresort@harborside.com; www.gbresort.com; south end of town.* よ

Inn at Nesika Beach / ★★★

33026 NESIKA RD, GOLD BEACH; 541/247-6434 Many visitors to this three-story neo-Victorian (built in 1992) call it the Oregon Coast's finest B&B. A jewel of a structure occupying a bluff in quiet Nesika Beach, the inn boasts lovely landscaping, a relaxing wraparound porch, and an enclosed oceanfront deck. The expansive interior, with hardwood floors and attractive area rugs, is grandly decorated. Four large upstairs guest rooms all enjoy fabulous ocean views, uncommonly comfortable (and large) feather beds, and private baths with deep whirlpool tubs. On the third floor, a suite-sized room has a fireplace and private deck overlooking the Pacific. Wine and nibbles are offered evenings in the Fireside Room and living room. Hostess Ann Arsenault serves a full breakfast (in a dining room facing the ocean) that might include crepes, scones, gingerbread pancakes, myriad egg dishes, and muffins. No small children or pets. *$$$; no credit cards; checks OK; www.goldbeachlodging.com; 5 miles north of Gold Beach.*

Tu Tu'Tun Lodge / ★★★★

96550 NORTH BANK ROGUE, GOLD BEACH; 541/247-6664 OR 800/864-6357 This lodgelike resort, named after a local Native American tribe, is one of the loveliest in the Pacific Northwest, though it's 7 miles inland from the ocean. Tall, mist-clouded trees line the north shore of the Rogue River, and hosts Dirk and Laurie Van Zante will help you get a line in for salmon, steelhead, or trout. The main building is handsomely designed, with lots of windows, fireplaces, private porches overlooking the river, racks for fishing gear, and stylish decor. The two-story main building holds 16 units, and the adjacent lodge has two larger kitchen suites, all with river views. In the apple orchard is the lovely Garden House, which sleeps six and features a large stone fireplace. The nearby two-bedroom and two-bath River House, open in summer, is the spendiest and most luxurious, with a cedar-vaulted living room, outdoor spa, satellite TV, and washer/dryer. Guests can swim in the heated lap pool, use the four-hole pitch-and-putt course, play horseshoes, relax around the mammoth rock fireplace in the main lodge, kayak, hike, or fish. A fire is lit every evening on the terrace, and you might spot two resident bald eagles. Breakfast and hors d'oeuvres are served. A four-course prix-fixe dinner (available for an additional fee, and only May 1–Oct 26) might include your own fish, or perhaps chicken breasts with a champagne sauce, or prime rib. *$$$; MC, V; checks OK; tututun@harborside.com; www.tututun.com; 7 miles up from Rogue River bridge (north road).*

Brookings

Situated 6 miles north of the California line, Brookings is bookended by breathtaking beauty and enjoys the state's mildest winter temperatures. To the north are **SAMUEL H. BOARDMAN** and **HARRIS BEACH STATE PARKS** (541/469-0224 or 800/452-5687). The verdant Siskiyou Mountains, deeply cut by the Chetco and Winchuck Rivers are located east, and ancient redwood groves lie to the south. Most of the **EASTER LILIES** sold in North America are grown in this favorable clime. Brookings also boasts the Oregon Coast's safest harbor—so it's busy. Retirees have inundated the area, and the hills hum with new housing.

At **AZALEA CITY PARK** (just east of Hwy 101 at the south end of town; 541/469-3181) fragrant western azaleas bloom in May, alongside wild strawberries, fruit trees, and violets; picnic amid the splendor on hand-hewn myrtlewood tables. **MYRTLEWOOD** (which grows only on the Southern Oregon Coast and in Palestine) can be seen in groves in **LOEB PARK** (8 miles east of town on North Bank River Rd; 541/469-2021). Drive 4 miles up curvy Carpenterville Road from N Highway 101 to visit the tasting room at **BRANDY PEAK DISTILLERY** (18526 Tetley Rd; 541/469-0194), a family-owned microdistillery producing fruit brandies, grappa, and eau-de-vie.

The **REDWOOD NATURE TRAIL** in Siskiyou National Forest winds through one of the few remaining groves of old-growth coastal redwoods in Oregon. See where a Japanese pilot dropped a bomb during World War II—the only place in the contiguous United States bombed by a foreign power—on **BOMBSITE TRAIL,** a pretty walk through the redwoods. Contact the **U.S. FOREST SERVICE** (555 5th St; 541/469-2196) for directions to trails.

FISHING is renowned here. The fleet operates from the south end of town. Stop in at **SPORTHAVEN MARINA** (16372 Lower Harbor Rd; 541/469-3301) for supplies and info, or at nearby **TIDEWIND CHARTERS** (16368 Lower Harbor Rd; 541/469-0337) for oceangoing fishing adventures. Soak up the harbor ambiance, and scarf an order of halibut-and-chips, at **CHETCO SEAFOOD CO.** (16182 Lower Harbor Rd; 541/469-9251).

LODGINGS

Chetco River Inn Bed and Breakfast Retreat / ★★

21202 HIGH PRAIRIE RD, BROOKINGS; 541/670-1645 OR 800/327-2688
Expect a culture shock: this secluded, alternative-energy retreat/farm planted with lavender sits on 35 forested acres of a peninsula formed by a sharp bend in the turquoise Chetco River, 17 mostly paved miles east of Brookings. Solitude is blissful; the five newly furnished bedrooms and cottage have no phones, and cellphone service is iffy at best. But you can read by safety propane lights and in the cottage watch TV via satellite (there's also a VCR). The large, open main floor—done

in lovely, deep-green marble—offers views of the river, myrtlewood groves, and wildlife. Full breakfast is included; make special arrangements for a deluxe sack lunch or exemplary five-course dinner. Guests who want it bring their own alcohol. Anglers and crack-of-dawn hikers (the Kalmiopsis Wilderness is nearby) are served early-riser breakfasts. *$$; MC, V; checks OK; chetcoriverinn@harborside.com; www.chetcoriverinn.com; off North Bank Rd, call for directions.*

South Coast Inn / ★★

516 REDWOOD ST, BROOKINGS; 541/469-5557 OR 800/525-9273 Twin gargoyles guard this handsome, 4,000-square-foot, Craftsman-style home designed in 1917 by renowned San Francisco architect Bernard Maybeck. Though it's two blocks above downtown, trees and shrubs—some of them flower all year in the mild climate—muffle the traffic noise. A spacious, partially covered deck, lighted in evening, extends around most of the lodging. Four luxurious guest rooms (two with ocean views) are appointed with antiques. The spacious, first-floor Maybeck Room has cherrywood decor, a gas fireplace, and a private patio. Downstairs, a stone fireplace and grand piano grace the parlor, while a workout room includes a weight machine, sauna, and hot tub. An unattached garden cottage (with kitchen) is outfitted with rustic log furniture. Innkeepers Ken Raith and Keith Popper will pick you up at the nearby Crescent City (California) airport. No children under 12; no pets. *$$; AE, DIS, MC, V; checks OK; innkeeper@southcoast inn.com; www.southcoastinn.com; 2 blocks above Hwy 101.*

SOUTHERN OREGON AND THE CASCADES

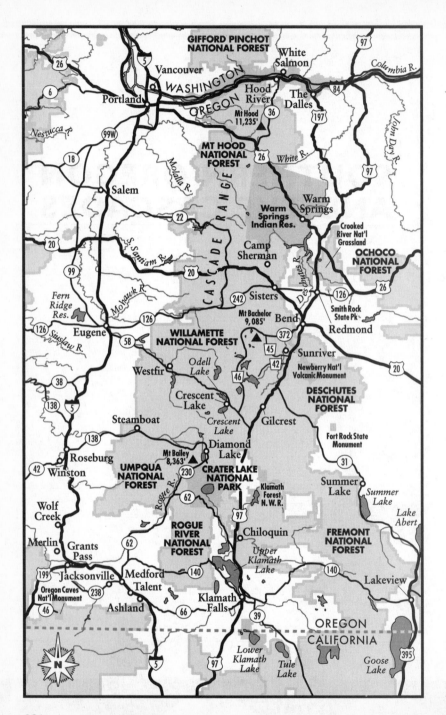

SOUTHERN OREGON AND THE CASCADES

Like a hastily dotted exclamation point, Southern Oregon sits at the end of the Cascade Range, a series of narrow valleys forming a unique ecological zone, through which Interstate 5 winds to California. Surrounding hills shelter each valley from the prodigious rains that flood the more wide-open Willamette Valley in the north, and make these pockets both warmer and drier than the rest of Western Oregon.

Just east of the Cascades, at 4,000-feet elevation, Oregon's high desert is less arid than deserts of the American Southwest and offers another unique ecological niche. Anchored at the north and south ends by Indian reservations, about 200 miles apart, the high desert is cut with deep canyons of running and dry rivers; it's scabbed with hardened lava flows and riddled with underground lava caves created by violent volcanic eruptions. Resplendent with stands of red-barked ponderosa pine, soft green juniper trees spackled with blue-gray berries, and an understory of manzanita bushes and sage, it looks and smells good.

Towering above this desert floor only a few miles from US Highway 97, the Cascade Range stands like a curtain, featuring the snowcapped peaks of Mounts Jefferson, Washington, and Bachelor, as well as the Three Sisters and Broken Top. The crown jewel in this setting is Crater Lake National Park, at the southernmost end.

ACCESS AND INFORMATION

A major north-south highway travels down each side of the Cascade mountains: **INTERSTATE 5** on the west, and **US HIGHWAY 97** on the east. **US HIGHWAY 26**, the main route between Portland and the desert, crosses Mount Hood southeast into the scenic Warm Springs Indian Reservation, where it soon connects with US Highway 97. Routes to Bend, the largest town on the east side, depart from Salem on **HIGHWAY 22**, from Albany on **US HIGHWAY 20**, and from Eugene on **HIGHWAY 126** (McKenzie Pass). From Eugene follow **HIGHWAY 58** (Willamette Pass) to US Highway 97 at the halfway point between Bend and Klamath Falls. The most scenic route to the east side of the mountains, open only in summer, is the narrow **OLD McKENZIE HIGHWAY** (Hwy 242) from Eugene. Farther south, Crater Lake is accessible from Roseburg on **HIGHWAY 138** (Diamond Lake) and from Medford on Highway 62. The most southerly routes are from Medford on Highway 140 and Ashland to Klamath Falls on Highway 66.

Flights between Portland and Bend/Redmond, Klamath Falls, and Medford are offered daily on **HORIZON AIR** (800/547-9308; www.horizonair.com) and other carriers. **AMTRAK** (800/USA-RAIL; www.amtrak.com), bound for California from Portland, crosses Willamette Pass into Klamath Falls, bypassing Southern Oregon with the exception of a stop in tiny Chemult.

Roseburg and the Umpqua Valley

The Willamette Valley and Interstate 5 corridor south of Eugene lead to Roseburg and the Umpqua River Valley. The "Wild and Scenic" North Umpqua River (so named under the Wild and Scenic River Act) is famed worldwide among serious fly-fishers, and the valley is gaining recognition for its wine-growing endeavors.

Roseburg

In the former timber town of Roseburg, you'll find the **DOUGLAS COUNTY MUSEUM OF HISTORY AND NATURAL HISTORY** (off I-5 at fairgrounds, exit 123; 541/957-7007; www.co.douglas.or.us/museum), which imaginatively displays the area's logging, mining, and pioneer history in a handsome contemporary structure.

Find picnic fixings at **KRUSE FARMS** (532 Melrose Rd; 541/672-5697), a family farm dating to 1923. Berries and tomatoes, Dillard cantaloupes, 45 varieties of veggies, and cherry, peach, prune, apple, pear, and walnut orchards keep the produce stand filled.

The Roseburg area now has seven wineries: **ABACELA VINEYARDS & WINERY** (12500 Lookingglass Rd; 541/679-6642; www.abacela.com); **CHAMPAGNE CREEK** (340 Busenbark Ln; 541/673-7901); **DENINO UMPQUA RIVER VINEYARDS** (451 Hess Ln; 541/673-1975); **GIRARDET** (895 Reston Rd; 541/679-7252; www.girardet wine.com); **HENRY ESTATE WINERY** (Hwy 9, Umpqua; 541/459-5120; www.henry estate.com); **HILLCREST** (240 Vineyard Ln; 541/673-3709 or 800/736-3709); and **LA GARZA CELLARS & GOURMET KITCHEN** (491 Winery Ln; 541/679-9654; www.winesnw.com/lagarza.htm). Henry Estate and HillCrest are open for tours and tastings all year; the others have limited winter hours. La Garza has a tasting-room restaurant, the first in the region.

WILDLIFE SAFARI (Hwy 99, 4 miles west of I-5, exit 119; 541/679-6761 or 800/355-4848; www.wildlifesafari.org) lets you drive through rolling country to see a quasi-natural wildlife preserve, with predators discreetly fenced from their prey.

THE SEVEN FEATHERS HOTEL AND CASINO RESORT (146 Chief Milwaleta Ln, Canyonville; 800/548-8461; www.sevenfeathers.com), owned by the Cow Creek Band of the Umpqua Tribe, is located about 25 miles south of Roseburg, and is the most luxurious hotel on Oregon's Interstate 5 corridor. Funded by hundreds of slots and gaming tables, the four-story, 156-room hotel (with pretty indoor swimming pool and spa) is one of the better bargains too, especially on weekdays. Golf packages include a room, breakfast for two, morning paper, and a round of golf for two (and cart rental) at the 18-hole **MYRTLE CREEK CHAMPIONSHIP COURSE** (541/863-GOLF). The dramatic crystal-chandeliered Camas Room offers fine Northwest cuisine dinners and a truly exceptional Sunday brunch.

RESTAURANTS

Roseburg Station Pub & Brewery / ★

700 SHERIDAN ST, ROSEBURG; 541/672-1934 The brothers McMenamin's familiar stamp of pub antiquities and peculiar art, which eerily reflects the past of whatever historic building they've "pub-icized," is repeated in this restoration of Roseburg's 90-year-old train depot. But we aren't complaining. The cozy bar and dining room look out onto the tracks over which the Southern Pacific Railroad's Shasta Route once ran. The brick depot's vaulted, 16-foot ceiling, tongue-and-groove fir wainscoting, and marble molding have been shined up and the roof replaced. The usual

OREGON CASCADES THREE-DAY TOUR

DAY ONE: Having overnighted at **KAH-NEE-TA LODGE,** take an early-morning soak in the swimming pool and spas filled with natural hot springwater (nonsulfurous); then have your coffee and a roll before visiting the award-winning **MUSEUM AT WARM SPRINGS** on the Warm Springs Indian Reservation. Head south to Bend, where you catch a huge lunch at the **ALPENGLOW CAFE.** Take Century Drive as it climbs out of Bend through the Three Sisters, Broken Top, and Mount Bachelor peaks, then returns to earth near Sunriver. Take a hike on any of the marked trails along the road, or if it's winter, ski **MOUNT BACHELOR's** downhill or groomed Nordic trails. Check in to **SUNRIVER LODGE** and have dinner on-site at the **MEADOWS** restaurant; then enjoy a hot soak.

    DAY TWO: Rise early and breakfast at the **TROUT HOUSE** at the Sunriver Marina (57235 River Rd; 541/593-8880), then buy picnic fixings at the local grocery store. Visit the **HIGH DESERT MUSEUM,** then drive to the **LAVA LANDS VISITOR CENTER.** There, walk into **LAVA RIVER CAVE,** a mile-long natural tube underground. Head south on US Highway 97 a short way to **NEWBERRY NATIONAL VOLCANIC MONUMENT** and picnic at Paulina or East Lake. Continue south on US Highway 97 to either Highway 138 in summer for the north entrance to **CRATER LAKE NATIONAL PARK,** or to Highway 62 just north of Klamath Falls in winter to the south entrance, and proceed on the 33-mile **RIM DRIVE** (closed in winter). Check in to **CRATER LAKE LODGE** (book months in advance) and make your dinner reservations for the dining room, then take a short hike or boat ride out to Wizard Island.

    DAY THREE: After breakfast at the lodge, drive west on Highway 62 to Medford and detour east to Jacksonville. Stroll California Street and visit the **JACKSONVILLE MUSEUM,** then continue the Gold Rush nostalgia with lunch at century-old **BELLA UNION.** Head south on Interstate 5 to Ashland, take a short walk in **LITHIA PARK,** then check in to the romantic **ROMEO INN** and enjoy afternoon refreshments. Slip into your glad rags, have a leisurely dinner at **CUCINA BIAZZI,** and take in a play at the **OREGON SHAKESPEARE FESTIVAL.** If you still have energy, have an after-theater drink at **CHATEAULIN,** or soak in the hot tub before bed.

McMenamins' beer (Hammerhead, Terminator Stout, and Ruby, infused with raspberry juice) is as good as ever, and the hearty menu is the same as in other McMs' pubs: Captain Neon and Communication Breakdown burgers, chicken Caesar salad, and cheesesteak sandwiches. *$; AE, DIS, MC, V; local checks only; lunch, dinner every day; full bar; reservations not necessary; www.mcmenamins.com; across from Village Bistro.* &

Village Bistro & Bakery / ★

500 SE CASS AVE, ROSEBURG; 541/677-3450 This is the sunniest spot in Roseburg, with a wide-open floor plan, and patio seating under umbrellas on the warmest days. Generous portions of down-to-earth bistro food are served here. The short breakfast menu includes home fries and biscuits and gravy. For lunch, try seared salmon and fresh spinach salad, topped with miso-ginger dressing. *$; AE, DIS, MC, V; local checks only; breakfast, lunch Mon–Sat, dinner Thurs–Sat; beer and wine; reservations not necessary; village@rosenet.net; just south of downtown.* &

LODGINGS

Steamboat Inn / ★★

42705 N HWY 138, STEAMBOAT; 541/498-2230 OR 800/840-8825 On the banks of a fly-only fishing stream is this plain-seeming lodge, run for many years by Jim and Sharon Van Loan. Linked by a long veranda paralleling the North Umpqua River are eight small cabins; adult-only rooms have knotty pine walls and just enough space, with Jacuzzi tubs in the rooms. Five secluded cottages in the woods have living rooms and kitchens, suitable for small families; two suites are by the river. Across the river, four three-bedroom houses are offered through an arrangement with the state of Oregon and the U.S. Forest Service. Remarkably good family-style dinners are served in the main building each night a half hour after dark, by reservation ($40 per person). The inn also serves breakfast and lunch every day, and is entirely nonsmoking. No pets; enjoy the Van Loans's instead. *$$$; MC, V; checks OK; closed Jan–Feb, weekends only Mar–Apr, Nov–Dec; www.thesteamboatinn.com; 38 miles east of Roseburg.*

Wolf Creek Inn / ★

100 FRONT STREET, WOLF CREEK; 541/866-2474 An 1880s stagecoach stop and the oldest inn in Oregon, this two-story clapboard inn was purchased by the state, restored in 1979, and refurbished to what it reportedly looked like in 1925. Nine nicely furnished guest rooms, including one suite, have comfortable antique beds. All have private, basic baths. Downstairs, true to tradition, are separate men's and ladies' parlors, and a cozy dining room featuring the fresh Nothwest fare. Children OK; no pets; no smoking. *$$; MC, V; local checks only; closed Mon–Tues, Oct–Apr; www.thewolfcreekinn.com; 25 miles north of Grants Pass, exit 76 off I-5.* &

The Rogue River Valley

The Rogue River is one of Oregon's most beautiful rivers. Running west from the Cascades, it's chiseled into the coastal mountains, protected by the million-acre Siskiyou National Forest, flecked with abandoned gold-mining sites, and inhabited by splendid steelhead. Many rustic lodges along the river cater specifically to fly-fishers and rafters, and are often only accessible via water. Grants Pass, along the upper reaches of the Rogue, offers the best access for fishing and rafting.

Grants Pass

Two companies offer guided tours of the Rogue River. **HELLGATE JETBOAT EXCURSIONS** (966 SW 6th St; 541/479-7204 or 800/648-4874; www.hellgate.com) departs from the Riverside Inn (971 SE 6th St; 541/476-6873 or 800/334-4567; www.riverside-inn.com) in Grants Pass. **ORANGE TORPEDO TRIPS** (209 Merlin Rd, Merlin; 541/479-5061; www.orangetorpedo.com) conducts popular whitewater trips on inflatable kayaks and rafts.

RESTAURANTS

Hamilton River House / ★

1936 ROGUE RIVER HWY/HWY 99, GRANTS PASS; 541/479-3938 Owner Doug Hamilton moved the restaurant from his childhood home to a new riverside location, and it's built for a crowd. Casual and colorful (bright yellow, green, and coral), with tiered seating inside and out, the restaurant still serves the same good food. Count on moist and exquisite salmon, and rich, creamy Jamaican jerk chicken over angel hair pasta. A daily fresh sheet might feature lingcod, snapper, halibut, and tri-tip steaks. Lunches include Milano-style wood-fired pizza, smoked-salmon ravioli, and great burgers. Grants Pass is noted for inexpensive dining, and Hamilton River House fits the mold. *$; AE, DIS, MC, V; checks OK; lunch, dinner every day (closed Feb–Mar); full bar; reservations recommended; Grants Pass exit off I-5.* &

Matsukaze

1675 NE 7TH ST, GRANTS PASS; 541/479-2961 This small Japanese restaurant offers fresh preparations in a calm setting, just off the interstate, and commercially bottles and sells its tasty sauces. There are fish, vegetable, and meat teriyakis; tempura; sukiyaki; king crab; Oregon lox sushi (of course); and plate lunches served with salad, rice, vegetables, and hot tea. Or try mahimahi in a light egg wash, sautéed. Finish up with refreshing green tea ice cream. *$; DIS, MC, V; no checks; lunch Mon–Fri, dinner Mon–Sat; beer and wine; reservations not necessary; corner of Hillcrest Dr.*

Summer Jo's / ★

2315 UPPER RIVER RD LOOP, GRANTS PASS; 541/476-6882 This bright garden room, owned by two retired *MacWorld* editors, sits on 6½ acres of flower, vegetable, and herb gardens and 100-year-old fruit trees. The gardens are lovely, with more than 200 varieties of roses, many of them climbing a series of trellises. The restaurant, overseen by Philip Accetta, who trained at the Hyde Park Culinary Institute, offers hearty sandwiches served with soup or salad, such as the popular roasted portobello mushroom with smoked-tomato relish and white cheddar. Afternoons (Tues–Sat), have tea with scones served with Devonshire cream, lemon curd, brown-sugar shortbread, fruit, and tea sandwiches. For sale in the adjoining pantry are fresh vegetables grown at Summer Jo's certified organic farm. *$; AE, MC, V; local checks only; lunch Tues–Sat, dinner Fri–Sat (closed mid-Dec–mid-Feb); beer and wine; reservations not necessary; www.summerjo.com; exit 58 off I-5.* &

LODGINGS

Flery Manor / ★★

2000 JUMPOFF JOE CREEK RD, GRANTS PASS; 541/476-3591 OR 541/471-2303 This classy two-story, 5,000-square-foot 1990s rural home on 7 acres of wooded mountainside became a B&B in 1996. Owners John and Marla Vidrinskas recently added waterfalls and ponds to the lower yard, complete with elegant black swans; guests can barbecue in the peaceful gazebo. The showpiece is the Moonlight Suite, favored by honeymooners and second-honeymooners. Its king-sized canopied bed sits in front of a fireplace. French doors open to a private balcony. The bath has a double vanity, double Jacuzzi, and glassed-in shower. A second suite offers the same luxury with a private first-floor patio. There are three additional guest rooms. Marla serves a three-course breakfast in a formal dining room, with baked goods, quiches, and frittatas (featured in several gourmet magazines). No pets; no smoking; no children under 10. *$$; MC, V; checks OK; flery@flerymanor.com; www.flerymanor.com; 10 miles north of Grants Pass, Hugo exit 66 off I-5.* &

Morrison's Rogue River Lodge / ★

8500 GALICE RD, MERLIN; 541/476-3825 OR 800/826-1963 Start your Rogue River rafting adventures here and you'll follow in the footsteps of former presidents George Bush and Jimmy Carter. This is the best of the Rogue River lodges favored by anglers and river runners. It is also easiest to reach. While others are accessible only by boat or plane, Morrison's is accessed via a paved road. The lodge, dating to the 1940s, has four guest rooms and nine riverview cottages (most guests prefer the latter, with fireplaces, private decks, and covered parking). One- or two-bedroom cottages and lodge rooms have private baths. Rates include breakfast and a four-course dinner, which might feature oven-poached salmon, spinach salad with chutney dressing, and homemade blackberry cobbler; the dining room is open to nonguests by reservation. *$$–$$$; DIS, MC, V; checks OK; closed Nov–Apr; info@morrisonslodge.com; www.morrisonslodge.com; 12 miles west of 1-5.*

Weasku Inn / ★★

5560 ROGUE RIVER HWY/HWY 99, GRANTS PASS; 541/471-8000 OR 800/493-2758 This 1924 log lodge where Hollywood actors once retreated to fish was resuscitated in 1999. Weasku Inn (pronounced "we-ask-you"), with its river-rock fireplace and broad lawn among giant trees, is an idyllic place to stay on the banks of the Rogue River. Better yet, book one of nine luxurious river cabins. Any potential traffic noise is drowned out by the rush of water over Savage Rapids Dam. A short trail from the cabins to the rocky shore below the dam brings you to a fabulous bird-watching spot for mergansers, mallards, osprey, and herons. River cabins have gas fireplaces, lodge-style furnishings, large baths that are well appointed, and decks for morning sun. Whirlpool tubs are in some cabins as well as in several lodge rooms. Complimentary continental breakfast is served in the lodge dining room, and evening wine and cheese next to the fireplace. *$$; AE, DIS, MC, V; no checks; www.weasku.com; exit 48 off I-5.*

Oregon Caves National Monument

Cave Junction is 28 miles southwest of Grants Pass on US Highway 199. The Cave Junction area is home to two of Oregon's better wineries: **FORIS VINEYARDS WINERY** (654 Kendall Rd; 541/592-3752 or 800/84FORIS; www.foriswine.com) and **BRIDGEVIEW VINEYARDS & WINERY** (4210 Holland Loop Rd; 541/592-4688 or 877/273-4843; www.bridgeviewwine.com). Both have tasting rooms open daily.

About 20 miles east of Cave Junction, on Highway 46, is **OREGON CAVES NATIONAL MONUMENT** (20000 Caves Hwy; 541/592-2100; www.nps.gov/orca), a group of intriguing formations of marble and limestone set among redwoods. Tours leave hourly every day, mid-March through November. They are a bit strenuous, and the caves remain a chilly 41°F; the tight spaces can get awfully packed with tourists. Part of the caves' walkway is wheelchair-accessible. Children must meet a height requirement. In summer, arrive early or you may have a long wait.

OREGON CAVES LODGE (541/592-2100; open May–Oct) is nothing fancy but a restful old wooden lodge with 22 rooms and a cafeteria-style dining room.

LODGINGS

Out 'n' About Treesort / ★

300 PAGE CREEK RD, CAVE JUNCTION; 541/592-2208 OR 800/200-5484 A nationally publicized battle with planning officials in the 1990s made this tree-house resort famous. Owner Michael Garnier, who got the official OK in 1998 for his out-on-a-limb B&B, now has 14 different structures swinging from the trees—tree houses, platforms, forts, ladders, swinging bridges, a ropes course, and a floating ship "piratree." Accommodations (there are seven units in all; some are open seasonally) range from the Tree Room Schoolhouse Suite, with a bathroom, kitchenette, and sitting area, to the Swiss Family Complex, a pair of tree houses connected by a swinging bridge. Full breakfast is included. Book early; summer reservations go fast. Children welcome. *$$; no credit cards; checks OK; treesort@treehouses.com; www.treehouses.com; 8 miles SE of Cave Junction near Takilma.*

Medford

Southern Oregon's largest city may not win any contests for prettiness, but it is the center of things in this part of the world. It's well known across the nation due to the marketing efforts of Harry and David's, a mail-order giant purveying pears, other fruit, and condiments. **HARRY AND DAVID'S COUNTRY VILLAGE** (1314 Center Dr; 541/776-2277; www.harry-david.com) offers "seconds" from gift packs and numerous other items; it's the departure point for tours (877/322-8000) of the corporate complex, also home to **JACKSON & PERKINS** (www.jackson-perkins.com), the world's largest rose growers.

The **CRATERIAN GINGER ROGERS THEATER** (23 S Central Ave; 541/779-3000; www.craterian.org) is Medford's showpiece, a downtown performing arts center with a 742-seat theater that opened in 1997. (The 1924 building was originally The Craterian, a vaudeville and silent-movie house.) Why Ginger Rogers? The actress owned a ranch on the nearby Rogue River for many years, once danced on The Craterian stage, and in the last couple of years before her death helped raise money for the theater's $5.3 million renovation.

Locals like lunch and dinner at **SAMOVAR** (101 E Main St; 541/779-4967), a Russian cafe; for Thai food they flock to **ALI'S THAI KITCHEN** (2392 N Pacific Hwy; 541/770-3104), a humble spot north of town with good, inexpensive fare.

LODGINGS

Under the Greenwood Tree / ★★★☆

3045 BELLINGER LN, MEDFORD; 541/776-0000 OR 800/766-8099
Innkeeper Renate Ellam—a Cordon Bleu chef—will have you relaxing in the lap of luxury amid green lawns and 300-year-old trees on her 10-acre farm with an orchard, beautiful rose gardens and gazebo, and antique farm buildings. The 1862 home has five guest rooms, each with private bath, Persian rugs, ironed pillowcases, fresh flowers, and amenities such as terry-cloth robes and hair dryers. Guests who arrive early might be greeted by lemon pound cake or hot scones with orange butter; Ellam's elaborate three-course breakfasts include dishes such as poached pears with Chantilly cream. Massages can be booked in-room or out in the rose garden. Popular for weddings, the B&B has a dance floor under the stars. *$$; no credit cards; checks OK; grwdtree@internetcds.com; www.greenwoodtree.com; exit 27 off I-5.* &

Jacksonville

The town, a few miles west of Medford on Highway 238, started with a boom when gold was discovered in Rich Gulch in 1851. Then the railroad bypassed it, and the tidy little city struggled to avoid becoming a ghost town. Much of the 19th-century city has been restored; Jacksonville now boasts more than 85 historic homes and buildings, some open to the public. The strip of authentic Gold Rush–era shops, hotels, and saloons along **CALIFORNIA STREET** has become a popular stage set for films, including the TV-movie version of *Inherit the Wind*. Jacksonville is also renowned for antique shops.

JACKSONVILLE MUSEUM (206 N 5th St; 541/773-6536; www.sohs.org), housed in the stately 1883 Italianate-style courthouse, follows the history of the Rogue River valley with photos and artifacts, and displays works by Peter Britt (see below). The adjacent **CHILDREN'S MUSEUM** lets kids walk through various miniaturized pioneer settings (jail, tepee, schoolhouse). Walking trails thread around old gold diggings in the hills; the longest (3 miles) is **RICH GULCH HISTORIC TRAIL** (trailhead off 1st and Fir St), an easy climb to a panoramic view. Also stroll through the 1875 "country gothic" **BEEKMAN HOUSE** and gardens (on east end of California St; 541/773-6536).

VALLEY VIEW WINERY (1000 Applegate Rd; 541/899-3124 or 800/781-WINE; www.valleyviewwinery.com) is at Ruch, 6 miles southwest of Jacksonville on Highway 238. The winery maintains another tasting room in town, in **ANNA MARIA'S** (130 W California St; 541/899-1001).

The **BRITT FESTIVAL** (541/773-6077 or 800/882-7488; www.brittfest.org; late June–Sept), an outdoor music-and-arts series, is held on the hillside field where Peter

Britt, a famous local photographer and horticulturist, lived. Listeners gather on benches or blankets to enjoy music ranging from jazz and bluegrass to folk, country, and classical, as well as musical theater and dance. Performance quality varies, but the series includes big-name artists. Begun in 1963, the festival now draws some 70,000 visitors each summer.

RESTAURANTS

Bella Union / ★★

170 W CALIFORNIA ST, JACKSONVILLE; 541/899-1770 This restaurant, in the original century-old Bella Union Saloon (half of which was reconstructed when *The Great Northfield, Minnesota Raid* was filmed in Jacksonville in 1969), has everything from pizza and pasta to elegant dinners to summer picnic baskets. Outdoor dining under a magnificent century-old wisteria is popular with guests. Proprietor Jerry Hayes, a wine fancier, pours a wide variety of labels by the glass as well as the bottle. *$$; AE, DIS, MC, V; checks OK; lunch, dinner every day, brunch Sun; full bar; reservations recommended for 6 or more; greatfood@bellau. com; www.bellau.com; downtown.*

Jacksonville Inn / ★★

175 E CALIFORNIA ST, JACKSONVILLE; 541/899-1900 OR 800/321-9344 Ask a native to name the area's best, and the answer is often the Jacksonville Inn. The staff is considerate, and the antique-furnished dining room, housed in the original 1863 building, is elegant and intimate. The inn's restaurant features steak, seafood, pasta—plus health-minded low-cholesterol fare and an expanded variety of vegetarian entrees. Dinners can be ordered as leisurely seven-course feasts or à la carte. Desserts are lovely European creations. Jerry Evans maintains one of the best-stocked wine cellars in Oregon, with more than 1,500 domestic and imported labels. Upstairs, eight rooms are decorated with 19th-century details: antique beds, patchwork quilts, and original brickwork on the walls. Modern amenities include private baths and air conditioning (a boon on 100-degree summer days). The inn has four honeymoon cottages nearby, all with king-sized canopied beds and two-person Jacuzzis; the newest one has a dining room where the inn's chef can prepare a meal. Guests enjoy a full breakfast. Reserve in advance, especially during the Britt Festival. *$$; AE, DC, DIS, MC, V; checks OK; breakfast, dinner every day, lunch Tues–Sat, brunch Sun; full bar; reservations recommended; jvinn@ mind.net; www.jacksonvilleinn.com; on main thoroughfare.*

McCully House Inn / ★★

240 E CALIFORNIA ST, JACKSONVILLE; 541/899-1942 OR 800/367-1942 McCully House, an elegant Gothic Revival mansion, was built in 1860 for Jacksonville's first doctor—and later housed the first private school in Southern Oregon. Inside, four intimate dining rooms draw raves for ambience and a menu crafted by Grants Pass native Derenda Hurst. The daily blue plate special, featuring such down-home favorites as Salisbury steak and chicken pot pie, complements the more sophisticated entrees—cutlets of pork tenderloin on a bed of balsamic glazed apples, for example. The best of the three guest rooms flaunts a fire-

SHAKESPEARE FESTIVAL TIPS

The Oregon Shakespeare Festival mounts plays in three theaters. In the outdoor **ELIZ-ABETHAN THEATER**, which seats 1,200, famous and authentic nighttime productions of Shakespeare are staged (three each summer). The festival opened a new indoor theater in 2002; it's the first time a venue has been added in 25 years. The season for the two indoor theaters, the New Theatre and the Angus Theatre, runs February through October and includes comedies, contemporary fare, and some experimental works. Visit the **EXHIBIT CENTER**, where you can clown around in costumes from plays past. There are also lectures and concerts at noon, excellent backstage tours each morning, and Renaissance music and dance nightly in the courtyard.

The best way to get current **INFORMATION AND TICKETS** (last-minute tickets in summer are rare) is through a comprehensive agency: Southern Oregon Reservation Center (541/488-1011 or 800/547-8052; www.sorc.com; Mon–Fri), or the festival box office (15 S Pioneer St, Ashland; 541/482-4331; www.osfashland.org).

Ashland is also home to a growing number of smaller theater groups—often called Off Shakespeare or Off Bardway—and worth watching. Festival actors often join in these small companies to have a bit of fun. **OREGON CABARET THEATER** (1st and Hargadine Sts; 541/488-2902; www.oregoncabaret.com), for example, presents musicals and comedies through much of the year, with dinners, hors d'oeuvres, and desserts for theater patrons. —*Jan Halliday*

place, huge claw-footed pedestal tub, and the original black-walnut furnishings that traveled 'round the Horn with J. W. McCully. Children welcome (with well-behaved parents); no pets. *$$; AE, DC, DIS, JCB, MC, V; checks OK; dinner every day, brunch Sun (closed Sun–Mon in winter); full bar; reservations recommended; mccully@wave.net; www.mccullyhouseinn.com; downtown.* ⅍

LODGINGS

TouVelle House / ★★

455 N OREGON ST, JACKSONVILLE; 541/899-8938 OR 800/846-8422 This stately mansion, one of Jacksonville's first, was built in 1855. Frank TouVelle and his bride remodeled and added to the three-story Craftsman-style house after moving to Oregon from Ohio. Today it's a Jacksonville landmark, which Steven Harris and Nick Williamson run as a six-room B&B. Period wallpapers and lighting fixtures (discovered in the owners' ongoing treasure hunts) flatter the extensive wood paneling and square-beamed ceilings. Two suites are large enough to accommodate three or four. The grounds feature a pond and a historical garden with old-fashioned roses, hedging, and pergolas. A modern swimming pool with a gazebo is out back. Breakfast is a gourmet, three-course affair. Corporate rates available. *$$; AE, DIS, MC, V; checks OK; touvelle@wave.net; www.touvellehouse.com; downtown.*

Talent

RESTAURANTS

New Sammy's Cowboy Bistro / ★★★

2210 S PACIFIC HWY/HWY 99, TALENT; 541/535-2779 Proprietors Vernon and Charleen Rollins rely entirely on word-of-mouth advertising and appear amused when you find them. There's no sign other than a flashing light at night, and the outside looks barely a cut above a shack. Inside, though, is as charming a dinner house as you're likely to find in Southern Oregon—and nowadays it even accepts credit cards. With just six tables, reservations are a must, and you may have to wait a couple of weeks. The French-inspired menu usually lists a handful of entrees, like duck breast with spinach, chicken with spicy couscous, and salmon with dill sauce and vegetables (perfectly cooked). The wines include more than 2,000 choices from Oregon, California, and France. *$$; MC, V; checks OK; dinner Thurs–Sun (Fri–Sat in midwinter); beer and wine; reservations required; halfway between Talent and Ashland.*

Ashland

The remarkable success of the **OREGON SHAKESPEARE FESTIVAL** (see "Shakespeare Festival Tips" in this chapter), now well over 50 years old, has transformed this sleepy town into one with, per capita, the region's best tourist amenities. The festival draws more than 360,000 people through the nine-month season, filling its theaters to an extraordinary 91 percent capacity. Visitors pour into this town of 18,000, and fine shops, restaurants, and bed-and-breakfasts spring up in anticipation. Amazingly, the town still has its soul: for the most part, it seems a happy little college town, set amid lovely ranch country, that just happens to house the largest repertory company in the nation.

Designed by the creator of San Francisco's Golden Gate Park, **LITHIA PARK**, Ashland's central park, runs for 100 acres behind the outdoor theater, with duck ponds, Japanese gardens, grassy lawns, playgrounds, and groomed or dirt trails for hikes and jogging; locals find it a pleasant place to play guitar or practice Qigong, a Chinese discipline said to reduce stress and anxiety. There's even an ice-skating rink in winter. **SCHNEIDER MUSEUM OF ART** (1250 Siskiyou Blvd; 541/552-6245) at the south end of the **SOUTHERN OREGON UNIVERSITY** campus is the best art gallery in town.

WEISINGER'S OF ASHLAND WINERY (3150 Siskiyou Blvd; 541/488-5989; wine@weisingers.com; www.weisingers.com) and **ASHLAND VINEYARDS** (I-5 exit 14; 541/488-0088; www.winenet.com) offer opportunities to sample Ashland vintages.

Nearby daytime attractions include river rafting, picnicking, and historical touring. The **ROGUE RIVER RECREATION AREA** has fine swimming on sizzling summer days, as does the lovely Applegate River. **HOWARD PRAIRIE LAKE RESORT** (3249 Hyatt Prairie Rd; 541/482-1979) is 22 scenic miles southeast of Ashland up Dead Indian Memorial Road. **SKI ASHLAND** (1745 Hwy 66; 541/482-2897), on nearby Mount Ashland 18 miles south of town, offers 22 runs for all classes of skiers, usually Thanksgiving to mid-April.

RESTAURANTS

Chateaulin / ★★★

50 E MAIN ST, ASHLAND; 541/482-2264 Less than a block from the theaters is a romantic cafe reminiscent of New York's Upper West Side. During Shakespeare season, the place bustles with before- and after-theater crowds gathered for fine French cuisine or drinks at the bar. House specialties are pâtés and veal dishes, but seafood and poultry are also impressive. Chef David Taub and co-owner Michael Donovan change the menu frequently. The cafe menu is a favorite of the after-show crowd: baked goat cheese in puff pastry with sundried tomatoes served on mesclun green salad with raspberry vinaigrette gets raves, as does a delicious onion soup; coffee and specialty drinks round out the menu. Service is polished and smooth even during the rush. The restaurant has an inside door to its sister business, a wine and gourmet-food shop. *$$; AE, DIS, MC, V; checks OK; dinner every day (closed Mon–Tues in winter); full bar; reservations recommended; www.chateaulin.com; down walkway from Angus Bowmer Theater.*

Cucina Biazzi / ★★

568 E MAIN ST, ASHLAND; 541/488-3739 Chef April Morehouse and proprietor Beasy McMillan have turned this pretty little house into a traditional Tuscan trattoria with a wisteria-covered patio. Four-course dinners are served on white linen in the former living room. Don't fill up on the delicious antipasto course alone (though it's tempting): asiago cheese, imported olives, marinated mushrooms, oven-roasted vegetables, and bean salad, with plenty of warm bread. Pasta portions, made with fresh pasta and creamy cheeses, are filling, followed by a full plate of fish or meat entree such as osso buco. Dinner finishes with a perfectly dressed green salad. Desserts might be lemon tarts or rich chocolate cake. *$$; MC, V; checks OK; dinner every day; full bar; reservations recommended; near fire station on E Main St.*

Firefly / ★★

23 N MAIN ST, 3RD FL, ASHLAND; 541/488-3212 Prepare for a visual feast as well as unusual fare at this dining room, the entire third floor (with elevator access) of Ashland's historic Masonic Temple. The room is simple, rich, and beautiful: plum and grape, hand-carved walnut, and two fireplaces. Chef-owners Tim and Dana Keller change the menu frequently, but entrees may include banana-wrapped swordfish with coconut rice and green sauce, or pork tenderloin rubbed with anise and curry, served with lentils and applesauce. *$$; AE, DIS, MC, V; checks OK; lunch, dinner every day; full bar; reservations recommended; on plaza.*

Monet / ★★★

36 S 2ND ST, ASHLAND; 541/482-1339 Pierre and Dale Verger have created a gentrified French restaurant that is the talk of Ashland (and even gets mentioned in Portland). Favorite dishes in this gracious house include shrimp sautéed in white wine and Pernod, and veal with wild mushrooms and Madeira. Pierre Verger goes out of his way to make interesting vegetarian choices—sautéed artichoke hearts with sundried tomatoes, olives, mushrooms, garlic, shallots, feta, and Parmesan over pasta, as well as a simple French-country dish called *la crique Ardechoise,* a kind of gourmet potato pancake with garlic and parsley. The wine list is extensive. Dine outdoors in summer. *$$; MC, V; local checks only; dinner every day (Tues–Sat off-season, closed Jan–mid-Feb); full bar; reservations recommended; ½ block from Main St.*

LODGINGS

Chanticleer Inn / ★★★

120 GRESHAM ST, ASHLAND; 541/482-1919 OR 800/898-1950 New owners Ellen and Howie Wilcox have freshened up the six guest rooms in one of Ashland's first B&Bs with a French-country decor face-lift. Each room has a view of the Cascade foothills or a private patio entrance with a garden view. The largest room has a gas fireplace; all have private baths and cotton robes for the trek to the Jacuzzi out back. A gourmet breakfast (orange eggs Benedict with smoked salmon is a favorite) is served in the dining room, and complimentary afternoon wine, sherry, port, and homemade cookies are available. Children over 12 OK; no pets. *$$; AE, MC, V; checks OK; innkeeper@ashland-bed-breakfast.com; www.ashland-bed-breakfast.com; 2 blocks from library, off Main St.*

Country Willows Inn / ★★★

1313 CLAY ST, ASHLAND; 541/488-1590 OR 800/945-5697 Set on 5 acres of farmland seven minutes from downtown, this rebuilt 1896 country home offers peace and quiet and a lovely view of the hills. Dan Durant and David Newton offer five rooms, three suites, and a separate cottage, with air conditioning and private baths, plus a swimming pool and a hot tub on the large back deck. The best room is in the barn: the Pine Ridge Suite has a bed/living room with a lodgepole pine king-sized bed, and a bath bigger than most bedrooms. Breakfast is organic juices and egg dishes, pumpkin pancakes or waffles, presented on a pretty sunporch. The grounds offer running and hiking trails into the adjacent foothills; the owners keep a small flock of ducks, a gaggle of geese, and even a couple of goats. Children over 12 OK; no pets. *$$; AE, DIS, MC, V; checks OK; www.willowsinn.com; 4 blocks south of Siskiyou Blvd.* &

Cowslip's Belle / ★★

159 N MAIN ST, ASHLAND; 541/488-2901 OR 800/888-6819 Named after a flower mentioned in *A Midsummer Night's Dream* and *The Tempest,* this home has a cheery charm, with its swing chair on the front porch, vintage furniture, and fresh flowers inside. A huge deck with redwood arbor overlooks a koi pond and lagoon. Two lovely bedrooms (one a suite) are in the main house—a 1913 Craftsman bungalow—and three more in a romantic carriage house in back; the newest one has a spa tub and a private balcony overlooking the mountains. Jon and Carmen Reinhardt, owners for 18 years, provide turndown service (with chocolate truffles) and full breakfasts such as cheese blintzes, walnut wheat-germ pancakes, and Jon's brioche, scones, and other baked goods (his wholesale bakery is on premises, so the inn always smells heavenly). No children under 10; no pets. *$$; no credit cards; checks OK; stay@cowslip.com; www.cowslip.com; 3 blocks north of theaters.* &

Mount Ashland Inn / ★★★

550 MOUNT ASHLAND RD, ASHLAND; 541/482-8707 OR 800/830-8707
Wind your way up Mount Ashland Road and you discover a huge, custom-made two-story log cabin, built in 1987, using some 275 cedar trees cut from the 160-acre property in the Siskiyous. Examples of the original owner's handiwork are seen throughout: stained-glass windows, a spiral cedar staircase with madrona railing. Chuck and Laurel Biegert have owned the inn for seven years. Each of the five suites has a gas fireplace and jetted or soaking tub, as well as a microwave and refrigerator. Spectacular views of Mounts Shasta and McLoughlin are visible from the dining room. An outdoor spa, cross-country skis, snowshoes, and mountain bikes are available for guests' use. The golden aromatic-cedar logs, high-beamed ceilings, large windows, and huge stone fireplace make this the perfect après-ski spot. Expect snow November through April. No children under 10; no pets. *$$$; DIS, MC, V; checks OK for deposits; www.mtashlandinn.com; follow signs to Mount Ashland Ski Area.*

Peerless Hotel / ★★

243 4TH ST, ASHLAND; 541/488-1082 OR 800/460-8758 Originally a hotel in Ashland's now-historic railroad district in 1900, the building fell into disrepair but was saved by Chrissy Barnett. She merged hotel rooms into six B&B units (two of them suites), and filled them with antiques collected from places as disparate as New Orleans and Hawaii. High ceilings and oversized bathrooms are trademarks. Suite 3 features a bath with two claw-footed tubs and a glassed-in shower. Several rooms have Jacuzzis. Breakfast is served in the adjoining restaurant (open to the public for dinner), across the garden; you can walk to the theaters. Children over 14 OK. *$$$; AE, DIS, MC, V; checks OK; www.peerlesshotel.com; between A and B Sts.* &

Romeo Inn / ★★★

295 IDAHO ST, ASHLAND; 541/488-0884 OR 800/915-8899 This imposing 1932 Cape Cod home has four plush guest rooms and two suites, some decorated in English country with antiques, some neoclassical. Spacious rooms have king-sized beds, phones, and private baths. The Stratford Suite is a separate structure with its own bedroom, bath, and kitchen; it features a vaulted ceiling with skylight, marble-tiled wood fireplace, and raised whirlpool tub for two. The Cambridge Suite has a fireplace, patio, and private entrance. The heated pool on the large back deck is open seasonally, and the hot tub is inviting year-round. Innkeepers Don and Deana Politis serve freshly squeezed orange juice, melon with blueberry sauce, eggs Florentine, sausage, and baked goods—plus afternoon refreshments and bedtime chocolate. No pets or children under 12. *$$$; DIS, MC, V; checks OK; innkeeper@romeoinn.com; www.romeoinn.com; downtown.*

Klamath Falls

This city of 17,000 people, the largest for 70 miles around, is so isolated that it once led a movement to secede from Oregon and become the state of Jefferson. Residents happily welcome tourists, bird-watchers, and sports enthusiasts from Oregon and California (25 miles south). Seemingly dormant for years, the geothermally heated town has bubbled to life in the past few years with a flurry of construction, including chain hotels and the $250-million **RUNNING Y RANCH RESORT** (5500 Running Y Rd; 888/850-0275; www.runningy.com), with its 85-room lodge, Arnold Palmer 18-hole golf course, restaurant, and condo development on 9,000 acres on Klamath Lake, 10 miles out of town. The Klamath Indian Tribe, a confederation of the Klamath, Modoc, and Yahooskin Natives who have occupied the region for thousands of years, opened their **KLA-MO-YA CASINO** (541/783-7529; www.klamoya.com) on US Highway 97 at Chiloquin, just a few miles north of the Klamath Falls Airport.

The **FAVELL MUSEUM OF WESTERN ART AND INDIAN ARTIFACTS** (125 W Main St; 541/882-9996; www.favellmuseum.com) is a true Western museum, with arrowheads, Native artifacts, and the works of more than 300 Western artists. **KLAMATH COUNTY MUSEUM** (1451 Main St; 541/883-4208) exhibits the volcanic geology of the region, regional Native artifacts, and relics from pioneer days. The **BALDWIN HOTEL MUSEUM** (31 Main St; 541/883-4207; open June–Sept), in a spooky 1906 hotel, retains many fixtures of the era. **ROSS RAGLAND THEATER** (218 N 7th St; 541/884-0651 or 888/627-5484; www.rrtheater.org), a onetime art deco movie theater, now presents more than 60 stage plays, concerts, and the like each year.

UPPER KLAMATH LAKE lies on the remains of a larger ancient lake system and, at 143 square miles, is the largest lake in Oregon; it's fine for fishing and serves as the nesting grounds for many birds, including white pelicans. The Williamson River, which flows into the lake, yields plenty of trout.

RESTAURANTS

Fiorella's / ★★

6139 SIMMERS AVE, KLAMATH FALLS; 541/882-1878 Fiorella and Renato Durighellois came here from a town near Venice, Italy, and 15 years ago opened one of the town's best restaurants. They've done their best to re-create rustic Italian ambience in a former residence with white tablecloths, fresh flowers, plastered walls, wooden-beamed ceilings, and a copper polenta pot nestled in the fireplace. Specials may include beef roll stuffed with sausage and served with grilled polenta, or osso buco. Homemade egg pastas are delicious, including ravioli stuffed with wild mushrooms. *$$; AE, MC, V; local checks only; dinner Tues–Sat (closed Jan); full bar; reservations not necessary; S 6th St to Simmers Ave.*

Lakeview

At nearly 4,300 feet elevation, Lakeview calls itself "Oregon's Tallest Town." Call the **LAKE COUNTY CHAMBER OF COMMERCE** (126 North E St, Lakeview; 877/947-6040) and ask if **OLD PERPETUAL,** Oregon's only geyser (at Hunter Hot Springs, on west side of US Hwy 395, 2 miles north of town), is open to the public.

WARNER CANYON SKI AREA (10 miles north of Lakeview; 541/947-5001) offers 17 weeks of skiing each year, beginning in mid-December, with no lines for the 700-foot vertical chair lift. A modest ski lodge has a fireplace and small restaurant.

For authentic campfire cuisine and Western-style cabins, visit the **WILLOW SPRINGS GUEST RANCH** (Clover Flat Rd, Lakeview; 541/947-5499; www.willow springsguestranch.com), a working cattle ranch that generates its own power. The wood-fired hot tub overlooks acres of meadows.

LAKE ABERT, 20 miles north of Lakeview on US Highway 395, is a stark, shallow body of water over which looms **ABERT RIM,** a massive fault scarp. One of the highest exposed geologic faults in North America, the rim towers 2,000 feet above the lake.

Summer Lake

From Summer Lake, continue north on Highway 31 and you'll pass **FORT ROCK STATE MONUMENT** (541/388-6055), where Klamath Indians found refuge when Mount Mazama exploded 6,800 years ago. Woven sandals found in one of Fort Rock's caves were carbon-dated to 9,000 years ago; archaeological studies have found Klamath-style artifacts that date back 13,000 years in the prehistoric lakebed. Summers, the mom-and-pop grocery store and the small pioneer museum nearby are usually open.

LODGINGS

Summer Lake Inn / ★★

47531 HWY 31, SUMMER LAKE; 541/943-3983 OR 800/261-2778 If you are looking for luxury in a remote setting, this is it—about 110 miles southeast of Bend on the edge of one of Oregon's largest bird refuges, Summer Lake Wildlife Refuge. From the inn's hot tub on the wide deck you can see 40 unmarred miles in all directions and, at night, more stars than you can count. Stay in one of their six new cabins, or in one of three cabin-style condos—all have kitchens, Jacuzzis, and fireplaces. All are equally attractive. Breakfast is served American style two or three days a week with continental-breakfast baskets available the rest of the time. The cedar-and-glass dining room serves dinner six days a week by reservation February through September—check with owners Darrell Seven and Jean Sage for the reduced winter schedule. The area has considerable natural charms, which you'll have mostly to yourself—hiking in the Gearhart Mountain Wilderness Area to the south, fly-fishing, birdwatching, and viewing petroglyphs. $$; AE, MC, V; checks OK; www.summerlakeinn.com; between mileposts 81 and 82.

Crater Lake National Park

Heading north from Klamath Falls on US Highway 97, then west on Highway 62, you'll reach the south entrance to **CRATER LAKE NATIONAL PARK.** Some 7,700 years ago, 10,000- to 12,000-foot Mount Mazama was the Mount St. Helens of its day. It blew up and left behind a 4,000-foot-deep crater—now a lake filled by rainwater and snowmelt. With the water plunging to 1,932 feet, it's the deepest lake in the United States. A prospector searching for gold found this treasure in 1853; it was designated a national park in 1902, the only one in Oregon.

Crater Lake National Park is extraordinary: the impossibly blue lake, eerie volcanic formations, a vast geological wonderland. The **STEEL INFORMATION CENTER** (near the south entrance at park headquarters; 541/594-3000) offers an information desk, books, and an interpretive video; in summer, a second visitors center operates in **RIM VILLAGE**. Visitors can camp at Mazama Village Campground or book a room at the 40-unit Mazama Village Motor Inn (541/830-8700); be sure to plan early, as space fills fast. The 33-mile **RIM DRIVE** along the top of the caldera offers many vistas, or take the two-hour boat ride from Cleetwood Cove out to Wizard Island and around the lake. There are dozens of trails and climbs to magnificent lookouts. In winter, when the crowds thin, only the south and west entrance roads are open. Then, cross-country skiing and snowshoe walks are popular.

LODGINGS

Crater Lake Lodge / ★★

RIM DR, CRATER LAKE NATIONAL PARK; 541/830-8700 Originally built in 1909, the historic wood-and-stone building, perched at 7,000 feet on the rim of the caldera, was weakened considerably by decades of heavy snowfall. The four-story summer lodge was restored in the mid-1990s with a $15-million taxpayer-funded makeover and features 71 rooms. Although only 26 rooms face the lake, all have great views. Best are the eight with claw-footed bathtubs in window alcoves. You won't find TVs or in-room phones here. The dining-room motif is 1930s lodge decor, but the menu (breakfast, lunch, dinner) is contemporary. Guests should reserve space in the tiny dining room up to 30 days before arrival. If the dining room is full, choose between two less-than-grand restaurants at Rim Village, 500 feet from the lodge. *$$$; DIS, MC, V; checks OK; open mid-May–mid-Oct; www.crater-lake.com/lodge.htm; via Hwy 138 (north) or Hwy 62.*

Diamond Lake and Mount Bailey

MOUNT BAILEY ALPINE SKI TOURS (off Hwy 138, just north of Crater Lake; 541/793-3348 or 800/446-4555; www.mountbailey.com) offers true backcountry skiing, with snow-cats instead of helicopters to take you to the top of this 8,363-foot ancient volcano, and experienced, safety-conscious guides. **DIAMOND LAKE RESORT** (800/733-7593; www.diamondlake.net) is headquarters for the guide service. Also popular in winter: snowmobiling, cross-country skiing, inner-tube and snowboard hills, and ice-skating. When the snow melts, the operation turns to mountain-bike tours, boating, swimming, and hiking.

Cascade Lakes Area

The 100-mile scenic **CASCADE LAKES HIGHWAY** (Hwy 58) tour needs several hours and a picnic lunch for full appreciation; stunning mountain views and a number of lakes and rustic fishing resorts are tucked along the way. Odell and Davis Lakes, near Willamette Pass on Highway 58, mark the southern end of the tour that winds its way north, eventually following the Deschutes River on Century Drive to Bend.

Odell Lake

LODGINGS

Odell Lake Lodge and Resort

E ODELL LAKE ACCESS OFF HWY 58, CRESCENT LAKE; 541/433-2540 This resort on the shore of Odell Lake is ideal for the fisher, hiker, and skier in all of us. The lake's a bit alpine for swimming; instead, cast for Mackinaw trout, rainbow, or kokanee. (Most sports equipment—fishing rods to snowshoes—is rentable here.) The small library is perfect for sinking into an overstuffed chair in front of the fireplace. Request a lakeside room, one of seven in the hotel (Room 3, specifically, is a corner suite warmed with knotty-pine paneling and lake and stream views). If you'd prefer one of the 12 cabins, the few additional dollars required to get one lakeside are well spent. Pets OK in cabins. The restaurant is open year-round for three squares a day. *$$; DIS, MC, V; checks OK; 2-night min holidays and weekends; www.odell lakeresort.com; from Oakridge on Hwy 58, head east for 30 miles, take E Odell Lake exit.* &

Westfir

This former logging town flanks the North Fork of the Middle Fork of the Willamette River, excellent for rainbow trout fishing. The **AUFDERHEIDE NATIONAL SCENIC BYWAY** winds west from the Cascade Lakes out to Westfir, meandering along the river, and is popular with bicyclists, although heavy snowfall closes the route November through early April.

LODGINGS

Westfir Lodge / ★★

47365 1ST ST, WESTFIR; 541/782-3103 Westfir Lodge has long anchored the tiny community of Westfir. For many years it housed the former lumber company offices, then Gerry Chamberlain and Ken Symons converted the two-story building into a very pleasant eight-room inn. The bedrooms ring the first floor; in the center are a living area, kitchen, and formal dining room where guests are served a full English breakfast (English bangers and fried potatoes, eggs, broiled tomato topped with cheese, and scones). Cottage gardens outside and a plethora of antiques inside lend an English country ambience. The longest covered bridge in Oregon—180-foot Office Bridge (1944)—is just across the road. *$$; no credit cards; checks OK; 3 miles east of Hwy 58 near Oakridge.* &

Bend and Mount Bachelor

Bend was a quiet, undiscovered high-desert paradise until a push in the 1960s to develop recreation and tourism tamed Bachelor Butte (later renamed **MOUNT BACHELOR**) into an alpine playground. Then came golf courses, an airstrip, bike trails, river-rafting companies, hikers, tennis players, rockhounds, and skiers. Bend's popularity—and population (now more than 53,000)—has been on a steady increase ever since.

Heading north from Summer Lake on Highway 31 or Klamath Falls on US Highway 97, the road to Bend passes through **NEWBERRY NATIONAL VOLCANIC MONUMENT** (between La Pine and Bend on both sides of US Hwy 97; 541/593-2421 or 541/383-4771), a 56,000-acre monument in the Deschutes National Forest that showcases geologic attractions tens of thousands of years old. **NEWBERRY CRATER,** 13 miles east of US Highway 97 on Forest Road 21, is the heart of the monument. Major attractions also include Paulina Peak, the Big Obsidian Flow, Paulina Falls, and East and Paulina Lakes, each with a small resort. Tour **LAVA RIVER CAVE,** a mile-long lava tube on US Highway 97 (13 miles south of Bend). As you descend into the dark and surprisingly eerie depths, you'll need a warm sweater. **LAVA LANDS VIS-ITOR CENTER** at the base of Lava Butte (12 miles south of Bend; closed in winter; 541/593-2421) is the interpretive center for the miles of lava beds. Drive or—when cars are barred—take the shuttle up Lava Butte, formed by a volcanic fissure, for a sweeping, dramatic view of the moonlike landscape. Seasons for Newberry attractions vary, depending on snow, but generally run May through October.

Bend

The main thoroughfare through Bend—US Highway 97's 10 miles of uninspired strip development—bypasses the historical town center, which thrives just to the west. **DESCHUTES HISTORICAL CENTER** (NW Idaho and Wall Sts; 541/389-1813) features regional history and interesting pioneer paraphernalia.

The **HIGH DESERT MUSEUM** (59800 S Hwy 97, 4 miles south of Bend; 541/382-4754; www.highdesert.org) is an outstanding nonprofit center for natural and cultural history. A "Desertarium" exhibits desert animals, including live owls, lizards, and Lahontan cutthroat trout. Twenty acres of natural trails and outdoor exhibits offer replicas of covered wagons, a sheepherder's camp, a settlers' cabin, and an old sawmill; three river otters, three porcupines, and about a half-dozen raptors are in residence (presentations daily). A new curatorial center and two new wings (one featuring an extensive collection of Columbia Plateau Indian artifacts, and the other focusing on birds of prey) are all just part of a recently completed $15-million expansion.

Part of Bend's charm comes from the blindingly blue sky and pine-scented air, the other part from its proximity to outdoor attractions. Mountain bike or hike for 9 miles along the **DESCHUTES RIVER TRAIL,** from downtown Bend past the Inn of the Seventh Mountain (see review) and a series of waterfalls. **PILOT BUTTE STATE PARK** (541/388-6055), just east of town on US Highway 20, is a red-cinder-cone park with a mile-long road to the top. It offers a knockout panorama of the city and the mountains beyond; look out for pedestrians on the road. Have a shake and a burger at the **PILOT BUTTE DRIVE-IN** (at Pilot Butte's base; 541/382-2972).

RESTAURANTS

Alpenglow Cafe

🌲 **1040 NW BOND ST, BEND; 541/383-7676** The glow they're referring to is probably the warm feeling you'll have after eating their mountain of breakfast (served all day). Orange juice is fresh squeezed and full of pulp, bacon and ham are locally smoked (salmon is brined and smoked in-house), and all breads are homemade. Chunky potato pancakes, made with cheddar and bacon, are served with homemade applesauce or sour cream. The salmon eggs Benedict is huge—two eggs on two English muffin halves, topped with smoked king salmon, fresh basil, tomatoes, and a rich, lemony hollandaise. Even the huevos rancheros have the Alpenglow touch—a generous dollop of cilantro pesto and fresh salsa on top. Entrees come with a pile of home fries and coffee cake or fresh fruit. *$; AE, DIS, MC, V; local checks only; breakfast, lunch every day; no alcohol; reservations not necessary; next to Deschutes Brewery.* &

Broken Top Restaurant / ★★

62000 BROKEN TOP DR, BEND; 541/383-8210 The 25,000-square-foot clubhouse of the Broken Top Golf Course captures an exceptional view of the Cascades beyond the course and lake. Make your reservation for a half hour before sundown, and if Mother Nature is accommodating, you'll see a spectacular sunset over the jagged Broken Top and Three Sisters. The food is equally sensational; try the rack of New Zealand lamb, oven roasted with mint pesto crust on mountain huckleberry sauce. New York steak is always on the menu, as are Northwest game and fish specials. This is central Oregon elegance. *$$; AE, MC, V; local checks only; lunch Tues–Fri, dinner Tues–Sat; full bar; reservations recommended; www.brokentop.com; just off Mount Washington Dr from Century Dr.* &

Cafe Rosemary / ★★★

222 NW IRVING AVE, BEND; 541/317-0276 Appreciative diners have been known to stand and applaud the food and chef-owner Bob Brown at this simple bistro. The bright room has a fireplace and Oriental carpets to complement white-tablecloth fine dining. Garlic-sausage sandwiches and huge salmon salads are popular lunch choices. The restaurant's trademark rosemary salad, prepared with Gorgonzola, fresh fruit, and homemade poppyseed dressing, introduces each dinner, and may be followed by crispy duck leg or veal chop with roasted mushrooms and portobello jus. *$$; AE, MC, V; checks OK; lunch Mon–Fri, dinner every night; beer and wine; reservations recommended; call for directions.* &

Hans / ★★

915 NW WALL ST, BEND; 541/389-9700 A casual, bright cafe with hardwood floors and big windows, Hans offers a fine selection of salads and interesting daily specials. Service is sometimes brisk, but the bustle is hospitable. Lunch menus have mix-and-match sandwiches with all kinds of breads, cheeses, and other ingredients. Dinner brings finer dining, ranging from grilled portobello appetizers, unique pizzas, and seafood pasta, to salmon in a lemon herb beurre blanc, and tenderloin, all with creative yet simple sauces and flavors. A case full of pastries and sweets tempts. *$; MC,*

V; checks OK; lunch Tue–Sat, dinner Wed–Sat; beer and wine; reservations recommended; near breezeway. ♿

Marz Planetary Bistro / ★★

163 MINNESOTA AVE, BEND; 541/389-2025 This lively, loud, and colorful bistro is a welcome change from standard central Oregon cuisine. An interesting but limited ethnic-fusion menu matches the bright decor, disco ball, and funky artwork. Often backed by jazz or blues, closely set tables create a metropolitan ambience. A wide selection of wines and a handful of microbrews accompany everything from Argentinian marinated skirt steak to Asian-style rice paper–wrapped fresh fish. *$–$$; DIS, MC, V; checks OK; dinner every day; beer and wine; reservations recommended for parties of 6 or more; between NW Bond and NW Wall Sts.* ♿

Pine Tavern Restaurant / ★★

967 NW BROOKS ST, BEND; 541/382-5581 Buttonhole four Bend citizens and tell them you're ready for a fancy night out, with good food, service, atmosphere, and a decent value for your dollar, and three out of four will recommend the Pine Tavern. This establishment has 56 years of history and a reputation for quality. Request a table by the window (overlooking placid Mirror Pond) in the main dining room and marvel at the tree growing through the floor; outdoor dining is now available, weather permitting. Naturally grown Oregon prime rib is the restaurant's forte. Don't miss the great honey butter and sourdough scones. *$$; AE, DIS, MC, V; checks OK; lunch Mon–Sat, dinner every day; full bar; reservations not necessary; www.pinetavern.com; foot of Oregon Ave downtown.*

LODGINGS

The Bend Phoenix Inn / ★

300 NW FRANKLIN AVE, BEND; 541/317-9292 OR 888/291-4764 Huge, spotless minisuites with leather couches, microwaves, refrigerators, coffeemakers, and other amenities make you feel at home in this establishment, which recently added 32 rooms for a grand total of 117. Request a room with a mountain view. The staff is informative and friendly. There's a pool, Jacuzzi, and fitness center. But the best thing about this inn is its downtown location—and local calls are free. The continental breakfast buffet in a comfortable dining room includes fresh pastries, fruit, and newspapers. *$$–$$$; AE, DC, DIS, MC, V; checks OK; downtown.*

Inn of the Seventh Mountain / ★★

18575 SW CENTURY DR, BEND; 541/382-8711 OR 800/452-6810 The Inn offers the closest accommodations to Mount Bachelor and is popular with families, no doubt due to the vast menu of activities built into the multicondominium facility and the reasonable prices. New owners expect a substantial renovation project to be complete by early 2003, but availability of some amenities may be affected in the meantime. An ice rink (which converts to a roller rink in April); huge coed sauna; three bubbling hot tubs; and two heated swimming pools vie for guests' attention, along with tennis, horseback riding, biking, skating, rafting—you name it. Josiah's restaurant offers fine dining, as well as breakfast and lunch, in the spacious lounge downstairs. *$$–$$$; AE, DIS, MC, V; checks OK; www.innofthe 7thmountain.com; 7 miles west of downtown.* &

Mount Bachelor Village / ★★

19717 MOUNT BACHELOR DR, BEND; 541/389-5900 OR 800/452-9846 What this development has over some of its more famous neighbors is spacious rooms. Every unit (130 in all) has a furnished kitchen, wood-burning fireplace, and private deck. We prefer the newer units, where the color scheme is modern and light, and sound-proofing helps mute the thud of ski boots. Some units look out to the busy mountain road, but the River Ridge addition looks out over the Deschutes River. Amenities include two outdoor Jacuzzis, seasonal outdoor heated pool, six tennis courts, a 2.2-mile nature trail, and complimentary access to an exclusive athletic club on the property. *$$$; AE, DIS, MC, V; checks OK; www.mtbachelorvillage.com; toward Mount Bachelor on Century Dr.* &

Pine Ridge Inn / ★★☆

1200 SW CENTURY DR, BEND; 541/389-6137 OR 800/600-4095 Perched on the edge of the river canyon on Century Drive, this 20-suite inn is smaller than neighboring resorts but big on privacy, luxury, and south-facing bird's-eye views of the Deschutes River. Suites have step-down living rooms with antique and reproduction furniture, and gas-log fireplaces, private porches, and roomy, well-stocked baths. The second-floor Hyde Suite is best, with luxurious king bedroom, living/dining room, Jacuzzi, adjoining powder room, and two decks. Complimentary full breakfasts are served in a small gathering room or delivered to your door. Well-behaved children are welcome; they can choose from a well-stocked library of videos, munch popcorn in their room, and get a special turndown treat of hot chocolate and cookies before bed (grown-ups get bottled water, ice, fresh towels, and a special pillow treat). Budget tip: Six rooms facing the parking lot are less expensive. *$$$; AE, DC, DIS, MC, V; checks OK; pineridge@empnet.com; www.pineridgeinn. com; just before Mount Bachelor Village.* &

Rock Springs Guest Ranch / ★★

64201 TYLER RD, BEND; 541/382-1957 From late June through late August and at Thanksgiving, the emphasis here is on family vacations. (The rest of the year, it's a top-notch conference center.) Counselors take care of kids in day-long special programs while adults hit the trail, laze in the pool, play tennis, or meet for evening hors d'oeuvres on the deck. Digs are comfy knotty pine two- and three-room cottages with fireplaces. Only 50 guests stay at the ranch at one time, so it's easy to get to know everyone, particularly since you eat family style in the lodge. The setting, amid ponderosa pines and junipers alongside a small lake, is secluded and lovely. The main activity here is riding, with nine wranglers and a stable of 70 horses. Summer season is booked by the week ($1,760 per person—kids for less, children under 2 free), which includes virtually everything. Look for lighted tennis courts, a free-form whirlpool, a sand volleyball court under the tall pines, guided canoe trips, golf with the general manager, mountain biking, and fishing in the ranch pond. It's ideal for weddings or reunions. *$$$; AE, MC, V; checks OK; info@rocksprings.com; www.rocksprings.com; 7 miles from Bend and 20 miles from Sisters.* &

Sunriver Lodge / ★★★

SUNRIVER; 541/593-1000 OR 800/547-3922 More than a resort, Sunriver is an organized community with its own post office, chamber of commerce, realty offices, outdoor mall, grocery store, and more than 1,500 residents. The unincorporated town sprawls over 3,300 acres, and its own paved runway for private air commuting does brisk business. Sunriver's specialty is big-time escapist vacationing, and the resort has all the facilities to keep families, couples, or groups busy all week long, year-round. A brand-new indoor spa offers a full slate of services, from massages to aromatherapy. Summer offers golf (three 18-hole courses), tennis (28 courts), rafting, canoeing, fishing, swimming (three pools, two complexes of hot tubs), biking (30 miles of paved trails), and horseback riding. In winter the resort is home base for skiing (Nordic and alpine), ice-skating, and snowmobiling. For the best bargain, deal through the lodge reservation service, request one of the large contemporary homes (often with hot tubs, barbecues, and decks), and split expenses with another family. If you want access to the pool and hot tub facility, request a house that has a pass. Even the bedroom units in the lodge village have small decks and fireplaces, and come with privileges such as discounted recreation, depending on the season. Four complexes hold 38 luxury River Lodges, each with a deck or balcony overlooking the Meadows golf course, slate-floored bathrooms with soaker tubs and separate showers, and gas fireplaces. Lodge dining includes the Meadows, a much-acclaimed showplace for lunch, dinner, and Sunday brunch. Elsewhere in the town of Sunriver, choose anything from Chinese to pizza. We like breakfast at the Trout House at the Sunriver Marina, too. *$$; AE, DIS, MC, V; checks OK; www.sunriverresort.com; 15 miles south of Bend.*

Mount Bachelor

MOUNT BACHELOR SKI AREA (22 miles southwest of Bend, on Century Dr; 541/382-7888 for ski report or 800/829-2442; www.mtbachelor.com) is now under the ownership of Park City, Utah–based Powdr Corp. It's one of the largest ski areas in the Pacific Northwest, with seven high-speed lifts (10 lifts in all) feeding skiers onto 3,100 vertical feet of groomed and dry-powder skiing. The tubing park is brand new, with a surface lift and five groomed runs. The **SKIER'S PALATE** (at midmountain Pine Marten Lodge) serves excellent lunches; **SCAPOLO'S** (on lodge's lower level) features Italian cuisine. Skiing closes Memorial Day and the slopes reopen July 1 for summer sightseeing. High-season amenities include ski school, racing, day care, rentals, and an entire Nordic program and trails.

Elk Lake

LODGINGS

Elk Lake Resort

CENTURY DR, BEND; 541/480-7228 This remote fishing lodge—reached by snow-cat or 10 miles of cross-country skiing in the winter (or by car in the summer)—consists of 10 self-contained cabins, with kitchens, bathrooms, and sleeping quarters for 2 to 12, and a small store. It's nothing grand, but the place is favored by Bend dwellers and the scenery is wonderful. A pair of primitive cabins open for summer visitors. The dining room has changing daily specials. Reserve in advance for cabins or dining, and bring bug juice in summer—mosquitoes can be ravenous. *$$; MC, V; no checks; www.elklakeresort.com; look for signs to Elk Lake.*

Sisters and the Deschutes River Area

From Bend, US Highway 20 heads northwest to Sisters, and from Sisters, Highway 126 goes east to Redmond; together with US Highway 97 these roads form a triangle in an area rich with rivers and parks. North from Madras on US Highway 26 is the Warm Springs Indian Reservation. And through it all runs the **DESCHUTES RIVER,** designated a scenic waterway north of Warm Springs.

Redmond

Often overlooked in favor of its big sister to the south (Bend), Redmond offers a nice alternative base for exploring the Sisters region. About 6 miles north of Redmond, east of Terrebonne, some of the finest rock climbers gather to test their skills on the red-rock cliffs of **SMITH ROCK STATE PARK** (off US Hwy 97; 541/548-7501). Year-round camping is available.

The **CROOKED RIVER DINNER TRAIN** (4075 NE O'Neil Rd; 541/548-8630; www.crookedriverrailroad.com) ambles up the 38-mile Crooked River valley between Redmond and Prineville with three-hour scenic excursions and white-table-cloth dinner service. Special events and theme rides are offered, from murder-mystery tours to champagne brunches. Reservations required.

LODGINGS

Inn at Eagle's Crest / ★★

1522 CLINE FALLS HWY, REDMOND; 541/923-2453 OR 800/MUCH-SUN Sisters has Black Butte, Bend has Sunriver, and Redmond has Eagle's Crest. The private homes at this full resort rim the 18-hole golf course, and visitors choose one of the 100 rooms in the hotel (best ones have decks facing the course) or a condominium. A new recreation center—the inn's second—has an indoor basketball court, swimming pool, and full day spa. The other sports center includes indoor tennis, squash, and racquetball courts, workout room, masseuse, tanning salon, heated outdoor pool, and tennis courts. The resort also has miles of biking and jogging trails, an equestrian center, and playfields. The food at the resort's formal Niblick & Greene (dinner only) is predictable for such a clubby atmosphere, with rancher-sized portions. The three-tiered deck outside provides a good view. *$$; AE, MC, V; checks OK; 5 miles west of Redmond.*

Sisters

Named after the three mountain peaks (Faith, Hope, and Charity) that dominate the horizon, this little community is becoming a mecca for tired urbanites looking for a taste of cowboy escapism. On a clear day (about 250 a year here), Sisters is exquisitely beautiful. Surrounded by mountains, trout streams, and pine and cedar forests, this little town capitalizes on the influx of winter skiers and summer camping and fishing enthusiasts.

There's mixed sentiment about the pseudo-Western storefronts that thematically organize the town's commerce, but then again, Sisters hosts 56,000 visitors for each of four shows during June's annual **SISTERS RODEO**. The town also has the world's largest outdoor quilt show, the longtime **SISTERS OUTDOOR QUILT SHOW** in July, with 800 quilts hanging from balconies and storefronts. Call the visitor center (541/549-0251) for information on either event.

In the early 1970s, Sisters developed the Western theme, but it's grown much more sophisticated. The town, built on about 30 feet of pumice dust spewed over centuries from the nearby volcanoes, has added minimall shopping clusters with courtyards and sidewalks to eliminate blowing dust. There are several large art galleries, good bakeries, an excellent fly-fishing shop, **THE FLY FISHER'S PLACE** (151 W Main Ave; 541/549-3474), and even freshly roasted coffee at **SISTERS COFFEE COMPANY** (273 W Hood Ave; 541/549-0527). Although the town population is about 1,000, more than 7,500 live in the surrounding area on miniranches.

RESTAURANTS

Bronco Billy's Ranch Grill and Saloon / ★

190 E CASCADE ST, SISTERS; 541/549-RIBS Formerly known as the Hotel Sisters Restaurant, this bar and eatery serves ranch cooking—good burgers and some Mexican fare. Seafood is fresh, filet mignon grilled perfectly, chicken and ribs succulent. The waitstaff is friendly and diligent. Owners John Keenan, Bill Reed, and John Tehan have succeeded in turning old friendships into a going business consortium, re-creating the look of a first-class 1900 hotel. The upstairs hotel rooms are now private dining rooms, perfect for banquets. The deck is a good place for drinks. *$$; MC, V; checks OK; lunch, dinner every day (lunch Sat–Sun only in winter); full bar; reservations recommended; at Fir St.* &

Royal Thai Cafe / ★★

291 E CASCADE ST, SISTERS; 541/549-3025 It doesn't look like much from the outside but this small, dark downtown establishment serves unbeatable traditional Thai cuisine. Run by Sineenat Spofford, from Thailand, and Mark Spofford, who ran a restaurant in Thailand, where he met his wife, the restaurant generally attracts a full house with good food and warm, efficient service. The house specialty is a coconut soup served with prawns, chicken, or tofu. The small, casual room is intimate enough to suit a date or feed a festive family. *$; MC, V; checks OK; dinner Mon–Sat; beer and wine; reservations recommended; at Spruce St.*

LODGINGS

Black Butte Ranch / ★★★

HWY 20, BLACK BUTTE RANCH; 541/595-6211 With 1,800 acres, this vacation and recreation wonderland remains the darling of Northwest resorts. Rimmed by the Three Sisters mountains and scented by a plain of ponderosa pines, these rental condos and private homes draw families year-round to swim, ski, fish, golf, bike, boat, ride horses (summer only), and play tennis. The best way to make a reservation is to state the size of your party and whether you want a home (most are large and contemporary) or simply a good-sized bed and bath (lodge condominiums suffice, though some are dark and dated, with too much orange Formica and brown furniture). The main lodge is handsome but not overwhelming, and serves as dining headquarters (breakfast, lunch, dinner). Tables at the Restaurant at the Lodge (closed Mon–Wed in Jan and Feb) are tiered so everyone can appreciate the meadow panorama beyond. *$$$; AE, DIS, MC, V; checks OK; info@blackbutte ranch.com; www.blackbutteranch.com; 8 miles west of Sisters.* &

Conklin's Guest House / ★★

69013 CAMP POLK RD, SISTERS; 541/549-0123 An expensive remodel of an old farmhouse makes this one of the best B&Bs in central Oregon. Each of five rooms is wallpapered and well appointed, with private bath. Rooms have no phones or TVs—just peace. The Forget-Me-Not, on the first floor, has a gas fireplace, sunset view, and deck. The second-floor Morning Glory Suite has a stunning view of the pond and gardens, pastures, and mountains. One room under the eaves has been remodeled into the Heather Room, with one queen bed and two singles. Large farm breakfasts are served with espresso on the glass-enclosed sunporch, or next to the outdoor heated pool. Guests are welcome to use laundry facilities, fish for trout from two ponds, and make themselves at home next to the stone fireplace. The pretty grounds are a perfect wedding backdrop. *$$; no credit cards; checks OK; www.conklinsguesthouse.com; across from Sisters airport.* &

Camp Sherman

This little settlement is on a road north of US Highway 20, about halfway between Sisters and Santiam Pass. Try **KOKANEE CAFE** (25545 SW Forest Service Rd 1419; 541/595-6420; April–Oct) for a quick bite.

LODGINGS

Metolius River Resort / ★★

25551 SW FOREST SERVICE RD 1419, CAMP SHERMAN; 541/595-6281 OR 800/81-TROUT Not to be confused with the lower-priced, worn and well-loved, circa-1923 Metolius River Lodges across the bridge, these 11 gracious cabins on the west bank are wood-shake with large decks and river-rock fireplaces. Most have river views, master bedrooms and lofts, furnished kitchens, and French doors leading to large river-facing decks. Because the pricey cabins are privately owned, interiors are luxurious but different; most have a CD player and TV/VCR with satellite dish. *$$$; MC, V; checks OK; reservations@metolius-river-resort.com; www.metolius-river-resort.com; 5 miles north of US Hwy 20.*

Warm Springs

Many travelers pass through the Warm Springs Indian Reservation on their way south to Bend or north to Mount Hood. If you're not spending a night at the Kah-Nee-Ta Resort and Village (see review), at least be sure to stop and visit the incredible

THE BIG GLASSY

One of the premier attractions of **NEWBERRY NATIONAL VOLCANIC MONU-MENT** is an enormous mound of volcanic glass that sits in the middle of Newberry Caldera, east of LaPine. The eruption of the Big Obsidian flow, just 1,300 years ago, is the most recent dated volcanic event in Central Oregon. The flow covers just over one square mile to an average depth of 300 feet.

The razor-sharp glassy shards of obsidian were put to good use by the area's early residents. Broken bits of glass were shaped into arrowheads, knives, and extraordinary cutting tools, as well as being used for barter. Obsidian from Newberry has been found in archaeology sites as far east as Missouri and as far north as Alaska. Older obsidian flows in Newberry Caldera may be one of the reasons the earliest North Americans chose to live here at least 9,500 years ago.

Today a one-mile **INTERPRETIVE TRAIL** leads up and into the obsidian flow; there you can see magnificent views of 7,984-foot-high Paulina Peak and topaz-blue Paulina Lake, one of two large "crater" lakes that fill the 100,000-year-old caldera floor. Follow Highway 97 about 15 miles south of Sunriver, and watch for Newberry Crater signs to the east.

For more information, contact the Deschutes National Forest Lava Lands Discovery Center (541/593-2421).   —*Jan Halliday*

MUSEUM AT WARM SPRINGS (541/553-3331). The award-winning facility includes a stunning exhibit of a Wasco wedding ceremony, a contemporary art gallery, and a gift shop.

LODGINGS

Kah-Nee-Ta Resort and Village / ★★

100 MAIN ST, WARM SPRINGS; 541/553-1112 OR 800/554-4786 The spring-water bubbling from the ground near the Warm Springs River is hot, sweet water—no sulfur—and the basis for Kah-Nee-Ta Resort and Village on the Warm Springs Indian Reservation. The 139-room lodge perches on the canyon wall, with sweeping southerly views, above the river where there's a huge pool complex, spa, and 20-tepee encampment (kid heaven). The resort also includes several houses with full kitchens and hot tubs, five RV spaces, a 30-room motel, gift shop, tennis courts, and 18-hole golf course. Popular Indian-style salmon bakes, sometimes with dance performances, are held Saturdays during summer. The main lodge's Juniper Room offers fine dining; a new buffet restaurant serves three meals daily. The resort is a peaceful getaway 11 miles from US Highway 26. *$$; AE, DC, DIS, MC, V; checks OK; www.kah-nee-taresort.com; 11 miles north of Warm Springs on Hwy 3.* ♿

EASTERN OREGON

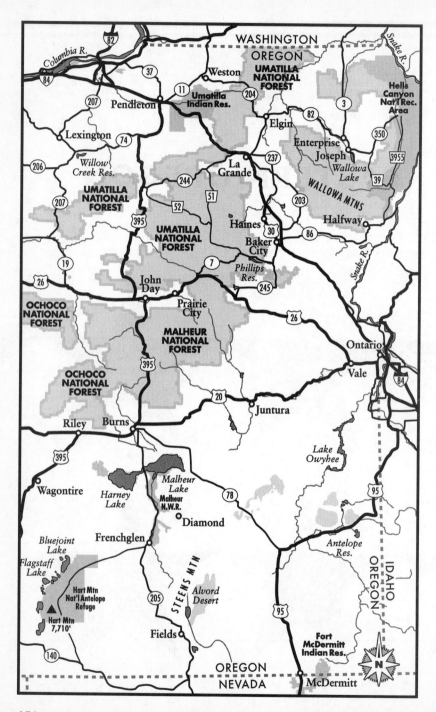

EASTERN OREGON

Eastern Oregon is as different from Western Oregon as it is from, say, Kansas, and it's commonly misrepresented by Western Oregonians, who refer to it as a "desert." Sure, some areas here are pretty dry, with about a million pickup loads' worth of sagebrush, but Eastern Oregon also has mountains galore, where winter snows pile up and springtime snowmelt feeds streams and wetlands. Lava flows and glaciers formed much of the landscape, including Steens Mountain, the world's largest fault block. The Wallowa Mountains, in the northeast corner of the state, are classic examples of glacial action—their crags and cirques and gemlike lakes were all formed by Ice-Age glaciers.

Oregon Trail pioneers got across this land as quickly as they could, but some returned after a short stay in Western Oregon. They became gold miners and cattle ranchers. Today, though the bulk of the gold has been grabbed, this is still cattle country, where a rugged Western spirit prevails.

ACCESS AND INFORMATION

INTERSTATE 84 is the main route across Eastern Oregon, connecting Pendleton, La Grande, and Baker City with Portland to the west and Boise, Idaho, to the east. The other east-west routes are **US HIGHWAY 26** through Prineville, John Day, and Prairie City, and **US HIGHWAY 20**, the route from Bend to Burns and Ontario. **US HIGHWAY 395** is the main north-south route, with Pendleton, John Day, and Burns along its route. Between Pendleton and La Grande, Interstate 84 crosses the Blue Mountains at 4,193 feet; this pass often closes down for a day or so after a heavy snow. For road conditions throughout the state, check in with the **OREGON DEPARTMENT OF TRANSPORTATION** (503/588-2941 outside of Oregon or 800/977-6368; www.odot. state.or.us/travel/); the online Travel Advisor (www. tripcheck.com) also has helpful, up-to-date information on road conditions.

HORIZON AIR (800/547-9308; www.horizonair.com) flies to Pendleton and Redmond from Portland. And even though you may not want to hear about it (we didn't, until our car broke down in La Grande), buses are another option out here. **GREYHOUND** (800/231-2222; www.greyhound.com) runs along Interstate 84 and stops in towns such as La Grande and Pendleton; **PEOPLE MOVERS** (541/575-2370 or 800/527-2370) travels between Prairie City and Bend; **WALLOWA VALLEY STAGE LINES** (541/569-2284) makes the trip between Wallowa Lake and La Grande.

Pendleton

Looking for the Wild West? Stop by Pendleton in mid-September, when the whole town puts on a party hat (the Stetson kind) for the **PENDLETON ROUND-UP** (1205 SW Court St; 800/457-6336 tickets and information). The event features a dandy rodeo and a crazy street scene.

PENDLETON WOOLEN MILLS (1307 SE Court Pl; 541/276-6911; www.pendleton-usa.com; tours Mon–Fri) sells woolen yardage and imperfect versions of its famous blankets at reduced prices. **PENDLETON UNDERGROUND TOURS** (37 SW Emigrant Ave; 541/276-0730) offers a 90-minute walk through Pendleton's subterranean history to view the remains of businesses that date back to the turn of the century: bordellos, opium dens, and Chinese jails. Reservations are necessary; make them at least 24 hours in advance; $12 per adult.

The Umatilla tribe's **TAMUSTALIK** (say "ta-MUST-ah-luck") **CULTURAL INSTITUTE** (72789 Hwy 331; 541/966-9748), on 640 acres behind the Wildhorse Gaming Resort, tells the story of Oregon from the Native point of view.

RESTAURANTS

Raphael's / ★★

233 SE 4TH ST, PENDLETON; 541/276-8500 OR 888/944-2433 You know you're well east of the Cascades when you walk in the front door and see the row of cowboy hats hanging from coat hooks. This also tells you that you're at a classy joint, where men actually remove their hats before sitting down at the table. The decor is simple, with Craftsman-style chairs and impressive art on the sage-colored walls. The menu ranges from light dinners, such as a salmon sauté, to an autumn selection of "Hunters' Specials," including rattlesnake and rabbit sausage tossed with sautéed vegetables and pasta, or Rocky Mountain elk osso buco. You'll likely find Raphael Hoffman, the owner and Nez Perce tribal member, behind the bar while her husband Rob does the cooking. *$$; AE, DIS, MC, V; checks OK; dinner Tues–Sat; full bar; reservations recommended; between Court Pl and Dorion Ave.* &

LODGINGS

Parker House Bed and Breakfast / ★★

311 N MAIN ST, PENDLETON; 541/276-8581 OR 800/700-8581 Don't underestimate Pendleton's capacity for grandeur. What seems, especially at Round-Up time, to be a fairly rough-and-tumble town, has some spectacular old houses, not the least of which is the pink stucco Parker House, just up the hill and across the Umatilla River from downtown. Built in 1917, the house is in great condition and retains many of its original fittings, including beautiful Chinese silk wall fabrics and, in the shared bathroom, what may be the world's most unusual shower. (It only *looks* like a torture chamber.) Of the five rooms, Gwendolyn is the grandest, with a fireplace and French doors. *$$; MC, V; checks OK; www.parkerhousebnb.com; north on Hwy 11, follow City Center signs to downtown, head north on Main St, cross Umatilla River to N Main St.*

The Working Girl's Hotel

17 SW EMIGRANT AVE, PENDLETON; 541/276-0730 OR 800/226-6398 Just upstairs from the Pendleton Underground Tours, this nonprofit hotel, designed to bring tourism to Pendleton, gets its name from its former incarnation as a bordello. The girls are gone, but the five spacious rooms (one long flight up) in this pretty brick building are just as welcoming. Each has 18-foot ceilings and antique furnishings. The plumbing's still the original stuff, so you'll need to cross a hall to the bath—but that's a small price to pay for such a fun night's stay. A full kitchen and dining area are available. Young children are discouraged. *$; MC, V; checks OK; between Main and SW 1st Sts.*

NORTHEASTERN OREGON THREE-DAY TOUR

DAY ONE: Start the day in La Grande with breakfast at **FOLEY STATION.** Wander around downtown and stop in at **SUNFLOWER BOOKS** (1114 Washington Ave; 541/963-8057), which has a cozy cafe and a wide selection of books. Then hop in the car and head east along Highway 82. Several antique stores make up the whole of small-town Elgin, and it's a nice place to get out of the car. By the time you reach Enterprise, the Wallowa Mountains dominate the scenery. Stop by the huge **WALLOWA MOUN-TAIN VISITORS CENTER,** on the bluff as you enter Enterprise, for information on hiking, mountain biking, or cross-country skiing. From Enterprise, it's just 6 miles to Joseph, where the **WILDFLOUR BAKERY** is a good lunch spot (pick up some baked goods here for tomorrow's breakfast). Spend the afternoon browsing the galleries and shops along Main Street. Head out toward **WALLOWA LAKE STATE PARK** and check into the **WALLOWA LAKE LODGE;** you can grab dinner at the lodge restaurant and spend the evening playing gin rummy in the lobby.

DAY TWO: Sleep in if you must, but an early start will make for the best hike or horseback ride; **EAGLE CAP WILDERNESS PACK STATION** can set you up with a horse and guide. For an easy ride (sans horse) to mountaintop views, hitch a ride on the **WALLOWA LAKE TRAMWAY.** Try to finish by lunch, when you'll want to eat a giant breakfast burrito at the **OLD TOWN CAFÉ.** Head east out of town, then turn south onto Forest Road 39, a paved road that takes you high above **HELLS CANYON** (be sure to take the 3-mile detour to the scenic overlook) to link up to Highway 86. Head west on Highway 86 into Halfway. Even though it's only 65 miles between Joseph and Halfway, allow at least two hours for the drive, and remember: This is remote country, with no restaurants, stores, or gas stations. (Forest Rd 39 is closed in winter.) In Halfway, stay and eat at **PINE VALLEY LODGE.**

DAY THREE: After breakfast at Pine Valley Lodge, backtrack east along Highway 86 to the **SNAKE RIVER.** Choose a noisy **JET-BOAT RIDE** or a quiet **HIKE.** If you opt for the latter, drive north from **OXBOW DAM** until the long, dusty dirt road ends. Park and walk. For lunch, grab a bite at the **COWBOY CAFE** (241 S Main St; 541/742-7777) in downtown Halfway. Then take Highway 86 west to the **NATIONAL HISTORIC OREGON TRAIL INTERPRETIVE CENTER** in Baker City for both the indoor exhibits and the trail to the wagon ruts. By late afternoon, leave the dusty trail behind and check into the **GEISER GRAND HOTEL** for a little rest before dinner downstairs in the **PALM COURT.**

Condon

LODGINGS

Hotel Condon / ★

202 S MAIN ST, CONDON; 541/384-4624 OR 800/201-6706 The highlight of a visit to Condon has, in the past, been a visit to Country Flowers, the local gift shop/lunch counter/Powell's Books outlet where all of Gilliam County checks in for local news. Now, with the renovation of the Hotel Condon, there's reason to stay the night. Condon is a good base for exploring the John Day country. The renovated hotel is— much like the people who live here—an attractive mix of country and sophistication. Rooms are spare and elegant, decorated with art that tends toward the modern—a far cry from the framed prints of horses and hunting dogs you might expect. *$$; AE, DIS, MC, V; checks OK; h-condon@oregonvos.net; www.hotel condon.com; downtown at corner of 2nd and Main Sts.* &

The Wallowas and Hells Canyon

This is the ancestral home of Chief Joseph; he fled from here with a band of Nez Perce to his last stand near the Canadian border. Although Chief Joseph's remains are interred far from his beloved land of the winding water, he saw to it that his father, Old Chief Joseph, would be buried here, on the north shore of Wallowa Lake (see also "The Wallowas' First Residents" in this chapter). **HELLS CANYON NATIONAL RECREATION AREA** (35 miles east of Joseph) encompasses the continent's deepest gorge, an awesome trench cut by the Snake River through sheer lava walls.

La Grande

RESTAURANTS

Foley Station / ★★

1011 ADAMS AVE, LA GRANDE; 541/963-7473 If you want to hang with the happening folks in La Grande, show up at Foley Station at 7am. That's when the doors open to Eastern Oregon's most sophisticated breakfast joint. Settle into a big wood booth or perch at the marble bar and get down to the formidable task of deciding what to eat. Try the potato pancakes topped with apple compote, or the Bay Shore Frittata, loaded with scallops, bacon, asparagus, and smoked Gouda cheese, and wash it all down with good coffee or a giant French-press thermos filled with delicious tea. Foley's does dinner too, with a menu that changes monthly and shows off chef-owner Merlyn Baker's culinary pedigree (he was chef at Jake's in Portland before opening Foley's in 1997). The focus is on locally grown, seasonal produce and local meats (providing an outlet for Eastern Oregon emu ranchers) prepared in a Northwest style, with Mediterranean influences. A nice touch is the attention to side dishes; pan-roasted pork chops with a green peppercorn sauce are accompanied by blue cheese chive mashed potatoes and stuffed delicata squash, for example. *$$; MC, V; checks OK; breakfast, lunch Wed–Sun, dinner*

Thurs–Sat; beer and wine; reservations recommended; foleystation@restaurant. com; www.restaurant.com/foleystation; between 4th and Chestnut Sts. &

Mamacita's

110 DEPOT ST, LA GRANDE; 541/963-6223 The menu here is standard but well-prepared Mexican fare, offered up in a friendly, easygoing way. House specials such as the Full Meal Steal (yummy corn soup, a salad, and a cheese quesadilla) are usually the best things out of the kitchen. In winter, try to catch Mamacita's on International Night (once a month) for a multicourse meal featuring foods of another nation; it sounds crazy, coming to a Mexican restaurant for Swiss food, but owner Sandy Sorrels makes it into a fun local event. *$; no credit cards; checks OK; lunch Tues–Fri, dinner Tues–Sun; beer, wine, and tequila; reservations not necessary; just west of Adams Ave.* &

Ten Depot Street

10 DEPOT ST, LA GRANDE; 541/963-8766 Ten Depot, a longtime local favorite, is a good place to get a feeling for this friendly town. The dining room, in an old brick building with antique furnishings, is nice but it's more fun to eat dinner in the bar, with its beautiful carved wooden-back bar. Bargain hunters look for the blue plate special; other dinners range from a two-fisted (half-pound) burger to chicken-and-pesto pasta to prime rib (the house specialty). *$$; AE, MC, V; checks OK; lunch, dinner Mon–Sat; full bar; reservations recommended; 2 blocks west of Adams Ave.* &

LODGINGS

Stang Manor Inn / ★

1612 WALNUT ST, LA GRANDE; 541/963-2400 OR 888/286-9463 This restored timber baron's house on the hill behind town lends a touch of elegance to La Grande. It's a huge place, with four bedrooms at the top of a sweeping staircase. The master suite is best, but even if you opt for the former maid's quarters, you won't have to lift a finger. The good-natured owners, Marjorie and Pat McClure, enjoy getting to know their guests (many of whom are business travelers). Kids over 10 welcome. One note: The McClures have put the B&B on the market, and it will eventually change hands. *$$; MC, V; checks OK; innkeeper@stangmanor.com; www.stang manor.com; at Spring St.*

Union

LODGINGS

Union Hotel

326 N MAIN ST, UNION; 541/562-6135 It's hard to miss the Union Hotel; the huge brick building dominates Main Street. Inside, room by room, it's turning into a darn nice place to stay in this small town on the back road between La Grande and Baker City. Built in 1921, it was neglected long enough for it to become something of an Eastern Oregon squat (a sheep was among the residents). Allen and Twyla Cornelius bought the place in 1996 and poured enormous amounts of energy into restoring it before turning it over to new managers in early 2002. The parlor's dark woodwork and wicker furniture evoke the 1920s; the rooms are all different and range from the modest, old-fashioned Original Room to the more modern Northwest Room, with a separate kitchenette and huge soaking tub. *$; DIS, MC, V; checks OK; info@theunionhotel.com; www.theunionhotel.com; 14 miles southeast of La Grande, at corner of Presbiterin.*

Joseph

Artists, especially bronze artists, thrive in Joseph. The many galleries include **MANUEL MUSEUM AND STUDIO** (400 N Main St; 541/432-7235), featuring the work of David Manuel, and **VALLEY BRONZE OF OREGON** (307 W Alder St; 541/432-7551), with a foundry, a showroom, and weekday tours.

WALLOWA LAKE STATE PARK (just south of Joseph on the edge of the lake) is full of campers and camper-friendly deer all summer, but it's near trailheads that lead into the **EAGLE CAP WILDERNESS AREA,** a rugged mountain wilderness that looks more Alpine than Oregonian. (This resemblance isn't lost on the Joseph tourist board; an **ALPENFEST** with music, dancing, and Bavarian feasts occurs in September.)

Scoot to the top of 8,200-foot Mount Howard on the **WALLOWA LAKE TRAMWAY** (59919 Wallowa Lake Hwy; 541/432-5331), a four-person summer gondola that shimmies you up to spectacular overlooks and 2 miles of hiking trails. Maps of the region's roads and trails, and information on conditions, are available at the **WALLOWA MOUNTAINS VISITOR CENTER** (88401 Hwy 82, Enterprise; 541/426-5546).

As you hike down into Hells Canyon or up to the lake-laden Eagle Cap Wilderness, let a llama lug your gear with **HURRICANE CREEK LLAMAS** (541/432-4455 or 800/528-9609; www.hcltrek.com; June–Aug). A day's hike takes you 4–8 miles, and hearty meals are included; reserve in advance. Sign up for a morning horseback ride or an extended wilderness pack trip at the **EAGLE CAP WILDERNESS PACK STATION** (59761 Wallowa Lake Hwy; 541/432-4145 or 800/681-6222; neoregon.net/wildernesspackstation).

Don't let winter stop you from exploring the Wallowas—head into the backcountry for a few days of guided telemark skiing with **WING RIDGE SKI TOURS** (541/426-4322 or 800/646-9050; www.wingski.com). Experienced backcountry ski guides lead you to accommodations in a rustic cabin or wood-floored tent shelters (conveniently located next to a wood-fired sauna tent).

RESTAURANTS

Old Town Café

8 S MAIN ST, JOSEPH; 541/432-9898 Locals and tourists pack this place, which has a modern-day, Western chat 'n' chew atmosphere. Breakfast burritos (eat 'em any time of day, smothered in homemade salsa) and artery-plugging desserts are among the favorites here. *$; MC, V; checks OK; breakfast, lunch Fri–Wed, dinner Fri–Sat; beer and wine; reservations not accepted; downtown.*

THE WALLOWAS' FIRST RESIDENTS

The beautiful Wallowa Valley is the homeland of the **NEZ PERCE TRIBE.** Outside town and off the main roads, little has changed since the tribe wintered in the canyon bottoms, dug camas on the prairies, and hunted at the base of the Wallowa Mountains.

LEWIS AND CLARK'S CORPS OF DISCOVERY were the first whites encountered by the Nez Perce. They had an exceptionally good relationship, and relations with whites remained good even as pioneers began to settle the valley. In 1877, the government ordered the Nez Perce to a reservation in north-central Idaho. The Wallowa Valley bands were reluctantly ready to comply, when a few young men lashed out by killing white settlers. Their band feared retribution and thus began one of history's great and tragic treks, as more than 800 Indians sought safety in Canada, east of the Continental Divide. The U.S. Army pursued the Nez Perce and suffered some defeats but ultimately wore them down, killing not only warriors but women and children as well. The Nez Perce finally surrendered in northern Montana, where Chief Joseph gained his fame as an orator.

Surviving Nez Perce were sent to Oklahoma, and eventually back to the Northwest, where they were split between reservations in Idaho and Colville, Washington. Chief Joseph is buried on the Colville reservation; his father, Old Chief Joseph, is buried at the northern end of Wallowa Lake. From Chief Joseph's surrender speech:

It is cold and we have no blankets.
The little children are freezing to death.
My people, some of them, have run away to the hills,
and have no blankets, no food;
no one knows where they are—perhaps freezing to death.
I want to have time to look for my children
and see how many I can find.
Maybe I shall find them among the dead.
Hear me my chiefs.
I am tired;
My heart is sick and sad.
From where the sun now stands,
I will fight no more forever.

—Judy Jewell

Wildflour Bakery / ★

600 N MAIN ST, JOSEPH; 541/432-7225 It's easy to cruise right by this glorified double-wide on the north side of downtown Joseph, but if you keep your eyes open, you'll see a bunch of happy noshers out on the front deck. Inside, the Wildflour Bakery is light and airy, staffed by friendly folks who are proud of their organic, slowly risen breads. If a loaf of bread isn't proper hiking fuel for you, grab a Marionberry turnover from the pastry case. Good sandwiches appear at lunch, and it's as easy to go vegetarian here as it is to order the delicious grilled sausage sandwich (the sausages are from Enterprise's Blue Willow Sausage Company). *$; no credit cards; checks OK; breakfast, lunch Wed–Mon; no alcohol; reservations not accepted; north end of town.* &

LODGINGS

Wallowa Lake Lodge / ★

60060 WALLOWA LAKE HWY, JOSEPH; 541/432-9821 This rustic lodge is like a scaled-down version of a great national park lodge. Many of the guest rooms are quite small, but that shouldn't matter; you're here to hike the trails, knock around downtown Joseph, and try for the perfect photo of Wallowa Lake. That said, the lakeview rooms with balconies have a little more space, and evenings are best spent sprawled in front of the big stone fireplace in the lobby. If you plan to stay longer than a night, the lakeside cabins, each with a living room, fireplace, and kitchen, allow for a bit more flexibility. Neither lodge rooms nor cabins have TVs or phones, which contributes to the quiet appeal. The lodge and its restaurant are open only on weekends and holidays from mid-October through Memorial Day, but cabins are available year-round. *$$; DIS, MC, V; checks OK; info@wallowalake.com; www. wallowalake.com; near Wallowa Lake State Park.*

Halfway

Once just a midway stop between two bustling mining towns, Halfway is now the quiet but quirky centerpiece of Pine Valley—stashed between the fruitful southern slopes of the Wallowa Mountains and the steep cliffs of Hells Canyon.

The continent's deepest gorge, **HELLS CANYON,** begins at **OXBOW DAM,** 16 miles east of Halfway. For spectacular views of the **SNAKE RIVER,** drive from Oxbow to Joseph (take Hwy 86 to Forest Rd 39; summers only). Maps of the region's roads and trails are available from the U.S. Forest Service ranger station in Pine (541/742-7511) 1½ miles outside Halfway. The folks at **WALLOWA LLAMAS** (36678 Allstead Ln; 541/742-2961; wallama@Pinetel.com; www.neoregon.com/wallowallamas.html) lead three- to seven-day trips into the pristine Eagle Cap Wilderness high in the Wallowas, while their surefooted beasts lug your gear and plenty of food. For those who would rather experience the raging river up close, **HELLS CANYON ADVENTURES** (4200 Hells Canyon Dam Rd; 541/785-3352) in Oxbow arranges jet-boat or whitewater raft tours leaving from Hells Canyon Dam.

LODGINGS

Pine Valley Lodge / ★★

N MAIN ST, HALFWAY; 541/742-2027 A wacky good spirit came to Halfway with Babette and Dale Beatty. They've put together an eccentric complex of lodgings on one side of Main Street and a restaurant and gallery across the street. Rent a room in the main lodge, the Love Shack, or the Blue Dog House—they're all comfortable and loaded with whimsy. And take the time to chat with Babette. Upstairs from the breakfast area, look for the inaugural *Sports Illustrated* swimsuit issue from 1963, where you'll recognize young Babette on the cover. Next to '60s fashion magazine covers, you'll see her extensive cookbook collection, and nearby is the art studio where she paints (mostly on silk) and Dale builds giant fanciful fishing rods and lures. If you visit on a weekend, dine at the Halfway Supper Club (part of the Pine Valley operation). On days when the restaurant is closed, Babette will make you a stunningly good dinner anyway, if you request it when you make room reservations. *$$; no credit cards; checks OK; neoregon.net/pinevalley lodge; downtown.*

Baker City and Haines

Baker City is still a cow town, albeit a sophisticated one. For proof, just stay over on a Saturday night when the streets (and bars) fill with hats, boots, and big belt buckles. Located in the valley between the Wallowas and the Elkhorns, it makes a good base for forays into the nearby mountain Gold Rush towns. The **NATIONAL HISTORIC OREGON TRAIL INTERPRETIVE CENTER** at Flagstaff Hill (Hwy 86, Baker City; 541/523-1843), 4 miles east of Interstate 84, is worth a detour. The multimedia walk-through brings the Oregon Trail experience to life. Open every day; admission is $5 per adult or $10 per carload.

Tour the Elkhorn Mountains, west of Baker City, flush with **MINING GHOST TOWNS**, on a 100-mile loop from Baker City (some on unpaved roads). The loop begins on Highway 7, then leads through the deserted towns of Bourne, Granite, Bonanza, and Whitney. A restored narrow-gauge steam train, the **SUMPTER VALLEY RAILWAY** (541/894-2268; www.svry.com), makes the short run between McEwen, just west of Phillips Lake, and Sumpter, from Memorial Day through September. **ANTHONY LAKES SKI AREA** (20 miles west of North Powder on Forest Rd 73; 541/856-3277) has good powder snow, one chairlift, cross-country trails, and snow-cat skiing.

RESTAURANTS

Haines Steak House / ★

910 FRONT ST, HAINES; 541/856-3639 There's no mistaking that you're in cattle country, so get ready to chow down on a giant steak. Some say this is the state's best steak house; it certainly is popular with Eastern Oregonians. Teenage boys in cowboy hats try to act suave at the salad bar to impress their dates, but the minute the meat is served, it's all eyes on the plate. Don't stray from beef here—it's well selected, well cut, and well cooked (rare, natch). *$$; AE, DC, MC, V;*

checks OK; lunch Sun, dinner Wed–Mon; full bar; reservations recommended; on old Hwy 30. &

LODGINGS

Geiser Grand Hotel / ★★

1996 MAIN ST, BAKER CITY; 541/523-1889 OR 888/434-7374 A $7-million restoration to this landmark downtown hotel made all of Oregon look up and pay attention to Baker City. A highlight of the restoration is the Palm Court, a dining area that rises three stories to a huge stained-glass skylight. If the biggest stained glass in the Pacific Northwest doesn't shed enough light, check out the bejeweled chandeliers—they're probably not what you would choose for your own house, but they fit right into this 1889 Italianate Renaissance Revival hotel. The rooms are large and comfortable—the cupola suites are a bit of a splurge but have great views of the mountains and downtown Baker City. All in all, a night at the Geiser Grand makes a trip to Baker City something special. Well-behaved dogs are welcome. *$$; AE, DIS, MC, V; checks OK; downtown at Washington Ave.* &

John Day

It looks like just another cow town, but John Day's surroundings are loaded with history. It's just off the Oregon Trail, and before the 1860s, the whole region was packed tight with gold (in 1862, $26 million in gold was mined down the road in Canyon City). **KAM WAH CHUNG MUSEUM** (250 NW Canton St; 541/575-0028; open May–Oct, closed Fri), was the stone-walled home of a Chinese herbalist early in the 20th century. A tour makes for an interesting glimpse of the Chinese settlement in the West: opium-stained walls, shrines, and herbal medicines are on display, as well as a small general store.

JOHN DAY FOSSIL BEDS NATIONAL MONUMENT lies 40 to 120 miles west, in three distinct groupings: the colorfully banded hillsides of the Painted Hills Unit, an ancient fossilized forest at the Clarno Unit, and fascinating geological layers at the Sheep Rock Unit. Stop by the visitor center and museum near the Sheep Rock Unit (on Hwy 19, 10 miles northwest of Dayville; 541/987-2333; open daily, 9am–5pm) for a look at the choicest fossils.

LODGINGS

The Ponderosa Guest Ranch / ★★★

PO BOX 190, SENECA; 541/542-2403 OR 800/331-1012 Been fantasizing about trading in your tennis shoes for pointy-toed boots? Checking out the cowboy web sites? Well, pardner, must be time for the Ponderosa. This isn't some big-shot developer's fluffed-up idea of a ranch—it's a real working cattle ranch, with all the buckaroos to prove it. Guests help staff cowboys manage 2,500 to 4,000 head of cattle—this can mean assisting with a bovine cesarean section, branding, or driving cattle to mountain pastures—all the little things that go into that nice steak dinner you're gonna get at the end of a long day's work. But nobody here is going to make you get on a horse. You can grab a field guide and rustle up some wild-flowers, or look for antelope, bear, groundhogs, eagles, sandhill cranes, cinnamon ducks, and sage hens. Hearty ranch fare (included in the price) is served family style. Guest operations are scaled back in winter. Ages 18 and up only. *$$$; MC, V; checks OK; 3-night min; seeyou@ponderosaguestranch.com; www.ponderosaguestranch.com; on Hwy 395, halfway between Burns and John Day.*

Prairie City

LODGINGS

Strawberry Mountain Inn

E HWY 26, PRAIRIE CITY; 541/820-4522 OR 800/545-6913 Anyone in Prairie City will tell you what a classy five-room B&B Linda Harrington runs, with prime views of the Strawberry Mountains, rising from the horse pasture across the road. Ask for one of the two rooms with mountain views—the backyard is nice, with a little orchard and a garden, but it's the mountains that give Prairie City its life. In addition to the requisite B&B reading room, there's a hot tub, a pool table, and plenty of videos and CDs. Unlike many B&B hosts, the Harringtons welcome kids, and have a play area in the yard. Breakfasts fuel you for a hike into the Strawberry Mountain Wilderness Area. *$$; AE, MC, V; checks OK; strawberry@moriah.com; www.moriah.com/strawberry; just east of downtown.*

Southeast High Desert

MALHEUR NATIONAL WILDLIFE REFUGE (37 miles south of Burns on Hwy 205; 541/493-2612) is one of the country's major bird refuges—187,000 acres of wetlands and lakes (see "Birds of the Malheur" in this chapter).

Burns

The town of Burns, once the center of impressive cattle kingdoms, is still a market town, but a pretty quiet one. Walking downtown, you can hear a luff as a flock of quail take flight from a parking lot.

CRYSTAL CRANE HOT SPRINGS (25 miles southeast of Burns on Hwy 78, Crane; 541/493-2312) is a good place to take a break from driving and swim in the hot-springs pond, or soak in a water trough turned hot tub.

RESTAURANTS

Pine Room Cafe / ★

543 W MONROE ST, BURNS; 541/573-6631 This may be Burns's fanciest restaurant, but that doesn't mean you have to take your cowboy hat off at the dinner table. It's a good-natured, chummy spot where locals call out to each other and comment, sotto voce, on who's dining with whom. But it's not cliquish, and the staff is eager to make out-of-towners feel like hanging around the bar after dinner. Besides the expected array of steaks, popular entrees include the Chicken Artichoke and fish dishes (though don't count on your halibut being flown in fresh). The bread is homemade, and the steaks hand-cut in the kitchen. *$$; MC, V; local checks only; dinner Tues–Sat; full bar; reservations recommended; at Egan Ave.* ♿

LODGINGS

Sage Country Inn / ★

351½ W MONROE ST, BURNS; 541/573-7243 Set well back from the main drag through Burns, the Sage Country Inn is the project of three longtime friends who rotate hostess duties. They're all ranch women, so they're friendly and welcoming without a lot of fuss. Likewise, the rooms in this 1907 Georgian Colonial house are comfortable but not cloying—they're filled with antiques and stacks of books on local history and ranchers' witticisms. Read up, and save your questions for breakfast—Carole, Georgia, and Susan can tell you all about life present and past in southeastern Oregon. $; MC, V; checks OK; pstick@centurytel. net; at S Court Ave.

Diamond

LODGINGS

Hotel Diamond

12 MILES EAST OF HWY 205, DIAMOND; 541/493-1898 When you drive into Diamond, the first thing you see are dilapidated stone buildings tucked under giant old poplar trees. Buzz by and you might mistake Diamond for a ghost town; however, its handful of residents keep the looming ghosts at bay. Shirley Thompson, David Thompson, and Gretchen Nichols, longtime Diamond Valley residents and owners of the nearby McCoy Creek Inn, bought the Hotel Diamond in 2001 and are bringing a surge of energy to the little hotel. The Diamond, which doubles as a general store (watch the pickups pull in at 5pm for the evening six-pack) has five small bedrooms upstairs sharing two baths and a sitting area; three larger rooms off the front porch have private baths. Dinners are available for hotel guests (a big family-style meal if the house is full; cheeseburgers when the crowds go away). $; MC, V; checks OK; closed approximately Nov 15–Mar 15 (call for exact dates); 12 miles east of Hwy 205.

Frenchglen

This beautiful little town (population 15) 60 miles south of Burns is a favorite stopover for those visiting the MALHEUR NATIONAL WILDLIFE REFUGE (see "Birds of the Malheur" in this chapter) or STEENS MOUNTAIN. Steens rises gently from the west to an elevation of 9,670 feet and then drops sharply to the Alvord Desert in the east. A road goes all the way to the ridge top (summers only), and another makes a long loop around Steens—passing the vast borax hardpan of the former Alvord Lake, numerous hot springs, and, near the northeastern end of the route, good fishing in Mann Lake. Contact the BUREAU OF LAND MANAGEMENT (Hwy 20 W, Hines; 541/573-4400) just southwest of Burns for information about Steens Mountain.

It's a rough but scenic ride from Frenchglen to the 275,000-acre HART MOUNTAIN NATIONAL ANTELOPE REFUGE (509/947-3315). Turn west off Highway 205 and follow Rock Creek Road to the visitor center, where you can learn about recent wildlife sightings. Pronghorn, of course, are frequently noted, and bighorn sheep live east of the headquarters on the steep cliffs that form the western boundary

BIRDS OF THE MALHEUR

MALHEUR NATIONAL WILDLIFE REFUGE is ground zero for Eastern Oregon birding—its 187,000 acres of wetlands make it a hospitable stop for migrating birds. Spring is the best time to see birds; more than 130 species nest on the refuge, and many more make rest stops. Sandhill cranes (with 8-foot wingspans) and tundra swans may show up as early as February, followed by waterfowl in March, shorebirds in April, and songbirds late in May, when other birds are beginning to fly off. During the hot summer months, trumpeter swans swim the refuge ponds. Sandhill cranes, ducks, and geese return in the fall, and then fly on to California, leaving the winter to eagles and hawks.

Start your trip to Malheur with a visit to the **REFUGE HEADQUARTERS** (32 miles southeast of Burns on south side of Malheur Lake; 541/493-2612), where you can pick up maps and brochures. Visit the **GEORGE BENSON MEMORIAL MUSEUM** (chock full of mounted birds), and spy on birds in the pond and in the trees around headquarters. From there, drive south on Central Patrol Road, a good gravel road that passes a number of ponds before ending at P Ranch, right near the Frenchglen Hotel. In order to protect the wildlife, most areas are closed to hiking, but if you need to burn off some energy, it's okay to mountain bike along Central Patrol Road.   —Judy Jewell

of fault-block Hart Mountain. No visit here is really complete without a prolonged dip in the local hot spring. It's south of the visitor center in the campground—very rustic and absolutely free.

LODGINGS

Frenchglen Hotel / ★

FRENCHGLEN; 541/493-2825 One of the handful of historical hotels owned by the Oregon State Parks system, the Frenchglen is a small, white-frame building that dates back to 1916. Upstairs, eight small, plain bedrooms share baths. Room 2 is the largest and nicest, and the only one with a view of Steens Mountain. Nothing's very square or level here, and that's part of the charm. Downstairs are a large screened-in front porch and the dining room, where guests mingle and compare travel notes. Many of the guests are birders, and the lobby is well stocked with field guides. John Ross, the hotel manager, and his local crew cook up good, simple meals for guests and drop-by visitors. Ranch-style dinner is one seating only (6:30pm sharp) and reservations are a must. $; MC, V; checks OK; closed mid-Nov–mid-Mar; fghotel@ptinet.net; on Hwy 205, 60 miles south of Burns.

SEATTLE AND ENVIRONS

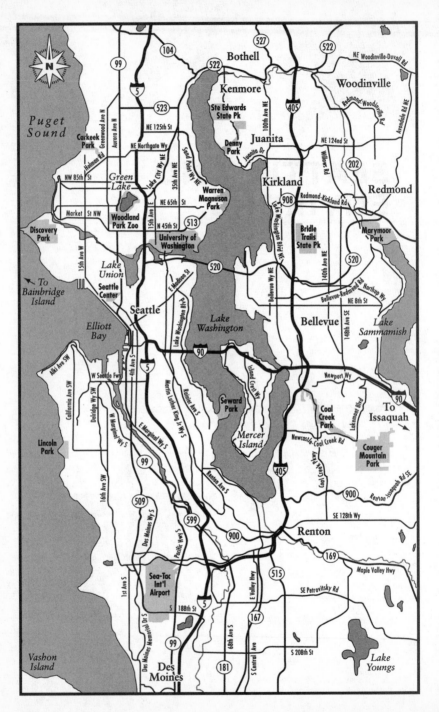

SEATTLE AND ENVIRONS

You know a city has achieved world-class status when it has its own shorthand. Seattle need only flash one of several names to be internationally recognized: Microsoft, Amazon.com, Starbucks.

Of course, Seattle is more than the sum of its slick corporate logos. (Though, except for Los Angeles, it's hard to imagine a more Nike-wearing, Starbucks-drinking, SUV-driving citizenry.) It's also a city of disarming optimism—fueled by hot technology and cool culture—and increasing confidence; a place where gray days far outnumber sunny ones, but sunglasses and sunroofs are big sellers.

The area's geography matches its expansive mood. A diverse obstacle course of bookend mountain ranges (Olympics on the west, Cascades on the east) and around-the-compass waterways (Elliott Bay, Lake Union, Lake Washington, and Lake Sammamish) make an exhilarating playground. And when the sun does shake its cover, the resulting Technicolor perfection makes it hard not to hum "the bluest skies you've ever seen are in Seattle" as you run, bike, kayak, sail, windsurf, or skate on your way. The lush landscape also creates a sense of expectation with something compelling—mountains, skyscrapers, water, floatplanes, boats, bridges—always visible in the near distance. This yin-yang pattern is repeated in the urban grid: historic Pike Place Market gives way to swanky retail on Fifth and Sixth Avenues; Fremont, Capitol Hill, and Belltown each claim a distinctive corner of the city's hip neighborhood triangle. Seattle's sibling suburbs are a study in divergent personalities: the minimetropolis glam of Bellevue, corporate sprawl of Redmond, charming waterfront styles of Kirkland and Bainbridge Island, and the wanna-be-village quaintness of Issaquah.

Once-resented newcomers have added an edge to the native low-key style. With the swell in population—and inflated traffic and housing prices—has come a welcome cultural spike, with hip hotels, restaurants, shops, and nightclubs springing up like so many espresso carts.

Even Seattle's longtime architectural conservatism has begun to bend. The Frank Gehry–designed, Paul Allen–owned Experience Music Project museum threatens to eclipse the adjacent Space Needle in attitude if not altitude. Its lumpy psychedelic exterior drew mews of dislike, but now the downtown public library set to open in fall 2003 has revealed a similarly ambitious blueprint for its new building. And when a city's *library* is cutting new architectural ground, a corner undeniably has been turned.

Optimism isn't always enough. In 1999, the high-profile hosting of the World Trade Organization devolved into a street spectacle tagged the "Battle in Seattle" by the national press; then, in 2001, Mardi Gras celebrations ended violently and Boeing shocked everyone by decamping its headquarters to Chicago. Nevertheless, Seattle is just hitting its 21st-century stride.

ACCESS AND INFORMATION

The nightmare traffic story has become something of a competitive sport in Seattle. It doesn't require dramatic license: a recent national study pegged Seattle as having the second-worst traffic jams in the nation (behind Los Angeles). And though a long-awaited light-rail system should alleviate some of the carbon-monoxide crush, it's not set to go online until 2009.

In the meantime, the best defense is a sense of humor and street smarts. The road basics: **INTERSTATE 5** is the main north-south arterial; two east-west arterials connect it to Eastside communities (such as Bellevue) via two floating bridges—**INTERSTATE 90** (south of downtown) and **HIGHWAY 520** (north of downtown); the major Eastside north-south highway is **INTERSTATE 405**. Downtown Seattle is divided into "avenues" (starting with First near the waterfront) running north-south, and "streets" running west-east. Many are one-way.

Getting to downtown from **SEATTLE-TACOMA INTERNATIONAL AIRPORT** (17801 Pacific Hwy S, SeaTac; 206/431-4444) is a 35-minute straight shot north on Interstate 5 (avoid peak rush hours 7–9:30am and 4:30–7pm). **GRAY LINE AIRPORT EXPRESS** (206/626-6088) runs airport passengers to and from major downtown hotels for about $8.50 one-way. **TAXIS** from the airport cost $30–$35. Thanks to a new law, however, taxis to the airport from downtown Seattle charge a flat fee of $25 (though some cabbies might need reminding). Large **CAR RENTAL** agencies have locations near the airport, in downtown Seattle, and in the outlying suburbs.

AMTRAK (3035 S Jackson St; 206/382-4126 or 800/USA-RAIL; www.amtrak. com) trains arrive at and depart from King Street Station, and **GREYHOUND** (811 Stewart St; 800/231-2222) also serves the city.

The city's **METRO TRANSIT** (206/553-3000; transit.metrokc.gov) serves the city, the Eastside, and connects with buses from greater Puget Sound to the north and south. Metro buses are free until 7pm in the downtown core (between the waterfront and I-5, and Jackson and Bell Sts). The **WATERFRONT STREETCAR** (part of Metro) serves the waterfront, Pioneer Square, and the city's Chinatown/International District. For off-road transport, ride the space-age **MONORAIL** (also part of Metro), which glides between downtown's Westlake Center (Pine St and 4th Ave, 3rd floor) and the Seattle Center in 90 seconds, or catch a **WASHINGTON STATE FERRY** (206/464-6400 or 800/843-3779; www.wsdot.wa.gov/ferries/) at Pier 52 to nearby islands, including Bainbridge.

The **SEATTLE-KING COUNTY CONVENTION AND VISITORS BUREAU** (800 Convention Pl, Galleria level; 206/461-5840; www.seeseattle.org) is a good source for information and maps. In summer, visit the outdoor kiosks at Seattle Center and Pioneer Square.

Seattle

Traditionalists yearn for Seattle's small-town *Pleasantville* past: those carefree—and, by comparison, car-free—days before our clothes, musicians, and hot beverages were hijacked as fashion statements, and the only jet set we knew built planes at Boeing. Seattle's sheltered location in the far corner of the national map afforded a blissfully long childhood, but the city has gained some of the more intriguing complications and entertaining perks of adulthood.

MAJOR ATTRACTIONS

Even first-timers can probably rattle off the big must-sees in Seattle: **PIKE PLACE MARKET** (Pike St and 1st Ave), **PIONEER SQUARE** (1st Ave and James St), the

SEATTLE THREE-DAY TOUR

DAY ONE: You'll find it's easy being car-less in Seattle. Don't bother with a sit-down breakfast on your first morning; just nibble on an apple fritter from **THREE GIRLS BAKERY** (1514 Pike Pl; 206/622-1045) as you meander through the bustling **PIKE PLACE MARKET.** After lunch at the **PINK DOOR,** a charming "hole-in-the-alley" trattoria, stroll through the **SEATTLE ART MUSEUM.** (On your way to SAM, swing by **TICKET/TICKET** in the Market to pick up half-price day-of-show tickets for that evening's entertainment). Back in your room at the **INN AT THE MARKET** (more moderately priced rooms can be had at the nearby **ACE HOTEL**), you'll have time for a shower and change before dinner at downstairs **CAMPAGNE.** Then it's a leisurely walk to Benaroya Hall and an evening of **SEATTLE SYMPHONY** music. Cab back for a nightcap at the romantic **CHEZ SHEA** lounge in the Market before tucking in for the night.

DAY TWO: Rise early, but indulge in a room-service breakfast from **BACCO** before descending the Pike Place Hillclimb to hop the vintage waterfront trolley for historic **PIONEER SQUARE.** After the Underground Tour of old Seattle, resurface to peruse the Square's collection of galleries and the **ELLIOTT BAY BOOK CO.,** then take a seat at **IL TERRAZZO CARMINE** for lunch. Cross the nearby pedestrian overpass to the ferry dock at Pier 52 and a 35-minute ferry ride to **BAINBRIDGE ISLAND.** After plumbing the antiques shops of the quaint town of Winslow, settle in for dinner at **CAFE NOLA.** No need to rush dessert: ferries to the city run late, and if you're lucky, a moonlit Seattle skyline will be your closing scene.

DAY THREE: Wake up like a local with a latte and pastry (or bowl of fresh fruit) at Belltown's **MACRINA BAKERY AND CAFE.** Then it's off for some serious shopping and people watching at the splashy **PACIFIC PLACE** mall and flagship **NORDSTROM.** (Take kids to the high-end **GAMEWORKS** video arcade.) Grab a bite at the Place's **GORDON BIERSCH BREWERY RESTAURANT** (4th floor; 206/405-4205). Or, if it's Sunday and the Mariners are in town, baseball fans can catch a bus to **SAFECO FIELD**—pregame activities should include partaking of a mess of ribs at **PECOS'S PIT BBQ** (2260 1st Ave S; 206/623-0629). If not, walk to **WESTLAKE CENTER,** where the **MONORAIL** will whisk you to **SEATTLE CENTER** for an afternoon of high-tech musical exploration at the **EXPERIENCE MUSIC PROJECT.** Before winding up your day and your stay with dinner at Belltown's **FLYING FISH,** say goodbye to the city from atop the landmark **SPACE NEEDLE.**

SPACE NEEDLE. The Needle actually anchors a corner of another major attraction, the **SEATTLE CENTER** (between Denny Wy and Broad St; 206/684-8582). Born out of the 1962 World's Fair, the 74-acre park is home to arts and athletics venues— such as the **OPERA HOUSE** and **KEY ARENA**—as well as the **PACIFIC SCIENCE**

CENTER (200 2nd Ave N; 206/443-2880), with cool hands-on science exhibits and an IMAX theater.

Water-based exhibits are the focus of **ODYSSEY, THE MARITIME DISCOVERY CENTER** (2205 Alaskan Wy, Pier 66; 206/374-4000) and the **SEATTLE AQUARIUM** (1483 Alaskan Wy, Pier 59; 206/386-4320), which boasts a 400,000-gallon Underwater Dome. Visitors and animals come breathtakingly close in the **WOODLAND PARK ZOO**'s (5500 Phinney Ave N; 206/684-4800) animal-friendly natural habitats.

In Pioneer Square, the hokey-but-fun **UNDERGROUND TOUR** (610 1st Ave; 206/682-4646) lets visitors take in the sights—and some of the smells—of old Seattle, preserved from the 1889 great fire that leveled much of the city. Downtown **ART GALLERIES** open new shows for the popular monthly **FIRST THURSDAY** art walks.

MUSEUMS

The striking street-corner Hammering Man sculpture directs patrons into the **SEATTLE ART MUSEUM** (100 University St; 206/654-3100), home to impressive Asian, African, and Northwest Native art collections, as well as national traveling exhibits. The **HENRY ART GALLERY** (15th Ave NE and NE 41st St; 206/543-2280), on the University of Washington campus, is known for its photography collection and more experimental shows, particularly video installations. First Hill's once frumpy **FRYE ART MUSEUM** (704 Terry Ave; 206/622-9250) has been redesigned inside and out, adding imaginative exhibits and music and film events.

The **CHILDREN'S MUSEUM** (Seattle Center; 206/441-1768) encourages exploration of other cultures with hands-on activities and inventive exhibits, such as a global village featuring child-sized dwellings from Japan, Ghana, and the Philippines. The **WING LUKE ASIAN MUSEUM** (407 7th Ave S; 206/623-5124) examines the Asian American experience in the Northwest, including an exhibit concerning the internment of Japanese Americans during World War II. Bankrolled by Microsoft cofounder Paul Allen, the eye-and-ear popping **EXPERIENCE MUSIC PROJECT** (Seattle Center; 206/770-2700; www.emplive.com) celebrates rock 'n' roll and its roots with high-tech installations. The **BURKE MUSEUM OF NATURAL HISTORY AND CULTURE** (17th Ave NE and NE 45th St; 206/543-5590) on the UW campus harbors the Pacific Northwest's only dinosaurs (snap a shot of Junior sitting on the 5-foot-tall sauropod thigh bone). Twenty-six full-sized airplanes are suspended in midair at the **MUSEUM OF FLIGHT** (9404 E Marginal Wy S; 206/764-5720).

PARKS AND GARDENS

Throw a rock, hit a park. Local favorites include **DISCOVERY PARK** (3801 W Government Wy; 206/386-4236), with 534 wild and woodsy acres, miles of trails, beach, and Sound views. **WASHINGTON PARK ARBORETUM** (2300 Arboretum Dr E; 206/543-8800) has 200 wooded acres, walking and running trails, and a Japanese garden. **VOLUNTEER PARK** (1247 15th Ave E; 206/684-4075) features a 1912 conservatory full of hothouse plants and a popular view from the top of the water tower; it's also home to the **SEATTLE ASIAN ART MUSEUM** (206/654-3100). **GAS WORKS PARK** (N Northlake Wy; 206/684-4075) is where Seattleites go fly a kite.

SHOPPING

NORDSTROM's downtown flagship store (500 Pine St; 206/628-2111) includes a spa and five floors of clothes and accessories. Connected to Nordie's via a glass sky-bridge is **PACIFIC PLACE** (600 Pine St; 206/405-2655), a splashy four-level com-mercial cathedral stocked with name retailers, restaurants, and a cinema. Other downtown malls include **WESTLAKE CENTER** (400 Pine St; 206/467-1600) and **CITY CENTRE** (1420 5th Ave; 206/624-8800).

Neighborhoods are where to find unusual or handmade goods, from funky jew-elry and artwork at Fremont's **FRANK AND DUNYA** (3418 Fremont Ave N; 206/547-6760) to shabby chic relics at Capitol Hill's **PRIVATE SCREENING** (1530 Melrose Ave; 206/839-0759). Pioneer Square has cutting-edge galleries and old-fashioned shops such as **WOOD SHOP TOYS** (320 1st Ave S; 206/624-1763), while the **PIKE PLACE MARKET** is justly famous for its fresh fruit, flower, and fish stalls, and authentic crafts, including **MILAGROS MEXICAN FOLK ART** (1530 Post Alley; 206/464-0490).

PERFORMING ARTS

THEATER/DANCE. The big three playhouses are **A CONTEMPORARY THEATRE (ACT)** (700 Union St; 206/292-7676), **INTIMAN THEATRE** (Seattle Center; 206/269-1900), and **SEATTLE REPERTORY THEATRE** (Seattle Center; 206/443-2222). The toasts of Broadway land at the **5TH AVENUE THEATRE** (1308 5th Ave; 206/625-1900) and **PARAMOUNT THEATRE** (911 Pine St; 206/443-1744), while wonderfully imaginative, and surprisingly sophisticated, productions play out at **SEATTLE CHILDREN'S THEATRE** (Seattle Center; 206/441-3322). Classics are at the core of the city's premiere dance company, the **PACIFIC NORTHWEST BALLET** (Seattle Center; 206/441-2424). An annual holiday favorite, *The Nutcracker,* fea-tures spectacular Maurice Sendak sets.

MUSIC. Grunge long ago earned a place on the "get over it" list locals would like to e-mail to the mass media (Seattle's coffee habits top the list). Music of all genres—from alternative rock and reggae to chamber and classical—is amply represented. The **SEATTLE SYMPHONY** (200 University St; 206/215-4747), under the baton of Gerard Schwarz, has an elegant downtown home, Benaroya Hall. The **SEATTLE OPERA** (Seattle Center; 206/389-7676), guided by Speight Jenkins, mounts its performances at the Mercer Arts Arena—better known for booking pop acts than divas—until the summer of 2003, when its refurbished permanent home, Marion Oliver McCaw Hall, reopens. First-rate jazz clubs include classy **DIMITRIOU'S JAZZ ALLEY** (2033 6th Ave; 206/441-9729) and cozy **TULA'S** (2214 2nd Ave; 206/443-4221).

Some of the city's most anticipated festivals revolve around music. The **NORTH-WEST FOLKLIFE FESTIVAL** (Seattle Center; 206/684-7300) showcases a melting pot of talent—from African marimba players to American fiddlers—on Memorial Day weekend. **BUMBERSHOOT** (Seattle Center; 206/281-8111), on Labor Day weekend, hosts headliner acts ranging from Beck to Tony Bennett. And jazz artists, repre-senting bebop to swing, make the rounds of local clubs for the **EARSHOT JAZZ FES-TIVAL** (206/547-9787) in October.

LITERATURE/FILM. Seattle's reputation for being well-read is reinforced by almost-daily author readings at the **ELLIOTT BAY BOOK CO.** (101 S Main St;

206/624-6600) in Pioneer Square and the heavily attended (though constantly relocating) annual **NORTHWEST BOOKFEST** (206/378-1883), which celebrates all things bookish—from authors to small presses—every October.

The **SEATTLE INTERNATIONAL FILM FESTIVAL** (various theaters; 206/324-9996) brings together world premieres, stars, filmmakers, and film buffs for a staggering three-plus weeks starting in late May.

Check the free weeklies, *Seattle Weekly* or *The Stranger,* for event listings. Most theater and event tickets are sold through **TICKETMASTER** (206-292-ARTS); **TICKET/TICKET** (401 Broadway Ave E and Pike Place Information Booth, 1st Ave and Pike St; 206/324-2744) sells half-price, day-of-show tickets.

NIGHTLIFE

It's still not a party-all-night kind of city, but Seattle's urban neighborhoods have definitely put more snap into nighttime. Some of the best see-and-be-seen nightspots are on Capitol Hill and in Belltown. Hot spots on the Hill, a favorite with Seattle's lesbian and gay population, range from the techno-cool of the **MANRAY** video bar (514 E Pine St; 206/568-0750) to the retro-chic of the **BALTIC ROOM** (1207 Pine St; 206/625-4444). Belltown counters with the cultured **AXIS** (2214 1st Ave; 206/441-9600) and funky hybrids like the live-music club/cafe **CROCODILE CAFE** (2200 2nd Ave; 206/441-5611) and the live-music club/cafe/laundromat **SIT & SPIN** (2219 4th Ave; 206/441-9484).

In Queen Anne, classy lounges—**PARAGON** (2125 Queen Anne Ave N; 206/283-4548) and **TINI BIGS** (100 Denny Wy; 206/284-0931)—easily coexist with colorfully cheesy hangouts such as **PESO'S TACO LOUNGE** (605 Queen Anne Ave N; 206/283-9353).

SPORTS AND RECREATION

Even when they don't win pennants, the **SEATTLE MARINERS** (206/622-HITS) have a hit on their hands with open-air Safeco Field (between Royal Brougham Wy and S Atlantic St; 206/346-4003), popular even with nonbaseball fans (public tours available). The as yet unnamed football stadium next door, opened in fall 2002, is the new home for the Paul Allen–owned **SEATTLE SEAHAWKS** (206/682-2800). While the **UNIVERSITY OF WASHINGTON HUSKIES** (Husky Stadium, 3800 Montlake Blvd NE; 206/543-2200) thrill rabid fans from their Lake Washington–backed gridiron. Seattle's pro women's basketball team, the WNBA's **SEATTLE STORM** (206/283-DUNK), tips off in the Key Arena (305 N Harrison St) in summer; the **SEATTLE SUPERSONICS** (206/283-DUNK) dominate the Key, November through April.

Plenty of outlets appeal to amateur athletes. In-line skaters and bikers work up a sweat on the **BURKE-GILMAN TRAIL,** a stretch of blacktop running from north Lake Union to the Eastside. Along the trail, the **BICYCLE CENTER** (4529 Sandpoint Wy NE; 206/523-8300) rents bikes and skates. For a map of Seattle **BIKE ROUTES,** call the City of Seattle Bicycle and Pedestrian program (206/684-7583). Kayakers, rowers, and canoeists ply the waters of Lake Union and Lake Washington. **MOSS BAY ROWING AND KAYAK CENTER** (1001 Fairview Ave N, Ste 1900; 206/682-2031) gives lessons and rents kayaks. Outdoor enthusiasts of all stripes flock to the two-level flagship **REI** (222 Yale Ave N; 206/223-1944), which, along with an abundance of equipment, houses an indoor climbing wall, an outdoor mountain bike/hiking test trail, and the U.S. Forest Service's Outdoor Recreation Information Center (206/470-4060) for trip planning.

RESTAURANTS

Andaluca / ★★★

407 OLIVE WY (MAYFLOWER PARK HOTEL), SEATTLE; 206/382-6999 Rosewood booths, fresh flowers, and textured walls create a romantic mood for lovers with an appetite. Begin with a glass of sherry at the half-moon bar, or share a few small plates from the lengthy tapas menu along with a bottle of wine from the extensive list. Chef Wayne Johnson's seasonal menu emphasizes Mediterranean conversant with Northwest seafood and produce. Try crispy duck cakes served with apricot chutney and cucumber yogurt; roasted mussels fragrant with garlic and rosemary; polenta cakes with almonds, pecorino, and oyster mushrooms; or spicy calamari with saffron aioli. *Cabrales*-crusted beef is a heartbreakingly rare tenderloin with grilled pears, blue cheese, and marsala glaze. Vegetarians love the ratatouille risotto, with artichokes, tomatoes, zucchinis, and crimini mushrooms. *$$$; AE, DC, DIS, MC, V; checks OK; breakfast, dinner every day, lunch Mon–Sat; full bar; reservations recommended; andaluca@andaluca.com; www.andaluca.com; downtown.* &

Anthony's Pier 66/ ★★★
Bell Street Diner / ★★
Anthony's Fish Bar / ★

2201 ALASKAN WY/PIER 66, SEATTLE; 206/448-6688 This handsome trio of restaurants at the Bell Street Pier is designed to suit any mood, appetite, or budget. The Asian-inflected menu of local and regional seafood offers selections such as ginger Penn Cove mussels steamed with sake, and Potlatch, an intoxicating mess of Northwest steamer clams, mussels, split snow crab legs, and half-shell oysters. Planked wild chinook salmon or Alaskan halibut are always reliable entrees. Pier 66, home to the most jaw-dropping view of Seattle's working waterfront, is open for dinner. For lunch or casual dinners, the boisterous Bell Street Diner downstairs offers an array of seafood, chowders, burgers, generous salads, rice bowls, and fish tacos. For a quick, no-frills bite, take the kids and join the gulls waterside at Anthony's Fish Bar for fish-and-chips, chowder, and blackened-rockfish tacos. *$$; $; $; AE, MC, V; checks OK; dinner every day (Pier 66); lunch, dinner every day (Bell Street Diner, Anthony's Fish Bar); 2 full bars; reservations recommended; www.anthonysrestaurants.com; on waterfront.* &

Brasa / ★★★★

2107 3RD AVE, SEATTLE; 206/728-4220 *Brasa*, translated from Portuguese, means "live coals," and you'll see why with its wide-open view of the kitchen and warmly inviting dining room of dark woods and toasty pinks and oranges. Executive chef-owner Tamara Murphy creates some of the most imaginative menus in town. The fragrance of Penn Cove mussels with curry, coriander, and coconut milk turns heads, as does hearty exotica such as suckling pig with chorizo, clams, and smoked hot paprika; or scallops with braised sweet Walla Walla onions, chive potato cake, a perfect little poached quail egg, and house-cured bacon. Owner-manager Bryan Hill's readable wine list is global and well considered. The bar is a great stop for a glass of wine from the formidable by-the-glass list and the affordable bar menu of tapas-like bites. *$$$; AE, DC, MC, V; checks OK; dinner every day; full bar; reservations recommended; seattle@brasa.com; www.brasa.com; Belltown.* &

Cafe Lago / ★★★

2305 24TH AVE E, SEATTLE; 206/329-8005 This little gem near the Montlake Bridge is filled nightly with locals who come for wonderful, unpresumptuous Italian fare. Start with the antipasto plate, stacked with eggplant, bruschetta with *olivata* (a purée of black olives), goat cheese, roasted peppers, mozzarella, roasted garlic bulbs, prosciutto, and Asiago cheese. City of Seattle Eggplant—grilled eggplant wedges marinated in olive oil, tomato, balsamico, and garlic, with a wedge of Gorgonzola—is served with thick slices of country Italian bread. The lasagne—made with impossibly thin pasta sheets layered with ricotta and béchamel so light it's like a soufflé—is so popular, you should order it before 8pm to make sure it isn't sold out. Try one of the thin-crust wood-fired pizzas or New York steak marinated in *basalmico* and herbs, covered with Gorgonzola, grilled onions, and radicchio. Finish with a slice of chocolate truffle cake in a puddle of espresso *crema inglese*. *$$; AE, DC, DIS, MC, V; checks OK; dinner Tues–Sun; full bar; reservations recommended; Montlake.* &

Campagne / ★★★★
Cafe Campagne / ★★★

86 PINE ST, SEATTLE; 206/728-2800 / 1600 POST ALLEY, SEATTLE; 206/728-2233 Set in a courtyard in the Pike Place Market, Campagne takes its cue from the cuisine of southern France. Owner Peter Lewis and some of Seattle's finest servers ensure you'll dine with grace and gusto. Northwest and French influences meet amorously in chef Daisley Gorden's creations, such as steamed halibut with fingerling potatoes, sweet Walla Walla onion, and artichokes on a salad of Picholine olives; or grilled king salmon on English pea and basil risotto. Housemade charcuterie includes a skillfully made lamb sausage. The dessert chef haunts the market as well, gathering local fruits and berries for tarts, ice creams, and granités. Not least among the joys of dining here is the carefully wrought wine list. A short, late-night menu is served in the bar—which, not unlike France, is smoky and romantic.

Cafe Campagne, located below its stylish sibling, offers a slice of French cafe life for breakfast, lunch, and dinner. Wherever you sit (cherrywood table or elegant counter) be sure to utter the most important words spoken here: garlic mashed potatoes. *$$$; $$; AE, DC, MC, V; no checks; dinner every day (Campagne), breakfast, lunch, dinner Mon–Sat, brunch Sun (Cafe Campagne); full bar; reservations recommended; Pike Place Market.* &

Canlis / ★★★★

2576 AURORA AVE N, SEATTLE; 206/283-3313 Cantilevered above Lake Union on Queen Anne Hill, this old establishment steak house has the best views of the lakes and Cascades of any nonrevolving joint in town. Chris and Alice Canlis brought the restaurant into modern times with a $1.5-million revamp and by hiring megachef Greg Atkinson, who has transformed it into an exciting regional restaurant. Atkinson kept longtime diners happy by honoring the former menu, and attracted a new bunch by seasonally enhancing classic Canlis fare. Dungeness crab cakes with orange-butter sauce are perfect and spicy with fresh ginger; fat Alaska weathervane scallops are barely cooked and set into little singing scallop shells with lime. Salads—such as the oil-free Mrs. C. Salad with greens, strawberries, and fresh basil—are wonderful. The famous copper broiler yields salmon, ahi, and New York cuts of Kobe beef. Broiler items are balanced with kabocha squash with ginger and soy; roasted garlic flan; or the mighty baked potato. The much-lauded wine list ranges from $30 to $1,000 a bottle. The dress code of yore has eased, but men are still asked to wear jackets. Expect to be treated like royalty, and to pay accordingly. *$$$$; AE, DC, DIS, MC, V; checks OK; dinner Mon–Sat; full bar; reservations required; canlis@canlis.com; www.canlis.com; south end of Aurora Bridge.* &

Carmelita / ★★★

7314 GREENWOOD AVE N, SEATTLE; 206/706-7703 Kathryn Neumann and Michael Hughes transformed a dilapidated retail space into a theatrically lit haven of color and texture, and introduced vegetarian fine dining to the north end. Chefs have come and gone, but the sophisticated, seasonal vegetarian menu remains enticing and food quality rarely wavers. Start with eggplant Rockefeller, a vegetarian version of the classic oyster dish with eggplant purée in little ramekins baked on rock salt and served with a spicy tomato marmalade. Little pizzas are great—especially grape pizza with goat cheese, blue cheese, grape halves, and walnuts. The wine list is short, with most bottles around $35. Teas, tisanes, juices, and a refreshing tamarind-ginger lemonade are best enjoyed in warm weather on the charming, plant-filled deck. *$$; MC, V; local checks only; dinner Tues–Sun; beer and wine; reservations recommended; carmaveggy@earthlink.net; www.carmelita.net; Greenwood.* &

Cascadia / ★★★

2328 1ST AVE, SEATTLE; 206/448-8884 Eat with French flatware off Limoges china and sip out of handblown glassware in this spare but elegant restaurant. An etched-glass wall separating dining room from kitchen has water sluicing through it like rain against a window. Chef-owner Kerry Sears celebrates "Cascadia," the region between our mountains and the Pacific, by using only indigenous foods and flavors. Prepare to spend a bundle here on exotica such as wild salmon on cedar fronds or white-truffled partridge baked in hay. Washington beefsteak in a tart crab-apple glaze is served with mustard vegetables and garlic fries. Choose from four menus or from one of the seven-course tasting menus. While the food can be quite exciting, presentation can border on precious. Sears has installed a lower-priced cafe menu, served in the bar or outside. The wine list has mostly premium bottlings; sommeliers are especially helpful. *$$$$; AE, DC, DIS, MC, V; no checks; dinner Mon–Sat; full bar; reservations recommended; cascadia@cascadiarestaurant.com; www.cascadia restaurant.com; Belltown.* &

Chez Shea / ★★★
Shea's Lounge / ★★☆

94 PIKE ST, 3RD FLOOR, SEATTLE; 206/467-9990 You might walk through Pike Place Market 100 times and not notice Sandy Shea's tiny, romantic hideaway, Chez Shea, perched above, looking out over Puget Sound. Dinner is a prix-fixe affair, with three of four courses preset and a choice of five entrees. Menus reflect the bounty of the season, employing ingredients fresh from the market stalls. A summer meal might begin with a savory tart of Walla Walla sweet onion, ricotta, Oregon blue cheese, and peach vinaigrette on a lighter-than-a-cloud pastry. The soup course may be a bisque of roasted corn tangy with ancho chiles and lime crème fraîche. Entrees may include pan-roasted wild king salmon with blueberry salsa; herb-crusted rack of lamb served with big white cannellini beans; or semolina gnocchi with parmigiana and a smooth saffron tomato sauce. Service is always gracious. Shea's Lounge next door is a sexy bistro with a Mediterranean-accented menu offering dishes like herb crepes with criminis and fontina, superb pizzas, and salads. *$$$; $$; AE, MC, V; no checks; dinner Tues–Sun; full bar; reservations recommended (Chez Shea); www.chezshea.com; Pike Place Market.*

Dahlia Lounge / ★★★★

2001 4TH AVE, SEATTLE; 206/682-4142 The Dahlia's trademark dining landscape of crimson, gold brocade, and papier-mâché fish lanterns is part of chefowner Tom Douglas's philosophy of keeping guests in comfortable zones while never letting them forget they're on the cutting edge. Menus change daily, but expect familiar dishes with innovative ingredients, from Tuscan bread salad with fresh mozzarella, luxurious lobster hot pot soup with rice noodles, and spunky ribeye steak with acorn–fava bean succotash and squash blossom fritter to grilled Copper River sockeye salmon with Yakima asparagus, fingerling potatoes, and caperberry vinaigrette. Dessert can be down-to-earth delectables, such as a bag of doughnuts fried to order with mascarpone and raspberry, plum, and apricot jams, or fluffy signature coconut cream pie. (For take-away yummies, swing by the next-door Dahlia Bakery; 206/441-4540.) Dahlia's recent location change and the release of Douglas's new cookbook have put him and his restaurants—the others are Etta's Seafood and Palace Kitchen (see reviews)—into an even higher stratum. *$$; AE, DC, DIS, MC, V; local checks only; lunch Mon–Fri, dinner every day; full bar; reservations recommended; maureen@tomdouglas.com; www.tomdouglas.com; downtown.* &

El Gaucho / ★★★

2505 1ST AVE, SEATTLE; 206/728-1337 El Gaucho is a swank Belltown remake of a '70s-era uptown hangout. The current version has dark, wide-open spaces where cooks scurry at a wood-fired broiler and servers deliver impaled conflagrations of meat to the well-heeled. The bar crowd sips martinis as a piano player coolly noodles jazz riffs on a baby grand. It's a ripe spot in which to see and be seen. Patrons seated at comfy banquettes in the theater-in-the-round-style dining room share chateaubriand for two or custom-aged steaks and huge baked potatoes with all the trimmings. Equally rich offerings include ostrich fillet, veal scaloppine, and venison chops. Seafood lovers can soak garlic bread in the sauce for buttery Wicked Shrimp, or suck saffron-scented broth from an artful bouillabaisse. Bananas Foster is a sublime capper to the evening. The formidable wine card is supplemented by a premium reserve list. Serious imbibers will be heartened by the lengthy single-malt Scotch list, and there are two cigar lounges. The Pampas Room downstairs, open for dancing and drinking on Friday and Saturday, offers the full El Gaucho menu. *$$$; AE, DIS, MC, V; checks OK; dinner every day; full bar; reservations recommended; www. elgaucho.com; Belltown.* &

Elliott's Oyster House / ★★★

1201 ALASKAN WY/PIER 56, SEATTLE; 206/623-4340 Dining at Elliott's is an in-city pleasure cruise. Ferries pull out of the terminal next door, wowing tourists and locals who know Elliott's for its slurpable oysters, outside dining, and mastery of fresh seafood. Try one of the rich chowders—the creamy, pink-tinged Dungeness crab chowder with a touch of cayenne is fantastic. Iced shellfish extravaganzas serve two, four, or six. Center-cut swordfish is firm yet tender, with a subtle butter–macadamia nut sauce. Mesquite-grilled ahi tacos at lunch are kicked with mango, lime, and wasabi. The Northwest cioppino includes cracked crab, scallops, salmon, Manila clams, Alaskan side-striped prawns, and Penn Cove mussels submerged in a dense herb- and saffron-scented tomato broth zingy with cayenne and red pepper. There's a safe, seafood-friendly wine list that features a trio sampler for tasting. *$$$; AE, DC, DIS, MC, V; checks OK; lunch, dinner every day; full bar; reservations recommended; www.elliottsoysterhouse.com; waterfront.* &

Etta's Seafood / ★★★

2020 WESTERN AVE, SEATTLE; 206/443-6000 Flamboyant chef-owner Tom Douglas created this exuberant seafood house and named it after his equally effervescent daughter. Etta's is in the same freewheeling style as its siblings, Dahlia Lounge and Palace Kitchen (see reviews). Seafood is perhaps what Douglas does best, and he does it with a light touch. For starters there are small half-shelled oysters—Kumomotos or Snow Creeks; mussels or clams in broth zesty with chorizo; and house-smoked salmon. Douglas's Dungeness crab cakes spiked with green tomato relish and his spice-rubbed pit-roasted salmon are Seattle's signature versions of these dishes. Lush desserts come from dessert central in the Dahlia Bakery. Lunch can be as simple as fish-and-chips with red cabbage slaw or more complicated, such as chilled peanut noodles with lemongrass chicken skewers. *$$$; AE, DC, DIS, MC, V; local checks only; lunch, dinner every day, brunch Sat–Sun; full bar; reservations recommended; maureen@tomdouglas.com; www.tomdouglas.com; Belltown.* &

Flying Fish / ★★★☆

2234 1ST AVE, SEATTLE; 206/728-8595 Flying Fish is a foodie's dream. That's because chef-owner Christine Keff not only knows her seafood, but has created a place where everybody seems to want to be. Order the small starter plates, two or three of which can make a meal. Keff encourages large parties to opt for the large sharing platters that are sold by the pound, such as whole fried rockfish or her famous Sister-in-law Mussels with chile-lime dipping sauce. Entree choices range from lobster ravioli with yellow-foot mushrooms in a puddle of lobster velouté to a pile of crispy fried calamari with a hot-sweet honey jalapeño mayonnaise, to shrimp and chicken rice noodles with Thai green curry and shiitakes. The servers are ultrafriendly, and the wine list is expansive, with lots of Northwest and California offerings. This is where Seattle goes for seafood without the distraction of a waterfront view and all that goes with that—it's a place for travelers, not tourists. $$; AE, DC, MC, V; local checks only; dinner every day; full bar; reservations recommended; www.flyingfishseattle.com; Belltown. &

The Georgian / ★★★☆

411 UNIVERSITY ST (FOUR SEASONS OLYMPIC HOTEL), SEATTLE; 206/621-7889 This grand old space got a grand old face-lift in 2001. The idea was to make The Georgian, which got an updated name as well as a brighter color scheme, more accessible. Her high ceilings, ornate chandeliers, and high prices are still here, but the stuffy dress code is not, and executive chef Gavin Stephensen has modernized the menu and made it more seasonal. The service remains uncompromisingly high, and a pianist tickles the ivories in the center of the room. Each dish is an objet d'art, beginning with the Dungeness crab salad with capsicum dressing, and a jumbo prawn with caviar. The intense, earthy flavors of baby beets and lentils, seared duck liver, and rosemary honey mustard give a broad flavor to crispy, rare-cooked duck breast; buttered Canadian lobster with roasted potato ravioli fairly sings of the sea. A vegetarian prix-fixe menu and à la carte selections are also available. The wine list includes domestic selections as well as imports. A short dessert list includes milk chocolate–topped polenta pound cake with Jack Daniels ice cream. The Garden Terrace is a civilized spot for a Cognac and a cigar. $$$; AE, MC, V; checks OK; lunch, dinner every day; full bar; reservations for large groups only; www.fourseasons.com/seattle/dining/dining_33.html; downtown. &

Harvest Vine / ★★★☆

2701 E MADISON ST, SEATTLE; 206/320-9771 It's hard to re-create the leisurely gusto with which the Spanish eat and drink—especially in soggy Seattle. But Joseph Jimenez de Jimenez and his crew do it every night in this rustic shoebox of a place, where it's standing room only for tapas and paella. Get a bottle or glass of wine and start ordering platitos from the more than two dozen tapas that make up most of the menu. Everything is shareable, including the salad of grilled escarole and black truffles circled by a slice of delightfully subtle smoky salmon; or the gratin of cardoons with a tomato sauce and mild but rich Idiazabel cheese. Skewered venison chunks, grilled rare and tender, rest in a mess of garlicky oyster mushrooms; sweet piquillo peppers stuffed with herbed Dungeness crab lie in a puddle of shellfish sauce. Whether seated at the copper-topped bar or at one of the few tables, a dinner-party atmosphere presides—with diners comparing dishes, pointing and yelling, "Give me one of those!" $$; MC, V; checks OK; dinner Tues–Sat; beer and wine; reservations not accepted; Madison Valley. &

I Love Sushi / ★★☆

1001 FAIRVIEW AVE N, SEATTLE; 206/625-9604 / 11818 NE 8TH ST, BELLEVUE; 425/454-5706 Don't let the have-a-nice-day name put you off. Chef Tadashi Sato has created a pair of bustling, bright, high-energy sushi bars with immaculately fresh fish, on both sides of Lake Washington. The staff at each place is friendly and helpful—making it a delicious place to learn for those unfamiliar with Japanese food. Sushi combinations are a bargain (particularly at lunch), while traditional Japanese specialties such as sea urchin, abalone, and fermented bean paste raise the stakes somewhat. À la carte dishes, like flame-broiled mackerel or salmon, the ubiquitous tempura, or geoduck *itame* sautéed with spinach, are excellent. *$$; AE, MC, V; no checks; lunch Mon–Fri, dinner every day (Seattle), lunch Mon–Sat, dinner every day (Bellevue); full bar; reservations not necessary; www.ilovesushi.com; South Lake Union (Seattle), east of I-405 (Bellevue).* ఉ

Il Terrazzo Carmine / ★★★

411 1ST AVE S, SEATTLE; 206/467-7797 Be prepared to spend an entire evening at Il Terrazzo. As you graze through the glistening array of antipasti, watch for Seattle's rich and famous, likely to be dining beside you to the strains of classical guitar. For a lusty starter, try calamari in padella, tender squid in a heady tomato garlic sauté, or a creamy soup of prawns and roast peppers. Deciding among pastas is a feat. Cannellonis are creamy and bubbly with ricotta and filled with veal and spinach, and fettuccine is tossed with in-house smoked salmon, mushrooms, and peas. The osso buco is braised in red wine and served with buttered fettuccine. The prime-cut tenderloin is roasted and served with a wine and pancetta sauce. Tiramisu and crème brûlée are well crafted, as are ever-changing choices— such as house-made gelati—that showcase local fruits in season. *$$$; AE, DC, DIS, MC, V; no checks; lunch Mon–Fri, dinner Mon–Sat; full bar; reservations recommended; Pioneer Square.* ఉ

Kingfish Cafe / ★★★

602 19TH AVE E, SEATTLE; 206/320-8757 The Coaston sisters have their restaurant just the way they want it—busy. It's a casual, contemporary space with blown-up sepia-tinted photos from the family album on the walls, including distant cousin Langston Hughes. Expect long lines for a taste of this sassy Southern soul food. It's kind of a party waiting at Kingfish, wine in hand—regulars, we're told, look forward to it. The buttermilk fried chicken is a huge favorite, as is Big Daddy's Pickapeppa Skirt Steak or the velvety pumpkin soup, crab and catfish cakes with green-tomato tartar sauce, or seafood curry with coconut grits. Lunch is a bargain: try the pulled pork sandwich with peach and watermelon barbecue sauce. At Sunday brunch, crab and catfish cakes are topped with a poached egg and hollandaise. *$$; no credit cards; checks OK; lunch Mon, Wed–Fri, dinner Mon, Wed–Sat, brunch Sun; beer and wine; reservations not accepted; kingfishcafe@aol. com; east Capitol Hill.* ఉ

Lampreia / ★★★★

2400 1ST AVE, SEATTLE; 206/443-3301 Scott Carsberg has a cultish following, and, like Sinatra, he does it his way. Raised in West Seattle, he headed east and was mentored by a master Tyrolean chef. Carsberg returned to open his spare ocher dining room, which is not unlike like his minimalist creations. For appetizers there's garden vegetables and pesto in a *cocotte* (little French iron casserole) with a poached egg; a silky sweet squash soup; or Walla Walla onion tart with osetra caviar, sweet and salty in a thin, buttery crust. The intermezzo course might be

HOW TO PASS FOR A LOCAL

Every city has its own set of idiosyncrasies. Visitors who want to mesh more naturally with the locals might benefit from these insights into Seattle's native style.

UMBRELLAS: Despite the city's rep, it doesn't rain buckets here daily (Miami has more rain annually). A sure way to spot a newcomer is to see an unfurled umbrella during a light shower.

SHADES: Residents have to combat cloud glare more than unfettered sunshine; as a result, sunglasses are de rigueur nearly year-round.

ATTIRE: While the Capitol Hill crowd favors black ensembles, body piercings, and Doc Martens, Green Lakers sport spandex, bare midriffs, and Nikes. Whatever the neighborhood, Seattleites are flexible about formality. A night at the opera here can mean evening gowns or jeans.

COOLNESS: This isn't a climate reference but an attitudinal one: we're not unfriendly, just politely reserved. Rumor has it that it takes two years to make a real friend here (unless, of course, the new friend is another lonely newcomer).

VOCABULARY: "Yeah" is as common a part of Seattle speech as "Oh my gawd!" is to a suburban teenager. Not to be confused with the intimidating interrogative "Oh yeah?!" favored by East Coasters, Seattle's "Yeah" is simply a laid-back form of assent or agreement. (In the more heavily Scandinavian section of the city, "Ya sure, you betcha" can be used as a synonym.)

JAYWALKING: That crowd on the corner isn't making a drug deal, they're waiting for the crosswalk sign to change. Natives are notorious sticklers for obeying these signs—and so are the police. Newcomers blithely crossing against lights may find themselves ticketed, at about $38 a pop.

BICYCLISTS: Some days they seem to outnumber cars. Observing the traditional politeness of the city, locals resist the urge to bump off cyclists who hold up traffic.

TRAVEL ESPRESSO CUPS: They're everywhere. Isn't that why car cup holders were invented? Besides, a swig of caffeine takes drivers' minds off dawdling cyclists.

—*Shannon O'Leary*

whipped potatoes set on a crispy, crepelike "tulip" of Reggiano Parmesan and piled with spot prawns covered in *tartufi bianchi,* the rare Piedmontese white truffles. Main courses include his famous veal chop with fonduta cheese sauce that has diners sucking the bones. Other triumphs are the matsutake, a prized wild mushroom, with grilled smoked salmon or the five-spice duck breast with fruit mustards and chanterelles. Servers bring a selection of handcrafted local cheeses, which make a fine and mellow end to a meal or a prelude to a delectable dessert. Service, as directed by Carsberg's wife, Hyun Joo Paek, is seamless and reverential. *$$$; AE, MC, V; no checks; dinner Tues–Sat; full bar; reservations recommended; Belltown.* &

Macrina Bakery and Cafe / ★★☆

2408 IST AVE, SEATTLE; 206/448-4032 / 615 W MCGRAW ST, SEATTLE; 206/283-5900 Seattle was a one-bread town until Leslie Mackie, originator of the rustic bread program at Grand Central Bakery, transformed it into a bread-lover's mecca. Her exceptional breads grace the tables of the city's finest restaurants—and homes. Mornings, Belltown regulars show up for warm buttery goods, bowls of fresh fruit, house-made granola, and creamy lattes to be enjoyed in the sunny Euro-chic cafe setting. Lunch brings simple, artful soups (try the corn chowder studded with Dungeness crab), salads, panini, and a classy meze trio of daily-changing Mediterranean-inspired noshes. Don't leave without one of the famous Rick's cookies—chewy with chocolate chunks, apricot, and espresso. *$; MC, V; local checks only; breakfast, lunch Mon–Fri, brunch Sat–Sun; beer and wine; reservations not accepted; Belltown and Queen Anne.* &

Marco's Supperclub / ★★☆

2510 IST AVE, SEATTLE; 206/441-7801 Ex-pat Chicagoans Marco Rulff and Donna Moodie opened their bistro in Belltown well before the neighborhood became the hippest food corridor in Seattle. They have created a sexy, noisy atmosphere that attracts regulars and tourists. The kitchen is adventurous and capable—don't miss the signature starter of fried sage leaves or the shiitake-stuffed spring rolls with holy basil. Moodie's family recipe for Jamaican jerk chicken is a perennial favorite, served with sweet potato purée and sautéed greens. Other exotica includes halibut with a Moroccan harissa rub and couscous, and pineapple-ginger pork loin served with fresh papaya sauce. An eclectic collection of European and Northwest wines is available by the bottle or glass. A bar running the length of the dining room is a great perch for solo diners, and in the fair-weather months, a deck out back doubles the seating. *$$; AE, MC, V; checks OK; dinner every day; full bar; reservations recommended; Belltown.* &

Matt's in the Market / ★★★

94 PIKE ST, 3RD FLOOR, SEATTLE; 206/467-7909 This spot in the Corner Market Building is hard to find if you're not looking for it. Our advice: Look for it. Matt's is curled up in a tiny space with an old tiled counter and stools. A handful of tables stand in the back of the room, looking out large-paned windows over Pike Place Market to Elliott Bay and the Olympic Mountains. The durable chef, Erik Canella, turns out food that's not only well crafted but some of the freshest, most innovative eats downtown. It's no wonder it's fresh—cooks shop the market twice a day. Seafood is the best bet here—rare-seared albacore is a mainstay; smoked catfish salad is pleasantly original. At lunchtime, the line of office workers forms early for oyster po'boys, heady filé gumbo, or clams and mussels in an ouzo-infused broth. There's also a quirky and wonderful wine list. Owner Matt Janke does everything else in this place—waiting, greeting, busing, prepping, and washing dishes. He sometimes even manages to squeeze in musicians to play live jazz. *$$; MC, V; no checks; lunch, dinner Tues–Sat; beer and wine; reservations not accepted after 6pm; Pike Place Market.*

Monsoon / ★★★

615 19TH AVE E, SEATTLE; 206/325-2111 Sister and brother Sophie and Eric Banh have brought a stylish addition to the city's diverse restaurant scene. They cook their seasonal Vietnamese dishes in a steamy open kitchen, which fronts a four-stool counter and an elegant dining room. Don't miss the tamarind soup with tiger prawns and chicken, a sweet and tangy mix with lotus root, pineapple, and bean sprouts. Compelling appetizers include cold shrimp-shiitake rolls, the *la lot* beef, and five-spice baby back ribs. Try sea scallops and crispy yams with spicy chile sauce, fresh halibut steamed with crunchy lily buds and shiitakes in a banana leaf, or grilled Asian eggplant, which can be ordered with green onions in coconut sauce or with snap peas and shiitakes. By all means order a pot of chrysanthemum tea. The dining room can be noisy when full; expect a wait at the door to be handled gracefully by another Banh sister, Yen. *$$; MC, V; no checks; lunch Tues–Fri, dinner Tues–Sun; beer and wine; www.monsoonseattle.com; east Capitol Hill.* &

Palace Kitchen / ★★★

2030 5TH AVE, SEATTLE; 206/448-2001 The palatial open kitchen and bar scene buzz until closing time. Catch the action from various vantage points: seated at the enormous tile-topped bar, beneath a huge painting of a lusty 17th-century banquet; in a private booth; at a storefront banquette; or in the glassed-in private room. Though this is essentially a bar, food from Tom Douglas—of Dahlia Lounge and Etta's Seafood (see reviews)—is always robust and innovative. Order shareable selections such as fat and spicy grilled chicken wings, bowls of clams, crispy-fried semolina-coated anchovies, or goat-cheese fondue with chunks of bread and apple slices. Or go all out and choose a special from the applewood grill, including pit-roasted lamb, chicken, or whole fish. The informative wine list is the most entertaining in town. *$$; AE, DC, DIS, MC, V; checks OK; lunch Mon–Fri, dinner every day; full bar; reservations recommended; maureen@tomdouglas.com; www.tom douglas.com; downtown.* &

The Pink Door / ★★☆

1919 POST ALLEY, SEATTLE; 206/443-3241 The low-profile entrance (just a pink door) underscores the speakeasy style of this Italian trattoria in the Pike Place Market. In winter, the dining room grows noisy around a burbling fountain. Come warmer weather, everyone vies for a spot on the trellis-covered terrace with its breathtaking view of the Sound. Inside or out, an arty, under-30 set happily noshes on garlicky black-olive tapenade and quaffs tumblers of wine from the reasonably priced, mostly Italian list. The menu features hearty, generously portioned pastas, daily risotto, excellent rack of lamb paired with mascarpone mashed potatoes, and lusty seafood-filled cioppino. Inventive salads are composed of mostly organic local produce. Desserts are a homey affair, such as apple crisp in a cereal bowl. Evenings often bring live music (and sometimes a tarot card reader). *$$; AE, MC, V; no checks; lunch Tues–Sat, dinner Tues–Sun; full bar; reservations recommended; Pike Place Market.*

Place Pigalle / ★★☆

81 PIKE ST, SEATTLE; 206/624-1756 Place Pigalle is the place if you want picture-postcard views of Elliott Bay and ambitious French-Northwest-Italian cooking. Hidden away in the market, the bistro is the perfect spot to sip an eau-de-vie, lunch with a friend, or engage in a romantic dinner. Ask for a window table and order something as simple as calamari sautéed with ginger, garlic, spinach, and creamy mustard sauce, or as sophisticated as a saddle of rabbit filled with apples, spinach, and blue cheese. Dessert options include rich pots de crème or brandied apricot-almond torte. On sunny days, a small deck appeals, but inside tables are within servers' sight lines. The little bar is ideal for dining solo—or just sipping from your choice of hundreds of wines. *$$$; AE, DC, MC, V; no checks; lunch, dinner Mon–Sat; full bar; reservations recommended; www.savvydiner.com; Pike Place Market.*

Ponti Seafood Grill / ★★★

3014 3RD AVE N, SEATTLE; 206/284-3000 What with its canalside perch, stucco walls and red-tiled roof, Ponti pulls off a nifty impersonation of Mediterranean style. The menu, however, borrows from an array of ethnic flavors, with more than a passing nod to Asia. Typical combinations are seared ahi in a ginger-jolted shoyu and sake sauce with coconut rice cake and cucumber-wasabi aioli. The lasting star power of head chef Tom Hollywood may rest with one dish: Thai curry penne (with broiled scallops, Dungeness crabmeat, spicy ginger-tomato chutney, and basil chiffonade). Savvy diners turn to the fresh sheet for offerings such as lobster and mussel stew in coconut broth, or red wine risotto with halibut cheeks, artichoke, asparagus, and chard. Tempting desserts include white chocolate crème caramel and seasonal fruit tarts. Dine outdoors in warm weather on balconies overlooking the Ship Canal. *$$$; AE, DC, MC, V; local checks only; lunch Sun–Fri, dinner every day, brunch Sun; full bar; reservations recommended; mnger@ponti.com; www.pontiseafoodgrill.com; south side of Fremont Bridge.* &

Ray's Boathouse / ★★
Ray's Cafe / ★★

6049 SEAVIEW AVE NW, SEATTLE; 206/789-3770 Ray's Boathouse is a Northwest icon. No wonder; it looks like a yacht club and has peerless views of Shilshole Bay and the Olympic Mountains. The landmark consistently turns out such Northwest fish-house staples as whole Dungeness crabs steamed fresh out of the live tank, or Manila clams in butter and dill broth. There's also Mediterraneanata such as savory roasted garlic cheesecake. Salmon is always great (Ray's was the first restaurant to acquire its own fish buyer's license), and fish is usually wild and always fresh. The rich black cod is a signature selection, which can be applewood smoked or marinated kasu style in sake lees. Expect an extensive Northwest wine list. Ray's Cafe upstairs serves lighter fare, such as fish-and-chips, burgers, or blackened red rockfish. Diehards sit on the cafe's outside deck, toddy in hand, year-round—servers bring blankets if you're chilled. *$$$; $$; AE, DC, DIS, MC, V; checks OK; dinner every day (Boathouse), lunch, dinner every day (Cafe); full bar; reservations recommended (Boathouse); rays@rays.com; www.rays.com; Ballard.* &

Rover's / ★★★★

2808 E MADISON ST, SEATTLE; 206/325-7442 Though chef-owner Thierry Rautureau has won the hearts of Seattleites, half his customers are out-of-towners making pilgrimages to his restaurant tucked into a garden courtyard in Madison Valley. His inspired hand in the kitchen has won him national renown. Choose from three prix-fixe *menus de dégustation* (one is vegetarian) served beautifully. Rautureau's forte is seafood, and he's adept at finding the best-quality ingredients. He's a master of sauces, using stocks, reductions, herb-infused oils, and purées to enhance breasts of quail, slices of sturgeon, steamed Maine lobster, wild mushrooms, Russian caviar, and foie gras. One knockout regular appetizer: eggs scrambled with garlic and chives, then layered with crème fraîche and lime juice in an eggshell cut into a tiny cup and topped with white sturgeon caviar. Expect professional service from Rautureau's servers, and sticker shock when perusing the extensive wine list. Dining in the courtyard, weather permitting, is enchanting. *$$$$; AE, DC, MC, V; checks OK; dinner Tues–Sat; beer and wine; reservations required; www.rovers-seattle.com; Madison Valley.* &

Sea Garden / ★★
Sea Garden of Bellevue / ★★

509 7TH AVE S, SEATTLE; 206/623-2100 / 200 106TH AVE NE, BELLEVUE; 425/450-8833 Live tanks with crabs and lobsters at the door are a clue to what's best in this busy Cantonese eatery in Seattle's Chinatown/International District and downtown Bellevue. Sip a Tsingtao while the waiter brings your lobster to the table for approval. It'll return soon, sliced in a black-bean sauce or wearing ginger and green onion. Don't miss the oysters with roast pork, or the double mushroom scallops. Try panfried sliced rock cod, or panfried squid in shrimp paste. Meats are great too—perhaps pork chops fried crispy and soaked in garlic honey sauce. Boneless duck steamed with eight kinds of meat and vegetables is a signature dish. Ask for chow fun noodles when ordering the Sea Garden special chow mein. *$; $$; AE, DC, MC, V; no checks; lunch, dinner every day; full bar; reservations recommended; Chinatown/International District (Seattle), at SE 2nd St (Bellevue).* &

Shiro's / ★★★½

2401 2ND AVE, SEATTLE; 206/443-9844 Shiro Kashiba introduced the concept of sushi to generations of Seattleites at his legendary Nikko, and they loved him for it. After 20 years, he sold Nikko to the Westin Hotel and then he opened Shiro's in 1995. In the simple, immaculate dining room, a small menu offers full-course dinner entrees including tempura, sukiyaki, and teriyaki. Kasu-style black cod is not to be missed. Hundreds of sushi variations are the main event, and the blond hardwood sushi bar is always jammed with an amazing mix of people: Japanese tourists, Belltown hipsters, business types—sushi fanatics all. There's a nice selection of sakes; desserts range from red bean ice cream to fresh peeled persimmon. *$$$; AE, MC, V; no checks; dinner every day; full bar; reservations recommended; Belltown.* &

Wild Ginger Asian Restaurant and Satay Bar / ★★★

1401 3RD AVE, SEATTLE; 206/623-4450 The wildly popular Wild Ginger has moved into larger, sleeker digs but still brings Seattle the best dishes from the streets and restaurants of Bangkok, Singapore, Saigon, and Djakarta. The new space features 100 more seats, private rooms, and a second-story cocktail lounge overlooking a bar below. Owners Rick and Ann Yoder bought the historic Mann Building in 1996 and spent millions renovating the decayed structure. Locals complain it lacks the coziness of the old space, but we'll have to get used to it. Service is as professional as always, and executive chef Jeem Han Lock has retained many old favorites including *laksa*, Malaysian seafood soup, and sliced fragrant duck breast to smear with plum sauce and tuck into little pillows of house-made bao. At the satay bar, order from a wide array of skewers: simple seared slices of sweet onion and Chinese eggplant, tender Bangkok boar seasoned with cumin and turmeric and basted with coconut milk, or lamb tenderloin with traditional peanut sauce. The wine list carries primarily West Coast producers. *$$$; AE, DIS, MC, V; no checks; lunch Mon–Sat, dinner every day; full bar; reservations recommended; downtown.* &

LODGINGS

Ace Hotel / ★★

2423 1ST AVE, SEATTLE; 206/448-4721 This newcomer to the lodgings scene (1999) offers futuristic—and surprisingly affordable—relief from dowdy hotel furnishings. The location (above Cyclops Cafe), owners (one a founder of Rudy's Barbershop), and press clippings (*Wallpaper** and *Details*) all lend the place hipster credibility. The 24 rooms (10 more rooms were being added at press time) are smartly stark: low beds adorned with wool French Army blankets, stainless-steel sinks and vanities, and funky art. Standard rooms (all have full-sized beds) share six large bathrooms down the hall. Those who don't relish communal washrooms can opt for more expensive deluxe rooms (15 of these) with private baths and king- or queen-sized beds. Amenities include small wall TVs, phones with data ports, and—in deluxes—CD players. No room service here, but there is an abundance of good eating in the area. Extras such as condoms and a copy of the *Kama Sutra* at the end of the bed distinguish the Ace as a grown-up getaway (although kids are welcome). For a quiet evening, avoid rooms on the noisy First Avenue side. Pets OK. *$$–$$$; AE, DC, DIS, JCB, MC, V; checks OK; reservation@theacehotel.com; www.theacehotel.com; Belltown.*

Alexis Hotel / ★★★

1007 1ST AVE, SEATTLE; 206/624-4844 OR 800/426-7033 The Alexis marries hedonism and elegance inside a turn-of-the-19th-century building. Even at 109 rooms (including 44 spacious suites), it has an intimate feel. (Request a room facing the inner courtyard, because rooms above First Avenue can be noisy.) Some suites include Jacuzzis or wood-burning fireplaces, but for sheer indulgence book one of the spa suites with two-person tubs. An on-site Aveda spa provides in-spa or in-room services (the hotel also has an on-call masseuse). Amenities range from voice mail, data ports, and complimentary morning tea and coffee to evening wine tasting, shoeshines, and a guest membership to the Seattle Club. Imaginative touches include in-line skating tours and a John Lennon suite, complete with original art. The Painted Table restaurant serves innovative Northwest cuisine; the Bookstore Bar is a cozy, though smoky, nook for libations. Pets OK. *$$$–$$$$; AE, DC, DIS, E, JCB, MC, V; checks OK; seattleres@kimptongroup.com; www.alexis hotel.com; downtown.* ♿

The Bacon Mansion Bed & Breakfast / ★★

959 BROADWAY E, SEATTLE; 206/329-1864 OR 800/240-1864 Built by Cecil Bacon in 1909, this Edwardian Tudor-style mansion is a B&B replete with old-world finery. Nine rooms in the main guest house (seven with private baths) are appointed with antiques and brass fixtures. Top of the line is the Capitol Suite, a huge second-floor room with a sunroom, fireplace, pine empress bed, and peep-hole view of the Space Needle (most visible during winter months when trees aren't in full bloom). The Emerald Suite sports a sleigh bed, fireplace, and claw-footed tub with shower. The Carriage House, a separate two-story building, is appropriate for a small family or two couples. A peaceful rose garden is in the courtyard, and Broadway's numerous restaurants and shops are a brief walk away. Proprietor Daryl King is an enthusiastic, friendly host. *$$–$$$; AE, DIS, MC, V; checks OK; info@baconmansion.com; www.baconmansion.com; Capitol Hill.*

Best Western Pioneer Square Hotel / ★★

77 YESLER WY, SEATTLE; 206/340-1234 OR 800/800-5514 This genteel four-story brick hotel doesn't flaunt its Best Western connection, which is probably an attempt to maintain an air of boutiqueness. Handsomely appointed, moderately priced, this is a boon for travelers intent on staying in the heart of historical Seattle. The 76 guest rooms (some scarcely larger than the bed) feature sturdy cherrywood furniture and, in some, small sitting alcoves. These surprisingly quiet rooms (the hotel is a block from the busy Alaskan Way Viaduct) come with a king or two doubles, or a queen in economy rooms. Guests in search of a view should avoid rooms on the south side, which face the back of another building. Sleepyheads will find the complimentary continental breakfast pretty picked over by 7:30am. Pioneer Square can be edgy, so timid travelers might opt for a more gentrified neighborhood, but those looking for an authentic urban experience will find it here. Kids under 12 stay free. *$$; AE, DC, DIS, JCB, MC, V; no checks; info@pioneersquare.com; www.pioneersquare.com; between 1st Ave S and Alaskan Wy.* ♿

Best Western University Tower Hotel / ★★

4507 BROOKLYN AVE NE, SEATTLE; 206/634-2000 OR 800/899-0251 It has lost its heritage moniker—Edmond Meany Hotel (named after a popular turn-of-the-19th-century University of Washington professor, mountaineer, and Seattle promoter)—but a $5-million renovation of this 15-story art deco tower has improved the place considerably. Hallways are trimmed in sunny yellows, reds, and blues, and rooms are brightly colored with plush feather beds, and modern amenities such as hair dryers, coffeemakers, ironing boards, and phones with data ports. The octagonal-tower design allows all 155 guest rooms (more than half of which contain king-sized beds) a view; those on the south side are sunny. There's no longer an on-site restaurant, but rates include a continental breakfast buffet, and the staff will order delivery from nearby restaurants. Mere blocks away are the UW campus and shopping on the Ave. *$$; AE, DC, DIS, MC, V; checks OK; www.universitytowerhotel.com; University District.* &

Chelsea Station on the Park / ★★

4915 LINDEN AVE N, SEATTLE; 206/547-6077 OR 800/400-6077 The neighborhood may not be near the city's major tourist destinations (with the exception of the superlative Woodland Park Zoo, just across the street), but this guest house has its own attractions. Situated in two 1929 brick homes in the Federal and Colonial Revival style, the inn is dressed in Craftsman-style furniture. Each of nine guest rooms comes with an antique king- or queen-sized bed and private bath. The topfloor Margaret suite offers three rooms and a view to the Cascades, the Sunlight suite features an endearingly retro kitchen, and the Morning Glory suite has a piano. Traffic is a little noisy on the north side, but this is mainly a quiet neighborhood. Generous gourmet breakfasts of stuffed French toast, Mexican scrambles, smokedsalmon hash, or banana nut pancakes are served downstairs. No children under age 6. *$$; AE, DC, DIS, MC, V; checks OK; 3-night min Apr–Oct; info@bandbseattle.com; www.bandbseattle.com; 1 block west of Hwy 99.*

Claremont Hotel / ★★★

2000 4TH AVE, SEATTLE; 206/448-8600 OR 877/448-8600 The light, airy rooms in this 1926 building enjoy prime downtown real estate: three blocks from Pike Place Market and Pacific Place, and a block and a half from the Monorail. Guest rooms offer one king- or queen-sized bed, two queens, or two doubles, as well as sitting areas and private bathrooms. Artsy touches include handmade glass pieces and framed botanicals on the walls. Junior Suites come with granite wet bars, while Executive Suites have separate living rooms and bedrooms. For longer stays, a few rooms with kitchens are available. Also available is an Apartment Suite, with a full kitchen, living room, and bedroom with two queen-sized beds. All rooms provide robes, hair dryers, irons and ironing boards, two-line phones with data ports, and voice mail. Upper floors boast views of downtown, Puget Sound, the Space Needle, Lake Union, and the Olympics. On the ground floor, Assaggio Ristorante is an excellent northern Italian eatery. *$$$; AE, DC, DIS, JCB, MC, V; checks OK; stay@claremonthotel.com; www.claremonthotel.com; Belltown.* &

The Edgewater / ★★★

2411 ALASKAN WY/PIER 67, SEATTLE; 206/728-7000 OR 800/624-0670 The Edgewater has its share of unusual claims to fame. It's the only Seattle hotel literally over the water (if watching whitecaps makes you dizzy, avoid firstfloor rooms). And, in 1964, the Beatles checked in and dropped fishing lines out their window (see the Fab Four photo in the gift shop). You can't fish from the windows anymore, but you can still breathe salty air and watch the ferry traffic. And now the 241-room hotel has a flashy new metal log-cabin exterior (aluminum shingles evoke silvery fish scales). The remodel extends to the lobby and rooms dressed in updated Northwest lodge: bark pillars with antlerlike branches, antler furniture, fireplaces, and log bed frames. The new Six Seven Restaurant & Lounge serves Northwest cuisine with pan-Asian influences, a sushi bar, and uninterrupted views of Elliott Bay,

Puget Sound, and the Olympics. It's a short walk to Bell Street Pier (Pier 66), with restaurants, the Odyssey Maritime Discovery Center, and an overpass to nearby Pike Place Market. Pets OK. *$$$; AE, DC, DIS, MC, V; checks OK; reservations@edge waterhotel.com; www.edgewaterhotel.com; waterfront.* &

Elliott Grand Hyatt Seattle / ★★★

721 PINE ST, SEATTLE; 206/774-1234 OR 800/233-1234 Seattle's newest megahotel opened in 2001 sporting an arsenal of high-tech extras, including bedside switches that raise and lower drapes. Adjacent to the convention center, the Elliott is poised to embrace a slew of conventioneers, with 425 guest rooms and 113 suites. An earth-tone Northwest motif runs from the expansive lobby to the backlit marble panels in hallways. Rooms begin on the 10th floor, so nearly every view reveals at least a sliver of water or mountain. All rooms have one king or two full beds, cotton linens, refrigerators, complimentary high-speed Internet access, and separate glassed-in marble showers and deep cast-iron bathtubs with cascading faucets. Huge 800-square-foot suites, with separate living and sleeping areas, add flat-screen televisions, wet bars, and dual-head showers to the list of features. The well-regarded 727 Pine restaurant serves "eclectic Northwest cuisine." Of course, any hotel guest can indulge in 24-hour room service. The hotel's first few months had a few new-hotel wobbles, but the place will no doubt evolve into a well-oiled part of the Hyatt machine. *$$$; AE, DC, DIS, JCB, MC, V; checks OK; sales@seaghp.hyatt.com; www.hyatt.com; downtown.* &

Four Seasons Olympic Hotel / ★★★★

411 UNIVERSITY ST, SEATTLE; 206/621-1700 OR 800/821-8106 Guests who want to be pampered and coddled spare no expense and book rooms at the Four Seasons. Smiling maids, quick-as-a-wink bellhops, and a team of caring concierges ensure round-the-clock comfort at this posh 1920s landmark. The hotel's old-world luxury extends from the newly updated 450 guest rooms and suites—furnished with king or two oversized twin beds; baths with showers and soaking tubs and terry-cloth robes; and freshly replaced carpets, drapes, and bedding—to its venerable The Georgian restaurant (see review). Executive suites feature down-dressed king-sized beds separated from elegant sitting rooms by French doors. Several refined meeting rooms and shops flank the lobby. Enjoy afternoon tea in The Georgian (or in The Garden during the holidays), work out in the health club, or relax in the solarium hot tub and pool (a massage therapist is on call). Four Seasons' prices are steep, but this is Seattle's one world-class contender. Deposits required for cash guests. The hotel goes out of its way for kids, right down to a toy in the crib and a step stool in the bathroom. Pets OK. *$$$$; AE, DC, DIS, JCB, MC, V; checks OK; www.fourseasons.com/seattle; downtown.* &

Hotel Monaco / ★★★

1101 4TH AVE, SEATTLE; 206/621-1770 OR 800/945-2240 It's nearly impossible to be depressed—even on Seattle's grayest days—when confronted by the sunny Mediterranean look of Hotel Monaco. The upbeat mood is set in the lobby—with its nautical mural of dolphins—and sealed in the boldly designed rooms. All 189 are decorated in a blend of eye-popping stripes and florals that may strike some as insanely busy, and others as utterly charming. All rooms come equipped with queen-

or king-sized beds; Mediterranean Suites feature deluxe bathrooms with two-person Fujijet tubs. As with many local hotels, views take a backseat to service and design (business travelers appreciate 6,000 square feet of meeting space). Monaco's campy principality extends to the Southern-inspired Sazerac restaurant. Pets OK (or ask for a loaner goldfish). *$$$$; AE, DC, DIS, JCB, MC, V; checks OK; seattleres@kimpton group.com; www.monaco-seattle.com; downtown.* &

Hotel Vintage Park / ★★★

1100 5TH AVE, SEATTLE; 206/624-8000 OR 800/624-4433 The Vintage Park takes its "vintage" theme to the limit: rooms are named after wineries, with updated Tuscany-inspired decor, and complimentary fireside wine tastings every evening. Part of the San Francisco–based Kimpton Group, the personable Park offers rooms facing inward or outward (exterior rooms have a bit more space, but forget about views) with two doubles or one king- or queen-sized bed. Rooms come with fax machines, hair dryers, irons and ironing boards, double phone lines with data ports, and phones in the bathrooms. Unfortunately, a nearby busy Interstate 5 on-ramp makes lower floors a bit noisy; soundproofing helps on upper floors. There's lightning-fast 24-hour room service, including lunch or dinner from the hotel's tasty Italian restaurant Tulio. Pets OK. *$$$; AE, DC, DIS, JCB, MC, V; checks OK; seattleres@kimptongroup.com; www.vintagepark.com; downtown.* &

Inn at Harbor Steps / ★★

1221 1ST AVE, SEATTLE; 206/748-0973 OR 888/728-8910 The Inn at Harbor Steps couples an in-the-thick-of it location with quiet-getaway ambience. Tucked inside a swanky retail-and-residential high-rise across from the Seattle Art Museum, rooms are shielded from the surrounding urban hubbub. The second Northwest property (after Whidbey Island's Saratoga Inn) from the California-based Four Sisters Inns, the inn offers 25 rooms with citified furnishings, garden views, fireplaces (excepting five of the rooms), air conditioning, king- or queen-sized beds, sitting areas, wet bars, refrigeratorss, data ports, and voice mail. Deluxe rooms include spa tubs. Amenities include 24-hour concierge/innkeeper services, room service from the Wolfgang Puck Cafe (4–10pm), complimentary evening hors d'oeuvres and wine, and full gourmet breakfast. Guests have access to an indoor pool, sauna, Jacuzzi, exercise room, and meeting rooms. *$$$; AE, DC, JCB, MC, V; no checks; www.foursisters.com; downtown.* &

Inn at the Market / ★★★★

86 PINE ST, SEATTLE; 206/443-3600 OR 800/446-4484 Perfectly positioned to capture all the wonders of bustling Pike Place Market, this 70-room brick inn remains unhurried and intimate. An ivy-draped courtyard wraps around its entrance and high-end retailers and restaurants, including country-French Campagne (see review). Newly updated rooms are handsomely dressed in a Biedermeier scheme of soft taupe, copper, and green (replacing Laura Ashley decor). Rooms above the fifth floor afford views, and those on the west have floor-to-ceiling windows that open to breezes off the Sound and unmatched vistas. Other amenities include in-room safes and refrigerators, and oversized bathrooms. Rise early to sample the market's fresh pastries and fruit. Or sleep late and indulge in room service from Bacco in the courtyard. In-room dinners come courtesy of Campagne (5–10pm). Campagne's bar is a snug, if smoky, spot for a nightcap. *$$$–$$$$; AE, DC, DIS, JCB, MC, V; checks OK; info@innatthemarket. com; www.innatthemarket.com; Pike Place Market.* &

MV Challenger Bunk & Breakfast / ★

1001 FAIRVIEW AVE N, STE 1600, SEATTLE; 206/340-1201 OR 877/340-1201 Rooms with water views aren't unusual in Seattle, but most don't come through a porthole. This perky red-and-white two-level 1944 tug moored on south Lake Union offers eight rooms, five with their own baths. The top-level Admiral's Cabin features a four-poster queen bed, soaking bath, and spectacular view. You won't find luxury on board; some quarters are tight, ladders between floors are steep, and the rooms are slightly worn. But this "bunk & breakfast" is filled with charming details: navigation charts as wallpaper, nautical brass fixtures, a comfy sitting room with a fireplace, a 300-plus videotape library. A full buffet breakfast is served in a cozy solarium, and there's 24-hour coffee and tea service. Eateries are steps away, as is the fascinating Center for Wooden Boats. Weather allowing, the tug takes a short daily cruise on Lake Union. Longer multiday trips on Puget Sound and to the San Juan Islands are also available—check the web site for schedule. *$$–$$$; AE, DC, DIS, JCB, MC, V; checks OK; www.tugboatchallenger. com; South Lake Union.*

Paramount Hotel / ★★

724 PINE ST, SEATTLE; 206/292-9500 OR 800/426-0670 The Paramount's relatively modest size—146 guest rooms, two small meeting rooms, and a tiny fitness center—appeals to those who eschew nearby megahotels. Standard guest rooms, though small, are prettily appointed, as are bathrooms. Each room includes phone with data port and voice mail, movie and game systems, coffeemaker, hair dryer, and iron. Consider splurging for a corner "executive king," roomier and outfitted with a fireplace and whirlpool tub. The adjoining pan-Asian-inspired Dragonfish Asian Cafe is trendy but tasty. *$$$; AE, DC, DIS, MC, V; checks OK; www.westcoasthotels. com/paramount; downtown.* &

Pensione Nichols / ★☆

1923 1ST AVE, SEATTLE; 206/441-7125 OR 800/440-7125 Bohemian atmosphere, a superb location (perched above Pike Place Market), and reasonable prices set Pensione Nichols apart from the crowd. Though some find the furnishings too well-worn, others are enchanted by the lovely antiques from the 1920s and '30s. Ten guest rooms share four bathrooms. Some rooms face noisy First Avenue; others don't have windows, but have bright skylights and are quieter. Also available: two spacious suites with private baths, full kitchens, and living rooms with jaw-dropping water views. A large, appealing common room on the third floor has a stunning view of Elliott Bay; it's here the bountiful breakfast—including fresh treats from the market—is served. Be warned—the stair climb from street level is a big one. No kids; well-behaved pets OK. *$$; AE, DC, DIS, MC, V; checks OK; 2-night min summer weekends; www.seattle-bed-breakfast.com; near Pike Place Market.*

Sheraton Seattle Hotel and Towers / ★★☆

1400 6TH AVE, SEATTLE; 206/621-9000 OR 800/325-3535 A megalith looming over the downtown convention center, the Sheraton goes all out for business travelers. While its 840 guest rooms are smallish and standard, emphasis is given to meeting rooms and restaurants. On the first floor are the lobby lounge and an oyster bar, as well as the casual Pike Street Cafe (home to a famous 27-foot dessert bar) and Andiamo's, a pizza and pasta place. (The Sheraton's former fine-dining restaurant, Fullers, was converted to a private dining facility in 2001.) Discriminating businesspeople head for the upper four Club Rooms (31–34), where they'll find their own lobby, concierge, private lounge, and complimentary continental breakfast and hors d'oeuvres. The 35th-floor health club features a heated pool and knockout city panorama (unfortunately, if you're not staying in the Club Rooms, you'll have to pay to use it—rates run $5 per day or $10 per stay). *$$$–$$$$; AE, DC, DIS, JCB, MC, V; checks OK; www.sheraton.com; downtown.* &

Sorrento Hotel / ★★★☆

900 MADISON ST, SEATTLE; 206/622-6400 OR 800/426-1265 Opened in 1909, the Sorrento is an Italianate masterpiece grandly holding court on its own corner east of downtown in Seattle's First Hill neighborhood. The beauty of the Sorrento is in the details: a softly lit lobby, elegant furnishings, rose petals left on your pillow in the evening (or hot water bottles in winter months). Despite their historic feel, the 76 tastefully decorated rooms include coffeemakers, direct TV, CD players, and dual-line cordless phones with data ports. There's also a small exercise room. Top-floor suites make posh quarters for meetings or parties—the showstopper being the 2,000-square-foot, $1,800-a-night penthouse, with a grand piano, fireplace, patio, Jacuzzi, and view of Elliott Bay. The Fireside Room off the lobby is a civilized place for taking high tea, or sipping Cognac while listening to jazz piano in the evening. The manly Hunt Club serves Mediterranean-influenced cuisine. Complimentary town-car service takes guests downtown. Some travelers consider the Sorrento's location—five blocks uphill from the heart of the city—inconvenient, but we find it quiet and removed. Small pets OK. *$$$$; AE, DC, DIS, JCB, MC, V; checks OK; mail@hotelsorrento.com; www.hotelsorrento.com; First Hill.* &

W Seattle Hotel / ★★★☆

1112 4TH AVE, SEATTLE; 206/264-6000 OR 877/W-HOTELS The W's see-and-be-seen lobby alone merits a cover charge—indeed, sometimes the staff pumps up techno dance music to give the place a nightclub feel. Colorful postmodern art adorns the walls, chocolate-velvet drapes run the length of the high windows, and plush modern furniture is situated between oversized chess sets and stylish magazines. Naturally, it's a magnet for black-garbed people with cell phones or froufrou drinks, as is the adjacent bar leading to the hotel's Earth and Ocean restaurant. The staff is also clad in black, but thankfully lacks the hipper-than-thou attitude. Rooms are chicly colored in taupe and black and outfitted with stainless-and-glass-appointed bathrooms, safes, irons and ironing boards, coffeemakers, desks, and Zen-inspired water sculptures. Many rooms (particularly higher corner rooms) have impressive downtown views; all have two double or one king-sized W Signature Bed sheathed in goose-down duvets and pillows, and 250-thread-count linens. Honor bars wittily yield mints, wax lips, and "intimacy kits." Room service is 24 hours, as is the fitness room; stylish meeting space totals 10,000 square feet. All W rooms are wired: each equipped with 27-inch TV with Internet access, CD and video player, two-line desk phone with high-speed Internet connection, voice mail, and a cordless handset. A Pet Amenity Program provides plush pet beds and treats for your pooch. *$$$$; AE, DC, DIS, JCB, MC, V; checks OK; www.whotels.com; downtown.* ⅏

Westin Hotel / ★★⯪

1900 5TH AVE, SEATTLE; 206/728-1000 OR 800/WESTIN-1 The Westin's twin cylindrical towers evoke all sorts of comparisons by local wits: corncobs, trash cans, mountain-bike handlebars. Nonetheless, they do provide spacious rooms with unbeatable views, particularly above the 20th floor. The hefty size of the hotel (891 rooms and 34 suites) contributes to some lapses in service: the check-in counter can resemble a busy day at Sea-Tac Airport. However, rooms are smartly furnished, and all beds (king or double) come with pillow-top mattresses and luxurious 300-thread-count linens. On the top floors are ritzy, glitzy suites. Hotel amenities are corporate-minded: business center, convention facilities spread over several floors, and a multilingual staff. You'll also find a large pool and Jacuzzi with city view, and an exercise room. The Westin's location, near Westlake Center and the Monorail station, is excellent, as are meals at Nikko, a Japanese restaurant, and Roy's (where gooey-in-the-center chocolate soufflés are reason enough to pay a visit). *$$$$; AE, DC, DIS, JCB, MC, V; checks OK; www.westin.com; downtown.* ⅏

The Eastside

The suburbs—and suburban cities—on the east side of Lake Washington across from Seattle are collectively known as "the Eastside." They include Bellevue, Redmond, Kirkland, Woodinville, and Issaquah. The **EAST KING COUNTY CONVENTION & VISITORS BUREAU** (425/455-1926; www.eastkingcounty.org) has the lowdown on Eastside goings-on.

Bellevue

Washington's fourth-largest city has been making noises for years about shaking its shopping-mall image. It has an impressive downtown skyline populated by thriving high-tech firms (including Attachmate and drugstore.com). The fairly new **MEYDENBAUER CENTER** (11100 NE 6th St; 425/637-1020) hosts myriad arts performances. Even the **BELLEVUE ART MUSEUM** (510 Bellevue Wy NE; 425/519-0770), long kidded about its former shopping-mall locale, has a new, boldly designed $23-million home across from its old site.

But shopping is still the main attraction. Consider the conglomeration of retail might: **BELLEVUE SQUARE** (NE 8th St; 425/454-8096), packed with a triple-decker Nordstrom store and new Crate & Barrel, plus 200 shops and restaurants; kitty-corner is glitzy **BELLEVUE PLACE** (10500 NE 8th; 425/453-5634); and, farther east, family-oriented **CROSSROADS SHOPPING CENTER** (15600 NE 8th; 425/644-1111). The new **BELLEVUE GALLERIA** along 106th Street is more strip-style tacky (read: Hooter's), but pulls in traffic with its cinemas, Rock Bottom Restaurant & Brewery, and Tower Records. The barn-sized **BARNES & NOBLE** bookstore (626 106th NE; 425/644-1650) is worth a look. And, the 19-acre **DOWNTOWN PARK**, possessed of a fine waterfall and promenade, in the southern shadow of Bellevue Square offers shoppers a nature break.

RESTAURANTS

Bis on Main / ★★

10213 MAIN ST, BELLEVUE; 425/455-2033 Joe Vilardi has successfully filled a gap in the Eastside dining scene. Using his knowledge and experience from Seattle's Il Terrazzo Carmine (see review), he created a serene respite from the franchised places so typical of the Eastside. Nothing on the dinner menu is too challenging, but everything is expertly executed and served, such as lamb roulade stuffed with spinach, hazelnuts, and mushrooms braised in red wine and finished with mustard. Mr. V's generous and crisp Dungeness crab cakes are accompanied by garlic tartar sauce and coleslaw tossed with apple cider vinaigrette. Dredge enough crusty bread through the brandy peppercorn sauce bathing pan-seared veal sirloin, and dessert becomes irrelevant. *$$; AE, DC, DIS, JCB, MC, V; checks OK; lunch Mon–Fri, dinner Mon–Sat; beer and wine; reservations recommended; www.bisonmain.com; 2 blocks west of Bellevue Wy.*

Noble Court / ★★

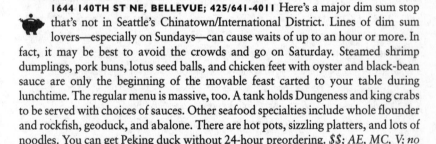

1644 140TH ST NE, BELLEVUE; 425/641-4011 Here's a major dim sum stop that's not in Seattle's Chinatown/International District. Lines of dim sum lovers—especially on Sundays—can cause waits of up to an hour or more. In fact, it may be best to avoid the crowds and go on Saturday. Steamed shrimp dumplings, pork buns, lotus seed balls, and chicken feet with oyster and black-bean sauce are only the beginning of the movable feast carted to your table during lunchtime. The regular menu is massive, too. A tank holds Dungeness and king crabs to be served with choices of sauces. Other seafood specialties include whole flounder and rockfish, geoduck, and abalone. There are hot pots, sizzling platters, and lots of noodles. You can get Peking duck without 24-hour preordering. *$$; AE, MC, V; no checks; lunch, dinner Mon–Fri, dim sum Sat–Sun; full bar; reservations recommended; off Bellevue-Redmond Rd.* &

LODGINGS

Bellevue Club Hotel / ★★★

11200 SE 6TH ST, BELLEVUE; 425/454-4424 OR 800/579-1110 From the sunken tubs in every room to original pieces by Northwest artists, the Bellevue Club's accommodations are some of the Eastside's most opulent. The 67 rooms are strikingly swathed in Asian-inspired colors—lots of soothing neutrals, browns, and grays—and furnished in cherrywood pieces custom-made on Whidbey Island. Many overlook tennis courts; Club Guest rooms' French doors open onto private terra-cotta patios. There's ample opportunity to work up a sweat at the extensive athletic facilities, including an Olympic-sized swimming pool; indoor tennis, racquetball, and squash courts; and

READ ALL ABOUT IT

Seattleites are bookworms. They spend double the national average on books every year, and are avid borrowers from the public library. Their page-turning proclivities ensure that you don't have to go far here to find a store selling new or used titles. Although they don't often write about the city, many well-known authors live and work in the area: Tom Robbins, Charles Johnson, Rebecca Wells, Jonathan Raban, Rebecca Brown, Brenda Peterson, and Pete Dexter, to name a few. Here's a short list of works that will help you learn more about Seattle and the Puget Sound region:

In *The Forging of a Black Community* (University of Washington Press, 1994), Quintard Taylor examines the often troubled evolution of Seattle's Central District from 1870 through the civil-rights struggles of the 1960s.

In *Rains All the Time: A Connoisseur's History of Weather in the Pacific Northwest* (Sasquatch Books, 1997), David Laskin recounts the history of this region's infamous relationship with "liquid sunshine."

Walt Crowley's *National Trust Guide Seattle* (John Wiley & Sons, 1998) gives a wonderful overview of the city's architecture and history that locals and visitors can enjoy.

Seattle City Walks (Sasquatch Books, 1999), by Laura Karlinsey, provides easy-to-use, detailed walking tours of various neighborhoods, with historical and cultural details.

Skid Road (Comstock, 1978), by Murray Morgan, is an irreverent look back at some of the events and eccentrics responsible for creating the Seattle we know today.

One of our most beloved regional books, *The Egg and I* (J. R. Lippincott Co., 1945), by Betty MacDonald, is a whimsical memoir of life on a Washington chicken ranch.

In *The Natural History of Puget Sound Country* (University of Washington Press, 1991), Arthur R. Kruckeberg offers insights into the region's environment.

A Voyage of Discovery to the North Pacific Ocean and Round the World (G. G. and J. Robinson, 1798), is explorer George Vancouver's recording of Northwest history.

Writer Sallie Tisdale (*Stepping Westward: The Long Search for Home in the Pacific Northwest;* Henry Holt, 1991) and *New York Times* correspondent Timothy Egan (*The Good Rain: Across Time and Terrain in the Pacific Northwest;* Alfred A. Knopf, 1990) offer contemporary perspectives on the region.

For more detailed touring information, pick up *Best Places Seattle* (Sasquatch, 2002).

—*J. Kingston Pierce*

aerobics classes. Oversized limestone-and-marble bathrooms—with spalike tubs—are perfect for postworkout soaks. The club offers fine dining at Polaris restaurant, and casual fare at the Sport Cafe. *$$$–$$$$; AE, DC, MC, V; checks OK; hotel@bellevueclub.com; www.bellevueclub.com; at 112th Ave SE.* &

Hyatt Regency at Bellevue Place / ★★

900 BELLEVUE WY NE, BELLEVUE; 425/462-1234 OR 800/233-1234 A platinum card's throw from Bellevue Square, this Hyatt is part of the splashy, sprawling retail-office-restaurant-hotel-health club complex called Bellevue Place. The 382-room, 24-story hotel offers many extras: pricier Regency Club rooms on the top three floors, some great views (particularly southside rooms above the seventh floor), two big ballrooms, several satellite conference rooms, use of the neighboring Bellevue Place Club (for $8), and a restaurant, Eques, serving Pacific Rim cuisine. *$$$–$$$$; AE, DC, DIS, JCB, MC, V; checks OK; www.hyatt.com; at NE 8th St.* &

Redmond

Once a bucolic valley farming community, Redmond today is a sprawling McTown of freeway overpasses, offices (Microsoft and Nintendo are headquartered here), subdivisions, and retail, including the open-air, 100-plus-shop **REDMOND TOWN CENTER AND CINEMAS** (16495 NE 74th; 425/867-0808). Some of Redmond's pastoral past remains. It's not dubbed the bicycle capital of the Northwest for nothing: bikers can pedal the 10-mile **SAMMAMISH RIVER TRAIL** or check out races on the 400-meter **MARYMOOR VELODROME** (2400 Lake Sammamish Pkwy; 206/675-1424; www.marymoor.velodrome.org). In summer, 522-acre **MARYMOOR PARK** (6046 W Lake Sammamish Pkwy NE; 206/296-2966) draws crowds for picnics and an annual horse show.

RESTAURANTS

Il Bacio / ★★

16564 CLEVELAND ST, REDMOND; 425/869-8815 Despite its Redmond strip-mall setting, an old-fashioned ambience—neoclassical statuary, tables set with maroon-on-white napery, tux-shirted servers—imbues this popular Italian bistro. Italian-born chef Rino Baglio (he's even cooked for two princesses) does his part by creating authentic dishes: antipasti such as chopped salad with cheese, salami, and mushrooms, or clams sautéed with garlic, white wine, and fresh tomatoes. A specialty is tenderloin of buffalo wrapped in prosciutto, with demi-glace of barolo wine. Try the herbed veal chop served with wild mushrooms, or Risotto di Novara, a peasant dish of Italian arborio rice, sausage, Tuscan beans, sage, and fresh tomato sauce. There are plenty of great pastas here, including penne puttanesca with olive oil, tomato, olives, capers, and anchovies, or Baglio's angel hair pasta with lobster meat in a fresh tomato sauce. *$$; AE, DC, DIS, JCB, MC ,V; no checks; lunch Mon–Fri, dinner every day; full bar; reservations recommended; ilbacioredmond@aol.com; www. ilbacio.com; across from Redmond Town Center.* &

Kirkland

Sure, there's a crunch of expensive condos and traffic, but this fetching town tucked into the eastern shore of Lake Washington has avoided the Eastside's typical strip-mall syndrome. People stroll here among congenially arranged eateries, galleries, and boutique retailers. In summer, sidewalks fill with locals and tourists, as do **PETER KIRK PARK** and the **KIRKLAND MARINA,** where you can catch an **ARGOSY**

(206/623-1445) boat for a lake cruise, April through September. Welcome downtown additions include the 402-seat **KIRKLAND PERFORMANCE CENTER** (350 Kirkland Ave; 425/893-9900). Even the obligatory mall, **KIRKLAND PARKPLACE** (6th St and Central Wy; 425/828-4468), doesn't spoil the townscape—it's several blocks east of the waterfront.

RESTAURANTS

Third Floor Fish Cafe / ★★★

205 LAKE ST S, KIRKLAND; 425/822-3553 It's a no-expectations, office-building elevator ride to dinner, but when you get to your third-floor destination, you'll be delighted. A set of stained-wood well-windowed rooms look out on Lake Washington. The signature grilled heart of romaine with apples, crispy bacon, and Roquefort is a must-sample. A Yukon Gold potato soup with Cougar Gold cheddar is a hearty choice when available. But, as the restaurant's name suggests, the best bet is fish, such as pan-seared salmon with fennel and red onion salad, or at least seafood, such as sea scallops with stewed organic vegetable ragout in a tarragon broth. Chef Greg Campbell makes five- and seven-course tasting menus with accompanying wines that are quite good, showing off his skills beyond fish. Desserts range from oven-roasted plum cake with plum caramel and whipped cream, to triple chocolate *semifreddo*. Service is unwaveringly polished and professional. The wine list of mostly domestics is carefully selected, but short at the low end, with just a bottle or two priced below $30. *$$$; AE, DC, DIS, MC, V; local checks only; dinner every day; full bar; reservations recommended; cafe@chaffeyhomes.com; www.fishcafe. com; on waterfront.* ᬫ

Yarrow Bay Grill / ★★★
Yarrow Bay Beach Café / ★★

1270 CARILLON POINT, KIRKLAND; 425/889-9052 (GRILL) OR 425/889-0303 (CAFÉ) These sibling restaurants stacked atop one another are joined at the hip—the Eastside casual hip, that is. Upstairs, the tony grill ranks in the upper echelons of price and quality among Kirkland places. New chef Felix Acosta continues the restaurant's pan-seared, pan-global approach with such diversities as Hawaiian sea bass, Cuban pork tenderloin, New England risotto, and Bangkok barbecue chicken. Every table has a lake view, the service is quite good, and there's a solid wine list. All of this makes the Grill a worthy destination. Downstairs, the Café has a clamorous Topsider-shod bar scene and Cameon Orel's riskier fare—get a shark quiche, tuna muffaletta, Vietnamese spring rolls with chorizo, or a burger. Delectable desserts range from Black Bottom Banana Cream Pie in the Café to, if you're lucky, Mexican Caramel Apple Flauta on the ever-changing upstairs Grill menu. *$$$; $$; AE, DC, DIS, JCB, MC, V; no checks; lunch Mon–Fri, dinner every day, brunch Sun (Grill), lunch, dinner every day (Café); full bar; reservations recommended; grillinfo@ybgrill.com, cafeinfo@ybbeachcafe.com; www.ybgrill.com, www.ybbeachcafe.com; Carillon Point.* ᬫ

LODGINGS

The Woodmark Hotel / ★★★

1200 CARILLON POINT, KIRKLAND; 425/822-3700 OR 800/822-3700 Still the only lodgings on the shore of Lake Washington, the Woodmark's singularity extends beyond its location. Despite its officelike exterior, this is one of the finest hotels in or out of Seattle. The Woodmark's 100 guest rooms (the best have lake views) all have one king- or two queen-sized beds, swim in cream-color furnishings and plush extras such as minibars and refrigerators, terry-cloth robes, and matchless service (from laundry to valet). Suites include the palatial Woodmark, with a lake-and-mountain view, dining space for six, lavish bathroom with Jacuzzi, 950 square feet of parlor space, entertainment center, and wet bar. Smaller suites feature varying parlor sizes. All guests get a complimentary newspaper and a chance to "raid the pantry" for late-night snacks and beverages. Downstairs is a comfortable Library Bar with a grand piano and a well-tended fire. The hotel's restaurant, Waters, features Northwest cuisine. *$$$–$$$$; AE, DC, JCB, MC, V; checks OK; mail@thewoodmark.com; www.thewoodmark.com; Carillon Point.* &

Woodinville

Oenophiles and hopheads (the microbrew kind) love this little Eastside town. **CHATEAU STE. MICHELLE** (14111 NE 145th St; 425/488-1133), the state's largest winery, offers daily tastings and tours and popular summer concerts on its lovely 87-acre estate. Across the street, **COLUMBIA WINERY** (14030 NE 145th St; 425/488-2776) has daily tastings and weekend tours. Or wet your whistle at one of the state's first microbreweries, **REDHOOK ALE BREWERY** (14300 NE 145th St; 425-483-3232), which, along with daily $1 tours (including a souvenir glass and plenty of samples), has a pub with tasty grub and live music Fridays and Saturdays.

RESTAURANTS

The Herbfarm / ★★★★

14590 NE 145TH ST, WOODINVILLE; 206/784-2222 The Herbfarm is a must-experience place for anyone who loves serious food and formal service, and can pay the freight. The nine-course prix-fixe dinner with accompanying wines costs around $175 per person. After a devastating fire, Ron Zimmerman and Carrie Van Dyke moved their foodie shrine to the Woodinville "wine country," near the Ste. Michelle and Columbia wineries, on the property of the posh Willows Lodge. Nationally renowned chef Jerry Traunfeld presides over menus that change with the seasons of local produce and herbs—much of which is grown in the Herbfarm's own gardens. This is the fastest five hours you'll ever spend. A night's repast could encompass tempura squash blossoms stuffed with goat cheese; crab salad with fennel and chives; sweet corn soup with smoked mussels and chanterelles; salmon smoked in basil wood; herb-crusted lamb; cheeses; a caramelized pear soufflé with rose geranium sauce; and a selection of small treats—lemon-thyme espresso truffles—to go with your coffee. Arrive a half hour before dinner for Van Dyke's tour around the gardens. This is a coveted, one-of-a-kind destination—reservations usually must be booked months in advance. *$$$$; AE, MC, V; checks OK; dinner Thurs–Sun; full bar; reservations required; reservations@theherbfarm.com; www.theherbfarm.com; next to Willows Lodge.* &

LODGINGS

Willows Lodge / ★★★✫

14580 NE 145TH ST, WOODINVILLE; 425/424-3900 OR 877/424-3930 This spectacular destination boutique hotel opened in September 2000 to unbridled accolades. The 88-room luxe lodge is surrounded by world-class wineries and voluptuous gardens, and features a lobby lined with 100-year-old reclaimed Douglas fir beams, a library, and an enormous stone-framed wood-burning fireplace. All rooms have fireplaces, king- or queen-sized beds, stereo-DVD-CD systems, high-speed Internet connections, lush bathrooms (some with jetted tubs and heated towel racks), and balconies or patios with views of the gardens, Chateau Ste. Michelle winery, the Sammamish River (and its popular bike trail), or Mount Rainier. The poshest of six suites ($750 per night) boasts a high-end Bang & Olufsen stereo, whirlpool bath, and flat-screen TV. Other amenities include a spa, 24-hour fitness room, and evening wine tastings. The gazebo in the herb garden shelters wedding ceremonies and other momentous events. The Barking Frog restaurant serves Mediterranean-influenced dinners and weekend brunch. Guests can also get reservations for nine-course meals at the renowned Herbfarm Restaurant (see review). *$$$–$$$$; AE, DC, DIS, JCB, MC, V; checks OK; mail@willowslodge.com; www.willowslodge.com; next to Redhook Brewery.* &

Issaquah

Though every so often a cougar shows up in this wealthy Cascade-foothills suburb 15 miles east of Seattle, Issaquah is pleasantly mild mannered. Historic **GILMAN VILLAGE** (317 NW Gilman Blvd; 425/392-6802), comprised of refurbished old farmhouses, offers an agreeable day of poking about in its 40 or so shops, and the **VILLAGE THEATRE** (120 Front St N and 303 Front St N; 425/392-2202) entertains with mostly original, mainly musical productions at two downtown theaters. Seattleites cross the Interstate 90 bridge in packs during summer weekends to "scale" the Issaquah Alps, which have miles of trails—from easy to challenging; the **ISSAQUAH ALPS TRAILS CLUB** (425/328-0480) offers organized hikes. For the ultimate in townfolk-wildlife bonding, drop in the first weekend of October for **ISSAQUAH SALMON DAYS** (425/392-7024), a celebration—including food, crafts, music, and a parade—marking the return of the salmon that surge up Issaquah Creek.

RESTAURANTS

Shanghai Garden / ★★★

80 FRONT ST N, ISSAQUAH; 425/313-3188 Shanghai Garden chef-owner Hua Te Su and family attract diners to this pink-hued restaurant with authentic Chinese dishes. Try the Shanghai favorite—soupy buns: flowery little packets of delicate dough twisted at the top containing combinations of minced pork, shrimp, or crab, each in a spoonful of hot broth. Prepare to be wowed by anything

made with pea vines or with the chef's hand-shaved noodles. Vivid green sugar pea tendrils resemble sautéed spinach and are tender and tasty, especially when paired with plump shrimp. The Shanghai emphasizes seafood. Especially memorable are pepper salted scallops, or pepper salted shrimp with a thin, crunchy M&M-like shell. This might be the only Chinese restaurant in town where desserts should not be missed. Su makes his own ice cream—try sour plum. *$; MC, V; no checks; lunch Mon–Fri, dinner every day; full bar; reservations recommended; at E Sunset Wy.* &

Bainbridge Island

Could these islanders be any friendlier? Spend a little time on Bainbridge and you'll soon understand why. They've got antique shops, galleries, and a perplexing number of good restaurants, not to mention stunning natural scenery: **FORT WARD STATE PARK** (2241 Pleasant Beach Dr NE; 206/842-4041) is perfect for picnics and the **BLOEDEL RESERVE** (7571 NE Dolphin Dr; 206/842-7631; open Wed–Sun by appointment) covers 150 gorgeous acres. Their commute is even stress-free: 35 minutes to Seattle on a seagull-chased ferry (see Access and Information). Fortunately, you can play native too.

RESTAURANTS

Cafe Nola / ★★☆

101 WINSLOW WY W, BAINBRIDGE; 206/842-3822 Cafe Nola is now run by Kevin and Whitney Warren, who bought the small, sunny corner cafe in 1999. Formerly a sous-chef at Marco's Supperclub in Seattle, Kevin creates pleasingly eclectic dishes. Popular with lunch crowds are hearty soups—from roasted eggplant to black-bean portobello—and the grilled salmon sandwich dressed with seasonal greens and sturdy Essential Bakery bread. Dinner brings forth Sichuan ribs basted with hoisin-pineapple sauce and sweet potato fries; pan-seared scallops served over yellow corn grit cakes with roasted pepper-garlic sauce; and not-to-miss desserts, such as triple-layer chocolate hazelnut torte. *$$; MC, V; checks OK; lunch Mon–Fri, dinner Wed–Sun, brunch Sat–Sun; beer and wine; reservations recommended; at Madison.* &

Ruby's on Bainbridge / ★☆

4569 LYNWOOD CENTER RD, BAINBRIDGE; 206/780-9303 With casual country-French style and ruby-colored walls warmed by candles, this is the sort of place you could spend half the day nursing a glass of wine and nibbling herb focaccia bread; fortunately, the wine list is extensive. Better yet, go for the slightly warmed spinach and sorrel torta puff-pastry appetizer with cucumber and dill relish. Affable owners Aaron and Maura Crisp offer a full menu that segues from wild mushroom fettuccine to rosemary chicken baked with Bosc pear, Riesling cream, and grapes. If all this leaves you feeling deliciously languid, settle down for a flick at the adorably retro movie house next door. *$$; AE, MC, V; checks OK; lunch Fri–Sat, dinner every day; beer and wine; reservations recommended; azen mama@hotmail.com; www.rubysonbainbridge.com; Lynwood Center.* &

LODGINGS

The Buchanan Inn / ★★☆

8494 NE ODD FELLOWS RD, BAINBRIDGE ISLAND; 206/780-9258 OR 800/598-3926 Close enough to Seattle for easy access but far enough to leave the city sounds behind, this beautifully renovated 1912 B&B (formerly an Odd Fellows Hall) is set in one of the island's most picturesque and sunny neighborhoods. Run by a friendly team of innkeepers, Judy and Ron Gibbs, the Buchanan features four spacious suites with large private baths and king- or queen-sized beds, separate sitting areas, CD players, coffeemakers, and minifridges stocked with complimentary beverages; two rooms have gas fireplaces. A short stroll away are Fort Ward State Park and the beach (ask Judy about other sights), and it's just steps to the inn's rustic cottage and a bubbling hot tub. Children over 16 OK. No pets (though dogs are on-site). *$$; AE, DC, DIS, JCB, MC, V; checks OK; jgibbs@ buchananinn.com; www.buchananinn.com; at W Blakely.*

Seattle-Tacoma International Airport

LODGINGS

Hilton Seattle Airport & Conference Center / ★★★☆

17620 PACIFIC HWY S, SEATAC; 206/244-4800 OR 800/HILTONS The recently completed $56-million redevelopment added about 218 rooms (for a total of 396, including seven suites), a fitness room, and a 39,000-square-foot, state-of-the-art banquet space. A cool, expansive lobby leads to rooms set around two landscaped courtyards with a pool and indoor/outdoor Jacuzzi. Inside are the expected complement of desks, computer hookups, high-speed Internet access, irons and ironing boards, and coffeemakers. Meeting rooms and a 24-hour business center cater to worker bees. The hotel's restaurant, Spencer's for Steaks and Chops, serves all meals. Complimentary airport shuttle. *$$–$$$; AE, DC, DIS, JCB, MC, V; checks OK; www.hilton.com; corner of S 176th St and Pacific Hwy S.* &

Seattle Marriott at Sea-Tac / ★★

3201 S 176TH ST, SEATAC; 206/241-2000 OR 800/228-9290 It's no surprise that this hotel one block from the airport attracts travelers who want to get in and out of town with a minimum of stress. The swift service at this 459-room megamotel makes transfer to and from Sea-Tac Airport virtually painless. Convenience doesn't come at the expense of enjoyment, though. The lobby, with its warm Northwest motif, opens into an enormous atrium complete with indoor pool and two Jacuzzis. For slightly higher rates than the standard rooms, five more spacious, handsomely appointed suites are available, and rooms on the concierge floor include turndown service, hair dryers, irons and ironing boards, and a lounge that serves continental breakfasts and nightly nibbles. All guests have access to a sauna and well-equipped exercise room. A casual dining room offers the usual hotel fare. Pets OK. *$$$; AE, DC, DIS, JCB, MC, V; checks OK; www.marriott.com; corner of S 176th St and 32nd Ave S.* &

PUGET SOUND

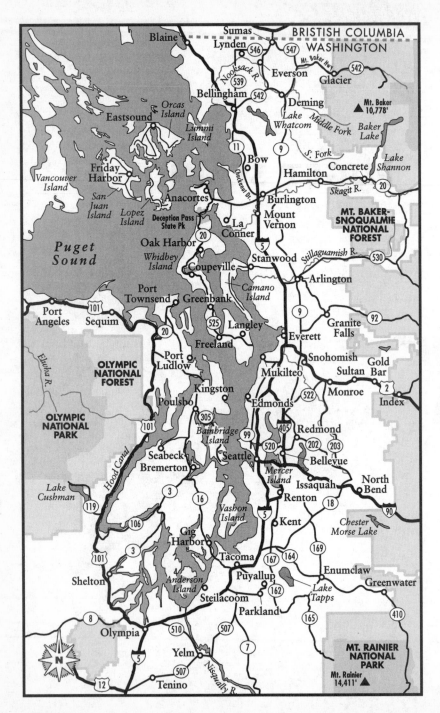

PUGET SOUND

From Olympia at the southern end of Puget Sound to Blaine at the border with Canada, Interstate 5 is flanked by a richly populated, verdant stretch of Washington State. Waterways, islands, farmlands and forest, and stunning mountain views dominate the landscape. This region is not only the cradle of the state's port, shipping, fishing, and naval industry, it also offers some of the area's most idyllic getaways.

Driving north from Seattle, the interstate carries you to the port city of Everett, the tulip town of Mount Vernon, and the university community of Bellingham. The area is best explored by leaving the freeway and traveling backroads, routes that lead to the state's most visited islands—including Whidbey and the San Juans—as well as to waterfront towns and villages—Langley, Coupeville, Anacortes, and La Conner—that invite travelers to linger and explore.

ACCESS AND INFORMATION

Fly into **SEATTLE-TACOMA INTERNATIONAL AIRPORT** (17801 Pacific Hwy S, SeaTac; 206/431-4444)—13 miles south of Seattle and 16 miles north of Tacoma— and you have easy access to Interstate 5. You'll need a car to best explore the region; most **CAR RENTAL** agencies have outlets at Sea-Tac.

Train travel offers a different view. **AMTRAK** (3035 S Jackson St, Seattle; 206/382-4125 or 800/USA-RAIL; www.amtrak.com) from King Street Station has daily runs between Portland and Seattle, and Seattle and Vancouver, with stops including Everett and Bellingham.

WASHINGTON STATE FERRIES (Pier 52, Seattle; 206/464-6400 or 800/843-3779; www.wsdot.wa.gov/ferries/) access the San Juan Islands, Whidbey, Vashon, and other islands in Puget Sound.

Everett Area

The Everett area extends from Edmonds on the south to Stanwood on the north. US Highway 2 heads east from Everett, and ferries head west from Mukilteo just south of Everett. Timber and fishing once supported this Snohomish County seat. Now, Boeing's Paine Field facility and the state-of-the-art U.S. naval base here add more to the area's growing economy and its ever-increasing population.

Everett

The redevelopment of the Monte Cristo Hotel—a historic landmark boarded up for 20 years—created the **EVERETT CENTER FOR THE ARTS** (1507 Wall St; 425/257-8380), a gorgeous home for the Everett Symphony, the Arts Council, and a stunning display of Pilchuck glass. The **EVERETT PERFORMING ARTS CENTER** (2710 Wetmore Ave; 425/257-8600 box office or 888/257-3722) hosts a variety of plays, concerts, dance, and other events.

The **EVERETT AQUASOX** (3802 Broadway; 425/258-3673; www.aquasox.com), the single-A short-season farm team for the Seattle Mariners, draws folks away from Seattle to enjoy baseball at the small, old-fashioned field. Don't miss the chili-dogs!

BOEING'S SOUTH EVERETT PLANT (exit 189 west from I-5 to Hwy 526, follow signs; 206/544-1264; www.boeing.com) offers 90-minute tours of the world's largest building (in volume), where you can watch the assembly of the aviation giant's 747s, 767s, and 777s. Tours (admission charge) run Monday through Friday, fill early, and have strict height requirements for children; a gift shop is on site.

Downtown Everett has an excellent bakery, **PAVÉ** (2613 Colby Ave; 425/252-0250), with sandwiches made fresh; however, the sour cherry and chocolate bread is reason enough to stop.

RESTAURANTS

Alligator Soul / ★

2013½ HEWITT AVE, EVERETT; 425/259-6311 Casual roadhouse atmosphere, exposed brick, Mardi Gras beads, hot-pepper lights and heaping portions of Southern smoked ribs with a hot barbecue sauce give this place its soul. The sides alone could make a meal: jalapeño cornbread, corn salad, and cool coleslaw. Other dishes—the Creole hot pot, crawfish étouffée, catfish gumbo (special order), fried catfish with hush puppies—have even diehard Northwesterners longing to go south. Bread pudding, packed with pecans and peaches, is served with a sweet bourbon sauce. *$$; MC, V; no checks; lunch, dinner every day; beer and wine; reservations recommended; near Broadway.*

The Sisters

2804 GRAND ST, EVERETT; 425/252-0480 This place is as popular as it is funky. Soups such as seafood chowder or beef barley can be outstanding. Sandwiches range from average deli stuff to a vegetarian burger made with chopped cashews and sunflower seeds. Morning favorites are pecan hotcakes or scrambled eggs wrapped in flour tortillas. Fresh-squeezed lemonade quenches your thirst; a big slice of marionberry pie cures what ails you. *$; MC, V; checks OK; breakfast, lunch Mon–Fri; no alcohol; reservations not accepted; in Everett Public Market.* &

LODGINGS

The Inn at Port Gardner / ★★

 1700 W MARINE VIEW DR, EVERETT; 425/252-6779 OR 888/252-6779 Industrial chic mixes with warm touches—an inviting lobby fireplace and colorful art accents—to create a stylish getaway or stay for the corporate traveler. The inn views the marina and is next to Lombardi's Italian restaurant. Thirty-three sophisticated rooms are done up in neutral tones. Suites have separate bedrooms, and fireplaces. Continental breakfast is included. *$$–$$$; AE, DC, DIS, MC, V; local checks; reservations@innatportgardner.com; www.innatportgardner.com; exit 193 off I-5.* &

Marina Village Inn / ★★

1728 W MARINE VIEW DR, EVERETT; 425/259-4040 OR 800/281-7037 The Puget Sound waterfront location of this 26-room inn on Port Gardner Bay can't be beat, even if lobby areas are looking a bit tired and dated. Rooms are contemporary with oak furnishings, satellite TV, handcrafted ceramic sinks, trouser presses, and refrigerators. Many have jetted tubs; most have telescopes. Book a room on the harbor side; sea lions might be lollygagging on the nearby jetty. Anthony's Home Port

NORTH PUGET SOUND THREE-DAY TOUR

DAY ONE: From Interstate 5, head into Everett for breakfast at **THE SISTERS,** then go west to the **MUKILTEO FERRY.** A 20-minute ferry ride puts you at Clinton, on the southeast end of **WHIDBEY ISLAND.** Exit off the main highway to Langley, a cliffside village overlooking Saratoga Passage. Between exploring First Street galleries, antiques shops, and boutiques, head to the **STAR BISTRO** for lunch, then complete your tour. Check into the **INN AT LANGLEY,** then seek out an order of the island's own Penn Cove mussels at **CAFE LANGLEY.** Enjoy a soak while watching boats in Saratoga Passage before bed.

DAY TWO: Breakfast at the inn gets you ready to head up-island to Coupeville. Drop by the **ISLAND COUNTY HISTORICAL MUSEUM,** tour the exhibits, and watch the informative video about island history. Pick up a map there for exploring **EBEY'S LANDING,** then have lunch at **TOBY'S 1890 TAVERN.** Go for a hike on the beach at **FORT EBEY STATE PARK,** particularly inspiring with views west to the water and setting sun. For a rustic, historical experience, overnight at the **CAPTAIN WHIDBEY INN,** where you also have dinner.

DAY THREE: Breakfast at the inn or at **KNEAD & FEED.** Continue north on the island, stop at **DECEPTION PASS STATE PARK** for a ground-level view of the furious waters in the pass, then cross the **DECEPTION PASS BRIDGE** and get a glimpse from above. Swing through Anacortes and browse at **MARINE SUPPLY AND HARDWARE** or the **ANACORTES MUSEUM.** Grab a bite at the **CALICO CUPBOARD,** then head south to La Conner where you can stroll through town and have an early dinner at **KERSTIN'S.** Take the back route out of La Conner and stop at **SNOW GOOSE PRODUCE,** then rejoin Interstate 5 at Conway, or stay on backroads to Stanwood. Check in at the **CAMANO ISLAND INN,** relaxing by the fireplace while watching the sun set behind Whidbey Island, where you began your journey.

restaurant is next door. *$$; AE, DC, DIS, MC, V; checks OK; mvi1728@aol.com; gtesupersite.com/marinavilinn; exit 193 off I-5.* &

Mukilteo

On the southwest edge of Everett, Mukilteo is, unfortunately, best known for the congestion caused by ferry traffic to Whidbey Island (see Access and Information). A block or two south of the ferry terminal (follow signs from freeway), however, a small waterfront park has a historical lighthouse worth seeing. You can also stroll the waterfront and fish off the docks.

RESTAURANTS

Charles at Smugglers Cove / ★★

8340 53RD AVE W, MUKILTEO; 425/347-2700 Chef Claude Faure and his wife, Janet, turned this landmark building (a 1929 speakeasy set on a bluff above Possession Sound) into an elegant restaurant. The atmosphere is country French, and a small terrace views the Sound. Dishes such as veal chop with tarragon and *poulet aux crevettes* (breast of chicken with prawns) grace the classically French menu. Save room for crepes suzette or Grand Marnier soufflé. For lunch try a tasty salad niçoise. *$$$; AE, MC, V; local checks only; lunch Tues–Fri, dinner Mon–Sat; full bar; reservations recommended; www.charlesatsmugglerscove.com; at Hwys 525 and 526.* &

LODGINGS

Silver Cloud Inn / ★★

718 FRONT ST, MUKILTEO; 425/423-8600 OR 800/311-1461 It's hard to beat the location of this new waterfront inn adjacent to the Mukilteo ferry. It's built over the water and half of the 70 guest rooms have spectacular Puget Sound views. Rooms are decorated in rich colors and traditional furniture; some have minikitchens, some view rooms have jetted tubs and gas fireplaces. A generous continental breakfast is included. *$$–$$$; AE, DIS, MC, V; checks ok; www.silvercloud.com; exit 189 from I-5.*

Snohomish

This small community southeast of Everett, formerly an active lumber town, now bills itself as the "Antique Capital of the Northwest." Plenty of antique shops fill the downtown historical district; the **STAR CENTER MALL** (829 2nd St; 360/568-2131) is the largest, with 175 dealers from all over the area. Gather with locals at **THE CABBAGE PATCH** (111 Avenue A; 360/568-9091) for soups, omelets, and other cozy food. For a slice of something sweet, visit the **SNOHOMISH PIE COMPANY** (915 1st St; 360/568-3589).

When you're through taking in the old, get a new perspective on Snohomish from the air: charter a scenic flight at **HARVEY FIELD** (9900 Airport Wy; 360/568-1541; www.snohomishflying.com), take a trip with **AIRIAL HOT AIR BALLOON COMPANY** (10123 Airport Wy; 360/568-3025; www.airialballoon.com), or enjoy a parachute adventure with **SKYDIVE SNOHOMISH** (9912 Airport Wy; 360/568-7703; www.letsgoskydiving.com).

Stanwood

North of Everett, Stanwood is a sleepy farm village with Scandinavian heritage, and one good reason for a sightseeing detour. Years ago, local daughter Martha Anderson started **ROSEMALING** (traditional Norwegian flower painting) and teaching it to fellow Stanwoodians. Now businesses are embellished in this genre—not for tourist show but out of an authentic impulse to express their heritage and decorate Main Street.

Founded in 1971 by local glass artist Dale Chihuly and Seattle art patrons John Hauberg and Anne Gould Hauberg, **PILCHUCK SCHOOL** (206/621-8422;

www.pilchuck.com) is an internationally renowned glass-art school. Students live and study on campus, in the midst of a country tree farm. A summer open house gives folks a chance to see artists at work; call for times and directions.

Camano Island

Many city folk have summer homes on this out-of-the-way island west of Stanwood and only an hour from Seattle. There's no ferry to catch, so this is a great spot for an easy island getaway. **CAMANO ISLAND STATE PARK** (360/387-3031) on the southwest side is a day-use park with a beach and picnic shelters.

LODGINGS

Camano Island Inn / ★★

1054 W CAMANO DR, CAMANO ISLAND; 360/387-0783 OR 888/718-0783
This luxurious waterfront inn has spectacular water views. Cozy up in the sitting room with its rustic river-rock fireplace; sink into king-sized feather beds. Six guest rooms (all with water views) have private waterfront decks and large bathrooms; some have jetted tubs. Kayaks are available for guests ($20 per use); massages can be arranged. *$$; AE, DIS, MC, V; checks OK (in advance); www.camanoislandinn.com; rsvp@camanoislandinn.com; exit 212 from I-5, follow Hwy 532 onto the island.*

Whidbey Island

Whidbey Island is one of only eight islands that make up Island County (with Camano, Ben Ure, Strawberry, Minor, Baby, Smith, and Deception). Named for Capt. Joseph Whidbey, a sailing master for Capt. George Vancouver, Whidbey Island was first surveyed and mapped by the two explorers in 1792. More than 200 years later, its largest employer is the government (thanks to the Oak Harbor navy base). The island boasts pretty towns, historical parks, sandy beaches, and pastoral rolling farmland.

Although they have no bike lanes, Whidbey's flat, relatively traffic-free roads make for good **BIKING**, especially if you stay off the main highway; call the South Whidbey Information Line (360/221-6765) for route ideas. Depart from the mainland at Mukilteo (see the Everett Area section), about 25 miles north of Seattle, for a 25-minute ferry ride (see Access and Information) to Clinton on the south end of the island. Expect long car waits on sunny weekends. You can also drive onto Whidbey at its north end, on Highway 20 south of Anacortes. Here the island is described from south to north.

Langley

The nicest town on Whidbey carries its small-town virtues well, though it may be getting a little too spit-and-polish for some. With the addition of **LANGLEY VIL-LAGE**, a charming collection of old-style shops on Second Street, it has grown into a two-street town.

Swap stories with Josh Hauser at **MOONRAKER BOOKS** (209 1st St; 360/221-6962), then head to the antique- and candy-filled gift shop **WAYWARD SON** (22 1st

St; 360/221-3911). For singular shopping, try **THE COTTAGE** (210 1st St; 360/221-4747) for heirloom lace and linens; and **WHAT A GIRL WANTS** (208 1st St; 360/221-5735), for unusual women's clothing.

Look for original Northwest paintings, pottery, sculpture, and glass at **GASKILL-OLSON GALLERY** (302 1st St; 360/221-2978); and stop to enjoy the Georgia Gerber sculpture of Reggie, a well-known town terrier, in front of the gallery. Next door at **HELLEBORE GLASS GALLERY** (308 1st St; 360/221-2067), you can watch glassblower George Springer at work. **MUSEO** (215 1st St; 360/221-7737) features regional and national glass art and handcrafts.

The **BRAEBURN** (197 2nd St; 360/221-3211) is a good spot for espresso and light breakfasts, lunches, and refreshments; the **DOG HOUSE** (230 1st St; 360/221-9825) for a microbrew (18 on tap) after a movie at **THE CLYDE** (213 1st St; 360/221-5525). The pesto pizza by the slice at **LANGLEY VILLAGE BAKERY** (221 2nd St; 360/221-3525) is a local favorite, as is the moist, Three Milk cake, also available by the slice. A few minutes south of town, the **WHIDBEY ISLAND WINERY** (5237 S Langley Rd; 360/221-2040) has a fine tasting room. Try the rhubarb wine.

RESTAURANTS

Cafe Langley / ★★

113 1ST ST, LANGLEY; 360/221-3090 Owners Shant and Arshavir Garibyan maintain the sparkling consistency that established this cafe as the town's best bet from the moment it opened. Make a reservation (especially weekends) and prepare for fine Mediterranean dining. Appetizers include hummus and warm pita bread, and Penn Cove mussels in saffron broth. The Greek salad is perfect before a feast of seafood stew, a lamb shish kebab, or a creative preparation of Northwest salmon or halibut, in season. Split the Russian cream for dessert. *$$; AE, MC, V; checks OK; lunch Wed–Mon, dinner every day (closed Tues in winter); beer and wine; reservations recommended; www.langley-wa.com/cl; on main street.* &

Star Bistro / ★

201½ 1ST ST, LANGLEY; 360/221-2627 An island favorite, the Star (above the Star Store) is a fun, color-splashed place that hops on weekends and after local events. Chef Paul Davina's menu includes pastry-enclosed French onion soup, creamy oyster stew, salads, pasta, and burgers, along with fancier daily specials. There's a breezy, sun-drenched deck. Pull up a stool at the red-topped bar for excellent martinis or margaritas. *$$; AE, DC, MC, V; no checks; lunch, dinner every day (dinner Tues–Sun in winter); full bar; reservations recommended; bistro@whidbey. com; www.whidbeynet.net/starbistro; on main street.*

Trattoria Giuseppe / ★

4141 E HWY 525, LANGLEY; 360/341-3454 Inside Trattoria Giuseppe—an unexpected discovery in a little strip mall on Highway 525—the scent of garlic and taverna decor are reminiscent of little places in the Tuscan countryside. Penn Cove mussels are prepared marinara. We like the fusilli primavera with prawns and scallops, and the *salmone con spinaci*—salmon on a bed of spinach with lemon butter sauce. Finish with a traditional Italian dessert like cannoli. Enjoy live music on

Friday or Saturday nights. *$$; AE, DIS, MC, V; checks OK; lunch Mon–Fri, dinner every day; full bar; reservations recommended; dine@trattoriagiuseppe.com; www. trattoriagiuseppe.com; at Langley Rd.*

LODGINGS

Boatyard Inn / ★★

200 WHARF ST, LANGLEY; 360/221-5120 The industrial siding and metal roofs of this inn mesh well with Langley's working waterfront. Big windows, pine accents, and back-to-basics Eddie Bauer-esque furnishings characterize 10 breezy suites (the smallest is 600 square feet), each with a gas fireplace, galley kitchen, queen-sized bed, sofa bed, cable TV, private deck, and water view. Loft units are suitable for small groups. *$$$; AE, DC, DIS, MC, V; local checks only; boat yard@whidbey.com; www.boatyardinn.com; take Wharf St downhill.* &

Chauntecleer House, Dove House, and Potting Shed Cottages / ★★

5081 SARATOGA RD, LANGLEY; 360/221-5494 OR 800/637-4436 Our only quibble with these gorgeous cottages on a quiet bluff north of downtown Langley is that it's too hard to choose one. Decorating these hideaways was a labor of love for transplanted Southerner Bunny Meals. We prefer Chauntecleer House, but only by a nose—or a beak (Chauntecleer is a Chaucerian term for "rooster")—for its sun-yellow walls, view of Saratoga Passage, wood-burning fireplace, and outdoor hot tub. Dove House doesn't share the view but is charmingly decorated with a mix of furniture and art (the bronze otter was sculpted by Georgia Gerber, Seattle's Pike Place Market Rachel-the-pig artist). A wood stove adds coziness, a second bedroom has bunks for the kids. The Potting Shed has a whimsical garden theme, "twig" bed, two-person jetted tub, and glass-front wood stove. A full breakfast is left in each kitchen. *$$$; AE, MC, V; checks OK; bunny@ dovehouse.com; www.dovehouse.com; take 2nd St north from town.*

Country Cottage of Langley / ★

215 6TH ST, LANGLEY; 360/221-8709 OR 800/713-3860 Innkeepers Kathy and Bob Annecone spiffed up this collection of five cottages on 2 acres overlooking downtown Langley. Largest is Cabernet Cottage with a burgundy carpet and wine-country theme; we also like the Captain's Cove with its nautical theme, and the pretty floral Whidbey. All cottages have water views, gas fireplaces, Jacuzzis, feather beds, TVs and VCRs, refrigerators, and coffeemakers. A full breakfast is served in the main house, a restored 1920s farmhouse, or may be brought to your room on request. *$$–$$$; AE, DIS, MC, V; checks OK; info@acountrycottage.com; www. acountrycottage.com; off Langley Rd.*

Inn at Langley / ★★★

400 1ST ST, LANGLEY; 360/221-3033 It's difficult to imagine a more idyllic getaway, or one more evocative of the Pacific Northwest, than Paul and Pam Schell's first private venture, built elegantly into the bluff over Saratoga Passage. Architect Alan Grainger combined three themes: Frank Lloyd Wright style, Northwest ruggedness, and Pacific Rim tranquility. Inside this rough-hewn, shingled building are 24 rooms with simple Asian-influenced furnishings, trimmings of three different woods, and quarry-tiled bathrooms with hooks made from alder twigs. Every room of the four-story inn views the water (you can watch boat traffic from the Jacuzzi); we prefer the upper-level rooms. Two townhouse cottages—with living room, bedroom, and master bath—just east of the inn offer more expansive and expensive options. Spa services are available on-site. Continental breakfast included. Five-course prix-fixe dinners—only occasionally flawed—that celebrate Northwest foods are served weekends (by reservation). Diners sip sherry while chef Steve Nogal delivers his appetite-whetting spiel. *$$$–$$$$; AE, MC, V; local checks only; www.innatlangley.com; edge of town.* &

Island Tyme / ★

4940 S BAYVIEW, LANGLEY; 360/221-5078 OR 800/898-8963 At Island Tyme, on a quiet 10 acres, 2 miles from downtown Langley, innkeepers Cliff and Carol Wisman raise pheasants and pygmy goats. Rooms in the Victorian-style inn are romantic retreats, especially the Heirloom Suite, with its fireplace, two-person jetted tub, and deck. All five rooms have private baths, TVs, and VCRs. One room allows pets. *$$; AE, MC, V; checks OK; islandty@whidbey.com; www.islandtymebb.com; call for directions.* &

Lone Lake Cottages and Breakfast / ★

5206 S BAYVIEW RD, LANGLEY; 360/321-5325 Dolores Meeks's place is still one of the most interesting B&Bs around. Rooms, decorated with Oriental antiques, have eccentric charm. One of the four is aboard the tiny *Whidbey Queen,* a stern-wheeler permanently moored on the lake. Guests enjoy the same extras in the lakeside cottages: fireplace, soaking tub for two, VCR, and CD player. The one-bedroom Terrace Cottage, which looks into a stunning aviary of rare birds, is the nicest of the landlubber's accommodations. A honeymoon suite in the main house has a grand lake view, fireplace, and double-jetted tub. Full kitchens are stocked with breakfast makings for your first two days, plus barbecue seasonings should you land a trout. Guests are welcome to use the private beach, canoes, and bikes. *$$$; no credit cards; checks OK; www.lonelake.com; 5½ miles from Clinton.*

Saratoga Inn / ★

201 CASCADE AVE, LANGLEY; 360/221-5801 OR 800/698-2910 It's a two-minute walk from downtown Langley to the Saratoga Inn, which has architectural touches reminiscent of New England. Each of 15 view rooms is festooned in warm plaids or prints and furnished with a gas fireplace, an armoire, and an entertainment center. Breakfast can be delivered to your chamber. Solitude seekers like the separate Carriage House, with a full kitchen, stone fireplace, and king-sized sleigh bed. Small conferences are held in the Library Boardroom; guests socialize in the tea room. The Four Sisters Inn group manages the property. *$$$; AE, DC, MC, V; no checks; www.foursisters.com; corner of 2nd St.*

Villa Isola / ★★★

5489 S COLES RD, LANGLEY; 360/221-5052 OR 800/246-7323 Tucked into a pine-studded pastoral landscape, Bob and Dora Thirsk's version of an Italian country villa re-creates the slow, sweet life of the Old Country on 4 landscaped acres. Guests have the inspired villa space—with floor-to-ceiling windows and modern European furnishings—to themselves. Six large, sumptuous suites have oversized baths (five have jetted tubs), queen-sized beds, and down comforters; two suites share a deck. The largest suite has skylights, a fireplace, and a wall of windows. Espresso and delicacies are served in the sunny dining room or on the adjacent deck. Borrow the inn's mountain bikes or try a game of boccie (Italian lawn bowling). Gwen keeps CDs and board games in the living room, and the kitchen stocked with Italian desserts. *$$–$$$; MC, V; checks OK; villa@villaisola.com; www.villaisola.com; 2 miles southeast of Langley.*

Freeland

The small, unincorporated town of Freeland is home to **NICHOLS BROTHERS BOAT BUILDERS** (5400 S Cameron Rd; 360/331-5500; www.nicholsboats.com), manufacturers of cruise boats and stern-wheelers, and the town's largest employer. **FREELAND PARK** on Holmes Harbor has picnic tables, a play area, and a sandy beach.

LODGINGS

Cliff House / ★★★

727 WINDMILL RD, FREELAND; 360/331-1566 Perched on a cliff above Admiralty Inlet, this extraordinary getaway, designed by Seattle architect Arne Bystrom, is full of light from lofty windows, centering on a 30-foot-high native plant–filled atrium, and a sunken living room with a wood-burning fireplace. For a staggering $425 a night, two can have use of the entire luxuriously furnished house and its 14 acres of woods. There are hammocks, benches, and a deck with a hot tub high on the cliff. The elfish Sea Cliff Cottage is more modestly priced ($175) and includes a queen-sized feather bed, a kitchenette, and a deck overlooking the water. Peggy Moore sets the country table (in both houses) with a continental breakfast. *$$$$; no credit cards; checks OK; 2-night min stay; wink@whidbey.com; www.cliffhouse.net; Bush Point Rd to Windmill Rd.*

Greenbank

Here on a narrow part of the island, stop by **WHIDBEY'S GREENBANK FARM** (765 E Wonn Rd; 360/678-7700), at one time the largest loganberry farm in the country. Now the grounds have picnicking spots.

LODGINGS

Guest House Log Cottages / ★★

24371 HWY 525, GREENBANK; 360/678-3115 We love this place, partly because playing house here fulfills long-lost storybook dreams. Six dwellings set in a woodland-fringed clearing include the pine-log Tennessee Cottage with a king-sized feather bed and river-rock fireplace. Comparatively modest and less expensive, but just as cozy, is the Farm Guest Cottage. Everybody's favorite is the Lodge, a $325-a-night log home-for-two at the edge of a spring-fed pond; a tall stone fireplace plays center stage in a space that combines the old (a wood stove) with the new (a dishwasher). Breakfast makings are left in the fully equipped kitchens. All accommodations have TVs and VCRs (the video library boasts 500 flicks), and whirlpool spas for two. An outdoor pool is seasonally heated. *$$$; AE, DIS, MC, V; checks OK; guesthse@whidbey.net; www.guesthouselogcottages.com; 1 mile south of Greenbank.*

Coupeville

The second-oldest incorporated town in the state dates back to the mid-1850s; no wonder the town has a strict agenda of historical preservation. Coupeville's downtown consists of a half-dozen gift and antique shops and several restaurants. A must-see gallery is the **JAN MCGREGOR STUDIO** (19 NW Front St; 360/678-5015; open weekends year-round, every day in summer). McGregor specializes in rare porcelain techniques and imports Japanese tansu chests. **ISLAND COUNTY HISTORICAL MUSEUM** (NW Alexander St and Front St; 360/678-3310) tells the story of Whidbey Island's early history. Community events include the **COUPEVILLE ARTS & CRAFTS FESTIVAL** the second weekend in August, **A DANCE BONANZA** the first weekend in November, and March's **PENN COVE MUSSEL FESTIVAL**; for information, contact the Central Whidbey Chamber of Commerce (302 N Main St; 360/678-5434; www.centralwhidbey chamber.com).

TOBY'S 1890 TAVERN (8 NW Front St; 360/678-4222) is a good spot for burgers, beer, mussels, and a game of pool. Homemade breads, pies, soups, and salads make a memorable meal at **KNEAD & FEED** (4 NW Front St; 360/678-5431), and real coffee lives at **GREAT TIMES ESPRESSO** (12 NW Front St; 360/678-5358). An immediate hit, **THE TORTUGA** (11 NW Front St; 360/678-8386; www.tortuga restaurant.com) is a new small bistro specializing in seafood; try the island mussels and oysters.

An extra bike lane follows Engle Road 3 miles south of Coupeville to **FORT CASEY STATE PARK** (360/678-4519), a decommissioned fort with splendid gun mounts, a lighthouse, beaches, and commanding bluffs. Explore the magnificent bluff and beach at the nearby 17,000-acre **EBEY'S LANDING NATIONAL HISTORIC RESERVE** and **FORT EBEY STATE PARK** (360/678-4636). The **KEYSTONE FERRY** (888/808-7977 in WA; www.wsdot.wa.gov/ferries/) connecting Whidbey to Port Townsend on the Olympic Peninsula leaves from Admiralty Head, just south of Fort Casey.

LODGINGS

Anchorage Inn / ★

807 N MAIN ST, COUPEVILLE; 360/376-8282 OR 877/230-1313 A modern Victorian, the Anchorage offers moderately priced lodgings on Coupeville's main street. Six rooms have private baths; we especially like the water-view room with the four-poster king-sized bed, the room in the turret, and the top-floor Crow's Nest suite with fireplace. All rooms have TVs, VCRs, and cable. Full breakfast (included) is served in the antique-filled dining room. *$$; DIS, MC, V; checks OK; crowsnest@ anchorage-inn.com; www.anchorage-inn.com; on Main St.*

Captain Whidbey Inn / ★

🌲 **2072 W CAPTAIN WHIDBEY INN RD, COUPEVILLE; 360/678-4097 OR 800/366-4097** Owner John Colby Stone has made sure that little changes at this 1907 Penn Cove inn, built of sturdy madrona logs. In such a beloved place, history sometimes outranks comfort; the thin walls seem to talk, sniffle, and sneeze. Upstairs, 12 small, almost shiplike original rooms (two are suites) have sinks and share two bathrooms, one for each gender. Avoid rooms above the bar, unless you're planning to be up until closing time. Four furnished cabins include fireplaces and baths, and three newer cottages have full kitchens, fireplaces, two bedrooms, and hot tubs. Best bets are 13 lagoon rooms, with private baths and inlet views. Feather beds and down comforters grace all beds. Public rooms include a lantern-lit dining room, warm-weather deck, woodsy bar, well-stocked library, and folksy fireplace lobby. The restaurant features Penn Cove mussels (you're looking out at the mussel beds), fresh seafood, and greens from the gardens. *$$; AE, DIS, MC, V; local checks OK; info@captainwhidbey.com; www.captainwhidbey.com; off Madrona Wy.*

Fort Casey Inn / ★

1124 S ENGLE RD, COUPEVILLE; 360/678-8792 OR 866/661-6604 Built in 1909 as officers' quarters for nearby Fort Casey, this row of nine houses offers tidy, no-frills accommodations with a historical bent. Houses are divided into two-bedroom duplexes with fully equipped kitchens (coffee is provided but bring your own breakfast fixings). Garrison Hall, with a small reception area and its own private bedroom and bath, can be rented for weddings or private parties. The inn welcomes kids. It's a ten-minute walk to the beach and there's plenty to explore in Fort Casey State Park, the bird sanctuary at Crockett Lake, or nearby Ebey's Landing National Historic Reserve. *$$; MC, V; checks OK; www.fortcaseyinn.com; 2 miles south of Coupeville.*

The Old Morris Farm / ★

105 W MORRIS RD, COUPEVILLE; 360/678-6586 OR 800/936-6586 Owners Mario Chodorowski and Marilyn Randock have transformed their 1909 farmhouse into an elegant B&B. Four guest rooms are individual in style and decor, yet reflect the home's colonial feeling. The Treehouse Suite has a sitting room and fireplace, two queen bedrooms and one bath, and balconies. Enjoy breakfast in the red dining room, and evening hors d'oeuvres in the sun-washed living room. Small dinners are available by arrangement. Stroll the gardens; a small gift shop includes locally made walking sticks. *$$; MC, V; checks OK; www.oldmorrisfarm.com; 3 miles from Coupeville overpass.*

Oak Harbor

Named for the thriving Garry oak trees, Oak Harbor is Whidbey's largest city and home to **NAVAL AIR STATION WHIDBEY ISLAND,** a large air base for electronic attack, patrol, and reconnaissance squadrons as well as Navy Search and Rescue; group tours are currently limited on a case-by-case basis by reservation (360/257-2286). For the most part, Oak Harbor is engulfed in new and retired military folk. Kids at heart should visit **BLUE FOX DRIVE-IN THEATER AND BRATTLAND GO-**

KARTS (1403 Monroe Landing Rd; 360/675-5667; www.bluefoxdrivein.com), 2 miles south of Oak Harbor.

RESTAURANTS

Kasteel Franssen / ★

33575 HWY 20 (AULD HOLLAND INN), OAK HARBOR; 360/675-0724 Owned and operated by Joe and Elisa Franssen, this motel with the trademark windmill is a shade close to the highway. However, it has a regal, European feel and a restaurant that is a delightful surprise. For more than 10 years, classically trained chef/co-owner Scott Fraser has maintained a solid reputation among locals for seafood, chicken, and game. Expect the unexpected—ostrich, for example. Or try a Northwest version of Hawaiian lau lau with red snapper, prawns, scallops, and julienne vegetables all steamed in ti leaves. Fraser also serves delicious, lean, buffalo short ribs, a favorite of recent visitor, the Galloping Gourmet, Graham Kerr. Catch live music Thursdays and most Saturdays. Some of the inn's upper-story rooms have antiques, and six have private hot tubs. There's a tennis court, hot tub, outdoor pool, and children's play area. Rates include continental breakfast. *$$; AE, DIS, DC, MC, V; local checks only; dinner every day (Mon–Sat in winter); full bar; reservations recommended; www.kasteelfranssen.com; ½ mile north of Oak Harbor, 8 miles south of Deception Pass.*

Lucy's Mi Casita

31359 HWY 20, OAK HARBOR; 360/675-4800 It doesn't look like much, lined up along a strip of fast-food joints and automotive stores, and decorated with beer-bottle-cap curtains and cutouts of flamenco dancers, but Al and Lucy Enriquez keep locals coming back with homemade Mexican food and a lively atmosphere. Don't miss the *entomatadas*—tortillas topped with tomato sauce, cheese, and onion—a dish from Lucy's hometown of Chihuahua. *$; AE, DIS, MC, V; local checks only; lunch, dinner every day; full bar; reservations recommended; on main drag.*

Deception Pass State Park

Beautiful, treacherous **DECEPTION PASS,** at the north end of the island, has a lovely, if crowded, park (41229 Hwy 20; 360/675-2417)—the state's most popular—offering 3,600 acres of prime camping land, forests, and beach. The park's centerpiece—a stunning steel bridge connecting Whidbey and Fidalgo Islands—is not to be missed. Park in the highway pullouts at either end and walk across. **STROM'S SHRIMP/FOUNTAIN AND GRILL** (1481 Hwy 20; 360/293-2531), north of the pass, sells fresh seafood. They also grill up a mean oyster burger.

The Skagit Valley

To travelers on Interstate 5, the Skagit Valley is little more than a blur—except in spring, when the lush farmlands are brilliantly swathed in daffodils (mid-Mar–mid-Apr), tulips (Apr–early May), and irises (mid-May–mid-June). The countryside is ideal for bicyclists, except during the annual **TULIP FESTIVAL** (360/428-5959; www.tulipfestival.org; usually late Mar–early Apr). Mount Vernon is the county seat of this food- and flower-growing valley. For information on **HARVEST FESTIVALS**—

June is strawberries, September apples—contact the Mount Vernon Chamber of Commerce (117 N 1st St, Ste 4; 360/428-8547).

Mount Vernon

Mount Vernon is the "big city" of surrounding Skagit and Island Counties. Browse **SCOTT'S BOOKSTORE** (121 Freeway Dr; 360/336-6181) in the historical Granary Building at the north end of town, then have a pastry at the **CALICO CUPBOARD** (121-B Freeway Dr; 360/336-3107) next door. Or drop into the **SKAGIT RIVER BREWING CO.** (404 S 3rd St; 360/336-2884) to sample house-brewed suds and pub grub, including pizza from a wood-fired oven. The **CHUCK WAGON DRIVE INN** (800 N 4th St; 360/336-2732) offers 50 different burgers and the world's largest collection of whiskey-bottle cowboys.

RESTAURANTS

Pacioni's Pizzeria / ★

606 S 1ST ST, MOUNT VERNON; 360/336-3314 Come here for pizza and to watch husband/wife team Andrew Glocker and Glenda Downs hand-toss the pizza dough (remember the mad Italian baker in *Moonstruck?*). Vegetarian pies include the Ala 'Biermann—roasted red peppers, sweet onions, and walnuts. *$; MC, V; checks OK; lunch Tues–Sat, dinner Mon–Sat; beer and wine; reservations not accepted; in old downtown.* &

La Conner

La Conner was founded in 1867 by John Conner, a trading-post operator, who named the town after his wife, Louisa A. Conner. Much of what you see today was built before railroads arrived in the late 1880s, when fishing and farming communities on Puget Sound traded largely by water. In an age of conformity, the town became a literal backwater, and a haven for nonconformists (Wobblies, WWII COs, McCarthy-era escapees, beatniks, hippies, and bikers), always with a smattering of artists and writers, including Mark Tobey, Morris Graves, Guy Anderson, and Tom Robbins.

This long-standing live-and-let-live attitude has allowed the neighboring Native American Swinomish community to contribute to the exceptional cultural richness of La Conner. Merchants here have created a unique American bazaar with shops like **COTTONS** (608 S 1st St; 360/466-5825) with comfortable clothing; **NASTY JACK'S ANTIQUES** (1st and Morris Sts; 360/466-3209); **TWO MOONS** (620 S 1st St; 360/466-1920) gallery; the **OLIVE SHOPPE** (101 N 1st St; 360/466-4101); and **O'LEARY'S BOOKS** (609 S 1st St; 360/466-1305).

GO OUTSIDE (111 Morris St; 360/466-4836) is a small but choice garden store. If all this shopping leaves you in need of respite, stop by the stylish **LA CONNER BREWING CO.** (117 S 1st St; 360/466-1415) for fine ales and tasty wood-fired pizzas. Kids like **WHISKERS CAFE** (128 S 1st St; 360/466-1008), a casual burger stop on the dock.

GACHES MANSION (703 S 2nd St; 360/466-4288), home to the not-to-be-missed **QUILT MUSEUM**, is a wonderful example of American Victorian architecture, with period furnishings and a widow's walk that looks out on the entire Skagit Valley.

ART'S ALIVE IN LA CONNER

Notice the quality of the light when you're in La Conner. Sometimes moody, sometimes bright, it has shaped the character of this town. In the 1940s, this picturesque waterfront village drew artists such as Mark Tobey, Kenneth Callahan, Morris Graves, and others, whose work was influenced by the Skagit Delta—its landscape, Native people, lifestyle, and especially its light. The artists became world famous and collectively are known as the **NORTHWEST SCHOOL**. Their work is on permanent, albeit rotating, display on the upper (second) floor of the Museum of Northwest Art (see below).

Since those days, La Conner has attracted artists, especially each November when the community hosts **ART'S ALIVE** (360/466-4778 or 888/642-9284)—a weekend festival with galleries and specialty stores such as the **WOOD MERCHANT** (709 1st St; 360/466-4741), showcasing the work of modern Northwest artists and artisans. The **MUSEUM OF NORTHWEST ART** (121 S 1st St; 360/466-4446; www.museumofnwart.org) preserves, collects, and shows the work of Northwest artists. And while it shows pieces from around the country and world, the quality of work displayed in the **LA CONNER QUILT MUSEUM** (703 S 2nd St; 360/466-4288), which sometimes appear to be paintings in fabric, is in keeping with the artistic spirit of the town.

—Jena MacPherson

The **MUSEUM OF NORTHWEST ART** (121 S 1st St; 360/466-4446; open Tues–Sun) is worth a visit. If you come into La Conner via Conway off I-5, stop at **SNOW GOOSE PRODUCE** (on Fir Island Rd; 360/445-6908) for an ice-cream cone in a homemade waffle cone. You can buy tulips in spring, local produce, specialty food items, and fresh seafood.

RESTAURANTS

Calico Cupboard / ★

720 S 1ST ST, LA CONNER (AND BRANCHES); 360/466-4451 Hearty waffle and omelet breakfasts are featured, but most folks come here for the pastries—delicious cinnamon rolls, hot apple dumplings, cranberry scones, triple berry Danishes, and more. Our advice for avoiding the weekend crowds: buy your goodies from the take-out counter and find a sunny bench by the water. Two other Calicos are in Anacortes (901 Commercial Ave; 360/293-7315) and Mount Vernon (121-B Freeway Dr; 360/336-3107). *$; MC, V; checks OK; breakfast, lunch every day (early dinner Fri–Sat in Mount Vernon); beer and wine; reservations not accepted; on main drag.*

Kerstin's / ★★

505 S 1ST ST, LA CONNER; 360/466-9111 The former location of Andiamo and The Black Swan, with its postage-stamp lower level and upstairs dining room viewing Swinomish Channel, has a duo at the helm that's likely to stay a while—especially considering local raves. Chef and co-owner David Poor (formerly of La Petite in Anacortes) and his wife, Kerstin, a former New York ballet dancer, have lightened up these charming old main street digs. While the menu changes seasonally, count on moist, fall-off-the-bone-tender lamb shank served with cabernet sauce over roasted-garlic risotto, and Samish Island oysters, baked in the shell with garlic cilantro butter, and a small kick of Tabasco. The vegetarian special is a savory, layered dish of roasted vegetables including portobello mushrooms, caramelized red onions, and eggplant. A small outdoor deck offers good-weather dining with a channel view. *$$; AE, DC, MC, V; local checks only; lunch, dinner Wed–Mon; full bar; reservations recommended; dpoor@fidalgo.net; east side of 1st St.*

Palmers at the Lighthouse / ★★

512 S 1ST ST, LA CONNER; 360/466-3147 In 2001, Thomas and Danielle Palmer's popular eatery moved from its former cozy location in the La Conner Country Inn into the former home of a less stellar restaurant on main street. Newly renovated, with sage green walls and high-gloss ivory woodwork, the spacious digs now have a Nantucket flair enhanced by expansive channel views. Regulars love the seasoned, slow-cooked prime rib. Breast of duckling with fresh ginger and raspberry demiglace shows the kitchen can work just as successfully with more exotic offerings. The restaurant is nonsmoking, but a wine and port bar, with its own entrance and separate ventilation, allows smoking. *$$; AE, MC, V; local checks OK; lunch, dinner every day; full bar; reservations recommended; left off Morris at 1st St.* &

LODGINGS

The Heron in La Conner / ★★

117 MAPLE AVE, LA CONNER; 360/466-4626 OR 877/883-8899 The Heron is one of the prettiest hostelries in town, with 12 jewel-box rooms. Splurge on Room 31, the Bridal Suite, with Jacuzzi and gas fireplace, or Room 32, with gas fireplace, spacious sitting area, and a wonderful view of the Skagit Valley and Cascades. Downstairs is an elegant living room with wing chairs and a formal dining room, where full breakfast is served. Out back, barbecue in the stone fire pit or slip into the hot tub. *$$; AE, MC, V; checks OK; www.theheron.com; heroninn@ncia.com; edge of town.*

Hotel Planter / ★

715 S 1ST ST, LA CONNER; 360/466-4710 OR 800/488-5409 A hotel since 1907, this Victorian-style brick establishment has known the most famous (and infamous) characters of La Conner's colorful past. Current owner Don Hoskins used his connoisseur's eye and artisan's care to create a tasteful blend of past (original woodwork staircase and entrance) and present (private baths and armoire-hidden TVs in every room). Four of the 12 rooms face the waterfront (and the often noisy main street); four others overlook a garden courtyard (guests reserve time in the hot tub); four have limited views. The staff, well versed on the Skagit Valley, is exemplary. *$$; AE, MC, V; checks OK; south end of main street.*

La Conner Channel Lodge / ★★

205 N 1ST ST, LA CONNER; 360/466-1500 OR 888/466-4113 The Channel Lodge is an urban version of its casual cousin, the La Conner Country Inn, a few blocks inland (see review) in a prime location at the edge of Swinomish Channel. Most rooms have channel views; watch boats ply the waterway from tiny decks. Some rooms have jetted tubs; if you're not splurging for a splash, request one that isn't directly below those with potentially noisy waterjets. Your gas fireplace is lit upon arrival. A continental breakfast includes fresh fruit, pastries, and homemade granola. *$$$; AE, DC, MC, V; checks OK; www.laconnerlodging.com; north end of town.* ᕙ

La Conner Country Inn / ★

107 S 2ND ST, LA CONNER; 360/466-3101 OR 888/466-4113 Despite its name, the La Conner Country Inn is more of a classy motel than a true country inn. All 28 rooms have gas fireplaces, country pine furnishings, pretty floral bedspreads, and armchairs. The inn is especially accommodating to families; rooms with two double beds are generously sized. Complimentary breakfasts are served in the library, where an enormous fieldstone fireplace and comfy couches beckon. *$$; AE, DC, MC, V; checks OK; www.laconnerlodging.com; downtown off Morris St.* ᕙ

Skagit Bay Hideaway / ★★

17430 GOLDENVIEW AVE, LA CONNER; 360/466-2262 OR 888/466-2262 A sybaritic and romantic spot, this Northwest shingle-style cottage, designed by architect Earlene Beckes and operated by her and partner Kevin Haberly, is a luxury waterfront hideaway with two 600-square-foot suites sporting minikitchens and double-headed showers. You can watch the sun set over the water from your rooftop spa, or enjoy a fire in your own cozy living room. Full breakfast served in your suite. *$$–$$$; AE, DIS, MC, V; checks OK; hideaway@skagitbay.com; www. skagitbay.com; 1½ miles west of La Conner across Rainbow Bridge.*

White Swan Guest House / ★★

15872 MOORE RD (FIR ISLAND), LA CONNER; 360/445-6805 "It reminds guests of Grannie's farmhouse," says affable host Peter Goldfarb of his classic, popular, 14-year-old Fir Island B&B, halfway between the La Conner exit (at Conway) off Interstate 5 and the town itself. Poplars line the driveway, Adirondack chairs dot the garden, and the grounds are full of perennials. Tranquil farm fields stretch beyond. The house is splashed with warm yellow, salmon, evergreen, and peach wall tones and fabric accents, and seems to soak up the sunlight—even in the rain. Pamper yourself with a soak in the large clawfooted tub (three guest rooms share two baths), or curl up on the sofa in front of the woodstove. Dog lovers enjoy meeting Goldfarb's three friendly canines. Goldfarb serves a country continental breakfast of fresh scones or muffins, fruit, and coffee; his wonderful chocolate chip cookies are waiting in the afternoons. Bring binoculars for bird-watching and bikes for touring the island's flat farmlands. A charming guest cottage out back provides an especially private accommodation, great for families or romantics; it has an open first floor with living/dining room and kitchen area, and a queen-bedded room upstairs. *$$; MC, V; checks OK; www.thewhiteswan. com; 6 miles southeast of La Conner, call for directions.*

The Wild Iris Inn / ★★

121 MAPLE AVE, LA CONNER; 360/466-1400 OR 800/477-1400 This romantic 19-room inn has spacious suites, each featuring a gas fireplace, oversized Jacuzzi, and panoramic Cascade views. Each is individually decorated, so specify white wicker and lace, or more masculine furnishings. Most standard rooms face the parking lot and seem a bit cramped. Dinner (not included) is served Tuesday through Saturday; make reservations, because it's open to the public. The intimate dining room has country charm, but the real magic is in the seasonally changing menu, which might include fresh salmon with peppercorn butter, or grilled duckling breast with mushrooms, sun-dried cherries, and marsala. The breakfast buffet can include hot spiced fruit soup, vegetable quiche, or baked pastry eggs. *$$$; AE, MC, V; checks OK; www.wildiris.com; edge of town.* &

Chuckanut Drive

This famous stretch of road (Hwy 11) between Burlington or Bow and Bellingham was once part of the Pacific Highway; now it is one of the prettiest drives in the state, curving along the Chuckanut Mountains and overlooking Samish Bay and its many islands. If you're in the driver's seat, however, you'll have to keep your eyes on the narrow and winding road. Take the Chuckanut Drive exit (231) off Interstate 5 northbound (or follow 12th St south out of Bellingham, exit 250 from I-5).

As you wend north to Bellingham through bucolic communities, it's hard to believe Interstate 5 is only minutes away. Removed from traffic and shopping malls, you'll discover orchards, oyster beds, slow-moving tractors, and fields of mustard. For an interesting detour, visit the **BREAZEALE-PADILLA BAY NATIONAL ESTU-ARINE RESEARCH RESERVE AND INTERPRETIVE CENTER** (1043 Bayview-Edison Rd; 360/428-1558; open Wed–Sun, 10am–5pm). Learn about the Padilla Bay estuary through displays, saltwater tanks, and a library. A 2-mile shoreline trail begins a short drive south of the center. Nearby **BAYVIEW STATE PARK** (360/757-0227) has overnight camping and beachfront picnic sites, perfect for winter bird-watching.

Permanent and part-time residents inhabit **SAMISH ISLAND,** as do numerous oyster beds. **BLAU OYSTER COMPANY** (11321 Blue Heron Rd; 360/766-6171; open Mon–Sat, 8am–5pm; 7 miles west of Edison via Bayview-Edison Rd and Samish Island Rd) has been selling Samish Bay oysters, clams, and other seafood since 1935. Follow signs to the shucking plant. If you're hungry or thirsty as you make your way through Edison, stop at the (smoky) **LONGHORN SALOON & GRILL** (5754 Cains Ct; 360/766-6330) for burgers, steaks, local oysters, crab dinners, and a full-service bar; new owner Steve Mains has fancied up the place and the menu (you can now get a hand-cut New York steak with oysters), but you can still get a delicious $4.95 burger.

LARRABEE STATE PARK (off Chuckanut Dr; 360/902-8844; www.parks.wa.gov; 7 miles south of Bellingham) was Washington's first state park. Beautiful sandstone-sculpted beaches and cliffs provide a backdrop for exploring abundant sea life. Picnic areas and camping are good. The **INTERURBAN TRAIL,** once the electric rail route from Bellingham to Mount Vernon, is now a 5-mile trail connecting three parks on Chuckanut Drive: Larrabee State Park to Arroyo Park to Fairhaven Park (in Bellingham).

TEDDY BEAR COVE is a lovely secluded beach along Chuckanut Drive just south of the Bellingham city limits. Watch for a parking lot on the east side of the road.

RESTAURANTS

The Oyster Bar on Chuckanut Drive / ★★★

2578 CHUCKANUT DR, BOW; 360/766-6185 A face-lift and new fireplace in recent years improved the appearance of this famed Chuckanut Drive restaurant, but little can improve upon the spectacular view of Samish Bay, gourmet fare, and award-winning wines—they're still tops. The frequently changing menu focuses on seafood and local bounty. Start with a half-dozen raw oysters fresh from the bay. Entrees might be a generous fillet of wild salmon or a perfectly cooked filet mignon. A creamy cheesecake is often on the menu—try the lemon for a light finish. No children under 10, please. *$$$; AE, MC, V; local checks only; dinner every day; beer and wine; reservations recommended; www.chuckanutdrive.com; north of Bow.*

The Rhododendron Cafe / ★

5521 CHUCKANUT DR, BOW; 360/766-6667 The Rhododendron Cafe is the perfect starting or ending point for a scenic trek on Chuckanut Drive. It may not have the view of other eateries, but the commitment to making everything from scratch—including basil and shallot buns for sandwiches—makes this a delicious stop. Once the site of the Red Crown Service Station in the early 1900s, the Rhody serves homemade soup (chowder is excellent) and a tasty portobello burger. Delicious, lightly breaded, and panfried Samish Bay oysters are available for lunch or dinner. Dinner also brings grilled pork loin and chicken Parmesan. A nightly seafood stew has an ethnic theme—check the blackboard for the country of the month. *$$; AE, MC, V; checks OK; breakfast Sat–Sun, lunch, dinner every day Apr–Aug (lunch Wed–Sun, dinner every day off-season, closed late Nov–Dec); beer and wine; reservations recommended; at Bow-Edison junction.*

LODGINGS

Benson Farmstead Bed & Breakfast

10113 AVON-ALLEN RD, BOW; 360/757-0578 OR 800/441-9814 Once part of a working dairy farm, this 17-room house, surrounded by English-style gardens, is packed with antiques and Scandinavian memorabilia. Four upstairs guest rooms (all with private baths) are outfitted with iron beds and custom quilts. Best are the Wildflowers and the English Garden Rooms. A cottage-style family suite is in the granary out back. Kids especially like the playroom and the three cats. In the evening, relax in the parlor, sharing Sharon Benson's desserts and coffee. Jerry and Sharon Benson cook a country breakfast. Don't be surprised to hear music in the air; the Bensons are talented pianists and violinists. *$$; MC, V; checks OK; bensonfarmstead@hotmail.com; www.bbhosts.com/bensonbnb; exit 232 west off I-5.*

Samish Point by the Bay / ★★

4465 SAMISH POINT RD, BOW; 360/766-6610 OR 800/916-6161 Theresa and Herb Goldston's tranquil getaway on their estatelike property at Samish Island's west end offers miles of wooded trails, a beach, mountain views, and solitude. Their three-bedroom cottage has a gas fireplace in the cozy living room and a hot tub on the back deck. It accommodates two to six (rates based on party size). The kitchen is stocked with continental breakfast fixings. *$$$; AE, MC, V; checks OK; hgtg@samishpoint.com; www.samishpoint.com; on Samish Island.*

Bellingham

Bellingham, the hub of northwestern Washington, is situated where the Nooksack River flows into Bellingham Bay. This community—full of fine old houses, award-winning university architecture, stately streets, and lovely parks—has been redis-covered in recent years. A new development on Squalicum Harbor, called **BELLWETHER**, with a park, outside amphitheater, shops, galleries, restaurants, shops, and a mini–grand hotel (see Hotel Bellwether, below) finally takes advantage of the town's waterfront location.

WESTERN WASHINGTON UNIVERSITY (on Sehome Hill south of downtown; 360/650-3000) is a fine expression of the spirit of Northwest architecture: warm materials, formal echoes of European styles, and respect for context and the natural backdrop. The visitor-parking kiosk on the south side of campus has maps of the university's outdoor sculpture collection.

The Old Town around Commercial and W Holly Streets hosts antique and junk shops and some decent eateries. **BELLINGHAM FARMERS MARKET** (downtown at Railroad Ave and Chestnut St, Sat, Apr–Oct; in Historic Fairhaven at 11th and Mill Sts, afternoons June–Sept; 360/647-2060; www.bellinghamfarmers.org) features produce—including the county's famed berry harvests—fresh seafood, herbs, flowers, and crafts.

The **WHATCOM MUSEUM OF HISTORY AND ART** (121 Prospect St; 360/676-6981; www.whatcommuseum.org) is a four-building campus. The main building is a massive Romanesque structure dating from 1892 and was used as a city hall until 1940. It has permanent exhibits on historic Bellingham as well as an adventurous exhibition schedule. Check out the presentations on local wildlife and Native Amer-ican culture in the **SYRE EDUCATION CENTER** (201 Prospect St) down the block, and the **WHATCOM CHILDREN'S MUSEUM** (227 Prospect St) a few doors farther north. Across the street, the **ARCO BUILDING** has changing art and history displays. One block from the main museum is **HENDERSON BOOKS** (116 Grand Ave; 360/734-6855), a 7,000-square-foot store with 250,000 volumes of used books in excellent shape (the staff is fanatical about the condition of the books) and a good collection of art books.

The summer **BELLINGHAM MUSIC FESTIVAL** (360/676-5997 or 800/335-5550; www.bellinghamfestival.org; late July–mid-Aug) has quickly become an institution, featuring more than two weeks of orchestral, chamber, and jazz performances. The **MOUNT BAKER THEATRE** (104 N Commercial St; 360/734-6080; www.mount bakertheatre.com), built in 1927 and renovated in 1995, is home to the **WHATCOM**

NO EXPERIENCE NECESSARY

SEA KAYAKING is an elegant, delightful way to explore the waterways, bays, and islands of Puget Sound. Miles of secluded coastline and engaging wildlife—including eagles and other birds, harbor seals, river otters, minke whales, even orcas—guarantee you're never bored. A real plus is that sea kayaking is surprisingly easy, even for novices. All you need is good health, an adventurous spirit, and a good teacher/guide. Half-day or shorter outings help you "get your feet wet." Ambitious overnight trips with provisions are like specialized backpacking/camping trips—by water—and become more of an adventure and an investment.

Several outfitters in Bellingham and the San Juan Islands offer short or long trips: **SAN JUAN SAFARIS** (San Juan Island; 360/378-6545; www.sanjuansafaris.com) trips leave from Roche Harbor and Friday Harbor; ask about whale-watching trips. **SHEARWATER KAYAK TOURS** (Eastsound, Orcas Island; 360/376-4699; www.shearwater kayaks. com) does half-day and longer trips from Eastsound and Rosario Resort. **MOONDANCE** (Bellingham; 360/738-7664; moondancekayak.com) offers half-day and longer outings, including exploring the petroglyphs of Bellingham Bay; as does **NORTH SOUND SEA KAYAK EXPEDITIONS** (Bellingham; 360/527-8714; www.northsoundkayaks.com). With **NORTHERN LIGHTS EXPEDITIONS** (Fairhaven; 800/754-7402), you can take an extensive trip (with gourmet meals) up the Inside Passage and in western Canada.

—*Jena MacPherson*

SYMPHONY ORCHESTRA (www.whatcomsymphony.com) and hosts other concerts, plays, films, and special events.

Bellingham has two attractive brewpubs: the **BOUNDARY BAY BREWERY** (1107 Railroad St; 360/647-5593) downtown, and the **ORCHARD STREET BREWERY** (709 W Orchard St; 360/647-1614), north of downtown in an office park. Boundary Bay serves a delicious lamb burger and other tasty pub grub; Orchard Street is popular among locals for its food and its beer. **MOUNT BAKER VINEYARDS** (11 miles east of Bellingham on Mount Baker Hwy/Hwy 542; 360/592-2300; open every day), in a cedar-sided, skylit facility, specializes in lesser-known varietals such as Müller Thurgau and Madeleine Angevine.

SEHOME HILL ARBORETUM (Bellingham Parks and Recreation; 360/676-6985; www.cob.gov), adjacent to WWU campus, sports more than 3 miles of trails, with prime views of the city, Bellingham Bay, and the San Juans. **WHATCOM FALLS PARK** (1401 Electric Ave; 360/676-6985) has more than 5 miles of trails overlooking several scenic falls. **BIG ROCK GARDEN PARK** (2900 Sylvan St, near Lake Whatcom; 360/676-6985; Apr–Oct) is a wonderful woodland site with a vast array of azaleas, rhododendrons, Japanese maples, and outdoor sculpture. **LAKE WHATCOM RAILWAY** (on Hwy 9 at Wickersham; 360/595-2218) makes scenic runs on July and August Saturdays using an old Northern Pacific engine. The **SKI-TO-SEA RACE**

(360/734-1330) attracts teams from all over the world to an annual seven-event relay on Memorial Day weekend.

South of the university, **FAIRHAVEN,** a once-separate town that was the result of a short-lived railroad boom in 1889–93, retains its old-time charm and offers plenty of exploring. The **MARKETPLACE** (Harris and 12th Sts), the grand dame of the attractive old buildings, was restored in 1988 and houses shops and dining options. The district is rich with diversions: crafts galleries, coffeehouses, bookstores, a charming garden/nursery emporium, and a lively evening scene. **VILLAGE BOOKS** (1210 11th St; 360/671-2626) carries an eclectic mix of new and used best-selling, children's, and regional titles, and has a knowledgeable staff. Downstairs is **THE COLOPHON CAFE** (360/647-0092; also downtown at 308 W Champion St, 360/676-6257), known for its African peanut soup and real cream pies. **TONY'S COFFEES** (1101 Harris St; 360/738-4710) is the local beanmeister. Stop at the **ARCHER ALE HOUSE** (1212 10th St; 360/647-7002) for a selection of brews, including hard-to-find Belgian beers, and tasty pizza and focaccia.

A handsome port facility in Fairhaven houses the southern terminus of the **ALASKA MARINE HIGHWAY SYSTEM** (355 Harris Ave; 360/676-8445 or 800/642-0066; www.state.gov/ferry); here travelers begin the long coastal journey through Alaska's famed Inside Passage. The **SAN JUAN ISLAND SHUTTLE EXPRESS** (355 Harris Ave, Ste 104; 360/671-1137) passenger-only ferry provides closer-to-home service to the San Juans, April though September; whale-watching and overnight cruises are also offered.

RESTAURANTS

Cafe Toulouse / ★

114 W MAGNOLIA ST, BELLINGHAM; 360/733-8996 Cafe Toulouse's claim to fame continues to be huge, well-orchestrated breakfasts and lunches for the local office crowd. Favorites include Greek and Provençal frittatas, huevos rancheros, hefty sandwiches, soups, and espresso drinks, all served up in a basic French bistro-style atmosphere. *$; AE, DIS, MC, V; checks OK; breakfast, lunch every day; no alcohol; reservations recommended for 5 or more; downtown near Cornwall Ave.* &

India Grill / ★

1215½ CORNWALL AVE, BELLINGHAM; 360/714-0314 The space is commercial looking—rectangular and glass-fronted—but music and decor put you in the mood. Delicious northern Indian cuisine, a long list of vegetarian choices, and a generous, inexpensive lunch buffet are the draws. Lamb saag, a spinach and lamb combo, and the Kadahi shrimp served in a wok are great choices for nonvegetarian newcomers. Dinner is a deal (with a 13-course offering under $15). *$; DIS, MC, V; checks OK; lunch, dinner every day; full bar; reservations not necessary; downtown between Holly and Chestnut Sts.* &

Pacific Cafe / ★★★

100 N COMMERCIAL ST, BELLINGHAM; 360/647-0800 A gastronomic leader in Bellingham for more than 17 years, the Pacific Cafe is still a relative "secret" outside the Northwest. Tucked into the Mount Baker Theatre building, its ambience is civilized and modern—with abstract watercolors and quiet jazz—and service is superb. Co-owner Robert Fong's Hawaiian background and years of travel in Europe, India, China, and Malaysia influence the sophisticated menu. Seafood dishes are specialties, but don't overlook the duck marinated with garlic, Thai chile, and fresh lemons. A current favorite is sizzling calamari with Thai basil. Expect wonderful desserts from pastry chef Wayne Kent, who's studied in New York with great American pastry chef Jacques Peyard. Made fresh, desserts include lilikoi (passion fruit) sorbet, butter pecan ice cream, and hand-dipped Belgian chocolate truffles. Quality vintages reflect a fine-tuned palate. Check on special wine dinners and food events. *$$; MC, V; local checks only; lunch Mon–Fri, dinner Mon–Sat; beer and wine; reservations recommended; near Champion St.* &

Pepper Sisters / ★★

1055 N STATE ST, BELLINGHAM; 360/671-3414 "We really try to rock the house," says owner Susan Albert, about the innovative, Southwestern fare served at Pepper Sisters. That attitude combined with cheerful, knowledgeable service, a great location in a vintage brick building, and a wide-awake kitchen have made the restaurant an institution. Seafood specials mix local provender with a "high desert" approach; the marinated grilled king salmon taco on soft blue corn tortilla with accents of kalamata olives, garlic, chipotle aioli, and fresh arugula is wildly popular. The kitchen shows the same verve with traditional favorites: delicious chiles rellenos are prepared with herbed chevre, jack cheese, cilantro, and blue cornmeal crust. For dessert, count on delicious traditional flan. *$; MC, V; checks OK; dinner Tues–Sun; beer and wine; reservations recommended for 5 or more; south of downtown.* &

LODGINGS

Best Western Heritage Inn / ★★

151 E MCLEOD RD, BELLINGHAM; 360/647-1912 OR 888/333-2080 Three tasteful, shuttered and dormered structures nestle amid a small grove of trees adjacent to Interstate 5 and a conglomeration of malls. This Best Western is one of the most professionally run hotels in the area. Rooms have a classic elegance with wing chairs in rich fabrics and cherrywood furnishings. Thoughtful touches include free newspapers, a guest laundry facility, an outdoor pool (in season), and indoor hot tub. Request a room away from the freeway. European-style continental breakfast is included. *$$; AE, DC, DIS, MC, V; checks OK; heritageinnbham@aol.com; www.bestwestern.com/heritageinnbellingham; exit 256 off I-5.*

The Chrysalis Inn & Spa / ★★★

804 10TH ST, BELLINGHAM; 360/756-1005 OR 888/ 808-0005 Perched on the water just north of Fairhaven, this new Northwest Craftsman–style hotel is a stylish, romantic retreat. All 43 guestrooms have oversized soaking or jetted tubs, fireplaces, and water views. We like the corner suites—pricey, but you could move in and be happy ever after. Spend an afternoon in the spa. Dine in Fino's, a sophisticated wine bar/restaurant with terrific water views,

and creative food beautifully presented—though with lots of wood, metal, and glass, it can be noisy. *$$$–$$$$; AE, DC, DIS, MC, V; checks OK; info@thechrysalis inn.com; www.thechrysalisinn.com; Old Fairhaven Pkwy exit off I-5.*

Fairhaven Village Inn / ★★

1200 10TH ST, BELLINGHAM; 360/733-1311 OR 877/733-1100 This new Victorian-style boutique hotel offers a great location in the heart of Fairhaven. Twenty-two large guest rooms have modern traditional furnishings, and bay or park views. Though not individually decorated, rooms are light-filled and appointed with traditional-style cherry wood furnishings and accents in crisp red and greens. The second-story terrace overlooks the bay and cruise terminal. Small conference rooms are also available. Continental breakfast is included. *$$–$$$; AE, DC, DIS, MC, V; checks OK; nwcinns@seanet.com; www.nwcountryinns.com/ fairhaven; exit 250 from I-5 and follow Old Fairhaven Pkwy.* &

Hotel Bellwether / ★★★★

ONE BELLWETHER WY, BELLINGHAM; 360/392-3100 OR 877/411-1200 Bellingham now has a perfect small "grand" hotel located in a perfect spot. Built at a cost of $10 million, the Hotel Bellwether on Squalicum Harbor opened in fall 2001. Many of the 68 rooms are on the waterfront overlooking Bellingham Bay and have terrific sunset views from private balconies or patios. Rooms have gas fireplaces, soaking tubs that can take in the view or be closed off (they also have separate glassed-in showers), and are richly decorated with furniture imported from Italy. A turndown service provides fine chocolates on your Hungarian down pillow (the dreamy beds are made up with Austrian bed linens). The dramatic Lighthouse Suite, a few steps from the hotel, offers three levels of seclusion and comes with its own private butler, champagne, and caviar. The hotel's friendly Harborside Bistro offers fine dining and views; breakfast and afternoon tea are served in the smaller, more intimate Compass Room. Enjoy a libation and watch the sun sink in the west from the Sunset Lounge. If you arrive by boat, you can "park" at the hotel's private dock. Security car parking is included. *$$–$$$$; AE, DC, DIS, MC, V; local checks only; reservations@hotelbellwether.com; www.hotel bellwether.com; exit 256 off I-5, turn right on Squalicum Wy.* &

North Garden Inn / ★

1014 N GARDEN ST, BELLINGHAM; 360/671-7828 OR 800/922-6414 This Victorian house (on the National Register of Historic Places) is popular with visitors to nearby WWU. Some of the 10 guest rooms (8 with private baths) have lovely views over Bellingham Bay and the islands. Rooms are attractive and have a bit more character than usual—due to the antique house and the influence of energetic, talented, and well-traveled hosts. Barbara and Frank DeFreytas are both musical: a piano is in one of the parlors for guests to use. *$$; AE, DIS, MC, V; checks OK; ngi@northgarden inn.com; northgardeninn.com/ngi; at E Maple St.*

Schnauzer Crossing / ★★★

4421 LAKEWAY DR, BELLINGHAM; 360/734-2808 OR 800/562-2808 Many of Donna and Monty McAllister's guests—romantic couples, business-people, discerning foreign travelers—return to this lovely contemporary home overlooking Lake Whatcom. The grounds include a meditation garden, wisteria arbor, hammock, koi pond, hot tub in a Japanese-style garden, and a miniature teahouse (handcrafted by Monty) in an idyllic glade. Three accommodations are available: the spacious and elegant Garden Suite, with fireplace, Jacuzzi, TV/VCR, and the separate cottage overlooking the lake are most luxurious. Guests in the simpler Queen Room enjoy the surroundings without the pricey amenities. A finely tuned sense of hospitality shows in small details: extra-thick towels, bathrobes and slippers, and gorgeous flowers year-round. Breakfast might include Triple-sec French toast or baked oatmeal served with ice cream "snowballs," summer fruits from the garden, and fresh-baked hazelnut scones. Children are welcome (breakfast is staggered for guests seeking quiet). Dog lovers take note—a new Schnauzer pup has joined the household—but please leave yours at home. *$$$; AE, MC, V; checks OK; schnauzerx@aol.com; www.schnauzercrossing.com; exit 253 off I-5.*

South Bay B&B / ★★

4095 SOUTH BAY DR, BELLINGHAM; 360/595-2086 OR 877/595-2086 You'll feel as if you've somehow fallen into an eagle's nest when you arrive at the top of this winding mountain road and get the bird's-eye views of Lake Whatcom. Privacy, views, forest—all offer a real getaway. Four guest rooms have lake views, queen beds with crisply ironed sheets, down comforters and pillows, and private baths with oversized jetted tubs for two; two rooms have gas fireplaces and one is a suite with living room and fireplace. Breakfast is an event—homemade granola, fruit, and an entree (perhaps crab in patty shells), enjoyed in the sunroom or lakeview dining room. Ask owners Dan and Sally Moore to tell the story of how their house came to this spot. *$$$; MC, V; checks OK; southbay@gte.net; www. southbaybb.com; 25 min south of Bellingham, I-5 exit 240.*

Stratford Manor / ★

4566 ANDERSON WY, BELLINGHAM; 360/715-8441 OR 800/240-6779 This rambling English Tudor–style home amid farmland northeast of Bellingham overlooks a half-acre pond, garden, and surrounding countryside. Three guest rooms occupy their own wing; all have jetted tubs and gas fireplaces. Our favorite is the Garden Room, with a spacious sitting area and tub overlooking the garden. The common area has a TV/ VCR with a selection of movies; outdoors is a hot tub. Wake-up coffee is delivered to your door; breakfast is served in the dining room, *$$$; MC, V; checks OK; llohse@aol.com; www.stratfordmanor.com; Sunset Dr exit off I-5.*

Lummi Island

Located just off Gooseberry Point northwest of Bellingham, Lummi is one of the most overlooked islands of the ferry-accessible San Juans. It echoes the days when the San Juan Islands were a hidden treasure, visited only by folks seeking bucolic surroundings. Private ownership has locked up most of this pastoral isle, so you won't find state parks or resorts. To stretch your limbs, bring bikes and enjoy the quiet country roads. Plan ahead; dining options are sparse. Not far from the ferry landing, the **BEACH STORE CAFE** (2200 N Nugent Rd; 360/758-2233) uses produce from the island or grown in its own garden; it's an island gathering place for pizza or clam chowder, but don't overlook daily specials. The **WILLOWS INN** (see below) has a small cafe with soups and sandwiches.

Lummi is serviced by the tiny **WHATCOM CHIEF FERRY** (360/676-6759 or 360/676-6730; www.co.whatcom.wa.us), which leaves Gooseberry Point at 10 minutes past the hour from 7am until midnight (more frequently on weekdays). It's easy to find (follow signs to Lummi Island from I-5, north of Bellingham), cheap ($4 round-trip for a car and two passengers), and quick (six-minute crossing). The ferry returns from Lummi on the hour.

LODGINGS

The Willows Inn / ★★☆

2579 W SHORE DR, LUMMI ISLAND; 360/758-2620 OR 888/294/2620 The torch was passed when longtime owners-innkeepers, Gary and Victoria Flynn sold this island icon to Judy Olsen and Riley Starks, of nearby Nettles Farm. The emphasis on good food is even stronger than before. Weekend dinners and Sunday brunch are served, and Willows has a small espresso cafe. The scones Australian chef Barry Forrester serves up, using his mother's recipe, are some of the best we've had. Cooking classes are offered (check web site). Four guest rooms with private baths in the main house include two on the main floor with private entrances. A private small cottage for two has a tiny kitchen and a terrific view; a two-bedroom guest house looks out to the water from a deck. For couples traveling together, the last is our favorite for its gas fireplace and whirlpool tub, and natural woodsy feel. Kitchens are stocked with basics. Judy has changed the decor to chic simple, sometimes spare but always restful. She and Riley are busy with their farm and are assisted by innkeepers Donna Baker and Lauren Rossano. *$$$; AE, MC, V; checks OK; willows@willows-inn.com; www.willows-inn.com; north on Nugent Rd for 3½ miles.* &

Lynden

This tidy community, with many immaculate yards and colorful gardens, adopted a Dutch theme in tribute to its early settlers. Visit the charming **PIONEER MUSEUM** (217 W Front St; 360/354-3675), full of local memorabilia, antique buggies, and motorcars.

RESTAURANTS

Hollandia

655 FRONT ST, LYNDEN; 360/354-4133 Chef Dini Mollink delivers authentic hearty fare imported from the Netherlands in a tasteful bistro setting that's a quiet oasis at the south end of Lynden's unique Dutch mini–shopping mall. Try the *Toeristen* menu: *Groentesoep* (firm, tasty meatballs in a luscious vegetable broth), Schnitzel Hollandia (lightly breaded chicken breast), and dessert (little almond tarts). *$; MC,*

V; local checks only; lunch Mon–Sat, dinner Thurs–Sat; beer and wine; reservations recommended; at Guide Meridian. &

LODGINGS

Dutch Village Inn / ★

655 FRONT ST, LYNDEN; 360/354-4440 One might question an inn located in a windmill in a Dutch-theme village. This inn, however, provides six tastefully furnished rooms to please all but the most jaded of travelers. Not surprisingly, rooms are named for Dutch provinces; the Friesland Kamer (Holland's northernmost province) room occupies the top of the windmill. Views are lovely, but interrupted as the giant blades of the windmill pass by (it turns, fully lit, until 10pm). Two rooms have extra beds fitted into curtained alcoves; two have two-person tubs. A continental breakfast is included. *$$; AE, DIS, MC, V; local checks only; dvinn@premier 1.net; off Guide Meridian.*

Blaine

The northernmost city along the Interstate 5 corridor, Blaine is the state's most popular—and most beautiful—border crossing into British Columbia. Home to the grand white **INTERNATIONAL PEACE ARCH MONUMENT,** which spans the U.S.-Canadian border, the surrounding park borders on Boundary Bay and is filled with lovely gardens and sculptures. Each June there's a Peace Arch celebration.

LODGINGS

Resort Semiahmoo / ★★★

9565 SEMIAHMOO PKWY, BLAINE; 360/318-2000 OR 800/770-7992 Nestled on a 1,100-acre wildlife preserve on Semi-ah-moo Spit, Resort Semiahmoo offers golf, waterfront, views west to the sea and the San Juans and east to Drayton Harbor, and acres of wooded trails. Amenities include a 300-slip marina; a house cruise vessel for San Juan excursions or fishing trips; a spa and salon; and a fitness center with heated indoor/outdoor pool, racquetball, tennis, and more. A multimillion-dollar renovation in 2001 added classy new earth-tone furnishings in the comfortably large rooms, art, and up-to-the-minute exercise equipment. Ask for a water-view room, with a fireplace; other rooms overlook the parking lot. Three restaurants provide views and a range of culinary alternatives; Stars is an award-winning fine dining eatery. The Arnold Palmer–designed golf course has long, unencumbered fairways surrounded by dense woods, and lovely sculptural sand traps. Adjacent is a convention center in revamped cannery buildings. *$$$; AE, DC, DIS, MC, V; checks OK; info@semiahmoo.com; www.semiahmoo.com; exit 270 off I-5.*

Anacortes and the San Juan Islands

There are 743 islands at low tide and 428 at high tide; 172 have names, 60 are populated, and only 4 have major ferry service. The San Juans are varied, remote, and breathtakingly beautiful. They lie in the rain shadow of the Olympic Mountains; most receive half the rainfall of Seattle. Of the main islands, three—Lopez, Orcas, and San Juan—have lodgings, eateries, and some beautiful parks.

ACCESS AND INFORMATION

The most obvious and cost-effective way to reach the San Juans is via the **WASH-INGTON STATE FERRIES** (206/464-6400 or 800/843-3779; www.wsdot.wa.gov/ferries/), which run year-round from Anacortes (see below). The sparsely populated islands are overrun in summer, and getting your car on a ferry out of Anacortes can mean a three-hour-plus wait. Bring a good book—or park the car and board with a bike. Money-saving tip: Cars pay only westbound. If you plan to visit more than one island, arrange to go to the farthest first (San Juan) and work your way east.

Other summer options for those who don't bring a car include the high-speed **VIC-TORIA CLIPPER** (2701 Alaskan Wy, Seattle; 206/448-5000; www.victoria clipper.com), which travels daily from downtown Seattle to Friday Harbor (with seasonal stops at Orcas Island's Rosario Resort); the passenger-only **SAN JUAN ISLAND SHUTTLE EXPRESS** (360/671-1137 or 888/373-8522) runs from Bellingham in summer. **KENMORE AIR** (425/486-1257 or 800/543-9595; www.kenmoreair.com) schedules five floatplane flights a day during peak season; fewer in off-season. Round-trip flights start at about $159 per person and leave from downtown Seattle at Lake Union and from north Lake Washington; luggage is weight-limited. **WEST ISLE AIR** (206/768-1945 or 800/874-4434; www.westisleair.com) offers scheduled daily flights from Boeing Field to the San Juan Islands, Anacortes, and Bellingham.

Anacortes

Anacortes, the gateway to the San Juans, is itself on an island: Fidalgo. Though most travelers rush through on their way to the ferry, this town adorned with colorful, life-sized cutouts of early pioneers is quietly becoming a place that warrants slowing down. Try **GEPPETTO'S** (3320 Commercial Ave; 360/293-5033) for Italian takeout; those with more time head to **GERE-A-DELI** (502 Commercial Ave; 360/293-7383), a friendly hangout with good homemade food in an airy former bank. And don't forget the **CALICO CUPBOARD** (901 Commercial Ave; 360/293-7315), an offshoot of the well-known cafe/bakery in La Conner.

For ferry reading material, stop by **WATERMARK BOOK COMPANY** (612 Commercial Ave; 360/293-4277). Seafaring folks should poke around **MARINE SUPPLY AND HARDWARE** (202 Commercial Ave; 360/293-3014); established in 1913, it's packed to the rafters with basic and hard-to-find specialty marine items. For the history of Fidalgo Island, visit the **ANACORTES MUSEUM** (1305 8th St; 360/293-1915; www.anacorteshistorymuseum.org).

Those who plan to kayak stop by **EDDYLINE WATERSPORTS CENTER** (1019 "Q" Ave; 360/299-2300 or 866/445-7506; www.seakayakshop.com), located at the **CAP SANTE MARINA** (just before Anacortes, take a right on "R" Ave off Hwy 20; 360/293-0694; portofanacortes.com). Test a kayak in the harbor, take a lesson, or rent one for a San Juan weekend; reservations necessary.

WASHINGTON PARK is less than a mile west of the ferry terminal. Here you'll find scenic picnic areas and a paved 2½-mile trail looping through an old-growth forest with great San Juan views.

RESTAURANTS

Bella Isola / ★★

619 COMMERCIAL AVE, ANACORTES; 360/299-8398 Owner Andy Ferguson and head chef Daniel Deer create traditional Italian specials that keep regulars coming back. The *penne con vodka*, penne pasta tossed in a creamy rose sauce with proscuitto and chile pepper vodka for spice, has lots of kick and is an unexpected offering. The grilled sirloin steak with balsamic glaze and Gorgonzola sauce is delicious. *$$; AE, DC, DIS, MC, V; checks OK; dinner every day; full bar; reservations recommended; between 6th and 7th Sts.* &

La Petite / ★★

3401 COMMERCIAL AVE, ANACORTES; 360/293-4644 OR 866/331-3328 Bela Berghuys, longtime owner of this restaurant at the Islands Inn motel, delivers French-inspired food with a touch of Dutch. Try lamb marinated in sambal, pork tenderloin with mustard sauce, or delicious chateaubriand when it's on the menu. Soup, salad, and fresh bread are included. A prix-fixe breakfast is intended for (but not exclusive to) motel guests. *$$; AE, DC, DIS, MC, V; local checks only; breakfast every day, dinner Tues–Sun; full bar; reservations recommended; www.islands inn.com; east end of Commercial Ave.*

Lopez Island

Lopez Island, flat and shaped like a jigsaw-puzzle piece, is a sleepy, bucolic place, famous for friendly locals (drivers always wave) and gentle inclines. The latter makes it the easiest bicycling in the islands: a mostly level 30-mile circuit suitable for the whole family. If you don't bring one, rent a bike from **LOPEZ BICYCLE WORKS** (2847 Fisherman Bay Rd; 360/468-2847; www.lopezbicycleworks.com); you can also rent kayaks there (www.lopezislandkayaks.com), mid-April through October.

Two day parks with beach access—**OTIS PERKINS** and **AGATE COUNTY**—are great for exploring. You can camp at 80-acre **ODLIN COUNTY PARK** (on right about 1 mile south of ferry dock; 360/468-2496) or 130-acre **SPENCER SPIT STATE PARK** (on left about 5 miles south of ferry dock; 888/226-7688; www.parks.wa.gov), both on the island's north side. Odlin has many nooks and crannies, and 30 grassy sites among Douglas firs, shrubs, and clover. Spencer Spit has about 50 campsites, 8 of them walk-ins on the beach. Both parks have water, toilets, and fire pits. Seals and bald eagles can often be seen from the rocky promontory off Shark Reef Park (off Shark Reef Rd), on the island's southwestern shore.

LOPEZ VILLAGE, 4 miles south of the ferry dock on the west shore near Fisherman Bay, is basic but has a few spots worth knowing about, such as **HOLLY B'S BAKERY** (Lopez Plaza; 360/468-2133; Apr–Dec), with fresh bread and pastries, and coffee to wash them down, and **THE LOVE DOG** (1 Village Ctr; 360/468-2150), for soups, sandwiches, and other choices.

RESTAURANTS

The Bay Cafe / ★★★

9 OLD POST RD, LOPEZ ISLAND; 360/468-3700 For years, the twinkling Bay Cafe has been reason alone to come to this serene isle. Its modern digs close to the beach (old fans remember its smaller, funkier location in the village) are spacious and retain the same rack of Fiestaware plates and rowboat suspended from the ceiling. A great sunset view of Fisherman Bay's entrance is a bonus. It's a come-as-you-are kind of place—and people do. The oft-changing menu might include steamed mussels in a Thai green chile coconut broth, Oregon bay shrimp cakes, or grilled tofu with chickpea-potato cakes (vegetarians never suffer). The daily seasonal fish special could be salmon, halibut, or fresh mahi mahi. Dinners include soup and local green salad. *$$; AE, DIS, MC, V; checks OK; dinner every day (Wed–Sun in winter); full bar; reservations recommended; baycafe@hotmail.com; www.bay-cafe.com; junction of Lopez Rd S and Lopez Rd N, Lopez Village.*

LODGINGS

Edenwild Inn / ★★

132 LOPEZ RD, LOPEZ ISLAND; 360/468-3238 OR 800/606-0662 This modern Victorian manse with a garden features eight individually decorated rooms, some with fireplaces, some with king-sized Victorian sleigh beds, all with private baths and beautiful hardwood floors. The inn is not on the water, yet front rooms upstairs have fine views: Room 6 features Fisherman Bay vistas. Owners Mary-Anne Miller and Clark Haley serve breakfast at individual tables in the dining room. Village restaurants and shops are within walking distance. *$$$; AE, MC, V; checks OK; edenwild@rockisland.com; www.edenwildinn.com; Lopez Village.* &

Inn at Swifts Bay / ★★★

856 PORT STANLEY RD, LOPEZ ISLAND; 360/468-3636 OR 800/375-5285 Nature and luxury blend charmingly in this Tudor retreat. You may be greeted by friendly deer or see rabbits cavorting in the yard. While the setting is "back to nature," accommodations are well above it. Five beautifully appointed rooms (three are suites with gas fireplaces and outside entrances) have queen-sized beds with down comforters—or lambswool, if you prefer—and are meticulously clean. On cool evenings, retreat to the living room, choose a book or magazine and sink into a wingback chair to enjoy a crackling fire. You can watch movies in the den (the video collection is impressive); make popcorn and help yourself to tea. True hedonists delight in the small cabin with a two-person sauna and outdoor shower. Reserve private time in the secluded hot tub, down a stone path at the edge of the forest. Guests are treated to fresh morning muffins, homemade jams, and the inn's secret fresh juice blend. You can drive, bike, hike, or get a ride (the innkeepers arrange this) from the ferry. *$$–$$$; AE, DIS, MC, V; checks OK; inn@swiftsbay.com; www.swiftsbay.com; 2 miles south of ferry landing.*

MacKaye Harbor Inn / ★

949 MACKAYE HARBOR RD, LOPEZ ISLAND; 360/468-2253 OR 888/314-6140 Bicyclists call this paradise after a sweaty trek from the ferry on the north end of the island to the little harbor on the south end. The tall white Victorian house, built in 1927, sits above a sandy, shell-strewn beach, perfect for sunset strolls or pushing off in a kayak. The Harbor Suite is our choice, with fireplace, private bath, and enclosed sitting area facing the beach. Rent kayaks or borrow mountain bikes; ask friendly innkeepers Mike and Robin Bergstrom to share their island secrets, and you're off to explore. Return later for fresh-baked cookies. If you do come by bike, be warned: the closest restaurant is 6 miles back in town. *$$$; MC, V; checks OK; 12 miles south of ferry landing.*

Orcas Island

Named not for the whales (the large cetaceans tend to congregate on the west side of San Juan Island and are rarely spotted here) but for a Spanish explorer, Orcas has a reputation as the most beautiful of the four main San Juan Islands. It's also the biggest (geographically) and the hilliest, boasting 2,407-foot **MOUNT CONSTITUTION** as the centerpiece of **MORAN STATE PARK** (800/233-0321). Drive, hike, or—if you're up to it—bike to the top; from the old stone tower you can see Vancouver, Mount Rainier, and everything between. The 4,800-acre state park, 13 miles northeast of the ferry landing, also has lakes and nice campsites, obtained through a central reservation service (888/226-7688; www.parks.wa.gov) at least two weeks ahead.

The man responsible for the park was shipbuilding tycoon Robert Moran. His old mansion is now the focal point of **ROSARIO RESORT & SPA** (see review), just west of the park. Even if you don't stay there, the mansion, decked out in period memorabilia, is worth a stop. Its enormous pipe organ is still used for performances.

Shaped like a pair of inflated lungs, with the cute little village of Eastsound running up the breastbone, Orcas has its ferry landing where it's most convenient for boats, 8 miles from town. Thus, most people bring their cars to the island; but you can walk on the ferry and rent a bicycle for the fairly level ride to town. Rent bicycles by the hour, day, or week from **DOLPHIN BAY BICYCLES** (at ferry landing; 360/376-4157), or **WILD LIFE CYCLES** (in Eastsound; 360/376-4708). Walk-ons can also stay at the historic **ORCAS HOTEL** (see review) at the landing.

RESTAURANTS

Bilbo's Festivo / ★

NORTH BEACH RD, EASTSOUND; 360/376-4728 Patrons speak of this cozy place with reverence. Its eclectic decor and setting—mud walls, Mexican tiles, fireplace, Navajo and Chimayo weavings, in a small house with generous garden courtyards—are charming. Note the highly varnished tables and wraparound bench fashioned from old-growth cedar. For more than 28 years, owner Cy Fraser has served up fare with Mexican and New Mexican flair; choose from enchiladas, burritos, chiles rellenos, and mesquite-grilled specials that include seafood and vegetarian options. Fraser broils the tomatoes, peppers, and other vegetables for his sauces to intensify flavors. Summer lunch is served taqueria-style, grilled-to-order outdoors. *$; MC, V; local checks only; lunch every day June–Sept and weekends Apr–May, dinner every day; full bar; reservations recommended; at A St.*

Cafe Olga / ★

OLGA JUNCTION (11 POINT LAWRENCE RD), OLGA; 360/376-5098 While you wait for your table at Cafe Olga, browse the adjoining Orcas Island Artworks, a sprawling crafts gallery in a renovated strawberry-packing barn. International home-style entrees at this popular midday island stop include a rich Sicilian artichoke pie and a chicken enchilada with black-bean sauce. For dessert, try the terrific blackberry pie. *$; MC, V; local checks only; lunch every day (closed Jan–Feb); beer and wine; reservations not necessary; at Olga Junction.* &

Christina's / ★★★

310 MAIN ST, EASTSOUND; 360/376-4904 Perched over Eastsound and built above a 1930s gas station, Christina's offers a bewitching blend of provincial locale and urban sophistication. And the water view from the dining room and deck doesn't hurt. Christina Orchid's classic continental food keeps patrons returning. After two decades alone at the helm, she now shares that role with talented head chef Jacob Angel. Local oysters are routinely on the menu. King salmon might come with scallops, sorrel, and Jack Daniels cream sauce; and the fillet of beef could arrive with a horseradish potato gratin and an apple shiitake demi-glace. These kinds of dishes have made Christina's reputation. Servings tend toward generous; appetizers are sized to share or enjoy as a light meal. *$$$; AE, DC, MC, V; checks OK; dinner every day (Thurs–Mon in winter); full bar; reservations recommended; www.christinas.net; at N Beach Rd.*

Ship Bay Oyster House / ★★

326 OLGA RD, EASTSOUND; 360/376-5886 Ship Bay has a reputation for fresh fish and local oysters: baked, stewed, panfried, or au naturel (try an oyster shooter with Clamato and sake). The Pacific Coast locale (a comfortable old farmhouse with a view of Ship Bay) belies the Atlantic Coast ambience. The New England clam chowder might be the best in the West, and the kitchen obviously never learned portion control (order a small slab of spicy-hot barbecue baby back ribs with black beans and salsa, and you'll get our drift). Locals swear the best deal on the island is appetizer fare in the lounge or outdoor patio. Eleven deluxe rooms (one an executive suite with whirlpool bath) have king beds, fireplaces, and bay views. *$$; AE, DC, DIS, MC, V; checks OK; dinner every day (Tues–Sun Mar–Apr and Oct–Nov, closed Dec–Feb); full bar; reservations recommended; shipbay@rockisland.com; www.innatshipbay.com; east of Eastsound on Olga Rd.* &

LODGINGS

Cascade Harbor Inn / ★★

1800 ROSARIO RD, EASTSOUND; 360/376-6350 OR 800/201-2120 Forty-eight modern units—some studios with Murphy beds, some two-queen rooms, some in-between—have decks and water views, and many configure into multi-unit suites with full kitchens. The inn shares its vistas of pristine Cascade Bay and beach access with sprawling Rosario Resort next door. Continental breakfast is included in summer. *$$$; AE, DIS, MC, V; checks OK; cascade@rockisland.com; www.cascade harborinn.com; just east of Rosario.*

Deer Harbor Inn and Restaurant / ★★

33 INN LN, DEER HARBOR; 360/376-4110 OR 877/377-4110 Over the years, owners Pam and Craig Carpenter have shored up this rustic old lodge, built in 1915 in an apple orchard overlooking Deer Harbor. Lodge rooms are small, with peeled-log furniture. Newer cabins have a beachy feel—knotty pine walls, log furniture, woodstoves or fireplaces, and private hot tubs; the two-bedroom, two-bath Pond Cottage is roomy with a full kitchen, fireplace, and deck. Beds are heaped with quilts. Breakfast is delivered to your door: freshly baked goods and plenty of hot coffee. Dinners are served nightly in the lodge's rustic dining room. *$$–$$$; AE, MC, V; checks OK; www.deerharborinn.com; from ferry landing, follow signs past West Sound to Deer Harbor.* &

Orcas Hotel / ★

 ORCAS FERRY LANDING, ORCAS; 360/376-4300 OR 888/672-2792 This pretty, romantic 1904 Victorian, originally built as a boardinghouse, has period pieces inside and white wicker on the deck overlooking the water. Best of the dozen accommodations are two new, larger rooms with private balconies and whirlpool tubs. This is the only hotel within walking distance of the ferry; the adjoining cafe and bakery with its grandstand deck is *the* place to wait with a beer or a sandwich. A full-service restaurant and bar are within the hotel. *$$$; AE, MC, V; checks OK; orcas@orcashotel.com; www.orcashotel.com; Orcas ferry landing.*

Outlook Inn / ★

171 MAIN ST, EASTSOUND; 360/376-2200 OR 888/688-5665 If you stay in Eastsound—Orcas's "big city"—stay at the legendary 1888 Outlook Inn. Like the proverbial hippies who once flocked here, the 45-room inn has traded its counter-cultural spirit for luxuries money can buy. Though the old portion with shared baths is still available, and affordable, newer swanky suites have bang-up views, fireplaces, decks, whirlpool baths, and heated towel racks—and command prices a hippie would surely protest. We remember its humble past so the renovated Outlook Inn feels a little soulless to us. But the bar and restaurant have a loyal local clientele: always a good sign. *$$–$$$; AE, DIS, MC, V; local checks only; info@outlook-inn.com; www.outlook-inn.com; downtown.* &

Rosario Resort & Spa / ★★★

1400 ROSARIO RD, ROSARIO; 360/376-2222 OR 800/562-8820 This historic, waterfront estate built by 1900s Seattle industrialist Robert Moran was converted to a resort in the 1960s and was popular with boaters. The resort has seen expensive renovation in recent years, to return the mansion to its former elegance. Teak floors, mahogany paneling, original furnishings, and Tiffany accents give a feel for the home's past. Now the ugly, obstreperous duckling is a dazzling swan. One thing can't be overcome: most of the guest rooms are perched on a hillside behind the mansion—a steep climb unless you take the resort's van service. Rooms have a cheery upscale country style; most offer bay views. The mansion itself houses a museum and music room (don't miss the organ recital by historian Christopher Peacock), gift shops, lounge, veranda, and restaurants. Spa services and a pool are on the lower level. Also on the grounds are a kayaking concession, dive shop, and conference facilities. *$$$–$$$$; AE, DC, DIS, MC, V; checks OK; info@rosarioresort.com; www.rosarioresort.com; from Eastsound drive east on Olga Rd for 3 miles.* &

Spring Bay Inn / ★★★

464 SPRING BAY TRAIL, OLGA; 360/376-5531 It's a long dirt road getting here, but rarely is a drive so amply rewarded. On 57 wooded seafront acres, the inn's interior reflects the naturalist sensibilities of innkeepers Sandy Playa and Carl Burger, a youthful pair of retired state park rangers. The angular great room, with fieldstone fireplace, showcases a stunning view. Upstairs, four thoughtfully decorated guest rooms have private baths and fireplaces; two have balconies. Downstairs, the Ranger's Suite has 27 windows and its own hot tub. Coffee, muffins, and fruit are delivered to each door—sustenance for a complimentary two-hour guided kayak tour. Return for a healthy brunch. The property, laced with hiking trails and teeming with wildlife, is adjacent to Obstruction Pass State Park. Ease tired muscles with a soak under the stars in the bayside hot tub. *$$$; DIS, MC, V; checks OK; info@springbayinn.com; www.springbayinn.com; Obstruction Pass Rd to Trailhead Rd, left onto Spring Bay Trail.*

Turtleback Farm Inn / ★★

1981 CROW VALLEY RD, EASTSOUND; 360/376-4914 OR 800/376-4914 Located inland amid tall trees, rolling pastures, and private ponds, Turtleback offers seven spotless rooms dressed in simple sophistication and stunning antiques. Turtleback's veteran innkeepers, Bill and Susan Fletcher, have thought of everything, from cocoa, coffee, and fresh fruit for nibbling, to flashlights for evening forays. We found our room—the Nook—aptly named. It's worth the extra $50 or more to go up a notch or two: choose either of the larger upstairs rooms, one of two downstairs rooms with private decks overlooking the meadow, or a luxury suite in the Orchard House. Susan cooks magnificent breakfasts and serves them on the deck in sunny weather. A barn-style building in the orchard houses four spacious suites with fir flooring, trim, and doors, each with a Vermont Casting stove, king-sized bed, bar-sized refrigerator, and spacious bath with large claw-footed tub and shower; all have private decks. Children are welcome in suites by prior arrangement. *$$$; AE, DIS, MC, V; checks OK; www.turtlebackinn.com; 6 miles from ferry on Crow Valley Rd.* &

San Juan Island

San Juan Island, the most populated in the archipelago, supports the biggest town, Friday Harbor. The **SAN JUAN HISTORICAL MUSEUM** (405 Price St; 360/378-3949) is filled with memorabilia from the island's early days. Another bit of history is hidden away at **ROCHE HARBOR RESORT** (see review). Here you'll find a mausoleum, a bizarre monument that may tell more about timber tycoon John McMillin than does all the rest of Roche Harbor. The ashes of family members are contained in a set of stone chairs that surround a concrete dining room table. They're ringed by a set of 30-foot-high columns, symbolic of McMillin's adherence to Masonic beliefs. At the entrance to Roche Harbor Resort Village, a new 19-acre preserve on Westcott Bay contains sculptural works by renowned artists.

Other attractions on the island include the mid-19th-century sites of the **AMERICAN** and **ENGLISH CAMPS** (360/378-2240; www.nps.gov/sajh/home), established when ownership of the island was under dispute. The conflict led to the infamous Pig War of 1859–60, so called because the sole casualty was a pig. Americans and British shared joint occupation until 1872, when the dispute was settled in favor of the United States. The English camp, toward the island's northwest end, is wooded and secluded; the American camp at the south end is open, windy prairie and beach. Either makes a fine picnic spot. So does beautiful **SAN JUAN COUNTY PARK** (50 San Juan Park Rd; 360/378-2992), on the island's west side, where it's possible to camp on 19 sites on a pretty cove (reservations recommended). Another camping option is **LAKEDALE RESORT** (2627 Roche Harbor Rd; 360/378-2350 or 800/617-2267; www.lakedale.com; reservations recommended), a private campground on 84 acres with three lakes for swimming and fishing, a 10-room lodge and six two-bedroom log cabins.

The best diving in the archipelago can be had here (some claim it's the best cold-water diving in the world); **EMERALD SEAS OUTFITTERS** (180 1st St, Friday Harbor; 360/378-2772; www.emeraldseas.com) has rentals, charters, and classes. Several charter boats are available for whale-watching (primarily Orcas); try the **WESTERN PRINCE** (1 block from ferry landing; 360/378-5315 or 800/757-ORCA). Those distrustful of their sea legs can visit the marvelous **WHALE MUSEUM** (62 1st St; 360/378-4710 or 800/946-7227; www.whalemuseum.com), with exhibits devoted to the resident cetaceans; or go to the nation's first official whale-watching park at **LIME KILN POINT STATE PARK** on the island's west side. Bring binoculars and patience.

Oyster fans happily visit **WESTCOTT BAY SEA FARMS** (904 Westcott Dr; 360/378-2489) off Roche Harbor Road, 2 miles south of Roche Harbor Resort, where you can help yourself to oysters at bargain prices.

RESTAURANTS

Duck Soup Inn / ★★

50 DUCK SOUP LN, FRIDAY HARBOR; 360/378-4878 Richard and Gretchen Allison are committed to a kitchen with an ambitious reach, using local seafoods and seasonal ingredients, and they've succeeded admirably. The arbor-fronted, shingled cottage is tucked into the woods overlooking ponds. The wood-paneled dining room, with stone fireplace, wooden booths, and high windows, is a charmer. The menu is all house specialties—succulent sautéed prawns in wild blackberry sauce, applewood-smoked Westcott Bay oysters, and grilled fresh fish. House-baked bread served with tangy anchovy paste and butter; a small bowl of perfectly seasoned soup, and a large green salad accompany ample portions. *$$; DIS, MC, V; checks OK; dinner Wed–Sun (closed in winter); beer and wine; reservations recommended; www.ducksoupinn.com; 5 miles northwest of Friday Harbor.* &

The Place Next to the San Juan Ferry Cafe / ★

I SPRING ST, FRIDAY HARBOR; 360/378-8707 Behind the unassuming name and waterside location is this striving concern, garnering much local praise. Chef-owner Steven Anderson features a rotating world of cuisines, focusing on fish and shellfish, from BC king salmon to Westcott Bay oysters. Salmon might come with gingery citrus sauce, or try black-bean ravioli topped with tiger prawns in a buttery glaze. In summer, crab cakes flavored with ginger and lemongrass are a sure bet. Servers know exactly how much time you have if your boat's in sight: with luck, enough to savor the sumptuous crème caramel. *$$; MC, V; local checks only; dinner every day; beer and wine; reservations recommended; at foot of Spring St.* &

LODGINGS

The Argyle House / ★★★

685 ARGYLE RD, FRIDAY HARBOR; 360/378-4084 OR 800/624-3459 Two blocks from downtown Friday Harbor, Argyle House is a vintage 1910 Craftsman home set on a gardened acre with fish pond, brick patio, and outdoor spa tub. Accommodations include three upstairs rooms with private baths, a downstairs two-bedroom suite with claw-footed tub, and a honeymoon cottage with private deck. The main house has lovely hardwood floors, high ceilings, and a cozy living area, where owners Bill and Chris Carli have been known to join guests in impromptu musical reveries (Bill plays guitar and harmonica). Immaculate bedrooms are nicely appointed; the honeymoon cottage has a beamed skylit ceiling, lace curtains, a hope chest with extra towels, and a kitchenette with microwave, minifridge, coffeemaker, and beverages—plus a private hot tub and shatter-proof champagne glasses. Listen to the Carlis, avid travelers and sailors, tell stories over breakfast of a sailing excursion to the Panama Canal, while you feast on exceptional French toast with berries, homemade granola, coffee cake, and fresh fruit (if you leave before breakfast, they'll pack you something to go). *$$; MC, V; checks OK; cmcarli@hotmail.com; argylehouse.net; 4 blocks from ferry.*

The Cabin of Two Bears / ★☆

153 LIMESTONE POINT RD, SAN JUAN ISLAND; 360/378-3190 OR 888/367-5211 A cheerful atmosphere and secluded location (not far from Roche Harbor Resort Village) make the Cabin of Two Bears a romantic weekend or honeymoon favorite. And you might not be able to fit more than two in this cabin. Peter and Michele DeLorenzi built it between 1991 and 1998 using extras from other projects to charming effect; natural wood touches complement country-style curtains and trimmings. The homey cabin is nestled in the woods and has a gas fireplace, full kitchen, gas grill, TV/VCR, CD player, and small dining table. The upstairs bedroom loft is warm and cozy—though you must climb the indoor ladder or use the outdoor staircase to reach it. A great wraparound deck features a private hot tub for a soak under the stars. The DeLorenzis have four other cabins (see web site). *$$$; MC, V; checks OK; 2-night min summer weekends; twobears@rockisland.com; www.sanjuanislandvacationrentals.com; about 9 miles from ferry.*

Duffy House / ★

4214 PEAR POINT RD, FRIDAY HARBOR; 360/378-5604 OR 800/972-2089
This 1920s farmhouse overlooks Griffin Bay and the Olympics, commanding a splendid, isolated site on the island's southeast side. Decorated with antiques, Duffy House offers five comfy guest rooms, all with private baths. The living room sports a bounty of island information. Even neophyte bird-watchers can't miss the bald eagles; they nest across the street near the trail to the beach. *$$; MC, V; checks OK; duffyhouse@rockisland.com; www.duffyhousebnb.com; take Argyle Rd south from town.*

Friday Harbor House / ★★★

130 WEST ST, FRIDAY HARBOR; 360/378-8455 Some shudder at the sore-thumb architecture of San Juan Island's poshest inn, a sister property of Whidbey Island's Inn at Langley. Others consider this stylish urban outpost a welcome relief from Victorian B&Bs. Either way, the interior is a bastion of spare serenity, a mood abetted by professional management. Twenty rooms are decorated in muted contemporary tones, have gas fireplaces and (noisy) Jacuzzis positioned to absorb both the fire's warmth and the harbor view. Some rooms have tiny balconies; not all offer full waterfront views. Breakfast is continental, with delicious hot scones. The view dining room maintains the inn's spartan cool, warming considerably under the influence of chefs Laurie Paul and Tim Barrette's cooking. *$$$; AE, DIS, MC, V; checks OK; fhhouse@rockisland.com; www.fridayharborhouse.com; from ferry, left on Spring St, right on 1st St, right on West St.* ♿

Friday's Historic Inn / ★

35 1ST ST, FRIDAY HARBOR; 360/378-5848 OR 800/352-2632 New innkeepers Adam and Laura Saccio have spruced up this 1891 historic building that's been a B&B-style inn for more than 10 years, adding more communal space and a garden terrace. Of the 15 rooms, the best is the Eagle Cove, a third-floor, water-view perch with a deck, kitchen, double shower, and Jacuzzi. Heated bathroom floors and occasional fresh-baked cookies are just two thoughtful touches. *$$; MC, V; checks OK; fridays@friday-harbor.com; www.friday-harbor.com; 2 blocks from ferry.* ♿

Harrison House Suites / ★★★

235 C ST, FRIDAY HARBOR; 360/378-3587 OR 800/407-7933 This crisply renovated Craftsman inn, run by the effusive Farhad Ghatan, features five impressive suites: all with kitchens and private baths, four with decks, four with whirlpool tubs. Rooms with views overlook the scenic sweep of Friday Harbor. A pretty water garden, plus flower, fruit, and vegetable gardens for guest use make this the only place we've seen in the islands where you can pick your own salad and toss it in your own kitchen. Great for families or groups. Fresh-baked breads are served each evening; mornings, it's fresh scones. Kayak and mountain bikes are available for guests. Ghatan also runs a little cafe—guests only—for private dinners and catered events. *$$; AE, DIS, MC, V; checks OK; hhsuites@rockisland.com; www.san-juan-lodging.com; 2 blocks from downtown.* ♿

Highland Inn / ★★★

WEST SIDE OF SAN JUAN ISLAND; 360/378-9450 OR 888/400-9850 The former owner of the famous Babbling Brook Inn in Santa Cruz, California, Helen King moved north and built the inn of her dreams on the west side of San Juan Island. Now she has just two lovely suites, one at each end of her house. Licensed for only two couples a night (no children), the Highland Inn is everything you could ask for in privacy and hospitality. Suites are huge, with sitting rooms, wood-burning fireplaces, marble bathrooms—each with a jetted tub for two and steam-cabinet shower—and views of the Olympic Mountains, Victoria, and Haro Strait from the 88-foot-long covered veranda. Afternoons, King serves tea and "Mrs. King's Cookies"—a white-and-dark-chocolate-chip cookie. *$$$; AE, MC, V; checks OK; helen@highlandinn.com; www.highlandinn.com; call for directions.*

Lonesome Cove Resort / ★

416 LONESOME COVE RD, FRIDAY HARBOR; 360/378-4477 A fixture on the island since the 1940s, this 10-acre resort offers classic log-cottage-in-the-woods charm. Six immaculate little cabins at the water's edge, manicured lawns, and domesticated deer that wander the woods make the place a favorite for lighthearted honeymooners. Sunsets are spectacular. No pets—too many baby ducks. *$$; MC, V; checks OK; 2-night min, 5-night min in summer; cabins@lonesomecove.com; www.lonesomecove.com; take Roche Harbor Rd 9 miles north to Lonesome Cove Rd.* &

Roche Harbor Resort / ★★

ROCHE HARBOR; 360/378-2155 OR 800/451-8910 The centerpiece of Roche Harbor Resort, the stately, ivy-clad Hotel de Haro is steeped in Northwest history. Built by Tacoma lawyer-industrialist John McMillin in 1886 (around foot-thick walls of a Hudson's Bay post), its creaky, uneven floorboards have felt the press of famous shoe leather, including Teddy Roosevelt. History buffs relish the piecework wallpaper and period furnishings, and remnants of McMillin's lime quarry, once the largest west of the Mississippi. From the hotel entry, gaze out at the trellised, cobblestoned waterfront and yacht-crammed bay. The hotel offers 20 rooms; only four have private bathrooms. Separate accommodations include four luxury view suites (in McMillin's old house) with claw-footed soaking tubs. A few nicely renovated cottages (ask for one viewing the water) and condos are available. A fine-dining restaurant, cafe, and casual eatery are on the grounds. Stroll the gardens, swim, kayak, play tennis, and visit the mausoleum (really). *$$$; AE, MC, V; checks OK; roche@rocheharbor.com; www.rocheharbor.com; on waterfront at northwest end of island.* &

Wharfside Bed & Breakfast / ★

K DOCK, #13, FRIDAY HARBOR; 360/378-5661 OR 800/899-3030 If nothing lulls you to sleep like the gentle lap of the waves, the Wharfside's for you. Two guest rooms on the 60-foot sailboat *China Girl* are nicely finished, with full amenities and the compact precision that only boat living can inspire. Staterooms, fore and aft, have queen-sized beds. Aft has its own bathroom; fore uses the bath in the main cabin. When the weather's good, enjoy the huge breakfast on deck and watch boaters head to sea. *$$; AE, MC, V; checks OK; slowseason@rockisland.com; www.slowseason.com; marina is north of ferry terminal.*

Tacoma, Olympia, and the South Sound

Going south, Interstate 5 takes you to the state's second-largest city, Tacoma, which is experiencing a renaissance, especially in the arts, and to the state's picturesque bay-side capital of Olympia.

Vashon Island

Faintly countercultural, this bucolic isle is a short ferry ride from downtown Seattle (foot passengers only), West Seattle (the Fauntleroy ferry), or Tacoma (Point Defiance ferry), all via **WASHINGTON STATE FERRIES** (206/464-6400 or 800/843-3779; www.wsdot.wa.gov/ferries/). It's a wonderful place to explore by bicycle, although the first long hill from the north-end ferry dock is a killer. Few beaches are open to the public, but some public spots invite a stroll and offer a view.

Vashon has several island-based companies that market goods locally and nationally, these include **K2 SKIS, INC.** (19215 Vashon Hwy SW; 206/463-3631) and **SEATTLE'S BEST COFFEE** (19529 Vashon Hwy SW; 206/463-5050). Stop and pick up fresh preserves, fruit syrups, and apple cider at **WAX ORCHARDS** (22744 Wax Orchards Rd; 206/463-9735). Island arts are displayed at the **BLUE HERON ART CENTER** (19704 Vashon Hwy SW; 206/463-5131). The **COUNTRY STORE AND GARDENS** (20211 Vashon Hwy SW; 206/463-3655) is an old-fashioned general store stocking many island-made products including Maury Island Farms jams (www.goodjam.com), natural-fiber apparel, housewares, and gardening supplies. **VASHON ISLAND KAYAK COMPANY** (Jensen Acres boathouse at Quartermaster Harbor; 206/463-9257 or www.pugetsoundkayak.com) offers instruction and day trips.

RESTAURANTS

Express Cuisine / ★

17629 VASHON HWY SW, VASHON; 206/463-6626 This storefront restaurant and catering company may not look like much, but locals line up for gourmet take-out dinners, or fill communal tables to enjoy tender prime rib, mouth-watering sirloin stroganoff, and smoked salmon over linguine with a mushroom Alfredo sauce. Dinners include soup or salad (if seafood chowder is on the list, choose it). Service is counter-style. Come early or call ahead for takeout; otherwise, you might have to wait. *$; no credit cards; local checks only; dinner Wed–Sat; beer and wine; reservations not accepted; near Bank Rd.* &

Tacoma

Flanked by Commencement Bay and the Narrows and backed by Mount Rainier, Tacoma is no longer just a blue-collar mill town, but a growing urban center with a thriving cultural core and a plethora of wonderful new and old, small and large, modest and grand museums. Perhaps the brightest star is the $63 million **MUSEUM OF GLASS: INTERNATIONAL CENTER FOR CONTEMPORARY ART** (on Thea Foss

Waterway, 253/396-1768; www.internationalglass.org), designed by famed architect Arthur Erickson and open in July 2002. Also new is **JOB CARR'S CABIN** (N 31st St; 253/627-5405), a tiny Old Town museum that marks the city's birthplace. The **COMMENCEMENT BAY MARITIME CENTER** (705 Dock St; 253/272-2750) is a work in progress with plenty of boats on display, and telling the story of the real-life Tugboat Annie. The free **KARPELES MANUSCRIPT MUSEUM** (407 South G St; 253/383-2575; kmuseumtaq@aol.com), with changing exhibits and signatures of famous figures, is located across from Wright Park (Division and I Sts), a serene in-city park with trees, a duck-filled pond, and a beautifully maintained glass-and-steel 1890 conservatory.

The **TACOMA ART MUSEUM** (12th St and Pacific Ave; 253/272-4258) has paintings by Renoir, Degas, and Pissarro, and the largest public collection in the country of glass art by Tacoma native Dale Chihuly. The museum is housed for the time being in a former bank; watch for its grand new home in 2003. The **WASHINGTON STATE HISTORY MUSEUM** (1911 Pacific Ave; 888/238-4373) occupies a handsome building just south of Union Station. A state-of-the-art museum experience, it provides history and innovation under the same roof; from the outside, the museum has been designed to complement the old train station. The **RUSTON WAY WATERFRONT** (between N 49th and N 54th Sts) is a popular 2-mile mix of parks and restaurants.

The **BROADWAY CENTER FOR THE PERFORMING ARTS** (901 Broadway Plaza; 253/591-5894) often does shows at both the Pantages and Rialto Theaters. The restored 1,100-seat **PANTAGES THEATER** (901 Broadway Plaza), originally designed in 1918 by nationally known movie-theater architect B. Marcus Priteca, is the focal point of the reviving downtown cultural life—dance, music, and stage presentations.

Historic buildings in the downtown warehouse district have been converted from industrial use to hip residential and commercial functions; the **UNIVERSITY OF WASHINGTON** (1900 Commerce St; 253/692-4000 or 800/736-7750) now has a branch campus here. Stately homes and cobblestone streets in the north end are often used as sets by Hollywood's moviemakers.

History and architecture buffs delight in **OLD CITY HALL** (625 Commerce St), with its coppered roof and Renaissance clock; the Romanesque **FIRST PRESBYTERIAN CHURCH** (20 Tacoma Ave S); the rococo **PYTHIAN LODGE** (925½ Broadway Plaza); and the one-of-a-kind **UNION STATION** (17th St and Pacific Ave), built in 1911 and now the much praised Federal Courthouse (with some spectacular Chihuly glass on public display). Also of note is the turreted chateau of Stadium High School (N 1st St and Stadium Wy), site of several Hollywood movie sets.

POINT DEFIANCE PARK (northwest side of Tacoma, call for directions; 253/305-1000) has 500 acres of untouched forest jutting out into Puget Sound and is one of the country's most dramatically sited and creatively planned city parks. The wooded 5-mile drive and parallel hiking trails open up now and then for sweeping views of the water, Vashon Island, Gig Harbor, and the Olympic Mountains. There are rose, rhododendron, Japanese, and Northwest native gardens; a railroad village with a working steam engine; a reconstruction of Fort Nisqually (originally built in 1833); a museum; a swimming beach; and the much acclaimed **POINT DEFIANCE**

ZOO & AQUARIUM (5400 N Pearl St; 253/591-5335). Watching the play of sea otters, polar bears, walruses, and white beluga whales from underwater vantage points is a rare treat.

The **TACOMA DOME** (2727 E "D" St; 253/572-3663), the world's largest wooden dome, is the site of trade, entertainment, and sports shows. Fans of baseball played outdoors in a first-class ballpark head to Cheney Stadium to watch the **TACOMA RAINIERS** (2502 S Tyler St; 253/752-7707), the triple-A affiliate of the Seattle Mariners.

Thirsty? **ENGINE HOUSE NO. 9** (611 N Pine St; 253/272-3435) near the University of Puget Sound is a friendly, beer-lover's dream tavern (minus the smoke). Other fun watering holes include **THE SPAR** (2121 N 30th St; 253/627-8215) in Old Town. The new **HARMON** brewpub (1938 Pacific Ave; 253/383-2739), across from the history museum, and the nearby **SWISS** (1904 S Jefferson Ave; 253/572-2821) are local favorites.

LAKEWOLD GARDENS (12317 Gravelly Lake Dr SW, Lakewood; exit 124 off I-5 to Gravelly Lake Dr; 253/584-3360; open Thurs–Mon, Apr–Sept, and Mon, Thurs, and Fri in winter), one of the area's largest estates, lies ten minutes south of Tacoma on a beautiful 10-acre site overlooking Gravelly Lake in Lakewood. Recognized as one of America's outstanding gardens, Lakewold Gardens offers guided and nonguided tours.

RESTAURANTS

Altezzo / ★★

1320 BROADWAY PLAZA (SHERATON TACOMA HOTEL), TACOMA; 253/572-3200 Atop the Sheraton (see review), this restaurant is "lofty" in space and attitude. Request a window table for great downtown and area views—and some of the best Italian cuisine in Tacoma. Chef James VandeBerg offers a delicious cioppino, or ravioli with spinach and chard in tomato cream sauce. Tiramisu is the real McCoy, and there's a wonderful fresh pear and berry tart with ice cream and cinnamon sauce. The bar is a great place to kick back with a glass of wine and a plate of antipasto and enjoy the view. *$$; AE, DC, MC, V; dinner every day; full bar; reservations recommended; between 13th and 15th Sts.* &

The Cliff House / ★★

6300 MARINE VIEW DR, TACOMA; 253/927-0400 Commanding views of Commencement Bay, Mount Rainier, and the Tacoma skyline, and its formal decor and "memory lane" desserts—cherries jubilee and crepes suzette flambéed tableside—make this a special occasion eatery for some. The addition of a new more casual restaurant downstairs is good news. *$$$; AE, DC, DIS, MC, V; no checks; lunch, dinner every day; full bar; reservations recommended; top of Marine View Dr (Highway 509).*

East & West Cafe / ★

5319 TACOMA MALL BLVD, TACOMA; 253/475-7755 What this restaurant lacks in location, it makes up for tenfold in great food and charm. It's a haven of Asian delights on the busy thoroughfare south of Tacoma Mall. Owner

Vien Floyd, a Saigon native, has gained a loyal local following and has remodeled and doubled her space *twice* in recent years. Her incomparable personality helps make meals here a treat. The emphasis is on Vietnamese and Thai cuisine; the Saigon Crepe is filled with chicken, prawns, and vegetables. Vegetables are crisp, bright, and full of flavor; sauces have character; meats are tender. For the price, it's hard to have a better meal in Tacoma. *$; AE, DIS, MC, V; local checks only; lunch, dinner Mon–Sat (closed daily from 3 to 4 pm); beer and wine; reservations not accepted; 56th St exit off I-5.* &

Fujiya / ★★

1125 COURT C, TACOMA; 253/627-5319 Absolute consistency is what attracts a loyal clientele from near and far to Masahiro Endo's stylish downtown Japanese restaurant for sushi and sashimi. Begin with *gyoza* (savory pork-stuffed dumplings). The real test of a Japanese restaurant is tempura, and Endo's is feathery-crisp. Those who prefer seafood cooked can try the *yosenabe* (seafood stew) served in a small cast-iron pot. The owner is a generous and friendly man; seldom an evening goes by that he doesn't offer a complimentary tidbit. *$$; AE, MC, V; checks OK; lunch Mon–Fri, dinner Mon–Sat; beer and wine; reservations recommended; between Broadway and Market St.*

Harbor Lights / ★

2761 RUSTON WY, TACOMA; 253/752-8600 Anthony's now owns Harbor Lights, but blessedly the only changes at Tacoma's pioneer Ruston Way waterfront restaurant have been new, generous containers of summer flowers and a general spruce-up. Decor is circa 1950, with glass floats, stuffed prize fish, and a giant lobster. Up-to-the-minute it may not be, but that doesn't bother seafood fans who regularly crowd the noisy dining room for buckets of steamed clams and mounds of perfectly cooked panfried oysters. Fillet of sole is grilled to perfection; halibut-and-chips are the best around, as are crisp hash browns. Portions are gargantuan. *$$; AE, DC, DIS, MC, V; checks OK; lunch Mon–Sat, dinner every day; full bar; reservations recommended; City Center exit off I-5.*

Katie Downs / ★

3211 RUSTON WY, TACOMA; 253/756-0771 Katie Downs's Philadelphia-style deep-dish pizza is a winner. Place your order at the counter for one of the classic combinations. Especially good is the Fearless, which recklessly matches smoked bacon and provolone with white onions, spicy peperoncini—and lots of fresh garlic. Since pizzas can take 30 minutes to make, order steamer clams to tide you over while you watch boat traffic on Commencement Bay. This tavern (no minors) is noisy, boisterous, and fun. *$; MC, V; local checks only; lunch, dinner every day; beer and wine; reservations not accepted; City Center exit off I-5.* &

The Primo Grill / ★★★

601 S PINE ST, TACOMA; 253/383-7000 Come here for great food and a hit of high energy. Belfast-born chef Charlie McManus (formerly at Altezzo) has created a contemporary, bistro-style restaurant in a developing district at Sixth and Pine. He's not afraid to use spices, and anything on the menu in this energetic art-filled spot is delicious. Try a "small bite" of crispy polenta with melted goat cheese and roasted pepper coulis; an entree of grilled pork chop with cinnamon caramelized onions or fire roasted prawns; or a special favorite of the house—warm bread salad with sausage, tomatoes, and onions. Finish with a warm hazelnut brownie and vanilla ice cream. Even when the restaurant isn't crowded, the vibrant colors, art, and design seem to radiate a kind of buzz you associate with San Francisco. *$$; AE, MC, V; local checks only; lunch Mon–Fri, dinner every day; full bar; reservations recommended; www.primogrilltacoma.com; off 6th St at Pine St.* &

Stanley and Seaforts Steak, Chop, and Fish House / ★★

115 E 34TH ST, TACOMA; 253/473-7300 Every seat in this restaurant has a panoramic view of Tacoma, its busy harbor, and, on a clear day, the Olympics. But the emphasis here is on quality meats and seafood simply grilled over applewood with flavorings of herbs and fruits. That and dependable preparation have made Stanley and Seaforts a favorite for two decades. The spacious bar features distinctive Scotch whiskeys—and a great sunset. *$$; AE, DC, DIS, MC, V; local checks only; lunch Mon–Fri, dinner every day; full bar; reservations recommended; City Center exit off I-5.* &

LODGINGS

Chinaberry Hill / ★★★

302 TACOMA AVE N, TACOMA; 253/272-1282 This 1889 grand Victorian (on the National Register of Historic Places) in Tacoma's historic Stadium District has been beautifully restored by Cecil and Yarrow Wayman. Now an eclectic B&B, it is richly inviting. Lovers of old homes delight in the detailed woodwork, stained glass, and period lighting. Three rooms are in the main house: we prefer the Pantages Suite, with its view of Commencement Bay and a Jacuzzi, or the Wild Rose Suite, which has a fireplace, a Jacuzzi, and bay windows overlooking the garden. Families enjoy the Catchpenny Cottage behind the main house; once the estate's carriage house, it has been made over into a lovely two-story retreat that sleeps up to seven. The Waymans serve full breakfast in the dining room or on the veranda. *$$$; MC, V; checks OK; chinaberry@wa.net; www.chinaberry hill.com; City Center exit off I-5.*

Sheraton Tacoma Hotel / ★★

1320 BROADWAY PLAZA, TACOMA; 253/572-3200 OR 800/845-9466 This is the best hotel in town. With the Tacoma Convention Center next door, it attracts conventioneers and corporate travelers. The updated decor includes lively red and gold fabrics and prints that grace the lobby and guest rooms in a sophisticated style similar to other properties managed by the highly regarded Kimpton Group (affiliated with such fine hotels as Seattle's Alexis and Vintage Park). Most rooms have views of Commencement Bay or Mount Rainier. For good Italian food, head to top-floor Altezzo (see review). *$$$; AE, DC, MC, V; checks OK; www.sheratontacoma.com; between 13th and 15th Sts.*

Thornewood Castle B&B Inn / ★★★

8601 N THORNE LN, LAKEWOOD; 253/584-4393 "B&B" and "Castle" may be contradictory terms, yet the two come together beautifully in this 28,000-square-foot Gothic tudor built by Chester A. Thorne in 1908. It once hosted Presidents Howard Taft and Theodore Roosevelt, and is now owned by innkeepers Wayne and Deanna Robinson. On four acres overlooking American Lake, the architecturally grand home has impressive reception rooms—a ballroom, music room, great hall, gentlemen's parlor, and more—with extensive wood paneling and medieval stained-glass window accents. Eight guest rooms are decorated with antiques; the impressive bridal suite is done in ivory tones. Some rooms have fireplaces, jetted tubs or antique soaking tubs; all have terry-cloth robes, TV/VCRs, and CD players. Roam the grounds, exploring the sunken Olmsted-designed English garden; fish, swim, or boat on the lake. Tours and high tea are available to nonguests (see web site). *$$$–$$$$; AE, MC, V; checks OK in advance; www.thornewood castle.com; take I-5 exit 123 south of Tacoma to Thorne Ln.*

The Villa Bed & Breakfast / ★★★

705 N 5TH ST, TACOMA; 253/572-1157 This Mediterranean villa–style home in the heart of Tacoma's historic residential North End stands out from the crowd. Built in 1925, it is open and airy, with high arched windows, tiled roof, and a palm tree out front. Becky and Greg Anglemyer's large and gracious B&B has been made even more spacious in recent years with the addition of a new wing so skillfully built and blended that it's hard to tell where old and new meet. Our favorite room is still the cozy Maid's Quarters in the older part of the house on the top floor—an utterly private hideaway, it has a grand view of Commencement Bay and the Olympics. Most spacious is the Bay View Suite, with a fireplace, a sitting area, and a view veranda. A CD player in every room is music to our ears. *$$; MC, V; checks OK; villabb@aol.com; www.villabb.com; City Center exit off I-5.*

Puyallup

At the head of the fertile Puyallup Valley southeast of Tacoma, this frontier farm town serves as one gateway to Mount Rainier, with Highway 410 leading to Chinook Pass, and Highways 162 and 165 leading to the Carbon River and Mowich Lake. The bulb, rhubarb, and berry farmland continues to be cultivated, but much of it has been strip-malled and auto-row-ravaged around the edges. Avoid the fast-food strip on Highway 161 to the south, and head east up the valley to Sumner and the White River (Hwy 410), or Orting, Wilkeson, and Carbonado (Hwys 162 and 165).

The **EZRA MEEKER MANSION** (312 Spring St; 253/848-1770; www.meeker mansion.org; open Wed–Sun, 1–4pm, mid-Mar–mid-Dec) is the finest original pioneer mansion left in Washington. Its builder and first occupant, Ezra Meeker, introduced hops to the Puyallup Valley. The lavish 17-room Italianate house (circa 1890) now stands beautifully restored in the rear parking lot of a Main Street furniture store.

Puyallup is big on old-time seasonal celebrations and hosts two of the Northwest's largest: April's **DAFFODIL FESTIVAL AND PARADE** (253/627-6176) and September's Western Washington Fair—better known as the **PUYALLUP FAIR** (110 9th Ave SW; 253/841-5045; www.thefair.com)—one of the nation's biggest fairs, with food, games, rides, and premier touring bands. The **PUYALLUP DOWNTOWN FARMERS MARKET** is held Saturday mornings at Pioneer Park (corner of Pioneer and Meridian Sts) and runs throughout the growing season (usually late May–Sept).

Parkland

RESTAURANTS

From the Bayou / ★★

508 GARFIELD ST, PARKLAND; 253/539-4269 Four former school friends from Opolosa, Louisiana, are at the helm of this Parkland restaurant that has everyone who comes here raving. The smoked-salmon cheesecake appetizer is unexpectedly addictive. Then there's a tantalizing array of soul food—étouffée, gumbo, alligator, po'boys—to satisfy you. Even stuffed halibut—or praline cream pie—is worth the trip. The setting is a bonus, too, with Zydeco music playing and black-and-white photos of Acadian villages gracing the walls. *$–$$; AE, DIS, V; checks OK; lunch, dinner Mon–Sat; beer and wine; reservations recommended; cajun@fromthe bayou.com; www.fromthebayou.com; take Hwy 512 E exit from I-5, then the Pacific Ave exit to Parkland.* &

Marzano's / ★

516 GARFIELD ST, PARKLAND; 253/537-4191 The reputation of Lisa Marzano's voluptuous cooking has people arriving from miles away. In fair weather, outside seating on two deck areas is an added plus to this large space. Meals begin with fresh-baked crusty bread, ready to be topped with shredded Parmesan and herbed olive oil. For entrees, try the stubby rigatoni, perfect for capturing the extraordinary *boscaiola* sauce made with mushrooms and ham; lasagne is sumptuous, as is elegant chicken piccata pungent with capers and lemons. Finish with the many-layered chocolate poppyseed cake floating in whipped cream. *$$; DIS, MC, V; checks OK; lunch Tues–Fri, dinner Tues–Sat; beer and wine; reservations required; adjacent to Pacific Lutheran University, Hwy 512 exit from I-5.* &

Gig Harbor

Once an undisturbed fishing village (and still homeport to an active commercial fleet) northwest of Tacoma across the Narrows Bridge on Highway 16, Gig Harbor is now part suburbia, part retirement destination, and quietly getting better and better as a weekend getaway. Boating is still important, with good anchorage and various moorage docks attracting gunwale-to-gunwale pleasure craft. When the clouds break, Mount Rainier holds court for all. An especially good view can been had from the new **ANTHONY'S HOMEPORT** (N Harborview Dr; 253/853-6353). A variety of interesting shops and galleries line Harborview Drive, which almost encircles the harbor. It's a picturesque spot for browsing and window-shopping. Sea-kayaking classes from **GIG HARBOR KAYAK CENTER** (8809 N Harborview Dr; 253/851-7987 or 888/429-2548) are fun and thorough; rental boats are available and you can explore the bay in a few hours, or sign up for a guided tour that takes you farther afloat.

Gig Harbor was planned for boat traffic, not automobiles (with resulting traffic congestion and limited parking), yet it's a good place for celebrations. An arts festival in mid-July, a maritime festival in June, and a Scandinavian fest in October are main events. The Saturday **GIG HARBOR FARMERS MARKET** (on Hunt St; May–Oct) features locally grown produce, plants, and Northwest gifts. For festival and other information, contact the **GIG HARBOR CHAMBER OF COMMERCE** (3302 Harborview Dr; 253/851-6865; www.gigharborchamber.com).

Two newly built 50-plus room inns dramatically increase lodging options, although both are a drive from downtown. The **BEST WESTERN WESLEY INN** (6575 Kimball Dr; 253/858-9690 or 888/462-0002; www.wesleyinn.com) is the only hostelry in town with a swimming pool (outdoor). The Northwestern-style **INN AT GIG HARBOR** (3211 56th St NW; 254/858-1111 or 800/795-9980; www.innat gigharbor.com) has an on-site restaurant featuring seafood specialties.

PARADISE THEATER (6615 38th Ave NW; 253/851-7529) and **ENCORE! THEATER** (253/858-2282), Gig Harbor's resident groups, mount enjoyable productions year-round. In winter there's dinner theater at Paradise and family theater at Encore. Summer shows are staged outside; theatergoers bring picnics and blankets and watch beneath the stars. It's turned into a wonderful small-town custom.

PENINSULA GARDENS NURSERY (5503 Wollochet Dr NW; 253/851-8115) southwest of town is fun to explore and has espresso available. Nearby **KOPACHUCK STATE PARK** (follow signs from Hwy 16; 253/265-3606) is popular, as are **PENROSE POINT** and **JOEMMA STATE PARKS** on the Key Peninsula (south of Hwy 302, west of Hwy 16 at Purdy), all with beaches for clam digging. Purdy Spit, right on Highway 302, is most accessible.

RESTAURANTS

The Green Turtle / ★★★

2905 HARBORVIEW DR, GIG HARBOR; 253/851-3167 At this fun and funky waterfront restaurant, with its undersea decor, owners Nolan and Sue Glenn, and chef Roman Aguillon, present a seafood-focused menu popular with community regulars and fun for visitors. A piquant pear-and-spiced-walnut salad is a nice starter. King salmon comes crusted with sesame seeds; spicy seafood sauté is dressed-up phad thai with shrimp, scallops, and clams. The Turtle Surf and Turf (jumbo scampi in creamy lemon sauce with filet mignon in cabernet demi-glace) is a little pricey but garners raves. Desserts—banana toffee or Key lime pie, crepes suzette, chocolate mousse, and more—are worth the extra calories. In fine weather, dine on the deck overlooking the harbor. *$$; AE, DIS, MC, V; checks OK; dinner Wed–Sun; beer and wine; reservations recommended; www.thegreenturtle.com; past Tides Tavern.* &

Marco's Ristorante Italiano / ★

7707 PIONEER WY, GIG HARBOR; 253/858-2899 Everyone in the area loves Marco's. It shows in the busy, crowded bustle of the place. The menu ranges from traditional (spaghetti and meatballs, handmade tortellini in fresh pesto) to more original specials (a dense, tender piece of tuna sautéed in red wine). Deep-fried olives are an unusual starter. Adjacent to the restaurant is Mimi's Pantry, a retail shop featuring Italian specialty goods. *$$; AE, MC, V; checks OK; lunch, dinner Tues–Sat; beer and wine; reservations recommended; 2 blocks from harbor.*

Tides Tavern

🌲 **2925 HARBORVIEW DR, GIG HARBOR; 253/858-3982** "Meet you at the Tides" has become such a universal invitation that this tavern perched over the harbor often has standing room only, especially on sunny days when the deck is open. People come by boat, seaplane, and car. Originally a general store next to the ferry landing, the Tides is a full-service tavern (no minors) with pool table, Gig Harbor memorabilia, and live music on weekends. Indulge in man-sized sandwiches, huge charbroiled burgers, a gargantuan shrimp salad, and highly touted fish-and-chips (pizzas are only passable). *$; AE, MC, V; checks OK; lunch, dinner every day; beer and wine; reservations not accepted; www.tidestavern.com; downtown Gig Harbor.*

LODGINGS

Aloha Beachside Bed and Breakfast / ★★★

🏹 **8318 STATE RTE 302; GIG HARBOR; 888/256-4222** It may take a while to get your bearings. Seductive Hawaiian music, an expansive beach, a waterfall tumbling over rocks, and a fishing pond (trout) make this feel like Maui. Creature comforts abound and include the sparkling smile of innkeeper Lalaine Wong, the dynamo who runs this two-room B&B with husband Greg. Lalaine loves desserts for breakfast—perhaps cheesecake or fruit crepes. The comfortable guest rooms, named Orchid and Pikake, claim the top (entry) floor and have queen-sized feather beds, water views, and private baths. A spacious balcony between the two overlooks the Sound. The kitchen and a sitting area, also with views, are one floor down. In good weather there's nothing better than breakfast on the deck, with the soothing waterfall and water view. *$$–$$$; MC, V; checks OK; lalaine@alohabeach sidebb.com; www.alohabeachsidebb.com; 7 miles west of Narrows Bridge, take exit 302 and turn left over Purdy Bridge.*

The Maritime Inn

3212 HARBORVIEW DR, GIG HARBOR; 253/858-1818 The Maritime Inn is well located in downtown Gig Harbor, walking distance to shops and restaurants and across from the waterfront. Fifteen rooms are comfortably appointed with queen-sized beds, gas fireplaces, and TVs; several "specialty rooms" offer themed decor (the Polo Room, the Victorian Room) and a bit more space, including sundecks, at slightly higher cost. Space or no, the price is a bit high considering the lack of conversational privacy in the rooms. Avoid rooms on the front of the inn closest to the street. *$$; AE, DIS, MC, V; checks OK; info@maritimeinn.com; www.maritimeinn. com; downtown.* ♿

Steilacoom and Anderson Island

Once a Native American village and later the Washington Territory's first incorporated town (1854), Steilacoom today is a quiet community of old trees and houses, with no vestige of its heyday, when a trolley line ran from Bair's drugstore northeast to Tacoma. October's **APPLE SQUEEZE FESTIVAL** and midsummer's **SALMON BAKE**, with canoe and kayak races, are popular. The **STEILACOOM TRIBAL MUSEUM** (1515 Lafayette St; 253/584-6308) is in a turn-of-the-century church overlooking the South Sound islands and the Olympic range. **CITY HALL** (253/581-1900) has tourist information.

PIERCE COUNTY FERRIES (253/798-2766 recording; www.co.pierce.wa.us/services/transpo/ferrysch.htm) run from here to bucolic off-the-beaten-path Anderson Island, with restricted runs to McNeil Island (a state penitentiary).

RESTAURANTS

The Bair Restaurant at the Bair Drug and Hardware Store

🌲 **1617 LAFAYETTE ST, STEILACOOM; 253/588-9668** Side orders of nostalgia are gratis when you step into Bair Drug. Except for the customers, little has changed since it was built in 1895. Products your grandparents might have used—cigars, washtubs, perfume, and apple peelers—are on display. Old post office boxes mask the bakery, which turns out pies and pastries, such as flaky apple dumplings. Best of all is a 1906 soda fountain, where you can still get a sarsaparilla, a Green River, or a genuine ice-cream soda. On weekday afternoons, by reservation, you can enjoy traditional high tea, complete with tiny tea sandwiches and tartlets. Friday and Saturday nights, dinners focus on seasonal fare such as crab-stuffed salmon, Northwest scallops, and halibut. The crab and artichoke dip appetizer is delicious. *$; MC, V; checks OK; breakfast, lunch every day, dinner Fri–Sat; beer and wine; reservations recommended; www.thebairrestaurant.com; at Wilkes St.* ᕳ

ER Rogers Mansion / ★

1702 COMMERCIAL ST, STEILACOOM; 253/582-0280 View restaurants on Puget Sound are not novelties, but views like this are still exceptional, particularly from a restored 100-year-old Queen Anne–style home. The Steilacoom special prime rib, first roasted and then sliced and quickly seared, is tops. The huge Sunday buffet brunch offers a selection of seafood: oysters on the half shell, cold poached or kippered salmon, flavorful smoked salmon, cracked crab, pickled herring, steamed clams, and fettuccine with shrimp. An upstairs bar has a widow's walk just wide enough for one row of tables. *$$; MC, V; checks OK; dinner every day, brunch Sun; full bar; reservations recommended; info@ERRogers.com; www.ERRogers.com; corner of Wilkes St.* ᕳ

LODGINGS

Anderson House on Oro Bay / ★★

12024 ECKENSTAM-JOHNSON RD, ANDERSON ISLAND; 253/884-4088 OR 800/750-4088 A short ferry ride from Steilacoom and a few miles from the dock is a large house on 200 acres of farmland and woods. Randy and B. Anderson operate this landmark home, with original artwork, antique furnishings, and four large guest rooms. While the hosts live on-site, use of the whole house can be arranged. Full farm breakfasts feature breads hot from the oven, fruit pizzas, and other treats. In addition, the Andersons rent an antique-furnished three-bedroom cedar fishing cabin (woodstove-heated, but updated with full kitchen, microwave, and washer/dryer) on Outer Amsterdam Bay with a deck, barbecue, hot tub, and sweeping Olympic-view deck. A short bike ride takes you to a mile-long secluded beach. Arrangements can be made to pick up guests from the ferry. B. offers weaving workshops; check the summer class schedule. A nine-hole golf course is nearby. Boaters and those with seaplanes have their own dock. *$$–$$$; MC, V; checks OK; ahouse@centurytel.net; www.non.com/anderson; call for directions.*

Olympia

The state capital's centerpiece—visible from the freeway—is the classic dome of the **WASHINGTON STATE LEGISLATIVE BUILDING** (416 14th Ave; 360/586-TOUR or 360/753-5000). Lavishly fitted with bronze and marble, this striking Romanesque structure houses the offices of the governor and other state executives. Damaged during an earthquake in February 2001, the building is undergoing repair and renovation, and is expected to open sometime in 2005 for tours. Meanwhile, take a virtual tour on the web (www.ga.wa.gov).

Opposite the Legislative Building rises the pillared **TEMPLE OF JUSTICE,** seat of the State Supreme Court. To the west is the red brick **GOVERNOR'S MANSION,** which also sustained exterior damage during the 2001 earthquake; it was expected to reopen for Wednesday afternoon tours in late 2002 (501 13th Ave SW; 360/586-TOUR; reservations required).

The **STATE CAPITOL MUSEUM** (211 W 21st Ave; 360/753-2580) houses a permanent exhibit that includes an outstanding collection of Western Washington Native American baskets. The **WASHINGTON STATE LIBRARY** has moved to Tumwater (6880 Capitol Blvd S; 360/753-5592) and is open to the public during business hours.

Downtown, on Seventh Avenue between Washington and Franklin Sts, is the restored **OLD CAPITOL,** whose pointed towers and high-arched windows suggest a late-medieval chateau. The **WASHINGTON CENTER FOR THE PERFORMING ARTS** (on Washington St between 5th Ave and Legion Wy; 360/753-8586) has brought new life to downtown. Across Fifth Avenue, the **CAPITOL THEATER** (206 E 5th Ave; 360/754-5378) provides a showcase for the active **OLYMPIA FILM SOCIETY** and locally produced plays and musicals. Toward the harbor, the lively **OLYMPIA FARMERS MARKET** (near Percival Landing; 360/352-9096; www.farmers -market.org; open Thurs–Sun during growing season—April–Oct—and weekends Nov–Dec up to Christmas) displays produce, flowers, and crafts from all over the South Sound. The waterfront park of **PERCIVAL LANDING** (700 N Capitol Wy) is a community focal point, the site of several harbor festivals. In another part of downtown, just off the Plum Street exit from Interstate 5 and adjacent to City Hall, is the serene **YASHIRO JAPANESE GARDEN,** honoring one of Olympia's sister cities.

The historic heart of the area (Olympia, Lacey, and Tumwater) is **TUMWATER FALLS** (exit 103 off I-5), where the Deschutes River flows into Capitol Lake. A nice walk along the river takes you past several waterfalls. This is the site of the chief local industry, the Tumwater Division of the **MILLER BREWING COMPANY** (exit 103 off I-5, follow signs; 360/754-5000), which brews Olympia Beer. For something sweet after strolling the falls, stop at **DESSERTS BY TASHA NICOLE** (2822 Capitol

Blvd SE; 360/352-3717; www.tashanicole.com) in Tumwater: chocolate-dipped cheesecake on a stick is to die for.

Olympia also has a triad of colleges: the Evergreen State College, west of Olympia on Cooper Point; St. Martin's, a Benedictine monastery and college in adjacent Lacey; and South Puget Sound Community College, across US Highway 101. The **EVERGREEN STATE COLLEGE** (2700 Evergreen Pkwy NW; 360/866-6000) offers a regular schedule of plays, films, experimental theater, and special events. Its library and pool are public.

The area's finest nature preserve lies well outside the city limits. This is the relatively unspoiled Nisqually Delta—outlet of the Nisqually River that forms at the foot of a Mount Rainier glacier and enters the Sound just north of Olympia. Take exit 114 off Interstate 5 and follow signs to the **NISQUALLY NATIONAL WILDLIFE REFUGE** and visitor's center (360/753-9467; www.nisqually.fws.gov). Five trails include a 5-mile hiking trail following an old dike around the delta through a wetland alive with birds, and a handicapped-accessible mile-plus boardwalk through freshwater wetlands. Just south, a rookery of great blue herons occupies the treetops. Between the delta and Tacoma to the north is Fort Lewis Military Reservation.

RESTAURANTS

Budd Bay Cafe / ★

525 N COLUMBIA ST, OLYMPIA; 360/357-6963 The Budd Bay Cafe, with its long row of tables looking out to Budd Inlet, is still a preferred after-hours haunt of many legislators, lobbyists, and state government movers and shakers. Don't look for elaborate dishes; the menu (seafood, steaks, salads, pasta) is designed for boaters and people to whom good talk matters more than haute cuisine. The bar is pleasant and lively, with wines by the glass and specialty beers. *$$; AE, DC, DIS, MC, V; checks OK; lunch Mon–Sat, dinner every day, brunch Sun; full bar; reservations recommended; bbaybcafe@olywa.net; www.buddbaycafe.com; between A and B Sts.* &

Capitale / ★★

609 CAPITOL WY S, OLYMPIA; 360/352-8007 In downtown Olympia, across Sylvester Square from the old courthouse, is a tiny, casual place serving up delicious food in a pleasant atmosphere. Walls are lined with local artwork; jazz music often complements meals. In good weather a few additional tables outside give a nice neighborhood feel. The menu is a mix of Mediterranean and pan-Pacific, with interesting variations. Consider handmade black-bean ravioli with chipotle and lime cream sauce, or satisfying chicken and shiitake mushroom lasagne with smoked gouda. The rectangular rustic pizzas are excellent. Wine tastings on weekends. *$$; AE, MC, V; checks OK; lunch Mon–Fri, dinner Mon–Sat; beer and wine; reservations recommended; at Legion St.* &

Gardner's Seafood and Pasta / ★★

111 W THURSTON ST, OLYMPIA; 360/786-8466 To loyal fans, Gardner's is the hands-down favorite in Olympia, with very good reason. This homey place with its wood floors and profusion of fresh flowers on all the tables makes you feel as though you're in the home of a friend who cooks like a dream. Owners Leon and Jane

Longan offer good, simple food that always hits the spot. During the right season, you might find a dozen Olympia oysters, each the size of a quarter, served on the half shell. Pastas are homemade but sometimes bland; appetizers, such as sautéed rock shrimp with garlic and lemon, never are. *$$; AE, MC, V; checks OK; lunch Mon–Fri, dinner Mon–Sat; beer and wine; reservations recommended; north on Capitol Wy to Thurston St.* &

Louisa / ★★

205 CLEVELAND AVE SE, TUMWATER; 360/352-3732 Located just south of downtown Olympia in Tumwater, Louisa continues to generate quite a buzz. Owner Jeff Taylor (formerly of Capitale) has fashioned pleasantly stylish dining rooms (on two levels) with lots of blond wood, Oriental rugs, and a few scattered antiques. Cuisine is primarily Mediterranean with Northwest and Pacific Rim influences: main dishes include seafood cannelloni stuffed with shrimp and baked in a saffron sauce, and chicken piccata; starters could be fresh spring rolls with soy and black vinegar dipping sauce, or local mussels in a coconut-lemongrass sauce. *$$; MC, V; checks OK; lunch Tues–Fri, dinner Tues–Sat; beer and wine; reservations recommended; Tumwater exit off I-5.*

Portofino / ★★

101 DIVISION ST NW, OLYMPIA; 360/943-8812 This tiny, converted 1890s farmhouse—overshadowed by a beetling office building—is a quiet, elegant refuge for Olympians seeking imaginative, skillfully prepared Northwest cuisine (the menu changes daily) and an extensive wine list. Their seafood emphasis features *cacciucco* (pronounced cash-chew-co), a lighter fish stew than cioppino made with mussels, clams, and calamari. Crab cakes are made fresh from shrimp and crab shucked on the spot. Garlic lovers must try their garlic and spinach purée soup; a house-made fresh ravioli changes daily. In spring or summer, sit on the restaurant's glassed-in porch—though the view of overtrafficked Division Street may make you long for the days when this place was a farm. *$$; AE, MC, V; checks OK; dinner Tues–Sun; full bar; reservations required; 1 block south of Harrison Ave.* &

The Spar

114 E 4TH AVE, OLYMPIA; 360/357-6444 Above the restaurant's old-fashioned booths are blown-up Darius Kinsey photos of old-time loggers with unbelievably mammoth trees they've just brought to earth. Indeed, some 60-odd years ago, the Spar used to be known as a workingman's hangout. Today it's egalitarian, with a mixture of students, attorneys, businesspeople, artists, politicians, fishermen, tourists, and retirees. The Spar's robust milk shakes and homemade bread pudding are locally acclaimed, although much of the menu is average. Willapa Bay oysters or fresh salmon from the farmers market are sometimes available; the prime rib dinner is popular on weekends. The Spar is known for its full-service cigar counter. *$; AE, DC, MC, V; local checks OK; breakfast, lunch, dinner every day; full bar; reservations not accepted; 1 block east of Capitol Wy.*

Sweet Oasis / ★

507 CAPITOL WY, OLYMPIA; 360/956-0470 This Capitol Way spot is particularly informal but offers some delicious Mediterranean foods. Among daily specials are spanakopita and homemade soup. Friday and Saturday you can get *kibby sineeyah,* a deliciously offbeat baked dish combining ground lamb with bulgur, pine nuts, and spices. Falafel, meat pies, and other traditional Mediterranean items are available too. House-made pastries are very good. On some Saturdays you can watch artful belly dancing, winding casually among the tables. *$; MC, V; local checks only; lunch Tues–Sat, dinner Wed–Sat; beer and wine; reservations recommended for 4 or more; at 5th Ave.* ᷃

LODGINGS

Harbinger Inn / ★★

1136 E BAY DR, OLYMPIA; 360/754-0389 Occupying a restored 1910 mansion, this B&B offers Mission-style furnishings, a fine outlook over Budd Inlet and the distant Olympic Mountains, and five choice guest rooms. Nicest is the top-floor Innkeeper's Suite, with its king-sized bed, sitting room, gas fireplace, and large bathroom with soaking tub. Rooms on the front of the house have views, but rooms on the back side are farther from the street, with only the sound of a small artesian-fed waterfall to disturb the tranquility. All have private baths (although the bath for the Cloisonné Room is on the main floor, directly below the room). The inn is situated near excellent routes for bicycle riding, and Priest Point Park is close by. Full breakfast is served. *$$; AE, MC, V; checks OK; www.harbingerinn.com; ½ mile north of State St.*

WestCoast Olympia Hotel

2300 EVERGREEN PARK DR, OLYMPIA; 360/943-4000 OR 866/896-4000 Few urban hotels around Puget Sound take such striking advantage of the Northwest's natural beauty as this one, dramatically perched on a bluff above Capitol Lake, with the capitol dome—illuminated at night—rising to the north. The hotel has 190 fairly large rooms cheerily decorated in tones of red and yellow, an American bistro-style restaurant on-site, and occasional music in the lounge. You'll also find a fitness center and a heated outdoor pool (seasonal). Request a waterside room; some rooms can be noisy. *$$; AE, DC, DIS, MC, V; checks OK; www.westcoasthotels.com; exit 104 from I-5.* ᷃

Tenino

This little burg south of Olympia on Highway 99 is known for **WOLF HAVEN** (3111 Offut Lake Rd; 360/264-4695; www.wolfhaven.org), an educational research facility that teaches wolf appreciation and studies the question of whether to reintroduce wolves into the wild. The public is invited to see the wolves or join them in a howl-in.

RESTAURANTS

Alice's Restaurant / ★

19248 JOHNSON CREEK RD SE, TENINO; 360/264-2887 Chef-owner Vincent de Bellis serves hearty five-course dinners at Alice's, a fine turn-of-the-century farmhouse on a lively little creek. All meals include cream of peanut soup, fresh greens with hot bacon dressing, trout, an entree (perhaps ham with pineapple glaze, homemade Gorgonzola ravioli with walnuts, catfish, local ostrich, or on-site aged rib-eye steak), and dessert, such as chocolate upside-down cake. Vincent also features prizewinning Northwest wines. Wedding parties by arrangement. *$$; AE, DC, DIS, MC, V; no checks; dinner Fri–Sun (or by arrangement); beer and wine; reservations recommended; call for directions.*

Yelm

RESTAURANTS

Arnold's Country Inn / ★

717 YELM AVE E, YELM; 360/458-3977 Long known as one of Olympia's most accomplished chefs, Arnold Ball established his latest restaurant just outside Yelm on the road to Mount Rainier. Steaks and meat dishes dominate, though fresh seafood is available. Besides steak Diane and French Pepper steak, familiar Arnold's specialties include chicken sautéed with raspberry brandy, and traditional escargots. Arnold is careful with small details: his house-baked rolls are warm and delicious, as are fine pies. His wine list is adequate; many patrons drive all the way from Olympia just for the food. *$$; AE, MC, V; no checks; breakfast Sat–Sun, lunch, dinner Tues–Sun; full bar; reservations recommended; Old Nisqually exit off I-5, follow Reservation Rd/Hwy 510.* &

OLYMPIC PENINSULA

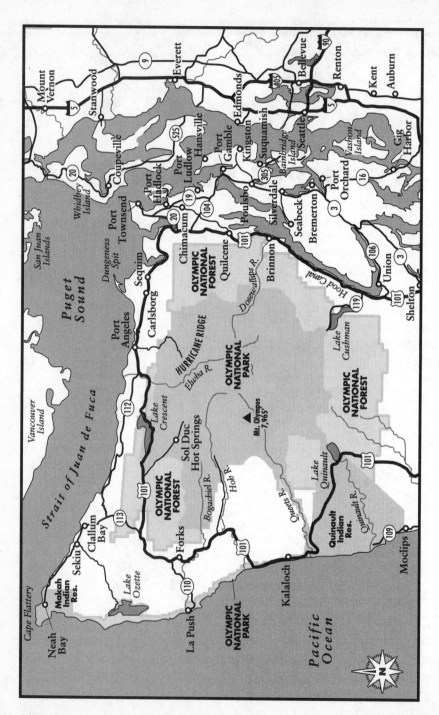

OLYMPIC PENINSULA

The scenery within the 5,000 square miles of the Kitsap and Olympic Peninsulas varies considerably. In Kitsap County, you'll see Silverdale's mall country with neon lights and fast-food joints, get caught up in Poulsbo's Scandinavian atmosphere, or ponder history through the dollhouse homes in the historic mill town of Port Gamble. Then cross the Hood Canal Bridge to the Olympic Peninsula's land of emerald farmland carpets, hulking forests of cedar and fir, crashing swells that pound the Pacific coast, and the Victoriana of Port Townsend.

With each change in topography comes a change in climate. You could bask in the sun in Sequim (popular with retirees, in the rain shadow of the Olympics), and two hours later find yourself pelted by hammering raindrops in Forks. The variations make planning a trip easy: bring everything. Good sturdy shoes and a water-repellent jacket are musts year-round. The only thing you probably won't need is formal wear—the Olympic Peninsula is fairly laid-back.

Countless opportunities exist here for picnicking, hiking, camping, photography, boating, fishing, shopping, and more. Residents are a hearty lot of artists and mill workers, loggers and entrepreneurs. They stay for tradition's sake, for the space, and for the opportunities.

And, of course, for the trees. US Highway 101 wraps snugly around an empire built and ruled by Mother Nature. In the center, Olympic National Park is home to some 1,200 plant species, 300 bird species, and 70 different kinds of mammals. More than 5 million people every year come to soak in the hot springs, wander the forest, hug the 250- to 500-year-old fir and cedar trees, and sneak a peek at wildlife adept at the art of camouflage. Visitor centers at Hurricane Ridge and the Hoh Rain Forest feature helpful rangers and interpretive, hands-on learning exhibits.

Perhaps the Olympic Peninsula's rainy winter weather (rainfall ranges from 24 inches a year in Port Angeles to more than 130 in the Hoh Rain Forest) is nature's way of keeping visitors just that. If you don't mind getting wet, though, you'll learn why 200,000 people call it home.

ACCESS AND INFORMATION

You could drive around Puget Sound to reach the Olympic Peninsula, but the scenic **WASHINGTON STATE FERRIES** (206/464-6400 or 800/843-3779; www.wsdot.wa.gov/ferries/) run regularly between downtown Seattle and Bremerton on the Kitsap Peninsula, or Bainbridge Island. Boats also dock in Port Townsend (from Keystone on Whidbey Island), on the Kitsap Peninsula in Kingston (from Edmonds), and in Southworth, near Port Orchard (from Fauntleroy in West Seattle).

Arriving in Port Angeles by boat is a snap from Victoria, British Columbia, with the **MV COHO,** operated by Black Ball Transportation (360/457-4491; twice daily year-round, except during Jan dry docking), and via the much quicker **VICTORIA EXPRESS** (360/452-8088 or 800/633-1589), a foot-passenger ferry that runs two or three times daily, summer and fall. In summer, **ROYAL VICTORIA TOURS** (888/381-1800; www.royaltours.com) offers guided bus trips to Victoria and Butchart Gardens.

PUBLIC BUS transportation between communities is available through Kitsap Transit (360/373-2877 or 800/501-RIDE), Jefferson County Transit (360/385-4777), West Jefferson Transit (800/436-3950), Clallam Transit System (360/452-4511 or 800/858-3747), and Mason County Transit Authority (360/426-9434 or 800/281-9434).

Small **PLANES** land at airports in Bremerton, Jefferson County, Shelton, Sequim, and Port Angeles. The largest airline to serve the peninsula is Horizon Air (800/547-9308; www.horizonair.com), which lands at Fairchild International Airport in Port Angeles.

Average temperatures on the Olympic Peninsula range from 45°F in January to 72°F in August. Rainfall averages 2–3 inches per month, less in Sequim and more—up to 121 inches annually—in Forks. For information on visiting the area, contact the **PORT TOWNSEND CHAMBER OF COMMERCE VISITOR INFORMATION CENTER** (2437 E Sims Wy, Port Townsend; 360/385-2722 or 888/ENJOYPT; www.ptchamber.org) or the **NORTH OLYMPIC PENINSULA VISITOR & CONVENTION BUREAU** (360/452-8552 or 800/942-4042; travel@olypen.com) in Port Angeles.

Kitsap Peninsula

Kitsap Peninsula sits between the larger Olympic Peninsula and the mainland, roughly defined by Puget Sound (and Bainbridge and Vashon Islands) on the east and Hood Canal on the west. Connected to the Olympic Peninsula by a small stretch of land at the southern end of Hood Canal, it links to the body of Western Washington via the Tacoma Narrows Bridge. The Hood Canal Bridge connects Kitsap's northern end to the Olympic Peninsula.

Port Orchard

The center of this small town hugs the southern shoreline of one of Puget Sound's many fingers of water: Sinclair Inlet. With its boardwalk and beach access, the waterfront area is a true gathering place. The **PORT ORCHARD FARMERS MARKET** (Marina Park, 1 block from Bay St; Sat, late Apr–Oct) offers a selection of cut flowers, fresh vegetables, baked goods, and crafts. Take home Hood Canal oysters or ask the oyster lady to grill a few. Antique shops abound, and the **SIDNEY ART GALLERY AND MUSEUM** (202 Sidney Ln; 360/876-3693) displays Northwest art.

HORLUCK TRANSPORTATION (360/876-2300), a privately owned foot ferry that runs every half hour, Monday through Saturday, provides an economical means of travel between downtown Port Orchard and the main ferry terminal at Bremerton. Otherwise, drive north on Highway 3.

LODGINGS

Reflections Bed and Breakfast Inn / ★★

3878 REFLECTION LN E, PORT ORCHARD; 360/871-5582 Every cliché that's used to describe an excellent Northwest B&B applies to this sprawling inn set on a hillside overlooking Sinclair Inlet, with the Olympic Mountains as backdrop. Former New Englanders Jim and Cathy Hall extend warm hospitality to their guests and serve a hearty breakfast of regional dishes. The Halls furnish four guest

OLYMPIC PENINSULA THREE-DAY TOUR

DAY ONE: Starting in Edmonds, grab breakfast on the ferry as you cruise to Kingston. On your way to Port Townsend, take a detour through charming little Port Gamble and grab an ice cream or a coffee at the **PORT GAMBLE GENERAL STORE.** Cross the Hood Canal Bridge to the Olympic Peninsula and follow signs to Port Townsend. Slow down on your way through the Chimacum Valley to drink in the bucolic splendor—this is dairy-farm country. Stop at the Harbormaster Restaurant at **PORT LUDLOW RESORT AND CONFERENCE CENTER** for a lunch of fish-and-chips. Once in Port Townsend, check in at the **QUIMPER INN,** then wander through the Uptown district, stopping at **ALDRICH'S** for coffee. Go downtown via the Taylor Street steps, built to accommodate ladies who took tiny steps in their tight Victorian skirts, to the **HALLER FOUNTAIN.** Window-shop downtown, finishing up with a wine tasting at the **WINE SELLER.** Then take dinner at the **SILVERWATER CAFÉ** and perhaps a movie at the **ROSE THEATER.**

DAY TWO: Head out of town after the Quimper Inn's breakfast and take Highway 20 to Highway 101 west toward Sequim. Take the Sequim exit for a roving **MURAL TOUR**—the main street is peppered with trompe l'oeil works. Continue down 101— it joins up with the main street as you head west—toward Port Angeles. Pick up a sandwich and a cranberry muffin at **SUNNY FARMS COUNTRY STORE** (261461 Hwy 101; 360/683-8003), between Sequim and Port Angeles. Follow signs to **HURRICANE RIDGE** in Olympic National Park, where in summer meadows are filled with wildflowers, and winter activities include free guided snowshoe tours and cross-country skiing. After playing all day, return to Port Angeles and check into the **TUDOR INN** and soak in a nice hot bath; then head to dinner at **C'EST SI BON.**

DAY THREE: The inn's breakfast prepares you for when Mother Nature beckons again. Continue west on Highway 101 to Forks, stopping at **RIVER RUN COFFEE HOUSE** for coffee or the **RAIN DROP CAFE** (111 S Forks Ave; 360/374-6612) for lunch. Then visit the **TIMBER MUSEUM** to learn about trees and the logging industry. Head east into the **HOH RAIN FOREST** to tromp rain-forest trails flanked by ancient trees dripping with lacy moss, and perhaps spy a herd of Roosevelt elk. On the way back to Forks, pick up some groceries and find your way to the **SHADY NOOK COTTAGE,** where you can cook your own dinner and relax for tomorrow's drive home.

rooms (two with private baths) with family antiques, including heirloom quilts. The largest has a private porch and a soaking tub. All have water views. The well-tended grounds include a hot tub, a gazebo, and birds eating and preening at various feeders. *$$; MC, V; no checks; jimreflect@hurricane.net; www.portorchard.com/ reflections; east of Port Orchard off Beach Dr.* &

Bremerton

Bremerton and its naval station have been entwined since the early 1890s, when a young German, William Bremer, sold close to 200 acres of bay front to the U.S. Navy for $9,587. The naval shipyards are still downtown, and rows of moth-gray ghost ships—silent reminders of past naval battles—loom offshore. Only the destroyer USS *Turner Joy* (300 Washington Beach Ave; 360/792-2457), which saw action off Vietnam, is open for self-guided tours (every day May–Sept, Thurs–Mon Oct–Apr). Adjacent to the ferry terminal and the *Turner Joy*, the **BREMERTON NAVAL MUSEUM** (360/479-7447) depicts the region's shipbuilding history back to bowsprit-and-sail days; open every day in summer, closed Mondays, Labor Day through Memorial Day.

Farther north on the Kitsap Peninsula is the **TRIDENT NUCLEAR SUBMARINE BASE** at Bangor. Occasionally a pod of orcas can be glimpsed escorting one of the mammoth submarines through the local waters to deep-sea duty. Since 1915, Keyport has been the major U.S. site for undersea torpedo testing. Now it also is home to the extraordinary **NAVAL UNDERSEA MUSEUM** (360/396-4148; open every day, closed Tues Oct–May), housing the first Revolutionary War submarine.

RESTAURANTS

Boat Shed / ★

101 SHORE DR, BREMERTON; 360/377-2600 This casual seafood restaurant overhanging the Port Washington Narrows is aptly named. Rough wood panels the walls inside and out, and a solitary fish tank serves as decor. Scaups and scoters patter along the water while boats of every size pass by. Local seafood is the main attraction here: rich clam chowder, popular Dungeness crab cakes, and seasonal seafood dishes adorned with a variety of homemade salsas and chutneys. Landlubbers choose the knockwurst piled with red onions and cheese on sourdough, or steak. *$; AE, MC, V; local checks only; lunch, dinner every day, brunch Sun; full bar; reservations recommended; east side of Manette Bridge.* &

Seabeck

LODGINGS

Willcox House / ★★★

2390 TEKIU RD, SEABECK; 360/830-4492 OR 800/725-2600 Col. Julian Willcox and his wife, Constance, once played host to such famous guests as Clark Gable at this copper-roofed, 10,000-square-foot, art deco manse on the east side of Hood Canal. Oak parquet floors, walnut-paneled walls, and a copper-framed marble fireplace—one of five fireplaces in the house—grace the front rooms. All five rooms have private baths and views of Hood Canal and the Olympics. One has a fireplace; one has a double soaking tub. Downstairs are a bar, a game room, and a clubby library. Comb the beach for oysters, fish from the dock, or hike the hillside trails. Owners Phillip and Cecilia Hughes serve a hearty breakfast, offer lunch to multinight guests, and provide a prix-fixe dinner (open to nonguests on weekends by reservation). Diners love the roasted pork tenderloin served Saturdays, and if you're lucky, you'll come on a night when Cecilia has made one of her famous chocolate truffle cakes. The place is about a half-hour drive from the Bremerton ferry, though some guests arrive by boat or floatplane. *$$$; DIS, MC, V; checks OK; www.willcoxhouse.com; 9 miles south of Seabeck, call for directions.*

Silverdale

RESTAURANTS

Bahn Thai / ★★

9811 MICKELBERRY RD, SILVERDALE; 360/698-3663 Fifteen years of cooking at Seattle's Bahn Thai put Rattana Vilaiporn in perfect position to take over operations at the Silverdale location. She's kept the menu and the same clean, exotic look of the place, with sunken tables and lots of Thai art. Come with a group to share a variety of the brightly flavored dishes of Thailand: *tod mun*—spicy, crisp patties of minced fish, green beans, and lime leaves; *tom yum goong,* a favorite soup of prawns and lemongrass; and six exotic curries, including *mussamun*—beef and potatoes sauced with a medium curry infused with coconut milk and cloves, nutmeg, and cinnamon. *$; AE, MC, V; local checks only; lunch, dinner weekdays, dinner on weekends; beer and wine; reservations not necessary; kbahnthai@excite.com; ½ block north of Bucklin Hill Rd.* &

Yacht Club Broiler / ★

9226 BAYSHORE DR, SILVERDALE; 360/698-1601 This simple restaurant has a water view and some elegant touches: copper-covered tables, walls lined with delicate rice-paper fish prints, and bare wood floors softened by Oriental-style rugs. As you might expect from its name and location (on Dyes Inlet), seafood is big here. More unexpected is the high quality of that seafood (as the commercial fishermen who eat here will attest), be it sweet, moist Dungeness crab cakes, halibut prepared in a variety of ways, or a bucket of plump steamed clams. *$$; AE, DC, DIS, MC, V; checks OK; lunch, dinner every day, brunch Sun; full bar; reservations recommended; Silverdale exit off Hwy 3.* &

LODGINGS

Silverdale on the Bay / ★

3073 NW BUCKLIN HILL RD, SILVERDALE; 360/698-1000 OR 800/544-9799 This tastefully designed resort hotel serves equally well for a conference or a getaway, although encroaching shopping malls are a distraction. Many of the 150 rooms and suites have balconies with sweeping views over Dyes Inlet; some have fireplaces. But this resort sports extras: indoor lap pool, large brick sundeck, sauna, weight room, and video-game room. The Mariner Restaurant offers white-linened tables, professional service, and nicely prepared meals that aren't too pricey. The crab chimichanga took first place in a local restaurant competition. Enjoy a breakfast of boardinghouse-style biscuits and gravy, or Belgian waffles piled with strawberries and cream. *$$; AE, DC, DIS, MC, V; checks OK; sdhotel@silverlink.net; www.westcoasthotels.com/silverdale; at Silverdale Wy.*

Poulsbo

Poulsbo was once a community of fishermen and loggers, primarily Scandinavian. Today it's full of gift shops, and its snug harbor is full of yachts. Scandinavian heritage, however, is still strong—**FRONT STREET** sports its "Velkommen til Poulsbo" signs, and the architecture is a dolled-up version of the fjord villages of Norway. Stroll the boardwalk along Liberty Bay, or rent a kayak from **OLYMPIC OUTDOOR CENTER** (360/697-6095).

ALLEN'S WATERFRONT DELI (18937 NE Front St; 360/779-2763) makes good sandwiches, soups, quiche, and desserts; or select something from the overwhelming choices at the famed **SLUY'S BAKERY** (18924 Front St NE; 360/779-2798). Too crowded? Walk south a block to **LIBERTY BAY BAKERY AND CAFE** (18996 Front St NE; 360/779-2828; closed Mon). **BOEHM'S CHOCOLATES** (18864 Front St NE; 360/697-3318) also has an outpost here.

RESTAURANTS

Benson's Restaurant / ★★★

18820 FRONT ST, POULSBO; 360/697-3449 White linen, clean lines, and walls dressed in Georgia O'Keeffe–style flower prints make an elegant first impression at Poulsbo's nicest downtown neighbor. Owners Kelly and Jeffrey Benson go out of their way to charm diners with suggestions for appropriate wines and specials, while the well-mannered waitstaff is friendly and efficient. The menu offers selections that rate high on the good-for-you scale: puffy homemade gnocchi under a tomato-basil and grilled-vegetable sauce; grilled fresh salmon with hazelnut butter; tender lamb shish kebabs sweetened by a subtle rosemary marinade. Mushrooms stuffed with crab and artichoke hearts could use a little more of both. For dessert try chocolate mousse torte, or lovingly presented apple tart under caramel glaze, with vanilla ice cream. Wednesdays are good for wine lovers; bottles and glasses are half price. *$$; AE, MC, V; checks OK; lunch, dinner Tues–Sat, brunch Sun; beer and wine; reservations recommended; bensons.restaurant@prodigy.net; from Lincoln St NE, head to water.* &

LODGINGS

Manor Farm Inn / ★★

26069 BIG VALLEY RD NE, POULSBO; 360/779-4628 A lavish retreat in the middle of nowhere, Manor Farm is a small gentleman's farm with horses, pigs, sheep, cows, chickens, and a trout pond—a beguiling mix of the raw and the cultivated that succeeds in spoiling even the city-bred. There are seven bright guest rooms; individual rooms might feature wood-burning fireplaces, private porches, and king-sized beds. Breakfast happens twice at Manor Farm: first a tray of hot scones and orange juice at your door, then breakfast for guests and the general public—fresh fruit, apple crepes, eggs Benedict (courtesy of resident hens), and rashers of bacon, for example. No kids under 16 at the inn or restaurant. *$$$; AE, MC, V; checks OK; information@manorfarminn.com; www. manorfarminn.com; off Hwy 305, half hour from Bainbridge ferry.*

Suquamish

In Suquamish, on the Port Madison Indian Reservation (follow signs past Agate Pass), the **SUQUAMISH MUSEUM** in the Tribal Center (15838 Sandy Hook Rd NE; 360/598-3311) is devoted to studying and displaying Puget Sound Salish Indian culture. Chief Sealth's grave is nearby, on the grounds of St. Peter's Catholic Mission Church. Twin dugout canoes rest on a log frame over the stone, which reads, "The firm friend of the whites, and for him the city of Seattle was named."

Port Gamble

Built in the mid-19th century by the Pope & Talbot timber people, who traveled here by clipper ship from Maine, this is the essence of the company town. Everything is still company owned and maintained—though the company is now Olympic Resource Management, not Pope & Talbot—and the dozen or so Victorian houses are beauties. The town, which was modeled on a New England village, also boasts a lovely church and a vital and well-stocked company store. The historic **PORT GAMBLE MUSEUM** (on Rainier Ave; 360/297-8074) is a gem, with an ideal presentation of a community's society and industrial heritage, designed by Alec James, a designer for the displays for the Royal Provincial Museum in Victoria. The lumber mill is no longer in operation.

Hansville

Just beyond the unassuming fishing town of Hansville are a couple of the prettiest, most accessible, and least explored beaches on the peninsula. To the east is **POINT NO POINT,** marked by a lighthouse, which is great for a family outing. Follow the road from Hansville to the west and you'll reach **CAPE FOULWEATHER.** The short trail through the woods is tough to find, so look for the Nature Conservancy sign on the south side of the road.

Hood Canal

Highway 101 hugs the west side of Hood Canal through tiny towns with names like Lilliwaup, Hamma Hamma, Duckabush, and Dosewallips, and vacation homes line the miles of scenic shoreline. In bays and inlets along the way, oyster and clam populations are making a comeback; stop at any roadside stand or store for fresh crab and oysters. Sample the wines at **HOODSPORT WINERY** (N 23501 Hwy 101; 360/877-9894; 10am–6pm, Mon–Fri), plus fine chocolates and gourmet treats, at the cottage tasting room.

Once serious timber country—the logging community of Shelton still sells thousands upon thousands of Christmas trees nationwide each year—this stretch of highway also serves as the jumping-off spot for many recreational areas in the Olympic National Forest, including **LAKE CUSHMAN** and its state park (7211 N Lake Cushman Rd; 360/877-5491). Numerous hiking trails lead to remote, cloud-draped alpine lakes and meadows.

Shelton

RESTAURANTS

Xinh's Clam & Oyster House / ★★

221 W RAILROAD AVE, STE D, SHELTON; 360/427-8709 Chef Xinh Dwelley knows her shellfish. For 20 years, she worked as the quality control manager (and did her fair share of shucking) at Taylor United Inc., a Shelton shellfish company. And there she won attention when she began cooking elaborate lunches for visiting shellfish buyers. Today, Xinh runs not only Shelton's finest seafood restaurant, but one of the best and freshest little clam and oyster houses on the Olympic Peninsula. Xinh herself picks out the best of each day's haul. Slide down a few Olympias or Steamboat Island Pacifics on the half shell and then see what she can do with a sauce. The menu sports an Asian twist, with a few Italian dishes. You won't find a better heaping plate of mussels in a Vietnamese curry sauce. *$$; MC, V; checks OK; dinner Tues–Sat; beer and wine; reservations recommended; www.taylorunited.com/xinhs; at 3rd St.* &

Union

RESTAURANTS

Victoria's / ★★

E 6790 HWY 106, UNION; 360/898-4400 The stone-and-log structure on the east bank of Hood Canal has been a stopover since the early 1930s. Locals remember its various functions as a lively dance hall and tavern, a drugstore, and a B&B, but in the past decade it has evolved into one of the area's better eateries. High-beamed ceilings, a fireplace, and large windows set the scene for equally appealing food. Seafood can be exceptional, and portions of prime rib are ample. Victoria's signatures include salmon with melted Brie, and medallions of beef. Desserts are imaginative and rich. Try the Hood Canal Pie with a thin chocolate layer over amaretto ice cream surrounded by an Oreo crust, laced with raspberry sauce and crème fraîche. *$$; MC, V; checks OK; dinner Wed–Sun; full bar; reservations recommended; ¼ mile west of Alderbrook Inn.* &

Quilcene

Every summer weekend, concerts are given by the internationally acclaimed, Seattle-based Philadelphia String Quartet and world-class guest artists at the **OLYMPIC MUSIC FESTIVAL** (11 miles west of Hood Canal Bridge on Hwy 104, then ¼ mile south from Quilcene exit; 360/732-4000). Music lovers sit on hay bales in a century-old Dutch Colonial barn or stretch out with a picnic on the gentle hillside while listening to chamber music.

Port Townsend and the Northeast Corner

During the early days of clipper ships, Port Townsend was the official point of entry to Puget Sound and it continues to be the main draw to this region.

Port Ludlow

LODGINGS

Heron Beach Inn / ★★

 1 HERON RD, PORT LUDLOW; 360/437-0411 The Heron Beach Inn (sister to the Inn at Langley and Friday Harbor House) guards the entry to Hood Canal. It exudes the atmosphere of a New England estate crammed onto one small point of land (near the harbor to the Port Ludlow Resort), but inside is a gorgeous, peaceful retreat with 37 big, well-appointed rooms—with fireplaces, great views, and deep tubs. Play chess in the common room, or hold a private wine tasting in front of a blazing fire. In the restaurant overlooking the water, a refined staff serves an ambitious and elegant collection of entrees. *$$$; AE, DIS, MC, V; checks OK; www.heronbeachinn.com; next to marina.* &

Port Ludlow Resort and Conference Center

200 OLYMPIC PL, PORT LUDLOW; 360/437-2222 OR 800/732-1239 The "biggest damn cabin on the Sound" is actually a splendid Victorian home that belonged to Pope & Talbot's sawmill manager and shared this site—overlooking the teardrop bay—with the busy Port Ludlow mill. It is now a popular resort facility, catering to groups, with a marina, tennis courts, 27-hole championship golf course, hiking and cycling trails, and year-round swimming pool on 1,500 developed acres. Individually decorated suites—privately owned by out-of-towners—are very livable, with fireplaces, kitchens, and private decks, many with views of the harbor. Stay away from standard rooms, which resemble budget motel rooms, complete with paper-thin walls, noisy heaters, and appliances and plumbing that just don't work quite right. The Harbormaster Restaurant has a pleasant bar and deck. *$$$; AE, MC, V; checks OK; resort@portludlowresort.com; www.portludlowresort.com; 6 miles north of Hood Canal Bridge on west side.*

Port Hadlock

The false-front, Old West–style buildings in Port Hadlock have been painted with the same hot pinks, blues, and purples that some supermarkets use to ice cakes—a new take on "local color." South of Hadlock on Highway 19, the **CHIMACUM CAFE** (9253 Rhody Dr; 360/732-4631) serves great homemade pie. A transplanted Frenchman and his American wife bake heartachingly delicious bread and pastries at the **VILLAGE BAKER** (10644 Rhody Dr; 360/379-5310). Heading north, at the Shold Business Park off Highway 19, buy a bag of superb fresh bagels (baked daily) and toppings to go at **BAGEL HAVEN BAKERY & CAFE** (227 W Patison St; 360/385-6788).

RESTAURANTS

Ajax Cafe / ★

271 WATER ST, PORT HADLOCK; 360/385-3450 The Ajax is an establishment with a rich history, and owners Tom and Linda Weiner will tell some almost-tall tales while they serve up big plates of seafood with fresh vegetables. The signature dish is a flavorful fishermen's stew: poached fish swimming in leek and saffron broth and served with garlic aioli. Locals crave Blackjack Ribs spiked with Jack Daniels that melt away from the bone. Live music (jazz, blues, folk) plays most nights. *$$; MC, V; local checks only; dinner Tues–Sun; beer and wine; reservations recommended; www.ajaxcafe.com; in lower Hadlock on waterfront, off Oak Bay Rd.* &

Marrowstone Island

Marrowstone Island faces Port Townsend across the bay. To get there from Port Ludlow or Hadlock, watch for signs directing you to Indian Island, Fort Flagler State Park, and Marrowstone from Oak Bay Road. **FORT FLAGLER STATE PARK** (10541 Flagler Rd; 360/385-1259), an old coastal fortification, has acres of trails, grassy fields, and miles of beaches to walk, as well as RV and tent camping. Seals hang out at the end of a sand spit, as do nesting gulls. Long ago, Marrowstone's enterprise was turkey farming; today, locals farm oysters and harvest clams. At the historic **NORDLAND GENERAL STORE** (5180 Flagler Rd; 360/385-0777), with its oiled floors and covered porch, you can pick up a bag of oysters or, in summer, rent a small boat to paddle on Mystery Bay. In winter, locals gather around the woodstove in the back of the store with espresso.

LODGINGS

Beach Cottages on Marrowstone / ★

10 BEACH DR, NORDLAND; 360/385-3077 OR 800/871-3077 Formerly known as The Ecologic Place, this gathering of eight rustic cabins in a natural setting is a great spot for families who'd rather spend more time out than in, though indoor offerings include books, puzzles, and games. The resort borders on a tidal estuary that flows into Oak Bay and then Puget Sound, and offers a view of the Olympics and Mount Rainier. The unique and very rustic cabins have everything you need to enjoy the simple beauty of the place—woodstoves, equipped kitchens, comfortable queen-sized beds, and fine-for-the-children bunks and twin beds. Bring bikes, boats, books, bathing suits, binoculars, children, and groceries. *$$; MC, V; checks OK; www.beachcottagegetaway.com; right at "Welcome to Marrowstone" sign.*

Port Townsend

Wealthy folk settled here and built more than 200 Victorian homes; foreign consuls off ships from around the globe added a cosmopolitan flavor to the port town's social life. When the mineral deposits petered out, the railroad never came, and the elite investors left, Port Townsend became a land of vanished dreams and vacant mansions. The restored buildings with wraparound views, now a National Historic Landmark District, lie at the heart of the town's charm. A **HISTORIC-HOMES TOUR** (888/ENJOYPT) happens the first weekend in May, and again the third weekend in September, and the **JEFFERSON COUNTY HISTORICAL SOCIETY** (210 Madison St; 360/385-1003) has a fascinating museum in the original city hall.

Colorful shops line Water Street. **ANCESTRAL SPIRITS GALLERY** (701 Water St; 360/385-0078) has an abundant and elegant collection of sculpture, prints, paintings, jewelry, and music by Native craftspeople across the country. **NORTHWEST NATIVE EXPRESSIONS ART GALLERY** (637 Water St; 360/385-4770), owned by the Jamestown S'Klallam tribe, holds a wide selection of Puget Sound, British Columbia, and Southeast Alaska prints, jewelry, and related books. There's **WILLIAM JAMES BOOKSELLER** (829 Water St; 360/385-7313), and **EARTHEN WORKS** (702 Water St; 360/385-0328), specializing in high-quality Washington crafts. You'll find the best antique selection is at the **PORT TOWNSEND ANTIQUE MALL** (802 Washington St; 360/379-8069). And check out the revitalized uptown, especially **ALDRICH'S** (Lawrence and Tyler Sts; 360/385-0500), an authentic 1890s general store with an international twist.

The best ice-cream cones can be had at **ELEVATED ICE CREAM** (627 Water St; 360/385-1156); the best pastries at **BREAD AND ROSES BAKERY** (230 Quincy St; 360/385-1044); and for picnic fare, coffee, homemade chocolates, and people watching, try **MCKENZIE'S** (221 Taylor St; 360/385-3961). At the **WINE SELLER** (940 Water St; 360/385-7673), proprietor and jazz guitarist Joe Euro stocks gourmet snacks, a selection of high-end beer, and wines from around the globe.

SIRENS (823 Water St; 360/379-1100), hidden up a flight of stairs in the historic Bartlett Building, is a delightful place to enjoy a glass of wine, shoot some pool, and listen to music from the deck overlooking the bay. **ROSE THEATER** (235 Taylor St; 360/385-1039), a beautifully restored arthouse, has red velvet curtains, ancient frescoed walls, and the world's best popcorn. It's also home to the annual **PORT TOWNSEND FILM FESTIVAL** (360/379-1333; www.ptfilmfest.com)

CHETZEMOKA PARK (Jackson and Blaine Sts), a memorial in the northeast corner of town to the S'Klallam Indian chief who became a friend of the first white settlers, has a charming gazebo, picnic tables, tall Douglas firs, and a grassy slope down to the beach. You can see the chief's likeness carved in the huge pillars in front of the post office, or in a bronze sculpture at the golf course. **HALLER FOUNTAIN** (Washington and Tyler Sts) is where Port Townsend's brazen goddess lives. Galatea, her voluptuous body draped beneath a diaphanous swag, has graced this intersection since 1906.

The **RHODODENDRON FESTIVAL** (888/ENJOYPT) in May, with a parade and crowning of the queen, is the oldest festival in town. The Wooden Boat Foundation (380 Jefferson St; 360/385-3628; info@woodenboat.org; www.woodenboat.org) presents the **WOODEN BOAT FESTIVAL,** at Point Hudson Marina on the weekend after Labor Day: a celebration of traditional crafts and a showcase for everything from kayaks to tugboats. The first weekend of October finds lunatic geniuses racing human-powered contraptions across town, on the water, and through a mud bog in the **KINETIC SCULPTURE RACE** (360/385-3741).

FORT WORDEN STATE PARK (200 Battery Wy; 360/385-4730), along with sister forts on Marrowstone and Whidbey Islands, was part of the defense system established to protect Puget Sound a century ago. The 433-acre complex overlooking Admiralty Inlet now incorporates turn-of-the-century officers' quarters, campgrounds, gardens, a theater, and a concert hall (see Lodgings). A huge central field, formerly the parade ground, is perfect for games or kite flying. The setting may look familiar to those who saw the movie *An Officer and a Gentleman,* most of which was filmed here. At the water's edge, an enormous pier juts into the bay—it's the summer home to the **MARINE SCIENCE CENTER** (360/385-5582), with touch tanks, displays of sea creatures, and cruises to nearby Protection Island, the region's largest seabird rookery. Also here are a safe, protected swimming beach and access to miles of beaches. On the hillside above, you can spend hours exploring deserted concrete bunkers.

Fort Worden is also home to Centrum, a sponsor of concerts, workshops, and festivals throughout the year. Many of these take place in the old balloon hangar, reborn as McCurdy Pavilion. The **CENTRUM SUMMER SEASON** (360/385-3102; www.centrum.org; June–Sept) is one of the most successful cultural programs in the state, with dance, fiddle tunes, chamber music, a writers' conference, jazz, blues, and theater performances.

The **PUGET SOUND EXPRESS** (431 Water St; 360/385-5288) runs a daily ferry in summer to Friday Harbor on San Juan Island.

RESTAURANTS

Fountain Cafe / ★★

920 WASHINGTON ST, PORT TOWNSEND; 360/385-1364 Kris Nelson, owner and local treasure, is passionate about great flavors. The menu, which now includes breakfast on weekdays, features a fine anchovy penne and a *pollo proscuitto*. Nelson uses organic, local produce whenever she can and it shows. Sandwiches are inventive (tapanade chicken) and robust (turkey Reuben), served on terrific bread from the Village Baker in Port Hadlock. There are only 10 tables, but it's well worth the wait. *$$; MC, V; checks OK; lunch (summer only), dinner every day; beer and wine; reservations not accepted; 1 block north of Water St.*

Lanza's / ★★

1020 LAWRENCE ST, PORT TOWNSEND; 360/379-1900 Lori, the youngest Lanza sibling (of five), and her partner, Steve, reclaimed a family legacy when they took over Lanza's from outside owners. There's no mistaking the Italian in these folks, but the addition of Northwest elements makes for delightful hybrid cuisine. Start with a Caesar; then move to ravioli or one of the best steaks in town. Family recipes include homemade sausage, and big calzone stuffed with smoked salmon, fat prawns, and pesto. The kitchen is stocked with organically grown local herbs and vegetables; pizza can be ordered to go. Catch live music Fridays and Saturdays. *$; MC, V; checks OK; dinner Mon–Sat; beer and wine; reservations recommended; www.olympus.net/lanzas/; uptown.* ⅃

Lonny's / ★★★

2330 WASHINGTON ST, PORT TOWNSEND; 360/385-0700 The film *Big Night* comes to mind, not just because of the decor, but because of the gregarious owner, Lonny Ritter, who has opened some of the Olympic Peninsula's best restaurants. In fact, when that movie opened at the local Rose Theater, Ritter and another chef replicated its outrageous dinner, complete with suckling pig, and tickets sold out in 12 minutes. Try the oyster stew, made with sweet cream, fennel, and diced pancetta—though the chargrilled prawns with mango salsa may be easier on the arteries. Paella combines the best of earth and sea—local clams and mussels, chicken, shrimp, and sausage—in fragrant saffron rice. Patrons make the trip from Seattle just to eat here.

$$; MC, V; checks OK; lunch Mon–Fri, dinner Wed–Mon; beer and wine; reservations recommended; lonnys@olypen.com; www.lonnys.com; adjacent to harbor. ぇ

Manresa Castle / ★★★

7TH AND SHERIDAN STS, PORT TOWNSEND; 360/385-5750 OR 800/732-1281 An actual castle outfitted in elegant Victoriana, this place was built in 1898 by Prussian baker and entrepreneur Charles Eisenbeis—and some swear they've seen ghosts from the place's previous incarnation as a Jesuit cloister. But the castle is now happily home to a B&B and the finest dining room on the Olympic Peninsula, under the exacting and creative leadership of Swiss-German chef Walter Santchi. He's cultivated an international menu of inventively prepared and artfully presented seasonal dishes. Favorites include king salmon rosette or exotic curry chicken Casimir. Sunday brunch is the best deal in town. It's impossible to leave hungry after Santchi's signature Swiss *roesti,* a heap of shredded potatoes browned with bacon and ham, then topped with Swiss cheese and two fried eggs. The Castle can accommodate banquets and weddings, with reception space for 80. *$$; DIS, MC, V; checks OK; dinner every day May–Oct (Wed–Sat Oct–May), brunch Sun; full bar; reservations recommended; www.manresacastle.com; heading into town on Sims Wy, take a left onto Sheridan St.*

The Public House / ★

1038 WATER ST, PORT TOWNSEND; 360/385-9708 A large space with soaring ceilings, the Public House is comfortable and casual. It features antique light fixtures, wood floors, dark green wainscoting, a nonsmoking bar, and is a great place for a big spicy bowl of gumbo, a Vermont cheddar burger, or creamy fennel-laced seafood stew. Owner Joann Saul also owns a local sushi restaurant, Sentosa, and adds select offerings delivered from there. Down a beer from the impressive list of drafts and watch the world go by through the big front windows, or catch live music on weekends. *$; AE, DIS, MC, V; checks OK; lunch, dinner every day; full bar; reservations not necessary; www.thepublichouse.com; north side of street.* ぇ

Silverwater Cafe / ★

237 TAYLOR ST, PORT TOWNSEND; 360/385-6448 Owners David and Alison Hero—he's a carpenter, potter, and baker; she's a gardener and cook—have run this restaurant of their dreams for the past 12 years. It's a warm, lovely gathering place combining 1800s architecture with satisfying food served on David's handmade plates with a carefully selected wine list. Start with artichoke pâté, fresh sautéed oysters, or a big spinach salad; lunches include filling salmon salad sandwiches, and hearty homemade soups. Local raves for dinner are green-peppercorn steaks, amaretto chicken in a tart and spicy lemon and curry sauce, and seafood pasta loaded with prawns and wild mushrooms and doused with brandy. *$$; MC, V; checks OK; lunch, dinner every day; full bar; reservations recommended; next to Rose Theater.* ぇ

FROM TIMBER TO TOURISM

Dennis Chastain passes his chain saw across a cubic yard of cedar, sawdust flying like sparks as he removes a corner. He switches to a smaller saw and gingerly shaves down rough edges with the care of a barber giving a young boy his first crew cut. After about 20 minutes, a cuddly-looking grizzly bear emerges from the block.

Chastain is a master chain-saw carver: he's won and placed in competitions all over the Northwest. People from around the world stop to admire and buy the works he creates from an outdoor shop, **DEN'S WOOD DEN,** behind his home a few miles south of Forks on Highway 101.

"When we moved here it was known as the last frontier," he says, recalling the virgin timber and big-money jobs.

That was three decades ago, when Chastain and his wife, Margaret, came from Salem, Oregon. He took a production job in a mill that eventually went belly-up. Others in the timber industry faced the same problem in the 1980s, when overlogging and new environmental rules sent a shock wave through the corridor of Highway 101: timber could no longer sustain the community.

"They wanted me to sit around on my butt and answer the telephone, and I just couldn't do that," Chastain says.

So in 1988, he turned his carving hobby into full-time work where he could gulp in the aroma of fresh cedar sawdust; Margaret takes care of sales and business. The Chastains' company is part of the Olympic Peninsula's evolution to a tourism-based economy. The towns of Port Angeles, Sequim, and Forks have stepped up efforts to bring in people to play in Olympic National Park, roam the rocky coast, and shop for antiques and local art.

The Chastains have seen some of their best friends leave town to pursue logging careers in other places, such as Alaska, Chastain says. But the Olympic Peninsula is his home.

"I have a funny feeling we may be planted here," he says.   —*Vanessa McGrady*

LODGINGS

Ann Starrett Mansion / ★★

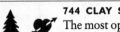 **744 CLAY ST, PORT TOWNSEND; 360/385-3205 OR 800/321-0644** The most opulent Victorian in Port Townsend, this multigabled Queen Anne hybrid was built in 1889 by a local contractor who just had to have himself a home with more of everything than his neighbors. He succeeded. The spiral stairway, octagonal tower, and "scandalous" ceiling fresco of maidens representing the four seasons are stunning. Rooms are furnished with antiques and have lovely decorative touches—hand-painted details or finely crafted ceiling moldings. The Drawing Room (with a tin claw-footed bathtub) opens to views of the Sound and Mount Baker, while the newer, romantic Gable Suite occupies the whole third

floor with a skylight, a knockout view, and a spacious seating area. For a heart-warming treat, book the Master Suite with its canopy bed and antique fainting couch. Breakfasts are ample. The house is open for public tours, noon to 3pm, when any unoccupied bedrooms are cordoned off for viewing. *$$; AE, DIS, MC, V; checks OK; edel@starrettmansion.com; www.starrettmansion.com; at Adams St.* &

Bay Cottage / ★★

4346 S DISCOVERY RD, PORT TOWNSEND; 360/385-2035 Susan Atkins turned two cottages on the shore of Discovery Bay into a delightful retreat. The cottages have good stoves and refrigerators, a tasteful mix of antique furniture, and comfy mattresses covered with feather beds. Direct access leads to a private sandy beach—marvelous for swimming, bonfires, and beach-combing. Atkins stocks the kitchens with basic breakfast necessities, and when the mood strikes, she has been known to bake cookies for guests. Each cottage has its own picnic basket, binoculars, and library. The rose garden is an enchantment. It's an ideal retreat for romantics or—some say—a great girl getaway. No pets. *$$; no credit cards; checks OK; www. olympus.net/biz/getaways/BC/index.htm; ½ mile west of Four Corners Grocery.*

Fort Worden / ★

200 BATTERY WY, PORT TOWNSEND; 360/344-4400 Fort Worden was one of three artillery posts built at the turn of the 20th century to guard the entrances of Puget Sound. The troops are long gone, and the massive gun mounts on the bluff have been stripped of their iron, but the beautifully situated fort is now a state park, a conference center, a youth hostel (especially for teenagers biking the peninsula), and the splendid Centrum, the Center for Arts and Creative Education, which presents the Centrum Summer Season. It's also an unusual place to stay. Twenty-four former officers' quarters—nobly proportioned structures dating back to 1904—front the old parade ground. These two-story houses are spacious lodgings, each with a complete kitchen, at bargain rates (great for family reunions; a few smaller homes suit couples). The most coveted of the one-bedroom lodgings is Bliss Vista, perched on the bluff, with a fireplace and plenty of romantic appeal. Alexander's Castle, a minimonument with a three-story turret, is charming in its antiquity, sequestered away from the officers' houses on the opposite side of the fort's grand lawn. RV and tent sites are near the beach and tucked into the woods. Make summer reservations well in advance. *$$; DIS, MC, V; checks OK; www. olympus.net/ftworden; 1 mile north of downtown, in Fort Worden State Park.*

Hastings House/Old Consulate Inn / ★★

313 WALKER ST, PORT TOWNSEND; 360/385-6753 OR 800/300-6753 This ornately turreted red Victorian on the hill is one of the most fre-quently photographed of Port Townsend's "painted ladies." It is also one of its most comfortable. In the enormous Master Suite (our favorite), you can soak in a claw-footed bathtub, sip coffee in the turret alcove overlooking the water, and warm up later in front of the antique fireplace. The third-floor Tower Suite, with a sweeping bay view and swathed in lace, is the essence of a Victorian-style romantic valentine. Owners Michael and Sue DeLong provide king-sized beds and private baths in each room and serve a great breakfast. A hot tub in the backyard sits in a glass gazebo. *$$$; AE, DC, MC, V; checks OK; www.oldconsulateinn.com; on bluff at Washington St.*

The James House / ★★★

1238 WASHINGTON ST, PORT TOWNSEND; 360/385-1238 OR 800/385-1238
The first B&B in the Northwest (1889) is still in great shape, though when a gale blows off the strait and hits the high bluff, you are glad to be in one of the three rooms that have a cozy fireplace or a wood-burning stove. This fine B&B rests in the competent hands of Carol McGough, who continually freshens the 13 rooms and delightful garden. Rooms in front have the best water views; not all rooms have private baths, but shared facilities are spacious and well equipped. The main floor offers two comfortable parlors, each with a fireplace and plenty of reading material. Breakfast is served either at the big dining room table, or in the kitchen with its antique cookstove. Ask about the bungalow on the bluff. *$$; AE, DIS, MC, V; checks OK; innkeeper@jameshouse.com; www.jameshouse.com; corner of Harrison St.*

Quimper Inn Bed and Breakfast / ★★☆

1306 FRANKLIN ST, PORT TOWNSEND; 360/385-1060 OR 800/557-1060
The Quimper Inn is nestled in all its Victorian splendor on Franklin Street. The dollhouse-like three-story home welcomes guests with a large open porch, and the open hearts of hosts Sue and Ron Ramage. In the cozy bay-windowed parlor, a fireplace crackles. Rooms are named for family members and each has its own distinctive mood. The Michelle Room, for example, has a soft rose tint and a large bathroom with a deep claw-footed tub. Even the most humble of rooms has surprising charm, and most have views of the gardens, mountains, or water. Breakfasts are well executed and the second-floor balcony is perfect for morning tea. The inn is within walking distance of town and the Ramages thoughtfully provide menus for most local restaurants. Trust their suggestions. *$$; MC, V; checks OK; www.olympus. net/quimper; thequimps@olympus.net; corner of Harrison St.*

Sequim and the Dungeness Valley

Sequim (pronounced "skwim") was once a carefully kept secret. The town sits smack in the middle of the rain shadow cast by the Olympic Mountains: the sun shines 306 days a year here, and annual rainfall is only 16 inches. Now Sequim has been discovered, especially by retirees, and is growing fast; golf courses sprout in what used to be pastures.

On Sequim Bay, near Blyn, the S'Klallam Indians operate the unique **NORTH-WEST NATIVE EXPRESSIONS** art gallery (1033 Old Blyn Hwy; 360/681-4640). Across the highway stands the **7 CEDARS** (270756 Hwy 101; 800/4LUCKY7), a mammoth gambling casino with valet parking and good food. **CEDARBROOK HERB FARM** (1345 Sequim Ave S; 360/683-7733; every day Mar–Dec 23), Washington's oldest herb farm, has a vast range of plants—including scented geraniums—fresh-cut herbs, and a pleasant gift shop. **OLYMPIC GAME FARM** (1423 Ward Rd, 5 miles north of Sequim; 360/683-4295) is the retirement center for Hollywood animal stars and endangered species. An hour-long guided walking tour is available mid-May through Labor Day; or take a driving tour year-round.

DUNGENESS SPIT (360/457-8451), 6 miles northwest of Sequim, is a national wildlife refuge for birds (more than 275 species have been sighted) and one of the longest natural sand spits in the world. A long walk down the narrow 5½-mile beach takes you to a remote lighthouse (check a tide table before you start).

Two small but notable wineries offer tastings: **LOST MOUNTAIN WINERY** (3174 Lost Mountain Rd; 360/683-5229; tastings by arrangement or chance) and **NEUHARTH WINERY** (885 S Still Rd; 360/683-9652; every day in summer, Wed–Sun in winter).

RESTAURANTS

Khu Larb Thai II / ★

120 W BELL ST, SEQUIM; 360/681-8550 Ever since the Itti family opened their second establishment (the first is in Port Townsend), Sequim residents are thrilled that they don't have to drive so far to savor the vibrant flavors of Thailand. Thai food stands out in the land of logger burgers, and the Ittis have perfected this aromatic cuisine. They do great business. Newcomers to Thai food should request the tried-and-true *tum kah gai* (a chicken soup with coconut milk and lime broth), the phad thai (sweet, spicy noodles stir-fried with egg, tofu, and vegetables), or the garlic pork. Aromatic curries appeal to more adventurous diners. *$; MC, V; local checks only; lunch, dinner Tues–Sun; beer and wine; reservations not necessary; at Sequim Ave.* &

Oak Table Cafe / ★

292 W BELL ST, SEQUIM; 360/683-2179 Breakfast (served until 3pm) is the thing at this cafe. It's a feast—huge omelets, fruit crepes, or legendary puffy apple pancakes. Service is friendly and efficient, and the place is noisy, boisterous, and chatty. Good old-fashioned lunch options (turkey sandwiches, soothing—but unexciting—soups) are mixed with a few enlightened salads (such as chicken sesame). It's owned by one of the Nagler family, who also own the Chestnut Cottage (see review) and First Street Haven in Port Angeles. *$$; AE, DC, MC, V; checks OK; breakfast every day, lunch Mon–Sat; no alcohol; reservations not necessary; www.oaktablecafe.com; at 3rd Ave.* &

LODGINGS

Groveland Cottage / ★

4861 SEQUIM-DUNGENESS WY, SEQUIM; 360/683-3565 OR 800/879-8859 At the turn of the century, this was a family home in Dungeness—a wide spot in the road, a short drive from the beach. Now the place has the comfortable salty-air feel of an old summer house with a great room where guests convene around the fireplace. Four cheerful guest rooms have private baths, two with whirlpool tubs. A one-room cottage out back may not be as special but has its own cooking space. The place fills up in summer with guests addicted to owner Simone Nichols's little luxuries like coffee in your room before sitting down to her four-course breakfast. No children under 6. *$$; AE, DIS, MC, V; checks OK; simone@olypen.com; www.sequimvalley. com; follow signs toward Three Crabs.*

Juan de Fuca Cottages / ★

182 MARINE DR, SEQUIM; 360/683-4433 Any of these five comfortable cottages—overlooking Dungeness Spit, or with a view of the Olympics—is special, whether for a winter weekend or a longer summer sojourn. A two-bedroom suite has both views and a welcoming fireplace. Each is equipped with a Jacuzzi, kitchen utensils, games, and reading material, as well as cable TV and VCR, and you can choose from a 250-video library. Outside is the spit, begging for beach walks and clam digging. *$$; DIS, MC, V; checks OK; 2-night min weekends and July–Aug; www.juandefuca.com; 7 miles north of Sequim.*

Toad Hall / ★

12 JESSLYN LN, SEQUIM; 360/681-2002 Named after Toad Hall from *The Wind in the Willows,* this B&B was quietly opened by Linda and Bruce Jennings to unexpected acclaim in 1997. The Jennings are happy to share their love of all things British—from proper tea and cakes in the afternoon, to a perfect scone at breakfast. Plush amenities—monogrammed robes, lavender sachets from the garden, morning coffee at your door—create a sense of abundance. Three rooms, two with private bath, are done up in white lace, burgundy, and deep green. The main room is great for quiet socializing. We wish it were farther from the road. No children. *$$; DIS, MC, V; checks OK; 2-night min; www.toadhall.tv; at N Sequim Ave, north of Old Olympic Hwy.*

Port Angeles and the Strait of Juan de Fuca

The north shore of the Olympic Peninsula was home to several thriving Native American tribes long before outside explorers laid claim to the area. Today this region is anchored by the blue-collar mill town known as Port Angeles—"where the Olympics greet the sea." Port Angeles Harbor, protected against wind and waves by Ediz Hook sand spit, is the largest natural deep-water harbor north of San Francisco. It is also a jumping-off point to Victoria, British Columbia, 17 miles across the Strait of Juan de Fuca on Canada's Vancouver Island.

Port Angeles

Port Angeles is primarily notable for being the northern gateway to **OLYMPIC NATIONAL PARK** (360/565-3130; www.nps.gov/olym/). The park, as big as Rhode Island, with a buffer zone of national forest surrounding it, contains the largest remaining herd of the huge Roosevelt elk, which occasionally create "elk jams" along Highway 101. Follow the signs to the park's visitor center, just south of town on Mount Angeles Road; then drive 17 miles along winding precipices to mile-high **HURRICANE RIDGE** and breathtaking views. Rest rooms and snack facilities are on the ridge, as well as plenty of hiking trails in summer, and good cross-country skiing and a weekend poma-lift downhill-skiing-and-tubing area in winter. Seasonal snowshoe rental and guided snowshoe nature walks are offered through March. Check road conditions before you go (24-hour recorded message: 360/565-3131).

OLYMPIC RAFT AND KAYAK SERVICE (360/452-1443 or 888/452-1443) offers easy floats and kayaking ventures on the Elwha and Hoh Rivers.

In downtown Port Angeles, **PORT BOOK AND NEWS** (104 E 1st St; 360/452-6367) sells a wide selection of magazines and daily newspapers like the *New York Times* and *The Wall Street Journal*. **MOMBASA COFFEE COMPANY** (113 W 1st St; 360/452-3238) serves excellent fresh-roasted coffee. **GINA'S BAKERY** (710 S Lincoln St; 360/457-3279), near the library, is a good place to buy picnic food, especially pastries, hulking cinnamon rolls, and freshly made sandwiches. Browse **SWAIN'S GENERAL STORE** (602 E 1st St; 360/452-2357) for everything else.

RESTAURANTS

C'est Si Bon / ★★

23 CEDAR PARK DR, PORT ANGELES; 360/452-8888 Yes, it *is* good—especially if you're yearning for classic French cooking with splendid sauces. Dine leisurely in an attractive setting: the best tables are in window bays that overlook the rose garden; a new glass conservatory is a favorite for large parties. If the food is slow in coming, host Juhasz Norbert regales waiting guests with tales of his musical experiences in France and Hollywood (and others, who've heard him, beg him to bring out his violin). A big bowl of onion soup, bubbling under a brown crust of cheese, can serve as a meal in itself, particularly when followed by a refreshing salad. The most popular dish here is Tournedos Royale: filet mignon topped with sautéed crab. To assure consistency, stick to simpler preparations, such as braised lamb, classic steak au poivre, or fresh halibut and salmon in season. The chocolate mousse is wickedly rich, and the wine list has good choices. *$$$; AE, DIS, MC, V; local checks only; dinner Tues–Sun; full bar; reservations recommended; 4 miles east of Port Angeles.* &

Chestnut Cottage / ★

929 E FRONT ST, PORT ANGELES; 360/452-8344 Owners Diane Nagler and Ken Nemirow are particular when it comes to quality food and service. And it shows. Their Chestnut Cottage is the place to go for an exceptional breakfast in delightful country Victorian–style surroundings smack in the middle of downtown. A custardy apple and walnut French toast is only one of several morning treats; others include Belgian waffles, pancakes, quiches, frittatas, or lemon blintzes drizzled with raspberry purée. Children are delighted by the breakfast pizza (ham and eggs on pita). Simple porridge and berries is another kid-friendly option. Nagler and Nemirow also own First Street Haven (107 E 1st St; 360/457-0352), an equally good place for more casual breakfasts and fresh lunches, where prices are reasonable. *$$; AE, DIS, MC, V; checks OK; breakfast, lunch every day; beer and wine; reservations not necessary; east of town center.* &

Hacienda del Mar / ★

408 S LINCOLN ST, PORT ANGELES; 360/452-5296 This is a reincarnation of a longtime favorite Mexican restaurant, and locals say the food is better than ever. Most of the charming staff has remained, but be warned: your waiter will have you saying *si* to another margarita and dessert before you know it.

Salsa gets points for being thick and zesty with a comfortable balance of cilantro and heat. The standards—fajitas, burritos, tacos—are all fine, but specialties are where the house shines. Try spinach-filled tamales with a cream cheese sauce, or seafood enchiladas. *$; AE, DIS, MC, V; checks OK; lunch, dinner every day; beer and wine; reservations not necessary; between 4th and 5th Sts.* &

Thai Peppers / ★★

222 N LINCOLN ST, PORT ANGELES; 360/452-4995 Consider the pepper: sweetly benign, audaciously hot, or sneakily sublime. It's also a fitting name for the best Thai food in Port Angeles. The menu offers an intriguing mix of flavors for both battle-ready and timid taste buds. *Po tak* soup takes a twist on *tom yum,* by adding assorted seafood to a broth enlightened with lemongrass, cilantro, Kaffir lime leaves, and mushrooms. Sizzling, succulent duck makes a grand appearance, basil beef combines a generous helping of both with chile-garlic sauce, and the curries (particularly red) do justice to fresh seafood. Thai Peppers comes from the same family who brought the Olympic Peninsula Khu Larb in Port Townsend and Sequim. When you're hot, you're hot. *$; MC, V; checks OK; lunch, dinner every day (Mon–Sat in off-season); beer and wine; reservations not necessary; thaipep@ olypen.com; between Front St and Railroad Ave.* &

LODGINGS

Five SeaSuns / ★

1006 S LINCOLN ST, PORT ANGELES; 360/452-8248 OR 800/708-0777 This huge 1926 Dutch Colonial house was home to only four families before owners Bob and Jan Harbick took over and turned it into a B&B in 1996. It has a well-kept interior with sunny rooms, elegantly crafted architectural details, and polished hardwood floors. A parlor outfitted with comfy couches gives guests a homey sitting space, and rooms are decorated to evoke the feeling of the four seasons. Pick of the lot is the Herfst (autumn) room, with private white-tiled bath, queen-sized brass bed, wicker furniture, well-placed antiques, and hats and hatboxes of a bygone era. The Carriage House is for rent, too, with rustic, wood-paneled decor and full kitchen. Breakfast—your choice of two sittings—is filling and artfully presented. *$$–$$$; AE, MC, V; checks OK; seasuns@olypen.com; www.seasuns.com; corner of E 10th St.*

Tudor Inn / ★★

1108 S OAK ST, PORT ANGELES; 360/452-3138 Jane Glass is a gracious host of one of the oldest—and best looking—B&Bs in town. This completely restored 1910 Tudor-style B&B is 12 blocks from the ferry terminal in a quiet residential neighborhood, and boasts a library, a fireplace, crisp linens, and well-chosen antiques. Five rooms are nattily decorated in turn-of-the-20th-century style; the best has a balcony with mountain view, fireplace, claw-footed tub, and shower. Glass serves a traditional full breakfast with none of the forced conviviality that sometimes afflicts B&Bs; she takes a healthy approach to cooking, using the freshest ingredients available. Well versed in Port Angeles political and cultural life, Glass will arrange fishing charters, horseback rides, winter ski packages, and scenic flights. *$$; AE, DIS, MC, V; checks OK; info@tudorinn.com; www.tudorinn.com; at 11th St.*

Lake Crescent

Highway 101 skirts the south shore of 600-foot-deep Lake Crescent with numerous scenic pullouts. The Fairholm store and boat launch are on the far west end of the lake, with East Beach 10 miles away. Lake Crescent is home to rainbow trout and steelhead, to Beardslee and the famous Crescenti trout, which lurk in its depths. Rental boats are available. Ask about the easy 1-mile hike that takes you to 90-foot Marymere Falls.

LODGINGS

Lake Crescent Lodge / ★

416 LAKE CRESCENT RD, PORT ANGELES; 360/928-3211 Built 85 years ago, the well-maintained Lake Crescent Lodge has been well worn since the days when it was known as Singer's Tavern. The historic main building has a grand veranda that overlooks the deep, crystal blue waters of Lake Crescent; a so-so restaurant; and a comfortable bar. Upstairs rooms are noisy and rustic—a euphemism that means, among other things, that the bathroom is down the hall. Motel rooms are the best buy, but the clutter of tiny basic cabins, with porches and fireplaces, can be fun—though bear in mind that they were built in 1937, when President Franklin Roosevelt came to visit. Service is fine—mainly enthusiastic college kids having a nice summer. It's true this side of the lake sees less sun than the north side, but you don't come to the rain forest to see sun, do you? *$$; AE, CB, DC, DIS, MC, V; checks OK; closed Nov–Apr; www.olypen.com/lakecrescentlodge; 20 miles west of Port Angeles.* &

Sol Duc Hot Springs

Whether you arrive by car after an impressive 12-mile drive through old-growth forests, or on foot after days of hiking mountain ridges, these hot springs are the ideal trail's end. The Quileute Indians called the area *Sol Duc*—"sparkling water." In the early 1900s, Sol Duc Hot Springs (28 miles west of Port Angeles; 360/327-3583; open every day mid-May–Sept, Thurs–Sun Apr–mid-May and Oct, closed Nov–Mar) became a mecca for travelers seeking relief from aches and pains. For $7.50, you can have a hot soak, followed by a swim in a cold pool. You can also opt for a lengthy massage ($55 for an hour). The hike to nearby **SOL DUC FALLS** passes through one of the loveliest stands of old-growth forest anywhere.

LODGINGS

Sol Duc Hot Springs Resort

SOL DUC RD AND HWY 101, PORT ANGELES; 360/327-3583 Surrounded by forest, 32 small cedar-roofed sleeping cabins are clustered in a grassy meadow. The favorites are those with river-facing porches. Up to four guests can share a cabin, which are carpeted and have private baths and double beds. Duplex units have kitchens, and in keeping with the natural serenity, there are no TVs anywhere (and a no-smoking policy everywhere). Camping and RV sites are available. The Springs Restaurant serves breakfast and dinner in summer, and a deli is open midday through the season. Use of the hot springs and the pool is included in the cabin rental fee. *$$; AE, DIS, MC, V; checks OK; open every day mid-May–Sept,*

*Thurs–Sun Apr–mid-May and Oct; pamsdr@aol.com; www.northolympic.com/
solduc/index.html; turn off a few miles west of Lake Crescent, then drive 12 miles
south of Hwy 101.*

Clallam Bay and Sekiu

Twenty-one miles south on Hoko-Ozette Road from Sekiu is **LAKE OZETTE,** the
largest natural body of freshwater in the state. At the north end of the lake is a campground and trails leading to several beaches where you can see the eerie, eroded
coastal cliffs. It was near here in the 1960s that tidal erosion exposed a 500-year-old
Native American village—once covered by a mud slide—with homes perfectly preserved. The archaeological dig was closed in 1981 after 11 years of excavation; artifacts are on display at the Makah Cultural and Research Center in Neah Bay (see
Neah Bay).

Neah Bay

This is literally the end of the road: Highway 112 ends at this small waterside town
on the northern edge of the **MAKAH INDIAN RESERVATION.** Two 8-mile-long
rutted roads lead to **CAPE FLATTERY**—take the west one coming and going. The
Makah allow public access across their ancestral lands—a ½-mile walk on a new
boardwalk to **LAND'S END,** the far northwestern corner of Washington's seacoast.
From these high-cliffed headlands, cow-calf pairs of gray whales can often be seen
migrating north in April and May. Salmon-fishing charters are available. Sandy
HOBUCK BEACH is open for picnics (no fires) and surfing, and farther on, the **TSOO-
YAS BEACH** (pronounced "sooes") is accessible (pay the landowners a parking fee).
Call the visitors center (360/452-0330) in Port Angeles for coastal access information. The **MAKAH CULTURAL AND RESEARCH CENTER** (Front St; 360/645-2711)
has a stunning exhibit of artifacts from the village discovered under Lake Ozette; it
also serves as an ad hoc tourist-information center.

Forks and the Hoh River Valley

The **HOH RAIN FOREST** in Olympic National Park is the wettest location in the con-
tiguous United States, with an average yearly rainfall of 133.58 inches. This steady
moisture nurtures dense vegetation—more than 3,000 species of plant life—
including the Rain Forest Monarch, a giant Sitka spruce more than 500 years old
towering close to 300 feet over the moss- and fern-carpeted forest floor. Take the
spur road off Highway 101, 13 miles south of Forks, to the visitors center and campground (30 miles southeast of Forks; 360/374-6925). For those with more time, one-
to three-day round-trip hikes up **MOUNT OLYMPUS** provide some of the best hiking
in the world. The longer trip to **GLACIER MEADOWS** is best mid-July through
October. Stop in at **PEAK 6 ADVENTURE STORE** (about 5 miles up the road to the
Hoh; 360/374-5254), a veritable miniature REI right where you need it most.

HOW TO EAT AN OYSTER

Despite their reputed powers as an aphrodisiac, oysters are not for everyone. But don't assume you won't like them just because they're ugly—especially if you've never tried one of the Northwest's famous shellfish.

Restaurants all over the region offer a multitude of preparations, from sautéing to frying, but purists insist the slippery mollusks are best raw; many chefs concoct special sauces to go with uncooked oysters as well. Xinh Dwelley of Xinh's Clam & Oyster House, in Shelton on Hood Canal, offers the following tips:

1. Place the oyster on a towel draped over your open palm, using caution to avoid the sharp edges (wear work gloves). Hold the oyster firmly with one hand, and in your dominant hand, hold an oyster knife.

2. Slip the blade between the top and bottom shell near the hinge.

3. Run the knife around the oyster until you get to the other side. This sounds easy, but be careful; people are most likely to cut themselves at this step.

4. Using a twisting motion, pry the top and bottom shells apart. Be gentle but firm so as not to spill the oyster "liquor" inside.

5. Cut the oyster free from the shell by slicing through tough connection membrane.

6. Eat your oyster. Slurp it plain, or add Tabasco, cocktail sauce, or a squeeze of lemon to dress up the ugly but lovable bivalve.

—Vanessa McGrady

Forks

From this little town on the west end of the Olympic Peninsula, you can explore the wild coastal beaches, hook a steelhead, or go mountain biking, camping, or hiking. The pristine waters of the Hoh, Bogachiel, Calawah, and Sol Duc Rivers all flow near Forks, making it a key fishing destination. Ask your innkeeper, the informative **FORKS VISITORS CENTER** (1411 S Forks Ave; 360/374-2531 or 800/44-FORKS), or **OLYMPIC SPORTING GOODS** (190 N Forks Ave; 360/374-6330), next to the liquor store, for information on recommended guides, licenses, or where to land the Big One.

On the outskirts of town, the **TIMBER MUSEUM** (1421 S Forks Ave; 360/374-9663) tells the story of the West End's logging heritage. Next door at the visitors center, pick up a map for Arttrek, a self-guided tour of nearly two dozen local studios and galleries; most are in artists' homes, but if the Arttrek sign is out, you're welcome. A delightful mingling of art, espresso, antiques, and books can be found where **TINKER'S TALES & ANTIQUES, RIVER RUN COFFEE HOUSE,** and the **ALLEY STUDIO** share space (71 N Forks Ave; 360/374-9433).

LODGINGS

Eagle Point Inn / ★★

 384 STORMIN' NORMAN LN, FORKS; 360/327-3236 Cradled on 5 acres in a bend of the Sol Duc River, this spacious log lodge was designed by Chris and Dan Christensen to perfectly combine comfort and style. And it has become one of the most impressive places to stay near the rain forest. Two downstairs bedrooms, each with a queen-sized bed covered with a thick down comforter, have commodious bathrooms. The open two-story common living quarters house Chris's collection of kerosene lamps and other interesting antiques but leave plenty of room for guests to spread out in front of the fireplace, made of rocks from the Sol Duc River. The Christensens live nearby in what was the original lodge, leaving you just the right amount of privacy. Even if you need to get up before dawn to fish, a hearty breakfast will be ready. You can barbecue your own dinner in a covered outdoor kitchen near the river. *$$; no credit cards; checks OK; 10 miles north of Forks.*

Huckleberry Lodge

1171 BIG PINE WY, FORKS; 360/374-6008 OR 888/822-6008 Avid outdoors enthusiasts Kitty and Bill Speery own Forks's most fun adventure lodge, and go the extra mile to accommodate guests, whether it's a 4:30am breakfast or arrangements for a full day of fly-fishing or ATV adventures. On request, the owners provide niceties (toiletries, hot tub under the evergreens, sauna) and naughties (poker chips, cigars, a heated outdoor smoking canopy). You can spend the night, have breakfast, and do your own thing, but this place works best if you come with friends for a weekend. The pool table in the family room, the buffalo head (among numerous other items) in the living room, and the display of Native American artifacts reflect the spirit of this place. The cabins, complete with kitchen, are a good choice for the more independently minded (or for longer stays). A couple of RV hookups accommodate those who want to get away from the hubbub of busy RV parks. *$$; MC, V; checks OK; hucklodg@olypen.com; www.huckleberrylodge.com; north end of Forks.*

Shady Nook Cottage / ★

81 ASH AVE, FORKS; 360/374-5497 You wouldn't expect to find an English garden tucked away only a few blocks from downtown Forks, but that's exactly the atmosphere innkeeper Deannie Hoien has created in her two guest cottages. Hoien, an accomplished stained-glass artist, continually updates the decor with her creations. Handmade quilts lend homespun charm to spaces equipped with full kitchens, microwaves, and TVs. Hoien has a gift for coaxing bright flowers and graceful foliage from the patch of garden surrounding the cottages—a refreshing place to sit. Continental breakfast is included. *$$; no credit cards; checks OK; open Apr–Nov, other times by arrangement; shadynook@northolympic.com; www.northolympic.com/shadynook; turn west at N Forks Ave, go 2 blocks, and turn right onto Ash Ave.*

La Push and Pacific Ocean Beaches

The Dickey, Quillayute, Calawah, and Sol Duc Rivers merge and enter the ocean near La Push. To the north and south extend miles of wilderness coastline—the last such stretch remaining in the United States outside of Alaska—much of which is protected as part of Olympic National Park. It is home to the Quileute Indians, and today the small community still revolves around its fishing heritage. The lure of wild ocean beaches, with jagged offshore rocks and teeming tide pools, brings those seeking adventurous solitude. The only nearby lodging is **OCEAN PARK RESORT** (360/374-5267) in La Push, which is too worn to recommend.

Several miles to the north, Mora Road leads to **RIALTO BEACH** and a three-day wilderness beach hike to **CAPE ALAVA** west of Lake Ozette. A shorter, more strenuous hike leads from **THIRD BEACH**, south of La Push, 16 miles to the Hoh River—an extraordinarily dramatic stretch. Warning: All ocean beaches can be extremely dangerous due to fluctuating tides and unfordable creeks during periods of heavy rain. Stop at the **RANGER STATION** (360/374-5460) in nearby Mora (2 miles north of Forks, take turnoff for La Push Rd; as it forks into Mora Rd, take Mora Rd about 5 miles to Mora Campground) to get information about use permits and tide tables.

Farther south along Highway 101 is **RUBY BEACH**—ideal for walking—a wide stretch named for the tiny garnet crystals that compose much of its sand. A mile farther is the viewpoint for Destruction Island, a wildlife sanctuary topped by a lighthouse. Nearby, a trail leads to the world's largest western red cedar.

Several more beaches make good explorations as you continue south—particularly at **KALALOCH**, which has a campground and a fine clamming beach. **KALALOCH LODGE** (157151 Hwy 101, Forks; 360/962-2271) is one of the most isolated beachside resorts in Washington. Unfortunately, accommodations are rudimentary and the food in the restaurant standard at best. If you're looking for a view, you can't beat it, but those in the know camp.

Lake Quinault

Lake Quinault, at the inland apex of the **QUINAULT INDIAN RESERVATION,** is usually the first or the last stop on Highway 101's scenic loop around the peninsula's Olympic National Park and Forest. The glacier-carved lake is surrounded by cathedral-like firs, the fishing is memorable, and there are several easy trails, including one to **CAMPBELL GROVE** with its enormous old-growth trees. The **RANGER STATION** (on lake's south shore; 360/288-2444) provides information on more strenuous hikes up the North Fork of the Quinault River, or to Enchanted Valley. A large 1930s log chalet at the end of the 13-mile trail can house 50–60 hikers.

LODGINGS

Lake Quinault Lodge / ★

S SHORE RD, QUINAULT; 360/288-2900 OR 800/562-6672 (WA AND OR ONLY) A massive cedar-shingled structure, this grand old lodge was built in 1926 in a gentle arc around the sweeping lawns that descend to the lake. The rustic public rooms are done up like grandma's sunporch in wicker and antiques, with a massive stone fireplace in the lobby; the dining room overlooks the lawns. Rooms in the main building are small but nice; half have lake views. Choice lodgings are the 36 newer lakeside rooms a short walk from the lodge. Amenities consist of a sauna, an indoor heated pool, a game room, canoes and rowboats, and well-maintained trails for hiking or running. It's a good idea to make summer reservations four to five months in advance, but winter is wide-open—and a great time to experience the rain forest. The dining room puts up a classy front. Lunches are classic national park (Monte Cristos and logger burgers), but dinners are a bit more creative, with entrees such as ginger-seared halibut or blackened salmon. On occasion, conventioneers abound, drawn by the spalike features of the resort, but somehow the old place still exudes the quiet elegance of its past. $$–$$$; AE, MC, V; checks OK; www.visitlake quinalt.com; from Hwy 101, turn east at milepost 125 onto S Shore Rd.

NORTH CASCADES

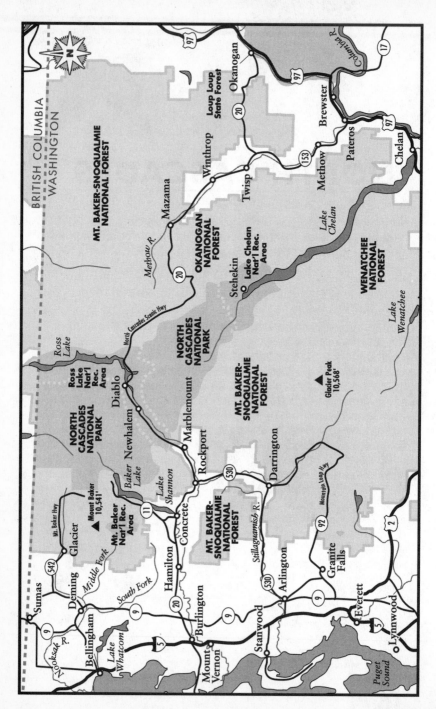

NORTH CASCADES

Few regions in Washington have the allure of the North Cascades. Settled squarely in the northwest part of the state, the mountainous area is world renowned for its ice-draped peaks, alpine meadows, and vast stands of old-growth forest. The crown jewel is North Cascades National Park, a cluster of magnificent peaks that are part of the Cascade Range. The park is surrounded by a jigsaw puzzle of federally protected wilderness areas, making the entire region nirvana for hikers and campers.

Broadly speaking, the North Cascades includes more than just the national park, encompassing Mount Baker to the north, the breathtaking North Cascades Scenic Highway that cuts across the park's center, the wide-open Methow Valley east of the Cascades, and, farther south, pristine and popular Lake Chelan.

The entire region remains relatively unscathed by development. The North Cascades contains no cities, few resorts, and little tourist-town sprawl. (Food and lodging aren't plentiful, either.) That may not last long, but for now, the towns scattered throughout the region still feel like small-town America (but with an espresso stand at almost every corner). These are friendly, hospitable spots, often with some interesting historical site or quirky attraction to merit a quick stop. But even locals concede the region's best feature is their backyards. Each is a gateway to the Great Outdoors, an invitation to hiking, camping, mountain biking, fishing, boating, and downhill and cross-country skiing. Just as nicely, there's still plenty of room for solitude.

ACCESS AND INFORMATION

Travelers tour the North Cascades via car (there are no airports or train service within this region) on the **NORTH CASCADES SCENIC HIGHWAY** (Hwy 20), an east-west corridor that links Sedro Woolley near Interstate 5 (exit 230, 65 miles north of Seattle) to the town of Twisp. East of the Cascades, the Twisp-Chelan leg is connected by Highway 153 and US Highway 97.

Generally, the best **WEATHER** for visiting the high country occurs mid-June to late September. Snow closes the North Cascades Highway—typically the stretch between Mazama on the east side and Diablo on the west—from approximately mid-November to mid-April, depending on the weather. In winter, Puget Sound visitors travel to the Methow Valley by crossing the Cascades via the longer, more southerly routes of US Highway 2 or Interstate 90.

For information, contact **NORTH CASCADES VISITOR CENTER** (502 Newhalem St, Newhalem, WA 98283; 206/386-4495) or **LAKE CHELAN VISITOR BUREAU** (PO Box 216, Chelan, WA 98816; 800/4-CHELAN; www.lakechelan.com).

Mount Baker

The **MOUNT BAKER HIGHWAY** (Hwy 542) rises from Bellingham, paralleling the sparkling Nooksack River and passing through little towns like Deming and Glacier, to reach two of the state's loveliest sights: 10,778-foot Mount Baker and 8,268-foot Mount Shuksan. Extreme skiers and snowboarders from all over the world journey to **MOUNT BAKER SKI AREA** (360/734-6771), 56 miles east of Bellingham. The mountain never lacks for snow—during the 1998–99 season, it set a world record for snowfall with 1,140 inches—and has the kind of steep terrain that satisfies avid boarders. The area typically is open mid-November to mid-May (the longest season in the state). In summer, enjoy beautiful vistas and exhilarating day hikes.

Deming

LODGINGS

Diamond Ridge / ★★

9216 MT BAKER HWY, DEMING; 360/599-3297 OR 800/424-1966 Set well away from the highway on an 80-foot ridge overlooking the Nooksack River, this new, luxurious B&B delivers a million-dollar view of Mount Baker. The English-style country gardens envisioned by proprietors Dawn and Dale Marr are still a work in progress, but the 400-year-old evergreens rising cathedral-like on 15 wooded acres make up for it. The 2,000-square-foot, new, log-style home aims for a lodge feel. The two guest rooms—both upstairs, one facing the river, the other the forest—are handsome, spacious accommodations, each offering separate balcony, private bath, and lush comforts (thick bathrobes, down comforter, a library of books) appreciated in these surroundings. No pets, smoking, or children under 16. *$$$; MC, V; checks OK; diamond ridge@bigplanet.com; www.diamondridgebb.com; first driveway on left following milepost 31, Hwy 542, 2 miles before Glacier.*

Glacier

RESTAURANTS

Milano's Restaurant and Deli / ★★

9990 MT BAKER HWY, GLACIER; 360/599-2863 This unassuming little restaurant within a market and deli doesn't initially look deserving of a stop. But slam on those brakes! To borrow the ski terminology used at nearby Mount Baker, there's black-diamond cuisine here in a blue-run atmosphere. The star offering at this informal Italian restaurant is freshly made pasta with creative fillings and sauces. The clam-packed *linguine vongole* and the chicken Gorgonzola, smothered in a rich, savory sauce, are mouth watering *speciale della casa*. They are nearly rivaled by a slew of tasty raviolis, stuffed with spinach, porcini mushrooms, or smoked salmon. Enjoy a beer or a glass of wine from the well-priced selection, or have coffee and tiramisu. The deli does a brisk business in take-out sandwiches for those headed to the mountains. *$$; MC, V; local checks only; breakfast Sat–Sun, lunch, dinner every day; beer and wine; reservations recommended; milanodeli@ aol.com; on Hwy 542 in Glacier.* &

LODGINGS

The Logs at Canyon Creek / ★

9002 MT BAKER HWY, GLACIER; 360/599-2711 Five log cabins nestled among dense stands of alder and fir at the confluence of the Nooksack River and Canyon Creek compose this rustic retreat. Comfortable cabins sleep up to eight in bunk-bedded rooms and on pullout couches. The centerpoint of each cabin

NORTH CASCADES THREE-DAY TOUR

DAY ONE: Start your day in the Puget Sound area and head eastbound on the **NORTH CASCADES SCENIC HIGHWAY** for a daylong drive. Pack a lunch or grab a burger at the cafe with the **GOOD FOOD** (59924 SR20; 360/873-9309) sign in Marblemount before making your first must-stop: the **NORTH CASCADES VISITOR CENTER** in Newhalem. Enjoy the center's exhibits, then take a short, easy hike to view the Picket Range. Back in the car, begin your drive across the mountains, allowing at least two hours for stops. **DIABLO LAKE** overlook and **WASHINGTON PASS** have sweeping, panoramic vistas. Continue your drive into the Methow Valley and collapse in the arms of luxurious comfort at either the **MAZAMA COUNTRY INN** in Mazama or **SUN MOUNTAIN LODGE** in Winthrop, where you'll have dinner.

DAY TWO: After breakfast at the lodge, take the morning to explore the frontier atmosphere of Winthrop. Mosey around the pioneer buildings of **SHAFER MUSEUM.** Poke through the main street's Old West storefronts, antique stores, and blacksmith shop. Stop for lunch nearby at the **DUCK BRAND RESTAURANT AND HOTEL,** where you can nibble virtuously at healthy salads or eat yourself into a coma on Mexican food, pasta, or steak. Use the afternoon to unwind at **PEARRYGIN LAKE STATE PARK.** Go for a swim, rent a boat, or simply relax with a book under one of the shade trees. Wrap things up with an elegant dinner at the **FREESTONE INN,** then return to your hotel.

DAY THREE: Head for Chelan, a 56-mile trip that takes about 1½ hours. Allow time to stop in Twisp to visit the **CONFLUENCE GALLERY** and small-town shops, and have lunch at the **FIDDLEHEAD BISTRO.** Once in Chelan, check into **CAMPBELL'S RESORT ON LAKE CHELAN** and settle into a lakeside lawn chair on the lodge's sandy beach to soak up the sun. If you get restless, saunter out to explore town; everything is within walking distance. Enjoy dinner at **CAMPBELL HOUSE CAFE** and wind up the day with an evening stroll through **RIVERWALK PARK.**

is the large fireplace (built from river cobbles and slabs of Nooksack stone), stocked with firewood. Each cabin has a fully equipped kitchen and a charcoal grill, but no phone or TV. In summer, enjoy the small pool or mosey along the riverbed. This is a great place to bring the kids and the family dog. *$$; no credit cards; checks OK; 3-night min in summer and holidays; thelogs@telcomplus.net; www.telcomplus.net/ thelogs; milepost 30.5, Hwy 542, 30 miles east of Bellingham.*

North Cascades Scenic Highway

The heart of this region is the North Cascades Scenic Highway (Hwy 20), frequently heralded as one of the nation's top scenic highways. The two-lane road, completed in 1972, slices through the mountains to provide stunning roadside mountain vistas, but almost as impressive are the brilliantly hued, jade-green and turquoise **DIABLO AND ROSS LAKES** created by a hydroelectric dam project.

The highway, the most northerly cross-state route, connects the wet, west, forested side of the Cascades to the semi-arid, sunlit world east of the mountains. More than 130 miles and a few hours' driving time, it climbs from peaceful farmland and lush, thick evergreens to rugged mountains and immense glaciers via **RAINY AND WASHINGTON PASSES**, then—*poof!*—it's a long hang-glide down into a wide-open pastoral valley and grassy meadowlands.

Marblemount

Hundreds of **BALD EAGLES** perch along the Skagit River from December through February, scavenging on spawned-out salmon. You can spy a number from the road, along Highway 20 between Rockport and Marblemount (bring binoculars). However, the best view is from the river, via a two- to three-hour **FLOAT TOUR**. Call **CHINOOK EXPEDITIONS** (800/241-3451), **WILDWATER RIVER TOURS** (800/ 522-WILD), or the **MOUNT BAKER RANGER DISTRICT** (2105 Hwy 20, Sedro-Woolley; 360/856-5700) for other float-trip operators.

LODGINGS

A cab in the woods / ★

9303 DANDY PL, ROCKPORT; 360/873-4106 They're nothing fancy, but these cozy cedar log cabins tucked into quiet, secluded woods off the main highway represent one of the best values in the area. Each of the five cabins sleeps four in a bedroom and living room, and has a fully equipped kitchen and gas fireplace. Owners Dave and Andie Daniels have given the cabins a good spit 'n' polish—reroofed them, upgraded furnishings, modernized the bathrooms—and tidied up the grounds for picnicking, playing badminton, or roasting marshmallows over a campfire. The marvelous Skagit River is within walking distance. *$$; MC, V; checks OK; www.cabinwoods.com; just past milepost 103 on Hwy 20, 3 miles west of Marblemount.*

North Cascades National Park

The North Cascades are often called America's Alps, which may be travel-writing hyperbole. If not that, they're certainly Washington's Alps. Like their European counterparts, the mountains possess extraordinary grandeur and majesty, along with a wild, elusive quality that makes them a worldwide draw.

In 1968, a 505,000-acre section immediately south of the U.S.-Canadian border won national park status. The huge park contains jagged peaks draped in ice, 318 glaciers, and unspoiled wilderness hidden from everyone but the most intrepid of hikers. Part of the Cascade Range, the peaks are not especially tall—the highest hover around 9,000 feet—but their vertical rise takes them from almost sea level into the clouds, making them steep-walled, enchanting to view, and, in many places, inaccessible.

This national park is not one you can zip into with your minivan and experience from a comfy lodge. Although the North Cascades Highway bisects the wilderness area and provides dramatic views, the inner sanctum contains no network of roads, no lodges or visitor centers. The park will not reveal its treasures easily; you have to discover them on foot. Fortunately, the adventurous have been given 386 miles of maintained trails in the territory to explore—and the rest can take solace in a stunning scenic drive.

Access to the park, about a three-hour drive from Seattle, is via the North Cascades Scenic Highway (Hwy 20). Food, lodging, and gas are minimal within the park. The main highway provides access to dozens of trails, including the **PACIFIC CREST NATIONAL SCENIC TRAIL**. Backpackers also hike into the park from Stehekin, located at the north end of Lake Chelan (see Stehekin). Hiking usually starts in June; snow commonly melts off from all but the highest trails by July. But summer storms are frequent; be prepared with rain gear. Expect four-legged company in the backcountry: black bears, elk, mountain goats, mountain lions, and a few grizzlies.

Backcountry camping requires a free permit, available at the **NORTH CASCADES NATIONAL PARK HEADQUARTERS** (2105 Hwy 20, Sedro-Woolley; 360/856-5700; www.nps.gov/noca/) or the **WILDERNESS INFORMATION CENTER** (7280 Ranger Station Rd, Marblemount; 360/873-4500). Both offices have park information.

Remember: Winter snow closes the park highway from approximately mid-November to mid-April, depending on the weather.

Diablo and Ross Lake

Since the only road access to Ross Lake is south from Hope, BC, the best way to get to the lake and its main attractions—campgrounds and the cabins built on log floats at **ROSS LAKE RESORT** (Rockport; 206/386-4437)—is on the **SEATTLE CITY LIGHT FERRY** (500 Newhalem St, Rockport; 206/386-4393) from Diablo. Here Seattle City Light built an outpost for crews constructing and servicing the dams on the Skagit River. The ferry leaves twice daily (8:30am and 3pm), running from mid-June through the end of October. Cost is $5 one-way; no reservations needed. Tours of the dams have been cancelled indefinitely due to the events of September 11, 2001; call Seattle City Light (206/684-3030) to find out when tours will run again.

The Methow Valley

Just east of the Cascades, Highway 20 descends into the Methow (say "MET-how") Valley. An ideal destination for recreators and a favorite with Puget Sounders, the Methow recalls the Old West, from the faux-Western storefronts of Winthrop to the valley's working ranches and farms, to the Big Sky-and-sagebrush landscape.

Mazama

There's little to do in tiny Mazama (say "ma-ZAH-ma") except fly-fish—or cross-country ski, depending on the season. If it's civilization you're after, head for the **MAZAMA STORE** (50 Lost River Rd; 509/996-2855). It has a sociable soup-and-espresso counter, products that range from Tim's Potato Chips to fine wines to Patagonia shirts, a picnic area (complete with grillmeister in summer), and the last gas pumps for more than 70 miles if you're traveling west across the mountains. In

CROSS-COUNTRY SKIING THE METHOW

Bright winter sunshine, dry powder snow, jaw-dropping views of mountain peaks—add almost 200 kilometers of well-groomed trails, and you have one of the nation's premier cross-country ski destinations. The **METHOW VALLEY SPORT TRAILS ASSOCIA-TION (MVSTA)** maintains this vast network of trails, the second largest in the United States. The system consists of four linked sections, many of which go directly past the valley's popular accommodations, so you can literally ski from your door. (In summer, the trails are used by mountain bikers.) Ski season usually begins in early December and continues through March. For updates on snow and trail conditions, contact the MVSTA (509/996-3287 or 800/682-5787; www.mvsta.com).

The largest section surrounds **SUN MOUNTAIN LODGE** in Winthrop, where 70 kilometers of trail cut through rolling hills. Below it, the **COMMUNITY TRAIL** snakes past farms and bottomland as it meanders from Winthrop to Mazama. Mazama's flat terrain and open meadows are ideal for novices.

The remaining section, called **RENDEZVOUS,** is recommended for intermediate / expert skiers only. Set above the valley at 3,500 to 4,000 feet, the trail passes through rugged forestland, where five huts are located at strategic points for overnight stays. Each hut bunks up to eight people and has a woodstove and a propane cookstove. Huts rent for $25 per person per night (or $150 for an entire hut). **CENTRAL RESERVATIONS** (800/422-3048; www.mvcentralres.com) has maps and information and makes reservations (required) for the **HUT-TO-HUT SYSTEM.** (For $70, Rendezvous Outfitters will lighten your load by hauling your group's gear and food to the huts.) Special trails are also set aside for **SNOWSHOERS.** Skiing on MVSTA trails requires trail passes, available at ski shops in the valley: $13 daily; $10 half-day; $30 three-day pass.

—*Nick Gallo*

summer, the town is home to the **METHOW MUSIC FESTIVAL** (800/340-1458), a classical-music series held in local barns and meadows.

If you've got the rig for it (four-wheel drive is best; trailers are allowed), jump off from Mazama on the Methow Valley Road (County Road 9140) for a 19-mile, knee-buckling sojourn up a steep, rough, one-lane road, complete with hairpin curves, no guardrails, and 1,000-foot drop-offs. Your reward: **HARTS PASS** and **SLATE PEAK,** the state's highest drivable point at 7,440 feet. Open only in summer, Harts Pass delivers spectacular views of the Cascades, hiking trails, campgrounds, and fragrant meadows of wildflowers.

RESTAURANTS

Freestone Inn / ★★★

17798 HWY 20, MAZAMA; 509/996-3906 OR 800/639-3809 A floor-to-ceiling river-rock fireplace stands in the center of the Freestone Inn (see Lodgings), and separates the lobby on one side from the dining room on the other. In this intimate room, diners sit at white-clothed, candlelit tables for dinners of Northwest specialties. The simple, elegant menu features ingredients grown by local purveyors and a wine selection heavy on Washington vintners. Start with gnocchi, chanterelles, crisped sage, and Gruyère—a wonderful combination of flavors and textures. The roasted beet, spinach, and candied pecan salad is also a standout. Chef Todd Brown's hearty entrees range from a noble panfried trout, to pepper-encrusted Angus steak, to divinely tender lamb chops on a bed of tomato and eggplant roulade. Finish with burnt lemon tart with whipped cream and strawberries, chocolate mousse with Grand Marnier, or a glass of muscat. *$$$; AE, DC, DIS, MC, V; local checks only; breakfast every day, dinner Tues–Sun; beer and wine; reservations recommended; info@freestoneinn.com; www.freestoneinn.com; 1½ miles west of Mazama.* &

LODGINGS

Freestone Inn and Early Winters Cabins / ★★★

17798 HWY 20, MAZAMA; 509/996-3906 OR 800/639-3809 Drive up to the 21-room log lodge that is the Freestone Inn, and you'll feel you've reached *Bonanza*'s Ponderosa. The inn sets an elegant, rustic tone for the 1,200-acre Wilson Ranch. The two-story lodge blends into the landscape, and gentle touches lend environmental appeal. A massive river-rock fireplace is the lobby centerpiece, and there's a little library nook nearby, stocked with Northwest books. The earth-toned rooms are subdued and classy, trimmed in pine with big stone fireplaces, large bathrooms, wrought-iron fixtures, and old photographs of Wilson Ranch. The ground-floor rooms are our favorites, opening onto the lakefront lawn or snowy banks. An outdoor hot tub is just between Freestone Lake—a pond enlarged into a lake and stocked with trout—and the lodge. Although views from the inn are more territorial than grand, activities here are as vast as the Methow Valley itself; Jack's Hut serves as a base camp for virtually anything you can dream of doing—from skiing to white-water rafting, fly-fishing to mountain biking. Additional lodging options include a luxurious Lakeside Lodge (complete with a kitchen and lots of room for families or friends) and 15 smaller Early Winters Cabins. Continental breakfast is complimentary for guests at the inn (but not in the cabins). *$$$; AE, DC, DIS, MC, V; local checks only; 1½ miles west of Mazama.* &

Mazama Country Inn / ★★

42 LOST RIVER RD, MAZAMA; 509/996-2681 OR 800/843-7951 (IN WA) With a view of the North Cascades from nearly every window, this spacious 6,000-square-foot lodge makes a splendid year-round destination (especially for horseback riders and cross-country skiers), with 14 good-sized rooms of wooden construction with cedar beams. Some of the guest rooms (all fairly standard) have air-conditioning, nice on hot summer Eastern Washington nights. Each room has a private bath, quilts on the beds, and futonlike pads that can be rolled out for extra guests. Four rooms behind the sauna have individual decks, two with views of Goat Peak and two looking out into the woods. In summer, breakfast, lunch, and dinner are offered in the lodge restaurant (best are meat selections such as beef tenderloin or spicy ribs); winter brings family-style breakfasts and dinners. Six cabins with kitchen and bath are available for families or groups of up to 10. No children under 13 in winter; no smoking; no pets. *$$; MC, V; checks OK; mazama@methow.com; www.mazamainn.com; 14 miles west of Winthrop.*

Mazama Ranch House / ★

42 LOST RIVER RD, MAZAMA; 509/996-2040 Owners Steve and Kristin Devin run this ranch house (which sleeps up to 13 guests) and the eight-room motel-style addition. The main house contains five beds and a full kitchen and is perfect for family retreats. The rooms in the addition open to a sunny deck that fronts the valley's trail system (so does the hot tub). An additional cabin, the rustic Longhorn, has its own kitchen, sleeping loft, and woodstove. There's no restaurant and no common lobby, but when you've got hundreds of miles of skiing, mountain-biking, and horseback-riding trails one step from your room, who needs anything but a firm bed and kitchenette? The rural ranch atmosphere is the real deal: the barn, corral, and arena are available for free to any overnighter who arrives with a horse—and in summer, many do. For the horseless, two excellent outfitters are located within a few miles: Rocking Horse Ranch (509/996-2768) and Early Winters Outfitting and Saddle Company (509/996-2659). *$$; MC, V; checks OK; just south of Mazama Country Inn, same entrance.* &

Winthrop

Most of the tourist activity in the Methow Valley is found in this Western-motif town where old-fashioned storefronts and boardwalks will have you looking for Gary Cooper. Stop in the **SHAFER MUSEUM** (285 Castle; 509/996-2712), housed in pioneer Guy Waring's 1897 log cabin on the hill behind the main street. Exhibits tell of the area's early history and include old cars, a stagecoach, and horse-drawn vehicles.

The valley offers fine white-water rafting, spectacular hiking in the North Cascades, horseback riding, mountain biking, fishing, and cross-country or helicopter skiing. After you've had a big day outside, quaff a beer at the **WINTHROP BREWING COMPANY** (155 Riverside Ave; 509/996-3183), in an old schoolhouse on the main street. **WINTHROP MOUNTAIN SPORTS** (257 Riverside Ave; 509/996-2886) sells outdoor-activity equipment and supplies, and rents bikes, skis, snowshoes, and ice skates. The **TENDERFOOT GENERAL STORE** (corner of Riverside Ave and Hwy 20; 509/996-2288) has anything else you might have forgotten. **PEARRYGIN LAKE STATE PARK** (509/996-2370), 5 miles north of town, offers good swimming and campsites.

METHOW VALLEY CENTRAL RESERVATIONS (303 Riverside Ave; 800/422-3048; www.mvcentralres.com) books lodging for the entire valley and sells tickets for major events, such as mid-July's **RHYTHM AND BLUES FESTIVAL.** For more info, contact the **METHOW VALLEY INFORMATION CENTER** (241 Riverside Ave; 888/463-8469; www.methow.com.)

RESTAURANTS

Duck Brand Restaurant and Hotel / ★

246 RIVERSIDE AVE, WINTHROP; 509/996-2192 OR 800-996-2192 "Meet you at the Duck" is a common refrain heard in these parts. For more than a decade, this funky, eclectic restaurant built to replicate a frontier-style hotel has been a popular gathering spot and provisioner of good, filling meals at modest prices. The menu includes everything from burritos to fettuccine to teriyaki chicken. American-style breakfasts feature wonderful cheesy Spanish potatoes and billowing omelets. The in-house bakery produces delicious baked goods, including biscotti, cinnamon rolls, and fruit pies. Beware: Lines form in summer. Upstairs, the Duck Brand Hotel has six sparsely furnished rooms, priced right. *$$; AE, DC, DIS, MC, V; local checks only; breakfast, lunch, dinner every day; full bar; reservations not accepted; duck brand@methow.com; www.methownet.com/duck; on main street in Winthrop.*

Sun Mountain Lodge / ★★

PATTERSON LAKE RD, WINTHROP; 509/996-2211 OR 800/572-0493 All tables have beautiful views of the Methow Valley, giving diners the impression they are eating in a fantastical tree fort. Executive chef James Best offers just what visitors to the lodge want: beautiful (to the point of being fussy) presentation of dishes, made from high-quality ingredients. The crab cakes come artfully arranged, two pillowy rich, perfectly cooked dreams with a rather modern orbit of capers amid swirls of infused olive oil. Many delights accompany the beef tenderloin—mashed Yukon Golds and a morel demi-glace, seared squash, and two elaborate horns of crispy turnip. The wild salmon cooked with lavender and citrus butter can feature asparagus, a risotto cake, and grilled tomatoes. The obsequious staff give good advice about the extensive wine list (focusing on many Northwest varietals) and provide seamless service. Overall the food is delicious, but prices are high for what you get, and a few items appear on the menu simply because they are expected—a rather bland sturgeon dish, for example. Still, the view, several nice touches like sorbet palate cleansers and chocolate truffles that accompany the bill make Sun Mountain Lodge very likeable. Lunch and breakfast are more simple, as is the menu in the adjoining Eagle's Nest Lounge. *$$$; AE, DC, MC, V; local checks only; breakfast, lunch, dinner every day; full bar; reservations recommended; smtnsale@methow.com; www.sun mountainlodge.com; 9.6 miles southwest of Winthrop.* &

LODGINGS

Sun Mountain Lodge / ★★★

PATTERSON LAKE RD, WINTHROP; 509/996-2211 OR 800/572-0493 The location of Sun Mountain Lodge is dramatic, high on a hill above the pristine Methow Valley and facing the North Cascades. Everything's big at the massive timber-and-stone lodge, from the hewn beams and stone fireplaces to the expansive views—and every space has a view. Guest rooms offer casual ranch-style comfort, with log furniture, wrought-iron sconces, glass coffee tables, and thick, soft

299

blankets. The newer, luxe Mount Robinson rooms are stunning, with towering views even from the whirlpool bath; more reasonably priced Gardner rooms aren't quite as large but still have fireplaces and private decks or patios; the older main lodge rooms offer many of the same amenities (robes, coffeemakers, fine toiletries). In addition, 13 appealing cabins—particularly good for families—are available just down the hill at Patterson Lake. (Children's play areas and child care/activity programs are available.) Much of the Sun Mountain experience stems from the outdoors, and a helpful activities/rental desk is waiting to get you out there. In summer, try tennis, horseback riding, swimming (two heated, seasonal pools), fly-fishing or rafting trips, golf (nearby), mountain biking, and more. In winter, resort trails are part of the valley's 175-kilometer cross-country trail system. Or you can arrange ice skating, snowshoeing, or a sleigh ride. Soak in one of two outdoor hot tubs, or splurge on a facial and massage. The restaurant in the lodge offers unbeatable views, with a menu that emphasizes regional cuisine (see Restaurants review). Reserve early for summer or winter ski-season dates. *$$$–$$$$; AE, DC, MC, V; checks OK; 2-night min on weekends; smtnsale@methow.com; www.sunmountainlodge.com; 9.6 miles southwest of Winthrop.* &

Wolfridge Resort / ★★

412-B WOLF CREEK RD, WINTHROP; 509/996-2828 OR 800/237-2388
Serenity reigns at this resort, which sits—literally and metaphorically—somewhere between the home-style Mazama Country Inn and the more showy Sun Mountain Lodge. Five log buildings contain 17 units divided into two-bedroom town houses, one-bedroom suites, hotel-style rooms, and a cabin. The lodgings are tastefully, if simply, furnished with handcrafted log furniture. But it's the 60-acre riverside setting that impresses. Lovely ponderosas blow in the wind, mountain peaks dance behind a curtain of green forest, a glorious meadow lets in the sun. For sybarites, there's an outdoor pool and a Jacuzzi in a river-rock setting. Cross-country skiers and mountain bikers, jump on the trail system that runs right outside your door. *$$–$$$; AE, MC, V; checks OK; www.wolfridgeresort.com; south of Winthrop head up Twin Lakes Rd for 1½ miles, turn right on Wolf Creek Rd, and travel 4 miles to entrance on right.*

Twisp

Eight miles away from Winthrop, ordinary-looking Twisp (the name is said to come from a Native American word for the noise made by a yellow jacket) doesn't possess any of its sister city's gussied-up Western ornamentation, but it's worth a stop. On Saturday mornings, the thriving **METHOW VALLEY FARMERS MARKET** operates next to the community center April 15 through October 15. Poke around Glover Street and you'll find local arts and crafts at the **CONFLUENCE GALLERY** (104 Glover St; 509/997-ARTS), theater performances during summer at the **MERC PLAYHOUSE** (101 Glover St; 509/997-PLAY), and wonderful pastries and fresh bread—served hot 9–11am—at **CINNAMON TWISP** (116 Glover St; 509/997-5030). For more info, contact the **TWISP VISITOR INFORMATION CENTER** (509/997-2926).

RESTAURANTS
Fiddlehead Bistro / ★★

201 GLOVER ST, TWISP; 509/997-0343 Alice Waters would approve of Fiddlehead. The warm bistro features locally produced, organic vegetables and fruit in a perfectly balanced seasonal menu, in addition to great bread from Anjou, an award-winning bakery located outside of nearby Cashmere. Dishes range from a braised lamb shank with apricot-balsamic glaze to grilled swordfish niçoise to the rich Penne TeTe—featuring Gorgonzola, pear, and topped with caramelized rosemary walnuts. The owner is on-site and welcomes all diners, and his staff is personable and knowledgeable. The wine list is relatively short but offers exquisite choices, great prices, and generously sized vessels (a glass of wine here is equivalent to two elsewhere). Desserts are rich—don't pass up the chocolate ecstasy cake. *$; MC, V; checks OK; breakfast Sun, lunch Sun–Tues and Thurs–Fri, dinner Thurs–Sun; beer and wine; reservations not necessary; downtown.* &

Pateros

LODGINGS
Amy's Manor Inn / ★★

435 HWY 153, PATEROS; 509/923-2334 Built in 1928, this enchanting manor is dramatically situated at the foot of the Cascades overlooking the Methow River. The setting is miragelike after you've traveled through the region's arid sagebrush: an impressive stand of maples, oaks, and large pines greets you. Stone fences line the property; 6 acres of flower gardens produce bursts of color. Three guest rooms, country French in character, have a quiet elegance. But the hidden treasures here are the culinary creations of owner Pamela Koehler, who has extensive training as a chef. Combine the seasonal harvest from her organic garden with her skills in the kitchen, and the table's bounty, be it breakfast or dinner, never disappoints. This is your best bet for miles. *$$; MC, V; checks OK; 5 miles north of Pateros.*

Lake Chelan

South of the Methow Valley, Lake Chelan sits with half a mind in the mountains and the other half in vacation playland. On one end, the 55-mile-long, fjordlike lake isolates itself in the Cascades—the remote community of Stehekin sits at this northern tip—and at the other, the lake turns sociable in the town of Chelan, happily splashing along as one of the state's most popular summer swimming, boating, and fishing destinations. The lake is never more than 2 miles wide (it's also one of the deepest in the nation), so you have a sense of slicing right into the Cascades.

Chelan

This resort area is blessed with the springtime perfume of apple blossoms, beautiful Lake Chelan thrusting into tall mountains, 300 days of sunshine a year, and good skiing, hunting, fishing, hiking, and sailing. It has been trying to live up to its touristic potential since C. C. Campbell built his hotel here in 1901, with mixed success. Now

MOUNTAIN LOOP HIGHWAY

The Mountain Loop Highway is one of Washington's less-recognized gems, overshadowed by the spectacular North Cascades Scenic Highway to the northeast. Located east of Everett, the Mountain Loop Highway is a 78-mile scenic drive that follows three swift rivers as it swings through the foothills of the western Cascades. The prime section is a 50-mile stretch past the town of Granite Falls that makes for an ideal weekend drive (especially in fall, when the colors are out). The highway also offers access to more than 300 miles of hiking trails, ranging from baby-stroller romps to rugged climbs into remote mountains. Note: Snow closes upper elevations of the highway during winter.

The highway consists of three roads: Highway 92, Forest Road 20, and Highway 530. It starts in **GRANITE FALLS,** 14 miles east of Everett (exit 194 off I-5), which isn't much to look at, but is the best spot to grab lunch or last-minute supplies. Choose from pizza places, diner fare, or ethnic-food restaurants.

Eastbound from Granite Falls, the highway retraces an old railway bed, passing through the town of Verlot; the **VERLOT RANGER STATION** (33515 Mountain Loop Hwy, Granite Falls; 360/691-7791) has information on hikes and sights. During the late 1880s, prospectors discovered gold, silver, and other metals in nearby mountains. Eastern investors built a railroad to haul ore to a smelter in Everett. But after a brief flurry of activity, the endeavor was undone by high costs, constant floods, and an economic depression. The mines closed in 1907.

that time-share condos and B&Bs have sprouted throughout the area, the amenities have greatly improved.

The top attraction is the cruise up Lake Chelan to Stehekin (see below) on **LADY OF THE LAKE II,** an old-fashioned tour boat, or one of its faster, more modern siblings. In summer, three boats are in operation. The *Lady II,* the largest of the vessels, holds 350 and provides a leisurely four-hour trip uplake, with a 90-minute layover in Stehekin. It departs Chelan daily at 8:30am and returns around 6pm ($22 per person round-trip; kids 6–11 years old travel half price). The faster, smaller *Lady Express* shortens the trip to just over two hours one-way, with a one-hour stop in Stehekin before heading back (round-trip tickets $41). The *Lady Cat,* a catamaran that whips across the lake at 50mph, makes the trip in 75 minutes; cost is $79 round-trip. Many travelers opt for the "combination trip," traveling uplake on the *Lady Express* and returning on the *Lady II,* which allows for a three-hour, 15-minute layover in Stehekin and a return by 6pm. Reservations are not needed for the *Lady II,* but the two faster boats almost always book up; advance purchase is necessary. During off-season—November 1 through May 1—the boat schedule cuts back drastically. For full details, contact the **LAKE CHELAN BOAT COMPANY** (1418 W Woodin Ave; 509/682-2224 or 509/ 682-4584; www.ladyofthelake.com).

Outside Granite Falls, the highway turns into a gravel road that plunges into thick forest as it follows the "Stilly"—the darting, fast-flowing South Fork of the Stillaguamish River. Campgrounds appear at regular intervals, offering convenient places to picnic. The following hikes make nice outings: **OLD ROBE TRAIL** (mile 9 from Granite Falls; easy; 3 miles round-trip) leads to two former railroad tunnels; **MOUNT PILCHUCK LOOKOUT** (mile 11; difficult; 6 miles round-trip) climbs 2,100 feet and scrambles over boulders to reach a 5,300-foot lookout tower; **BIG FOUR ICE CAVES** (mile 25; easy; 2 miles round-trip), popular with families, leads to year-round ice caves (don't go inside the caves; ice crashing down from the ceiling makes it dangerous); and **MONTE CRISTO** (mile 31; easy; 8.6 miles round-trip) goes to a former gold-mining town, but there's little there except for a few shacks.

At **BARLOW PASS,** the highway pavement ends and a 14-mile stretch of winding gravel on Forest Road 20 drops down from the mountains before it emerges in farmland near the timber town of **DARRINGTON. The COUNTRY COFFEE & DELI** (1180 Cascade St, Darrington; 360/436-0213) will replenish you with sandwiches, ice cream, and espresso. At Darrington, the Mountain Loop Highway swings west on Highway 530 and loops back to Arlington near Interstate 5; you can also go north 19 miles on Forest Road 20 to connect to the North Cascades Scenic Highway in Rockport.

—Nick Gallo

Alternatively, **CHELAN AIRWAYS** (1328 W Woodin Ave; 509/682-5065 or 509/682-5555) offers daily seaplane service to Stehekin ($120 round-trip), as well as scenic tours of the mountains. **CHELAN BUTTE LOOKOUT,** 9 miles west of Chelan, also provides a view of the lake, the Columbia River, and the orchard-blanketed countryside.

The best reason for going to Chelan is Lake Chelan itself, where some of the best accommodations are **SHORESIDE CONDOS.** Chelan Quality Vacation Properties (888/977-1748; www.lakechelanvacationrentals.com), a rental clearinghouse, has listings for condos and private vacation homes in the area. Each condo or house is privately owned so furnishings and taste vary greatly. **CONDOS AT WAPATO POINT** (1 Wapato Point Wy, Manson; 509/687-9511 or 888/768-9511; www.wapatopoint.com), a full-fledged resort in neighboring Manson, are rented directly through its office.

Chelan's hot summer weather and the lake's clear, cool water beg you to get waterborne. Waterskiing, windsurfing, pleasure boating (personal watercraft, kayak, motorboat), and swimming—stick close to the lake's lower end for the warmest water—are popular activities. Rent boats and water-ski gear at **CHELAN BOAT RENTALS** (1210 W Woodin Ave; 509/682-4444). Popular public boat docks in the area are Don Morse Park (the city park), Riverwalk Park, Lake Chelan State Park, 25 Mile Creek State Park, and Old Mill Park. **SLIDEWATERS** (102 Waterslide Dr; 509/682-5751), one of the Northwest's largest waterslide parks, keeps the kids happy.

Fishing for steelhead, rainbow, cutthroat, and chinook is very good in Lake Chelan, with special emphasis on the chinook fishery. Stocked in the lake since the mid-'70s, chinook are the lake's prized catch. **GRAYBILL'S GUIDE SERVICE** (509/682-4292) is a reputable outfit; check with the **LAKE CHELAN CHAMBER OF COMMERCE** (800/4-CHELAN) for more guides.

RESTAURANTS

Campbell House Cafe / ★★

104 W WOODIN AVE, CHELAN; 509/682-4250 The decor is somewhat dowdy and the menu sticks to safe, predictable choices, but this is where you'll find Chelan's freshest seafood, dependable steaks, and acceptable pastas. A solid wine list is a plus. Breakfast is popular, with apple pancakes, biscuits and gravy, and other standards leading the way. Upstairs, you can find casual fare—burgers, fish-and-chips, salads—at the Second Floor Pub & Veranda. The outdoor deck is a choice spot to catch a bite on a warm evening. *$$$; AE, MC, V; checks OK; breakfast (Cafe), lunch, dinner every day; full bar; reservations recommended (Cafe), reservations not accepted (Pub); downtown, facing main street near lake.* &

Deepwater Brewing & Public House / ★

225 HWY 150, CHELAN; 509/682-2720 Brewmaster Scott Dietrich's likable brewpub features a strong lineup of microbrews and tasty pub food to match its gregarious mood. The ribs are crowd favorites, pasta servings are generous, and the familiar appetizer fare (nachos, fried mozzarella, calamari) is good enough. Grab a seat at the outdoor terrace on a warm evening and enjoy sunset dining under a big sky. Live music on summer weekends. *$$; AE, MC, V; checks OK; lunch, dinner every day; full bar; reservations recommended; deepwaterbrewing@msn.com; www.deepwaterbrewing.com; 2 miles outside Chelan on N Manson Hwy.* &

LODGINGS

Best Western Lakeside Lodge / ★

2312 W WOODIN AVE, CHELAN; 509/682-4396 OR 800/468-2781 This 65-unit complex, sharp-looking in a green sage and cedar trim exterior, offers spacious rooms (vaulted ceilings on the top floor), a cheerful indoor pool, and complimentary breakfast in an airy, gazebo-shaped conference room with full-length windows facing the lake. The biggest reason to stay might be the backyard; nicely landscaped grounds slope down to a small, adjoining park fronting the water, where uplake views of the North Cascades's snowy peaks are delightful. *$$$; AE, DC, DIS, MC, V; checks OK; info@lakesidelodge.net; www.4-westview.com; 2 miles south of Chelan on Hwy 97A.* &

Campbell's Resort on Lake Chelan / ★★

104 W WOODIN AVE, CHELAN; 509/682-2561 OR 800/553-8225 Chelan's landmark resort continues to be the most popular place for visitors. Its major draw is prime lakeside property—and a sandy 1,200-foot beach. The resort's 170 rooms, many with kitchenettes, are spread out in five buildings of varying vintage. The majority are more comfortable than plush, with the most attractive in one

of the new or recently remodeled buildings—Lodge 1 or 4. Amenities include two heated outdoor pools, two outdoor hot tubs, and boat moorage. With a conference center that holds 300 people, Campbell's is undeniably a large-scale operation, but it still has an amiable, personable quality, thanks to the fact that the same family who built the resort still owns and operates it four generations later. Reservations are scarce in high season. *$$$; AE, MC, V; checks OK; res@campbellsresort.com; www.campbellsresort.com; on lake at end of main street near downtown.*

Kelly's Resort / ★★

12801 S LAKESHORE RD, CHELAN; 509/687-3220 OR 800/561-8978 Kelly-owned for half a century, this longtime getaway qualifies as a "find" for urban escapees. It's a peaceful retreat, though it's also like summer camp for families who return year after year to claim the same cabin. You can walk on woodland trails or take a boat out on the water, but most people seem happy to sunbathe on the sunny deck. The 11 cabins set back in the woods are a bit dark, shaded by the forest, but they're fully equipped with kitchens, fireplaces, and TVs. A great feature is an outdoor heated pool in the woods. Kelly's also offers modern condo units on the lake (from the lower units, you can walk right off the deck into the water), a three-bedroom house for rent, a convenience store, and a Ping-Pong table. The only off note: The budget prices have gone up. *$$–$$$; AE, MC, V; checks OK; www.kelly resort.com; 14 miles uplake on south shore.*

Stehekin

A passage to Stehekin, the little community at the head of Lake Chelan, is like traveling back in time. This jumping-off point for exploring rugged and remote North Cascades National Park is reached only by a four-hour boat trip from Chelan on *Lady of the Lake II* or one of its faster counterparts (see Chelan, above), by **CHELAN AIRWAYS** floatplane (see Chelan), by hiking, or by private boat. For a shorter boat ride, catch one of the boats uplake at Field's Point. At Stehekin, you can take a bus tour, eat lunch, enjoy close-up views of the North Cascades's rugged peaks, and be back onboard the boat in time for the return voyage. The **STEHEKIN PASTRY COMPANY** (summer only), a pleasant stroll from the boat landing, fills the mountain air with fresh-from-the-oven, sugary smells of cinnamon rolls.

Exploration is the prime reason for coming here. Good day hikes include a lovely one along the lakeshore and another along a stream through the **BUCKNER ORCHARD**; numerous splendid backcountry trails attract serious backpackers. In winter, fine touring opportunities for cross-country skiers or snowshoe enthusiasts abound, though the town pretty much shuts down for the season. The **RANGER STATION** at Chelan (428 W Woodin Ave, Chelan; 509/682-2576), open year-round, is an excellent information source. A National Park Service shuttle bus (509/682-2549) provides transportation from Stehekin to trailheads, campgrounds, fishing holes, and scenic areas mid-May through mid-October.

Part of the national park complex near the Stehekin landing, **NORTH CASCADES STEHEKIN LODGE** (at head of Lake Chelan; 509/682-4494; www.stehekin.com) is a year-round lodge featuring 28 rooms, a full-service restaurant, a general store, and a rental shop for bikes, boats, skis, and snowshoes.

The Courtney family will pick you up at Stehekin in an old bus and take you to their **STEHEKIN VALLEY RANCH** (800/536-0745; www.courtneycountry.com) at the farthest end of the valley, where you can enjoy river rafting and hiking or opt for seclusion. Open in summer, the ranch rents 12 units, 7 of which are rustic tent-cabins offering the basics (screened windows, a kerosene lamp, showers in the main building). The price is decent ($75–$85 per night per person), considering it includes three hearty, family-style meals and valley transportation. **CASCADE CORRALS** (509/682-7742), also run by the family, arranges horseback rides and mountain pack trips.

LODGINGS

Silver Bay Inn / ★★

10 SILVER BAY RD, STEHEKIN; 509/682-2212 OR 800/555-7781 (WA AND OR ONLY) The Silver Bay Inn, at the nexus of the Stehekin River and Lake Chelan, is a gracious, memorable retreat. Friendly Kathy and Randall Dinwiddie welcome guests to this passive-solar home and spectacular setting: 700 feet of waterfront with a broad green lawn rolling down to the lake. Formerly a B&B, the inn has changed its configuration slightly. The main house now rents out as a single unit. The two-bedroom, two-bath house, decorated with antiques, has a 30-foot-long sunroom, two view decks, a soaking tub, and a faraway view. The house includes an apartment-sized unit with a private entrance, rented separately. Two lakeside cabins are remarkably convenient (dishwasher, microwave, all linens) and sleep four and six. Bicycles, canoes, croquet, and hammocks are available. The hot tub has a 360-degree view of the lake and surrounding mountains. During summer, units have a two- to five-night minimum stay and kids under 9 are not allowed (though they're welcome other months). $$–$$$; MC, V; checks OK; stehekin@silverbayinn.com; www. silverbayinn.com; 1½ miles up Stehekin Valley Rd from landing.

CENTRAL CASCADES

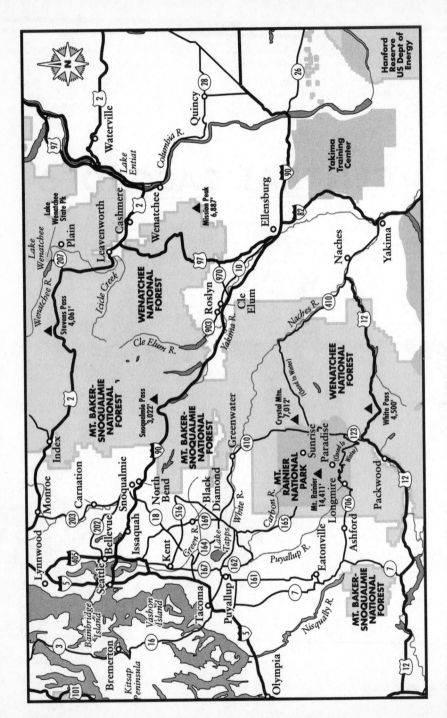

CENTRAL CASCADES

The soaring, snowcapped mountains of the Central Cascades contain not only the main arteries between Western and Eastern Washington—Interstate 90 and US Highways 2 and 12—but also the state's best recreation destinations. In summer, these thoroughfares are jammed with those seeking fir- and pine-perfumed air, pristine lakes, mountain trails, rock walls to climb, and campsites in forested glades. In winter, the routes can be choked with snow, and skiers and snowboarders flock to the summits of Snoqualmie, Stevens, and White Passes to schuss the slopes.

The mountains around the Bavarian-style village of Leavenworth, and north to the tiny village of Plain, contain countless all-season mountain getaways. Leavenworth's many festivals draw visitors year-round. The Central Cascades are also home to quite probably the world's most beautiful mountain—Mount Rainier. In summer, many Northwesterners make a tradition of picnicking amid wildflower meadows, an experience that on a sunny day feels like a fat slice of heaven. No wonder it's called Paradise. The mountain is an easy day trip—or overnight in one of the B&Bs or lodges nearby.

ACCESS AND INFORMATION

One of the Northwest's most beautiful drives, the 400-mile **CASCADE LOOP** follows US Highway 2 from Everett, takes in Leavenworth and Wenatchee, and heads north (see North Cascades chapter) to Lake Chelan, Winthrop, and the North Cascades Scenic Highway. The route can be accessed from Interstate 90 at Cle Elum by taking Highway 970 to US Highway 97 north. It joins US Highway 2 just east of Leavenworth. A brochure is available from the **CASCADE LOOP ASSOCIATION** (PO Box 3245, Wenatchee, WA 98807; 509/662-3888; www.cascadeloop.com).

INTERSTATE 90 is an elegant multilane freeway, designated a National Scenic Byway in 1998, which roughly traces the South Fork of the Snoqualmie River east into the Cascade foothills, cutting through the verdant Snoqualmie Valley and fir-thick hillsides like a wide boulevard. A map of outings and activities along the route and a heritage tour map are available from the **MOUNTAINS TO SOUND GREENWAY TRUST** (1011 Western Ave, Ste 606, Seattle; 206/382-5565; MTSGreenway@tpl.org; www.mtsgreenway.org).

US Highway 2 and Stevens Pass

Highway 2 heads east-west across the state, from Interstate 5 at Everett to Spokane, winding up to Stevens Pass along the Skykomish River. **STEVENS PASS** itself (exit 194 off Hwy 2; 206/812-4510; www.stevenspass.com) is a favorite destination of Seattle area skiers, offering downhill and cross-country (the **NORDIC CENTER** is located 5 miles east of the summit). Day lodges at the summit house half a dozen casual eateries. From the pass, Highway 2 drops down to the Wenatchee River. Along the way, the towns of Leavenworth, Cashmere, and Wenatchee give travelers reason to stop.

Index

Challenging cliffs loom just behind this tiny town, where rock climbers go to climb the **TOWN WALL**. The modest **BUSH HOUSE COUNTRY INN** (300 5th St; 360/793-2312), first established during the mining boom of 1898, now has 11 pretty (and simple) sleeping rooms; the on-site restaurant features steaks and fancier choices, such as Cajun jambalaya, and there's a pub garden out back.

Lake Wenatchee

Lake Wenatchee, about 5 miles north of Highway 2 on Highway 207 at Coles Corner (and the same distance northwest of Plain), has a state park at one end, with a large, sandy public swimming beach and campsites (overnight fee; 888/226-7688; www.parks.wa.gov) in the woods closer to the Wenatchee River and lake. There are also lakeside campsites at the Forest Service's **GLACIER VIEW CAMPGROUND**, 5 miles west on Cedar Brae Road. Here you'll also find the trailhead to **HIDDEN LAKE** (a ½-mile family hike to a small alpine lake). Ask at the **RANGER STATION** (22976 Hwy 207, Leavenworth; 509/763-3103) on the north side of the lake about other day hikes in the area. Play golf or tennis at **KAHLER GLEN GOLF AND SKI RESORT** (20890 Kahler Dr, Leavenworth; 509/763-2121 or 800/440-2994; www.kahlerglen.com).

Plain

LODGINGS

Mountain Springs Lodge / ★★

19115 CHIWAWA LOOP RD, PLAIN; 509/763-2713 OR 800/858-2276 This mountain retreat with lots of open space lets in the sun—in any season. Check in at Beaver Creek Lodge, which houses two spacious Ralph Lauren–style suites upstairs, and a restaurant (meals available by reservation) and a full-time espresso bar. Two 20-person-plus lodges and two smaller A-frame chalets face a sprawling lawn, good for volleyball, croquet, or cartwheels. Follow the brook to the barn, where events as special as weddings or as down-home as a family reunion chuck-wagon barbecue take place. This is a good place for anyone anytime but is best when you've got an energetic group and rent one of the lodges. Hot tubs and massive rock fireplaces become magnets after a day of snowmobiling (available here), in the saddle (horses for rent nearby), or on sleigh rides (on-site in winter). *$$$; AE, DIS, MC, V; checks OK; info@mtsprings.com; www.mtsprings.com; 14 miles northwest of Leavenworth, then 1 mile north of Plain.*

Natapoc Lodging / ★★★

12348 BRETZ RD, LEAVENWORTH; 509/763-3313 OR 888/NATAPOC For any city dweller who's dreamed of a weekend home on the Wenatchee River, Natapoc is the next best thing. Each log house—from small romantic ones to a rambling abode that sleeps 20—claims 1 to 5 piney acres and at least 200 feet of riverfront. The bigger homes are good for groups (extra bedding, two living areas, and large out-of-the-way hot tubs). All are stocked with everything from VCRs to microwaves. Activities include fly-fishing and cross-country skiing, but

CENTRAL CASCADES THREE-DAY TOUR

DAY ONE: Head east on Interstate 90 from Seattle. Take exit 22, past Preston, a turn-of-the-century Scandinavian mill town, and Fall City, the final upstream landing for early steamboats. Highway 202 takes you to dramatic 270-foot **SNOQUALMIE FALLS,** where you have lunch at **SALISH LODGE & SPA** in fancy surroundings with views of the falls. Then tour the little town of Snoqualmie. At North Bend, where the rocky face of Mount Si rises to the north, return to Interstate 90 and continue east to **SNO-QUALMIE PASS.** The terrain begs you to stop for a view—or a hike. East of the summit, in historic Roslyn, grab a burger at the **ROSLYN CAFE;** then on to Cle Elum to spend the night at the **IRON HORSE INN B&B.**

DAY TWO: After breakfast at your B&B, stock up on road snacks in town: choose goodies at the **CLE ELUM BAKERY** or pick up beef jerky at **OWEN'S MEATS.** Follow signs north to Blewett/Swauk Pass (US Hwy 97), a scenic drive that drops along Peshastin Creek to Highway 2; head east. Swing through Cashmere and visit the **PIO-NEER VILLAGE** and **LIBERTY ORCHARDS** for fruit candy samples, then continue to Wenatchee. Watch for the **ANJOU BAKERY** sign and stop for a macaroon or fudgy chocolate cookie. Your destination on a clear spring or summer day is **OHME GAR-DENS,** just north of town. Have a late lunch at **THE WINDMILL,** then head west on Highway 2 to Leavenworth. Check into **RUN OF THE RIVER** or **HAUS LORELEI INN** and relax before dinner, enjoying river and mountain views. A romantic Austrian-style dinner at **RESTAURANT OSTERREICH** ends your day.

DAY THREE: Have a leisurely breakfast, then explore Leavenworth's **FRONT STREET** shops. Enjoy lunch in the calm atmosphere of **CAFE MOZART**—or, if it's sunny, eat on the patio at **LORRAINE'S EDEL HOUSE INN.** If you want to burn more calories, check in at the ranger station for suggested **HIKES.** Stay a second night in Leavenworth and take in a concert at the **ICICLE CREEK MUSIC CENTER** (9286 Icicle Rd, Leavenworth; 509/548-6347; call ahead). Or take Highway 2 west, enjoying the views at Stevens Pass, and head to Index for an overnight stay at the **BUSH HOUSE COUNTRY INN** before returning to the Seattle area.

frankly, all we really want to do is soak in the hot tub and make snow angels. *$$$; AE, MC, V; checks OK; info@natapoc.com; www.natapoc.com; 4 miles south of Lake Wenatchee.*

Leavenworth

Once a railroad yard and sawmill town, Leavenworth recast itself in the 1960s as a Bavarian-style village with tourism as its primary industry. The architecture sets the tone, and while some cringe at the dirndls-and-lederhosen decor, beyond the facade most find an appealing town suited to its stunning alpine setting. Popular festivals are held in fall and spring and before Christmas. Call the Leavenworth Chamber of Commerce (see below) for information.

FRONT STREET is the strolling, shopping, and festival showcase street. **DIE MUSIK BOX** (933 Front St; 800/288-5883; www.musicbox.com) has a dazzling—sometimes noisy—array of music boxes; **ALPEN HAUS MINIATURES** (807 Front St; 800/572-1559) features dollhouse furniture and miniatures; and **A COUNTRY HEART** (821 Front St; 509/548-5719) sells country for the urban home. Away from Front Street, one of our favorites is **CABIN FEVER RUSTICS** (923 Commercial St; 509/548-4238), offering cabin-style accessories for the Western bungalow. A good stop with kids is the **GINGERBREAD FACTORY** (828 Commercial St; 509/548-6592) for cookies and houses (near the holidays).

For a respite from shopping, **CAFE MOZART** (829 Front St; 509/548-0600) offers European charm, tasteful German-style foods, and afternoon tea. **VISCONTI'S** (636 Front St; 509/548-1213; and in Wenatchee at 1737 N Wenatchee Ave; 509/662-5013; www.viscontis.com), an Italian-style restaurant adjacent to the **LEAVEN-WORTH BREWERY** (509/548-4545), has a beer sampler, great with their savory, thin-crust pizzas.

Outdoor activities abound here; check with the **LEAVENWORTH RANGER STA-TION** just off Highway 2 (600 Sherbourne St, eastern edge of town; 509/548-6977) or the **LEAVENWORTH CHAMBER OF COMMERCE** (220 9th St; 509/548-5807; www.leavenworth.org) for maps and information on hiking, fishing, skiing, mountain biking, rafting, and horseback riding. Tour the **LEAVENWORTH NATIONAL FISH HATCHERY** (12790 Fish Hatchery Rd, off Icicle Rd; 509/548-7641; www.leavenworth.fws.gov or www.salmonfest.org) on Icicle Creek to watch the chinook salmon run late-May through July, and spawn in late August, or walk the mile-long nature trail. Golf at the scenic 18-hole **LEAVENWORTH GOLF CLUB** (9101 Icicle Rd; 509/548-7267; www.leavenworthgolf.com).

SCOTTISH LAKES BACK COUNTRY CABINS (High Country Adventures; by reservation; 425/844-2000 or 888/9-HICAMP; www.scottishlakes.com), 8 miles into the backcountry west of Leavenworth, is a cluster of eight cabins and a small day lodge at the edge of the Alpine Lakes Wilderness Area.

RESTAURANTS

Lorraine's Edel House Inn / ★★

320 9TH ST, LEAVENWORTH; 509/548-4412 OR 800/487-3335 Edel House got its start as a B&B. Although it has a few pretty upstairs guest rooms, and a cottage suite next door with whirlpool tub and gas fireplace, today it's best known for fine dining. Schnitzel is on the menu, but you'll find vegetarian choices too, such as plump portobello mushrooms with goat cheese. There's a perfect puttanesca, or meat specials such as a grilled pork tenderloin topped with caramelized Asian pears. The ambitious menu changes frequently. Lorraine's doesn't serve breakfast but gives overnight guests a 50 percent discount on dinner. *$$; DIS, MC, V; checks OK; dinner every day; beer and wine; reservations recommended; www.lorrainesedelhouse.com; between Commercial St and the river.* &

Restaurant Osterreich / ★★★

633A FRONT ST, LEAVENWORTH; 509/548-4031 Make your way to the cellar of the Tyrolean Ritz Hotel, and you'll find one of Leavenworth's finest Austrian restaurants. It's dim, devoid of windows, but gently flickering candlelight warms the room. Talented Austrian chef Leo Haas serves flavorful yet lighter-than-German fare. Come hungry. Appetizers, especially crayfish strudel with a tart sorrel salad, are outstanding. Entrees include a robust braised lamb shank or duck breast with port wine–berry sauce, as well as nightly seafood and game specials. The wine list boasts rarely seen Austrian wines. Desserts, such as honey ice parfait with port wine cherries, are excellent, but we doubt you'll have room. Upstairs, the friendly hotel offers 16 standard, streetfront rooms. *$$; AE, DIS, MC, V; local checks only; dinner Wed–Sun; beer and wine; reservations recommended; www.leavenworthdining. com; below Tyrolean Ritz Hotel.* &

LODGINGS

Abendblume Pension / ★★★

12570 RANGER RD, LEAVENWORTH; 509/548-4059 OR 800/669-7634 Come here to leave everything behind (especially the kids). It's one of the most elegant, sophisticated inns in town, run by the most gracious host. A beautiful sweeping staircase leads upstairs. The two best rooms have wood-burning fireplaces, Italian marble bathrooms with whirlpool tubs discreetly opening to the rooms, and sun-drenched window seats with views. Every room (each with its own VCR) is an escape, regardless of size. Outside is a patio hot tub. Breakfast at your own pace in the pine-trimmed morning room. *$$$; AE, DIS, MC, V; checks OK; abendblm@rightathome.com; www.abendblume.com; north on Ski Hill Dr at west end of town.*

All Seasons River Inn / ★★★

8751 ICICLE RD, LEAVENWORTH; 509/548-1425 A new porch adds country appeal to this modern two-story cedar house, in keeping with its relaxing riverside location. Six cheery rooms (all have river views and whirlpools; some have sitting rooms; several have fireplaces), antique furnishings, amenities such as chocolates and evening treats, and attention to detail by owners Kathy and Jeff Falconer offer comfort that soothes the spirit. An adult retreat; no TVs in rooms. *$$; MC, V; checks OK; allriver@rightathome.com; www.allseasonsriverinn.com; 1 mile south of Hwy 2.*

Bosch Garten / ★

9846 DYE RD, LEAVENWORTH; 509/548-6900 OR 800/535-0069 Friendly hosts and stylish, homey comfort make this newly built two-story home, in a residential area at the eastern outskirts of town, a good choice. Three rooms with private baths are perfect for those traveling in small groups—then the house is yours. A garden gazebo hot tub and a tiny orchard make this particularly relaxing on warm summer evenings. Children over 14 OK. *$$; MC, V; checks OK; innkeeper@nwi.net; www. boschgarten.com; east of town.*

Haus Lorelei Inn / ★★

347 DIVISION ST, LEAVENWORTH; 509/548-5726 OR 800/514-8868 Here's a rarity: a B&B that welcomes kids. The 10 comfortable European-style rooms here are not indestructible, but not overly precious, and each is large enough to set up a spare bed or so. Those who don't want the kids so close could stash them in the clubby little Hansel and Gretel Room. The Prinzessin, an octagonal main-floor room with a canopy bed overlooking the river, is stunning. At the 2-acre site fronting the Wenatchee River, each of Elisabeth Saunders's rooms affords gorgeous views of the Cascades; at night you can hear the river rushing over boulders. A tennis court and hot tub are on-site; a sandy swimming beach isn't far. *$$; no credit cards; checks OK; www.hauslorelei.com; 2 blocks from downtown.*

Mountain Home Lodge / ★★★☆

8201 MOUNTAIN HOME RD, LEAVENWORTH; 509/548-7077 OR 800/414-2378 This lodge is a mile above Leavenworth in a breathtaking mountaintop setting. Reach it in summer driving 3 miles of dirt road; in winter, a heated snow-cat picks you up from the parking lot at the bottom of Mountain Home Road. Borrow cross-country skis to enjoy miles of tracked cross-country ski trails outside the back door; you can snowshoe and sled, or try the 1,700-foot toboggan run. Summer activities include hiking, horseshoes, badminton, and tennis; the hot tub and swimming pool overlook a broad meadow and mountains. Ten charming rooms are decorated with quilts and outdoor-themed accessories. Gourmet meals in the view dining area might include squash soup, pheasant, or a decadent chocolate tart; top Northwest offerings grace the wine list. Two private pine cabins nearby offer solitude and views. No kids. Meals included in winter. *$$$; DIS, MC, V; checks OK; info@mthome.com; www.mthome.com; off E Leavenworth Rd and Hwy 2.*

Run of the River / ★★★★

9308 E LEAVENWORTH RD, LEAVENWORTH; 509/548-7171 OR 800/288-6491 This elegant log inn on the bank of the Icicle River just keeps getting better. Monty and Karen Turner used their "wish list" accumulated over 15 years as extraordinary innkeepers as their guide to renovate the inn in 2001. They didn't add rooms, but added space and quality. Now each of the six rooms is a luxurious suite with river-rock fireplace, hand-hewn four-poster burlwood log bed, jetted tub for two surrounded by river rock, and work by local artists. We like the cozy log-cabin ambiance, warm colors, and privacy (there's a separate entrance) of the Kingfisher. Some rooms have reading lofts. All suites boast solitude, comfort, and attention to detail. Spend the day on large, private decks, reading or watching wildlife in the refuge across the river (binoculars provided). You'll also find cable TV, robes, and a bubble kit, in case stargazing from the hot tub isn't enough entertainment. New amenities include vintage typewriters with stationery for romantic missives or notes for the guest book. Hearty breakfasts emphasize seasonal produce. Bikes are available. The Turners have printed an excellent array of area-specific activity guides. This is a must-stay place. Our only regret is that room rates have inevitably spiked; check for Internet value packages. *$$$$; DIS, MC, V; checks OK; info@runoftheriver; www.runoftheriver.com; 1 mile east of Hwy 2.*

Sleeping Lady Retreat and Conference Center / ★★★

🌲 **7375 ICICLE RD, LEAVENWORTH; 509/548-6344 OR 800/574-2123** This is exactly the kind of place Leavenworth needed—a quintessential Northwest retreat with an acute awareness of the environment. A former Civilian Conservation Corps camp, the place is well set up for conferences; buildings—from a dance studio to a spacious 60-person meeting house—are comfortably elegant, with touches such as Oriental rugs and woodstoves, but all are high-tech-ready. The old fieldstone chapel is now a 200-seat performing arts theater (and home to the Icicle Creek Music Center, and its own resident string ensemble; 509/548-6347). The guest rooms—with log beds and additional beds in alcoves or lofts—are set in six different clusters. Two separate cabins include the romantic, secluded Eyrie, with a woodstove and whirlpool bath. Two woodland-style rock pools include a large heated pool used May through September, and a small heated soaking pool (year-round). Conferences have first dibs, but there's flexibility for other guests as space allows. Chef Damian Browne serves an excellent meal in a (slightly disconcerting) buffet style. Look for the outdoor glass "icicle" sculpture by Dale Chihuly. *$$; AE, DIS, MC, V; checks OK; info@sleepinglady.com; www.sleepinglady.com; 2 miles southwest of Leavenworth.*

Cashmere

This little orchard town gives cross-mountain travelers who aren't in a Bavarian mood an alternative to Leavenworth. The main street has put up Western storefronts; the town's bordered by river and railroad.

The **CASHMERE MUSEUM** (600 Cottage Ave; 509/782-3230) has an extensive collection of Native artifacts and archaeological material; the adjoining **PIONEER VILLAGE** puts 21 old buildings, carefully restored and equipped, into a nostalgic grouping. The waterwheel is on the National Register of Historic Places.

Aplets and Cotlets, confections made with local fruit and walnuts from an old Armenian recipe, have been produced in Cashmere for decades. You can tour the plant at **LIBERTY ORCHARDS** (117 Mission St; 509/782-2191)—and sample a few. In an orchard off Highway 2, 1 mile east of Cashmere, is **ANJOU BAKERY** (3898 Old Monitor Hwy; 509/782-4360), a great stop for rustic breads, streusel-topped apple pies, macaroons, chocolate cookies, and other baked goods. A premade selection of sandwiches and soups is available for takeout; a handful of tables are available.

Wenatchee

You're in the heart of apple country, with an **APPLE BLOSSOM FESTIVAL** the end of April; call the Wenatchee Valley Convention & Visitors Bureau (116 N Wenatchee Ave; 800/572-7753; www.wenatcheevalley.org). **OHME GARDENS** (just north of town on US Hwy 97A; 509/662-5785; www.ohmegardens) is a 9-acre alpine retreat with cool glades and water features. It sits on a promontory 600 feet above the Columbia River, offering splendid views of the valley, river, city, and mountains. The **RIVERFRONT LOOP TRAIL** on the banks of the Columbia makes for a pleasant evening stroll—or an easy bike ride; the 11-mile loop traverses both sides of the river (and crosses two bridges) from Wenatchee to East Wenatchee. The best place to join the trail is via a pedestrian overpass at the east end of First Street.

BLOOMIN' WONDERFUL FRUIT

The Wenatchee Valley is one of the state's most famous and picturesque fruit regions, with climate-perfect hot summers and cold winters to produce crisp, juicy apples. Spring and fall are the best times to visit.

Bloom time is usually around the end of April. Side roads between Leavenworth and Wenatchee offer grand blossom-touring opportunities. East from Leavenworth along Highway 2, exit at the tiny villages of Peshastin or Dryden, and meander through orchard country. Since the valley is cozy and intimate in scale—roads usually loop back to the main highway—it's hard to get lost, and fun to try. Wenatchee's **WASHINGTON STATE APPLE BLOSSOM FESTIVAL**—the state's oldest major fest—coincides with peak bloom, normally the last week in April and first week of May, weather cooperating.

Apples ripen in September and early October, which is a great time to travel here, stopping by fruit stands to buy boxes of apples, pears, or other tree fruits. Try **SMALL-WOOD HARVEST** (1 mile east of Leavenworth on Hwy 2; 509/548-4196; Apr–Oct) for fruits, wines, and specialty foods. **PREY'S FRUIT** (just east of Leavenworth on Hwy 2; 509/548-5771) is another good stop. Top apple varieties include Delicious, Jonagold, Gala, and Criterion.

The **WASHINGTON APPLE COMMISSION VISITORS CENTER** (2900 Euclid Ave, Wenatchee; 509/663-9600; www.bestapples.com; weekdays year-round, weekends May–Dec) offers bloom-time information, as well as displays, apple gift items for sale, and free juice or fruit samples. *—Jena MacPherson*

MISSION RIDGE (13 miles southwest on Squilchuck Rd; 509/663-6543; www.missionridge.com) offers some of the region's best powder, served by four chairlifts; ask for ski-and-lodging package info. On the second or third Sunday in April, the **RIDGE-TO-RIVER RELAY** (509/662-8799; www.r2r.org)—participants compete in six events, including skiing, running, biking, and paddling—is impressive.

RESTAURANTS

Garlini's Ristorante Italiano / ★

810 VALLEY MALL PKWY, EAST WENATCHEE; 509/884-1707 It's nothing fancy outside, but inside, this niche restaurant's dim lighting, dark wood, and festive music bring Italy to the senses. Craig Still makes sure the Garlini family's old Italian favorites—seafood fettuccine, chicken and veal parmigiana, and lasagne—are cooked just like Mamma's, and he's added lighter nightly specials. Good for families and large parties. *$; AE, DIS, MC, V; checks OK; lunch Tues–Fri, dinner Tues–Sun; beer and wine; reservations recommended; 1 block north of Wenatchee Valley Mall.*

John Horan's Steak & Seafood House / ★★

2 HORAN RD, WENATCHEE; 509/663-0018 Many of the orchards once surrounding this 1899 Victorian farmhouse, built by Wenatchee pioneer Mike Horan, are gone. Yet the roundabout drive to the house, near the confluence of the Wenatchee and Columbia Rivers, sets the tone for an evening that harkens back to more gracious times. Proprietor Inga Peters offers country hospitality; chef Brad Myers, makes his mark with seasonally fresh seafood—perhaps Columbia River sturgeon in season—but you'll be equally impressed with his Angus beef preparations. The Carriage House & Prime Rib next door—a friendly stop for a glass of wine, a Northwest microbrew, or a game of cribbage—offers casual fare. *$$–$$$; AE, DIS, MC, V; checks OK; dinner Mon–Sat in summer (off-season, call for hours); full bar; reservations recommended; johninga@johnhoranhouse.com; www.johnhoranhouse.com; just south of K-Mart plaza.* &

Shakti's / ★★★

218 N MISSION, WENATCHEE; 509/662-3321 Shakti Lanphere (formerly a chef in Seattle and Methow Valley restaurants) and her mother, Renee, have partnered to create this welcome newcomer. A luscious deep purple dining room with maple touches is a stylistic mix of Asia and Tuscany. With linen tablecloths and romantic lighting, it feels like a slice of Seattle. The food—such as braised rabbit, nightly risotto, or pasta specials—has more in common with rustic northern Italian cuisine. The fish—perhaps swordfish or salmon, according to season—is wild, not farm raised. You can get a great steak, too—pan-seared with pancetta, shallots, and rosemary, alongside fresh spinach lightly sautéed in garlic, lemon juice, and olive oil. Bread from Anjou Bakery arrives with herbs, and spiced oil for dipping; the bread also goes into pudding that may be the best we've had. Reasonably priced wine selections are well-matched to the menu. A bonus is talented table help well above the norm. Refreshing for Wenatchee is a full-service, nonsmoking lounge—stop for calamari and a martini or glass of wine. In warm weather, try the back patio. *$$–$$$; AE, MC, V; checks OK; lunch Tues–Fri, dinner Tues–Sat; reservations recommended; in Mission Sq, downtown.* &

The Windmill / ★★

1501 N WENATCHEE AVE, WENATCHEE; 509/665-9529 This former roadside diner is offbeat-looking, but a better tenderloin we've never tasted in Wenatchee. Although the owners have changed once (in a dozen years—Mary Ann and Greg Johnson started running it in early 1997), the waitresses stay and stay. Meals are western American classics; there's seafood, but don't be a fool—stick with the meat. Ritual dictates you finish with a piece of magnificent pie made daily on premises—the fat apple double crust or coconut cream are our picks. *$$; DIS, MC, V; checks OK; dinner Mon–Sat; beer and wine; reservations not accepted Fri–Sat; 1½ miles south of Hwy 2 exit.*

LODGINGS

The Warm Springs Inn / ★

1611 LOVE LN, WENATCHEE; 509/662-8365 OR 800/543-3645 The Wenatchee River is a perfect backdrop, and the pillared entrance and dark-green-and-rustic-brick exterior lend majesty to Jim and Kathy Welsh's B&B, which has six guest rooms with private baths. A lower room with outside access is suitable for children and some pets; check first. A path behind the two-story inn (which served as a hospital in the 1920s) leads through landscaped gardens and woods to the river. Guests can relax in the sitting room or on the veranda. *$$; AE, DIS, MC, V; checks OK; warmsi@warmspringsinn.com; www.warmspringsinn. com; turn south off Hwy 2 onto Lower Sunnyslope Rd, then right onto Love Ln.*

WestCoast Wenatchee Center Hotel / ★

201 N WENATCHEE AVE, WENATCHEE; 509/662-1234 OR 800/325-4000 This is the nicest hotel on the strip (a very plain strip, mind you), with a city and river view. The nine-story hotel has five nonsmoking levels. Recently renovated, rooms are classic in style with floral accents. Rates may rise if most rooms are already booked the day you call, so make advance reservations and ask about package rates. The Wenatchee Roaster and Ale House, on the top floor, has live entertainment Tuesday through Saturday and serves breakfast, lunch, and dinner daily. The city's convention center, next door, is connected by a skybridge. Swimmers enjoy outdoor and indoor pools. *$$; AE, DC, DIS, MC, V; checks OK; www.westcoasthotels.com; center of town.*

Interstate 90 and Snoqualmie Pass

The most popular east-west route across Washington, Interstate 90 connects Interstate 5 at Seattle with Ellensburg, Moses Lake, and Spokane (and beyond). Highway highlights include Snoqualmie Falls, the ski areas at Snoqualmie Pass, and towns such as Cle Elum and Roslyn.

Carnation

Carnation is a lovely stretch of cow country nestled in the Snoqualmie Valley along bucolic Highway 203 (which connects I-90 to Hwy 2 at Monroe). At MACDONALD MEMORIAL PARK (Fall City Rd and NE 40th St; 425/333-4192), meandering trails and an old-fashioned suspension bridge across the Snoqualmie River provide a great family picnic setting (for group reservations, call 206/296-2966).

The sky's the limit for your favorite fruits and vegetables at REMLINGER FARMS U-pick farm (on NE 32nd St, off Hwy 203; 425/333-4135), south of Carnation. The STRAWBERRY FESTIVAL in mid-June starts the season. Throughout summer, choose the best in raspberries, apples, corn, and grapes. In October, kids love tromping through the fields in search of the perfect jack-o'-lantern-to-be.

Snoqualmie

The lovely SNOQUALMIE VALLEY, where the mountains unfold into dairy land, is best known for its falls and its scenery, once the setting for the TV series *Twin Peaks*. THE 268-FOOT SNOQUALMIE FALLS, just up Highway 202 from Interstate 90 (parking lot adjacent to Salish Lodge & Spa; see review), has always been a thundering spectacle. Use the observation deck or, better yet, take a picnic down the 1-mile trail to the base of the falls.

The **NORTHWEST RAILWAY MUSEUM** (38625 SE King St; 425/888-3030; www.trainmuseum.org) runs a scenic tour to Snoqualmie Falls gorge from Snoqualmie and North Bend most Saturdays and Sundays, April through October.

LODGINGS

The Salish Lodge & Spa / ★★★★☆

 6501 RAILROAD AVE SE, SNOQUALMIE; 425/888-2556 The spectacular 268-foot Snoqualmie Falls may be the initial draw, but since you really can't see much of them from many of the rooms, it's a good thing the rooms themselves are so nice. Each offers a tempered country motif: light, clean-lined wood furnishings, pillowed window seats (or balconies), flagstone fireplaces (with full woodboxes), and armoires. Little things are covered: TV cleverly concealed, bathrobes, even a phone in the bathroom. Jacuzzis are separated from bedrooms by a swinging window. Tea is served to lodging guests daily, 4–6pm in the main-floor library. On the fourth level is an extensive spa, with beautifully appointed Asian-style massage and treatment rooms and hydrotherapy soaking spas. The Attic offers casual meals for lunch and dinner on the top floor. The excessive multicourse brunch lives on—though we can live without it, opting instead for dinner and praying for a table with a view of the falls. Chef Mike Davis's menu emphasizes fish, game, and Northwest produce. With more than 1,000 labels, the wine list is almost legendary. $$$; AE, DC, DIS, MC, V; checks OK; www.salishlodge.com; take exit 25 off I-90.

Snoqualmie Pass

Four associated ski areas—**ALPENTAL, SUMMIT WEST, SUMMIT CENTRAL,** and **SUMMIT EAST** (52 miles east of Seattle on I-90; 425/434-7669; www.summit-at-snoqualmie.com)—offer the closest downhill and cross-country skiing for Seattlites (with a free shuttle that runs between them on weekends). Alpental is most challenging; Summit West, with one of the largest ski schools in the country, has excellent instruction for beginners through racers; Summit Central has some challenging bump runs; and the smallest, Summit East, is a favored spot for cross-country skiers, with lighted, groomed cross-country tracks and many miles of trails.

In summer, the relatively low-lying transmountain route is a good starting point for many hikes. Contact the **NORTH BEND RANGER STATION** (425/888-1421; www.fs.fed.us/r6/mbs) for more information; the **BEST WESTERN SUMMIT INN AT SNOQUALMIE PASS** (603 Hwy 906; 425/434-6300 or 800/557-STAY; www.bw summitinn.com), a simple hotel, tastefully done, is your only choice for year-round lodging at the pass.

Roslyn

Modest turn-of-the-century homes in this onetime coal-mining town have become weekend places for city folk. But the main intersection still offers a cross section of the town's character. Once the stage set for the hit TV series *Northern Exposure,* fans will recognize the old stone tavern, inexplicably called **THE BRICK** (100 W Pennsylvania Ave; 509/649-2643), with a water-fed spittoon running the length of the bar. Down the road, behind the town's junkyard, you'll find **CAREK'S MARKET** (510 S "A" St; 509/649-2930), one of the state's better purveyors of fine specialty meats and sausages.

RESTAURANTS

Roslyn Cafe

201 W PENNSYLVANIA AVE, ROSLYN; 509/649-2763 Owners Karen and Bob Hembree have turned this former funky eatery into a family stop with home-style cooking—burgers, meatloaf, homemade soups, steaks, and a sizable vegetarian menu; for dessert, cobblers and pies. The Breakfast Special is a grilled mix of veggies, cheese, and herbs, with a special sauce. *$; MC, V; local checks only; breakfast, lunch every day, dinner Fri–Mon; no alcohol; reservations recommended; khembree@inlandnet.com; at 1st St.* &

Cle Elum

This small mining town of about 20,000 parallels Interstate 90. Freeway access, at either end of town, leads to First Street, Cle Elum's main thoroughfare, making it a handy stop when you need to grab a burger and fill your gas tank. **CLE ELUM BAKERY** (1st St and Peoh Ave; 509/674-2233) is a longtime local institution, also popular with travelers. From one of the last brick-hearth ovens in the Northwest come delicious *torchetti* (an Italian butter pastry rolled in sugar), cinnamon rolls, and old-fashioned cake doughnuts. **OWEN'S MEATS** (502 E 1st St; 509/674-2530), across the street, is an excellent stop for fresh meats, and beef and turkey jerky.

LODGINGS

Hidden Valley Guest Ranch / ★★

3942 HIDDEN VALLEY RD, CLE ELUM; 509/857-2322 OR 800/5-COWBOY A short hour from Seattle is the state's oldest dude ranch on 300 beautiful, private acres. Bruce and Kim Coe have spruced up some of the old cabins: the floors may still be a bit uneven, but touches include homemade quilts and potbelly stoves. Of the 13 cabins, our favorites are the older ones, particularly Apple Tree and Spruce Number 5. New ones, though fine, trade some charm for separate bedrooms and kitchenettes. Miles of trails, horseback riding (packages can include daily rides), nearby trout fishing, a pool, hot tub, and basketball hoop make up for the basic accommodations. Look for indoor fun in the ranch house (table tennis, pool table). Meals (included) are taken in the cookhouse dining room. *$$; MC, V; checks OK; open mid-April–Oct; info@hvranch.com; www.hvranch. com; off Hwy 970 at milepost 8.*

Iron Horse Inn B&B / ★

526 MARIE AVE, SOUTH CLE ELUM; 509/674-5939 OR 800/2-2-TWAIN This B&B was built in 1909 to house employees of the Chicago, Milwaukee, St. Paul & Pacific Railroad. Now on the National Register of Historic Places, the bunkhouse, with 10 guest rooms and a honeymoon suite, is pleasantly furnished with reproduction antiques. Railroad memorabilia—vintage photographs, model trains, schedules, and more—is on display. Two cabooses in the side yard are equipped with baths, refrigerators, queen-sized beds, and private decks. Owners Mary and Doug Pittis are railroad buffs (Mary's father was a Milwaukee railroad man). They'll rev up the outdoor hot tub for you. Kids OK; no pets. *$$; MC, V; checks OK; maryp@ironhorseinnbb.com; www.ironhorseinnbb.com; adjacent to Iron Horse State Park Trail.*

Mount Rainier National Park

The majestic mountain is the abiding symbol of natural grandeur in the Northwest, and one of the most awesome mountains in the world. Its cone rises 14,411 feet above sea level, several thousand feet higher than other peaks in the Cascade Range. The best way to appreciate Rainier is to explore its flanks: 300 miles of backcountry and self-guiding nature trails lead to ancient forests, dozens of massive glaciers, waterfalls, and alpine meadows lush with wildflowers during the mountain's short summer.

Chinook and Cayuse Passes are closed in winter; you can take the loop trip or the road to Sunrise late-May through October. The road from Longmire to Paradise remains open during daylight hours in winter; carry tire chains and a shovel and check current road and weather conditions by calling a 24-hour information service (360/569-2211). Obligatory backcountry-use permits for overnight stays can be obtained from any of the ranger stations. Of the five entrance stations (entrance fee is $10 per automobile or $5 per person on foot, bicycle, or motorcycle), the three most popular are described here; the northwest entrances (Carbon River and Mowich Lake) have few visitor facilities and unpaved roads.

Highway 410 heads east from Sumner to Enumclaw, the **WHITE RIVER ENTRANCE** to the park, and Sunrise Visitors Center, continuing on to connect with Highway 12 near Naches. Note that the road beyond the Crystal Mountain spur is closed in winter, limiting access to Sunrise, and Cayuse and Chinook Passes. Highways 7 and 706 connect the main **NISQUALLY ENTRANCE** with Tacoma and Interstate 5; Nisqually is open year-round to Paradise. The **STEVENS CANYON ENTRANCE** (southeast corner) on Highway 123, which connects Highways 410 and 12, is closed in winter; in summer, Ohanapecosh is a favorite stop.

You can climb the mountain with **RAINIER MOUNTAINEERING, INC.** (PO Box Q, Ashford, WA 98304; 360/569-2227; www.rmiguides.com)—the concessionaire guide service—or in your own party. Unless you are qualified to do it on your own—and this is a big, difficult, and dangerous mountain on which many people have been killed—you must climb with the guide service. If you plan to climb with your own party, you must register and pay a fee ($15 per person) at one of the **RANGER STATIONS** in Mount Rainier National Park (Paradise Old Station, and White River or Wilkeson Wilderness Information Centers; 360/569-2211). Reservations are required for summer climbing; solo climbs must be approved in advance. Generally, the best climbing time is late June through early September.

Black Diamond

This relatively quiet, former coal-mining town is located on Highway 169, in Maple Valley, about 10 miles north of Enumclaw. **BLACK DIAMOND BAKERY** (32805 Railroad Ave; 360/886-2741) boasts the last wood-fired brick oven in the area; the bread that comes out is excellent—26 different kinds, including cinnamon, sour rye, potato, and garlic French—and perfect for a Rainier excursion.

Greenwater

RESTAURANTS

Naches Tavern / ★

58411 HWY 410E, GREENWATER; 360/663-2267 Now this is the way to do a country tavern. The wall-long fireplace roars all winter to warm the Crystal Mountain après-ski crowd, hunters, loggers, and locals, who all mix peaceably. Homemade food—sandwiches, deep-fried mushrooms, chili, burgers, four-scoop milk shakes—is modestly priced. There's a countrified jukebox, pool tables, a lending library (take a book, leave a book) of yellowing paperbacks, and comfy furniture. Play cribbage, stroke the roving housepets, or nod off in front of the hearth. *$; MC, V; no checks; lunch, dinner every day; beer and wine; reservations not accepted; at Greenwater.* ♿

Crystal Mountain

CRYSTAL MOUNTAIN SKI RESORT (off Hwy 410 just west of Chinook Pass, on northeast edge of Mount Rainier National Park; 360/663-2265; www.skicrystal. com), southeast of Enumclaw, is the state's best ski area. It has runs for beginners and experts, plus fine backcountry skiing. Less well-known are summer facilities: you can ride the chairlift and catch a grand view of Mount Rainier and other peaks, and **SUMMIT HOUSE**, on the mountain, is open for lunch. Rent condominiums, hotel rooms, or cabins from **CRYSTAL MOUNTAIN LODGING** (on-mountain condos; 360/663-2558; www.crystalmtlodging-wa.com), **CRYSTAL MOUNTAIN HOTELS** (360/663-2262; www.crystalhotels.com; often closed in summer), or **ALTA CRYSTAL RESORT** (cabins; 360/663-2500; www.altacrystalresort.com). Although big plans (an almost $60-million project) are in the works to redo the resort, for now, there's just a grocery store, a sports shop, and **RAFTERS,** the bar-and-buffet restaurant atop Crystal's lodge.

LODGINGS

Silver Skis Chalet / ★★

CRYSTAL MOUNTAIN BLVD, CRYSTAL MOUNTAIN; 360/663-2558 OR 888/668-4368 These condos are your best bet if you want to stay right on the mountain. Pick and choose among 60-or-so options for details such as a fireplace (all have kitchens). Great for families, with the perk of a pool heated to 95°F, they're nonsmoking and have one or two bedrooms. Nonholiday midweek packages offer extra value. *$$$–$$$$; AE, MC, V; checks OK; crystalmtlodging@tx3.com; www.crystalmtlodging-wa.com; off Hwy 410, at end of Crystal Mountain Rd.*

Sunrise

Open only during summer, Sunrise (6,400 feet) is the closest you can drive to Rainier's peak. The old lodge has no overnight accommodations but does offer a **VISITOR CENTER** (northeast corner of park, 31 miles north of Ohanapecosh; 360/569-2177, ext. 2357; www.nps.gov/mora/), snack bar, and mountain exhibits. Dozens of trails begin here, such as the short one to a magnificent view of **EMMONS GLACIER CANYON.**

Eatonville

At Eatonville, just east of Highway 7, 17 miles south of Puyallup, the big draw is **NORTHWEST TREK** (on Meridian, Hwy 161; 360/832-6116; www.nwtrek.org), where animals roam free while people tour the 600-acre grounds in small open-air trams. The buffalo herd steals the show. Open daily mid-February through October, weekends the rest of the year; group rates available.

RESTAURANTS

Between the Bread

311 CENTER ST E, EATONVILLE; 360/832-3777 When you first step into Between the Bread, you immediately feel as if you are one of the locals. The small restaurant is cozy (eight tables), the staff extremely friendly, and the service makes you feel at home. Between the Bread offers everything from typical breakfast fare and wonderful desserts to weekly specials and a children's menu. Lunch includes sandwiches, soups, and salads; dinner ranges from pasta to seafood to steaks. There's outside seating in summer. *$–$$; MC, V, D; checks OK; lunch Tues–Sat, dinner Wed–Fri; beer and wine; reservations not necessary; in downtown Eatonville.*

Ashford

If Ashford is the gateway to Paradise, then **WHITTAKER'S BUNKHOUSE** (30205 Hwy 706E; 360/569-2439; www.welcometoashford.com) is the place to stop on the way to the very top—of Mount Rainier, that is. A good place to meet the guides, climbers, hikers, and skiers of the mountain. Rooms are basic and cheap (bunks available) but plush compared to camping.

MOUNT TAHOMA SKI HUTS, run by Mount Tahoma Trails Association (360/569-2451; www.skimtta.com), is Western Washington's first hut-to-hut ski trail system. It offers more than 90 miles of trails, three huts, and one yurt, in a spectacular area south and west of Mount Rainier National Park.

LODGINGS

Mountain Meadows Inn and B&B / ★★

28912 HWY 706 E, ASHFORD; 360/569-2788 If seclusion near the base of one of Washington's busiest tourist destinations is what you're after, you'll find it here. Just off the main road, the inn is privately situated on 11 landscaped acres, with a trout pond, nature trails, an outdoor fire pit, and a cedar grove hot tub. Three large guest rooms in the main house are filled with a hodgepodge of antiques. There's nothing kitschy here; just a tasteful home filled with John Muir memorabilia, a nature library, and some Native American baskets. A guest house has three studio apartments. *$$; MC, V; checks OK; mtmeadow@mashell.com; www.mt-rainier.net; 6 miles west of Nisqually park entrance.*

Nisqually Lodge / ★

31609 HWY 706 E, ASHFORD; 360/569-8804 Reasonably priced and clean, this 24-room, two-story lodge just west of the Nisqually entrance to Mount Rainier National Park offers welcome respite to those willing to trade some charm for a phone, satellite TV, and air-conditioning. Though walls are somewhat thin, returnees like the lobby's stone fireplace and the outdoor hot tub. Coffee and pastries are served for breakfast; conference and laundry facilities are available. *$$; AE, DC, MC, V; no checks; www.escapetothemountains.com; 5 miles from park entrance.*

Wellspring / ★★

54922 KERNAHAN RD, ASHFORD; 360/569-2514 For more than a decade, Wellspring has quietly greeted outdoor enthusiasts with two spas nestled in a sylvan glade surrounded by evergreens. A soothing hour or two at Wellspring has become almost de rigueur for folks coming off Mount Rainier. Three log cabins have an in-the-woods feel (no kitchens, TVs, or phones—just woodstoves, refrigerators, and queen-sized feather beds with down comforters). A fourth board-and-batten building holds our two favorites: Tatoosh, with a river-stone fireplace and waterfall-like shower, and The Nest, a tiny room with a swinging bed below a skylight. Three Bears is a four-room cottage with full kitchen and washer and dryer; children are OK here. Make an appointment for an hour massage, and you'll tuck in perfectly. *$$; MC, V; checks OK; 3 miles east of Ashford.*

Longmire

A few miles inside the southwestern park border, the village of Longmire has the 25-room (six without private bath) **NATIONAL PARK INN** (360/569-2275; www.guest services.com/rainier), renovated charmingly in 1990 with tasteful, hickory-style furnishings. A small museum with wildlife exhibits, a **HIKING INFORMATION CENTER** (360/569-2211, ext. 3317), and snowshoe and cross-country **SKI RENTAL** (360/569-2411) is nearby.

Paradise

At 5,400 feet, Paradise is the most popular destination on Rainier. You'll catch wonderful views of Narada Falls and Nisqually Glacier on the way to the paved parking lot and the **HENRY M. JACKSON MEMORIAL VISITOR CENTER** (just before Par-

FROM A WAGON ROAD TO THE PACIFIC CREST TRAIL

Hikers can access a portion of one of the nation's most famous trails, the **PACIFIC CREST NATIONAL SCENIC TRAIL**—a 2,600-plus-mile route through high country from Mexico to Canada—at Snoqualmie Pass. North from the pass, the trail leads through the Alpine Lakes Wilderness Area, a truly beautiful "hikers dream" destination. This area can be experienced on an overnight, or it can take at least five days to hike the Pacific Crest Trail segment from Interstate 90 north to Highway 2.

Shorter hikes, such as the Wagon Road Trail, take much less planning. Beginning near the Denny Creek Campground 3 miles off Interstate 90 (exit 47), it follows the original Snoqualmie Pass Wagon Road on an easy 2-mile loop winding through mostly old-growth forest.

For more information, contact the North Bend Ranger Station (425/888-1421) or check out web sites for the Washington Trails Association (www.wta.org) or the Pacific Crest Trail Association (www.pcta.org).

—*Jena McPherson*

adise; 360/569-2211, ext. 2328). The center, housed in a flying saucer–like building, has a standard cafeteria and gift shop, extensive nature exhibits and films, and a superb view of the mountain from its observation deck. Depending on the season, you could picnic (our advice is to bring your own) among the wildflowers, explore the trails (rangers offer guided walks), let the kids slide on inner tubes in the snow-play area, try a little cross-country skiing, or even take a guided snowshoe tromp. Reserve one of the 118 (30 without private bath) rooms at **PARADISE INN** (at the end of the road, 20 miles from the southwest—Nisqually—entrance; 360/569-2275; www.guestservices.com/rainier), a massive 1917 lodge with a wonderfully nostalgic feel, and comfortably spend the night in one of the most unique locations in the state.

LODGINGS

Stormking Spa at Mt. Rainier / ★★

37311 SR 706E, ASHFORD; 360/569-2964 OR 360/569-2339 Just a mile from the entrance to Mount Rainier National Park, the Stormking Spa offers a wonderful option for those who don't want to rough it. Built in the 1890s by the Mesler family, this rustic B&B has three rooms, each with a different theme (floral, wildlife, and Native Northwest), along with two cabins: the Eagle, romantic with a two-person greenhouse shower and private outdoor hot tub, and the Bear, perfect for large groups with three bedrooms and a fully equipped kitchen (and located over a mile from the main house). Enjoy nature trails, an outdoor hot tub, and massage and spa treatments. Whether you are looking for a good meal, the best place to rent a video, or where to find groceries, the proprietors have the answer. Complimentary breakfast is included for guests of the B&B (but not cabins). Children over age 12 and pets OK in the B&B but not cabins. It's hard to find at night; get detailed directions. *$$–$$$; MC, V; checks OK; stormking@storm kingspa.com; www.stormkingspa.com; 4½ miles east of Ashford.*

White Pass

WHITE PASS (509/672-3101; www.skiwhitepass.com) is an off-the-beaten-path ski destination offering downhill (with a high-speed quad lift) and cross-country skiing, located 12 miles southeast of Mount Rainier National Park at the summit of Highway 12. Its base is the highest on the Cascade crest, at 4,500 feet. A Nordic center near the day lodge serves cross-country skiers with about 18 miles of trails. Summer hiking can be found in adjacent William O. Douglas and Goat Rocks Wilderness Areas.

LODGINGS

Hotel Packwood / ★

104 MAIN ST, PACKWOOD; 360/494-5431 A couple of motels in Packwood may have more modern appliances, but this spartan lodge (open since 1912) remains a favorite. The aroma from the lobby woodstove makes you feel as if you're in the middle of the forest, even though you're in downtown Packwood. A narrow staircase climbs to the simple rooms; seven guest rooms share baths, two have private bathrooms. *$; DIS, MC, V; checks OK; just off Hwy 12 at Main St.*

SOUTHWEST
WASHINGTON

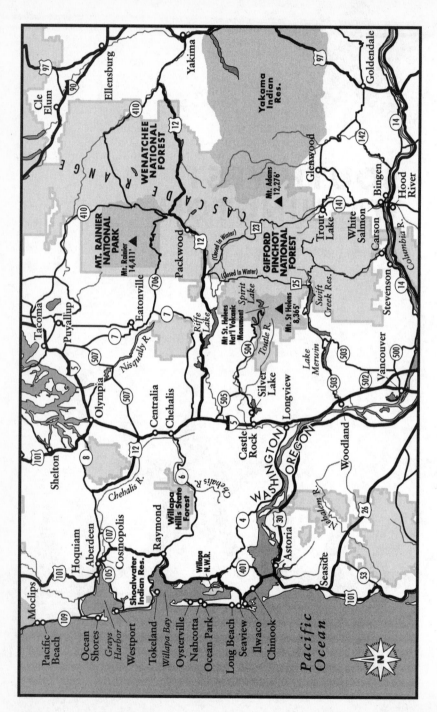

SOUTHWEST WASHINGTON

Nearly all of the varied terrain, scenery, and weather that make up the Pacific Northwest are on display in Southwest Washington. You can play on flat, sandy beaches that spread for miles along the Pacific coast, basking in an often wet but always mild marine climate. Or trek up the slopes of geologically young mountains—including one devastated by the same volcanic forces that built its neighbors. Across the mountains, following the gorge cut by one of the country's mightiest rivers, you can experience long, hot, arid summers.

History looms large here too. Since pre-Columbian times, Native Americans have used the ocean to travel from what is today Pacific Beach to the mouth of Grays Harbor, and on to Willapa Bay and the Long Beach Peninsula. The natural bounty of the coast—salmon and other fish, clams and oysters, plus wild berries and mushrooms—still figure prominently in the region's economy (and diet). In 1792, American sea captain Robert Gray sailed into Grays Harbor (a replica of his ship homeports at Aberdeen), staking important claims to the region for the fledgling United States. After the United States asserted its control below the 49th parallel in 1846, loggers came to harvest timber that would supply nearly half the world, and lumber barons built mansions in places such as Hoquiam and Cosmopolis.

The great Columbia River had tempted many explorers in search of a Northwest Passage, but the then-untamed river was extremely difficult to navigate. The broad mouth where the river crashes into the Pacific became the graveyard of countless big vessels, and can still be treacherous sailing. But by the 1820s, the British had established in Fort Vancouver a headquarters for the Hudson's Bay Company, which would control a vast trading empire that extended up to Alaska.

American explorers Meriwether Lewis and William Clark blazed a trail overland to the region almost 200 years ago; the mouth of the Columbia marked their journey's end in 1805. The explorers' party traveled this last leg of their trek through the beautiful Columbia River Gorge, both by canoe and on foot. Today's traveler finds signs and other interpretive monuments that mark their trail.

ACCESS AND INFORMATION

Most travelers exploring Southwest Washington via car approach from **INTERSTATE 5**, the multilane freeway between Seattle and Portland. Between the two metropolises, you'll find Vancouver just north of the Columbia and Longview a half-hour's drive farther north.

Other major highways that provide access in the region include **US HIGHWAY 12** (traveling through sleepy, tree-filled coastal mountains to Aberdeen/Hoquiam); **US HIGHWAY 101** (running south from Aberdeen to the Columbia at Astoria); and **HIGHWAY 14** (from Vancouver into the Columbia River Gorge), which frequently crosses the trail of Lewis and Clark, and enters rugged cliffs and sloping grasslands to connect with **US HIGHWAY 97** north to Goldendale.

AMTRAK's (800/USA-RAIL; www.amtrak.com) Coast Starlight route runs between Seattle and Portland, with stops at Kelso-Longview (501 S 1st Ave; 360/578-1870) and Vancouver (1301 W 11th St; 360/694-7307). **GREYHOUND**

BUS SERVICE (800/231-2222) is available to Castle Rock, Kelso-Longview, Woodland, Vancouver, and Goldendale.

Grays Harbor and Ocean Shores

Grays Harbor has attracted folks since Captain Robert Gray first sailed in on his 1792 expedition. Generations of loggers have begun to give over to retirees drawn by bargain-priced real estate—and the natural beauty of the region. A half-million Arctic-bound shorebirds migrate to the area from as far south as Argentina, and congregate on the tidal mudflats at the wildlife refuge of **BOWERMAN BASIN** (just beyond the Hoquiam airport, Airport Wy off Hwy 109) each spring from about mid-April through the first week of May. At high tide, the birds rise in unison in flocks that shimmer through the air, twisting and turning, and then drop again to feed. The **GRAYS HARBOR NATIONAL WILDLIFE REFUGE** (Hwy 109, 1½ miles west of Hoquiam; 360/753-9467) has more information.

Aberdeen and Hoquiam

The timber industry brought riches to these twin towns. Evidence can be seen in numerous mansions and the splendid **7TH STREET THEATRE** (313 7th St; 360/532-0302), a restored turn-of-the-20th-century edifice that hosts a variety of productions. Logging and sawmilling are just a shadow of their early-1900s heyday, but tourism is slowly rising to take their place. One attraction is the **GRAYS HARBOR HISTORICAL SEAPORT** (east side of Aberdeen; 360/532-8611), home to a full-scale replica of Captain Robert Gray's *Lady Washington,* a 105-foot floating museum. The ship, available for onboard tours and cruises, is often at other ports of call, so phone ahead.

RESTAURANTS

Billy's Bar and Grill / ★

322 E HERON ST, ABERDEEN; 360/533-7144 Billy's aims to recall Aberdeen's bawdy past and is named for the infamous Billy Gohl, who terrorized the waterfront in 1907. Gohl shanghaied sailors and robbed loggers, consigning their bodies to the murky Wishkah River through a trapdoor in a saloon just one block away from the present-day Billy's—where you get a square-deal meal (thick burgers and seasoned fries) and an honest drink, without much damage to your pocketbook. *$; AE, DC, MC, V; local checks only; breakfast, lunch, dinner every day; full bar; reservations not accepted; corner of G St.* ᴄ

Mallard's Bistro & Grill / ★

118 E WISHKAH ST, ABERDEEN; 360/532-0731 A local favorite, Mallard's has a cozy atmosphere to complement its outsized menu, which runs the gamut from French to Italian to Asian to American cuisine, with a natural emphasis on seafood. Tiger prawns in Pernod make a tasty opener before moving onto entrees such as rosemary and garlic pork tenderloin or coquille St.-Jacques. *$$; MC, V; local checks only; lunch Tues–Fri, dinner Tues–Sat; beer and wine; reservations recommended; between S "I" and S Broadway.*

SOUTHWEST WASHINGTON THREE-DAY TOUR

DAY ONE: Start the day from the Puget Sound area with a drive to Ocean Shores. Take lunch at the **GALWAY BAY RESTAURANT & PUB,** then spend the afternoon beach-combing, or perhaps go for a horseback ride on the beach. Check into the **CAROLINE INN** for a comfortable night in a Southern-inspired two-story suite, then head back into Ocean Shores proper for dinner at **ALEC'S BY THE SEA.** After dinner, relax in your Jacuzzi with a view.

DAY TWO: Enjoy a breakfast you make yourself in your full kitchen, then make dinner reservations at the Shoalwater in Seaview before checking out. Head south down Highway 101 about 90 miles to the **LONG BEACH PENINSULA.** In Long Beach, make a visit to **MARSH'S FREE MUSEUM** to ogle the oddities, then shop for a kite to fly on the beach. After a light lunch at the **HERON AND BEAVER PUB** in Seaview, fly your kite for a while and then check in at **CASWELL'S ON THE BAY BED & BREAKFAST** in Ocean Park and get ready for dinner at the **SHOALWATER** in Seaview.

DAY THREE: After a healthy breakfast at Caswell's, pack a picnic lunch and drive down to Ilwaco and **FORT CANBY STATE PARK,** where you can visit the **LEWIS AND CLARK INTERPRETIVE CENTER** and the **CAPE DISAPPOINTMENT LIGHTHOUSE.** Afterward, drive Highway 4 east along the Columbia River to Longview, where you can have dinner at **HENRI'S** (4545 Ocean Beach Hwy; 360/425-7970) if you're running late, or head north up Interstate 5 to Castle Rock, then east on Highway 503 to the **BLUE HERON INN**—make it by 7pm to enjoy the dinner included in the price of your room.

LODGINGS

Hoquiam's Castle Bed & Breakfast / ★★☆

515 CHENAULT AVE, HOQUIAM; 360/533-2005 If you've ever wished you could slip under the ropes at a museum and lounge on the antiques in Victorian splendor, Hoquiam's Castle Bed & Breakfast gives you your chance. Previously open only to tours, the mansion was purchased by David and Linda Carpenter in 1999, extensively renovated, and debuted in 2000 as an inn. Guests can relax by the rosewood grand piano in the parlor beneath a cut-crystal chandelier, watch the sun set on Grays Harbor from the panoramic Turet Room, or twirl across the Ball Room floor on their way to the Den, as the snug saloon with the ornate bar and custom stained-glass windows installed by timber potentate Robert Lytle (who built the mansion) is now known. All five guest rooms have private baths. Kids under 12 are discouraged. *$$–$$$; AE, DC, MC, V; no checks; info@hoquiam castle.com; www.hoquiamscastle.com; west on Emerson, right on Garfield St, uphill to Chenault Ave.*

Ocean Shores

Despite the best efforts of real estate speculators and celebrity investors in the 1960s, Ocean Shores did not develop into a Las Vegas of the North. Instead, residents managed to wrest control from the land barons, build schools, and create a real town, albeit one with strangely broad urban streets (a legacy of its pie-in-the-sky city planning).

That isn't to say building isn't booming. In addition to numerous hotels, Ocean Shores boasts a big convention center, busy year-round. An annual June **PHOTOGRAPHY SHOW** and November **DIXIELAND JAZZ FESTIVAL** (800/762-3224) are some of the events that draw visitors. Outside the downtown hubbub, consider reserving one of the **PRIVATE BEACH COTTAGES** (reservations: 888/702-3224; www.oceanshores.com) that owners make available.

The long, flat beach is great for **CLAMMING**—for seasons and license requirements, check with the Department of Fish and Wildlife (48 Devonshire Rd, Montesano; 360/249-4628)—beachcombing, and even driving if you dare. A fun way to explore is on horseback—**NAN-SEA STABLES** (360/289-0194) brings a string of horses to the beach in front of the Shilo Inn (see review); and **CHENOIS CREEK HORSE RENTALS** (just show up on the beach) has mounts available at the end of Damon Road, across from the Best Western Lighthouse Suites Inn (see review).

RESTAURANTS

Alec's by the Sea / ★

131 E CHANCE A LA MER BLVD NE, OCEAN SHORES; 360/289-4026 Alec's by the Sea heads a list of otherwise uninspiring dining options in Ocean Shores. Choices include fresh seafood (such as an oven-broiled seafood platter of salmon, scallops, prawns, crab, oysters, and more), steaks, pasta (smoked-salmon fettuccine is a winner), poultry, burgers, and sandwiches (try the Philadelphia prime sandwich with grilled onions, bell peppers, and Swiss cheese), as well as a thick, rich, buttery clam chowder. Alec's has three hallmarks of the family restaurant: large portions, early-bird specials (4–6pm), and crayons for kids. *$$; AE, DC, DIS, MC, V; local checks only; lunch, dinner every day; full bar; reservations not necessary; off Point Brown Rd.* &

Galway Bay Restaurant & Pub

676 OCEAN SHORES BLVD NW, OCEAN SHORES; 360/289-2300 Take off the chill in the best Irish fashion in this pub with a small but tasty traditional menu. Order a pint of Guinness (on tap), then dine on Irish stew (browned lamb, potatoes, carrots, and sautéed onions in a rich, creamy sauce), chicken and mushroom pasty, Limerick sausage roll, or Forfar bridies (chopped steak with sautéed onions, carrots, and potatoes baked in puff pastry). Finish with a tot of 16-year-old single-malt whiskey. If you're ready to cut a reel, there's live Irish music most weekends. *$$; AE, DIS, MC, V; checks OK; lunch, dinner every day; full bar; reservations not accepted; www.galway-bay.com; ½ block from Shilo Inn.* &

LODGINGS

Best Western Lighthouse Suites Inn / ★

491 DAMON RD NW, OCEAN SHORES; 360/289-2311 OR 800/757-SURF One of the sights you'll see as you head into Ocean Shores is a lighthouse—which turns out to be the five-story, 360-degree observation tower of the Best Western Lighthouse Suites Inn. Rooms are large and nicely decorated, and each has an ocean view as well as a fireplace, wet bar, microwave, refrigerator, coffeemaker, cable TV, and VCR. Recent expansion added a third-floor restaurant as well as 18 guest rooms. Things are quieter here on the north end of town, and the hotel lights the beach at night for contemplative walks. *$$$; AE, DC, MC, V; checks OK; manager@bwlighthouse. com; www.bwlighthouse.com; at north city limits.* &

The Caroline Inn / ★★

1341 OCEAN SHORES BLVD SW, OCEAN SHORES; 360/289-0450 Down a long road, at the end of the peninsula, is the Caroline Inn—a gleaming white Southern Gothic minimansion rising above the sea grass. Each of four two-story suites has a first-floor living room with a fireplace and a balcony facing the ocean, a dining room, and a fully outfitted kitchen (you're well removed from the restaurants and entertainment in town, but that's much of the appeal). In the upstairs bedroom, you can relax in the Jacuzzi while gazing out at the beach, or step onto another balcony for a better view. These tastefully furnished suites are popular year-round; reserve at least a month in advance for weekends. A much-requested second Southern-style mansion nearby with facilities for small weddings—the Judith Ann—is set to open at press time. *$$$; MC, V; checks OK; oceanshores.com/lodging/ caroline; toward end of peninsula, near Cutlass Ct.*

The Shilo Inn / ★★

707 OCEAN SHORES BLVD NW, OCEAN SHORES; 360/289-4600 OR 800/222-2244 Something of a crown jewel in the nation's largest privately owned hotel chain, the Shilo Inn at Ocean Shores delivers a lot for your money. Every one of its 113 rooms is a junior suite: sitting room, bedroom, and oceanview balcony, plus microwave, refrigerator, wet bar, four phones, three TVs with free cable—even one in the bathroom—fireplace, and free newspaper. Downstairs is a guest laundry, 24-hour indoor pool, spa, sauna and fitness center, a surprisingly good restaurant, and a beautiful 3,000-gallon aquarium. *$$$; AE, DC, MC, V; checks OK; www.shiloinns.com; at Chance a la Mer Blvd.*

Pacific Beach

LODGINGS

Sandpiper / ★★

4159 HWY 109, PACIFIC BEACH; 360/276-4580 The large, clean Sandpiper is perfect for a family reunion, or just some peaceful quality time with the nuclear family at the ocean. Two four-story complexes have suites with amenities including sitting rooms, kitchens, baths with heated towel bars, small porches, and real log-burning fireplaces. No phones or TV (or restaurant—you'll whip up the haute cuisine in the kitchen or on the outdoor barbecue), but there's a nice kids' play area, plus a gift shop that sells board games, kites, and sand pails. Pets are welcome with advance notice and deposit. Many units are reserved months in advance. *$$–$$$; MC, V; checks OK; min stays weekends and summer; oceanshores.com/ lodging/sandpiper; 1½ miles south of town.*

Moclips

LODGINGS

Ocean Crest Resort / ★

HWY 109 N, MOCLIPS; 360/276-4465 The tremendous view the Ocean Crest Resort commands from its cliffside perch among the spruce—as well as amenities such as an indoor pool and spa, exercise room, tanning bed, and a massage therapist—have made this inn a perennial hit, with minimum stays required during peak periods. Rooms run from bargain studio units with no view to kitchen and fireplace units to two-bedroom suites (logs provided free). Rates are reasonable even in summer. Best views are from the large suites in Building 5. The resort's somewhat pricey view restaurant, serving fresh seafood, pasta, steaks, and more, is the best dining within a half-hour's drive. *$$–$$$; AE, DIS, MC, V; checks OK; ocean shores.com/lodging/oceancrest; 18 miles north of Ocean Shores.*

Westport

A spate of oceanfront condos proves that retirees and urban escapees have begun to flock to Westport, just as fishers have for years. **CHARTER FISHING** is still the town's lifeblood, as the cluster of motels near the docks (and the fact you can eat breakfast at just about any restaurant before 5am) attests. Changes in the salmon fishery have resulted in more charter bottom-fishing trips (for halibut and snapper, among other catches), and popular whale-watching cruises. Gray whales migrate off the coast, March through May, on their way toward Arctic feeding waters, where they'll fatten up for the trip back down to their breeding lagoons in Baja come fall.

Some of the best charters include **CACHALOT** (2511 Westhaven Dr; 360/268-0323), **NEPTUNE** (2601 Westhaven Dr; 360/268-0124), **OCEAN** (2315 W Westhaven Dr; 360/268-9144), and **WESTPORT** (2411 W Westhaven Dr; 360/268-9120 or 800/562-0157).

If you're not enthused about catching your own, Westport has plenty of places to buy seafood. Try **BRADY'S OYSTERS** (3714 Oyster Pl, Aberdeen; 360/268-0077), just east of town on Highway 105; **MERINO SEAFOODS** (301 E Harbor St; 360/268-2510), near the docks; or **WESTPORT SEAFOOD** (609 Neddie Rose Dr; 360/268-0133).

The **WESTPORT LIGHTHOUSE** (turn left at the town's only stoplight) towers 100 feet over the dunes; call the Coast Guard (360/268-0121) for a guided tour. A scenic 2.5-mile (round-trip) trail leads through the dunes from Westport Lighthouse State Park to **WESTHAVEN STATE PARK**; it's paved and wheelchair-accessible. In town, exhibits at the **WESTPORT MARITIME MUSEUM** (2201 Westhaven Dr; 360/268-0078) trace seafarers back to the 1700s; it also shows collections of local Coast Guard, industry, and whaling artifacts.

LODGINGS

Chateau Westport / ★

710 W HANCOCK, WESTPORT; 360/268-9101 OR 800/255-9101 The Chateau Westport is '60s-boxy on the outside but pretty comfy and vaguely continental on the inside. Some of the more than 100 rooms and suites have fireplaces, kitchens, and balconies. Ocean-facing views (especially from the third and fourth floors) are quite lovely. An indoor heated pool and hot tub are available, as is free continental breakfast. Bargain winter rates apply during prime whale-watching months. *$$; AE, DC, MC, V; no checks; chateau@tss.net; www.chateau westport.com; at S Forest St.* &

Long Beach Peninsula and Willapa Bay

The ocean conjures up restful visions of soothing waves lapping the shore, but too many "destination" beach areas offer a shrill edge instead. Though the Long Beach Peninsula has its share of bumper boats and seashell tchotchkes—and the population triples in July and August—it delivers the real deal: beautiful, serene beaches blessed by a gentle marine climate. Beyond scenery and souvenirs, the peninsula offers renowned kite flying, cranberry bogs, famous Willapa Bay oysters, rhododendrons, and some excellent small-town dining.

With its 37-mile-long stretch of flat beach, the peninsula's topography and attractions make it perfect for a lengthy exploration by bicycle, though you're allowed to drive your car on the beach as well. If you really want to get away from it all, visit Willapa Bay's Long Island (accessible only by boat) and its 274-acre old-growth cedar grove, part of the **WILLAPA NATIONAL WILDLIFE REFUGE** (10 miles north of Seaview on Hwy 101; 360/484-3482). Campsites are available; check at the refuge's headquarters.

Chinook

Fishing has always loomed large in Chinook, located just south of the peninsula on US Highway 101. Occupants of the original Chinook (a few miles away) were Natives who fished the Columbia River until European diseases decimated the population. Late in the 1800s, the superefficient salmon traps of Chinook's white residents made the town the richest per capita in the United States until the traps were outlawed. The town is still a major Southwest Washington fishing center, and boasts thousands of feet of beautiful riverfront. **THE SANCTUARY** (794 Hwy 101; 360/777-8380, reservations recommended), a former Methodist church, serves delicious, eclectic dinners Wednesday through Saturday that take advantage of the local bounty.

On nearby Scarborough Hill, **FORT COLUMBIA STATE PARK** (2 miles southeast of Chinook on Hwy 101; 360/777-8221; open daily, mid-May–Sept) hosts a collection of restored turn-of-the-20th-century wooden buildings that once housed soldiers guarding the river mouth. The former commander's house is now a military museum; nearby is the youth hostel. For a fun getaway, rent the fully furnished Steward's House (two bedrooms) or Scarborough House (five bedrooms); advance reservation required (800/360-4240).

Ilwaco

Despite the vagaries of the salmon fishery in recent years, Ilwaco, the first town on the Long Beach Peninsula, is still the center of **CHARTER FISHING** on the lower Columbia River. Two popular sport-fishing operators, both located at the port docks, are **A COHO CHARTERS** (237 Howerton Wy SE; 360/642-3333) and **SEA BREEZE CHARTERS** (185 Howerton Wy SE; 360/642-2300). Many charter operators also offer eco-tours. The **ILWACO HERITAGE MUSEUM** (115 SE Lake St; 360/642-3446) does a wonderful job illuminating the area's history, with exhibits of Native American artifacts, cranberry agriculture, logging, fishing, and more. The old **ILWACO RAILROAD DEPOT,** which linked the Long Beach Peninsula's "Clamshell Railway" with steamers out of Astoria, has been incorporated into the museum.

Nearby **FORT CANBY STATE PARK** (2½ miles south of Ilwaco off Hwy 101; 360/642-3078 or 800/233-0321) is a hugely popular attraction (reserve camping spots well in advance for summer stays), with 2,000 acres stretching from the picturesque lighthouse at North Head to Cape Disappointment's equally stately lighthouse at the Columbia's mouth. Hiking trails take you to the shore sentinels, as well as the 2-mile-long North Jetty and Beard's Hollow beach. Open all year, the park even has yurts available for comfortable winter stays. It's also home to the **LEWIS AND CLARK INTERPRETIVE CENTER** (360/642-3029), offering visitors a fresh and vivid retelling of the explorers' monumental journey that began in St. Louis and ended on the Pacific shore. Fascinating displays cover the history of Cape Disappointment, construction of the **CAPE DISAPPOINTMENT LIGHTHOUSE**, local shipwrecks, and the early Coast Guard. The site boasts a stirring view of the mouth of the Columbia. High winds can occasionally close the center, otherwise open daily.

LODGINGS

Inn at Ilwaco / ★

120 WILLIAMS ST NE, ILWACO; 360/642-8686 Located on a quiet, dead-end street overlooking town, this B&B is housed in the 1928 former Ilwaco Presbyterian Church. Full breakfast is served in what was the sanctuary, transformed into a spacious dining area backed by a fireplace. All nine guest units—once Sunday-school classrooms and a nursery—have private baths and are decorated in shades of blue and white, with plush bedding, lacy curtains, and handsome furnishings. The two-room Admiral Suite has a massive captain's bed from the Hamburg-American ship line, as well as a fireplace and a small refrigerator. A roomy parlor has myriad comfy chairs and couches, watercolor seascapes, sea charts, and a ship's binnacle. Owner Ed Bussone says "well-behaved, under-control children are OK." *$$; MC, V; checks OK; www.longbeachlodging.com; off Spruce St E.*

Seaview

Touted as an ocean retreat for Portlanders early in the 20th century, Seaview now enjoys a legacy of older, stately beach homes, a pretty beachfront, and some of the best dining and lodging on the peninsula. Nearly every road headed west reaches the ocean, and you can park your car and stroll the dunes. You can also stroll the arts scene: **CHARLES MULVEY GALLERY** (46th Pl and "L" St; 360/642-2189) is owned by the noted watercolorist; **CAMPICHE STUDIOS** (504 Pacific Ave S; 360/642-2264) features watercolors, sculptures, and photography.

RESTAURANTS

The 42nd Street Cafe / ★★☆

4201 PACIFIC HWY, SEAVIEW; 360/642-2323 Locals going out for a nice dinner usually head to the 42nd Street Cafe, saving the tonier Shoalwater (see review) down the street for special occasions. The menu is mostly Americana, with steaks, poultry, and fresh seafood predominating, but includes pastas as well, with some unusual sauces (port wine and cranberry, for example). A house salad with honey–celery seed dressing makes a great starter. *$$; MC, V; checks OK; breakfast, lunch, dinner every day; beer and wine; reservations not necessary; at 42nd St.* &

The Heron and Beaver Pub / ★

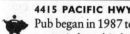 **4415 PACIFIC HWY, SEAVIEW; 360/642-4142** The tiny Heron and Beaver Pub began in 1987 to serve as a bar to its big brother across the hall, the Shoalwater (whose kitchen it shares; see review), while offering up simple snacks. Slowly, though, the pub (with 30 beers, a full bar, and more than 400 wines) began to poach items off the Shoalwater's menu (panfried Dungeness crab and shrimp cakes, Cajun-style "blackened" Willapa Bay oysters, to name a couple of yummy choices) until it became a dining destination for lunch or a light dinner in its own right. A deck overlooks the Victorian gardens of the Shelburne Inn (the historic hotel whose space the pub shares; see review), so you can enjoy your oyster shooters and wild mushroom–goat cheese lasagne outside on balmy days. *$$; AE, DC, MC, V; checks OK; lunch Mon–Sat, dinner every day, brunch Sun; full bar; reservations not accepted; www.shoalwater.com/pub.html; at N 45th St.* &

The Shoalwater / ★★★

4415 PACIFIC HWY, SEAVIEW; 360/642-4142 This is one of the splendid mainstays of Northwest cuisine. Native ingredients such as fresh Willapa Bay oysters, salmon, wild mushrooms, and Dungeness crab are employed in artful meals that fill a seafood-heavy menu. A fabulous selection of wines from the Northwest and beyond is available, pulled from a lovely antique wine closet. The Northwest bouillabaisse is heavenly, combining shellfish, crustaceans, and fresh fish in a saffron-infused fish broth and served with *rouille* (garlic mayonnaise) and garlic crostini. The roast herb-encrusted duck breast, served with a Marionberry-cranberry and truffle butter sauce on a bed of couscous, is also excellent. A special winter treat is the Shoalwater's popular annual winemakers' dinner series, featuring seven-course meals designed around wines from a visiting winemaker; reserve well in advance. *$$$; AE, DC, MC, V; checks OK; lunch, dinner every day, brunch Sun; full bar; reservations recommended; www.shoalwater.com; at N 45th St.* &

LODGINGS

The Shelburne Inn / ★★★

4415 PACIFIC HWY S, SEAVIEW; 360/642-2442 Well-worn, warm, and filled with antiques and friendly charm, the Shelburne Inn is listed in the National Register of Historic Places, and in the hearts of many a romantic traveler. The 1896 inn has 15 rooms filled with lovely quilt-covered four-poster beds, stained-glass windows, hand-braided rugs, and other Victorian furnishings. All have private baths, and many have decks. Owners David Campiche and Laurie Anderson prepare memorable breakfasts with fresh seasonal ingredients (including herbs from the Victorian garden). Possible treats: razor-clam cakes, scrambled eggs with smoked salmon and Gruyère cheese, and oysters prepared any number of ways—not to mention pastries. Lunch and dinner are available downstairs at the Shoalwater restaurant or Heron and Beaver Pub (under separate ownership; see reviews). Busy Highway 103 is right out front—request a west-facing room for maximum quiet. Best-value rooms are on the third floor, if you're up for the stairs. $$$; AE, MC, V; checks OK; www.theshelburneinn.com; at N 45th St. &

Long Beach

Long Beach is the center of peninsula tourist activity and host to throngs of summer visitors. You'll find the largest collection of gift shops, amusement arcades, and other attractions here, as well as the beach boardwalk—a pedestrian-only half-mile stroll with night lighting (wheelchairs and baby-strollers welcome, too).

A big draw is August's **INTERNATIONAL KITE FESTIVAL**. Visit the **LONG BEACH WORLD KITE MUSEUM AND HALL OF FAME** (112 3rd St NW; 360/642-4020), or get in on the fun yourself by shopping at **LONG BEACH KITES** (104 Pacific Ave N; 360/642-2202) or **OCEAN KITES** (511 Pacific Ave S; 360/642-2229). For a tastier museum, check out the **CRANBERRY MUSEUM AND GIFT SHOP** (Pioneer Rd W and Washington St N; 360/642-3638; Wed–Sun Apr–Dec); call ahead to arrange a tour of the bogs. **ANNA LENA'S PANTRY** (111 Bolstad Ave; 360/642-8585) has more than 30 gourmet cranberry products, including cranberry fudge, but is a quilters' destination too, with a huge assortment of supplies and a schedule of quilting retreats. **MILTON YORK CANDY COMPANY** (107 S Pacific St; 360/642-2352) has been around since 1882, and offers treats and simple meals.

No visit to the peninsula would be complete without a visit to **MARSH'S FREE MUSEUM** (409 S Pacific Ave; 360/642-2188). In addition to an enormous selection of knickknacks for sale, Marsh's has many antique coin-operated arcade machines and music boxes, as well as the museum's star attraction, Jake the Alligator Man. The mummified half-man, half-alligator has inspired a line of "Believe It Or Not"–style sportswear.

RESTAURANTS

Las Maracas / ★

601 S PACIFIC AVE, LONG BEACH; 360/642-8000 North of the border, you'll find that the glitzier the Mexican restaurant, the farther the food is from Mexico. The no-frills trappings of inexpensive Las Maracas is a good indicator of its authenticity. A huge menu offers such *platos típicos* as *pollo en adobo* (spicy chicken marinated with green peppers and onions), carne asada (slices of skirt steak braised over charcoal, served with guacamole), burritos, enchiladas, and a number of dishes that take advantage of the area's fresh seafood (the *camarones al mojo de ajo* are great—prawns sautéed with mushrooms in wine, butter, and garlic). In true Mexican style, most dishes are not picante—if you want the hot stuff, dab on delicious homemade salsa. Almost everything at Las Maracas is made from scratch in the restaurant's kitchen—even the tortilla chips. A full bar serves potent drinks with words like *loco* in their names. *$; AE, DC, MC, V; checks OK; lunch, dinner every day; full bar; reservations not accepted; on Hwy 103.*

LODGINGS

Boreas Bed & Breakfast / ★★

607 NORTH BLVD, LONG BEACH; 360/642-8069 Owners Susie Goldsmith and Bill Verner have polished their inn into a romantic gem. Each of five guest rooms in the 1920s beach house has a private bath, including the Dunes Suite with its Impressionist wall mural and private Jacuzzi. The living room, with large windows facing the ocean, is graced with a marble fireplace and baby grand piano. Masterful work is apparent in the delicious breakfasts. Possibilities include omelets filled with wild mushrooms and smoked salmon, ginger pancakes with lime sauce, French toast topped with Grand Marnier and almonds, and braised bananas, with organic coffee, hot chocolate, or one of dozens of teas. *$$; AE, DC, MC, V; checks OK; boreas@boreasinn.com; www.boreasinn.com; 1 block west of Hwy 103.*

Ocean Park

Ocean Park was once a Methodist retreat, which offered summers free of vice. But the senses are in for a bigger shock nowadays—at least during the June **GARLIC FESTIVAL**, which features a Northwest Wine Tasting and Brew Garden. Call the Ocean Park Chamber of Commerce (800/451-2542) for current dates.

The **WIEGARDT WATERCOLORS GALLERY** (2607 Bay Ave; 360/665-5976) displays Eric Wiegardt seascapes in a restored Victorian house. Nearby, the **SHOALWATER COVE GALLERY** (25712 Sandridge Rd; 360/665-4382) exhibits nature scenes in soft pastels. **JACK'S COUNTRY STORE** (Hwy 103 and Bay Ave; 360/665-4989) dates from 1885 and can supply almost every need—even some you didn't know you had.

LODGINGS

Caswell's on the Bay Bed & Breakfast / ★★★

25204 SANDRIDGE RD, OCEAN PARK; 360/665-6535 OR 888-553-2319 Take the long driveway off quiet Sandridge Road and prepare to be stunned by the gleaming yellow neo-Victorian mansion that sits at its foot, surrounded by rhododendrons. Inside you'll find five spacious rooms furnished in antiques (each with private bath), a large parlor offering an amazing panorama of Willapa Bay and distant mountains, a library, and a sunroom complete with spyglass, where you'll enjoy afternoon tea with cookies and sweets (feast on a full breakfast in the morning). This B&B on 3 acres next to the bay is earning a reputation as possibly the most romantic spot on the peninsula; you're close to the attractions, but far from traffic and noise. The premium Terrace Suite has a view of Willapa Bay, a balcony, and a lovely sitting room. No children. *$$$; MC, V; checks OK; www.caswellsinn.com; ½ mile south of Bay Ave–Sandridge Rd intersection.*

Shakti Cove Cottages / ★

ON 253RD PL, OCEAN PARK; 360/665-4000 Though the Shakti Cove Cottages are just off Highway 103, you'll feel miles from the outside world. Ten small cedar-shingled cabins stand in a semicircle around a gentle green, each funky-cozy, with its own carport, bath, and kitchen facilities. Amble a quarter mile down a private gravel road to the beach, likely passing black-tailed deer grabbing a meal along the way. Shakti Cove is popular with gays and lesbians, as well as travelers with dogs (even large ones), but "covekeepers" Celia and Liz Cavalli make all visitors feel at home. *$$; MC, V; checks OK; info@shakticove.com; www.shakti cove.com; 1 block west of Pacific Hwy 103.*

Nahcotta

A healthy population of seagulls attests to Nahcotta's tenure as a center for oysters. Several stands and storefronts purvey the tasty bivalves, including **JOLLY ROGER SEAFOODS** (273rd and Sandridge Rd, on old Nahcotta dock; 360/665-4111). On the same pier you can visit the **WILLAPA BAY INTERPRETIVE CENTER** (273rd and Sandridge Rd, next to the Ark restaurant; 360/665-4547; summer weekends) to learn the history of the 150-year-old oyster industry.

RESTAURANTS

The Ark / ★★☆

273RD AND SANDRIDGE RD, NAHCOTTA; 360/665-4133 The Ark has garnered rave reviews for years, and even got a thumbs up from former First Diner, President Bill Clinton. Owners Nanci Main and Jimella Lucas have co-authored several cookbooks and take advantage of the bounty of fresh ingredients nearby: oysters (lightly breaded and panfried), salmon, sturgeon, wild blackberries, Oregon blue cheese, and more. The season may determine your choices, but if possible, try calamari dijonnaise, oysters Italian, or chicken scallops and tarragon. Save room for Main's dessert pastries, then stretch with a walk through the Ark's vegetable and herb gardens. *$$$; AE, MC, V; checks OK; dinner Tues–Sun (Thurs–Sun in winter), brunch Sun; full bar; reservations recommended; www.arkrestaurant. com; on old Nahcotta dock, next to oyster fleet.*

Oysterville

Oysterville is a picture postcard of a tiny 19th-century sea town, and its double row of wooden houses with picket fences is listed as a Historic District with the National Register. The photogenic 1892 Baptist church no longer holds services but is open for visitors.

OYSTERVILLE SEA FARMS (1st and Clark; 360/665-6585 or 800/CRAN-BERRY) is the sole industry here, with a retail store that sells a variety of fresh and vacuum-packed oysters in flavors ranging from smoked to habanero, as well as Anna Lena preserves, dried fruits, baking mixes, and more.

LEADBETTER POINT STATE PARK (3 miles north, on Stackpole Rd) is a large wildlife refuge that attracts thousands of birds. Miles of hiking trails lead to interpretive signs and nearly untouched beaches along Willapa Bay; no camping.

Longview

Longview serves as a handy crossroads for travelers headed north to Seattle, south to Portland, or west to the Long Beach Peninsula. For a relaxing walk, stroll through the park surrounding Lake Sacajawea.

RESTAURANTS

Country Village Nutrition Shoppe and Cafe

711 VANDERCOOK WY, LONGVIEW; 360/425-8100 A good place to pick up organic foods before heading off to ocean beaches or Mount St. Helens, this is also a great stop for a tasty, filling, and inexpensive lunch. The special pairs a cup of homemade soup with a tender mixed green salad or a hearty half sandwich. Scared of "healthy" food? Opt for a baked potato stuffed with cheese and bacon. *$; DIS, MC, V; checks OK; lunch Mon–Sat; no alcohol; reservations not accepted; just off Washington Wy.* &

Mount St. Helens National Volcanic Monument

The May 18, 1980, explosion of Mount St. Helens's volcanic fury created a drastically changed landscape, as well as an attraction for the attention of hundreds of scientists and thousands of visitors from around the world. While the region can be explored via Randle in the north (on US Hwy 12) or Cougar in the south (off Hwy 503), most visitors opt to travel Highway 504, also known as **SPIRIT LAKE MEMORIAL HIGHWAY,** which heads east from Interstate 5 at Castle Rock. Five excellent visitor centers dot its length, and the route ends with a bird's-eye view of the volcano's still-steaming crater at **JOHNSTON RIDGE OBSERVATORY** (mile 52; 360/274-2151). A fee ($8 per person) lets you visit the three centers run by the U.S. Forest Service (www.fs.fed.us/gpnf/mshnvm), including Johnston Ridge. The **HOFFSTADT BLUFF REST AREA AND VIEWPOINT** (run by Cowlitz County) and the **WEYERHAEUSER FOREST LEARNING CENTER** (run by Weyerhaeuser) are free to visit.

Castle Rock

This small town at the intersection of Highway 504 and Interstate 5 is a gateway to Mount St. Helens. **THE CINEDOME THEATER** (1238 Mount St. Helens Wy NE/Hwy 504; 360/274-9844) boasts that "Mount St. Helens erupts here every 45 minutes!" and shows the Omnimax film *The Eruption of Mount St. Helens* every day (a great introduction to your mountain tour). The theater also shows first-run theatrical movies in the evening, employing the three-story, 55-foot screen and its seat-rumbling sound system). Plenty of souvenirs—from kitschy ash creations to valuable interpretive guides—can be found in town.

MOUNT ST. HELENS AND THE
COLUMBIA GORGE THREE-DAY TOUR

DAY ONE: Spend the day touring **MOUNT ST. HELENS.** You won't want to miss any of the five visitor centers spaced along the 50-mile drive, which offer various views of the landscape and pieces of the region's development since the blast more than 20 years ago. Once you've had your fill of volcanic activity, seismographs, and more, head south on Interstate 5 to Vancouver to check in at the **HEATHMAN LODGE.** Enjoy dinner at the **CHART HOUSE** (make reservations in advance), then return to the Heathman to sip a glass of wine by the stone fireplace in the lobby before bed.

DAY TWO: Have a tasty breakfast at **HUDSON'S BAR & GRILL,** then explore historic Vancouver—visit the re-created **FORT VANCOUVER,** walk along the riverfront and visit **OLD APPLE TREE PARK,** then explore **OFFICERS ROW,** where you have lunch at **SHELDON'S CAFE** at the Grant House. Afterward head east on Highway 14 and take in the magnificent scenery along the **COLUMBIA RIVER GORGE.** Stop for an authentic Mexican dinner at **FIDEL'S** in Bingen, then turn north onto Highway 141 for the short drive to the **INN OF THE WHITE SALMON** for the night.

DAY THREE: After a tremendous breakfast at the inn, you're ready to enjoy the gorge. If you're feeling adventurous, how about a **RAFTING TRIP** down the White Salmon River? If you prefer something calmer, opt for a picnic lunch at **WIND RIVER CELLARS.** Then drive back down to Highway 14 and head east to the **MARYHILL MUSEUM OF ART,** where you spend the afternoon investigating art treasures. A little farther down the road you'll find the **STONEHENGE REPLICA** (see "Art Treasures of the Columbia Gorge" in this chapter). Pack a dinner and enjoy it while you watch the sun set in the Columbia River Gorge. Continue east and then north to your night's lodging in Goldendale at **TIMBERFRAME COUNTRY INN B&B.**

LODGINGS

Blue Heron Inn / ★

2846 SPIRIT LAKE HWY, CASTLE ROCK; 360/274-9595 The Blue Heron Inn makes a comfy base of operations from which to explore Mount St. Helens. Built in 1996 by John and Jeanne Robards, the inn is a lodge-style log-and-stone retreat located next to Seaquest State Park, just across from the U.S. Forest Service Mount St. Helens Visitors Center. Each of the six rooms (and the Jacuzzi Suite) has a private bath, as well as a balcony with marvelous views of the volcano and Silver Lake. Included is a substantial breakfast served family style, as well as a 7pm dinner served with local wines. *$$$$; MC, V; checks OK; www.blueheroninn.com; Hwy 504 about 5 miles east of I-5 and just west of U.S. Forest Service Mount St. Helens Visitors Center.* &

Vancouver

One of the oldest white settlements in the Pacific Northwest, Vancouver is looking at a bright future, as a rapidly growing high-tech industry draws people to the area (the population grew half-again during the 1990s). The British Hudson's Bay Company ensconced itself in **FORT VANCOUVER** (1501 E Evergreen Blvd; 360/696-7655) in the early 19th century, until the territory passed to the United States, when the fort became an American military base. The stockade wall and some of the buildings of the fort have been reconstructed, and the visitor center features a museum and heirloom garden.

Another gem of Vancouver's large Central Park area is **OFFICERS ROW** (E Evergreen Blvd, between I-5 and E Reserve St), a leafy street of restored homes where officers billeted in bygone days; the Heritage Trust of Clark County (360/737-6066) gives tours. Grant House on Officers Row houses the **FOLK ART CENTER** (1101 Officers Row; 360/694-5252), a tribute to regional art. The **CLARK COUNTY HISTORICAL MUSEUM** (1511 Main St; 360/695-4681) reproduces pioneer stores and businesses. **COVINGTON HOUSE** (4201 Main St; 360/695-6750) is the oldest log house (1846) in the state; call to make tour arrangements.

A lovely 4-mile waterfront walk along Columbia Way begins just under the Interstate 5 bridge (next to the Red Lion Inn at the Quay), and passes the Northwest's oldest apple tree. Saturday's **VANCOUVER FARMERS MARKET** (Apr–Oct) takes up several blocks at the south end of Main Street with local produce, flowers, and food vendors. The **WATER RESOURCES CENTER** (4600 SE Columbia Wy; 360/696-8478) has exhibits and a superb view of the Columbia River, at the east end of Columbia Way on the edge of Marine Park.

RIDGEFIELD NATIONAL WILDLIFE REFUGE (3 miles west of I-5, exit 14; 360/887-3883) has nature trails leading to the bird refuge on the lowlands of the Columbia River. **MOULTON FALLS** (NW Lucia Falls Rd near County Rd 16; 360/696-8171) has a three-story-high arched bridge spanning the East Fork of the Lewis River, a 387-acre park, and two waterfalls. It's 2 miles south of Yacolt and 9 miles east of Battle Ground.

RESTAURANTS

Beaches Restaurant & Bar / ★

1919 SE COLUMBIA RIVER DR, VANCOUVER; 360/699-1592 A boisterous, bustling contemporary restaurant with a tremendous view of the Columbia, Beaches offers a panoply of whole-meal salads, burgers, steaks, ribs, seafood, and pastas in an effort to please the business crowd as well as families—and succeeds. Daily fresh fish specials always shine, and the cioppino is a great starter for seafood lovers. The bar keeps rollicking after the kitchen closes at 10pm (9pm Sun–Mon). *$$; AE, MC, V; local checks only; lunch, dinner every day; full bar; reservations not necessary; exit 1A off Hwy 14.* &

Chart House / ★★☆

101 E COLUMBIA WY, VANCOUVER; 360/693-9211 Chart House restaurants comprise a small national chain of fine restaurants, more than half of which occupy historical sites with water views. Vancouver's Chart House resides in a former Coast Guard station overhanging the Columbia. Though the view is fantastic, the food is more than its equal. Fresh seafood and aged beef dominate the menu; the grilled ahi tuna chop with black beans and mango relish is a knockout, while the herbed prime rib with creamed horseradish and Kona onions melts in your mouth. If you think you're up for it, order dessert when you order your dinner—the Chocolate Lava Cake (with a molten center of Godiva chocolate liqueur, vanilla ice cream, and warm chocolate sauce) takes 30 minutes to prepare. *$$–$$$; AE, DC, DIS, MC, V; no checks; lunch Mon–Fri, dinner every day; full bar; reservations recommended; just south of downtown.* &

Hudson's Bar & Grill / ★★☆

7805 GREENWOOD DR (HEATHMAN LODGE), VANCOUVER; 360/816-6100 A tremendous Pacific Northwest take on American comfort food, combined with the rich woods and native basalt of its rustic decor, make Hudson's Bar & Grill a destination for a soul-warming meal. Breakfasts and lunches are excellent, but dinner is where Hudson's shines. Try venison wrapped with apple bacon served with sweet-potato hash and candied shallots; the poached salmon fillet with acorn squash, shiitake mushrooms, and lemon chile butter; or the grilled pork medallions on black-bean cake with poblano rings and salsa verde. Fresh seasonal ingredients, plus breads and pastries baked daily, complement a modest selection of Northwest wines. *$$–$$$; AE, DC, DIS, MC, V; checks OK; breakfast, lunch, dinner every day; full bar; reservations not necessary; near Thurston Wy exit off Hwy 500.* &

Sheldon's Cafe at the Grant House / ★★

1101 OFFICERS ROW, VANCOUVER; 360/699-1213 In Vancouver's historic Officers Row, Sheldon's Cafe can be the culinary high point of a day's wander though the park or a summer evening stroll. Using the lower floor of a house named for Ulysses S. Grant (once a quartermaster at Fort Vancouver), Sheldon's shares space with a folk art museum. American cuisine is the emphasis, with some nice Northwest touches—Willapa Bay oysters and other fresh seafoods are especially good. The menu has plenty of other temptations among its salads, pastas, quiches, game birds, and house-smoked meats. *$$; MC, V; checks OK; lunch, dinner Tues–Sat; beer and wine; reservations recommended; midtown Vancouver, off Evergreen Blvd.*

Thai Orchid / ★★

1004 WASHINGTON ST, VANCOUVER; 360/695-7786 Using fresh, healthy ingredients (and no hydrogenated oils), Thai Orchid has garnered a slew of awards. The huge selection of curried, stir-fried, seafood, rice, and specialty dishes may require the helpful staff's assistance on choices. For both its name and its flavor, you can't go wrong with the Evil Jungle Prince curry (your choice of vegetables, beef, chicken, or pork on a bed of steamed cabbage and broccoli, all topped with curry sauce). Spicy dishes are marked on the menu and can be ordered to suit your courage. *$$; AE, DIS, MC, V; checks OK; lunch, dinner every day; full bar; reservations not necessary; www.thaiorchidrestaurant.com; at Evergreen Blvd.* &

LODGINGS

Heathman Lodge / ★★☆

7801 GREENWOOD DR, VANCOUVER; 360/254-3100 OR 888/475-3100 As you walk through the massive arched timber portico of the Heathman Lodge, you'll immediately forget you're in the 'burbs, a stone's throw away from the Vancouver Mall. You might think instead—as you take in peeled-log balconies draped with Pendleton blankets, a massive basalt gas fireplace, and other details—that you're in a luxurious high-mountain retreat. The Heathman Lodge features rooms that combine rustic furnishings with modern necessities—two-line phones, data ports, refrigerators, microwaves, coffeemakers, and ironing boards, as well as an indoor pool and fitness center downstairs. Suites offer wet bars, Jacuzzis, and gas fireplaces. With a great restaurant just off the lodge's lobby (Hudson's Bar & Grill; see review), you can stay inside over a rainy weekend and never break the illusion that you're tucked away in an alpine haven. *$$–$$$; AE, DC, DIS, MC, V; checks OK; www.heath manlodge.com; near Thurston Wy exit off Hwy 500.* ⌖

Mount Adams and the Columbia River Gorge

The **COLUMBIA GORGE INTERPRETIVE CENTER** (990 SW Rock Creek Dr, Stevenson; 509/427-8211 or 800/991-2338), just west of Stevenson, spins an evocative tale of the region's natural and cultural history, with a nine-projector slide show that re-creates the gorge's cataclysmic formation; plus exhibits on timber, fur trading, hydroelectric power, and more.

Mount Adams and its surrounding area, 30 miles north of the Columbia, offer natural splendor largely overlooked by visitors, who seldom venture in from the gorge. Besides climbing to the summit of the 12,276-foot mountain—greater in mass than any of the five other major volcanic peaks in the Northwest—hikers and skiers can explore miles of wilderness trails in the **MOUNT ADAMS WILDERNESS AREA** and **GIFFORD PINCHOT NATIONAL FOREST**. Contact the Mount Adams Ranger Station (2455 Hwy 141; 509/395-3400) in Trout Lake to register for ascents and area activities.

Stevenson

A small town blessed by scenery, Stevenson lies within the beginnings of the **GORGE SCENIC HIGHWAY** (Hwy 14) and marks the unofficial boundary of windsurfing country.

LODGINGS

Skamania Lodge / ★★

1131 SKAMANIA LODGE WY, STEVENSON; 509/427-7700 OR 800/221-7117 Skamania Lodge was designed to resemble a national park lodge, and it does, with lots of wood and stone, Mission-style furniture, Native American–style rugs, and beautiful views from its perch above the Columbia River Gorge. The differences are an award-winning 18-hole golf course, an indoor fitness center, a pool, saunas, and a spa. If you don't golf, opt to use one of two tennis courts, or rent a bike and follow the map of trails. A formal dining room offers fine cuisine, and the

River Rock Lounge serves lunch, appetizers, and light dinners. The lodge is huge—195 rooms, including 34 deluxe rooms with fireplaces, and 5 suites—and, with the two-state Columbia River Gorge Commission keeping a tight rein on regional construction, is likely to remain unique for the foreseeable future. *$$$; AE, DC, MC, V; checks OK; www.dolce.com/skamania/dolce_skamania.html; turn north onto Rock Creek Dr just west of Stevenson.*

Carson

"Funky" is the word most often used to describe **CARSON MINERAL HOT SPRINGS** (Hot Springs and St. Martin Ave; 509/427-8292). This historic resort has been around since 1897, and while the sheets have been changed since then, not much else has. Reserve ahead for its renowned old-style "treatment"—a (non-coed) hot mineral bath, followed by a rest while swathed in towels and blankets, which you can follow with a professional massage. If you decide you want to stay at this rustic, well-worn resort, TV- and phone-free rooms and cabins are available, as well as a restaurant and an 18-hole golf course.

White Salmon

Perched above the Columbia River with lovely views of Mount Hood and Mount Adams, White Salmon is a great base from which to enjoy the gorge. The **WHITE SALMON RIVER**, with its Class II–IV rapids, serene pools, and verdant canyon, is one of the state's most popular **RAFTING** destinations, April through October. Two of the best outfitters are **PHIL'S WHITE WATER ADVENTURES** (38 Northwestern Lake Rd; 509/493-2641 or 800/366-2004; www.gorge.net/philswwa) and **AAA RAFTING** (860 Hwy 141; 509/493-2511 or 800/866-7238). **RAY KLEBBA'S WHITE SALMON BOAT WORKS** (105 Jewett Blvd; 509/493-4749) can teach you how to make your own woodstrip-construction sea kayak or canoe; buy a kit to take home, or have the skilled crafters build one for you. **NORTHWESTERN LAKE STABLES** (126 Little Buck Creek Rd; 509/493-4965) offers backcountry horseback-riding packages ranging from one-hour rides to overnight adventures.

If a less strenuous outing is in order, visit **WIND RIVER CELLARS** (196 Spring Creek Rd; 509/493-2324). Enjoy complimentary sips in a tasting room with a stunning view of Mount Hood, and bring lunch to enjoy in the pretty grape-arbor picnic area.

RESTAURANTS

Fidel's

120 E STUBEN ST, BINGEN; 509/493-1017 Lively Mexican music sets the mood at Fidel's in nearby Bingen, so why not start with an enormous margarita to go with the salsa and tortilla chips fresh from the fryer? The menu offers carne asada, chile verde, chile colorado, and omelets machaca (with shredded beef, chicken, or pork). Portions are generous (often big enough for two), and the chile relleno—encased in a thick layer of egg whites so it resembles a big pillow—is good stuff. *$; MC, V; checks OK; lunch, dinner every day (call ahead in winter); full bar; reservations not accepted; 1 mile east of Hood River toll bridge.*

LODGINGS

Inn of the White Salmon / ★★

172 W JEWETT BLVD, WHITE SALMON; 509/493-2335 OR 800/972-5226 Janet Holen, who, with her husband, Roger, owns the Inn of the White Salmon, rightly says their inn offers the privacy of a hotel with the comfort of a B&B. This 1937-vintage jewel is a standout—each room has a large, comfy antique bed, as well as private bath, phone, cable TV, and air-conditioning; several are two-room suites. Just down the hall is a relaxing parlor where you can read or listen to music, or take a dip in the hot tub at the end of the hall. Breakfast serves up a real groaning board: 20 kinds of pastries and breads, juice, tea and coffee, and your choice among entrees such as Italian or artichoke frittatas, Hungarian *flauf,* quiche, and more. Fido can stay for a small extra fee. *$$; MC, V; checks OK; innkeeper@gorge.net; www.inn ofthewhitesalmon.com; Hwy 141, 1½ miles north of Hwy 14.*

Trout Lake

Trout Lake, about 25 miles north of the gorge on Highway 141, follows the White Salmon River toward its mountain source. Volcanic activity long ago left the Mount Adams area honeycombed with caves and lava tubes, including the **ICE CAVES** (509/395-3400) near Trout Lake, with stalactites and stalagmites formed by dripping ice. Southwest of Trout Lake is **BIG LAVA BED** (509/395-3400), a 12,500-acre lava field filled with cracks, crevasses, rock piles, and unusual lava formations. Late summer ripens the wild huckleberries growing in abundance in the nearby **INDIAN HEAVEN WILDERNESS AREA.**

LODGINGS

Serenity's Village / ★

MILE 23, HWY 141, TROUT LAKE; 509/395-2500 OR 800/276-7993 These four chalet-style cabins set among the firs and pines are a good base for exploring the Trout Lake valley below Mount Adams. All are tastefully finished, warmed by gas fireplaces (or cooled by air-conditioning), and equipped with basic kitchen facilities, plus outdoor barbecues. Two larger units have lofts and Jacuzzis, but smaller units are set farther back from the highway. A TV and VCR can be requested. Kids are OK, but not pets. *$$; MC, V; checks OK; www.gorge. net/serenitys; 23 miles north of White Salmon.* &

Glenwood

LODGINGS

Flying L Ranch / ★

25 FLYING L LN, GLENWOOD; 509/364-3488 OR 888/MT-ADAMS If you never went to camp as a kid, the 100-acre Flying L Ranch gives you the chance. Poised at the foot of Mount Adams, the ranch has trails for exploring on foot in summer or on skis in winter. Accommodations are rustic but comfortable. You have three options: five rooms in the main lodge house (some with their own fireplaces); five rooms in the Guest House (with a small shared kitchen); and cabins

ART TREASURES OF THE COLUMBIA GORGE

Wealthy eccentric Sam Hill left an indelible mark on the Columbia River Gorge. With dreams of establishing a Quaker agricultural town on the shores of the river early in the 20th century, Hill started construction on his own house, named Maryhill. After his land company failed and his visions of a utopian community died, Hill decided to make the isolated mansion perched on a lonely bluff into a museum.

Today the **MARYHILL MUSEUM OF ART** (35 Maryhill Museum Dr, Goldendale; 509/773-3733; www.maryhillmuseum.org; Mar–Nov) houses an eclectic mix of collections—Native American artifacts, European paintings, American Classical Realist canvases, the royal regalia of Hill's good friend Queen Marie of Romania, the Théâtre de la Mode French fashion mannequins, and, perhaps the greatest treasure, a large group of watercolors and sculptures by Auguste Rodin. In addition to other exhibits, the museum also houses the **CAFÉ MARYHILL**, a small deli that serves hot and cold sandwiches, desserts, espresso, and other beverages.

Hill's other monumental legacy in the region is a life-sized replica of England's neolithic **STONEHENGE** (about 2 miles east of the museum). Erroneously informed during World War I that the original Stonehenge was used for pagan sacrifices, Hill built his new version to honor fallen World War I soldiers from Klickitat County and as a memorial against war. Hill, who also built the Peace Arch at the U.S.-Canadian border at Blaine, rests in his crypt on a river bluff not far from his replica. —*Les Campbell*

about 200 feet from the main buildings (each with its own kitchen, woodstove, and electric heat). Everyone has access to the spacious living room with its stone fireplace, piano, stereo, and wonderful view, as well as to the kitchen and pantry in the main house, and the hot tub in the gazebo. Full ranch breakfasts are served in the Cookhouse dining room; lunch and dinner you'll make yourself, or see what you can find in tiny "downtown" Glenwood. *$$; AE, MC, V; checks OK; flyingl@mt adams.com; www.mt-adams.com; east through Glenwood about ½ mile toward Goldendale, turn north and proceed ½ mile to driveway on right.*

Goldendale

Though Goldendale is the seat of Klickitat County, it's not a case of bright lights, big city. This makes it the perfect location for the **GOLDENDALE OBSERVATORY STATE PARK** (602 Observatory Dr; 509/773-3141; goldobs@gorge.net; Wed–Sun in summer, weekends in winter), 1 mile north of Goldendale just off Columbus Avenue. Visitors can look through the 24½-inch telescope (one of the largest in the nation available to the public) or borrow a portable telescope to gaze at skies largely clear of air and light pollution. Lectures, slide shows, and films are also offered. On the way to visit nearby **MARYHILL MUSEUM OF ART** (see "Art Treasures of the Columbia Gorge" in this chapter), stop at the new **MARYHILL WINERY** (877/627-

9445) next door. In addition to a tasting room and deli, the winery plans concerts for its new 2,500-seat amphitheater. Goldendale is 10½ miles north of Highway 14 on US Highway 97.

LODGINGS

Timberframe Country Inn B&B

223 GOLDEN PINE RD, GOLDENDALE; 800/861-8408 The Timberframe is surrounded by ponderosa pines and meadows in the Simcoe Mountains. Each of the two suites has a private entrance, bath, TV, and VCR. The Tree Top room has a sundeck with a spa. B&B owner Dor Creamer provides information on local activities from windsurfing to the Goldendale Observatory and serves a full country breakfast. No smoking, children, or pets. *$$; no credit cards; checks OK; business.gorge. net/timberinn/; Broadway/Hwy 142 exit off Hwy 97.*

SOUTHEAST
WASHINGTON

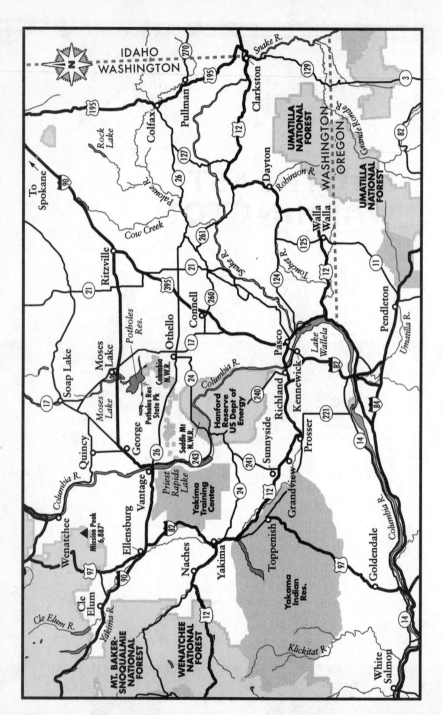

SOUTHEAST WASHINGTON

The central-to-southeast corner of the Evergreen State—from Ellensburg to Pullman—isn't very green, but it's rich in history. Here, rain is unusual, old-growth sagebrush is protected, and agriculture mixes with high-tech, making the region the heart of Washington's wine industry, and the bread basket of the Pacific Northwest.

The Southeast is its own melting pot, with strong influences from Mexican and Native American cultures. Residents are farmers, nuclear scientists, cowboys, college students, entrepreneurs, and good ol' boys. They enjoy a slower, more casual pace than in urban areas.

Of course, each city has bragging points. Ellensburg is famous for its lamb and Labor Day rodeo. Yakima is known for fruit trees, wineries, and outdoor activities. The Tri-Cities claim 300 days of sunshine annually, a Lewis and Clark campsite, and discovery of the 9,200-year-old Kennewick Man bones. (He's not available for public viewing due to government legal wranglings, and the discovery spot is unmarked to prevent vandalism. The best way to see the bones is at a "virtual interpretive center"; www.kennewick-man.com.) Washington State University in Pullman is famous for its Cougar Gold cheese. Walla Walla's resume includes sweet onions, world-class wine, and pioneers.

Appreciating the shrub-steppe landscape might take a conscious effort if you're accustomed to snowcapped mountains, green hills, and humidity. But the earth-toned palette reveals its own majestic geological formations, like the Palouse Falls 198-foot waterfall and Wallula Gap basalt pillars. Out here, spaces are wide-open, the clouds—if there are any—are high above your head, and you feel like you can see a million miles in the clear, dry air.

ACCESS AND INFORMATION

Most people visiting central and Southeast Washington drive. Even if you fly, you'll want to have a car. Numerous highways lead through often sparsely populated country to this dry, sunny corner. Take advantage of rest areas and be sure your gas tank is full. In summer, bring sunblock and a light sweater (for overactive air-conditioners and cool evenings); in winter, a turtleneck and warm, wind-proof jacket will keep you toasty.

INTERSTATE 90 is the most practical route from Puget Sound, connecting at Ellensburg with **INTERSTATE 82**, which leads through the Yakima Valley to the Tri-Cities at the confluence of the Yakima, Snake, and Columbia Rivers. From there, Walla Walla is an easy trip via Interstate 82 and **US HIGHWAY 12**.

From Portland, **INTERSTATE 84**—or the two-lane **HIGHWAY 14** on the Washington side—leads to Eastern Washington. If you're heading to Ellensburg or Yakima, turn north on **US HIGHWAY 97**. If your destination is the Tri-Cities, take Interstate 82/**US HIGHWAY 395**. Note: The Tri-Cities includes Kennewick, Richland, and Pasco, and freeway signs usually name one of those instead of the region's nickname.

The **TRI-CITIES AIRPORT** (3601 N 20th Ave, Pasco; 509/547-6352) is served by Horizon Air, Delta, United Express, and SkyWest. **HORIZON AIR** (800/547-9308;

www.horizonair.com) also serves the region's smaller airports, in Walla Walla, Yakima, and Moses Lake.

Most major **CAR RENTAL** companies operate out of the Tri-Cities Airport. The Pasco train station (535 N 1st Ave) serves **AMTRAK** (509/545-1554 or 800/USA-RAIL; www.amtrak.com) and **GREYHOUND** (800/231-2222). The local public transit company is **BEN FRANKLIN TRANSIT** (509/735-5100). The **TRI-CITIES VISITOR AND CONVENTION BUREAU** (6951 W Grandridge Blvd, Kennewick; 800/254-5824; www.visittri-cities.com) is a good source of information.

Columbia Basin

The Columbia Plateau is a vast tableland that stretches across the center of the state, much of it rich agricultural lands irrigated by the Columbia River Basin. More than 2,000 miles of canals and secondary canals water more than a million acres of fields.

Vantage and George

Situated on a splendid stretch of the Columbia just north of Interstate 90, Vantage doesn't have much food and lodging—but it has incredible scenery. **GINKGO PETRIFIED FOREST STATE PARK** (exit 136 off I-90; 509/856-2700) takes you back to the age of dinosaurs. The interpretive center is open daily in summer, by appointment otherwise. It's a great picnic spot.

The small town of George, Washington, also just off Interstate 90, boasts the naturally terraced **GORGE AMPHITHEATER** (www.barstop.com/gorge) with a westward view over the Columbia Gorge. Big names of all musical genres play here—from Aerosmith and Radiohead to Bob Dylan and the Dave Matthews Band. Arrive early to avoid country-road traffic jams. You can bring food, but packs are searched and alcohol is not allowed. Rest rooms are scarce, and locals have become less tolerant of rowdy concert-goers. Ticketmaster (206/628-0888; www.ticketmaster.com) handles most ticket sales. George is a three-hour drive from Seattle and two hours from Spokane. Nearest accommodations are in Vantage, Ellensburg, Quincy, Ephrata, or Moses Lake. The **GORGE CAMPGROUND** (509/785-2267) charges $35 per vehicle per night.

Ellensburg and Yakima Valleys

The Ellensburg and Kittitas Valleys stretch from the eastern foothills of the Cascades toward the Columbia at Vantage. The region is a key producer of cattle and hay, and it provides a natural gateway along the Yakima River to Yakima and its upper and lower valleys, separated by Union Gap.

The Yakima Valley has more fruit trees than any other county in the United States and is first in production of apples, mint, winter pears, and hops. Not surprisingly, the importance of agriculture and the outdoors overflows into area tourist attractions, including the **AMERICAN HOP MUSEUM** (22 S "B" St; 509/865-4677) in Toppenish, and the **CENTRAL WASHINGTON AGRICULTURAL MUSEUM** (4508 Main St, Fullbright Park; 509/457-8735) in Union Gap. The **YAKIMA VALLEY VISITORS AND CONVENTION BUREAU** (10 N 8th St; 800/221-0751; www.visityakima.com) has information on enjoying the region's natural beauty.

SOUTHEAST WASHINGTON THREE-DAY TOUR

DAY ONE: Grab coffee and some moist coffeecake at Ellensburg's **FOUR WINDS BOOKSTORE AND CAFE** (200 E 4th Ave); then stroll around downtown and get a feeling for the town. Head south on Interstate 82 to Yakima, then stretch your legs with a nature walk on **THE GREENWAY** or window-shop in the North Front Street Historical District. Sample the region's Mexican heritage with lunch at **EL PASTOR.** Drive to Toppenish to see the western art murals, then visit the **YAKAMA NATION CULTURAL HERITAGE CENTER,** one of the few Native American–designed and –operated museums in the state. Get back in the car and head to Sunnyside to **DARIGOLD'S DAIRY FAIR** for a self-guided tour of the cheese factory. Drive over to Grandview and check into the charming **COZY ROSE PRIVATE COUNTRY SUITES.** End the day with a lovely dinner at **DYKSTRA HOUSE RESTAURANT,** a quaint 1914 mansion with scrumptious desserts.

DAY TWO: After a romantic candelit breakfast, dress for the outdoors and head for the Tri-Cities and the roaring Columbia River. Bring sunblock, a hat, sneakers, and a bottle of water, and spend the morning on a Columbia River Journeys **JET-BOAT TOUR** through Hanford Reach. Eat lunch and quaff a Half-life Hefeweizen back in Richland at the **ATOMIC ALE BREWPUB & EATERY;** then hit the **COLUMBIA RIVER EXHIBITION OF HISTORY, SCIENCE & TECHNOLOGY.** Head over to Kennewick to the **PLAYGROUND OF DREAMS** and **FAMILY FISHING POND,** where kids can learn how to catch-and-release. Have dinner at **CEDARS PIER 1** and enjoy the view of the lighted cable bridge. Cross the bridge and end the day at Pasco's **DOUBLETREE HOTEL.**

DAY THREE: After a buffet breakfast at the Doubletree, hit the road for Walla Walla. Your first stop is the **WHITMAN MISSION,** where 19th-century missionaries and Native Americans clashed. Next, visit the historic buildings of the **FORT WALLA WALLA MUSEUM.** Lunch in downtown Walla Walla at chic but casual **GRAPEFIELDS;** then drive through rolling hills to Dayton, home of 88 buildings on the historic register. Check into the **WEINHARD HOTEL** and have dinner at the **WEINHARD CAFE.**

The Yakima Valley's agricultural industry has drawn migrant workers from Mexico, Texas, and California, resulting in a large Hispanic population and a culturally rich community. Over the years, many migrant families have settled in the area, bringing their native culture—and cuisine—with them.

Ellensburg

Once a contender to be Washington's state capital, Ellensburg now is a combination college-cowboy town. The **ELLENSBURG RODEO** (800/637-2444; www.ellensburgrodeo.com), started in 1923, is held at the county fairgrounds on Labor Day weekend: three days of competition, food, games, country-western music, and the Budweiser Clydesdales.

At **CENTRAL WASHINGTON UNIVERSITY** (400 E 8th Ave; 509/963-2244; www.cwu.edu), visit the serene **JAPANESE GARDEN**, designed by Masa Mizuno; and the **CHIMPANZEE AND HUMAN COMMUNICATION INSTITUTE** (14th and "D" Sts; 509/963-2244; www.cwu.edu), where humans and chimps communicate through American Sign Language. Workshops are offered for a fee, March through November.

A surprising amount of art can be found in this small town. The **SARAH SPUR-GEON GALLERY** in CWU's fine-arts complex (Randall Fine Arts Bldg; 509/963-2665) holds regional and national art exhibits year-round. The **CLYMER MUSEUM AND GALLERY** (416 N Pearl St; 509/962-6416) honors John Clymer, Ellensburg's chronicler of the western frontier whose work appeared in the *Saturday Evening Post*. **GALLERY ONE** (408½ N Pearl St; 509/925-2670) sells regional crafts and displays contemporary art.

Because the city is at the foot of the Cascades, it's also a popular base for skiing, rafting, and hiking along the Yakima River. Outdoors aficionados enjoy canoe or raft trips through the Yakima River's deep gorges, or fly-fishing for trout. Call the **ELLENSBURG CHAMBER OF COMMERCE** (801 S Ruby St, Ste 2; 509/925-3137).

RESTAURANTS

The Valley Cafe / ★★☆

105 W 3RD AVE, ELLENSBURG; 509/925-3050 Who would expect to find this gourmet gem in the cowboy town of Ellensburg? The Valley Cafe's atmosphere, cuisine, and wine selection would stand out anywhere. The decor is authentic art deco, with mahogany booths and a circa 1930s back bar. Lunch favorites are sandwiches and salads—the lemon tahini dressing is marvelous—and quiche is a specialty. Dinners are more gourmet, with fresh seafood and Ellensburg lamb. The wine list (including many Washington selections) has won awards from international wine publications. Yummy desserts include crème brûlée and fresh fruit pies. Top off the experience with some of Central Washington's best espresso. *$$; AE, DC, DIS, MC, V; checks OK; lunch, dinner every day; beer and wine; reservations not necessary; near Main St.*

LODGINGS

The Inn at Goose Creek

1720 CANYON RD, ELLENSBURG; 800/533-0822 Ten theme rooms, all with private baths, allow you to pick your mood, from romantic to sports to year-round Christmas. Each features a goose-down comforter, spa tub, TV, and VCR. Innkeepers Gary and Ylwa Mabee serve a continental breakfast. No smoking; no pets. *$$; AE, MC, V; checks OK; www.innatgoosecreek.com; exit 109 off I-90.* ⅙

Yakima

This is the preeminent city of Central Washington and the seat of county government. Hit the **NORTH FRONT STREET HISTORICAL DISTRICT,** including Yakima

Avenue and E "B" Street, where a 22-car train houses restaurants and shops selling everything from women's clothing to stationery and children's toys. The **YAKIMA VALLEY MUSEUM** (2105 Tieton Dr; 509/248-0747) appeals to all ages with recently renovated space with exhibits of pioneer equipment, a children's "underground" museum, a display on Yakima native Supreme Court Justice William O. Douglas, and an old-fashioned soda fountain.

THE GREENWAY (509/453-8280; www.yakimagreenway.org) is a 10-mile-long path along the Yakima and Naches Rivers for bicyclists, walkers, runners, and in-line skaters. The paved path has nature trail offshoots—sometimes allowing a view of bald eagles or blue herons—plus playgrounds. The Greenway hosts an annual summer blues and jazz festival. Entrance points are at Sarg Hubbard Park (111 S 18th St), Sherman Park (E Nob Hill Blvd), Rotary Lake ("R" St), Harlan Landing (west side of I-82 between Selah and Yakima), and the east end of Valley Mall Boulevard.

RESTAURANTS

Birchfield Manor / ★★

2018 BIRCHFIELD RD, YAKIMA; 509/452-1960 Birchfield Manor offers country-French dining, plus lodging. Owners Wil and Sandy Masset have filled the historical home with antiques. Trained in Europe, Wil offers six entrees—perhaps double breast of chicken Florentine or an authentic bouillabaisse—and a good list of Washington wines. The restaurant features a homey atmosphere in a relaxed, pastoral setting, and has a separate cigar room. Five B&B rooms ($99–$200) are above the restaurant, with six more in a separate building. Many have fireplaces or whirlpools, and guests have access to an outdoor pool. Personalized wine tours are available. *$$$; AE, DC, DIS, MC, V; checks OK; dinner Thurs–Sat; beer and wine; reservations not necessary; www.birchfieldmanor.com; 2 miles from Yakima, exit 34 off I-82 onto Hwy 24.* &

Deli De Pasta / ★

7 N FRONT ST, YAKIMA; 509/453-0571 This intimate Italian-influenced cafe is in the North Front Street Historical District. The original owners sold to their daughter and son-in-law, Melissa and Ron Richter, who haven't changed the recipes or the red-and-white classic decor. Though the menu is primarily Italian—with good pastas such as the popular smoked-salmon ravioli—it includes some international recipes. Entrees might feature steak, salmon, or duck. The wine list has many local selections. *$; AE, MC, V; checks OK; dinner Mon–Sat; beer and wine; reservations recommended; ½ block off Yakima Ave.*

El Pastor / ★

315 W WALNUT ST, YAKIMA; 509/453-5159 The Garcia family surprises visitors with a rare and reasonably priced dining experience. Flavorful Mexican fare starts with softball-sized bowls of cilantro-laden salsa and guacamole. Selections include chicken enchiladas, taquitos rancheros, arroz con pollo, tacos al carbon, steak *a la chicana,* and fajitas. The family partnership creates a friendly, casual feeling, and good customer service. *$; MC, V; checks OK; lunch, dinner Mon–Sat; beer only; reservations not necessary; at 4th Ave.*

Gasperetti's Restaurant / ★★☆

1013 N FIRST ST, YAKIMA; 509/248-0628 Linen tablecloths and fresh flowers accent the two dining rooms in this 35-year-old restaurant. Walls are painted in an aged stucco style, reminiscent of old Tuscany. Brad Patterson, who helped owner John Gasperetti open the place, has returned as chef, after working in Seattle's four-star Lampreia restaurant. Appetizers such as smoked-salmon cheesecake complement a range of entrees, from pastas to Washington filet mignon in a sauce of marsala wine and Gorgonzola. The award-winning wine list offers a solid selection from Washington, California, and Italy. This is the place to be seen in Yakima. *$$; AE, DIS, MC, V; checks OK; lunch Tues–Fri, dinner Tues–Sat; full bar; reservations recommended; N 1st St exit off I-82.* ♿

Grant's Brewery Pub / ★

32 N FRONT ST, YAKIMA; 509/575-2922 In 1982, Bert Grant opened the first brewpub in the United States since Prohibition was repealed. Located in Yakima's old train station, the pub is rich with atmosphere and thick with memories, especially now that Grant has passed on. There's seating at the bar, booths, and a few tables. Live music, including folk, can be enjoyed most weekends. Beer ranges from hefeweizen to stouts to cask-conditioned Scottish ales. Food is typical pub fare, with fish-and-chips a favorite. *$; AE, MC, V; checks OK; lunch, dinner every day (Mon–Sat in winter); beer and wine; reservations not necessary; in old depot building, from N 1st St head west on Yakima Ave.*

Santiago's Gourmet Mexican Cooking / ★

111 E YAKIMA AVE, YAKIMA; 509/453-1644 Dramatic brick walls, Southwestern art, and a huge mural in the bar are highlights of this downtown Yakima Mexican restaurant. In 1999, owners Jar and Deb Arcand added an outside scene of the Yakima River canyon, one of the largest murals in the state. Santiago's opened in 1980 and cheerfully continues to serve popular gourmet chalupas, fish tostadas, and tacos Santiago with beef, guacamole, and two cheeses. *$; MC, V; checks OK; lunch Mon–Fri, dinner Mon–Sat; full bar; reservations not necessary; downtown near 1st St.*

LODGINGS

Oxford Inn

1603 E YAKIMA AVE, YAKIMA; 800/521-3050 Each of the 96 basic rooms at this chain hotel is enhanced by a small balcony overlooking the Yakima River. Moderately priced, the former Rio Mirada Motor Inn has an outdoor heated pool (open in summer), and guests have easy access to the 10-mile Greenway path along the river. Pets OK. *$; AE, DC, DIS, MC, V; checks OK; exit 33-B off I-82.* ♿

A Touch of Europe B&B / ★★

220 N 16TH AVE, YAKIMA; 888/438-7073 This Queen Anne Victorian house, built in 1889, wins rave reviews. Owners Jim and Erika Cenci opened in 1995 with three elegant rooms tastefully filled with antiques. All rooms have private baths and air-conditioning; the Prince Victorian Mahogany Room has a gas fireplace. Erika, the chef, was raised in Germany and has written several cookbooks. Her European-style breakfast is served in the dining room, or privately in the turret by candlelight and classical music. Gourmet lunches, afternoon high tea, and dinners for up to 20 are available by arrangement. No smoking, pets, or children. *$$; AE, MC, V; checks OK; www.winesnw.com/toucheuropeb&b.htm; exit 31 off I-82, west on US Hwy 12.*

Naches

LODGINGS

Whistlin' Jack Lodge / ★★

20800 SR 410, NACHES; 800/827-2299 You can almost fish from the front porch of some cabins, but this 1957 mountain hideaway is also ideal for hiking, alpine and cross-country skiing, or just escaping civilization. Weekend rates vary by type of room: cottage, bungalow, or motel unit. Cottages have full kitchens and hot tubs, and are close to the river (some as little as 10–20 feet away)—and make great private retreats. Guests who come with bigger plans—and want to dine out—opt for motel rooms or bungalows. Some catch their own dinner—but Whistlin' Jack also serves panfried trout in its restaurant, with live music Thursday through Saturday nights. The lodge also has a convenience store and a 24-hour gas pump. *$$; AE, DIS, MC, V; local checks OK; www.whistlin-jacklodge.com; 40 miles west of Yakima.*

Toppenish

The town's best-known son, Western artist Fred Oldfield, has turned Toppenish's streets into an art gallery with more than 50 historical murals—and a new one is painted each June. Such efforts by the **TOPPENISH MURAL SOCIETY** (5A Toppenish Ave; 509/865-6516) complement stores selling Western gear, antiques, and art, making this a nice place for a walking tour—and giving an authentic feel to summer rodeos.

The **YAKAMA NATION CULTURAL HERITAGE CENTER** (off US Hwy 97 and Buster Rd; 509/865-2800) includes a Native American museum and restaurant, reference library, gift shop, theater, and the 76-foot-tall Winter Lodge for banquets. Nearby is the tribal-run **LEGENDS CASINO** (580 Fort Rd; 509/865-8800; www.yakamalegendscasino.com). **FORT SIMCOE STATE PARK** (open May–Sept), a frontier military post built in 1865, stands in desolate grandeur 30 miles west of Toppenish on Highway 220, on the Yakama Indian Reservation.

RESTAURANTS

El Ranchito / ★★

1319 E 1ST AVE, ZILLAH; 509/829-5880 El Ranchito, just across the river from Toppenish, is the perfect midday stop for tortillas. Servings are generous and authentic, from burritos to *barbacoa*—a mild, slow-barbecued mound of beef served in a tortilla shell. Don't expect anything fancy: order cafeteria style and sit at plastic-covered tables inside or out; it's like eating in a Mexican market. Tortillas are fresh from the adjoining factory, and the minimercado sells Mexican spices and pottery. *$; MC, V; checks OK; breakfast, lunch, dinner every day; beer only; reservations not necessary; exit 54 off I-82.*

Sunnyside and Grandview

This is true farm country, and it's famous for its wine grapes, Concords, hops, corn, apples, cherries, cucumbers, onions, peaches, pears, peppers, garlic, and dairy products—with all the accompanying aromas. If you need a snack or want to stretch your legs, stop at **DARIGOLD'S DAIRY FAIR** (400 Alexander Rd, Sunnyside; 509/837-4321). It's open daily for sandwiches, old-fashioned ice cream, free cheese-tasting, and self-guided tours of the factory.

RESTAURANTS

Dykstra House Restaurant

114 BIRCH AVE, GRANDVIEW; 509/882-2082 Dykstra House—a 1914 mansion—makes bread and rolls from hand-ground whole wheat grown in the surrounding Horse Heaven Hills. Owner Linda Hartshorn also takes advantage of local in-season produce—like asparagus—in her entrees, but her specialty is dessert. Favorites are apple caramel pecan torte and Dykstra House chocolate pie, served since Hartshorn opened the place in 1984. *$$; AE, DC, DIS, MC, V; checks OK; lunch Tues–Sat, dinner Fri–Sat; beer and wine; reservations recommended; exit 75 off I-82.*

Snipes Mountain Microbrewery & Restaurant / ★

905 YAKIMA VALLEY HWY, SUNNYSIDE; 509/837-2739 A huge stone fireplace and exposed rafters make Snipes feel like a mountain lodge in the center of the Yakima Valley. The tasty beer brewed on the premises, good-quality steak-house fare, and friendly service make it a good stop for lunch or dinner. Meals can be as fancy as you like, ranging from wood-fired pizza (try the Mountaineer—"beer-b-q" chicken, ale-caramelized onions, smoked Gouda, and pine nuts) to hazelnut-crusted rack of lamb with mustard demi-glace. *$; AE, DIS, MC, V; checks OK; lunch, dinner every day; beer and wine; reservations not necessary; exit 63 or 69 off I-82.* &

Taqueria la Fogata

1204 YAKIMA VALLEY HWY, SUNNYSIDE; 509/839-9019 The small, simple Mexican taqueria was remodeled in 1999, although its menu still reflects local tastes. The Michoacán specialties include posole—a stew of pork back, feet, and hominy—and menudo, a tripe-and-cow's-feet stew in a spicy sauce. Less adventurous diners can stick with tacos and burritos. *$; MC, V; checks OK; breakfast, lunch, dinner every day; full bar; reservations not necessary; middle of town.*

LODGINGS

Cozy Rose Private Country Suites / ★

1220 FORSELL RD, GRANDVIEW; 800/575-8381 Owners Mark and Jennie Jackson are dedicated to perfecting the B&B experience; they offer four rooms, each with a private entrance, bathroom, fireplace, cable TV, and stereo. Splurge and get the Secret Garden Suite with a two-person Jacuzzi and "king-sized wonder bed." Breakfast is delivered to your room; typical fare includes French toast, omelets, and pecan pancakes. The Jacksons grow their own strawberries, herbs, and apples. They keep llamas on the property and are near a vineyard for a romantic walk. No smoking; well-behaved children over 12 OK. *$$–$$$; no credit cards; checks OK; exit 69 off I-82.*

Prosser

Who can resist a quick stop in Prosser, the self-purported "pleasant place with pleasant people"? Every day, the tasting room at **CHUKAR CHERRIES** (321 Wine Country Rd; 509/786-2055) gives out samples of the local Bing and Rainier cherries—especially good once they're dried and covered in chocolate.

LODGINGS

The Vintner's Inn at Hinzerling Winery / UNRATED

1524 SHERIDAN AVE, PROSSER; 800/727-6702 OR 509/786-2163 If you'd like an insider's view of life in wine country, the Vintner's Inn is the place. Although the winery is one of the region's oldest, the bed-and-breakfast is a new endeavor and still being perfected. Located next to Hinzerling Winery, the Vintner's Inn came into being when owners Mike and Frankie Wallace purchased the 1907 Victorian-style house, loaded it onto a truck, and relocated it next to their winery. Accommodations are quaint but comfortable, with two bedrooms with private bathrooms upstairs. Dinner is available by reservation Fridays and Saturdays for $23.95 per person. The five-course meal is a gourmet treat, from the Tapenade Noir and Verde, to the chicken tarragon in sherry-caper cream sauce, to the Wallace '94 vintage port. A wine bar with patio seating is available on weekends. Mike's organic garden grows most of the herbs and vegetables used in the kitchen. A continental breakfast prepares guests for a strenuous day of wine touring. No smoking; call ahead to clear pets; no children. *$; DIS, MC, V; checks OK; www.hinzerling.com; just off Wine Country Rd.*

The Tri-Cities

The Tri-Cities's main attractions are the rivers (the Yakima, Snake, and Columbia converge here), wineries (more than a dozen between Prosser and Walla Walla), and golf courses (nine public or private). But the area also has an intriguing history, from Lewis and Clark's stop at what is now Sacajawea State Park in Pasco to Kennewick's annual summer hydroplane races to Richland's role in ending World War II with top-secret atomic research at Hanford. The region is made up of three cities (although Richland now sports "suburbs" of North and West Richland) and two counties (Benton and Walla Walla), but the **TRI-CITIES VISITOR AND CONVENTION BUREAU** (6951 W Grandridge Blvd, Kennewick; 800/254-5824; www.visittri-cities.com) pulls them together to provide a seamless visit.

Richland

Richland was once a secret city, hidden away while the atomic-bomb workers did research in the 1940s. "Atomic City," with a highly educated population, is proud of its nuclear past—the local high school features a mushroom cloud in its school

LEWIS AND CLARK TRAIL BICENTENNIAL

Exploring the Pacific Northwest is nothing new: the concept was made famous about 200 years ago by Meriwether Lewis and William Clark.

The bicentennial celebration of Lewis and Clark's Corps of Discovery runs from 2003 to 2006. Washington, Oregon, and the nine other states along the trail are preparing for "historical tourists" following all or part of the 3,700-mile route that led to the non-Native settlement of the Northwest. The trail is clearly outlined with signs (featuring the forward-looking silhouettes of Lewis and Clark), historical markers, parks, and interpretive centers. Many sites also delve into the other side of the story: the Corps's long-term effect on the region's Native tribes. What started as friendly relations built on trading and exploring led to great tragedy for many tribal people.

Lewis and Clark started along the Missouri River from Illinois in May 1804, sent out by President Thomas Jefferson to find an overland link to the Pacific Ocean. Five months later, they entered what is now the southeast corner of Washington State on the Snake River. The Alpowai Interpretive Center in **CHIEF TIMOTHY STATE PARK** (on Silcott Rd, 8 miles west of Clarkston; 509/758-9580) focuses on the white explorers' meeting with the Nez Perce Indians. **LEWIS AND CLARK TRAIL STATE PARK** (on Hwy 12, 4½ miles west of Dayton; 509/337-6457) features camp sites, picnic areas, and a 1-mile interpretive trail.

The Tri-Cities is the farthest point upriver on the Columbia explored by Lewis and Clark. **SACAJAWEA STATE PARK** (off Hwy 12 near Pasco; 509/545-2361), at the confluence of the Snake and Columbia Rivers, is the only park along the trail honoring

sign. The **COLUMBIA RIVER EXHIBITION OF HISTORY, SCIENCE & TECHNOLOGY** (95 Lee Blvd; 509/943-9000; www.crehst.org) displays the region's history from Ice Age through nuclear age. Hands-on exhibits explain how the Tri-Cities area sprang up during World War II, when the federal government created Hanford.

COLUMBIA RIVER JOURNEYS (1229 Columbia Park Trail; 509/734-9941; May–Oct 15) offers jet-boat tours through **HANFORD REACH,** an ecologically preserved section of the Columbia River. Beautiful **HOWARD AMON PARK** (509/942-7529) lies along the Columbia, with a paved path for bicycling, walking, or in-line skating.

ALLIED ARTS GALLERY (89 Lee Blvd; 509/943-9815) displays the work of local artists and sponsors an annual July art festival. For a quick bite, there's the **TASTE CAFE** (701 George Washington Wy; 509/946-4142), serving creative pasta salads, gourmet sandwiches, homemade soups, and large cookies.

the Indian woman guide. The 284-acre park includes the **SACAJAWEA INTERPRE-TIVE CENTER** (509/545-2361), housing a collection of Native artifacts; it is run by volunteers and open by appointment for group tours.

Paddling down the Columbia, the explorers talked with Natives near what is now **MARYHILL STATE PARK** (off Hwy 14, Goldendale; 509/773-5007; open year-round). **MARYHILL MUSEUM** (35 Maryhill Museum Dr, Goldendale; 509/773-3733; open Mar 15–Nov 15), on the hill across from Biggs, Oregon, has an outstanding display of Indian baskets and stone tools. **BEACON ROCK STATE PARK** (35 miles east of Vancouver on Hwy 14; 509/427-8265 or 800/233-0321) was where the explorers first noticed the effects of the Pacific Ocean's tide.

From the site of what is now **LEWIS AND CLARK CAMPSITE STATE PARK** (2 miles southeast of Chinook on Hwy 101), the 33 weary travelers first saw the Pacific Ocean. Washington State's **LEWIS AND CLARK INTERPRETIVE CENTER** (2½ miles southeast of Ilwaco, off Hwy 101; 360/642-3029) is on Cape Disappointment, where the explorers officially reached the Pacific.

After being pounded by cold and wet winds, they turned south to establish a winter campsite, however, at what is now **FORT CLATSOP NATIONAL MEMORIAL** (92343 Fort Clatsop Rd; 503/861-2471; open daily), 5 miles southwest of Astoria, Oregon. The visitor center includes a replica of Lewis and Clark's winter quarters.

Those wanting to know more should consult the national park's **LEWIS AND CLARK NATIONAL HISTORIC TRAIL** website (www.nps.gov/lecl) or the nonprofit **NATIONAL LEWIS AND CLARK BICENTENNIAL COUNCIL** (888/999-1803; www.lewisandclark200.org). —*Melissa O'Neil*

RESTAURANTS

Atomic Ale Brewpub & Eatery / ★

1015 LEE BLVD, RICHLAND; 509/946-5465 The microbrews are too good for Homer Simpson's taste in beer, but he'd appreciate their names: Half-life Hefeweizen and Plutonium Porter, for example. The standard pub food—pizza, salads, and soups—is good, and the house specialty is wood-fired gourmet pizzas made with garlic, basil, shrimp, and other flavorful morsels. Finish with a B Reactor brownie. *$; AE, DIS, MC, V; checks OK; lunch, dinner Mon–Sat; beer and wine; reservations not necessary; George Washington Wy exit off I-82.*

The Emerald of Siam / ★

1314 JADWIN AVE, RICHLAND; 509/946-9328 Thai-born Ravadi Quinn is known for sharing her native culture, through community school classes and in a cookbook. Her authentic recipes include curries, satays, noodles, and black-rice pudding. Lunch is a buffet. Dinner includes a full vegetarian menu—most popular is the sweet-and-sour tofu. The ambience is a bit scruffy, but if you need to get your Thai fix in the Tri-Cities, this is pretty much the only place to do so. *$; AE, DIS, MC, V; local checks only; lunch, dinner Mon–Sat; beer and wine; reservations not necessary; Uptown Shopping Center.*

Samovar's

1340 JADWIN AVE, RICHLAND; 509/946-6655 To the delight of the people of Richland, the Ukrainian and Russian people who work here have brought the tastes of the mother country to the Tri-Cities. Decorated with a colorful, faux-Siberian cabin theme, this is the place to find the best latkes this side of the mountains. The dinner and lunch menu can be hit or miss and slightly expensive for what you order, but the uniqueness of experience makes it worth a visit. Try the *pelmeni* (dumplings with beef or pork) or the *golubtze* (stuffed cabbage leaves), but not the *vareniki* (dumplings stuffed with bland potatoes). Samovar's bakery next door is devoted exclusively to items like *piroshki* (stuffed pastries filled with fruit or meat), Russian *khala* bread, and *blinis*. *$$; AE, DIS, MC, V; checks OK; lunch, dinner Tues–Sat, brunch Sun; full bar; reservations recommended; rsamovar@hotmail.com; www. samovar.net; Uptown Shopping Center.*

LODGINGS

Red Lion Hanford House / ★

802 GEORGE WASHINGTON WY, RICHLAND; 509/946-7611 OR 800/733-5466 With its 150 rooms remodeled in 1999, Hanford House remains one of the most popular places to stay—although the Tri-Cities area has no shortage of hotels. What makes this one special is its prime location on the Columbia River, select view rooms, and easy access to riverfront Howard Amon Park. If you can't get a room on the river, ask for one facing the grassy courtyard and swimming pool. Visit the fitness center if it's too hot to exert yourself outside. The casual-dining restaurant—serving steaks, hamburgers, and the like—also has a great view. *$$; AE, DC, DIS, MC, V; checks OK; Hwy 240 to George Washington Wy.* &

Kennewick

Kennewick is the largest of the Tri-Cities, sharing a border with Richland and an architecturally magnificent **CABLE BRIDGE** (lighted at night) with Pasco. The city is known as Southeast Washington's retail center and has several malls, including Columbia Center, but the place to visit is **COLUMBIA PARK** (between Hwy 240 and Columbia River; 509/585-4293). At the park's east end, near the US Highway 395 blue bridge, volunteers in 1999 built the wooden castle-like **PLAYGROUND OF DREAMS** with climbing structures and twisty slides. It's next to the **FAMILY FISHING POND**, where adults can teach children to catch-and-release. Both are handicapped-accessible. The park has a Frisbee golf course and is the site of the annual Columbia Cup unlimited **HYDROPLANE RACES** (509/547-2203; www. hydroracing.com) in late July. Winter sports fans focus on the **TRI-CITY AMERICANS** hockey team (509/736-0606), which plays at the **COLISEUM** (7100 W Quinault Ave; 509/783-9999).

RESTAURANTS

Casa Chapala / ★

107 E COLUMBIA DR, KENNEWICK; 509/586-4224 / 2100 N BELFAIR PL, KENNEWICK; 509/783-8080 Owners Lupe and Lucina Barragan are known throughout the community for their friendly smiles, and for organizing Tri-Citians in 1999 to make the world's largest burrito. Mexican food here is reasonably authentic and quite filling. The menu has kid-sized choices and several low-fat options. Beware: "Large" margaritas are huge. *$; AE, DIS, MC, V; checks OK; lunch, dinner every day; full bar; reservations not necessary; www.casachapala.com; east end of Kennewick, beside Hwy 240 on-ramp (Columbia Dr), at Hwy 12 and Columbia Center Blvd (Belfair Pl).*

Cedars Pier I / ★

355 CLOVER ISLAND DR, KENNEWICK; 509/582-2143 A step above "Tri-Cities casual," Cedars is frequented by boaters who dock here after a jaunt on the Columbia River. The cuisine is high-quality surf-and-turf, with various delicious cuts of meat including sirloin and T-bone. The seafood menu might include grilled ahi with a variety of sauces, salmon, and crab—both Dungeness and Alaskan king. The wine list is good, with many excellent regional choices, including the Hogue Genesis series and Glen Fiona syrahs. *$$; AE, DC, DIS, MC, V; checks OK; dinner every day; full bar; reservations recommended; www.cedarsrest.com; follow signs to Clover Island.*

Chez Chaz Bistro / ★

5011 W CLEARWATER AVE, KENNEWICK; 509/735-2138 Don't let the building's outward appearance make you hesitate; inside the decor is tasteful, if whimsical, and the food is good. Chez Chaz offers an enormous tapas menu in addition to ever-changing dinner selections. The tapas, perfect snacks to pair with wine, include traditional Mediterranean choices like *dolmas* (rice-stuffed grape leaves) and smoked garlic sausage with polenta and romesco sauce, and fusion choices like spicy sweet chili chicken wings or masa-crusted fried oysters. Entrees include oven-roasted duckling with cherry brandy and grilled rack of Colorado lamb. The Washington wine list is solid. Chez Chaz's sister restaurant and wine bar, Aioli's (94 Lee Blvd, Richland; 509/942-1914; lunch Mon–Sat, dinner Tues–Sat), serves the same tapas menu, plus tasty soups and salads, panini sandwiches, and specialties such as paella and lasagna. *$$; DIS, MC, V; checks OK; lunch Mon–Sat, dinner Tues–Sat; beer and wine; reservations recommended; between Union and Edison Sts.*

Sundance Grill / ★

413 N KELLOGG ST, STE B, KENNEWICK; 509/783-6505 The casual, business-lunch atmosphere here segues into dinner with tablecloths and live music Monday through Saturdays. The menu changes every three months, and features seasonal fish and produce, such as Copper River salmon, stuffed portobellos, lamb chops, and seared duck breast. Standing specialties include chicken marsala, prime beef, and crème brûlée. The wine list has more than 100 choices,

SOUTHEAST WASHINGTON THREE-DAY WINE TOUR

Washington is the second-largest wine-producing state in the nation (behind California), and more than half of its wineries are in Eastern Washington, where 99 percent of the grapes are grown. The state's wine industry saw incredible growth in the late 1990s—with nearly 50 new wineries opening in 1999 alone—bringing the total to about 140. Most, though not all, of these have tasting rooms open for visits year-round.

DAY ONE: Start in Yakima and drive to Zillah and the **WINEGLASS CELLARS** (260 N Bonair Rd, Zillah; 509/829-3011) tasting room. Next sample a few wines at **PORT-TEUS** (5201 Highland Dr, Zillah; 509/829-6970). Take a break with an authentic Mexican lunch at **EL RANCHITO** before heading south on Interstate 82 to the Outlook exit, where you follow the signs to **TEFFT CELLARS** (1320 Independence Rd, Outlook; 509/837-7651). Then drive to Prosser for tasting at **HOGUE CELLARS** (Wine Country Rd, Prosser; 509/786-4557). Take an afternoon drive to the Red Mountain growing area near Benton City. Taste at **KIONA** (44612 N Sunset Rd NE, Benton City; 509/588-6716); then see the underground barrel-storage tunnels at **TERRA BLANCA** (34715 N DeMoss Rd, Benton City; 509/588-6082). In Prosser, check in at the **VINTNER'S INN,** and enjoy their prix-fixe dinner.

DAY TWO: After breakfast at the inn, shop in Prosser for picnic fixings and take Highway 221 south to the Northwest's largest winery, **COLUMBIA CREST** (Columbia

most from Washington. *$$; AE, DIS, MC, V; checks OK; lunch, dinner Mon–Sat; full bar; reservations recommended; between Clearwater Ave and Canal Dr.*

Pasco

Pasco has the most diverse population of the three cities—about half the residents are Hispanic—and an economy based on light manufacturing and food processing. Historically a railroad town, Pasco is home to the **WASHINGTON STATE RAIL-ROADS HISTORICAL SOCIETY MUSEUM** (122 N Tacoma St; 509/543-4159; Sat Apr–Sept), which features old motorcars, railcars, and steam locomotives, including the state's oldest—the Blue Mountain, circa 1877.

Downtown is the **PASCO FARMERS MARKET** (4th Ave and Columbia St; 509/545-0738; Wed and Sat May–Nov), one of the state's largest open-air produce markets. **SACAJAWEA STATE PARK** (off Hwy 12) honors the remarkable Native American woman (see "Lewis and Clark Trail Bicentennial" in this chapter).

LODGINGS

Doubletree Hotel / ★★

2525 N 20TH AVE, PASCO; 509/547-0701 OR 800/222-8733 The Doubletree is the Tri-Cities's largest hotel, with 279 rooms, and its huge ballroom is popular for conventions and festivals. It's conveniently located next to the Tri-Cities Airport, as well

Crest Dr, Patterson; 509/875-2061), right on the Columbia. Taste the wine, take the tour, and then eat lunch on the grounds by the fountain. Return to the Tri-Cities on a loop route east on Highway 14 and north on Interstate 82, and visit Kennewick's **POWERS WINERY/BADGER MOUNTAIN VINEYARD** (1106 Jurupa St, Kennewick; 800/643-9463). Drive toward Walla Walla on US Highway 12, stopping en route to taste award-winning wines at **WOODWARD CANYON WINERY** (11920 W Hwy 12, Touchet; 509/525-4129) and **L'ECOLE NO. 41** (41 Lowden School Rd, Lowden; 509/525-0940). Check in at the **MILL CREEK INN** and dine at **WHITE-HOUSE-CRAWFORD** in Walla Walla.

DAY THREE: Fortified by breakfast in the inn's charming barn, and a walk in the grape fields, head to historic downtown Walla Walla and be sure to stop at the bright-yellow storefront of **CAYUSE VINEYARDS** (17 E Main St, Walla Walla; 509/526-0686). Eat a simple lunch across the street at **GRAPEFIELDS**. Stroll down Main Street and stop at a few more tasting rooms: **WATERBROOK WINERY** (31 E Main St, Walla Walla; 509/522-1262) and **CANOE RIDGE VINEYARD** (1102 W Cherry St, Walla Walla; 509/527-0885). Then head to **WALLA WALLA VINTNERS** (Mill Creek Rd, Walla Walla; 509/525-4724) for the tasting appointment you made two weeks ago. Finish the tour in Dayton with a swim in the pool at your night's lodging, the **PURPLE HOUSE B&B INN,** followed by a gourmet dinner at the highly rated **PATIT CREEK RESTAU-RANT**—having made reservations well in advance.

as Sun Willows Golf Course and Columbia Basin College. The hotel, formerly a Red Lion, has two outdoor pools and an exercise facility. The restaurant was upgraded in 1999 to the Vineyards Steak House, featuring vintages from Tri-Cities wineries; the Grizzly Bar is one of the town's hottest nightspots. *$$; AE, DC, DIS, MC, V; checks OK; exit 12 off I-82/US Hwy 395.* &

Walla Walla and the Blue Mountains

The Walla Walla Valley is an important historical area: the Lewis and Clark Expedition passed through in 1805, fur trappers began traveling up the Columbia River from Fort Astoria in 1811 and set up a fort in 1818, and in 1836 missionary Marcus Whitman built a medical mission west of the present town. But when a virulent attack of measles hit area tribes in November 1847, a group of enraged Cayuse men killed the missionaries. The incident came to be called the Whitman Massacre. The excellent interpretive center at the **WHITMAN MISSION NATIONAL HISTORIC SITE** (7 miles west of Walla Walla along US Hwy 12; 509/529-2761) sketches out the story of the mission and the massacre; there aren't any historic buildings, but the simple outline of the mission in the ground is strangely affecting. A hike up an adjacent hill to an overlook offers the best impression of what the area looked like to the Whitmans and their fellow settlers. The mission became an important station on the

Oregon Trail, and the Whitman party included the first white women to cross the continent overland.

Agriculture is important to the namesake county, known worldwide for its sweet onions and, more recently, its fine wines (see "Southeast Washington Three-Day Wine Tour" in this chapter). The **WALLA WALLA VALLEY CHAMBER OF COMMERCE** (29 E Sumac St; 877/998-4748; www.wwchamber.com) has additional information.

Walla Walla

Infused with tourism centered around some of the best wines in the country, restored downtown Walla Walla bustles with restaurants, wine-tasting rooms, and galleries. The community is strong on the arts, and the **WALLA WALLA SYMPHONY** (509/529-8020; www.wwsymphony.com) is the oldest symphony orchestra west of the Mississippi. Performances are held in Cordiner Hall (345 Boyer Ave) on the grounds of private **WHITMAN COLLEGE** (509/527-5176), which anchors the town and has a lovely campus. **FORT WALLA WALLA** (The Dalles Military Rd; 509/525-7703) has a museum featuring 14 historic buildings and a collection of pioneer artifacts. The adjacent city park features a skateboard park and BMX riding area.

RESTAURANTS

Grapefields / ★★

4 E MAIN ST, WALLA WALLA; 509/522-3993 A relative newcomer to Main Street's selection of cafes and restaurants, Grapefields has a sophisticated bistro attitude, from the art deco bar to tasty tapas. The latter include toast manchego—bread grilled with manchego and served with a tomato-onion herb salsa—and Spanish sardines (not fishy at all) marinated in citrus, vinegar, garlic, and olive oil. The cafe menu offers a traditional charcuterie plate featuring a selection of cured and preserved meats; a perfectly dressed salad verte topped with toasted walnuts, Gorgonzola, and Anjou pear; and hand-tossed pizzas. The dazzling selection of premium wines is both local and international. *$; AE, MC, V; checks OK; lunch Tues–Sat, dinner Tues–Sun; beer and wine; reservations not necessary; just off 2nd Ave.* &

Merchants Ltd. / ★★

21 E MAIN ST, WALLA WALLA; 509/525-0900 Brothers Bob and Mike Austin traded in their upstairs dining room for more ground-level space, now seating 300 people across three storefronts downtown and serving healthy morning and midday meals. A full, in-house bakery makes treats like chocolate croissants and pizzas, while the well-stocked imported cheese and meat case serves your picnic needs. One wall is dedicated to international groceries, gourmet food stuffs, and organic coffee beans, another to wines. Merchants has been a mainstay—especially for upscale liberal-arts college students who thrive on Wednesday-only spaghetti dinners—since 1976. *$; AE, DIS, MC, V; checks OK; breakfast, lunch Mon–Sat, dinner Wed; beer and wine; reservations not necessary; 2nd St exit off US Hwy 12.* &

Paisano's Italian Restaurant & Catering / ★★☆

26 E MAIN ST, STE 1, WALLA WALLA; 509/527-3511 Chef Jennifer Parent teams with mom and dad—Judy and Lewis Parent—to serve tasty, generous portions in an inviting setting. Creative sandwiches—pesto chicken or Italian burger with prosciutto, mozzarella, and sun-dried tomatoes—come with pasta salad and fresh bread to dip in herb-infused olive oil. It's more than enough to prepare for an afternoon of wine tasting. Dinner creations might include smoked-duck capellini, scampi Paisano's, and angel hair pasta tossed with fresh herbs and olive oil. *$$; MC, V; checks OK; lunch, dinner Mon–Sat; beer and wine; reservations not necessary; 2nd St exit off US Hwy 12, across from Merchants.* &

Whitehouse-Crawford / ★★★

🌲 **55 W CHERRY ST, WALLA WALLA; 509/525-2222** A former planing mill from 1905 has been rescued and restored to house this airy, chic restaurant that plays host to wine tourists and Carhart-wearing winery owners. Tasty appetizers—try spicy calamari with ginger—pair well with many local wines on the extensive wine list. Entrees are the usual suspects—salmon, steak, and pork tenderloin—but with unexpected twists like southwest-style salmon with black beans, corn, and squash in a piquant tomato sauce, or pork smoked and served with grilled fresh figs, shallots, and spaetzle. Desserts are divine, including lemon verbena crème brûlée and award-winning twice-baked chocolate cake—a marriage of dense cake and chocolate souffle. *$$–$$$; AE, MC, V; checks OK; dinner Wed–Sun; full bar; reservations recommended; downtown, at 3rd Ave.* &

LODGINGS

Green Gables Inn / ★★

👫 **922 BONSELLA ST, WALLA WALLA; 888/525-5501** The title character from L. M. Montgomery's *Anne of Green Gables* series loved staying in guest rooms. Margaret and Jim Buchan incorporate that spirit in five rooms named for topics in the popular books, like Idlewild, with a fireplace and Jacuzzi, and Dryad's Bubble, with a small balcony. The Carriage House is good for families because it is separate from the main house and gives kids more room to run around. Full breakfast is served on fine china by candlelight. A wraparound porch and air-conditioning make for pleasant summer evenings. *$$; AE, DIS, MC, V; checks OK; greengables@ hscis.net; www.greengablesinn.com; Clinton St exit off US Hwy 12.*

Inn at Blackberry Creek / ★

1126 PLEASANT ST, WALLA WALLA; 509/522-5233 Just around the corner from Pioneer Park and Whitman College is the charming Inn at Blackberry Creek. The 1912 farmhouse has been lovingly restored by innkeeper Barbara Knudson, whose attention to detail—fresh cookies in the evening, flawlessly decorated rooms— makes for a very pleasant stay. The three rooms available, Cezanne's Sanctuary, Monet's Retreat, and Renoir's Studio, all feature king-sized beds, private bath with shower, and peaceful views of the tree-lined property. The light-filled common area overlooks the lawns and invites you to play chess, thumb through design magazines, or read in the comfortable chairs. Breakfast might include freshly baked pastries, eggs, yogurt, and fresh fruit. No smoking or children under 12. *$–$$; MC, V; checks OK; bknud@hscis.net; www.innatblackberrycreek.com; 4 blocks southeast of Pioneer Park.*

Marcus Whitman

6 W ROSE ST, WALLA WALLA; 866/826-9422 One of the largest structures in downtown Walla Walla, the newly restored Marcus Whitman offers 91 clean, comfortable rooms. Best are the suites in the original portion of the hotel (the West Wing was added in the 1960s). Decorated in handsome, almost masculine colors with cherry molding, new carpets and furnishings, the suites are a good place to stay if you're on business or want to hold a large meeting in one of their conference centers or ballroom. If you don't feel like going out, grab dinner at the Marc restaurant down below for serviceable steaks, salmon dishes, or chicken. *$–$$; AE, MC, V; www.marcuswhitmanhotel.com; at 2nd Ave.*

Mill Creek Inn / ★★★

2014 MILL CREEK RD, WALLA WALLA; 509/522-1234 More than 100 years old, this 22-acre farmstead doubles as a working winery and luxurious retreat. Located outside town, surrounded by the rolling Palouse and the Blue Mountains, visitors can experience the tranquility of the country. All of the cottages and suites have been taken from their practical uses—chicken house, carriage house, haylofts—and transformed into accommodations with playful good taste. The Chicken House Cottage has vaulted ceilings, a slate-tiled walk-in shower for two, and an airy full kitchen. Best is the two-story Summer Kitchen Cottage, with a deck overlooking the vineyards, sky-lit bathroom, and full kitchen and living room. The small Hay Loft Suites in the remodeled barn are charmingly rustic, offering full run of the barn common space, which includes a crackling fireplace and leather couches, and plays host to the hearty gourmet breakfast served to all guests in the morning. Welcome touches include lit candles when guests arrive, high-quality soaps and shampoo, and ice water by the beds. No smoking or children under 12; pets allowed in Chicken House Cottage only. *$$–$$$; AE, DIS, MC, V; checks OK; www.mill creekbb.com; 1.6 miles outside downtown.*

Dayton

Dayton is a small farming town northeast of Walla Walla and one of the first communities established in Washington State. Small wonder it's full of historical buildings—almost 90 Victorian-era structures. The **DAYTON CHAMBER OF COMMERCE** (166 E Main St; 800/882-6299; www.historicdayton.com) offers information for self-guided walking tours. **THE DAYTON HISTORICAL DEPOT** (222 E Commercial St; 509/382-2026; tours Tues–Sat), built in 1881, is the state's oldest remaining railroad station, now a museum.

Dayton is also known for easy access to **BLUEWOOD SKI RESORT** (22 miles south of Dayton via US Hwy 12; 509/382-4725; www.bluewood.com), in Umatilla National Forest in the Blue Mountains. It has clear skies, dry powder, and the second-highest base elevation (4,545 feet) in the state.

RESTAURANTS

Patit Creek Restaurant / ★★★

725 E DAYTON AVE, DAYTON; 509/382-2625 This small-town restaurant is known regionwide for its consistent continental cuisine and is one of the most highly rated restaurants this side of the mountains. Bruce and Heather Hiebert turned a 1920s service station into a 10-table restaurant famous for fillet steaks in green peppercorn sauce, chèvre-stuffed dates wrapped in bacon, fresh vegetables, and huckleberry pie. The wine list is strong on Walla Walla selections. Patit Creek is a classic off-the-beaten-path discovery and a classy place to end a day of valley wine touring or skiing at Bluewood. Just don't drop in and expect a table; reservations are recommended at least two weeks in advance. *$$; MC, V; local checks only; lunch Wed–Fri, dinner Wed–Sat; beer and wine; reservations recommended; north end of town.* &

LODGINGS

The Purple House B&B Inn

415 E CLAY ST, DAYTON; 800/486-2574 This 1882 house really is purple, a B&B since the late 1980s. Four rooms have modern amenities, including air-conditioning. Two have private baths, while the others share one large bathroom. Innkeeper Christine D. Williscroft is a native of southern Germany, which shows in the inn's decor, as does her passion for Chinese antiques and Oriental rugs. Williscroft has two small dogs and welcomes other small pets—or children—with advance warning. Full breakfast might include strudel or crepes, served in a walled-in courtyard next to the private swimming pool. Lunch and dinner can be arranged for in-house guests and groups of six or more. *$$–$$$; MC, V; checks OK; 1 block off US Hwy 12.* &

The Weinhard Hotel / ★

235 E MAIN ST, DAYTON; 509/382-4032 Fresh flowers and fruit in each room greet guests—a pleasant surprise for those skeptical of finding uptown style in tiny Dayton. Owners Dan and Ginny Butler restored the old Weinhard building (built as a saloon and lodge hall in the late 1800s) and filled it with elegant Victorian antiques that they collected from across the country. The 15 rooms are furnished with antique dressers, desks, and canopied beds. (Tall people, however, should ask for one of the longer beds.) All rooms have private baths, and the Signature Room has a Jacuzzi. Inside the hotel is The Weinhard Cafe (lunch, dinner Tues–Sat), serving tasty fare in a casual bistro setting. Entrees range from homemade tamales to sockeye salmon with shiitake mushrooms and roasted garlic sauce. No smoking. *$$–$$$; AE, MC, V; checks OK; www.weinhard.com; downtown.* &

Pullman and the Palouse

Washington's golden Palouse region, next to Idaho and north of the Blue Mountains, is made up of seemingly endless, rolling hills covered with wheat, lentils, and other crops. The area also boasts rivers, including the Snake, and several geological wonders.

KAMIAK BUTTE COUNTY PARK (13 miles north of Pullman on Hwy 27) is a good place for a picnic with a view of the undulating hills. STEPTOE BUTTE STATE PARK (about 30 miles north of Pullman on US Hwy 195) is great for a panoramic view or stargazing, but windy.

At PALOUSE FALLS STATE PARK (2 miles off Hwy 261 between Washtucna and Tucannon; 509/646-3252 or 800/233-0321), the Palouse River roars over a basalt cliff higher than Niagara Falls, dropping 198 feet into a steep-walled basin on its way to the Snake. A hiking trail leads to an overlook above the falls, most spectacular during spring runoff. Camping and canoeing are allowed in LYONS FERRY STATE PARK (on Hwy 261, 7 miles north of Starbuck; 509/646-3252 or 800/233-0321), at the confluence of the Palouse and Snake Rivers; the park also has a public boat launch.

Pullman

The heart of the Palouse beats in Pullman, at the junction of U.S. Highway 195 and Highway 27 near the Idaho border, and the heart of Pullman is WASHINGTON STATE UNIVERSITY (visitor center: 225 N Grand Ave; 509/335-8633; www.wsu.edu). WSU started in 1892 and is where 17,000 die-hard Cougars live during the academic year. Campus tours are available weekdays. A trip through town wouldn't be complete without sampling the ice cream or Cougar Gold cheese made at the WSU creamery, FERDINAND'S (inside Agriculture Science Bldg; 509/335-2141; weekdays).

Pullman also is known for its historical buildings, with brick masonry and early 1900s classical and Georgian architecture. Find more information at the PULLMAN CHAMBER OF COMMERCE (415 N Grand Ave; 800/365-6948; www.pullman.com).

RESTAURANTS

Hilltop Restaurant

920 NW OLSON ST, PULLMAN; 509/334-2555 This steak house has an incredible view of the university and surrounding hills, a romantic vista complemented by linens and attentive service. Red meat is the specialty, from prime rib and steaks to Sunday's midday roast-beef family dinner. Homemade desserts include cheesecakes, mud pie, and chocolate truffles. Hilltop is connected to the three-story, 59-room Hawthorne Inn & Suites, where it offers room service. *$$; AE, DIS, MC, V; checks OK; lunch Mon–Fri, dinner every day; full bar; reservations not necessary; hilltop@completebbs.com; on Davis Wy.*

Swilly's Cafe & Catering / ★★

200 NE KAMIAKEN ST, PULLMAN; 509/334-3395 The renovated historic Hutchison Photography studio maintains its dedication to art, with local artwork displayed on the dining room's exposed-brick walls. Opened in 1986 by Jill Aesoph, Swilly's overlooks Paradise Creek in downtown Pullman. Casual warmth translates into homemade soups, salads, sandwiches, and burgers, plus more sophisticated dinner entrees such as Moroccan lamb, Thai shrimp, grilled tenderloin, and various pastas. Microbrews are on tap, and a moderately priced wine list is strong on Washington choices.

WINE TOURING TIPS

Wine-touring tips are the same whether you're visiting Washington's Walla Walla Valley, Oregon's Willamette Valley, or British Columbia's Okanagan Valley.

- Call ahead for tasting-room hours, especially in winter. And get accurate directions, because wineries are often in rural areas with few road signs.
- Limit your visits to no more than six wineries per day. Otherwise your taste buds will be too overwhelmed to appreciate the wines.
- Take three basic steps to fully enjoy each wine. (1) Hold the glass up to the light to admire the wine's color. (2) Put the glass on the counter and carefully swirl the wine to release its aromas—stick your nose in the glass and inhale. (3) Take a large sip and swish it around your mouth so it coats all your taste buds.
- You don't have to taste every wine in the tasting room, and you don't have to finish each sample. Most tasting bars have a "dump bucket," and it's perfectly acceptable to pour—or even spit—out wine, whether you like it or not.
- Ask questions: part of the experience is learning what went into the wine and how to enjoy it now.
- Experiment. Washington wineries produce more than 30 styles of wine. Try something new in addition to your favorites. You might surprise yourself.
- Buy a wine if you like it, because many are hard to find in stores. Bring an empty cooler to insulate the wines in your car—especially between May and September when it's hot in wine country. When you get home, let the bottles rest for a couple of weeks before drinking them, so the wine recovers from the shock of travel.

—Melissa O'Neil

$; AE, MC, V; checks OK; lunch, dinner Mon–Sat; beer and wine; reservations not necessary; at NW Olson St. &

LODGINGS

The Churchyard Inn B&B / ★

206 ST. BONIFACE ST, UNIONTOWN; 509/229-3200 The Churchyard Inn is next door to the historic St. Boniface Catholic Church in tiny Uniontown, 16 miles south of Pullman on US Highway 195. The three-story house was built as a parish in 1905, converted to a convent in 1913, then turned into a B&B by Linda and Marvin Entel in 1995. Each of seven uniquely decorated rooms has a private bath. The top-floor 1,200-square-foot Palouse Suite has a great room big enough for seminars or wedding receptions, a kitchen, dining area, gas fireplace, views from every window, two queen-sized hide-a-beds, and a separate room with a king-sized bed. Breakfast and beverages are served in the dining room with a view of the Palouse farmlands. No smoking, pets, or children under 14. *$$–$$$; MC, V; checks OK; pullman-wa. com/housing/chrchbb.htm; 2 blocks west of US Hwy 195.* &

Paradise Creek Quality Inn

1400 SE BISHOP BLVD, PULLMAN; 800/669-3212 Within walking distance of WSU, this motel is just far enough off Highway 270 (the route to Moscow, Idaho) to avoid traffic noise. The 66 rooms are standard but convenient. It's situated literally over the meandering creek for which it's named. *$; AE, DIS, MC, V; checks OK; www. qualityinn.com; ¼ mile east of campus.*

SPOKANE AND NORTHEASTERN WASHINGTON

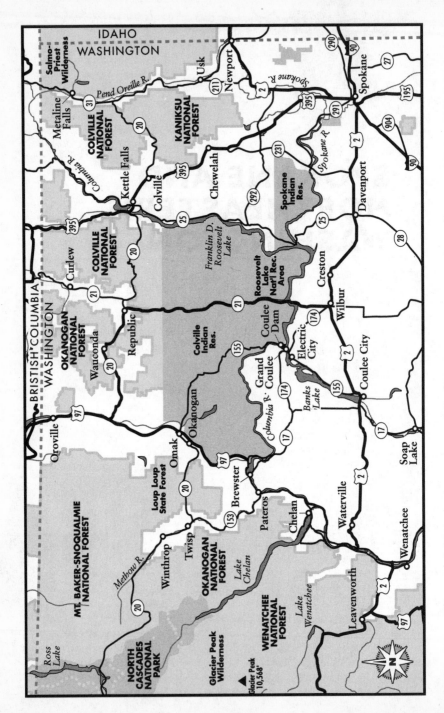

SPOKANE AND NORTHEASTERN WASHINGTON

It's natural to think of Washington State as equal parts yin and yang: the lush, green west side of the Cascades and the arid, desertlike landscape of Eastern Washington. But that image isn't exactly accurate. The state can be divided into neat quarters—with the northeastern quadrant a study in contrasts. The upper-right corner of Washington starts in the sleepy spa town of Soap Lake and runs north to the Canadian border near Oroville; along this imaginary north-south line lie the towns of Grand Coulee, Okanogan, and Omak. To the east are the vast Channeled Scablands—the most visible reminder of the great floods that poured from glacial Lake Missoula thousands of years ago. That flat, featureless terrain bumps up against the gorgeous and little-explored Kettle River Range to the north, and near Colville you'll find the spectacular Selkirks, an outlying range of the Canadian Rockies.

The image of everything east of the Cascades being dry couldn't be farther from reality when you consider that one of the nation's most powerful rivers—the Columbia—runs through this region, though it is much dammed and sedated. Its tributaries include the Pend Oreille, Colville, Spokane, and Okanogan, all of which create riparian areas in an otherwise sere shrub-steppe environment.

Spokane, in the far-eastern reaches of the state near Idaho, is famous for its tree-lined neighborhoods. The city is forested as well, with the spiky ponderosa pines of drier climes rather than the fir-dominated forests of Western Washington. Northeastern Washington years ago was dubbed the Inland Empire, and Spokane is its largest city, some 300 miles from the burgeoning Puget Sound region.

ACCESS AND INFORMATION

The fastest, most direct route to Spokane from Seattle is **INTERSTATE 90; US HIGHWAY 2** is another east-west route through Northeastern Washington. North-south routes include **US HIGHWAY 97** on the eastern slope of the Cascades and **US HIGHWAY 395**, which runs from Spokane through Colville. The **SPOKANE AREA VISITOR INFORMATION CENTER** (201 W Main Ave; 509/747-3230; www.visit spokane.com) can provide details about special events, as well as a list of accommodations and restaurants in the city.

Nine airlines—Alaska, America West, Big Sky, Canadian, Delta, Horizon, Northwest, Southwest, and United—serve **SPOKANE INTERNATIONAL AIRPORT** (W 9000 Airport Dr; 509/455-6455), a 10-minute drive west of downtown.

AMTRAK's (509/624-5144 or 800/USA-RAIL; www.amtrak.com) Empire Builder between Seattle and Chicago rumbles through the city, stopping in the middle of the night at Spokane's **INTERMODAL CENTER** (221 W 1st Ave). The **TRAILWAYS** bus system (509/838-5262) and **GREYHOUND** (509/624-5251) also use that depot; buses also serve nearby Cheney.

Spokane

Water is the reason for Spokane's existence. Native American tribes gathered at the massive, thundering falls of the Spokane River every August to harvest salmon. The city was founded in 1879 because of the mill-power provided by the falls, which today are the centerpiece of a spacious downtown oasis, Riverfront Park, built on the site of Expo '74. The river is home to rainbow trout and osprey, including birds that nest within the city limits. It also provides a scenic backdrop for horseback riding, hiking, and golf.

After more than a decade of decline, Spokane's urban core has been revitalized with the opening of a stylish mall that houses upscale retailers. **RIVERPARK SQUARE** (808 W Main Ave; 509/363-0304) is home to a state-of-the-art multiplex, Nordstrom, Williams-Sonoma, Restoration Hardware, and the Gap, among others. The venerable 281-room **DAVENPORT HOTEL** (807 W Sprague Ave; 509/455-8888), which dates back to the early 1900s, is scheduled to reopen in fall 2002 after a massive renovation; call for information.

On the South Hill, the stylish **ROCKWOOD BAKERY** (315 E 18th Ave; 509/747-8691) is a favorite sweet spot. In summer months, breakfast and lunch (sandwiches, soups, pastries, and espresso) are offered under towering trees at **THE PARK BENCH** (1928 S Tekoa St; 509/456-8066).

Museum-goers can duck inside to view Bing Crosby memorabilia at the **CROSBY LIBRARY** (Gonzaga University campus, 502 E Boone; 509/328-4240; www.foley. gonzaga.edu/spcoll/specbcc.com), the singer's gift to his alma mater. While on the Gonzaga campus, don't miss the **JUNDT ART MUSEUM** (202 E Cataldo Ave; 509/323-6611; www.gonzaga.edu) and its eclectic lineup of exhibits. The city's dramatically renovated **NORTHWEST MUSEUM OF ARTS & CULTURE**, the MAC (2316 W 1st Ave; 509/456-3931; www.northwestmuseum.org), reopened in 2001 after a $28-million expansion that includes a new 43,000-square-foot building.

Brazilian-born **SPOKANE SYMPHONY ORCHESTRA** conductor Fabio Machetti directs diverse programs such as a pops series—guest artists include native son and internationally known baritone Thomas Hampson—and the free Labor Day concert at Comstock Park (800 W 29th Ave; 509/624-1200). The **SPOKANE CIVIC THEATRE** (1020 N Howard St; 509/325-2507) offers a mixed bag of amateur performances, including productions geared for kids, and with occasional performances by the likes of Coeur d'Alene, Idaho, resident Patty Duke; **INTERPLAYERS ENSEMBLE THEATRE** (174 S Howard St; 509/455-7529) is a professional company with a full season featuring well-known works. The 12,000-seat **SPOKANE VETERANS ARENA** (720 W Mallon Ave; 509/324-7000) occasionally attracts major entertainers and bands; most tickets are sold through a local agency, **G&B SELECT-A-SEAT** (509/325-7328 or 800/325-7328; www.ticketswest.com).

Civic leaders still point to the development of **RIVERFRONT PARK** as one of the turning points in the city's history. Formerly railroad yards, this expansive space is full of meandering paved paths and attractions such as an IMAX theater and a mint-condition 1909 carousel built by Charles Looff. From here you can also access the wonderful **CENTENNIAL TRAIL**, which runs from downtown through the park to Coeur d'Alene, Idaho. (A 2-mile loop passes near the pretty campus of Spokane's Gonzaga University.)

On the city's South Hill, **MANITO PARK** (at Grand Blvd and 18th Ave) has a busy duck pond, a lovely rose garden filled with heirloom varieties, a peaceful Japanese

NORTHEASTERN WASHINGTON THREE-DAY TOUR

DAY ONE: Wake up in Spokane with Torrefazione coffee and stellar cranberry-orange scones at **ROCKWOOD BAKERY.** Afterward, explore nearby **MANITO PARK,** admiring the park's greens. Then lunch on a plate-sized pizza or refreshing salad combo at **LUNA** or the mostly vegetarian fare downtown at **MIZUNA.** Check out the shopping at spiffy **RIVERPARK SQUARE,** which includes a 20-screen cinema. Later, rent in-line skates or a bike at **RIVERFRONT PARK** and head out on the **CENTENNIAL TRAIL,** which runs along the scenic Spokane River. After a dinner of innovative fare at **PAPRIKA,** attend a **SPOKANE SYMPHONY ORCHESTRA** or local theater performance. Return to your room at **WAVERLY PLACE BED & BREAKFAST** to rest up for tomorrow.

DAY TWO: For a fine eye-opener, try the veggie frittata at the **CANNON STREET GRILL,** then head north on US Highway 395 toward Colville. Golfers can stop in Chewelah to play a round at the **GOLF AND COUNTRY CLUB;** skiers can hit the ski slopes at **49 DEGREES NORTH.** In Colville, explore Main Street shops and stop for a velvety cappuccino and a snack at **TALK AND COFFEE.** Check into **MY PARENT'S ESTATE;** then drive about 10 miles back to Colville for dinner at **CAFÉ ITALIANO.**

DAY THREE: Enjoy breakfast at the B&B, and then head west on **HIGHWAY 20** through the Okanogan over Sherman Pass to Republic. On the scenic drive between Kettle Falls and Grand Coulee, stop for coffee and pastries at Republic's **LOOSE BLUE MOOSE** (1015 S Clark Ave; 509/775-0441). From here, head south on Highway 21 to cross **LAKE ROOSEVELT** on the **KELLER FERRY;** then drive northwest on Highway 174 to the famous **GRANDE COULEE DAM.** Gape at the mammoth structure FDR built, walk in the historic town of **COULEE DAM,** or try your luck at the **CASINO.** For dinner, go Mexican at **LA PRESA;** then check in at luxurious **VICTORIA'S COTTAGE** and watch the summer laser light show at the dam from the garden gazebo.

garden, and the ever-changing **GAISER CONSERVATORY**—with displays that include coffee plants, exotic orchids, and prickly flowering cactus.

Two natural areas just a short drive from Spokane offer fine places to hike and see wildlife. The suburban **RIVERSIDE STATE PARK** (509/456-3964) extends from residential northwest Spokane to the Little Spokane River, and offers hiking and picnicking as well as the interesting Bowl and Pitcher basalt formations. The **LITTLE SPOKANE NATURAL AREA** at Riverside State Park is a calm, meandering 6-mile stretch of the Little Spokane River—one of the area's premiere paddling spots. It can be accessed off Waikiki Road near St. George's School in north Spokane; a well-marked parking lot is at the canoe launch, a half mile past the school. The area offers prime bird-watching and has one of the nation's highest diversities of nesting song-birds, as well as great blue heron, wood ducks, and wigeons.

Each spring, the city hosts one of the country's largest foot races. More than 60,000 runners (including a handful of world-class athletes) and walkers turn out on the first Sunday in May for the 7.46-mile **LILAC BLOOMSDAY RUN** (509/838-1579). The Spokane Arena is home to the Western Hockey League **SPOKANE CHIEFS** (509/328-0450). Skiing can be sublime with powdery snow the Inland Northwest is famous for: **MOUNT SPOKANE** (509/443-1397), 31 miles north of the city on Highway 206, is upgrading its terrain under new ownership. Or try 17 kilo-meters of groomed cross-country trails with two warming huts (a Sno-Park pass is required), 3 miles up the road.

RESTAURANTS

Café 5-Ten / ★★

2727 S MOUNT VERNON ST, SPOKANE; 509/533-0064 The short menu at this intimate spot focuses on flavorful steak, seafood, pasta, and chicken dishes. The "feast of the senses" changes seasonally. At dinner, the heavenly angel hair is spiked with a citrusy wine sauce paired with jumbo prawns and pesto. Smoked manchego cheese risotto is topped with grilled marinated chicken. The sirloin steak is rubbed with chili and served with a spicy house steak sauce. There's also an upscale burger and other sandwiches. Pay close attention when the server describes the daily seafood specials. Chef-owner Michael Waliser gets adventurous with exotics such as Hawaiian ono. *$$$; MC, V; checks OK; lunch Tues–Sat, dinner Tues–Sun; full bar; reservations recommended; in Lincoln Heights Shopping Center.* &

Cannon Street Grill / ★

144 S CANNON ST, SPOKANE; 509/456-8660 There are plenty of good greasy spoons in Spokane, but this cozy little spot in the Browne's Addition neighborhood is a cut above the average breakfast place. The coffee is from Craven's, a local roaster. Morning meals include a stellar frittata made with sautéed mushrooms, red peppers, and sweet onions; plate-filling pancakes; and thick French toast. On Sundays, not-to-be-missed brunch fare includes huevos rancheros with black beans, and house-smoked lox with bagels. Lunch consists of simple sandwiches and salads. *$; MC, V; checks OK; breakfast, lunch Mon–Fri, brunch Sun; beer and wine; reservations not accepted; from Maple St exit, north to 2nd Ave, west on Cannon St.* &

Chicken-n-More / ★

502 W SPRAGUE AVE, SPOKANE; 509/838-5071 Spokane's sole soul-food joint is located in a small corner storefront downtown. Owner Bob Hemphill is a Texas native who slow-cooks brisket and ribs in a smoker and tops them with his signature sauce. The deep-fried catfish sandwich—slathered with red pepper sauce and ketchup—takes 15 minutes but is worth the wait. Southern-style fried chicken is digit-licking good, especially alongside an order of jo-jo potatoes. Try a side of red beans and rice, or some braised greens; the coleslaw and baked beans are nothing special. The tiny dining room has a half-dozen tables and some counter space. *$; no credit cards; checks OK; lunch, dinner Mon–Fri; no alcohol; reservations not accepted; across from Ridpath Hotel.*

The Elk Public House / ★

1931 W PACIFIC AVE, SPOKANE; 509/363-1973 This lively neighborhood watering hole has an ever-changing selection of microbrews on tap and a menu designed to complement them. The Wisconsin bratwurst is slow-simmered in beer. A grilled lamb sandwich, slathered with tzatziki, is a three-napkin meal. And the 74th Street gumbo (inspired by a Seattle alehouse) is wickedly hot. The weekly fresh sheet offers global fare such as Spanish-style cod, Asian-inspired pork chops topped with gingery apricot chutney, or Southern-fried catfish with spicy grits. Vegetarians appreciate the option of subbing grilled tofu in any of the entrees or salads. Be patient; service can be slow. *$; MC, V; checks OK; lunch, dinner every day; beer and wine; reservations not accepted; at Cannon St.* &

Hill's Someplace Else / ★★

518 W SPRAGUE AVE, SPOKANE; 509/747-3946 Walk in the front door of this dark, smoky spot and it feels more like a bar than a restaurant, but chef-owner Dave Hill cranks out top-notch food in this casual atmosphere. Everything on the menu is made in-house, from the too-good-to-eat-just-one potato chips and spicy beef jerky to the sinful New York–style cheesecake. The lengthy menu includes sandwiches (house-smoked-salmon panini and the Reuben are standouts), meal-sized salads, and an eclectic lineup of house favorites: duck breast with green peppercorn sauce, chicken satay, beer-batter fish-and-chips, fiery shrimp creole, pork tenderloin with sundried-cherry chutney. Specials change twice daily (lunch and dinner), and the Culinary Institute of America–trained Hill has a way with seafood. *$$; AE, MC, V; checks OK; lunch, dinner Tues–Sat; full bar; reservations recommended; across from Ridpath Hotel.* &

The Italian Kitchen / ★

113 N BERNARD ST, SPOKANE; 509/363-1210 Italian is the cuisine du jour for many restaurants, but this trattoria turns out the most authentic fare in Spokane. The tender ravioli—filled with spinach and ricotta or Italian sausage—is handmade. Try it with rich Gorgonzola cream sauce. Lasagne is also built on a foundation of hand-rolled pasta, layered with beef and veal, béchamel, and marinara. Veal piccata is nicely done, as is the scaloppine—pan-seared with prosciutto and sage. The stylish dining room, done up in warm wood accents and big windows on the street side, dates back to the 1900s. In the lounge, a late-night menu is served until 11:30pm. *$$; AE, DIS, MC, V; checks OK; dinner every day; full bar; reservations not accepted; 2 blocks south of Opera House.* &

Lindaman's Gourmet-to-Go / ★

1235 GRAND BLVD, SPOKANE; 509/838-3000 Spokane's first coffeehouse, this South Hill cafe remains one of the city's most popular places to sip a latte. Lunch and dinner menus are written on a board that hangs above the bustling open kitchen, but the food's also on view in a display case where you order. The casual fare runs the gamut from flavorful wraps and roasted cornish game hens to comforting, cheesy

SPOKANE VALLEY WINE TOURING

While few grapes grow in Spokane itself, the area has a healthy wine industry. Seven wineries welcome visitors, especially during the annual spring barrel-tasting (usually the first weekend in May) and holiday open house (the weekend before Thanksgiving).

MOUNTAIN DOME (16315 Temple Rd; 509/928-2788; www.mountaindome. com)—largely recognized as Washington's finest producer of sparkling wine—is a family-run operation in the foothills of Mount Spokane.

There's no nicer spot for a picnic than **ARBOR CREST CLIFF HOUSE** (4705 Fruithill Rd; 509/927-9894), a historic home that sits high above the Spokane Valley. In summer, enjoy Sunday evening concerts and art exhibits. The family winery has a reputation for fine merlot and sauvignon blanc.

At **LATAH CREEK** (13030 E Indiana Ave; 509/926-0164), winemaker Mike Conway is almost always on the premises to answer questions about his merlots, cabernets, chardonnay, or the popular huckleberry Riesling. **KNIPPRATH CELLARS** (5634 E Commerce Ave; 509/534-5121), now in the former headquarters of Hale's Ale, specializes in varietals crafted in a European style, including pinot noir, chardonnay, and lemberger. Knipprath also produces a port. Tasting-room hours are limited.

In an odd juxtaposition, **CATERINA WINERY** (905 N Washington St; 509/328-5069) sits on the ground floor of the Broadview Dairy. Gregarious vintner Mike Scott jokes that's what makes his chardonnays so rich and creamy. At **WYVERN CELLARS** (7217 W 45th Ave; 509/455-7835), west of downtown, the friendly tasting-room staff is glad to pour from an extensive lineup that ranges from Riesling to merlot. The latest addition is **TOWNSHEND CELLAR** (16112 N Greenbluff Rd, Colbert; 509/238-4346), which produces chardonnay, merlot, cab, and a huckleberry port.

—Leslie Kelly

casseroles. The house salad with a creamy garlic dressing is not to be missed; same goes for the decadent pastries. Temptations include cheesecake, chocolate sin, and— in summer months—fine fruit pies. The wine selection is exceptional and affordable. *$; AE, MC, V; checks OK; breakfast, lunch, dinner every day; beer and wine; reservations not accepted; www.lindamans.com; near Sacred Heart Medical Center.* &

Luna / ★★★

5620 S PERRY ST, SPOKANE; 509/448-2383 If this classy neighborhood spot reminds you of a sun-drenched dining room in California, that's no happy accident. Owners Marcia and William Bond solicited advice from Alice Waters, the queen of nouvelle California cuisine, before they launched their restaurant in 1994. It shows—from the warm welcome to the ever-evolving menu that focuses on fresh ingredients, including herbs and vegetables harvested from a garden just outside the kitchen. First plates might include chipotle-grilled quail, yellowfin tuna tartare or house-cured Norwegian salmon, sliced paper thin and paired with grilled red onions. Main plates offer contemporary takes on classics. Coconut curry prawns are a customer favorite. Light eaters can split a plate-sized pizza from the wood-fired oven. Luna has one of the region's best wine lists, with extensive and affordable international selections. For brunch, indulge in rich smoked-salmon hash or French toast with caramelized bananas and pecans. *$$$; AE, DIS, MC, V; checks OK; lunch Mon–Fri, dinner every day, brunch Sat and Sun; full bar; reservations recommended; corner of 56th St.* &

Mizuna / ★★

214 N HOWARD ST, SPOKANE; 509/747-2004 Spokane's upscale vegetarian restaurant has added seafood to its innovative lineup, in which all dishes feature fresh, seasonal ingredients. In fall, it could mean pumpkin-filled ravioli served with sautéed apples, toasted hazelnuts, and a smoky Chilean pie with ancho chile sauce, or forest mushroom croquettes paired with braised grapes. Don't miss the Asian lettuce-wrap starter, with crunchy iceberg leaves enveloping a savory sauté of shiitakes, seitan, ginger, and garlic. At lunch, Cajun Caesar, tofu-stuffed salad rolls with a peanut dipping sauce, and a meatless Reuben—made with marinated, grilled seitan—are popular choices. A cozy bar adds to this inviting venue's appeal. *$$$; AE, DIS, MC, V; checks OK; lunch Mon–Fri, dinner Tues–Sat; beer, wine, and specialty cocktails; reservations not necessary; just south of Riverfront Park.* &

Niko's II Greek and Middle East Restaurant / ★★

725 W RIVERSIDE AVE, SPOKANE; 509/624-7444 The heart of this downtown restaurant is its sophisticated yet cozy wine bar. Take a tasting tour—several samples of one varietal or a famous wine region—and order the appetizer combo (hummus, tzatziki, baba ghanouj) while studying the extensive Mediterranean menu. Solid bets are lamb souvlaki, beef kebabs, tomato chutney–topped calamari steak, and chicken curry. Steer clear of dishes with pasta, which can be overcooked. House-made desserts include traditional baklava, velvety chocolate decadence, and elegant crème brûlée. The kitchen stays open until 11pm, with a late-night menu on weekends. *$$; AE, DIS, MC, V; checks OK; lunch Mon–Fri, dinner Mon–Sat; beer and wine; reservations not necessary; downtown, at Post St.* &

Paprika / ★★★

1228 S GRAND BLVD, SPOKANE; 509/455-7545 Across the street from the gothic spires of St. John's Cathedral on Spokane's South Hill, this little dining room has the most imaginative food in town. Offerings change seasonally: fall brings warming fare such as elk picatta, sautéed escolar with braised heirloom tomatoes, and rack of pork swimming in a puddle of hard cider sauce. Spring and summer focus on tender greens from local growers and whimsical presentations such as Bloody Mary gazpacho served in a martini glass with a plump prawn. For variety, try chef-owner Karla Graves's weekday bite nights: mini portions at mini prices. The walls at this cozy spot are bathed in the warm tones of the spice for which the restaurant is named. Striking art is painted by the sous-chef, who also prepares some of the desserts. Seasonal creations include updated classics such as a baked Alaska with a creamy Italian meringue. *$$$; AE, MC, V; checks OK; dinner Tues–Sat; beer and wine; reservations recommended; across from St. John's Cathedral.* ౬

LODGINGS

Angelica's Bed & Breakfast

1321 W 9TH AVE, SPOKANE; 509/624-5598 OR 800/987-0053 Renowned architect Kirtland Cutter designed this 1907 Arts and Crafts mansion with a European sensibility in the lower South Hill neighborhood, a mix of older homes and apartments. The dramatic entryway draws guests into the inviting living room or dining room, or up the stately wooden staircase. Past the cozy sunroom on the mezzanine, all four guests rooms (with private baths) are on the second level and are named for family members. Yvonne is a standout with a four-poster bed, a gas fireplace, a walk-in closet, and spiffy wood floors. Nice touches throughout include quality linens, guest robes, reading lamps, and early morning coffee in the sunroom. *$$; AE, DIS, MC, V; checks OK; info@angelicasbb.com; www.angelicasbb.com; just south of downtown, off Cedar St.*

Fotheringham House / ★★

2128 W 2ND AVE, SPOKANE; 509/838-1891 From the first cup of fresh-ground coffee in the morning to tea and treats at night, pampering of guests is a hallmark of owners Irene and Poul Jensen, who took over in spring 2001. The couple welcome guests to the beautifully restored Queen Anne–style mansion in the Browne's Addition neighborhood. The entire house is tastefully appointed with period antiques. You don't have to be a politician to enjoy the Mayor's Room, adorned with a four-poster bed draped in delicate lace, a piano desk, and a love seat; it also has a private bath. The Garden Room overlooks an urban bird sanctuary. It shares a bath with the Museum Room and the Mansion Room, named for the historic Patsy Clark's restaurant across the street. The summer garden bursts with color and fragrance, especially the lovely lavender display that lines the front walkway. *$$; MC, V; checks OK; innkeeper@fotheringham.net; www.fotheringham.net; just across from Cowley Park.*

Marianna Stoltz House / ★

427 E INDIANA AVE, SPOKANE; 509/483-4316 OR 800/978-6587 This 1908 foursquare home is on a tree-lined street near Gonzaga University, a 5-minute drive from downtown. The inviting parlor and living room are filled with elegant velvet couches and brocade armchairs. Three of the four rooms (two with private baths) are named for color schemes. The Blue Room is lit with an ornate chandelier that dates back to when the house was built, and the Green Room has an antique settee. Or try the Ivy Suite, one of our favorites. All have cable TV and air-conditioning. Hostess Phyllis Maguire's attention to detail includes robes, free local calls on the guest phone, a refrigerator to stash beverages, and a ready supply of coffee, tea, and cookies. Breakfast is served in courses: peach-melba parfait, homemade granola, and Dutch Baby pancakes or scrambled eggs tucked into a croissant. *$$; AE, DIS, MC, V; checks OK; info@mariannastolzhouse.com; www.mariannastolzhouse.com; Hamilton St exit off I-90.*

Waverly Place Bed & Breakfast / ★★

709 W WAVERLY PL, SPOKANE; 509/328-1856 Marge Arndt is the gracious hostess at this pretty 1902 Victorian located in a neighborhood just north of downtown. In summer, guests are invited to linger over afternoon lemonade on the expansive veranda with a view of nearby Corbin Park, or take a dip in the pool. The four rooms are on three levels, the grandest quarters being the two-story master suite, with its own sitting room and claw-footed tub in the luxurious bath. Of the two rooms that share a bath, Anna's Room has a window seat that overlooks the park. Breakfast specialties include Swedish pancakes with Idaho huckleberries. *$$; MC, V; checks OK; waverly@waverlyplace.com; www.waverlyplace.com; Division St exit off I-90.*

Westcoast Grand Hotel / ★

303 W NORTH RIVER DR, SPOKANE; 509/326-8000 OR 800/843-4667 This hotel makes a fine base for exploring downtown Spokane and Riverfront Park on foot. It sits on the bank of the Spokane River, and runners appreciate its proximity to the scenic Centennial Trail. A big draw is the large outdoor swimming pool, complete with a couple of water slides. Request a room—decorated in standard motel motif—with a city view. The hotel has more than 300 rooms and conference facilities, including 17 meeting rooms and exhibit halls (the largest is 9,800 square feet). A business center is available for guests; the airport shuttle is free. *$$; AE, DC, DIS, MC, V; checks OK; just north of downtown, off Washington St.*

Pend Oreille and Colville River Valleys

The wild terrain, the wildlife, and the region's wide river, the Pend Oreille (pronounced "pon-der-RAY"), which flows north to Canada, where it dumps into the Columbia just north of the border, deserve more attention than they get; and the sparsely populated Colville River valley is home to tiny farming and logging communities. But outdoor recreation, from fishing and boating to cross-country skiing and hunting, draws many to this pristine region.

The Pend Oreille

This northernmost corner of the state is generally considered a place to drive through on the way to Canada. In fact, it's nicknamed "the forgotten corner." (Although movie buffs might remember the scenery around Metaline Falls from *The Postman,* Kevin Costner's 1997 postapocalyptic box-office bomb. Film crews invaded Metaline Falls one summer and gave the town a new "old" look.)

Highway 20 heads north from US Highway 2 at Newport, following the Pend Oreille River. The surrounding **SALMO-PRIEST WILDERNESS AREA** is home to grizzly, caribou, and bald eagles, among other elusive wildlife. Its 38 miles of hiking trails traverse 7,300-foot Gypsy Peak. To the west of Metaline Falls, north of Highway 20 on Highway 31, hikers can trek to the **KETTLE CREST.** Considered one of the best hikes in the region, this 42-mile trek offers opportunities to view wildlife such as black bear, deer, coyotes, and a variety of birds. The Colville branch of the U.S. Forest Service (765 S Main St, Colville; 509/684-7000) has also developed some shorter loop trails that access the crest; the forest service's summer guided wildflower tours here have become so popular that reservations are essential.

Colville and Kettle Falls Area

This area has the working-class feel of a lumber town. Colville and Kettle Falls are tight-knit blue-collar communities, where you're likely to see "Cream of Spotted Owl" bumper stickers on the logging trucks that barrel down the road. Kettle Falls is a jumping-off spot for exploring Lake Roosevelt to the south and the Okanogan to the west.

CHEWELAH, 52 miles north of Spokane on US Highway 395, is home to the 18-hole challenging (and inexpensive) **GOLF AND COUNTRY CLUB** (Sand Canyon Rd; 509/935-6807). To the east is tiny but friendly **49 DEGREES NORTH** ski area (3311 Flowery Trail Rd; 509/935-6649), 58 miles northeast of Spokane, which offers free beginner lessons.

Continuing north on US Highway 395, reach Colville, with a quaint Main Street of antique shops and the friendly **TALK AND COFFEE** (119 E Astor Ave; 509/684-2373). When the weather's warm, head for the retro-cool **AUTOVUE DRIVE-IN** (444 AutoVue Rd; 509/684-2863) for first-run movies and special Sunday prices for carloads.

CHINA BEND WINERY (3596 Northport-Flatcreek Rd; 509/732-6123), north of Kettle Falls, grows organic grapes and has the northernmost vineyards in the state. In summer, catered lunches can be arranged (48-hour advance notice; around $10 per person); the menu focuses on the freshest ingredients from the winery's half-acre organic pea-patch.

West from Kettle Falls, Highway 20 is a little-traveled two-lane road that is one of the finest spots for fall foliage, lined with birch and maple trees. Near **SHERMAN PASS** are dramatic remnants of a 1988 forest fire. Beyond is the mountain town of **REPUBLIC.**

From Republic, Highway 21 heads south to Lake Roosevelt in the Grand Coulee area. If you're hankering to get out and explore the pretty landscape on horseback, head to **K-DIAMOND-K GUEST RANCH** (15661 Hwy 21 S; 509/775-3536 or 888/345-5355; www.kdiamondk.com). A working dude ranch, it specializes in guided mountain trail rides and down-home hospitality (everyone eats at the family table).

RESTAURANTS

Café Italiano

153 W 2ND AVE, COLVILLE; 509/684-5957 This inviting restaurant, with several dining rooms and an outdoor courtyard for summer seating, is run by the Karatzas family. Their Greek heritage shows up on the expansive menu with dishes such as sautéed scampi finished with feta, and filet mignon sautéed with Greek peppers. But the fare is mostly traditional Italian: pastas, pizzas, antipasto, and spumoni. Signature dishes include veal marsala, chicken sautéed with spicy capicolla ham, and eggplant Parmesan. The house cheesecake is made fresh daily, featuring different toppings. $$; AE, MC, V; checks OK; lunch Mon–Fri, dinner every day; beer and wine; reservations recommended; 2 blocks west of US Hwy 395.

INLAND NORTHWEST GOLF

When *Golf Digest* named Spokane one of the best places in the country to play on public links, some of the city's duffers were perturbed. It wasn't that they disagreed; they simply didn't want to share their secret.

The good news is, with so many courses in the area—40 within a half-day drive of Spokane—no one should have trouble getting a tee time. And most of those courses are still reasonably priced, averaging less than $30 for 18 holes.

The venerable **INDIAN CANYON** (4304 W West Dr; 509/747-5353) is considered the most beautiful links around—its sweeping fairways are lined with majestic evergreens. The 19th hole is especially appealing (sit on the deck and enjoy the view) after uphill jaunts on the 17th and 18th holes.

The newest city course, the **CREEK AT QUALCHAN** (301 E Meadowland Rd; 509/448-9317), is rife with water hazards. **ESMERALDA GOLF COURSE** (3933 E Courtland Ave; 509/487-6291) is one of the oldest courses and has become more challenging in recent years as growing trees have become a vexing obstacle.

County and municipal courses include a couple of beauties that sit side-by-side east of Spokane. **LIBERTY LAKE** (24403 E Sprague Ave, Liberty Lake; 509/255-6233) nestles up against a wooded hillside, which comes into play on several holes. Golfers are rewarded for their efforts with a fine view of the lake on the 18th green. The neighboring **MEADOWWOOD** (24501 E Valleyview Ave, Liberty Lake; 509/255-9539), which was given *Golf Digest*'s four-star seal of approval, is long and rambling with open fairways lined with tricky roughs.

Another county course, **HANGMAN VALLEY** (2210 E Hangman Valley Rd; 509/448-1212), has an almost desertlike landscape, with some fine valley views from elevated par 5s. —*Leslie Kelly*

LODGINGS

My Parent's Estate / ★

HWY 395, COLVILLE; 509/738-6220 Pull into the rambling driveway and say hello to hostess Bev Parent's pet llamas. This 43-acre historic spot was the St. Francis-Regis Mission in 1869, then a Dominican convent in the early '30s. Since 1989, it's been a B&B. Recently, Parent closed off the guest quarters in the main house and opened a large suite in a separate building. From the tiny deck, guests might spot an amazing array of wildlife—from resident deer to the occasional barn owl—or just a herd of cows grazing (and mooing) nearby. Inside are a fireplace, a pretty bathroom with a claw-footed tub, and a tiny kitchen area where guests can eat the breakfast Parent delivers each morning. A two-bedroom caretaker's cottage is available only for weekly or monthly rental. *$$; MC, V; checks OK; closed Oct–May; 7 miles north of downtown Colville.*

Grand Coulee Area

Grand, yes—this is a wonderful area from which to appreciate the outsized dimensions of the landscape and the geological forces that made it. The **COLUMBIA RIVER** slices through Northeastern Washington with a quiet power, as the water rushes by in silky strength through enormous chasms. In prehistoric times, glacier-fed water created a river with the largest flow of water ever known. Today it's the second-largest river in the nation, traversing a plateau of equally staggering scale.

Some 15 miles upstream of Grand Coulee Dam, the tiny **KELLER FERRY** (on Hwy 21; 509/324-6015) shuttles across the Columbia dozens of times a day at no charge. The *Martha S.*, operated by the state Department of Transportation, holds just a dozen cars. The crossing—which lasts only 15 minutes—is the waterborne section of Highway 21, between the Colville Indian Reservation to the north of the river and the Columbia Plateau on the south. On the Grand Coulee side is a small store run by the Colville Tribe that sells fishing licenses and some groceries, and rents boats.

For many years **LAKE ROOSEVELT,** the massive 150-mile-long reservoir created by Grand Coulee Dam, was untapped by the RV-on-pontoon fleets. Now several companies offer weekly (or weekend, for a hefty price) **HOUSEBOAT RENTALS.** Some of these vessels have deluxe features such as on-deck hot tubs, stereo systems, gourmet kitchens, and outdoor rinse-off showers. For rates and reservations, contact Roosevelt Recreational Enterprises (PO Box 5, Coulee Dam; 800/648-LAKE).

Grand Coulee Dam

Clustered around Grand Coulee Dam are the towns of Grand Coulee, Coulee Dam, and Electric City. The **GRAND COULEE DAM AREA CHAMBER OF COMMERCE** (319 Midway Ave; 800/268-5332; www.grandcouleedam.org) has information. Take a self-guided historical walking tour in Coulee Dam or try your luck at the **COULEE DAM CASINO** (515 Birch St; 509/633-0766). But the biggest attraction here, of course, is the dam itself. Grand Coulee Dam—sometimes referred to as the seventh wonder of the world—was conceived as an irrigation project, and now supplies water to more than 500,000 acres of farmland. World War II gave it a new purpose, producing power for the production of plutonium at Hanford and aluminum for aircraft. As tall as a 46-story building and the length of a dozen city blocks, the dam was completed in 1942, nearly 10 years after construction began.

Since September 11, 2001, tours have been suspended. Call first to determine if and when they will be reinstated. A summer laser light show illuminates a portion of the 12-million cubic yards of concrete used to build the dam. For tour and light show times, call the U.S. Bureau of Reclamation **VISITORS ARRIVAL CENTER** (Hwy 155, Grand Coulee; 509/633-9265; light show Memorial Day–Sept).

RESTAURANTS

La Presa / ★

515 E GRAND COULEE AVE, GRAND COULEE; 509/633-3173 The Hernandez family doesn't make a big deal about calling its food "authentic Mexican," but it is. Most authentic are the carne asada (cooked over a charcoal fire), the chorizo with eggs, or the dark, cinnamon-scented chicken mole. The menu is huge, with all sorts of steaks and seafood dishes. There's even (oddly enough) chicken teriyaki. Stick with traditional favorites such as the enchilada verde, made with fresh tomatillos. The decor is strictly velvet paintings and wool blankets, but the welcome is warm and the margaritas are icy cold. *$; MC, V; checks OK; lunch, dinner every day; beer, wine, and tequila; reservations recommended; on Hwy 21, just up from dam.* &

LODGINGS

Victoria's Cottage / ★★

209 COLUMBIA AVE, COULEE DAM; 509/633-2908 This isn't your average B&B. It's more like your own wing of one of the most impressive homes in Coulee Dam, where hosts Dave and Bonnie Schmidt respect their guests' privacy. This cottage includes a large living room with skylights over an oversized Jacuzzi. There's a sound system, two TVs with VCRs (one is in the bedroom), along with a sizable selection of CDs and movies. In the well-equipped pantry are drinks and everything you need to make s'mores over the portable gas "campfire" outside. The one-unit cottage can sleep four, with a pullout sleeper in the living room. Guests can help themselves to veggies from the owners' garden. Other thoughtful details include a well-stocked medicine cabinet (Tums, aspirin, etc., along with lotion and shampoo), plush robes, a supply of board games, and mountain bikes to borrow. Fresh-baked scones and fruit are delivered each morning with the newspaper. *$$; MC, V; checks OK; victoriascottage@excite.com; www.reitpro.com/victoriascottage; next to tiny Douglas Park.*

Soap Lake

Soap Lake earned its name on a windy day, when frothy whitecaps dotted the surface of this lake. Many believe the lake, known for its high content of soft minerals (which also give it a soapy feel), has healing properties. Contact the **SOAP LAKE CHAMBER OF COMMERCE** (300 N Daisy St; 509/246-1821; www.soaplakecoc.org) for information on renting canoes and sailboats.

DRY FALLS, off Highway 17 north of town, is an example of the power of ice. When glacial Lake Missoula overflowed its Ice-Age dam some 12,000 years ago, torrential floods headed west to the Pacific. The force of the water carved out what is now this ancient waterfall, 3-½ miles wide and 400 feet high (by comparison, Niagara Falls is 1 mile wide and 165 feet high). The **DRY FALLS INTERPRETIVE CENTER** (inside Sun Lakes State Park, 4 miles southwest of Coulee City on Hwy 17; 509/632-5583), at the top of the canyon a half mile from the scenic overlook, is open May through September, 10am–6pm daily.

SUN LAKES STATE PARK (800/233-0321; www.parks.wa.gov), downstream from the falls, offers all kinds of outdoor activities: hiking, canoeing, camping, swimming, boating, fishing, golf, horseback riding, and simple picnicking.

LODGINGS

Notaras Lodge

236 E MAIN ST, SOAP LAKE; 509/246-0462 Soap Lake's renowned mineral waters are on tap in the bathrooms, several of which have Jacuzzis. Though the lodge was rebuilt after a 1998 fire, and the 14 rooms are still decorated with Western history, some of the most popular—and quirkiest (like the Norma Zimmer Room, named after the bubble lady on the *Lawrence Welk Show*)—didn't make the transition. All four lodge buildings are log-cabin style and are right on the lake; six rooms have lake views. Owner Marina Romary also runs Don's Restaurant (14 Canna St; 509/246-1217; lunch, dinner every day), which specializes in steak, seafood, and Greek entrees. *$$; MC, V; checks OK; notaras@televar.com; www.notaraslodge.com; Soap Lake exit off Hwy 28, at Canna St.* &

Omak

Omak is a town of 4,000, located 50 miles north of Grand Coulee on Highway 155. The famous—and controversial—Suicide Race is the climax of the **OMAK STAMPEDE** (509/826-1002 or 800/933-6625; stampede@televar.com; www.omakstampede. org), the popular rodeo held here the second weekend of August on the banks of the Okanogan River. During the Stampede, Omak's population swells to 30,000.

LODGINGS

The Rodeway Inn

122 N MAIN, OMAK; 509/826-0400 OR 888/700-6625 This basic hotel has the distinction of being the closest lodgings to the Stampede grounds. Its 61 rooms include remote-control satellite TV, several Jacuzzi suites, and a few units with kitchens. There are smoking and nonsmoking rooms and an outdoor swimming pool; pets OK. *$; AE, DIS, MC, V; checks OK; next to movie theater.*

VANCOUVER AND ENVIRONS

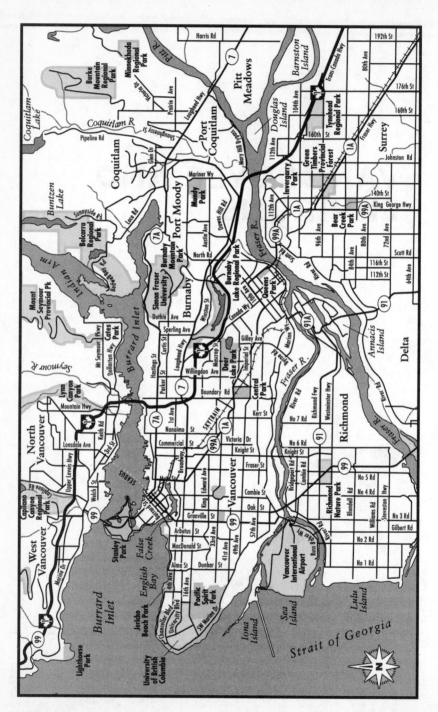

VANCOUVER AND ENVIRONS

The Vancouver area is Canada's fastest-growing metropolis and a city of magical contradictions—from rough-and-tumble Hastings Street, where timeworn brick-work exudes a wild, seaport-town atmosphere, to trendy Robson Street, with its futuristic Japanese noodle houses and haute couture. This city nestled between mountains and ocean has long touted itself as Canada's gateway to the Pacific Rim, and British Columbia is fortunate to be plugged into one of the world's fastest-growing economies. The city seems living proof that a benign environment will produce an easygoing disposition.

ACCESS AND INFORMATION

VANCOUVER INTERNATIONAL AIRPORT (9 miles/15 km south of downtown on Sea Island, Richmond; 604/207-7077; www.yvr.ca) is a major international airport with flights daily to every continent. Renovations to the domestic terminal were scheduled to be completed by July 2002. Several **CAR RENTAL** agencies, including Avis (604/606-2847), Budget (604/668-7000), and National (604/273-3121), are on the ground floor of the three-level parkade.

Weathered but still-graceful, **PACIFIC CENTRAL STATION** (1150 Station St) is the local terminus of several regional, national, and international bus and rail services. **GREYHOUND CANADA** (604/482-8747 or 800/231-2222; www.greyhound. ca) operates five buses daily between Vancouver and Seattle. **PACIFIC COACH LINES** (604/662-8074 or 800/661-1725; www.pacificcoach.com) operates a modern bus service between Vancouver and Victoria via **BC FERRIES** (250/386-3431 or 888/223-3779; www.bcferries.bc.ca). **VIA RAIL** (800/561-8630 or 888/VIA-RAIL; www.viarail.ca) is Canada's national passenger rail service. **AMTRAK** (800/USA-RAIL; www.amtrak.com) trains make daily runs between Vancouver and Seattle. **BC RAIL** (1311 W 1st St, North Vancouver; 604/984-5246 or 800/663-8238; www.bc rail.com/bcrpass), the provincial railway service, provides comfortable passenger transportation between North Vancouver and the central interior city of Prince George, as well as excursions to Squamish along scenic Howe Sound.

Travelers by car choose between two major highways. **HIGHWAY 99,** the main north-south highway connecting Vancouver to Seattle, leads south from the city across the fertile delta at the mouth of the Fraser River and connects with Washington State's Interstate 5. Highway 99 also connects Vancouver to the ski resort town of Whistler, about two hours north, and is known as the **SEA TO SKY HIGHWAY.** Transcontinental **HIGHWAY 1,** the main east-west highway, arrives from the east through the lower BC mainland and terminates in Vancouver; it runs along the south shore of the Fraser River. **HIGHWAY 7** runs east-west along the north shore.

Western British Columbia is blessed by a temperate maritime climate, and Vancouver's **WEATHER** is the mildest in Canada, thanks to ocean currents and major weather patterns that bring warm, moist air in waves from the Pacific year-round. Spring comes early (by mid-March, usually); July and August are warmest; late-summer and autumn days (through October) tend to be warm and sunny, with the occasional shower. Winter is rainy season—roughly November through March—but rain usually falls only as showers or drizzle.

Vancouver

Vancouver, its residents are fond of saying, is one of the few cities in the world where you can go snowboarding and sailing on the same day. How remarkable, then, that it should also be one of the few where, sitting outside a Neapolitan cafe, you can eavesdrop on an impassioned argument in Hungarian and see graffiti in Khmer. It's also a festive city, with art everywhere, and a fashionable shopping strip—Robson Street—often compared to Beverly Hills's posh Rodeo Drive. Yet glance away from the opulence of the shops as you saunter along Robson and at the end of a side street the peaceful waters of Burrard Inlet lap at the shore. Beyond, the mountains on the North Shore glitter with snow for half the year.

No city is homogenous, least of all Vancouver. It's really an amalgam of 23 neighborhoods, each with its own unique character and stories. **YALETOWN,** a whirling high-tech zone that's a case of gentrification gone right, looks across to the glittering condos on the south shore of False Creek. Home to one of the largest urban redevelopment projects ever attempted in North America, the **FALSE CREEK BASIN** has its natural center in the bustling market area and arts community on Granville Island. Equally dynamic alternative cultures of different sorts flourish in **KITSILANO** (a funky, former low-rent haven for hippies that has been yuppified by baby boomers and young families), across False Creek, and the **WEST END** (home to Canada's most densely populated neighborhood and western Canada's largest gay and lesbian community), just south of Stanley Park. The cultural mix along **COMMERCIAL DRIVE** is the contemporary home of bohemian subculture, where members of Vancouver's lesbian community can be seen alongside the graying curmudgeons of an older generation, all sipping espresso outside one of the many cafes. If the High Street style of British society is more to your liking, amble over to **AMBLESIDE** and rub shoulders with the sensible-shoe set browsing the private art galleries and lunching on pork pies.

The city's public transit system is an efficient way to get around town; **COAST MOUNTAIN TRANSLINK** (604/521-0400; www.translink.bc.ca) covers more than 695 square miles (1,800 square km) with three forms of transit: bus, SeaBus, and SkyTrain. More information is available from the **VANCOUVER TOURIST INFO-CENTRE** (200 Burrard St; 604/683-2000; www.tourismvancouver.com).

MUSEUMS AND GALLERIES

Francis Rattenbury's elegant old courthouse downtown is now the **VANCOUVER ART GALLERY** (750 Hornby St; 604/662-4719; www.vanartgallery.bc.ca), holding more than 20 major exhibitions a year. Its permanent collection includes works by Goya, Emily Carr, Gainsborough, and Picasso. Many of the city's commercial galleries are located on the dozen blocks just south of the Granville Bridge; art galleries here represent internationally renowned painters and photographers. Granville Island, site of the **EMILY CARR INSTITUTE OF ART AND DESIGN** (1399 Johnston St; 604/844-3800; www.eciad.bc.ca), has a number of pottery and craft studios. The avant-garde is most often at spaces such as the **MONTE CLARK GALLERY** (2339 Granville St; 604/730-5000).

The **MUSEUM OF ANTHROPOLOGY** at the University of British Columbia (6393 NW Marine Dr; 604/822-3825; www.moa.ubc.ca) has an extensive collection of artifacts from Native American cultures of coastal British Columbia (including an

VANCOUVER THREE-DAY TOUR

DAY ONE: Start your day at the **GRANVILLE ISLAND PUBLIC MARKET.** It opens at 9am and is a good place to turn breakfast into a progressive meal: an americano at **JJ BEAN,** apple focaccia from **TERRA BREADS,** candied salmon from **SEAFOOD CITY.** After exploring the shops, studios, and galleries, check in to the luxurious **SHERATON VANCOUVER WALL CENTRE** in Yaletown or the **YWCA HOTEL/RESIDENCE** (where you can work out for free in their high-end fitness facility). Next stop: **CHINA-TOWN,** for dim sum at **HON'S WUN TUN HOUSE** and a guided tour through the **DR. SUN YAT-SEN CLASSICAL CHINESE GARDEN,** before walking the frenzied streets looking for jade treasures or tasting steamed buns from one of Chinatown's many bakeries. Return to your room and change for a run along the **STANLEY PARK SEA-WALL** before heading to dinner (with a sunset) at the **RAINCITY GRILL.**

DAY TWO: After your first cup of strong coffee at the hotel, head west to **KITSI-LANO** for breakfast—big portions of eggs, pancakes, and waffles are on deck at **SOPHIE'S COSMIC CAFE.** Next, head to the University of British Columbia and the **MUSEUM OF ANTHROPOLOGY** to see its jaw-droppingly impressive First Nations artifacts, and the **UBC BOTANICAL GARDEN,** the oldest and one of the finest gardens in Canada. Leave time to freshen up at your hotel before you walk over to the **SUTTON PLACE HOTEL** for high tea or Japanese tea in Fleuri. Then stroll **ROBSON STREET,** a trendy boulevard of pret-a-porter boutiques and swank eateries. If you'd like to see a live show—pop, jazz, or an evening at the symphony—walk over to **GRANVILLE STREET,** where the Commodore Ballroom, Orpheum Theatre, and Vogue Theatre sometimes have last-minute tickets available before 8pm. Afterward, treat yourself to a late-night snack of "tapatizers" at **BIN 941 TAPAS PARLOUR.**

DAY THREE: Start the morning in West Vancouver with raspberry scones and coffee at the **SAVARY ISLAND PIE COMPANY.** After breakfast, leisurely browse the shops in Ambleside and Dundarave. Then it's off to **LIGHTHOUSE PARK'S** 1914 lighthouse (Marine Dr at Beaton Ln, West Vancouver) and the rocky outcrop of Point Atkinson—and its stunning city view. Back in Yaletown, have chowder and a beer at **RODNEY'S OYSTER HOUSE** or sushi and sake at **BLUE WATER CAFE** before browsing upscale boutiques. For dinner, go all out with a four-star meal at **LUMIÈRE** or **OUEST.**

impressive display of totem poles and two Haida houses), as well as artifacts from Africa and Asia. Tucked behind the imposing facade of Cathedral Place is the **CANA-DIAN CRAFT MUSEUM** (639 Hornby St; 604/687-8266), Canada's first national museum devoted to crafts.

The **GRANVILLE ISLAND MUSEUMS** (1502 Duranleau St; 604/683-1939; www. granvilleislandmuseums.com) are actually three museums in one building, and the place to while away a rainy afternoon. Catch the world's biggest public display of recreational fishing artifacts at the **SPORT FISHING MUSEUM**, while at the **MODEL SHIP MUSEUM**, miniature watercraft—from tugs to battleships to working model subs—are featured. For landlubbers, there's an impressive collection of toy and model trains at the **MODEL TRAIN MUSEUM**, along with a diorama of the Fraser Valley Canyon done in stunning detail—right down to 5,000 handmade trees. Admission to any one of the museums covers all three.

PARKS AND GARDENS

The city is blessed with a climate—similar to Britain's—well suited for flowers and greenery. Take a walk through the quiet rain forest in the heart of **STANLEY PARK** (west end of Beach and W Georgia Sts to Lions Gate Bridge; 604/257-8400). This 1,000-acre in-city park is within walking distance of the trendy shops of Robson Street but feels worlds away; its appeal includes the seawall, formal rose gardens, Vancouver Rowing Club, Vancouver Aquarium, restaurants, painters, totem poles, horse-drawn tours, and numerous wilderness trails. At **QUEEN ELIZABETH PARK** (Cambie St and 33rd Ave; 604/257-8570), dramatic winding paths, sunken gardens, and waterfalls skirt the **BLOEDEL CONSERVATORY**. Near Queen Elizabeth Park, **VANDUSEN BOTANICAL GARDEN** (5251 Oak St; 604/878-9274; www.vandusen-garden.org) stretches over 55 acres.

The **UNIVERSITY OF BRITISH COLUMBIA** (6804 SW Marine Dr; 604/822-9666; www.hedgerows.com/UBCBotGdn/index.htm) boasts superb gardens—the Botanical Garden, Nitobe Memorial Gardens, and Totem Park—along with the Physick Garden, which re-creates a 16th-century monastic herb garden. The **CHINESE CLASSICAL GARDEN** (578 Carrall St; 604/662-3207; www.vancouverchinesegarden.com) within Dr. Sun Yat-Sen Park is a spectacular reconstruction of a Chinese scholar's garden, complete with pavilions and water walkways. **KITSILANO BEACH** (Cornwall Ave and Arbutus St, bordering English Bay) is a year-round haven for joggers, dog-walkers, and evening strollers.

SHOPPING

Vancouver has always been bursting with storefronts. In **YALETOWN** (bordered by Pacific Blvd and Nelson, Cambie, and Seymour Sts), brick warehouses have been transformed into loft apartments, offices, chic shops housing ultrahip clothing stores and high-end home furnishings, and the city's most vibrant restaurants. **ROBSON STREET** (between Beatty St and Stanley Park) is the meeting place of cultures and couture, as *tout le monde* strolls among its many boutiques and restaurants. Weekends are crowded, but there's a lot to see, from art books, jewelry, and gifts by local artists at the **GALLERY SHOP** in the Vancouver Art Gallery to a string of flagship stores for international fashion companies (Zara, Banana Republic, Nike, French Connection, Gap, Club Monaco), and local fashion chains (Aritzia, Zioni, Boys' Co.). At Robson and Homer Streets, you'll find the main branch of the Vancouver Public Library (350 W Georgia St; 604/331-3600), designed by world-renowned architect Moshe Safdie and inspired by the Roman Coliseum. Its store, **BOOKMARK** (604/331-4040), has gifts for literary folk.

Downtown is full of outstanding shops. In poor weather, head underground to **PACIFIC CENTRE** (700 W Georgia St to 777 Dunsmuir St; 604/688-7236; www.

pacificcentre.ca), downtown's biggest and busiest mall, with over 140 outlets including name retailers **HOLT RENFREW** and **SEARS,** which connects to **VANCOUVER CENTRE** (604/688-5658). Also downtown is **SINCLAIR CENTRE** (757 W Hastings St; 604/659-1009), a striking example of the reclaimed-heritage school of architecture. It contains the high-end designer department store Leone, as well as Plaza Escada.

South Granville, from Granville Bridge toward 16th Avenue, borders on the prestigious **SHAUGHNESSY NEIGHBORHOOD** and caters to the carriage trade. Impressive is a new crop of Occidental antique stores—to supplement the existing British ones—that import treasures from Japan, Indonesia, and India. Under the Granville Bridge on Granville Island, warehouses and factories have been transformed into a public market and craft shops. Some of the best local designers are located in the Net Loft building, and there are more than 50 shops catering to the marine industry. At the **GRANVILLE ISLAND PUBLIC MARKET** (1689 Johnston St; 604/666-5784; www.granvilleisland.bc.ca), you can get everything from ocean-caught, candied salmon to artisan cheese to the best doughnuts in the city.

The oldest and biggest of Vancouver's ethnic communities is **CHINATOWN** (off Main St, on Pender and Keefer Sts). The Chinese groceries and apothecaries have been there for generations, and many display remnants of Vancouver's recent-past status as a neon mecca. For jade treasures, don't miss **CHICOCHAI ANTIQUES** (539 Columbia St; 604/685-8116). During the summer, there's an open-air night market, which runs from 6pm to midnight on weekends at Main and Keefer Streets.

Vancouver's 60,000 East Indian immigrants have established their own shopping area, called the **PUNJABI MARKET** (in south Vancouver at 49th and Main Sts), where you can bargain for a custom-fit *salwar kameez,* Rajastani jewelry, or the latest blockbuster from Bollywood on videotape.

In West Vancouver, **PARK ROYAL** has the distinction of being Canada's first shopping mall as well as the North Shore's largest and most prestigious shopping center. It straddles Marine Drive in West Vancouver, just across Lions Gate Bridge. (Out-of-town visitors note: It's too far to walk from downtown Vancouver, so take the bus or drive.)

PERFORMING ARTS

THEATER. The **VANCOUVER PLAYHOUSE THEATRE COMPANY** (Hamilton and Dunsmuir Sts; 604/873-3311; www.vancouverplayhouse.com; Oct–May) explores contemporary and classical theater. In the heart of lively Granville Island, the **ARTS CLUB THEATRE** (1585 Johnston St; 604/687-1644; www.artsclub.com) and neighboring **ARTS CLUB NEW REVUE STAGE** (604/687-1644) have become local institutions. Contemporary theater in Vancouver is largely centered in the **VANCOUVER EAST CULTURAL CENTRE** (1895 E Venables St; 604/251-1363; www.vecc.bc.ca), known to locals as the Cultch.

MUSIC. Over the past decade, the city has witnessed a renaissance in the proliferation of classical, jazz, and world music. Under the leadership of music director Bramwell Tovey, the 74-member **VANCOUVER SYMPHONY ORCHESTRA** (884 Granville St; 604/876-3434; www.vancouversymphony.ca) should continue to pursue artistic heights. The **VANCOUVER OPERA** (Hamilton at W Georgia St;

WHISTLER NORTHWIND TRAIN:
THREE-DAY TRIP TO PRINCE GEORGE

For train buffs, gourmands, or those who prefer a leisurely pace when traveling, the Whistler Northwind passenger rail service is an ideal getaway. Harking back to the days of rail romance, the coaches hug the cliff edges of the coast from North Vancouver to the northern city of Prince George, offering the best of train travel and luxury hotel accommodation along the way.

The first stop is **WHISTLER,** where guests can golf, hike, mountain bike, or simply luxuriate in the spa at the sumptuous Westin Resort. Next, the train passes through Seton Portage (watch for mountain goats) and the Fraser Canyon on its way to **100 MILE HOUSE,** deep in the heart of cowboy country. In the morning, guests can choose to walk off the previous night's BBQ dinner, go for a hay-ride, or even take a class in horse whispering at the Hill's Health Ranch. The final leg of the journey ends in **PRINCE GEORGE,** a northern university town known for its wide range of cultural and outdoors activities. From P.G., as locals call it, you either fly back to Vancouver (airfare not included in package) or carry on northward with an additional tour of horseback riding or a spa stay.

While both the Panorama and the Summit class feature 180-degree views from the passenger dome cars, the slightly more expensive Summit class is recommended for its separate dining car service. Prices vary, depending on the service you choose. Summit class is CAN $1,350–$1,450 for a three-day Northbound journey and runs May through October (604/984-5246 or 800/663-8238; www.whistlernorthwind.com).

—Anya MacLeod

604/683-0222; www.vanopera.bc.ca) presents four to five productions a year at the Queen Elizabeth Theatre. The **VANCOUVER INTERNATIONAL JAZZ FESTIVAL** (604/872-5200; www.jazzvancouver.com) attracts crowds of more than 250,000 each June, and the annual mid-July **VANCOUVER FOLK MUSIC FESTIVAL** (604/602-9798; www.thefestival.bc.ca) is extremely popular too. Ticketmaster (604/280-4444; www.ticketmaster.ca) has more information.

NIGHTLIFE

On an evening out in Vancouver, you can enjoy just about every clubbing experience imaginable, from an old-time rock 'n' roll bender to a no-holds-barred striptease show to a till-dawn rave in a factory warehouse. A piano player rules the roost weekends at tony **BACCHUS LOUNGE** (845 Hornby St; 604/608-5319). Live pop, world music, and electronica are the lures that attract schools of new-music aficionados to the **COMMODORE BALLROOM** (868 Granville St; 604/739-SHOW). For live jazz, head to the **CELLAR JAZZ CAFE** (3611 W Broadway; 604/738-1959; www.cellar jazz.com). The best sources for up-to-date listings are the *Georgia Straight* (www. straight.com) and the Thursday entertainment section of the *Vancouver Sun* (www.

vancouversun.com). For daily concert updates, contact Ticketmaster (604/280-4444; www.ticketmaster.ca).

SPORTS AND RECREATION

Cycling, running, hiking, and water sports are all popular here. A good in-city route for runners or in-line skaters is along the 6½-mile (10.5 km) **STANLEY PARK SEAWALL**. A good one-stop source for bicycling information, including maps and guidebooks, is **CYCLING BRITISH COLUMBIA** (332-1367 W Broadway; 604/737-3034; www.cycling.bc.ca). Contact the **OUTDOOR RECREATION COUNCIL OF BRITISH COLUMBIA** (334-1367 W Broadway; 604/737-3058; www.orcbc.ca) to reach the Canoeing Association, Whitewater Kayaking Association, or Sea Kayaking Association of British Columbia, or for more information on other sports.

For fans of spectator sports, your best bet is the NHL's **VANCOUVER CANUCKS**, playing at General Motors Place (800 Griffiths Wy; 604/899-7400; www.canucks.com). The faithful stick with the team through good times and bad, and that makes getting tickets a challenge. Closer to downtown, the Canadian Football League's **BC LIONS** play at BC Place Stadium (777 Pacific Blvd; 604/589-7627; www.bclions.com). Vancouver's diverse ethnicity has created a ready-made audience for soccer, especially among homesick Brits, Portuguese, and Italians. Swangard Stadium (intersection of Boundary Rd and Kingsway; 604/899-9823) hosts the **VANCOUVER WHITECAPS**. Tickets for most sporting events are available at the gates or through Ticketmaster (604/280-4444; www.ticketmaster.ca). Thoroughbreds race at **HASTINGS PARK** (Hastings St and Renfrew St; 604/254-1631; www.hastingspark.com; mid-Apr–Nov) on the grounds of the Pacific National Exhibition.

RESTAURANTS

Aqua Riva / ★★

30-200 GRANVILLE ST, VANCOUVER; 604/683-5599 Aqua Riva boasts an outstanding view of the harbor and, being adjacent to Canada Place, it gets the North Shore mountains, too. Executive chef Deb Connors rattles the pots and pans and tends the wood-fired oven and rotisserie. Prices are reasonable for alder-grilled salmon, oven-baked pizzas, and slow-smoked barbecued ribs. Service is unfailingly friendly, and the stunning decor is especially soothing when you're settled into a booth with Dana Irving's Art Deco wraparound mural above you. *$$; AE, DC, E, MC, V; no checks; lunch, dinner every day, brunch Sun May–Oct; full bar; reservations not necessary; dinner@aquariva.com; www.aquariva.com; at Howe St.* ♿

Bacchus Ristorante / ★★★

845 HORNBY ST (THE WEDGEWOOD HOTEL), VANCOUVER; 604/608-5319 Wonderfully romantic, this richly decorated room is a triumph for Eleni Skalbania. Dark wood paneling and deep burgundy velvet couches are accented by huge bouquets of flowers, creating private niches. At lunch, Bacchus attracts the legal beagles from the courthouse for roast of the day, pizza Bacchus, or the superb tortellini of sweet white corn. Afternoon tea (2–4pm) in front of the fireplace also hits the spot. Chef Frank Dodd's changing dinner menu might include pastrami of salmon lobster rolls with mango and mint, roasted loin of peppered venison, or a classic coq au vin. Hope that the mango tarte Tatin happens to be on the menu, or surrender to the opera cake. Best of all, Bacchus offers fine French cheese, fine wines, and servers who cater to your every whim. Monday through Saturday, a pianist tickles the ivories. Stogie aficionados have free rein in the cigar room. *$$$; AE, DC, MC, V; no checks; breakfast, lunch, dinner every day, brunch Sat–Sun; full bar; reservations required; info@wedgewoodhotel.com; www.wedgewoodhotel. com; between Robson and Smithe Sts.* &

Bin 941 Tapas Parlour/ ★★★
Bin 942 Tapas Parlour / ★★★

941 DAVIE ST, VANCOUVER; 604/683-1246 / 1521 W BROADWAY, VAN-COUVER; 604/734-9421 Pretty people pack both Bins long into the night, engaged in deep conversation (beneath muscular yet unoppressive music), while nibbling on a progression of small, well-executed plates. The shoebox-sized restaurants are funky and madcap, but chef-owner Gord Martin designs dazzling food at amazing prices. A pound of mussels done (superbly) any of four ways costs just $10. So does a fat crab cake with burnt orange–chipotle sauce and charred bok choy. Beef and fowl appear as well, none over $10. Shoestring *frites*—a $3 haystack of hand-cut Yukon Golds, seasoned after frying—are the city's best-tasting potato bargain. Martin headlines his menu "tapatizers" because everything can be shared or enjoyed solo (sharing's best!) while rubbing shoulders, unavoidably, with the next table. *$$; MC, V; no checks; dinner every day; beer, wine, liqueurs; reservations recommended; www.bin941.com; between Burrard and Howe Sts (Bin 941), between Fir and Granville Sts (Bin 942).* &

Bishop's / ★★★★

2183 W 4TH AVE, VANCOUVER; 604/738-2025 There's no better place to eat than in this simple two-level restaurant, long a fixture on busy W Fourth Avenue. John Bishop warmly greets his guests (celebrity and otherwise) and, assisted by the most professionally polished young staff in the city, proceeds to demonstrate that he understands personal service, hovering over each table, serving, pouring, and discussing. Chef Dennis Green's entrees are uncomplicated. Dungeness crab is bathed in a saffron tomato broth, and wild salmon is grilled and brushed with a sesame ginger glaze. The rack of lamb with truffle and goat cheese mashed potatoes, and the pan-roasted halibut on a warm new-potato salad are standouts. So are the pan-seared scallops in a sweet red pepper and chive bisque, topped with a crisp potato pancake. Everything bears the Bishop trademark of light, subtly complex flavors and bright, graphic color. Desserts such as the moist ginger cake pooled in toffee sauce, and the Death by Chocolate are legendary. Manager Abel Jacinto oversees an eclectic list of fine wines including a selection of more than 50 half bottles. *$$$–$$$$; AE, DC, MC, V; no checks; dinner every day (closed for two weeks in Jan); full bar; reservations required; inquire@bishopsonline.com; www.bishops online.com; between Yew and Arbutus Sts.*

Blue Water Cafe / ★★★

1095 HAMILTON ST, VANCOUVER; 604/688-8078 This is a long, cool drink of a room—a pleasure for both the eye and palate. The open kitchen running along the

North Wall leans heavily toward seafood dishes, like local sockeye salmon with pumpkin seed gnocchi and rock shrimp with spinach. At the Eastern Bar, Masanori Katsuno creates elaborate sushi rolls, while executive chef James Walt presides over the Western Bar, applying a deft hand to delicacies such as ceviche, caviar, and his formidable seafood tower (priced by the tier). For dessert, you might want to go light with one of the homemade fruit sorbets, or belly up to the Ice Bar to choose a concoction of chilled vodka and freshly squeezed juices. There's a heated terrace outside. *$$$–$$$$; AE, DC, E, MC, V; no checks; lunch Mon–Fri, dinner every day, brunch Sat–Sun; full bar; blueh2ocafe@look.ca; www.bluewatercafe.net; Yaletown.*

Bridges / ★★

1696 DURANLEAU ST, VANCOUVER; 604/687-4400 One of the city's most popular hangouts has a superb setting on Granville Island. Seats on the outdoor deck, with sweeping views of downtown and the mountains, are at a premium on warm days. Bridges is actually three separate entities: a casual bistro, a pub, and a more formal second-story dining room. The bistro's seafood Caesar is the best bet; upstairs, the kitchen takes its seafood seriously, but expect to pay top dollar for it. *$$–$$$$; AE, E, MC, V; no checks; lunch, dinner every day, brunch Sun; full bar; reservations recommended (dining room); info@bridgesrestaurant.com; www.bridgesrestaurant.com; Granville Island.* &

C / ★★★★

1600 HOWE ST, VANCOUVER; 604/681-1164 Be prepared to spend an entire afternoon or evening on the patio at C, because lunch or dinner is always an event at Harry Kambolis's restaurant. C offers contemporary and exotic seafood in Zen-like surroundings with an unbeatable view across False Creek to Granville Island. Chef Rob Clark creates dishes that are as dramatic on the palate as on the plate. Start with a taster box filled with green tea–cured gravlax, warm lobster salad, ahi tuna tartare, and five-spice roasted duck breast. And don't miss C's signature starters: caviar in a gold-leaf pouch, lobster tail sashimi bathed in Cognac, or octopus-wrapped scallops. A dim sum–style menu is served at lunch, featuring tasty portions of spicy crab dumplings, subtle steamed lobster, and macadamia nut miso buns, as well as crisp scallop and ahi tuna spring rolls. Wine service is correct and informative without being pretentious or intrusive. *$$$–$$$$; AE, DC, E, MC, V; no checks; lunch, dinner every day; full bar; reservations recommended; info@crestaurant.com; www.crestaurant.com; at Beach Ave.*

The Cannery Seafood House / ★★★

2205 COMMISSIONER ST, VANCOUVER; 604/254-9606 Frederic Couton's culinary artistry makes the trek out to this relatively remote east-end dockside location unquestionably worthwhile. Serving "salmon by the sea" for more than 25 years, the Cannery resides in a building that has been cleverly refurbished to look and feel even older than that. On any given day, you'll find a baker's dozen of honestly prepared, high-quality seafood choices on the fresh sheet, including a delicate arctic char, a juicy grilled swordfish, and a meaty tuna. (You can order a trio of shellfish for $39.) Salmon Wellington has been a house specialty here since 1971; recently rematched with a pinot noir sauce, it's still a winner, yet our favorite is the buttery steamed Alaskan black cod. Those who don't go for fish dine on herb-crusted rack of lamb, or a simple grilled beef tenderloin. The award-winning wine list is one of the city's best. Service is enthusiastic and friendly. *$$$; AE, DC, MC, V; no checks; lunch Mon–Fri, dinner every day; full bar; reservations recommended; info@canneryseafood.com; www.canneryseafood.com; at Victoria Dr.*

Chartwell / ★★★★

791 W GEORGIA ST (THE FOUR SEASONS), VANCOUVER; 604/689-9333
Chartwell remains in the bold forefront of excellent hotel dining with the arrival of star whisk Fabrice Rossmann from the Four Seasons Berlin. Offering a decidedly French take on local organic ingredients, you will find the taste of Paris in his par-tridge *demi-deuil* with *cèpes* lasagne, and the flavor of Burgundy in a cheese course of Epoïsses melted in a Yukon Gold potato. Rossmann's version of oxtail confit is a rich triumph sided with a tender roast beef tenderloin on a parsnip purée. For dessert, we wholeheartedly endorse the citrusy chocolate kalamansi wave and white chocolate–lime mousse. Service at Chartwell is warm, discreet, and attentive. A pretheater dinner menu is an outstanding value. The wine list is an award winner, and the winemaker dinners are the most popular in the city. *$$$$; AE, DC, DIS, JCB, MC, V; no checks; breakfast, dinner every day, lunch Sun–Fri; full bar; reservations recommended; www.fourseasons.com; at Howe St.* &

CinCin Restaurant & Bar / ★★★

1154 ROBSON ST, VANCOUVER; 604/688-7338 CinCin is a hearty Italian toast, a wish of health and good cheer in a sunny Mediterranean space. The Italian- and French-inspired dishes are boldly flavored by talented chef Romy Prasad. Launch your meal with his antipasto platter, which might include house-smoked trout, stuffed Prince Edward Island mussels, or a tomato and bocconcini crostini draped with Parma prosciutto. For entrees, savvy diners order Prasad's veal osso buco with fresh sage gnocchi or the 42-ounce T-bone with roasted vegetables. Wine takes center stage at CinCin, with a 10,000-bottle cellar and good values because of a reduced markup. Linger at the bar over a Mandorla Martini or the best margarita in town, or sip wine in the lounge (food's served until midnight). Dine outdoors on the heated terrace overlooking Robson Street. *$$$; AE, DC, MC, V; no checks; lunch Mon–Fri, dinner every day; full bar; reservations recommended; cincin@direct.ca; www.cincin.net; between Bute and Thurlow Sts.*

Cioppino's Mediterranean Grill / ★★★★
Cioppino's Enoteca / ★★★★

1133 HAMILTON ST, VANCOUVER; 604/688-7466 Talented Pino Posteraro's French-inspired Mediterranean dishes—foie gras and sea bass casserole, sautéed wild chanterelles and morels, spaghettini with truffles—have earned him a loyal fol-lowing. Stick to a tasting menu ($55 and up) and you'll have one of the most bril-liant meals in town for the price. Celestino Posteraro and Massimo Piscopo preside over a friendly bar and a serious wine list. And there's a wonderful private dining room for up to 24. Next door, Posteraro has opened Enoteca, a comfortable low-key wine bar with a rotisserie. *$$$–$$$$; AE, DC, MC, V; no checks; lunch*

Mon–Fri, dinner Mon–Sat; full bar; reservations recommended; pino@cioppinosyale town.com; cioppinosyaletown.com; between Helmcken and Davie Sts.

Circolo / ★★★

1116 MAINLAND ST, VANCOUVER; 604/687-1116 Umberto Menghi set out to capture his favorite cities, and one look at the chic decor in his Yaletown restaurant and you'll imagine yourself at a bustling oyster bar in Manhattan, a romantic bistro in Paris, or a classic restaurant in Florence. One look at the reasonable bill, however, and you'll know you're not in those cities. We suggest starting with fresh oysters and sharing the escargot de Bourgogne. Then order the *bistecca alla Fiorentina* for two, 32 ounces of grilled porterhouse sliced off the bone, chased with a bottle of Bambolo, Menghi's upscale Tuscan red. Everything makes us feel rich and a long way from home. It's easy to get in at the beginning of the week, tougher toward the weekend. *$$$–$$$$; AE, DC, E, MC, V; no checks; dinner Mon–Sat; full bar; reservations recommended; Yaletown.* &

Diva at the Met / ★★★☆

645 HOWE ST (METROPOLITAN HOTEL), VANCOUVER; 604/602-7788 Former executive chef Michael Noble is a hard act to follow, but executive chef Chris Mills and restaurant chef Andrew Springett are pulling it off in this airy, multitiered space with an exhibition kitchen. The Alaskan smoked black cod with herb gnocchi is a standout, and the vegetarian tasting menu is creative and makes you feel virtuous. If you can't make a decision, you can choose the unique tasting menu and select any three items on the menu for $60. Brunchers swoon over the black cod hash topped with poached eggs. Thomas Haas's desserts are the best in North America, and Diva's cheese program is one of the best in town. Food and beverage manager Matthew Opferkuch stocks a deep cellar with a strong Pacific Northwest focus. Don't pass on the opportunity to attend a wine-maker dinner. *$$$–$$$$; AE, DC, JCB, MC, V; no checks; breakfast, lunch, dinner every day, brunch Sat–Sun; full bar; reservations recommended; reservations@divamet.com; www.metropolitan.com; between Dunsmuir and W Georgia Sts.* &

Ezogiku Noodle Cafe / ★

1329 ROBSON ST, VANCOUVER; 604/685-8606 This is a small gem of a place operated for the benefit of Asian-food lovers who don't want to spend a lot of money. This tiny place (70 seats) displays only a modest awning saying "Noodle Cafe," but regulars would say that doesn't start to describe its value. Several varieties of ramen noodle, many representing a clever combination of Japanese and Chinese culinary tastes, come in huge, filling quantities. There's also fried rice, fried noodles, and wonderfully tasty *gyoza*. Be prepared to wait for a seat. Other branches are in Honolulu and Tokyo. *$; cash only; lunch, dinner every day; no alcohol; reservations not accepted, between Jervis and Bute Sts.*

Gotham Steakhouse & Cocktail Bar / ★★★

615 SEYMOUR ST, VANCOUVER; 604/605-8282 Meat is the main course here, or USDA prime, to be precise. The stand-alone steaks (vegetables are à la carte) are even more beautiful than the people. From the New York strip to the splendid 24-ounce porterhouse, it's a cattle drive for the taste buds. You can share mashed potatoes, creamed spinach, or crispy french fries. For sheer entertainment value, take a seat at the bar and engage in some of the best people watching Vancouver has to offer. Beware: This place prices under the assumption that everyone has a Swiss bank account. *$$$$; AE, DC, MC, V; no checks; lunch, dinner every day; full bar; reservations recommended; www.gothamsteakhouse.com; at Dunsmuir St.* &

Habibi's / ★★

7-1128 W BROADWAY, VANCOUVER; 604/732-7487 Richard Zeinoun cooks from the heart at this casual Middle Eastern spot. There are all sorts of surprises, starting with a complimentary meze that whets the appetite for *shinkleesh,* an aged goat cheese; *balila,* warmed chickpeas in garlic-infused oil; or *warak anab,* stuffed grape leaves. There are also falafels and both Lebanese- and Israeli-style hummus. Wines chosen to go with the food make Habibi's an unbeatable dining experience. Food is downright cheap; service is friendly and enthusiastic. *$; V; local checks only; dinner Mon–Sat; beer and wine; reservations not necessary; www.habibis.com; between Spruce and Oak Sts.*

Hon's Wun Tun House / ★

1339 ROBSON ST, VANCOUVER (AND BRANCHES); 604/688-0871 By serving the just-plain-good, basic Chinese specialties you'd find in street-corner restaurants in Hong Kong, and keeping prices to a minimum, what was once a steamy Chinatown noodle house has become a restaurant empire with six branches. Wonton is one of more than 90 varieties of soup available, and there's a seemingly endless list of noodle specialties. The trademark pot-sticker dumplings, fried or steamed, are justly famous. Hon's also offers delivery, takeout, and a full line of frozen dim sum. One more thing: Those addictive candied walnuts are available on your way out. *$; cash only (except Robson St, New Westminster, Coquitlam locations); lunch, dinner every day; beer and wine; reservations not necessary; hons@shinnova.com; www.shinnova.com; between Jervis and Bute Sts.*

Imperial Chinese Seafood Restaurant / ★★★☆

355 BURRARD ST, VANCOUVER; 604/688-8191 The Imperial may lay claim to being the most opulent Chinese dining room around. There's a feeling of being in a grand ballroom of eras past: a central staircase leads to the balustrade-lined mezzanine, diplomatic dignitaries and rock stars dine in luxurious private rooms, and two-story windows look out onto the panorama of Burrard Inlet and the North Shore mountains. The food can be equally polished—lobster in black-bean sauce with fresh egg noodles, panfried scallops garnished with coconut-laced deep-fried milk, sautéed spinach with minced pork and Chinese anchovies, a superb pan-smoked black cod, and the addictive beef sauté in chiles with honey walnuts. Dim sum is consistently good; service is ever courteous, informative, and helpful; and the wine list is exceptional for an Asian restaurant. *$$$–$$$$; DC, MC, V; no checks; lunch, dinner every day; full bar; reservations recommended; www.imperialrest.com; between Cordova and Hastings Sts.*

Le Crocodile / ★★★★

100-909 BURRARD ST, VANCOUVER; 604/669-4298 France without a passport—that's Le Crocodile. It was named after chef-owner Michel Jacob's favorite restaurant in his hometown of Strasbourg. Everyone wants to order Jacob's savory onion tart served with chilled Alsace Edelzwicker. Entrees of marvelously sauced classics such as duck (crisp outside, moist inside) in a reduction with olives, calf's liver with garlic spinach butter, and rabbit in a pinot noir sauce all pay their respects to tradition. He grills salmon "skin on" and panfries Dover sole to remember. Jacob's treasury of French cheeses makes a fine end to a meal or prelude to a tangy lemon tart with house-made raspberry sorbet. The wines of Alsace are proudly poured but so are many others. France's Loire Valley, Bordeaux, and Burgundy are well represented, as is California. The ever-professional service and chic European atmosphere make dinner at Le Crocodile an event. *$$$; AE, DC, MC, V; no checks; lunch Mon–Fri, dinner Mon–Sat; full bar; reservations recommended; info@lecrocodile. com; www.lecrocodile.com; at Smithe St.* &

Lucy Mae Brown / ★★★

862 RICHARDS ST, VANCOUVER; 604/899-9199 Vancouver's busiest restaurant, once a boardinghouse and brothel owned by Lucy Mae Brown, is now a cool blue triumph with high ceilings. Park yourself on a banquette and savor chef Andrey Durbach's complimentary starter of green olives and white bean dip with crusty bread. Pumpkin soup is a standout—blended with truffle oil and adorned with a dollop of almond cream. A pair of pine-crusted Saltspring Island lamb shanks perch on a pond of red currant reduction and roasted garlic, a small sage quiche poking shyly out from underneath. Ahi tuna is awash in capers, brown butter, and apple cider vinaigrette, and finds refuge on a bed of crushed new baby potatoes and roasted red peppers. For dessert, choose a generous portion of crème brûlée or Chocolate Nemesis cake with cherry-berry coulis. The wine list is short but well chosen. Pay a visit to the cellar bar downstairs—tucked behind an unmarked door, it's the closest thing around to a secret clubhouse for grown-ups. *$$$; AE, MC, V; no checks; dinner Mon–Sat; full bar; reservations recommended; between Robson and Smithe Sts.* &

Lumière / ★★★★

2551 W BROADWAY, VANCOUVER; 604/739-8185 Rob Feenie's restless energy fuels the passion for perfection that is Lumière, and he arguably creates the city's best food. Once a tad austere, the main room's second upgrade/expansion is complete—carpeting calms the sound level, and a new bar serves as main entry. Food luxuriates in the skill of Feenie's contemporary French kitchen—he always seems to achieve a perfect balance of flavors and textures. In the dining room choose from a large three-course prix-fixe selection, or one of four seasonally driven tasting menus Three of the four comprise eight small dishes, the Signature menu has 12, and all are designed to make diners swoon: garlic velouté with cauliflower purée; fricassée of baby beets; veal medallion and sweetbreads with white asparagus, swiss chard, and thyme-veal jus. The sublime vegetarian menu can win converts to the no-meat cause. For a relaxed, quicker-meal alternative, the bar offers a dozen scaled-down versions of Lumière classics. Angie Opanukij creates masterful desserts for both rooms—items such as tropical fruit soup with coconut jelly, and chocolate mousse with peanut butter sauce and sour cherry compote. The now-substantial wine list is always being improved; service is informed and attentive. *$$$$; AE, DC, MC, V; no checks; dinner Tues–Sun; full bar; reservations recommended; lumiere@relaischateaux.com; www.relaischateaux.com; between Trafalgar and Larch Sts.* &

Memphis Blues Barbeque House / ★★★

1465 W BROADWAY, VANCOUVER; 604/738-6806 Get your butt here early. Memphis Blues has been an instant success since restaurateur George Sui and wine nut Park Heffelfinger opened their authentic Southern baah-be-cue in the fall of 2001. All the Memphis favorites—ribs, beef brisket, pulled pork, rib ends, and smoked sausage—are perfectly prepared with sides of coleslaw, cornbread, potato salad or fries, and BBQ pit beans. The brisket is unsurpassed, spread out in thick, melting tender slices. Cornish hen is tender and juicy and, as the signature dish, definitely deserves its John Hancock. Just give up on the niceties and eat with your fingers. Heffelfinger posts a wine list, selected to whistle Dixie with smoked pork treats and available by glass or bottle. *$; AE, MC, V; no checks; lunch, dinner every day; beer and wine; reservations not accepted; West Side.* &

Montri's Thai Restaurant / ★★★

3629 W BROADWAY, VANCOUVER; 604/738-9888 Why go anywhere else for Thai food when Montri's is simply the best in town? Everything is good. *Tom yum goong* is Thailand's national soup, a lemony prawn broth, and it lives up to its name—yum. The *tod mun* fish cakes blended with prawns and chile curry are excellent, as is the beef or prawn spicy stir-fry served on panfried spinach. Montri Rattanaraj's Thai *gai-yang*, chicken marinated in coconut milk and broiled, is a close cousin to the chicken sold on the beach at Phuket. Have it with *som tum*, a green papaya salad served with sticky rice and wedges of raw cabbage; the cabbage and the rice are coolants, and you'll need them (Singha beer also helps). For a group of six or more, splurge for the *pla lard prig*, a whole rockfish or red snapper slashed to allow flavorings to penetrate and then quickly deep-fried. *$$; MC, V; no checks; dinner every day; full bar; reservations recommended; near Alma St.* &

Nat's New York Pizzeria / ★★

2684 W BROADWAY, VANCOUVER; 604/737-0707 / 1080 DENMAN ST, VANCOUVER; 604/642-0777 Nat and Franco Bastone learned how to create Naples-style pizza at their uncle's pizza parlor in Yonkers and now serve up some of the best thin-crust pizza around. Take out or pull up a chair under the Big Apple memorabilia and sink your teeth into pies loaded with chorizo and mushrooms, or artichokes and pesto, or capicollo and hot peppers. Try the Fifth Avenue (sweet onion, spinach, tomato, and feta cheese) or the Hot Veg (sun-dried tomatoes, hot peppers, and mushrooms). Top it off with oven-baked garlic shavings or other condiments. Avoid Nat's on weekdays between 11:30 and 12:15 during the local Kits High School student rush. If you're there before they leave, you'll notice students squeezing honey on leftover crusts for dessert. *$; no credit cards; no checks;*

lunch, dinner Mon–Sat; no alcohol; reservations not accepted; between Stephens and Trafalgar Sts (Broadway), at Helmcken St (Denman).

Ouest / ★★★★

2881 GRANVILLE ST, VANCOUVER; 604/738-8938 Returning west to his Vancouver roots after working alongside many of London's leading chefs, David Hawksworth is the city's best European-trained chef. His sophisticated contemporary French menu offers sensual dishes with intense reductions. Start with Ouest's signature of foie gras and chicken liver parfait on apple gelée—it's so perfect you don't want to ruin it with a fork. There are many successes here—panfried sole or halibut crusted with mushrooms, breast of squab with macaroni, even pig's trotter. A beautifully designed room with a cherry and marble bar seats 10 against the backdrop of a ceiling-high "wall of wine." The "wall" includes a custom-built refrigeration system that keeps wines within two degrees of their optimum temperature. You'll be impressed with any of Thierry Busset's fruit desserts and the fine cheese selection from Les Amis du Fromage. The wine list offers an impressive selection of French wines and champagnes, as well as new-world and BC wines. Service is seamless. Of course, all this comes at a price, but it's worth every penny. *$$$$; AE, DC, E, MC, V; no checks; dinner every day; full bar; reservations recommended; www.ouest restaurant.com; between W 12th and W 13th Aves.* &

Quattro on Fourth / ★★★☆

2611 W 4TH AVE, VANCOUVER; 604/734-4444 Patrick Corsi runs one of the most comfortable Italian restaurants in the city, and you're pampered the minute you walk through the door. An impressive antipasto platter includes no less than a dozen items (including grilled tiger prawns, crab and salmon cakes, salmon gravlax). The razor-thin-sliced raw swordfish is superb; so are the grilled radicchio bocconcini and portobello mushrooms. Kudos for the grilled beef tenderloin cloaked in aged balsamic syrup, the pistachio-crusted sea bass, and the spicy deboned Cornish game hen. Spaghetti Quattro ("for Italians only") rewards with a well-spiced sauce of chicken, chiles, black beans, and plenty of garlic. The mostly Italian wine list is stellar and the Corsi family also has the largest selection of grappa in Vancouver. The heated patio seats 35. *$$$; AE, DC, MC, V; no checks; dinner every day; full bar; reservations recommended; 4th@quattro.ca; www.quattrorestaurants.com; at Trafalgar St.* &

Raincity Grill / ★★★

1193 DENMAN ST, VANCOUVER; 604/685-7337 Grape nuts love the extensive list of Pacific Northwest wines (more than 120 by the glass), but that's only one reason to visit this bright, contemporary restaurant. Situated at the happening Davie-Denman intersection, Raincity dazzles diners with excellent views year-round of English Bay (in summer, loll on the patio). Beyond that dazzle lies a deep-rooted commitment to use the best ingredients BC has to offer, and to work with growers to produce them. Sean Cousins has taken command of the narrow, open kitchen after a stint at Harry Kambolis's other restaurant, C. To start, order the grilled Caesar, roasted duck breast, or verbena-scented gravlax. Move on to venison with morel mushrooms, or smoked-tomato grilled salmon served, in season, with grilled Okanagan peaches. Each menu item carries a wine suggestion. A glass of dessert wine and the day's tart or pastry make a perfect finish. Expect ever-professional service. *$$$; AE, DC, MC, V; no checks; dinner every day, brunch Sat–Sun; full bar; reservations recommended; info@raincitygrill.com; www.raincitygrill.com; at Morton St.* &

Rodney's Oyster House / ★★

1228 HAMILTON ST, VANCOUVER; 604/609-0080 It's hard to find a spot at the bar as gamins of all persuasions eye the forearms of the young shuckers at Rodney's. A team of experts makes careful checks of temperature, freshness, and quality of more than a dozen briny bivalves (many from the East Coast). While the slogan here is "The lemon, the oyster, and your lips are all that's required," you'll be catered to even if you don't take them straight. Rodney's makes four sauces—you'll want the seawich if you grew up with cocktail sauce on your shrimp. There's also a choice of creamy chowders, steamed mussels and clams, local Dungeness crab, and East Coast lobsters. *$$–$$$; AE, E, MC, V; no checks; lunch, dinner Mon–Sat; full bar; reservations not necessary; between Davie and Drake Sts.*

Savary Island Pie Company / ★★

1533 MARINE DR, WEST VANCOUVER; 604/926-4021 It's worth the trip over the Lions Gate Bridge to the homey Savary Island Pie Company. It opens at 6:30am and during the day it's a hangout for West Van moms and their preppie pups. Everything is good here, but the Savary is famous for strawberry rhubarb and lemon buttermilk pies, raspberry scones, cranberry-pecan muffins, vegetarian pizza foccacia, and multigrain bread. They also serve homemade soups (tomato Parmesan is a must), sandwiches, chicken potpie, and shepherd's pie. Eat in or take out. *$; V; no checks; breakfast, lunch, dinner every day; beer and wine; reservations not accepted; between 15th and 16th Sts.*

Shanghai Chinese Bistro / ★★

1128 ALBERNI ST, VANCOUVER; 604/683-8222 Consistently good food and cheerful servers have made this tasteful "bistro moderne" a popular haunt. The unique and magical nightly noodle show provides another excuse to bring visitors along for a good nosh before heading next door for a bellow of karaoke. Hand-pulled noodles Shanghai-style are a must, of course, and so are the chile wontons. Both the panfried live spot prawns with chile paste and soy, and the salt-and-chile crab, are finger-licking good. For a balanced meal, try a plate of pea shoots lightly touched with garlic, or drop in for a late-night snack of dim sum (from 10:30pm). *$$; AE, JCB, MC, V; no checks; lunch, dinner every day; full bar; reservations not necessary; between Bute and Thurlow Sts.*

Sophie's Cosmic Cafe / ★★

2095 W 4TH AVE, VANCOUVER; 604/732-6810 The walls of this funky Kitsilano diner are the flea market of a kitsch collector's dreams. So don't worry about the wait—there's plenty to look at, including Sophie's collection of colorful lunch boxes and hats. Evenings, people are drawn by burger platters, pastas, and boffo spicy mussels. Chocolate shakes are a balm for the tummy and hell on the diet (give in). On weekends, fans queue in the rain for stick-to-the-ribs breakfasts, especially the potent Mexican eggs (with sausage, peppers, and onions, spiced with hot-pepper sauce). Plenty of vegetarian choices are offered all day. A covered deck accommodates all-weather puffers. *$–$$; MC, V; no checks; breakfast, lunch, dinner every day, brunch Sat–Sun; full bar; reservations not accepted; at Arbutus St.* &

Stepho's Souvlakia / ★★☆

1124 DAVIE ST, VANCOUVER; 604/683-2555 Known as much for its lineups as for its cheap and delicious Greek food, Stepho's remains a fixture in Vancouver's West End, and for good reason. Huge portions of chicken, lamb, or beef brochettes fight for space on a plate loaded with rice pilaf, buttery roast potatoes, and a Greek salad, all served with pungent tzatziki and hot pita bread. The hummus appetizer is outstanding. Check the specials for tender and toothsome baby back ribs. Prompt and polite service, generous portions at cheap prices, and a well-priced wine list make Stepho's the budget eater's mecca for Mediterranean meals. *$; AE, MC, V; no checks; lunch, dinner every day; full bar; reservations not accepted; between Bute and Thurlow Sts.* &

The Teahouse / ★★

7501 STANLEY PARK DR, VANCOUVER; 604/669-3281 OR 800/280-9893 This stunning location in Stanley Park is a magnet for tourists and locals, with its series of airy and light dining rooms, park setting, and spectacular view of English Bay. Appetizers range from Teahouse stuffed mushrooms (crab, shrimp, and Emmenthaler) to steamed mussels in a lime and chipotle butter. Salmon is always a good bet, served with seasonal sauces, and the rack of lamb in a fresh-herb crust is a perennial favorite. Desserts include a dark- and milk-chocolate torta Milano with mascarpone mousse as well as a lemon meringue tart. *$$$–$$$$; AE, MC, V; no checks; lunch Mon–Fri, dinner every day, brunch Sat–Sun, afternoon tea Mon–Sat; full bar; reservations recommended; info@sequoia restaurants.com; www.teahouserestaurant.com; Ferguson Point.* &

Tojo's / ★★★★

202-777 W BROADWAY, VANCOUVER; 604/872-8050 Hidekazu Tojo is Tojo's. One of the best-known sushi maestros in Vancouver, this beaming mustachioed Japanese chef has a loyal clientele that regularly fills his spacious upstairs restaurant, though most people want to sit at the 10-seat sushi bar. He's endlessly innovative, surgically precise, and committed to fresh ingredients. Try the Tojo tuna or "special beef" (very thin beef wrapped around asparagus and shrimp) or suntan tuna with plum sauce. Tojo-san created the BC roll (barbecued salmon skin, green onions, cucumber, and daikon) now found in almost every Japanese restaurant in Vancouver. Japanese-menu standards like tempura and teriyaki are always reliable, and specials are usually superb: pine mushroom soup in the fall, steamed monkfish liver from October to May, and cherry blossoms with scallops and sautéed halibut cheeks with shiitake in spring. Cold Masukagami sake is hot at Tojo's. *$$$$; AE, DC, JCB, MC, V; no checks; dinner Mon–Sat; full bar; reservations recommended; www.tojos.com; between Heather and Willow Sts.* &

Vij's / ★★★☆

1480 W 11TH AVE, VANCOUVER; 604/736-6664 This is where food writers impress informed eaters from out of town. Bombay native Vikram Vij dishes up imaginative home-cooked Indian fare that evolves at a whim. His seasonal menu almost always includes a mean curry (lamb chops in a fenugreek-and-cream curry with turmeric potatoes) or a killer saag. The decor is minimalist, casual, and modern. Start with a glass of Vij's refreshing fresh-ginger-and-lemon libation, and don't pass on the standout appetizer, small samosas filled with ricotta and served with a Bengali sauce containing a mixture of five spices called *panchpooran*. Courtesy and simplicity rule as Vij waits carefully on all who arrive early enough to get in, greeting them with a glass of chai before discussing the menu. The wine list is small but excellent and the prices are civilized, too. *$$–$$$; AE, DC, MC, V; no checks; dinner every day; beer and wine; reservations not accepted; between Granville and Hemlock Sts.* &

Villa del Lupo / ★★★☆

869 HAMILTON ST, VANCOUVER; 604/688-7436 Chef Julio Gonzalez Perini's dazzling experiments with flavor bring off-duty local chefs to this elegant Victorian townhouse. Order the veal steak, and marvel at the delicate blending of tastes and textures found in a sautéed morel stuffed with rich foie gras. Prices tend to be high, but so is the quality, and the portions are generous. Almost everything on the northern Italian menu is wonderful. The roasted sea bass wrapped with Parma ham, prosciutto, and sage is remarkable. The osso buco is a hearty house specialty and a consistent favorite. The wine list goes far beyond the Italian border. Grappa and eaux-de-vie are available as well. Service is always amiable and correct. *$$$; AE, DC, MC, V; no checks; dinner every day; full bar; reservations recommended; between Robson and Smithe Sts.*

LODGINGS

The Fairmont Hotel Vancouver / ★★★

900 W GEORGIA ST, VANCOUVER; 604/684-3131 OR 800/441-1414 One of the grand French chateau–style hotels once owned by the Canadian Pacific Railway, the Hotel Van dates back to 1887. The steeply pitched, green-patina copper roof of its current incarnation has dominated the city's skyline since 1939. Stone arches, friezes, and other design elements hidden by earlier remodeling have been restored or re-created in the past few years. The Lobby Bar with oversized club chairs and the elegantly casual 900 West Restaurant (lunch only) and Wine Bar replaced the original main-floor lobby. A shopping arcade includes a Canadian Pacific Store, featuring private-label goods reminiscent of the early days of Canadian travel. Spacious guest rooms retain their elegance with dark-wood furnishings and comfortable seating areas. The health club has a lap pool beneath skylights. Try to get a room high above the street noise. *$$$–$$$$; AE, DC, DIS, E, JCB, MC, V; checks OK; concierge@fairmont.com; www.fairmont.com; at Burrard St.* &

The Four Seasons / ★★★★

791 W GEORGIA ST, VANCOUVER; 604/689-9333 OR 800/268-6285 (CANADA), 800/332-3442 (U.S.) Guests wallow in luxury at this upscale hotel, which offers meticulous attention to detail. It's a modern tower that's connected to more than 140 shops in the Pacific Centre mall below. Although the hotel is in the middle of the high-rise downtown core, many guest rooms offer surprising views of the city as well as peeks at the harbor. Amenities include bathrobes, hair dryers, VCRs, shoe shines, 24-hour valet and room service, and complimentary morning coffee and tea in the lobby. Housekeeping takes place twice daily. Facilities include a year-round indoor/outdoor pool, a complimentary health club (with iced towels), and a rooftop garden. Kids are welcomed not only with milk and cookies on arrival, but also with a teddy bear in their crib, a step stool in the bathroom, and their own plush bathrobes. There's also a Dog Recognition Program. Business travelers appreciate phones with voice mail in English, French, or Japanese; modular phone jacks for computer hookup; and full business services. Chartwell (see review) is the best hotel dining room in the city. The Garden Terrace Bar, just off the lobby, is a place to see and be seen. *$$$$; AE, DC, DIS, JCB, MC, V; no checks; vcr.sales@fourseasons.com; www.fourseasons.com; at Howe St.* ⅃

Johnson Heritage House / ★★★

2278 W 34TH AVE, VANCOUVER; 604/266-4175 To say that owners Ron and Sandy Johnson are fond of antiques is an understatement. They have restored a 1920s Craftsman-style home on a quiet street in the city's Kerrisdale neighborhood and turned it into one of Vancouver's most intriguing B&Bs. Everywhere in the three-story house are relics of the past: coffee grinders, gramophones—even carousel horses. The porch light is a genuine old Vancouver street lamp. Top-floor and basement rooms are cozy; the Carousel Suite, with its mermaid-themed bath and antique slate fireplace, is grandest. Breakfast is served in a bright, airy, cottage-style room. Children 12 and over OK; no pets. *$$; no credit cards; checks OK; fun@johnsons-inn-vancouver.com; www.johnsons-inn-vancouver.com; at Vine St, in Kerrisdale.*

Listel Vancouver Hotel / ★★⯪

1300 ROBSON ST, VANCOUVER; 604-684-8461 OR 800/663-5491 Art is the show at Listel. A superb location on trendy Robson, this boutique property features $1.5 million worth of paintings and sculptures on two of its six floors. The Gallery Floor showcases furniture and artwork handpicked from two of the city's fine-art galleries (Buschlen Mowatt and Keith Alexander). Thanks to the Museum of Anthropology, the Museum Floor has distinctive contemporary furniture made of hemlock and cedar, highlighting Northwest Coast art. There's an exercise room and Jacuzzi on the premises and guests can also use Fitness World (Bute and W Georgia Sts) at no charge. Ask about special rates, packages, and upgrades. The hotel's O'Doul's Restaurant and Bar features jazz nightly. *$$$; AE, DC, DIS, JCB, MC, V; no checks; reservations@listel-vancouver.com; www.listel-vancouver.com; at Jervis St.* ⅃

Metropolitan Hotel / ★★★

645 HOWE ST, VANCOUVER; 604/687-1122 OR 800/667-2300 Located in the heart of the downtown business and financial district, this red-brick tower offers outstanding concierge service, private Jaguar limousine service, nightly turndown service on request, 24-hour room service, a full-scale business center, and one of the city's finest hotel health clubs. There are 18 palatial suites; all other rooms are deluxe, offering elegant contemporary appointments with European duvets and Frette bathrobes. Technologically enhanced business guest rooms include modem hookups, laser printers, and in-room faxes that deliver the latest-breaking news from *The Wall Street Journal* and Japan's *Yomiuri Report*. The hotel's bar and restaurant, Diva at the Met (see review), has talented chefs rockin' on the pans. *$$$; AE, DC, MC, V; no checks; reservations@metropolitan.com; www.metropolitan.com; between Dunsmuir and W Georgia Sts.* &

"O Canada" House / ★★★

1114 BARCLAY ST, VANCOUVER; 604/688-0555 OR 877/688-1114 This beautifully restored 1897 Victorian home in the West End is where the national anthem, "O Canada," was written in 1909. Filled with the comfort and grace one would expect in such a setting, the front parlor and dining room harken back to gentler times. Potted palms nestled in Oriental urns; a welcoming fireplace; large, comfy chairs; and soft lights greet you at every turn, along with a glass of sherry in the evenings. A wraparound porch looks out onto the English-style garden. The late-Victorian decor continues into the six guest bed-cum-sitting rooms, which have private baths and modern conveniences. The South Suite has an adjoining sitting room. The Penthouse Suite offers two gabled sitting areas, skylights, and a view of downtown. The diminutive guest cottage, a new addition, has a gas fireplace and private patio. *$$$; MC, V; no checks; info@ocanadahouse.com; www.ocanadahouse.com; at Thurlow St, 1½ blocks south of Robson St.*

Pan Pacific Hotel / ★★★★

300-999 CANADA PLACE WY, VANCOUVER; 604/662-8111 OR 800/663-1515 (CANADA), 800/937-1515 (U.S.) No hotel in Vancouver has a more stunning location, a better health club, or a more remarkable architectural presence. As part of Canada Place, with its five giant white sails, the Pan Pacific juts out into Vancouver's inner harbor—the sails are actually the roof for a huge convention center. The pier, which is also the embarkation point for summer's thriving Alaska cruise ship market, hasn't achieved the fame of Sydney's architecturally similar Opera House, but Canada Place's five sails are gradually becoming the city's signature landmark. It's a little confusing when you first enter the hotel: check-in is on the third floor; guest rooms start on the eighth. Standard rooms are small, but suites are spacious. The decor is flawlessly understated and intentionally muted, in tones of cream and beige. Nothing deters from the spectacular views. The best views face west, but you can't beat a corner room (with views from your tub). Watch ships sail into the sunset from the Cascades Lounge. *$$$$; AE, DC, E, JCB, MC, V; no checks; concierge@panpacific-hotel.com; www.pan pacific.com; at foot of Burrard St.* &

Sheraton Suites le Soleil / ★★★

567 HORNBY ST, VANCOUVER; 604/632-3000 OR 877/632-3030 Outside, it's easy to walk right by the bland facade of Sheraton Suites le Soleil ("the sun"). But inside, the decor demands attention. The high-ceilinged lobby is a study in gilded opulence. It features original oil paintings, a grand fireplace, and a cozy sitting area. Like the lobby, the 112 guest suites are on the small side. But with their efficient layouts, the loss of space is not as noticeable as the value for the price. Besides, the suites are beautifully decorated and furnished in tones of regal red and gold, focusing on le Soleil's solar theme. Guests have access to the state-of-the-art YWCA fitness center next door. *$$$$; AE, DC, MC, V; no checks; info@lesoleilhotel.com; www.lesoleil hotel.com; near Dunsmuir St.* &

Sheraton Vancouver Wall Centre Hotel / ★★

1088 BURRARD ST, VANCOUVER; 604/331-1000 OR 800/663-9255 Just a few blocks from Robson Street, these stunning glass towers house a wonderful addition to Vancouver's wide-ranging luxury-lodging scene. What distinguishes the Wall Centre from the competition is its stylish, avant-garde decor. The lobby area features furnishings in playful primary colors and dramatic marble, as well as blown-glass chandeliers and a gold-leaf staircase. Standard double rooms are small, although expansive views from the higher floors make them feel larger. Check into a one-bedroom corner suite with a two-vista view; floor-to-ceiling windows face north up Burrard Street, with Grouse Mountain in the distance, and west to English Bay and the Coast Mountains beyond. Most suites feature wet bars, microwaves, and deep soaker tubs in the marble bathrooms. The complex has a full health club with a 15-meter (50-foot) lap pool and a hair salon. *$$$–$$$$; AE, DC, JCB, MC, V; no checks; concierge@wall centre.com; www.sheratonvancouver.com; at Helmcken St.* &

The Sutton Place Hotel / ★★★★

845 BURRARD ST, VANCOUVER; 604/682-5511 OR 800/961-7555 With its elegant interior and understated beige facade, Sutton Place would rank as a top hotel in any European capital. Each of the 397 soundproofed rooms and suites in this sumptuous residential-style hotel has all the amenities one could want. Housekeeping tidies rooms twice daily. Beds are king-sized; furnishings are museum-quality reproductions of European antiques (and plenty of spectacular original pieces are in the hotel's public spaces). Eleven floors are nonsmoking, elevators are the fastest in town, and the concierge and bellhops snap to attention when you arrive, whether you're wearing blue jeans and driving a beat-up truck or emerge in black-tie from a limo. Sutton Place's Fleuri restaurant and its lounges have long been popular with locals. Elegant meals, a civilized tea, and a chocolate buffet await. The richly paneled Gerard Lounge is ranked as one of the Northwest's best watering holes. Le Spa is replete with a swimming pool, a fitness room, and beauty salons. Sutton Place also provides the best wheelchair-accessible rooms in the city. High-end rental condominiums at La Grande Residence are located in a separate building connected to the hotel. *$$$$; AE, DC, DIS, E, JCB, MC, V; no checks; info@vcr.sutton place.com; www.suttonplace.com; between Robson and Smithe Sts.* &

Sylvia Hotel / ★

 1154 GILFORD ST, VANCOUVER; 604/681-9321 This is a favorite for price and location, more than for attentive service. The English ivy–covered, eight-story historic brick hotel is a landmark adjacent to English Bay Beach, Vancouver's most popular sand-and-strutting grounds. Try for a south-facing room. A low-rise addition was built to accommodate guests in the busy summer season, when you might have to settle for any available room. Weekend reservations are required well in advance. All 119 rooms, some of which are quite small, have private baths. Families or small groups should request the one-bedroom suites, which can sleep four and include a kitchen and living room. Covered parking—with no security (and that can be a problem)—is available for an extra charge. The hotel also offers room service, a restaurant, and a lounge. Legend has it that the first cocktail bar in Vancouver opened here in 1954. (On some winter afternoons, it looks as though the original clientele is still in situ.) The outstanding variety of cuisines available on Denman Street are more alluring. But the view of the bay at sunset makes a predinner cocktail in the lounge a rewarding experience. *$; AE, DC, MC, V; checks OK; www.sylviahotel.com; corner of Gilford and Beach Sts.*

The Wedgewood Hotel / ★★★

845 HORNBY ST, VANCOUVER; 604/689-7777 OR 800/663-0666 Eleni Skalbania's Wedgewood Hotel is a place you will want to return to time and again. It offers old-world charm and scrupulous attention to every detail. From the ideal downtown location just off Robson Street to its renowned Bacchus Ristorante (see review), this 93-room hotel is all that a small urban luxury hotel should be. The finely appointed rooms, which are surprisingly large and decorated with vibrant colors and genuine English antiques, have the feel of a grand home. Though the views are lost to taller buildings in the neighborhood, this is the place to spend your honeymoon—and many do. For that matter, any weekend at the Wedgewood is a weekend to savor. *$$$; AE, DC, DIS, E, JCB, MC, V; no checks; info@wedgewoodhotel.com; www.wedgewoodhotel.com; between Robson and Smithe Sts.* &

West End Guest House / ★★

1362 HARO ST, VANCOUVER; 604/681-2889 Don't be put off by the blazing-pink exterior of this early-1900s Victorian home. Owner Evan Penner runs a fine eight-room inn (each room with private bath), and during summer a vacancy is rare. Rooms are generally small but nicely furnished, and there are antiques throughout the house. The staff have all worked in major hotels and know hospitality. Sherry or iced tea is served in the afternoons on the covered back deck overlooking the verdant English-style garden. Nightly turndown service, feather beds and lambskin mattress covers, robes, telephones—even teddy bears—are provided in every room. The bountiful breakfast is served family style or delivered to your room. The guest parking is a rarity in the West End. Families with children are accepted, but be careful with the antiques. Take a stroll along the garden paths in Barclay Square, one block to the west, for a quick impression of how the neighborhood looked in the early 1900s. *$$–$$$; AE, DIS, MC, V; checks OK; info@westendguesthouse.com; www.westendguesthouse.com; at Broughton St, 1 block off Robson St.*

YWCA Hotel/Residence / ★★

733 BEATTY ST, VANCOUVER; 604/895-5830 OR 800/663-1424 Built in 1995, the YWCA is close to theaters, sporting venues, and the library. Rooms are functional, immaculately clean, and reasonably priced for a downtown location. All rooms have sinks; some have private baths and televisions; others share baths. The residence is remarkably quiet, and although it might not be quite the thing for those accustomed to amenities (no tissues, clocks, or coffeemakers here), it provides meeting rooms, kitchen and laundry facilities, and communal lounges. You can work out for free at the YWCA Fitness Centre at 535 Hornby Street. *$; MC, V; checks OK for deposit only; hotel@ywcavan.org; www.ywcahotel.com; between Georgia and Robson Sts.* ⎣

Richmond

This Vancouver suburb is south of the city, between the North Arm and the main Fraser River. The airport is between Richmond and Vancouver. Many Asians have moved into Richmond, as evidenced by the increasing number of outstanding Chinese restaurants and the Asian malls.

RESTAURANTS

Sun Sui Wah Seafood Restaurant / ★★★

4940 NO. 3 RD, RICHMOND; 604/273-8208 / 3888 MAIN ST, VANCOUVER; 604/872-8822 Simon Chan brought the proven track record and signature dishes of this successful Hong Kong group to Richmond and Vancouver and his team has been playing to packed houses ever since. Reasons are legion: crispy, tender roasted squabs and sculpted Cantonese masterpieces such as luscious broccoli-skirted steamed chicken interwoven with black mushrooms and Chinese ham; deftly steamed scallops on silky bean curd topped with creamy-crunchy *tobikko* (flying-fish roe) sauce; Alaskan king crab in wine and garlic; lobster hot pot with egg noodles; giant beach oysters steamed in black-bean sauce; and lightly sautéed geoduck paired with deep-fried "milk"—fragrant with sweet coconut in a fluffy crust. Reserve early; these are wedding hot spots. *$$; AE, MC, V; no checks; lunch, dinner every day; full bar; reservations recommended; www.sunsuiwah.com; Alderbridge Plaza (Richmond), at E 23rd Ave (Vancouver).* ⎣

LODGINGS

Fairmont Vancouver Airport Place / ★★★

3111 GRANT MCCONACHIE WY, VANCOUVER INTERNATIONAL AIRPORT, RICHMOND; 604/207-5200 OR 800/676-8922 While most airport hotels simply cater to harried business travelers, here is an oasis of tranquillity. Rising above the international terminal, it is the closest hotel to the airport. A waterfall in the lobby and floor-to-ceiling soundproof glass on all floors eliminate outside noise. The Globe at YVR is a reasonably priced restaurant with a full menu. Even if you're not a guest, it's a perfect spot to while away spare boarding time, in front of large fireplaces or

VANCOUVER HERITAGE WALK

Once visitors get over gawking at Vancouver's dramatic natural setting, they start noticing the richness and depth of its architectural landscape. Because Vancouver is a young and rapidly changing city, buildings constructed in the 1950s and 1960s are as vital to its architectural heritage as those from the late 1800s. Getting a sense of all this history is as easy as taking a walk.

A good place to start is Vancouver's oldest standing church, **CHRIST CHURCH CATHEDRAL** (690 Burrard St), completed in 1895 and now an island of antiquity amid a sea of traffic and glass high-rises. Christ Church is worth a visit for its beautiful stained-glass windows and the recent renovations to its exposed-beam, Gothic Revival structure. Just across the street, **HOTEL VANCOUVER** (900 W Georgia St) opened for business in 1939: its richly detailed, chateau-style exterior (complete with verdigris roof) is matched by an equally lavish interior restoration. Also nearby is the old **VANCOUVER PUBLIC LIBRARY** (corner of Burrard and Robson). Although it hasn't vanished like so many of the city's other modernist landmarks, this clean-lined 1957 building has had a recent makeover as a Virgin Megastore, the studios of local station VTV, and a Planet Hollywood location. For comparison's sake, it's worth a look at **LIBRARY SQUARE** (350 W Georgia St), which—no matter what anyone says—bears a strong resemblance to the Roman Colosseum.

From the corner of Georgia and Burrard Streets, head south to the **MARINE**

at the bar. Nonguests can use workout facilities, plus workout clothes and robes, for $15. This might be Canada's most technologically advanced and environmentally sound hotel. The room heat turns on when you check in; lights turn on when you insert your key in the door—and turn off when you leave; the "do not disturb" sign illuminates from a central control panel on the nightstand (which also shuts off the doorbell and routes calls to voice mail). *$$; AE, DC, E, MC, V; checks OK; fvares@fairmont.com; www.fairmont.com; on departure level of Vancouver International Airport.*

North Vancouver

Across Burrard Inlet at Second Narrows, North Vancouver is backed by mountains that are Vancouver's playground. Grouse Mountain, the Capilano Suspension Bridge, Capilano Regional Park, and the Capilano salmon hatchery are popular. The public market at **LONSDALE QUAY** (123 Carrie Cates Ct; 604/985-6261), lesser-known than the one at Granville Island, boasts two levels of shops and produce, its open stalls filled with everything from toys and crafts to produce and smoked salmon. A large Iranian population has settled in North Vancouver, as the many **IRANIAN MARKETS** and saffron-scented restaurants attest.

BUILDING (355 Burrard). From a distance, this 21-story art deco treasure, built in 1929–30, looks like something out of Gotham City. But comic-book analogies fail when you examine the exterior, inlaid with richly detailed terra-cotta friezes, and the opulent green- and blue-tiled foyer. Several blocks east on Hastings Street, the **GENERAL POST OFFICE** building (757 W Hastings St), completed in 1910, is now part of the Sinclair Centre retail complex; its corner clock tower makes dramatic use of double columns and arcades, finishing with a dome and weather vane. Close by, the colon-naded former **CANADIAN PACIFIC RAILWAY** station (601 W Cordova St), whose airy 1914 hall houses shops, offices, and the entrance to the Waterfront Sky Train and SeaBus stations. From here it's a short walk east to **GASTOWN**. Along Water Street you'll find some of the city's oldest hotels and warehouses, many of them refurbished as lofts and offices. Another promising route lies south on **GRANVILLE MALL**, home to numerous heritage buildings, including the **ORPHEUM THEATRE** (884 Granville St). Finished in 1927—and rescued from demolition during the 1970s—this onetime vaudeville theater has a low-key facade but houses a spectacular mix of baroque styles.

If you want an expert guide, July through September the **ARCHITECTURAL INSTI-TUTE OF BC** offers six rotating walking tours of Vancouver neighborhoods, including downtown, Chinatown, the West End, and Strathcona. Tours depart from the institute's offices (101–440 Cambie St; 604/685-8588; www.aibc.bc.ca).

--Nick Rockel

RESTAURANTS

Gusto di Quattro / ★★☆

1 LONSDALE AVE, NORTH VANCOUVER; 604/924-4444 Gusto makes a great excuse for a minicruise via the SeaBus. There's an air of festivity at all Quattro restaurants and the intimate Gusto is no exception. "La cucina leggera"—the "healthy kitchen"—is the motto here. Start with an antipasto platter. Pastas are beautifully balanced—an outstanding choice is the pappardelle Fagiano—thin rib-bons tossed with pheasant and chanterelles in a pheasant reduction. We loved the pistachio-crusted sea bass in a roasted sweet pepper sauce, but if you're really hungry, order the *l'abbuffata* menu for four or more big appetites. Distinctive Italian bottlings and well-chosen international favorites join a handful of top domestic vin-tages on the wine list. *$$–$$$; AE, DC, MC, V; no checks; dinner every day; full bar; reservations recommended; gusto@quattro.ca; www.quattrorestaurant.com; across from Lonsdale Quay Market.* &

The Tomahawk / ★

1550 PHILIP AVE, NORTH VANCOUVER; 604/988-2612 Step inside this 70-year-old Vancouver institution and be greeted by garden gnomes in a fountain. The menu names are a match for the kitschy decor. Try the legendary, massive all-day Yukon breakfast, or if you can say it with a straight face, a Big Chief Skookum Burger: a double beef-patty burger topped with a hot dog plus all the fixings, and a mountainous side order of fries, a pickle, and slaw. Cap your feast with baked-on-the-premises pie (lemon meringue, Dutch apple, or banana cream). *$; AE, DC, MC, V; no checks; breakfast, lunch, dinner every day; no alcohol; reservations not accepted; info@tomahawkrestaurant.com; www.tomahawkrestaurant.com; at Marine Dr.* &

LODGINGS

Thistledown House / ★★★

3910 CAPILANO RD, NORTH VANCOUVER; 604/986-7173 OR 888/633-7173 This Craftsman-style home was built in 1920 from timber cut on the nearby mountain and has been completely restored and luxuriously furnished. Antiques and period pieces intermingle with eclectic international art. Six soundproofed guest rooms have private baths, thick terry-cloth robes, and down duvets. Two rooms have gas fireplaces and separate sitting areas. Our favorite, Under the Apple Tree, has a two-person Jacuzzi and a private patio. Ideal innkeepers, owners Rex Davidson and Ruth Crameri are a genial former restaurateur and an expert on Scottish history, and a professional interior designer from five generations of Swiss hoteliers, respectively; service is flawless. Afternoon tea, with sherry and fresh pastries, is served on the porch overlooking the flower garden or in the living room by the fireplace. Guests linger to exchange travel stories over sumptuous four-course breakfasts. *$$$; AE, DC, E, MC, V; no checks; davidson@helix.net; www.thistle-down.com; across from Capilano Suspension Bridge.* &

LOWER MAINLAND
BRITISH COLUMBIA

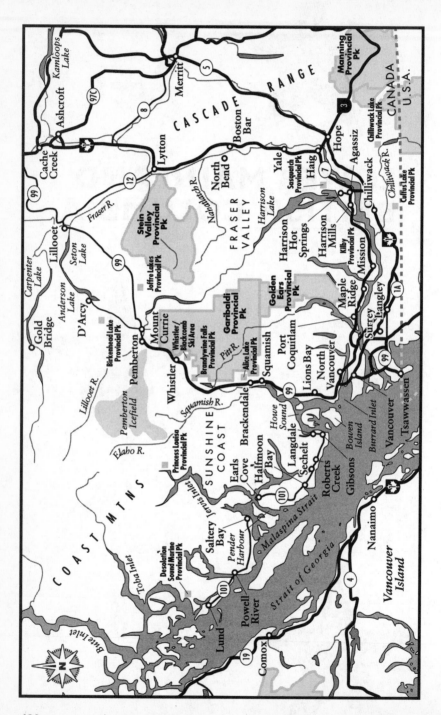

LOWER MAINLAND
BRITISH COLUMBIA

The term "Lower Mainland" came into currency among Vancouver Island settlers in the 19th century. Early immigration into what was then the Crown Colony of British Columbia spilled over from Vancouver Island into the lush farmland of the Fraser River estuary and Fraser Valley. Vancouver Islanders used the term "mainlanders" to emphasize their separation from these new communities. The Strait of Georgia that divides the island from the Lower Mainland represents as much a psychological schism as it does a physical split. It didn't help when, by the end of the 1800s, the upstart city of Vancouver and the burgeoning Lower Mainland had stolen Victoria's limelight.

Today the Lower Mainland has grown well beyond the Fraser River basin to encompass Greater Vancouver, the Sunshine Coast, the Sea to Sky corridor, as well as the Fraser Valley regions. The success of Vancouver's 1986 World Exposition, and Whistler's ascendancy as one of the world's hippest resorts, have thrown a halo around the hinterland. Visitors come for a look around, and keep coming back—or stay. Who wouldn't want to live where eagles drop by at supper or where you can ski in the morning and golf in the afternoon? Drawn by such a magnetic landscape, a new breed of entrepreneurs has set out to offer food and lodging in the midst of it all. In many cases the neighbors, if not the world, beat a path to their doors.

ACCESS AND INFORMATION

Border crossings (and customs) link Washington State and the Lower Mainland at four locations. The busiest are the crossings at Blaine, Washington, where Interstate 5 links with Highway 99 at the Peace Arch, and at Douglas, where BC's Highway 15 begins. The others are located just south of Aldergrove, British Columbia, and at Huntingdon-Sumas just south of Abbotsford, British Columbia. After September 11, 2001, security was tightened: allow two to five hours to make the crossing at peak hours, and carry a passport as proof of citizenship. The nearest major airport is **VANCOUVER INTERNATIONAL AIRPORT** (9 miles/15 km south of downtown on Sea Island, Richmond; 604/207-7077; www.yvr.ca).

HIGHWAY 1 (Trans-Canada Hwy) runs east-west and links the south Fraser Valley with Vancouver. **HIGHWAY 17** links the BC Ferries' Tsawwassen terminal with **HIGHWAY 99**. The North Shore is reached by traveling west on Highway 1 across the Ironworkers Memorial Second Narrows Bridge. Highway 1 (or the Upper Levels Hwy, as it is called on the North Shore) crosses North and West Vancouver to Horseshoe Bay, site of the BC Ferries terminal that connects the North Shore with Nanaimo on southern Vancouver Island, Langdale (and Highway 101) on the Sunshine Coast, and nearby Bowen Island. From Horseshoe Bay, Highway 99 (the Sea to Sky Highway) links the North Shore with the upcountry communities of Squamish, Whistler, Pemberton, and Lillooet.

Sea to Sky Highway (Highway 99)

The scenic Sea to Sky Highway crosses paths with two historic routes—the Pemberton Trail and the Gold Rush Heritage Trail—that linked the coast with the interior in the days before automobiles. Along these ancient pathways, generations of Coast Salish people traded with their relations in the Fraser Canyon, and in the 1850s, prospectors stampeded north toward the Cariboo gold fields. In 1915, the Pacific Great Eastern railway began service between Squamish and the Central interior, providing an ideal way to reach trailheads in **GARIBALDI PROVINCIAL PARK** (604/898-3678; wlapwww.gov.bc.ca/bcparks) and fishing camps such as Alta Lake's Rainbow Lodge, at the foot of London Mountain.

By the mid-1960s, the prospect of skiers heading from Vancouver to the fledgling trails on London Mountain—by this time renamed Whistler Mountain—prompted the provincial government to open a road north from Horseshoe Bay to Whistler. Space being at a premium along steep-sided Howe Sound (North America's southernmost fjord), road and railway parallel each other for much of the 28 miles (45 km) between Horseshoe Bay and Squamish, at the head of the sound.

The railway (which now departs from its southern depot in North Vancouver) and Highway 99 helped introduce visitors to the region's backcountry. Certainly, Whistler's success has propelled development, both commercial and recreational, in other parts of the region, particularly Squamish and Pemberton. So too has the popularity of the mountain bike and the sport utility vehicle—both of which make the backcountry more accessible.

Along the Sea to Sky Highway, at the **TANTALUS RANGE VIEWPOINT** (15 miles/25 km north of Squamish), you can see a dozen or more peaks. **BRANDYWINE FALLS PROVINCIAL PARK** (21 miles/34 km north of Squamish) south of Whistler features Brandywine Falls, Daisy Lake, and views of the Black Tusk's volcanic snaggletooth high above in Garibaldi Provincial Park. Shannon Falls Provincial Park in Squamish, site of BC's third-highest waterfall, and **NAIRN FALLS PROVINCIAL PARK** (2 miles/1.2 km south of Pemberton) near Pemberton also feature waterfalls. Contact BC parks (604/898-3678; wlapwww.gov.bc.ca/bcparks) for information.

ACCESS AND INFORMATION

GREYHOUND CANADA (604/482-8747 in Vancouver, 604/898-3914 in Squamish, 604/932-6236 in Whistler, or 800/231-2222; www.greyhound.ca) offers frequent daily service between Vancouver, Squamish, Whistler, Pemberton, and Mount Currie. **BC RAIL** (604/984-5246 or 800/663-8238; www.bcrail.com) offers regular passenger service between North Vancouver and Lillooet on the Cariboo Prospector day liner. In summer, BC Rail operates excursions between North Vancouver and Squamish, and a boat/train excursion between the two (water travel is via the MV *Britannia*). Call BC Rail or **HARBOUR CRUISES** (604/688-7246 or 800/663-1500 outside BC) for information.

The **SQUAMISH CHAMBER OF COMMERCE AND VISITOR INFO CENTRE** (37950 Cleveland Ave, Squamish; 604/892-9244; info@squamishchamber.bc.ca; www.squamishchamber.bc.ca) and **TOURISM WHISTLER** (4010 Whistler Wy, Whistler; 604/932-3928 in Whistler, 604/664-5625 in Vancouver, or 800/944-7853; www.tourismwhistler.com) are good resources for the area.

SEA TO SKY THREE-DAY TOUR

DAY ONE: After breakfast in Vancouver, head north on Highway 99 to Squamish, pausing at **SHANNON FALLS PROVINCIAL PARK** to view the cascade. Lunch at the nearby **ROADHOUSE DINER** (Shannon Falls, Hwy 99; 604/892-5312) at Klahanie, then continue on into Squamish. Stroll the hour-long **SQUAMISH ESTUARY TRAIL,** then visit **RAVEN SUN GALLERY** and the **BRACKENDALE ART GALLERY** (604/898-3333). Check in at the **HOWE SOUND INN & BREWING COMPANY;** in the pub, admire the view of Stawamus Chief Mountain, and quench your thirst from an arm's-long list of microbrews. Time to freshen up before dinner at the inn's **RED HEATHER GRILL.** Get an early night.

DAY TWO: Have breakfast at the inn, and make sure there's film in your camera for the breathtaking drive to Whistler. Nonstop, the drive is only 45 minutes, but take your time. Pause at the **TANTALUS RANGE VIEWPOINT** to see a dozen or more peaks, and at **BRANDYWINE FALLS PROVINCIAL PARK** to view the falls and the Black Tusk. Lunch in Whistler at **HOZ'S PUB,** where insiders have been heading for decades. Just outside is the beginning of the 12-mile (20 km) **VALLEY TRAIL.** Check into your room at the **EDGEWATER LODGE** on Green Lake before heading into Whistler Village, where you can catch happy hour at the **DUBH LINN GATE IRISH PUB** (604/905-4047) in the Pan Pacific Lodge. Head back to Green Lake for the sunset on Blackcomb and Whistler Mountains and dinner at the Edgewater; otherwise, treat yourself to dinner at **ARAXI'S.**

DAY THREE: Rise early for a quick breakfast delivered to your room before heading north. Stop at **NAIRN FALLS PROVINCIAL PARK** for a quick jaunt to the falls, then into Pemberton and to **GRIMM'S GOURMET & DELI** to pick up picnic supplies. Poke your head in the **PEMBERTON PIONEER MUSEUM** before beginning the two-hour drive to Lillooet; pause at **DUFFEY LAKE PROVINCIAL PARK,** or one of several BC Forest Service recreation sites beside **CAYOOSH CREEK,** to enjoy your picnic. Just before Lillooet, stop at the **BC HYDRO RECREATION AREA** on Seton Lake to walk the beach, then climb to the viewpoint. In Lillooet check into your room at the **4 PINES MOTEL,** then stroll over to **DINA'S PLACE** for dinner. Catch the sunset from the patio as the smell of sagebrush rises in the air.

Squamish

Squamish (population 16,000), or "Squish," as it's affectionately known, is a relief. Far smaller than Vancouver, larger than Whistler, and equidistant from both, Squamish is the envy of the south coast. It has so many things going for it—location, geography, wildlife, weather—that as forestry declines as the town's major employer, tourism and outdoor recreation have taken on greater importance. Travelers have always been drawn to Squamish, from the days of the Coast Salish people, who journeyed between Burrard Inlet and Stawamus (pronounced "STA-a-mus") at the mouth of the Squamish River, to more recent times when steamships began ferrying anglers, climbers, and picnickers here over a century ago. Things have only intensified since then.

Two blocks west of downtown Squamish is the hour-long **SQUAMISH ESTUARY TRAIL** (west end of Vancouver St). Bring binoculars: this is bald eagle country. If you want to take one home with you, you might find an authentic carved replica at **RAVEN SUN GALLERY** (Stawamus Reserve; 604/892-3133) or **BRACKENDALE ART GALLERY** (41950 Government Rd, Brackendale; 604/898-3333).

RESTAURANTS

Red Heather Grill / ★

37801 CLEVELAND AVE (HOWE SOUND INN), SQUAMISH; 604/892-2603 OR 800/919-2537 The most elegant dining room in Squamish features tastefully understated decor that matches the indoor/outdoor feel of the inn. Pull up a Craftsman chair to a sturdy wooden table, or plunk down in an oversized couch beside the fireplace next to the bar. Artwork by local painters fairly leaps off the walls. Some entrees may suffer from an over-the-top blend of ingredients, but you can't go wrong with the appetizers, often a meal in themselves. Try Cajun Fanny Bay oysters or peppered, seared yellowfin tuna. The Salmon Sampler—smoked, candied, barbecued tips with mango salsa, red pepper mayonnaise, and assorted relishes—is good with house bread, such as whole wheat focaccia or herb-and-cheese. (Loaves are available for purchase.) The grill has its own wood-fired pizza oven from which inventive creations emerge. *$$; AE, MC, V; no checks; breakfast, lunch, dinner every day, brunch Sat–Sun; full bar; reservations recommended; hsibrew@howesound. com; www.howesound.com; downtown Squamish.* &

LODGINGS

Howe Sound Inn & Brewing Company / ★

37801 CLEVELAND AVE, SQUAMISH; 604/892-2603 OR 800/919-2537 This 20-room inn with its massive fieldstone chimney is part brewpub, part restaurant (see listing for Red Heather Grill), and part roadhouse. Owner Dave Fenn not only fashioned a two-story traveler's hotel, he also created a meeting place for local outdoor enthusiasts. Guests can pick up information on climbing and kayaking routes, or get the latest road report. Simply appointed rooms are modestly sized. The upstairs reading lounge is perfect for planning the next day's outing. Other amenities include a sauna and bouldering wall. *$$; AE, MC, V; no checks; hsibrew@howesound.com; www.howesound.com; downtown Squamish.* &

SunWolf Outdoor Centre / ★

70002 SQUAMISH VALLEY RD, BRACKENDALE; 604/898-1537 OR 877/806-8046 When exploring the outdoors around Squamish, make this your base of operations. Ten cabins sit on the shaded 5½ acre-property at the confluence of the Cheakamus and Cheekye Rivers, whose constant voice drowns out the sound of everything else. Formerly a fishing lodge, each of the high-ceilinged cabins has been renovated and comes equipped with a gas fireplace, fir floor, pine furnishings, a double and a single bed. Some cabins have kitchens. Meals are also available from a cafe in the center's main building. Whitewater rafting and eagle-viewing float trips are two of the center's specialties. Mountain bikes, canoes, and kayaks are available for rent. BC Rail runs past the center, so hop the day liner to Whistler for some sightseeing: the Cheakamus River canyon just north of the lodge is a must-see. *$$; MC, V; checks OK; sunwolf@sunwolf.net; www.sunwolf.net; 4 km (2½ miles) west of Hwy 99 on Squamish Valley Rd.*

Whistler

The summit of the narrow Whistler Valley contains the Resort Municipality of Whistler (population 9,500), above which hundreds of runs crisscross Blackcomb Peak and Whistler Mountain. At the heart of Whistler lies Alta Lake. No other valley in the Sea to Sky region has such a wealth of small and medium-sized lakes. And no other lakes have quite the scenery to mirror. Above the tree line, remnants of the most recent Ice Age persist in glaciers on the highest peaks of surrounding Garibaldi Provincial Park.

Whistler's layout is a collection of 10 "villages." Roads and the recreational Valley Trail link them to the hotels and restaurants. Hop one of the Whistler Wave buses; it's often easier than trying to park in Whistler Village, and the trip only takes a few minutes.

WHISTLER MOUNTAIN (elevation 7,160 feet/2,182 m) and **BLACKCOMB** (elevation 7,494 feet/2,284 m) were rivals for two decades before merging in 1997. They comprise what many skiers and snowboarders consider the premier North American winter resort. You can just as easily explore one as the other; each offers a complimentary perspective on its companion and has a loyal following of ski and snowboard devotees. They have been around long enough (Whistler since 1965, Blackcomb since 1980) to have developed trails over a total of 7,071 acres that have been shaped, groomed, and gladed to hold snow and reduce obstacles. For information on **LESSONS AND RENTALS,** as well as ticket prices, contact guest relations (604/932-3434 in Whistler, 604/664-5614 in Vancouver, or 800/766-0449; www.whistler-blackcomb.com). Call for current **SNOW CONDITIONS** (604/932-4211 in Whistler, 604/687-7507 in Vancouver).

Whistler Village's **LOST LAKE PARK** features a 20-mile (32 km) network of packed and tracked trails for **CROSS-COUNTRY SKIERS** and snowshoers. At the log chalet near the start (on Valley Trail north of Lorimer Rd; 604/905-0071; www.crosscountryconnection.bc.ca), pay your fee (about $10 during the day, $4 in the evening, no charge after 9pm) for use of the trails. Skiing around the lake takes 60 to 90 minutes. Trails are marked for beginners to experts; the 2-mile (4 km) Lost Lake Loop Trail is lit for night skiing. A designated cross-country ski trail in winter and a hiking loop in summer, the 12-mile (20 km) **VALLEY TRAIL'S** access points include the Whistler Golf Course (on Hwy 99 in Whistler Village), the Meadow Park Sports Centre (on Hwy 99 in Alpine Meadows), and Rainbow Park (on Alta Lake Rd).

SNOWMOBILING is big at Whistler; try Cougar Mountain Wilderness Adventures (36-4314 Main St; 604/932-4086; www.cougarmountainatwhistler.com).

HELI-SKIING/BOARDING in Whistler can be arranged with Whistler Heli-Skiing (3-4241 Village Stroll; 604/932-4105; www.whistlerheliskiing.com) and Blackcomb Helicopters (9990 Heliport; 604/938-1700; www.blackcombhelicopters.com). **SNOWCAT SKIING/SNOWBOARDING** can also get you into Whistler's untracked backcountry; contact Backcountry Snowcats (9615 Emerald Pl; 604/932-2166 or 888/246-1111).

If you can walk, you can **SNOWSHOE**. Some of the most inviting trails in Whistler are those in the forest surrounding Olympic Station on Whistler Mountain. Canadian Snowshoe Adventures (604/932-0647; www.iias.com/outdoors) offers rentals and guided tours, including evening outings on Blackcomb.

Although diehards can ski Horstman Glacier until early August, come summer, do what the locals do: head for the hills (many consider the area to be the best **MOUNTAIN BIKING** terrain on the West Coast), the lakes (this is where **WINDSURFING** started in Canada), or the rivers (by **RAFT, CANOE,** or **KAYAK**). The **VALLEY TRAIL,** a mostly level 12-mile (20 km) loop that passes many of Whistler's neighborhoods and Lost Lake, takes you through cool forest to Alpha, Nita, Alta, and Green Lakes.

GOLFERS can try the scenic Arnold Palmer–designed Whistler Golf Club (4001 Whistler Wy; 604/932-3280), or the equally esteemed Robert Trent Jones Jr. link course at Chateau Whistler (4599 Chateau Blvd; 604/938-2092), or Nicklaus North (8080 Nicklaus N Blvd; 604/938-9898), a Jack Nicklaus–designed course in the Green Lake area.

Tourism Whistler's **ACTIVITY AND INFORMATION CENTRE** (4010 Whistler Wy; 604/932-2394) can offer advice and arrangements for any winter or summer recreation. Whistler has achieved such a high level of international popularity that on some weekends, rooms cannot be had for love nor money. With more than two million ski visits alone each winter, advance reservations are recommended for all lodging and restaurants. Many rooms in the area, as well as condos, are owned by different management companies. All may be reached through Tourism Whistler's **CENTRAL RESERVATIONS** (604/932-4222 in Whistler, 604/664-5625 in Vancouver, or 800/944-7853 from the United States and Canada, except BC).

RESTAURANTS

Araxi Restaurant & Bar / ★★★★

4222 WHISTLER VILLAGE SQ, WHISTLER; 604/932-4540 Araxi is one of Whistler's culinary cornerstones. In a town with so many restaurants per square foot, that means something. Araxi is located in the center of Whistler Village Square, with sought-after summer patio dining. Chef Scott Kidd's surprising starters include diver-caught octopus-and-squid salad with plums, toasted sesame, pickled ginger, sweet peppers, organic greens and jicama, or soup *di verdure*, a sorrel, leek, and spinach soup with black truffle oil and nasturtiums. Main courses run a gamut of aqua- and terra-sourced selections, such as a Hecate Strait halibut "succotash" of basil, chanterelles, sweet corn, toasted pine nuts, and oven-roasted organic tomatoes, or pan-seared calf's liver with Lyonnaise potatoes, spinach, double smoked bacon, portobello mushroom, and aged balsamic jus. Two somme-

EAGLE EYES

The largest gathering of bald eagles in southwestern British Columbia occurs along the banks of the Squamish River as it flows past Brackendale. Each year, from November until mid-February, thousands of these majestic birds come from points north and east to feast on a late-fall salmon run. Vast numbers of them roost along the river during the winter.

In 1996, the BC government created the **BRACKENDALE BALD EAGLE SANC-TUARY** (an hour's drive north of Vancouver, along Hwy 99), an act that recognized the importance of this area. It's a bit surprising to find a bird recently taken off the endangered species list in such abundance. Indeed, if you walk the trails or riverbanks here in the predawn darkness and wait for the first rays of sunlight, you'll be rewarded by the sight of 10–20 eagles in a single tree. (As crowds of bird-watchers and sightseers gather later in the day, the eagles start roosting farther away.) Because the peak viewing period is in winter, the cottonwood trees are bare of leaves, making for easy sightings. Additionally, a flock of trumpeter swans can often be seen near the mouth of the Squamish.

The **SUNWOLF OUTDOOR CENTRE** (604/898-1537) offers naturalist-guided raft tours of the Squamish River during winter. The **BRACKENDALE ART GALLERY** (604/898-3333) pays homage to the eagles by hosting an official eagle count in January each year (dates vary from one year to the next). In 1994, a record 3,769 eagles were counted. —*Steven Threndyle*

liers ensure that Araxi's big, changeable, and impressive wine cellar is yours to explore every night. Dessert? Share rich chocolate espresso mousse served with mascarpone cream and delicate butter biscuits, or ginger-scented crème brûlée. *$$$; AE, DC, MC, V; no checks; lunch May–Dec, dinner every day; full bar; reservations recommended; info@araxi.com; www.araxi.com; heart of Whistler Village.* ⅙

Caramba! / ★★

12-4314 MAIN ST, WHISTLER; 604/938-1879 This fun, boisterous, Mediterranean-influenced restaurant reflects owner Mario Enero's ability to wow even those who are on a modest budget. He's combined high-energy service with big, soul-satisfying portions of down-home pasta, pizza, and roasts. Start with the savory baked goat cheese served with a tomato coulis and garlic toast points. Then delve into the Fettuccine Natasha, accented with chunks of fresh salmon and a peppery vodka-and-tomato cream sauce. Munch on a Melanzana pizza heaped with roasted eggplant, roma tomatoes, and goat cheese. Or try the mouth-watering grilled bay trout with bacon-and-onion mashed potatoes. The open kitchen, earthen hues, and alderwood-burning pizza ovens lend a warm, casual tone to the room. Can't stay? They'll whip up a take-out meal in 15 minutes. Kids and adults both love the platter of three-cheese macaroni after a strenuous day on the slopes. *$; AE, MC, V; no checks; lunch every day in winter and summer only, dinner every day; full bar; reservations recommended; Village North, at Town Plaza Square.* ⅙

Chef Bernard's Café / ★

1-4573 CHATEAU BLVD, WHISTLER; 604/932-7051 Chateau Whistler's former executive chef, Bernard Casavant, is now Whistler's foremost caterer. When you walk into Chef Bernard's, you enter Casavant's kitchen. Fortunately, he included a few wooden tables and a take-out counter. With an emphasis on farm-fresh local produce, Casavant creates a flawless fusion of classic French and Pacific Northwest cuisines. Start with Brie-and-carrot soup, or organic field lettuce salad with herb-crusted chicken breast. Try pan-seared wild salmon fillet in a lemongrass and star anise marinade served with basmati rice and a spicy orange-ginger sauce. Chef Bernard keeps locals coming back for his fried free-range egg sandwich made with aged cheddar and bacon on a toasted granola bun. Fresh pies are a dessert treat. *$; AE, MC, V; no checks; breakfast, lunch every day, dinner every day in winter and summer only; beer and wine; reservations not accepted; Upper Village, at Blackcomb Wy.* &

Hoz's Pub & Creekside Grillroom / ★★

2129 LAKE PLACID RD, WHISTLER; 604/932-4424 Good basic fare in a down-to-earth atmosphere might seem hard to find in Whistler, but the locals know a spot that pleases almost every palate. From deluxe burgers, barbecued chicken, and ribs (served with beans, hand-cut fries, and slaw) to cod or salmon fish-and-chips, Hoz's satisfies. Surprises include Rahm Schnitzel (pork cutlet topped with mushroom and port sauce) and New York Neptune (charbroiled strip steak topped with white asparagus, baby shrimp, and hollandaise). Wear your best flannel shirt, and check pretensions at the door. If you're in the mood for steak, check out Ron "Hoz" Hosner's Creekside Grillroom next to the pub, where first-rate boneless prime rib and pepper steak are featured. The wine list offers a good West Coast selection. *$; AE, DC, MC, V; no checks; breakfast, lunch, dinner every day; full bar; reservations recommended; thebar@hozspub.com; www.hozspub.com; 1 block west of Hwy 99, Creekside area.*

La Rúa Restaurante / ★★★

4557 BLACKCOMB WY (LE CHAMOIS), WHISTLER; 604/932-5011 This stylish but comfortable restaurant in Le Chamois hotel prides itself on snap-of-the-finger service and a great wine list. Chef R. D. Stewart has devised some superb dishes served in ample portions. Start with a pyramid of bocconcini cheese or a seafood tower constructed with layers of Dungeness crab, salmon tartar, avocado salsa, smoked salmon and finished with caviar. No one makes better lamb, serving a rack with caramelized garlic sauce and mint dumplings or a shank set atop a mound of root vegetables and lentils. Exotic pastas, such as *lumache* shells stuffed with spinach, Dungeness crab, and ricotta cheese in a baked shrimp Mornay sauce, are sure to win your heart. Save room for mango-raspberry Napoleon made with layers of fresh berries, mango mousse, and vanilla phyllo crisp. *$$$; AE, DC, MC, V; no checks; dinner every day; full bar; reservations recommended; www.larua-restaurante.com; Upper Village, Lorimer Rd and Blackcomb Wy.* &

Quattro at Whistler / ★★★

4319 MAIN ST (PINNACLE INTERNATIONAL HOTEL), WHISTLER; 604/905-4844 Carbo-loading skiers *live* to slide into Antonio Corsi's restaurant at the Pinnacle International Hotel. Quattro at Whistler is upbeat, vibrant, and innovative. "La cucina leggera," or "the healthy kitchen," is the motto of Quattro, a concept that fits West Coast sensibilities like a good set of ski boots. Fungi fanciers love carpaccio featuring sliced portobello mushrooms topped with flavorful white truffle oil and shaved Asiago. Try *gnocchi al Gorgonzola,* an idyllic marriage of tender potato and semolina dumplings and sharp Gorgonzola topped with roasted pecans. Entrees of braised lamb shank simmered with root vegetables and porcini mushrooms served over a creamy polenta, or roasted lean duck breast accompanied by sun-dried cherry and grappa syrup, are irresistible. Portions are generous; the mainly Italian wine list is stellar; the staff is knowledgeable, friendly, and attentive. Stunning desserts change daily. *$$$; MC, V; no checks; dinner every day (closed mid-Oct–mid-Nov); full bar; reservations recommended; quattro@telus.net; www.quattrorestaurants. com; Village North, at Library Square.* &

Rim Rock Cafe and Oyster Bar / ★★★

2117 WHISTLER RD (HIGHLAND LODGE), WHISTLER; 604/932-5565 OR 877/932-5589 Filled to the rafters with a hip local crowd, this cozy cafe with a stone fireplace has been dishing out great food for years. Manager Bob Dawson and chef Rolf Gunther's restaurant is remarkable proof that fresh seafood and wondrous cuisine are not anomalies in the mountains. The fresh sheet features starters such as raw Fanny Bay oysters topped with vodka, crème fraîche, and caviar. Main events range from herb-infused salmon to panfried mahi mahi in an almond-ginger crust to a mouth-watering grilled filet mignon topped with fresh herb butter or creamy tricolored peppercorn sauce. The Death by Chocolate dessert can make grown men cry. In summer, book a table on the cozy back patio and dine amid fresh herbs in the chef's garden. Service is top-drawer—knowledgeable but not arrogant. *$$$; AE, MC, V; no checks; dinner every day (closed mid-Oct–mid-Nov); full bar; reservations recommended; rimrock@direct.ca; www.rimrockwhistler.com; 2 miles (3.5 km) south of Whistler Village, at Creekside.*

Splitz Grill / ★

4369 MAIN ST (ALPENGLOW), WHISTLER; 604/938-9300 It's been a long time since a hamburger (or any of its '90s-style chicken, salmon, or lentil cousins) has been this thick, juicy, and tantalizing. Splitz struck the right chord with locals and visitors by offering a not-so-humble grilled sandwich on a crusty bun with your choice of umpteen toppings. A satisfying meal is less than $10, including thick, house-cut fries and soft drink. Maybe that's why more than 44,000 burgers were sold in its first year. Sweet temptations include ice-cream sundaes, floats, shakes, cones, and a caramelized banana split. *$; V; no checks; lunch, dinner every day; beer and wine; reservations not accepted; Village North, across from 7-Eleven.*

Trattoria di Umberto / ★★★☆

4417 SUNDIAL PL (MOUNTAINSIDE LODGE), WHISTLER; 604/932-5858 Two large, romantically lit dining rooms separated by a massive open kitchen welcome you to this busy, lively, very northern Italian establishment. Animated conversation is as much a part of the atmosphere as the potted plants and sculptures, the pool-side view, and the rustic Italian decor. Service is fast and friendly. Classic Tuscan starters include beef carpaccio topped with shaved Parmesan, accompanied by a mélange of aromatic vegetables, and a hearty bean soup. But it's entrees like the grilled quail with sage, or the cioppino (a saffron- and fennel-laced stew combining crab, prawns, mussels, and a variety of fish in a rich tomato broth) that will leave you singing the kitchen's praises. The requisite pasta and risotto dishes include smoked duck-and-portobello risotto, and penne with pesto and smoked salmon. A respectable wine list, desserts large enough to share, and cappuccino complete the experience. *$$$–$$$$; AE, DC, MC, V; no checks; lunch, dinner every day; full bar; reservations recommended; inquire@umberto.com; www.umberto.com; Whistler Village, at Blackcomb Wy.* &

Val d'Isère / ★★★★

4314 MAIN ST (BEAR LODGE), WHISTLER; 604/932-4666 Val d'Isère offers a grand combination: fine dining and an intimate interior. The Provençal motif is tastefully executed in muted tones of blue and gold, illuminated by table lamps. Superchef Roland Pfaff presides over this French kitchen with overtones of Alsace, offering palate-pleasing delicacies such as a signature onion tart. His starter of Queen Charlottes smoked herring and Granny Smith apple salad served in a buttery potato mille-feuille with smoked-mussel vinaigrette is heart-warming. For entrees, try the delicately seared Alaskan scallops, served with champagne sauce and couscous, or the richly flavored braised duck legs, enhanced by duck stock and rosebud reduction, paired with bulgur risotto. French, American, and Canadian wines grace the impressive cellar list. Pfaff's trademark dessert is a chocolate cream–centered chocolate cake on a custardy crème anglaise. *$$$; AE, DC, MC, V; no checks; lunch, dinner every day (closed mid-Oct–mid-Nov); full bar; reservations recommended; valdiser@direct.ca; www.valdisere-restaurant.com; Village North, at Town Plaza Square.* &

LODGINGS

Brew Creek Lodge / ★★

1 BREW CREEK RD, WHISTLER; 604/932-7210 Originally built as a private home in the 1970s, Brew Creek Lodge became a quiet hideaway B&B on the road to Whistler in the 1980s. Brew Creek itself flows through the lodge's 12 acres to nearby Daisy Lake. The massive post-and-beam main lodge features six spacious rooms on its top floor, all with bathrooms en suite. Elsewhere on the property, accommodations include two family-size suites that adjoin the Guest House (sleeps eight), the Trappers Cabin (sleeps four), and the Treehouse (sleeps two). Fanciful architectural flourishes attest to the original owner's enthusiasm, though it would be hard to improve on the site's natural beauty. Cross-country trails lead from the lodge, and Whistler is 20 minutes north. The lodge has its own creekside hot tub and swimming pond. No TV; no phones. *$$–$$$; AE, MC, V; no checks; www.brewcreek.com; 12 miles (16 km) south of Whistler.* ♿

Delta Whistler Resort / ★★

4050 WHISTLER WY, WHISTLER; 604/932-1982 OR 800/268-1133 As the first major hotel to open in Whistler Village at the base of the dual mountain operations in the 1980s, the Delta Whistler Resort nabbed a prime location. Further development has added a year-round tennis facility, a heated outdoor lap pool, as well as a spa and fitness center. The resort's standard rooms are surprisingly ordinary. Deluxe studios are worth the extra expense, equipped with balconies and fireplaces, full kitchens, Jacuzzis or soaking tubs, and clothes dryers. Also convenient are bike and ski rental shops in the 300-room, pet-friendly hotel. The Delta's West Coast cuisine–themed Evergreen Restaurant was one of the first in Whistler to use local organic produce. *$$$$; AE, DC, DIS, JCB, MC, V; checks OK; reservations@delta-whistler.com; www.delta-whistler.com; Whistler Village.* ♿

Durlacher Hof Alpine Country Inn / ★★★

7055 NESTERS RD, WHISTLER; 604/932-1924 OR 877/932-1924 Erika and Peter Durlacher have a reputation as Whistler's most welcoming and generous innkeepers. Their Austrian pension commands a view of both Blackcomb and Whistler and is minutes from the slopes. Painstaking attention to detail is evident in the cozy après-ski area (where complimentary afternoon tea is served) and immaculate rooms with hand-carved pine furniture, comfortable beds, and goose-down duvets; some suites feature whirlpools. A groaning sideboard holds lavish breakfasts. From the moment you get up to the last cup of *glüwein* late at night (the guest lounge is also a licensed bar), sharing the Hof with the Durlachers is a joy. *$$$–$$$$; MC, V; checks OK; info@durlacherhof.com; www.durlacherhof.com; Nesters neighborhood.* ♿

Edgewater Lodge / ★★

8841 HWY 99, WHISTLER; 604/932-0688 OR 888/870-9065 The 12-room Edgewater Lodge sits in solitude on its sylvan 45-acre Green Lake estate. For all its potential, owner Jay Simmons keeps the place low-key. It has no lobby; rooms are small, with picture windows featuring great views. Half of the rooms have dens with pullout beds. As well as a lakeside Jacuzzi, guests can use a small beach area with summer canoe and kayak rentals. Immediate access to the outdoors is what sets the lodge apart—at the confluence of the River of Golden Dreams and aptly named Green Lake. Whistler's recreational Valley Trail connects the property with the rest of Whistler. Meadow Park Sports Centre—complete with indoor skating rink, fitness center, and swimming pool—is adjacent, as is the Nicklaus North golf course. Pets are welcome. Whistler insiders laud the lodge's 45-seat lakefront restaurant for its service, fine food, and stellar location. *$$–$$$; AE, DC, MC, V; local checks only; jays@direct.ca; www.edgewater.lodge.com; across from Meadow Park Sports Centre.* ♿

Fairmont Chateau Whistler Resort / ★★★★

4599 CHATEAU BLVD, WHISTLER; 604/938-8000 OR 800/606-8244
The largest resort hotel built in Canada in the past century, the 12-story, 563-room Chateau Whistler is arguably *the* place to experience Whistler, a pleasant five-minute walk from the buzz of the village, at the base of Blackcomb. Its sun-drenched east side takes in sweeping views of the mountains from slopeside suites, the hotel's main dining room and lounge, or the indoor/outdoor pool and spa complex. West-facing accommodations are priced slightly lower, and offer views of Rainbow Mountain. All the pampering touches one would expect are provided. Given the grand impression of the chateau's foyer, however, standard rooms—particularly junior suites—are only adequately sized; but public areas are some of the most pleasant in Whistler. Hooked rugs soften the slate slab floor, and two mammoth limestone fireplaces are accented by folk-art and twig furniture. *$$$$; AE, DC, DIS, MC, V; checks OK; reservations@chateauwhister.com; www. fairmont.com; at foot of Blackcomb.* &

Pan Pacific Lodge / ★★★☆

4320 SUNDIAL CRES, WHISTLER; 604/905-2999 OR 888/905-9995 At the Pan Pacific, a deer-antler chandelier and Morris chairs arranged beside a river-rock fireplace evoke the spirit of classic mountain lodges. But on the eight floors above, 121 studio, 1-, and 2-bedroom suites with floor-to-ceiling windows give the impression you're floating among the peaks. Whistler Mountain dominates the southeastern skyline, while Sproat and Rainbow Mountains provide the panorama to the northwest. All rooms have fireplaces, soaker tubs, plush robes, Internet hookups, full kitchens, and private balconies. Pan Pacific Hotels are renowned for their subtle blend of Japanese and western interior designs; fin de siècle touches abound here. A heated outdoor pool and hot tubs grace the lodge's second-floor terrace, with a spa, fitness center, and steam room tucked inside. In spring, après-ski action on the adjacent plaza heats up. *$$$$; AE, DC, MC, V; no checks; whistler@panpacific-hotel.com; www.panpac.com; off Blackcomb Wy.* &

Whistler Village Inn & Suites / ★★

4429 SUNDIAL PL, WHISTLER; 604/932-4004 OR 800/663-6418 When Blackcomb opened in 1980, Whistler Village began to take shape. It was as much a joy to stay at the Whistler Village Inn then as it is today, especially as it was completely renovated in 2000 with further touches added in 2001. Just around the corner from the base of the lifts for both mountains, the inn's view suites, with full kitchens, wood-burning fireplaces, patios, and cozy sleeping lofts provide a comfortable experience. There's also a heated outdoor pool, a steaming hot tub, and a sauna. Complimentary continental breakfast is served in the lobby under the baleful gaze of a regal moose head. The Whistler Village Inn sits in the heart of the village, so you can walk everywhere. *$$–$$$$; AE, DC, DIS, MC, V; no checks; wvi@direct.ca; www.whistlervillageinn.bc.ca; in Whistler Village.* &

Pemberton and Mount Currie

For over a century, Pemberton (population 855) was isolated from the rest of the Lower Mainland because travel in and out of its broad valley was regulated by the railway. When a highway was finally completed from Whistler in 1975, the long period of separation ended. At first, there was only a trickle of traffic along this stretch of Highway 99—logging trucks southbound for Squamish, and the occasional carload of climbers headed north to **JOFFRE LAKES PROVINCIAL PARK**, with its three turquoise alpine lakes and an ice- and rock-encrusted skyline. In the past decade, the pace of tourism has accelerated. The 1986 World Exposition in Vancouver kick-started bus tours to Whistler and beyond when a paved highway between Pemberton and Lillooet completed the corridor.

Today, this agriculturally and recreationally rich valley is experiencing phenomenal growth in visitors and new residents. Quick access to golfing, hiking, climbing, mountain biking, and backcountry snow touring is one reason for the surge. Not incidentally, this region is also the traditional territory of the Lil'wat people, who today are headquartered in the towns of Mount Currie and nearby D'Arcy. Everyone is welcome at First Nation events such as the **LILLOOET LAKE RODEO**, held each May in Mount Currie (population 1,400), and the August salmon festival in D'Arcy. The quaint **PEMBERTON PIONEER MUSEUM** (Camus and Prospect, Pemberton; 604/894-6135) offers a glimpse of pioneer life. **PEMBERTON CHAMBER OF COMMERCE TOURISM INFORMATION** (604/894-6175) can provide info on all activities; a Pemberton visitor info booth is open May 15 through September 30 on Highway 99 and Portage Road.

In Pemberton, seek out small cafes such as **PONY ESPRESSO** (1426 Portage Rd; 604/894-5700) and **GRIMM'S GOURMET & DELI** (7433 Frontier Ave; 604/894-5303). **WICKED WHEEL PIZZA** (2021 Portage Rd; 604/894-6622), in nearby Mount Currie, is packed on all-you-can-eat nights.

Lillooet

As the Sea to Sky Highway winds between Pemberton, Lillooet, and Hat Creek, it passes through the most notably varied terrain of its entire length. Much of this area lies in the rain shadow of the Coast and Cascade mountains. By the time the last moisture in the clouds has been raked off by the peaks around Cayoosh Pass, there's little left to water the countryside to the east. Ponderosa pine and sage take over from western hemlock and devils club. This section of Highway 99 is also called the Duffey Lake Road. Cayoosh Creek runs east from Duffey Lake and accompanies the highway for most of its 62 miles (100 km). Just before Lillooet, BC Hydro's recreation area at **SETON LAKE** has a viewpoint where pit homes once housed a First Nation community.

Lillooet (population 2,060) was the staging ground for the Cariboo Gold Rush of the late 1850s. Summer temperatures here are among the hottest in Canada. From May to October, the **LILLOOET INFO CENTRE** (790 Main St; 250/256-4308) is located in an A-frame former church, which it shares with the town museum. While in town, be sure to check out the **LILLOOET BAKERY** (719 Main St; 250/256-4889);

the **4 PINES MOTEL** (108 8th Ave; 250/256-4247 or 800/753-2576) is a good place to rest your head, particularly after an extended backcountry trip.

RESTAURANTS

Dina's Place / ★

690 MAIN ST, LILLOOET; 250/256-4264 A whitewashed Greek restaurant suits Lillooet's often scorching summer days. Dina's patio is the place to be in early evening, as long shadows begin to overtake the sun-drenched hillside above the Fraser River. Zesty panfried *saganaki* made with Kefalotiri goat cheese neatly sums up the owners' northern Greek roots. Plenty of fresh oregano in the *keftedhes scharas* (spicy meatballs) suits Lillooet's sagebrush environment. Twenty-six kinds of pizza keep one oven going, while creamy moussaka and *paithakia* lamb chops and other entrees keep another busy. Halibut steaks and calamari are a must-try recommendation. *$$; MC, V; no checks; lunch Mon–Sat, dinner every day; full bar; reservations not necessary; on east side of Main St.* &

LODGINGS

Tyax Mountain Lake Resort / ★★

TYAUGHTON LAKE RD, GOLD BRIDGE; 250/238-2221 The largest log structure on the West Coast, affable owner Gus Abel's Tyax Mountain Lake Resort is set beside Tyaughton Lake with the newly minted 173,000-acre South Chilcotin Provincial Park at its doorstep, about 60 miles (100 km) west of Lillooet. In summer, float-planes are an alternate mode of reaching the resort. Tyax also operates a shuttle service that picks up guests at the Lillooet train station—a 90-minute scenic drive via Highway 40. Floatplanes take anglers up to the Trophy Lakes; a helicopter lifts thrill-seekers to enjoy skiing, hiking, mountain biking, and even fossil hunting. But it's not all a high-tech adventure; you can simply canoe, gold pan, ice-skate, or ride horses. Twenty-nine suites in the spruce-log lodge have beamed ceilings, balconies, and down quilts. Five chalets each have kitchen, loft, and balcony overlooking Tyaughton Lake. Other amenities include a sauna, outdoor Jacuzzi, and game and workout rooms. *$$$; AE, MC, V; no checks; fun@tyax.bc.ca; www.tyax.bc.ca; 56 miles (90 km) west of Lillooet on Hwy 40, then 3 miles (5 km) north on Tyaughton Lake Rd.* &

Fraser Valley

The wide, fertile Fraser Valley runs 93 miles (150 km) inland from the Pacific to the small town of Hope. The Fraser River—broad, deep, and muddy—flows down the middle of the valley. River crossings are limited, forcing travelers to choose the north (Hwy 7) or south (Hwy 1) side. Except for the cities of Maple Ridge and Mission on the north side of the Fraser, and Abbotsford and Chilliwack on the south, this mostly rural, fertile valley supports a blend of farming and forestry, with outdoor recreation (cycling, camping, hiking) high on everyone's list.

Fort Langley

Several historic 19th-century forts in British Columbia serve as reminders of the West's original European settlers. In Fort Langley (population 2,600), on the south side of the Fraser off Highway 1, **FORT LANGLEY NATIONAL HISTORIC SITE** (23433 Mavis St; 604/513-4777) is a preserved and restored Hudson's Bay Company post. The **LANGLEY CENTENNIAL MUSEUM** (across from fort; 604/888-3922) houses a permanent collection of memorabilia, as well as rotating displays of contemporary arts and crafts. Glover Road, Fort Langley's main street, features shops, cafes, and restaurants, many in heritage buildings. The large community hall has been lovingly preserved.

Harrison Lake

All of 12 miles (18 km) long, the Harrison River, which drains south from Harrison Lake into the Fraser River, is among BC's shortest yet most significant waterways. Throughout fall, major runs of spawning salmon make their way upstream into numerous tributaries of the Harrison watershed. This quiet backwater is anchored by **KILBY PROVINCIAL PARK** (604/824-2300; wlapwww.gov.bc.ca/bcparks) at the crossroads community of Harrison Mills on Highway 7, on the north side of the Fraser. The beach at Kilby is popular with water-skiers with wet suits; water temperatures in Harrison Bay are influenced by outflow from chilly Harrison Lake, and rarely rise above 70°F (20°C). The beach is also popular with anglers, trumpeter swans, and a thousand or more bald eagles, which come in late autumn to feast on the annual salmon run.

    KILBY HISTORIC STORE (604/796-9576; open May–Oct, and at Christmas), adjacent to Kilby Provincial Park, has a wonderful pioneer history. The restored boardinghouse, post office, and general store give a feel for life on the Fraser River at the turn of the 20th century, when stern-wheelers linked small towns with the docks downstream at Mission and New Westminster.

    Bigfoot (Sasquatch, locally) is said to frequent the southern end of Harrison Lake—perhaps itching for a soak in the **HARRISON HOT SPRINGS** fabled waters. The indoor public bathing pool (224 Esplanade Ave; 604/796-2244) is one of the most inviting places in this lakefront town (population 1,060). **HARRISON LAKE** is too cold for most swimmers, but a constructed lagoon at the south end of the lake is rimmed by a wide swath of sand, and a small, quiet row of low buildings. In summer, rent sailboats or bikes, or hike nearby trails. Annual events include June's long-running **HARRISON FESTIVAL OF THE ARTS,** focusing on arts and cultures of the Third World, especially Africa and Latin America, and the **WORLD CHAMPIONSHIP SAND SCULPTURE** competition, on the second weekend in September. Contact the **HARRISON HOT SPRINGS VISITOR INFO CENTRE** (499 Hot Springs Rd; 604/796-3425; harrison@uniserve.com; www.harrison.ca) for details.

LODGINGS

Fenn Lodge Bed and Breakfast Retreat / ★

15500 MORRIS VALLEY RD, HARRISON MILLS; 604/796-9798 OR 888/990-3399 Once the home of a local lumber baron, the 1903 Victorian classic now has seven guest rooms on the upper floor, each with its own bathroom. Decor is understated and bright: creamy wallpaper, brass beds, overstuffed duvets. Owners Diane Brady and Gary Bruce are world travelers and art collectors. It shows in touches such as the harem bed in the bridal suite, and Chinese artwork displayed throughout the rambling main floor. Two life-sized herons preside over the sitting room with its granite fireplace. In the formal dining room, Chinese bamboo instruments are arranged around a grand piano. Breakfast is served at a large kitchen table and features tasty French toast, pancakes, fresh fruit, jams, muffins, eggs—whatever suits you. The estate grounds contain a heated spring-fed swimming pool, a labyrinth based on that of San Francisco's Grace Cathedral, and a children's playground. Kayaks are available for guest use. In autumn, the Chehalis River on the north side of the 90-acre property runs red with spawning salmon. Dinner is offered by prior arrangement. *$$–$$$; MC, V; no checks; info@fennlodge. com; www.fennlodge.com; 2 miles (4 km) northeast of Hwy 7 on Morris Valley Rd.*

The Harrison Hot Springs Hotel / ★★

100 ESPLANADE, HARRISON HOT SPRINGS; 604/796-2244 OR 800/663-2266 This legendary hotel on the south shore of beautiful Harrison Lake was originally built in 1885 but burned down in 1920. The current establishment was built in 1926 and extensively renovated in the 1950s. A new wing was added in the 1990s. Avoid the old wing, where noise seeps between the walls. A maze of hot-spring pools are steps away from the new wing; ask for a pool walk-out room. Two indoor pools are available only for use by hotel guests. Spacious grounds that surround the hotel are lovingly landscaped, with tennis courts and an exercise circuit. In addition, there is a full spa. Food and service at two hotel restaurants, the Lakeside Terrace and Copper Room, and a bar are excellent. In the off-season, a roaring hearth in the large foyer takes the chill from the damp air. Children are made welcome with a water park and special menus. *$$–$$$; AE, DC, DIS, MC, V; checks OK; info@harrisonresort.com; www.harrisonresort.com; west end of Esplanade Ave on lake.* ⅋

Hope

Hope (population 7,100) is a pretty little Fraser River town with a pioneer past. Hope's two main streets are lined with service centers, because it's an important highway junction, but the heart of town is frequently overlooked. Make a point of spending a few minutes here, if for no other reason than to breathe the incredibly fresh air that characterizes Hope. The **HOPE VISITOR INFO CENTRE** (919 Water Ave; 604/869-2021; www.hopechamber.bc.ca/)—and the **HOPE MUSEUM**—at the south end of Water Street that fronts the Fraser River is a font of up-to-date news and directions to other sights within the Hope area, including popular **MANNING PROVINCIAL PARK** (16 miles/26 km east of Hope on Hwy 3; 250/840-8836;

wlapwww.gov.bc.ca/bcparks), with its basic but classic, family fun **MANNING PARK LODGE** (Hwy 3, Manning Provincial Park; 250/840-8822 or 800/330-3321).

RESTAURANTS

Pinewoods Dining Room / ★

HWY 3 (MANNING PARK LODGE), HOPE; 250/840-8822 Pinewoods Dining Room—with porch posts carved with likenesses of black bears—offers three happily coexisting dining choices beneath its cedar roof: the Bear's Den Pub, the Cascade Cafe, and the Pinewoods Dining Room. The time of day, your culinary inclination, and your appearance (i.e., how recently you've been camping) will determine your choice. Pinewoods's log-and-pine-paneled interior makes this the cheeriest building at the resort. Walls are covered (but not cluttered) with prints and photographs of wildlife and adorned with vintage snowshoes, skis, toboggans, and oars, brightly lit by windows that look out on Cascade peaks. Specials include vintage skier's breakfasts, homemade jumbo cinnamon buns, burgers and fresh salads, personal pizzas and pastas, wraps and wings. Fresh-sheet entrees and daily soups in the Pinewoods always please. *$–$$; AE, MC, V; checks OK; breakfast, lunch, dinner every day; full bar; reservations not necessary; info@manningparkresort. com; www.manningparkresort.com; adjacent to lodge on Hwy 3, 37 miles (60 km) east of Hope.* &

The Sunshine Coast

The world's longest highway, the Pan-American (Hwy 1 and 101 in parts of the United States and Canada), stretches 9,312 miles (15,020 km) from Chile to Lund on BC's Sunshine Coast. The 87-mile (140 km) stretch of Highway 101 between Langdale and Lund leads to dozens of parks with biking, hiking, and ski trails; canoe and kayak routes; beaches; and coastal viewpoints.

Much of the Sunshine Coast is naturally hidden. Side roads with colorful names like Red Roof and **PORPOISE BAY** lead to places that don't announce themselves until you all but stumble upon them, such as **SMUGGLER COVE MARINE PARK** near Sechelt and **PALM BEACH PARK** south of the town of Powell River.

The Sunshine Coast lives up to its name. With an annual total of between 1,400 and 2,400 hours of sunshine, bright days outnumber gloomy ones by a wide margin. The area benefits from a rain shadow cast by the Vancouver Island mountains, which catch most of the moisture coming off the Pacific (though clouds regroup in the Coast Mountains to the east and provide sufficient winter snow to coat trails for cross-country skiing).

The region is split into two portions, on either side of Jervis Inlet. Roughly speaking, the southern half between the ferry slips at Langdale and Earls Cove occupies the **SECHELT PENINSULA**, while the northern half between the ferry slip at Saltery Bay and Lund sits on the **MALASPINA PENINSULA**. The coastline is deeply indented by the Pacific at Howe Sound, Jervis Inlet, and Desolation Sound. Jervis and Desolation attract a steady stream of marine traffic in summer.

ACCESS AND INFORMATION

The Sunshine Coast is only accessible from the rest of the Lower Mainland by boat or floatplane. Travelers aboard **BC FERRIES** (604/669-1211; www.bcferries.bc.ca/) leave Horseshoe Bay in West Vancouver aboard one of eight daily sailings for a 45-minute ride to Langdale on the Sechelt Peninsula. Highway 101 links Langdale with Earls Cove, 50 miles (80 km) north. Another ferry crosses Jervis Inlet to Saltery Bay, a 60-minute ride. Highway 101 makes the second leg of this journey 37 miles (60 km) north to Lund. BC Ferries also connects Powell River on the Malaspina Peninsula with Comox on the east side of central Vancouver Island.

One of the best parts about enjoying the northern Sunshine Coast in the off-season (Sept–May)—particularly midweek—is being able to catch ferries without experiencing interminable lineups. You'll still have to allow four hours to reach the Malaspina Peninsula from Horseshoe Bay, but you can do it without hurrying, enjoying the travel time just as much as the play time once you arrive. Ferry connections are scheduled to allow adequate time to make the drive from one dock to the next. Those traveling up the entire coast or returning via Vancouver Island should ask at the Horseshoe Bay terminal about special fares (saving up to 30 percent) for the circle tour (four ferry rides).

Gibsons

Gibsons (population 3,900) is a small waterfront community 2 miles (4 km) west of the BC Ferries dock in Langdale. Stop at the **GIBSONS VISITOR INFO CENTRE** (668 Sunnycrest Rd; 604/886-2325; gibsons_chamber@sunshine.net) to stock up on maps and brochures. Check out the nearby federal wharf, where there's often fresh seafood for sale. A short walk along the harbor seawall leads past a plaque commemorating the arrival of George Gibson and his two sons in May 1886. The trio came ashore from the family boat, the *Swamp Angel,* and promptly took up residence. A cairn at **CHASTER PARK** (on Gower Point Rd; 604/886-2325; www.scrd. bc.ca/park_sites.html) honors an even earlier arrival: Capt. George Vancouver camped here in June 1792.

RESTAURANTS

Chez Philippe / ★★

1532 OCEAN BEACH ESPLANADE (BONNIEBROOK LODGE), GIBSONS; 604/886-2188 Parisian Philippe Lacoste trained in Normandy before coming to Vancouver, where he worked at the prestigious Le Crocodile and Le Gavroche restaurants, then moved to Gibsons in the early 1990s. French-inspired with Northwestern influences, the menu features both à la carte selections as well as four-course prix-fixe table d'hôte, with entrees ranging from trout, red snapper, grilled prawns, and scallops in polenta shells to seafood ragout in Natua sauce, New York steak, chicken with wild mushrooms, rack of lamb, and duck à l'orange. Though limited, the wine list offers reasonably priced selections. In winter, a crackling fireplace lights up the dining room with the old-country ambience of a French relais. In summer, catch the sunset while finishing with profiteroles, filled with ice cream and topped with hot chocolate sauce. *$$$; AE, DC, MC, V; no checks; dinner* *every day (Fri–Mon in winter); full bar; reservations recommended; info@bonnie brook.com; www.bonniebrook.com; follow Gower Point Rd from downtown.*

LODGINGS

Bonniebrook Lodge / ★★

 1532 OCEAN BEACH ESPLANADE, GIBSONS; 604/886-2887 OR 877/290-9916 As of 2001, upstairs rooms in this popular B&B have been completely renovated and now have en suite baths. In addition to four rooms in the yellow clapboard house on the water (a guest house since 1922), three "romance" suites have been added. These are equipped with gas fireplaces, Jacuzzi tubs, overstuffed couches, wrought-iron queen bed frames, terry-cloth robes, and wooden armoires. Breakfast (perhaps a pesto omelet, fresh strawberry jam, and muffins) is served in the lodge's Chez Philippe restaurant or delivered to suites—following an early thermos of coffee. Explore the lodge's stretch of beach that leads to nearby Chaster Park. *$$; AE, MC, V; no checks; info@bonniebrook.com; www. bonniebrook.com; follow Gower Point Rd from downtown.* &

Rosewood Country House Bed and Breakfast / ★★

575 PINE ST, GIBSONS; 604/886-4714 In 1990, owner Frank Tonne felled and milled the timber growing on his steep slope overlooking the Strait of Georgia and built a Craftsman-style mansion, using classic doors and windows rescued from older Vancouver houses. The result harkens back to the spacious elegance of earlier times. White walls and blond wood give the house a warm, honeyed glow, a perfect setting for Oriental rugs and period furniture. Rosewood features two self-contained ground-floor suites with fireplaces, stained-glass windows, and French doors that open onto the garden. One has an antique bath by an oceanview bay window. Wake up to champagne and orange juice in the airy sunroom. Guests can request breakfast in bed, rolled in on a silver tea service. Co-owner Susan Tonne handles all the details. Romantic dinners (book in advance) are a specialty, served in a private dining room. Reserve several months in advance for weekends, May through October. *$$–$$$; V; checks OK; rosewood@uniserve.com; www.rose woodcountryhouse.com; 4 miles (6.4 km) west of Gibsons.* &

Roberts Creek

Follow Highway 101 north from Gibsons 4 miles (7 km) to the artistic community of Roberts Creek (population 2,250). Your first stop should be **MCFARLANE'S BEACH,** a sandy crescent where the creek meets the ocean at the south end of Roberts Creek Road. Early in the 19th century, Harry Roberts operated a freight shed here. On its side he painted "Sunshine Belt"—and visitors ever since have been referring to Sechelt Peninsula as the Sunshine Coast. From here, look north toward the sandy beaches at **ROBERTS CREEK PROVINCIAL PARK** (Hwy 101, 9 miles/14 km north of Gibsons; 604/898-3678; wlapwww.gov.bc.ca/bcparks), popular for summer picnics. On **BC DAY** (604/886-2325; first weekend in Aug), the community hosts an annual Gumboot parade and the Creek Freak contest.

REACHING THE PEAKS

The Coast Mountains, which begin in Vancouver and sweep north along the BC coast and through Alaska, are the tallest range in North America and among the most heavily glaciated. An imposing palisade of these peaks defines much of BC's Lower Mainland region. Some of the most rugged terrain in the province was uplifted here by a combination of glacial and volcanic activity about 12,000 years ago. Reaching the tallest peaks, such as **WEDGE MOUNTAIN** in Garibaldi Provincial Park near Whistler, requires advanced mountaineering skills. At 9,527 feet (2,904 m), Wedge is the highest peak in a park that is characterized by massive expanses of rock and ice.

If you're willing to settle for something less than the view from the loftiest pinnacles, there are less challenging approaches that still provide breathtaking panoramas. On a clear day, few skylines can compete with the six peaks—Black, Strachan, Hollyburn, Grouse, Fromme, and Seymour mountains—on Vancouver's North Shore. Roadways climb from sea level to viewpoints in **CYPRESS PROVINCIAL PARK** and **MOUNT SEYMOUR PROVINCIAL PARK.** For more information and to request maps of Cypress Park and Mount Seymour Park, contact **BC PARKS** at Mount Seymour Provincial Park (604/929-4818 or 604/924-2200; wlapwww.gov.bc.ca/bcparks).

If you don't have a vehicle, leave the driving to someone else and ride the Grouse Mountain Skyride gondola up **GROUSE MOUNTAIN** (604/980-9311 or 604/986-6262), at the north end of Capilano Road in North Vancouver. It's readily accessible by public transit via Coast Mountains Translink (604/521-0400; www.translink.bc.ca). The gondola takes visitors on a thrilling ascent up the slopes of Grouse Mountain and

RESTAURANTS

The Creekhouse / ★★

1041 ROBERTS CREEK RD, ROBERTS CREEK; 604/885-9321 Yvan Citerneschi's restaurant, in a house with a view of a tree-filled garden, is decorated simply with white walls, light wood floors, flowers on tables, and original contemporary art. On any given night you may choose from 10 seasonal entrees, such as wild boar, rack of lamb Provençal, sautéed prawns, or locally caught rabbit. Mango mousse lights up the evening. Afterward, walk down to the beach to see the twinkle of distant lights on the mainland and Vancouver Island. *$$; MC, V; local checks only; dinner Wed–Sun; full bar; reservations recommended; creekhouse@uniserve.com; www. robertscreekgetaways.com; at Beach Ave.* &

Gumboot Garden Café

1057 ROBERTS CREEK RD, ROBERTS CREEK; 604/885-4216 Just around the corner from the Creekhouse is an old maroon house with a simple sign: "Cafe." Inside, a terra-cotta sun on the brightly painted yellow wall radiates warmth, as do painted linoleum table mats. The menu shines with a strong Mexican deposits them at 4,100 feet (1,250 m). From there, moderate hiking trails lead off from Grouse Mountain Chalet to a variety of viewpoints.

No matter which approach you choose, the views will all be dominated by the local landscape's most impressive feature: snow-covered Mount Baker (12,906 feet/3,279 m). Though this semidormant volcano is in the Cascade mountains of nearby Washington State, its skyraking presence rears up above the Lower Mainland like none other. Just as sensational are sweeping views of Greater Vancouver, the Strait of Georgia, and Vancouver Island.

Farther inland, gondolas and chairlifts at Whistler take visitors to lofty heights on **WHISTLER MOUNTAIN** (7,160 feet/2182 m) and **BLACKCOMB PEAK** (7,494 feet/2,284 m). These are the same lifts that deposit skiers, snowboarders, snowshoers, and sightseers at **THE ROUNDHOUSE LODGE** on Whistler in winter. Come summer, once the snow has melted, an extensive network of moderate-to-challenging walking and hiking trails leads off into the surrounding landscape that borders on Garibaldi Provincial Park. Here, the peaks stand out in such sharp relief that they seem to be papercut against the backdrop of a Pacific blue sky. Chubby hoary marmots (whose distinctive warning call provided the inspiration for Whistler's name) sun themselves on warm rocks while ravens and eagles circle overhead. For more information and maps of sight-seeing trails on Whistler Mountain, contact guest relations (604/932-3434 in Whistler, 604/664-5614 in Vancouver, or 800/766-0449; www.whistler-blackcomb.com).

—*Jack Christie*

influence. Try the Huevos Gumboot, a hearty breakfast dish available all day. Breads and cheesecakes are baked daily, and produce is often organic. Locals come to hang out and listen to music Friday nights. In keeping with the community and clientele, service is laid back. The building that houses the cafe shares quarters with a juice bar, bookstore, hair salon, and clothing store. *$; MC, V; checks OK; breakfast, lunch every day, dinner Thurs–Sat; beer and wine; reservations recommended; www.heart ofthecreek.com/gumboot; junction of Lower Rd and Roberts Creek Rd.* &

LODGINGS

Country Cottage B&B / ★★

🌲 **1183 ROBERTS CREEK RD, ROBERTS CREEK; 604/885-7448** Philip and Loragene Gaulin's 2-acre farm includes the vintage Rose Cottage tucked inside the front gate, and the more recently constructed Cedar Cottage next to the sheep pasture. The first is a one-room fantasy, complete with fireplace, small kitchen, and quilt-covered bed. Farther back on the property is Cedar Cottage, a tree house for grownups. Wood and stonework set the tone, as does a chandelier fashioned from deer antlers and a loft bed. Skylights brighten the interior on even the gloomiest days. A wood-burning river-rock fireplace occupies one corner. On Sundays in winter, guests are welcome to accompany Philip on his weekly backcountry ski outing in nearby Tetrahedron Park. Get ready with a breakfast of fresh eggs scrambled with smoked salmon, or Belgian waffles that Loragene cooks up on her wood-burning stove. Dogs welcome. Reserve well in advance. *$$–$$$; no credit cards; checks OK; 9 miles (14 km) from Langdale ferry, off Hwy 101.*

Sechelt

If it weren't for a small neck of land less than a half mile wide, a large portion of the peninsula north of Sechelt would be an island. This wedge of sand backs ocean water, which flows in from the northwestern entrance to the Sechelt Inlet near Egmont. Nestled on the wedge is Sechelt (population 7,750), one of the fastest-growing towns in Canada, and home to the Sechelt First Nation whose **HOUSE OF HEWHIWUS** (5555 Hwy 101; 604/885-8991)—House of the Chiefs—is both a cultural and art center. Ask for a tour. **SECHELT VISITOR INFO CENTRE** (5755 Cowrie St; 604/885-0662; sechelt_chamber@sunshine.net) fills you in on the rest.

RESTAURANTS

Blue Heron Inn / ★★

5521 DELTA RD, SECHELT; 604/885-3847 OR 800/818-8977 One of the most consistently pleasant places to dine on the Sunshine Coast is the Blue Heron. Partly for the waterfront views of the Sechelt Inlet (complete with blue herons, of course), partly for the food (fresh clams, a carpaccio-style roast loin of veal, grilled wild salmon with fennel, smoked black cod with hollandaise, halibut fillet with red onion and strawberry salsa, creamy Caesar salad, bouillabaisse), and partly for the relaxed vacationlike atmosphere (fresh flowers, local art). Gail Madeiros makes sure you're comfortable while her husband, Manuel, makes sure you're well fed. Presentations are stunning, and food rolls out of the kitchen like clockwork. In winter, a fieldstone hearth warms the solid wood-beam interior. *$$; AE, MC, V; local checks only; dinner Wed–Sun; full bar; reservations recommended; blueheron@uniserve. com; west of Hwy 101 on Wharf St, right along Porpoise Bay Rd for 1 mile (1.6 km), watch for sign on left side.* &

Halfmoon Bay

The scenery gets wilder as you proceed north. **SMUGGLER COVE PROVINCIAL MARINE PARK** (just west of Halfmoon Bay; 604/898-4678; wlapwww.gov.bc. ca/bcparks) is a wonderful way to experience the coastal wilderness firsthand. Trails lead through an enchanting stand of old-growth forest and around the cove's indented shoreline.

LODGINGS

Lord Jim's Resort Hotel / ★

5356 OLE'S COVE RD, HALFMOON BAY; 604/885-7038 OR 877/296-4593 This former big-game sports lodge now caters just as readily to those in search of nature. Owner Hugh Gatsby's nest of simple cottages clings to the sun-splashed slopes above Ole's Cove. The location has a prime ocean view; the best place to enjoy it in summer is from the resort's freshwater pool. Newly renovated suites are attractive, with handsome furnishings and colorful bedspreads. Motel-style cabins (refurbished in 2000) are simply appointed and harken back to the 1970s, when Lord Jim's aspired to be *the* resort on the Sunshine Coast. Cabin 11 (Maple) enjoys the most secluded (and sunny) location. Great paddling is to be had from the resort's wharf and small pebble beach. The restaurant's menu is appetizing, but the bar has a tiki-tiki ambience—complete with stuffed lynx, cougar, and trophy-sized chinook salmon. *$$$; AE, MC, V; no checks; lordjims_resort@dccnet/com; www.lordjims.com; west on Mercer Rd off Hwy 101.*

Pender Harbour

It's hard to tell where freshwater lakes end and saltwater coves begin at the north end of the Sechelt Peninsula, a confused, puzzle-shaped piece of geography. Narrow fingers of land separate the waters around Agamemnon Channel from a marvelous patchwork of small and medium-sized lakes. Three oceanside communities comprise Pender Harbour: **MADIERA PARK, GARDEN BAY,** and **IRVINES LANDING.** As you head north of Pender Harbour, Highway 101 winds around Ruby Lake and climbs above it, allowing a good view of the jewel-like setting and beyond.

An impressive natural show occurs twice daily in **SKOOKUMCHUK NARROWS PROVINCIAL PARK** (Hwy 101; 604/898-3678; wlapwww.gov.bc.ca/bcparks) in Egmont, about 7 miles (12 km) north of Ruby Lake: one of the largest saltwater rapids on Canada's West Coast boils as tons of water force their way through Skookumchuk Narrows at the north end of Sechelt Inlet. A 2.5-mile (4 km) walking/cycling trail leads from the outskirts of Egmont to viewing sites at North Point and nearby Roland Point. At low tide, the bays around both points display astonishingly colorful and varied forms of marine life: giant barnacles, colonies of sea stars, sea urchins, and sea anemones.

LODGINGS

Ruby Lake Resort / ★

RUBY LAKE, MADIERA PARK; 604/883-2269 OR 800/717-6611 An engaging family from Milan—the Cogrossis—bought Ruby Lake Resort in 1993 and rebuilt the 10 cedar cottages, now nicely furnished with full kitchens and TVs; they added two new cottages in 2002. It's a great place to bring the kids; paddleboats are available, and you can rent canoes. The family's restaurant draws accolades for its northern Italian cuisine and fresh seafood. Waterfowl by the hundreds flock to the resort's private lagoon. Eagles drop by for their daily feeding at 6pm. In his spare time, chef Aldo Cogrossi builds birdhouses, more than 40 of which adorn the sides of cabins, telephone poles, rooftops, and the neighboring Suncoaster Trail, a lengthy mountain-bike and hiking trail. *$$; MC, V; no checks; closed Dec–Feb; talk2us@rubylakeresort.com; www.rubylakeresort.com; 6 miles (10 km) south of Earls Cove.*

Powell River

Travelers looking to experience the smooth, sedate pace of ferry sailings will enjoy the journey between Earls Cove and Saltery Bay on Jervis Inlet. Get out your binoculars: the hour-long sailing is an eye-opening coastal experience. Powell River (population 14,150) is a pleasant drive 19 miles (31 km) north of the ferry terminal at Saltery Bay. Look for the **VISITOR INFO CENTRE** (4690 Marine Ave; 604/485-4701; prvb@prcn.org) located in a storefront downtown. Just down the street is the **ROCKY MOUNTAIN PIZZA & BAKERY** (4471 Marine Ave; 604/485-9111), where you can perch on a stool and people watch while enjoying organic coffees, chunky soups, pizza-sized cinnamon buns, salads, wraps, pizza by the slice, and deli sandwiches.

RESTAURANTS

jitterbug café / ★

4643 MARINE DR, POWELL RIVER; 604/485-7797 Walk through Haida-born landscape artist April White's Wind Spirit Gallery, and you'll find one of Powell River's most enduring eateries. The jitterbug café's a stylishly renovated 1920s home typical of the BC coast, with solid oak tables in a sunny room. Gallery art adorns the walls, and sweeping views of islands in the Strait of Georgia open up to the west from the back deck. Simple meals are based on local ingredients—and some wonderful homemade breads. Shrimp season begins in April; blackberries appear on the menu in August. At lunch, try a chicken sandwich on warm cheese bread, or smoked salmon pasta. Dinners offer sautéed chicken breast with an Asiago cheese sauce, and a delightful and delicious lemon linguine. Try one of the house crepes for dessert. True to its name, the cafe features live music on Friday and Saturday evenings. *$$; AE, MC, V; no checks; lunch, dinner Tues–Sat; full bar; reservations recommended; allofus@windspirit.com; www.windspirit.com; downtown.* &

LODGINGS

Beach Gardens Resort & Marina / ★★

7074 WESTMINSTER AVE, POWELL RIVER; 604/485-6267 OR 800/663-7070 Sitting on a protected section of Malaspina Strait, the Beach Gardens Resort caters to divers, who come for the near-tropical clarity of the water and the abundant marine life (a dive shop is on-site). Tennis courts and a fitness center with steam rooms, saunas, and large indoor pool back on a lawn that slopes down to a sizable marina. Rooms are pleasantly comfortable, bright, clean, and painted with soft marine hues. Tiled bathrooms with full tubs are their crowning feature. Request a room in the new wing; from the balconies are views of Texada Island to the west. Divers prefer the less expensive, viewless cabins. *$$–$$$; AE, MC, V; no checks; bgardens@www. coc.powell/river.bc.ca/; www.beachgardens.com; off Marine Ave.* &

Lund

Little ports don't come more well hidden than Lund at the north end of the Sunshine Coast. The Malaspina Peninsula narrows to a thin finger of land here, wedged between Malaspina Strait on the west and Okeover Arm to the east. Lund retains much of the wilderness charm that drew a family of settlers from Finland here a cen-

GOLFING YOUR WAY UP THE SEA TO SKY HIGHWAY

The completion of several world-class golf courses in the 160-kilometer (100-mile) Sea to Sky corridor has been good news for duffers and scratch players alike. It's not Arizona or California, but once the clouds dissipate, the breathtaking mountain scenery more than makes up for the rainy weather.

Between a rock and a wet place might be the best way to describe **FURRY CREEK GOLF AND COUNTRY CLUB** (604/894-2224; 888/922-9462), located 48 kilometers (30 miles) north of downtown Vancouver on Highway 99. Built on a mountainside that slopes (none too gently in some places) to the briny depths of Howe Sound, the course must be seen to be believed. The course is short—6,001 yards from the gold tees—but requires the legs of a mountain goat to walk it. Carts are mandatory.

No less a golfing legend than Arnold Palmer himself ushered in the modern era of Whistler golf when he took a local nine-hole executive course and redesigned it into the **WHISTLER GOLF CLUB** (604/932-4544) in 1982. From the back tees, this superb recreational layout is just under 6,400 yards, with a slope rating of 128.

Palmer was followed to Whistler by the great architect Robert Trent Jones Jr., who built the stunning **FAIRMONT CHATEAU WHISTLER GOLF CLUB** (604/938-2095). Situated away from the village on the Blackcomb benchlands, the course is challenging; from the back tees, it's 6,635 yards, with a slope rating of 142. The clubhouse is an architectural marvel that goes well beyond the typical "19th Hole."

Fairmont Chateau Whistler fairly screamed "Can you top this?" to course architects, a challenge met by none other than the design team of Jack Nicklaus. Nicklaus has had a hand in planning more than 150 courses worldwide, but **NICKLAUS NORTH AT WHISTLER** (604/938-9898; 800/386-9898) is the only one he's ever lent his name to. Alongside the gurgling waters of Fitzsimmons Creek and adjacent to Green Lake, the course has water hazards on 15 of 18 holes. Nonetheless, it has been built with the recreational golfer in mind, with generous landing areas for well-placed drives.

Thirty-eight kilometers (24 miles) north of Whistler, in Pemberton, designer Bob Cupp took advantage of a broad, flat, sunny valley hemmed in by mountain peaks. Many golfers who play all of the Sea to Sky tracks on a regular basis think that **BIG SKY GOLF AND COUNTRY CLUB** (800/668-7900) is the most scenic of the lot. Two municipal tracks are worth mentioning as well. The **SQUAMISH GOLF AND COUNTRY CLUB** (604/898-9961 or 888/349-3688) is the oldest golf course in the region. The view of nearby Mount Garibaldi is striking. So are the views at the **PEMBERTON GOLF AND COUNTRY CLUB** (604/894-6197 or 800/390-4653). Both clubs welcome visiting players of all handicaps and are memorable for their scenery and playability.

—Steven Threndyle

tury ago. Recently the **LUND HOTEL** (1436 Hwy 101; 604/414-0474) has undergone a complete face-lift under new owners, the Sliammon First Nation. Flowers cascade from hanging baskets and carpet the hotel's garden. **NANCY'S BAKERY** (on wharf; 604/483-4180) is loaded with goodies like blackberry cinnamon rolls, and the **STARBOARD CAFÉ** (on Lund harbor) serves espresso in a breezy little bistro. A jolly looking red **WATER TAXI** (604/483-9749), the *Raggedy Anne,* ferries passengers and supplies to nearby Savary Island. **OKEOVER ARM PROVINCIAL PARK** (off Hwy 101, 3 miles/5 km east of Lund; 604/898-3678; wlapwww.gov.bc.ca/bcparks) is the choice of kayakers exploring Desolation Sound.

RESTAURANTS

The Laughing Oyster Restaurant / ★★

10052 MALASPINA RD, POWELL RIVER; 604/483-9775 Seek out the Laughing Oyster Restaurant. Its waterfront location, coupled with a split-level design, means everyone has a good view of Okeover Arm, particularly from the large patio. On dark and stormy evenings, you may prefer a corner table beside the fireplace. Start with a microbrew and smoked salmon-and-spinach Caesar or BC mussels, cooked to perfection. Large portions reflect nearby Powell River's mill town influence. Even those who aren't big oyster fans rave about the flavor of these—fresh off the restaurant dock to the table. A signature plate of Laughing Oysters is prepared with sun-dried tomatoes and red peppers under a drift of feta cheese. The staff is unwaveringly friendly, with the right degree of attentiveness. The reasonably priced wine list isn't deep but is thoughtfully chosen. *$$$; AE, MC, V; no checks; lunch, dinner every day, brunch Sun (closed Mon–Tues Oct–Mar); full bar; reservations recommended; falk@prcn.org; www.laughing-oyster.bc.ca; 20 minutes north of Powell River.* ♿

LODGINGS

Desolation Resort / ★★

MALASPINA RD, POWELL RIVER; 604/483-3592 Desolation Resort opened on the steep hillside above Okeover Arm in 1998. Seven uniquely designed wooden chalets perch on pilings. Fir floors flow into patterned pine walls and ceilings below steep-pitched cedar-shake roofs. Wide verandas offer sweeping views, and stairs lead to a floating dock. Carved figures of herons, gulls, and an ancient mariner sit on pilings. The quiet is broken only by the lapping of waves on the shore or the awk of a raven as it swoops among ramrod-straight firs flanking the cabins. Rental canoes and kayaks are available at the resort. Cabins are simply furnished; duvets spread atop flannel sheets provide the coziness you'd expect of a warm bed—but inadequate bedside lighting makes reading difficult. Chalets feature full kitchens. *$$; AE, MC, V; no checks; desolres@prcn.org; www.desolationresort.com; 20 minutes north of Powell River.* ♿

VICTORIA AND VANCOUVER ISLAND

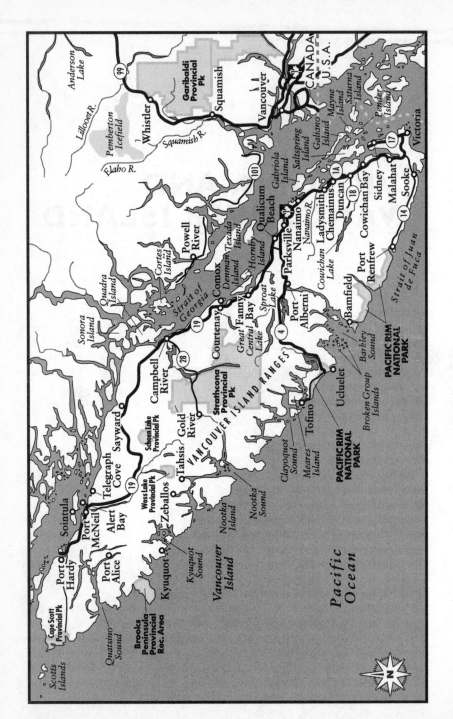

VICTORIA AND VANCOUVER ISLAND

Canadians throng to Vancouver Island because the Pacific Ocean moderates the climate to the mildest in the country: in winter, rain substitutes for snow. Wilder and less inhabited than other parts of the Pacific Northwest, this is a utopia of outdoor pursuits, from sea kayaking to mountain biking. All's not empty wilderness, of course. The island's east coast is booming with tourists and snow-weary retirees—and plenty of golf courses, marinas, restaurants, and good hotels. Victoria, a city of gardens subscribing to a whimsical "more English than the English" character, is the capital of British Columbia and most visitors' first taste of Vancouver Island.

ACCESS AND INFORMATION

It's an island, so most people get there by boat. From Seattle, the **VICTORIA CLIPPER** (206/448-5000 in Seattle, 250/382-8100 in Victoria, or 800/888-2535 elsewhere; www.victoriaclipper.com) zips to downtown Victoria via a high-speed passenger-only catamaran in two or three hours. You can also choose a cruise via the scenic San Juan Islands on **WASHINGTON STATE FERRIES** (206/464-6400 in Seattle, 250/381-1551 in Victoria, or 800/843-3779; www.wsdot.wa.gov/ferries/). A two-to three-hour trip runs year-round, once or twice daily, from Anacortes to Sidney, British Columbia, 17 miles (27 km) north of Victoria by highway. Reserve at least one day prior to departure. Cars should arrive at least one hour early at Anacortes; check-in times at Sidney can be longer, call ahead for details. **BLACK BALL TRANS-PORT** (360/457-4491 in Port Angeles, 206/622-2222 in Bellevue, or 250/386-2202 in Victoria; www.northolympic.com/coho) operates the MV *Coho* car-and-passenger ferry from Port Angeles on the Olympic Peninsula to Victoria, a 95-minute trip across the Strait of Juan de Fuca. There are one to four sailings daily; reservations are not accepted but call ahead for wait times. **VICTORIA SAN JUAN CRUISES** (360/738-8099 or 800/443-4552; www.whales.com) makes a three-hour, passenger-only cruise—including whale-watching and a salmon dinner—between Bellingham and Victoria's Inner Harbour. The service runs between mid-May and mid-October.

    BC FERRIES (for information: 250/386-3431, or 888/223-3779 in BC; for car reservations: 604/444-2890, or 888/724-5223 in BC; www.bcferries.bc.ca) runs car ferries from the British Columbia mainland (Tsawwassen terminal) into Swartz Bay, 20 miles (32 km) north of Victoria. Car reservations cost $15 in addition to the fare. Staterooms are available on some sailings for an extra $25.

    The fastest way to travel is straight to Victoria's Inner Harbour by air. **KENMORE AIR HARBOR** (425/486-1257 or 800/543-9595; www.kenmoreair.com) makes regular daily flights from downtown Seattle. From Sea-Tac International Airport, **HORIZON AIR** (800/547-9308; www.horizonair.com) flies into **VICTORIA INTER-NATIONAL AIRPORT** (1640 Electra Blvd; 250-953-7500), 15 miles (25 km) north of the city. From downtown Vancouver, Vancouver International Airport, and Boeing Field, Seattle, **HELIJET INTERNATIONAL** (604/273-1414 or 800/665-4354; www.helijet.com) gets you to Victoria by helicopter. Seaplanes for **HARBOUR AIR** (604/688-1277 or 800/665-0212; www.harbour-air.com) carry passengers from

Vancouver. From Vancouver International Airport, fly with **AIR CANADA** (888/247-2262; www.aircanada.ca).

In peak season (May–Aug), crowds are thickest, prices are highest, and tourist services are best. Gardens and greenery are freshest in May and June; days are sunniest July and August. April and September are pleasant months for quieter, reduced-rate travel (note that some hotel rates do not drop until mid-Oct). Rates are often quite low December through February, especially for U.S. travelers, who have enjoyed a favorable exchange rate in recent years. The **VANCOUVER ISLAND VISITOR INFO CENTRE** (250/754-3500) and the **VICTORIA VISITOR INFO CENTRE** (800/663-3883) have more information.

Victoria

Ever since Rudyard Kipling's hallowed turn-of-the-20th-century visit, Victoria has been selling itself as a wee bit of Olde England. The fancy is an appealing one, conjuring red double-decker buses and high tea as keynote themes in the Garden City. Kilted bagpipers rub shoulders with Victoria's annual 3.65 million tourists, who come from America and Japan—and elsewhere in Asia and Latin America—to walk along the waterside causeway, sit for caricatures, marvel at jugglers, and tap their feet to the one-man blues band of Slim Chance. In the harbor, Barbra Streisand's sleek, modern yacht may rest within hailing distance of an antique three-masted sailing ship.

The great thing about Victoria—rated among the world's top 10 cities by numerous upscale travel magazines—is that in the historic downtown, everything from the elegant Parliament Buildings to old Chinatown are within walking distance. In recent years Victoria has seen an explosion of whale-watching tours, and outdoor enthusiasts can sea kayak or mountain bike from the city's doorsteps. Minutes from downtown, seaside Dallas Road and Beach Drive meander through the city's finest old residential districts, offering a view of the spectacular Olympic Mountains of Washington State to the south across the Strait of Juan de Fuca.

ACCESS AND INFORMATION

A horse-drawn carriage ride is a romantic favorite: catch **VICTORIA CARRIAGE TOURS** (251 Superior St; 250/383-2207) at the corner of Belleville and Menzies Sts; the larger **TALLY-HO** carriages (8615 Eber Terrace; 250/383-5067) at the same corner offer rides at a family rate. The Inner Harbour is the locus of numerous popular maritime excursions. **VICTORIA HARBOUR FERRIES** (250/708-0201) offer tours of local waterways. Perched on the Inner Harbour, **TOURISM VICTORIA** (812 Wharf St; 250/953-2033; www.tourismvictoria.com) is brimful of brochures and helpful staff.

MAJOR ATTRACTIONS

Stroll through the main-floor hallways and shops of the venerable **FAIRMONT EMPRESS HOTEL** (721 Government St; 250/384-8111 or 800/441-1414), a postcard doyen since 1908. The elegant Rattenbury-designed 1898 provincial **PARLIAMENT BUILDINGS** (501 Belleville St; 250/387-3046) has frequent historical tours. The **VICTORIA BUG ZOO** (1107 Wharf St; 250/384-2847) fascinates children and

VICTORIA THREE-DAY TOUR

DAY ONE: Breakfast at the **BOARDWALK CAFÉ,** at the Delta Victoria Ocean Pointe Resort and Spa, with window and patio seating overlooking the attractive Inner Harbour. Proceed on a walking and shopping tour of downtown, and lunch at **KAZ JAPANESE.** Reaching the Inner Harbour, flag down a horse-drawn carriage for a tour of **BEACON HILL PARK.** Leave the meter running at the **BEACON DRIVE-IN RESTAURANT** to grab an ice cream, and then swing by gracious **EMILY CARR HOUSE.** After the tour, check into the view-blessed Windsor Suite at the swish **PRIOR HOUSE BED & BREAKFAST INN.** Return to the Inner Harbour to catch a pint-sized **VICTORIA HARBOUR FERRY** to the dock at Songhees Park, a five-minute meander along the waterfront to **SPINNAKERS** brewpub. Spend the afternoon quaffing Mount Tolmie Darks, and laze into a casual pub dinner with a view.

DAY TWO: Get bagels and cream cheese at **MOUNT ROYAL BAGEL FACTORY,** and then drive to Mile Zero and follow Dallas Road to Clover Point. Fly your **KITE** on the windy embankment, as the locals do, and enjoy bagels by the sea. Continue along Beach Drive, stop at Willows Beach, and pass through the Uplands to gaze at million-dollar heritage homes. Lunch at the outdoor tables of **OLIVE OLIO'S** (3840 Cadboro Bay Rd; 250/477-6618); then drive out to **BUTCHART GARDENS,** deservedly world famous for its more than one million blooms. Continue your drive north to the end of the Saanich Peninsula to dine at the **DEEP COVE CHALET;** then head back to your room at **ABIGAIL'S.**

DAY THREE: Savor hot coffee, croissants, and fruit salad at **DEMITASSE COFFEE BAR** for breakfast. Visit **CRAIGDARROCH CASTLE,** and see the stately signature manor of a Scottish coal baron. Back downtown, people watch at **TORREFAZIONE ITALIA** and grab a sandwich at **SAM'S DELI.** Then examine the fine First Nations arts at the **ROYAL BRITISH COLUMBIA MUSEUM.** Take in the turn-of-the-20th-century grandeur—at high tea—of the **EMPRESS HOTEL.** Relax, perhaps in the quiet orchard of St. Ann's Academy (835 Humboldt St; 250/953-8828). Later, dine on fine West Coast cuisine at **CAFE BRIO.** Have a change of scenery by staying the night at the **MAGNOLIA HOTEL & SPA** to conclude your Victoria tour.

adults, with features such as a surprisingly cute miniature apartment, scaled to its cockroach denizens.

CRAIGDARROCH CASTLE (1050 Joan Crescent; 250/592-5323), once visited only by 19th-century socialites, is now open to the public to take in the ballroom, grand foyer, and parlors of Victoria's richest resident, coal baron Robert Dunsmuir. Inside, fine wood banisters and paneling still glow with old money, while the quaint turret sunroom reveals the fine views the elderly Mrs. Dunsmuir enjoyed while doing needlework or plotting advantageous marriages for her 10 children. Heritage home connoisseurs enjoy **POINT ELLICE HOUSE** (2616 Pleasant St; 250/380-6506), an early Victoria residence in tasteful Italianate style, and **EMILY CARR HOUSE** (207 Government St; 250/383-5843), the birth home of admired West Coast artist and writer Emily Carr.

MUSEUMS AND GALLERIES

Across the street from the Fairmont Empress Hotel, the **ROYAL BRITISH COLUMBIA MUSEUM** (675 Belleville St; 250/387-3014; www.royalbcmuseum.bc.ca) delights with its extensive collection of Canadian indigenous art—from a traditional big-house to whaling hats and Haida masks—and the Old Town display, a reconstructed 19th-century streetscape. Kids are drawn to the Open Oceans exhibit, a simulated submarine ride, and the Imax theater. The **ART GALLERY OF GREATER VICTORIA** (1040 Moss St; 250/384-4101) is notable for its select collection of Asian art; the calming courtyard garden is home to North America's only Shinto shrine.

PARKS AND GARDENS

On the southern edge of downtown, the city's beloved **BEACON HILL PARK** boasts 184 acres of manicured gardens interspersed with some natural forest and meadows. The rightfully renowned **BUTCHART GARDENS** (800 Benvenuto Ave; 250/652-5256) are 13 miles (21 km) north. This 1904 country estate is crowded with blossoms, in the manicured precincts of the Italian Garden, Rose Garden, and the delicate Japanese Garden. For nondrivers, take city bus No. 75 Central Saanich; it stops on Douglas Street in front of Crystal Gardens.

SHOPPING

For those seeking English goods, Government Street north to Yates Street offers the best selection of tweeds and china. For men's suits and casual wear, **BRITISH IMPORTERS** (1125 Government St; 250/386-1496) will please, as will upscale **W & J WILSON** (1221 Government St; 250/383-7177), featuring fine women's wear. Irish goods are available at **IRISH LINEN STORES** (1019 Government St; 250/383-6812). **MURCHIE'S TEA & COFFEE** (1110 Government St; 250/383-3112) has the finest teas, from green Chinese Gunpowder to classic Empress blend. The **BRITISH CANDY SHOPPE** (638 Yates St; 250/382-2634) offers British treats like barley sugar and lemon acid drops. Chocolate lovers head to **ROGER'S CHOCOLATES** (913 Government St; 250/384-7021), and **CHOCOLATERIE BERNARD CALLEBAUT** (621 Broughton St; 250/380-1515), which sells Belgian-style chocolates. Shops such as **SASQUATCH TRADING** (1233 Government St; 250/386-9033) and **COWICHAN TRADING** (1328 Government St; 250/383-0321) offer hand-knit Cowichan sweaters, a specialty of Vancouver Island First Nations peoples. **OLD MORRIS TOBACCONISTS** (1116 Government St; 250/382-4811) sells pipes, Cuban cigars, and flasks in an authentic 19th-century shop, and stately **MUNRO'S BOOKS** (1108 Government St; 250/382-2464) offers discerning reading pleasures. In summer, buy a kite at **KABOODLES TOY STORE** (1320 Government St; 250/383-0931).

    BEACON DRIVE-IN RESTAURANT (126 Douglas St; 250/385-7521) has the city's best soft ice cream. Fresh Montreal-style bagels and cream cheese are found at **MOUNT ROYAL BAGEL FACTORY** (1115 N Park St—entrance is on Grant;

250/380-3588). At **DEMITASSE COFFEE BAR** (1320 Blanshard St; 250/386-4442) breakfast is the thing. Outdoor seating, along with espresso, is popular at **TORREFAZIONE ITALIA** (1234 Government St; 250/920-7203).

A section of Government Street (between View and Johnson Sts) has recently become a posh shopping mecca; Johnson Street (between Government and Wharf Sts) has quirky independent stores, highlighted by the welcoming enclosure of historic **MARKET SQUARE** (Johnson St, between Government and Store Sts). Victoria's **CHINATOWN** (Fisgard St between Government and Store Sts), is the oldest in Canada and worth visiting, especially to see narrow, shop-lined **FAN TAN ALLEY**. Outside of Old Town, **ANTIQUE ROW** (Fort St east of downtown from Blanshard to Cook Sts) beckons connoisseurs of 18th- to 20th-century goods.

PERFORMING ARTS

The **MCPHERSON PLAYHOUSE** (3 Centennial Square; 250/386-6121) is Victoria's leading live-theater venue. The **ROYAL THEATRE** (805 Broughton St; 250/386-6121) is home to a range of performances, from **PACIFIC OPERA VICTORIA** (1316B Government St; 250/385-0222) to the **VICTORIA SYMPHONY ORCHESTRA** (846 Broughton St; 250/385-6515). One of the most-anticipated public events of the year is the sunset **SYMPHONY SPLASH**, an Inner Harbour concert held the first Sunday of August. The free weekly *Monday Magazine*, available downtown in yellow boxes, has the best entertainment listings.

SPORTS AND RECREATION

The wittily named **PRINCE OF WHALES** (812 Wharf St; 250/383-4884) outfits participants in orange survival suits for a three-hour Zodiac-boat tour of local sea life; chances of orca sightings are best May through September. Launch a self-propelled ocean adventure from the **GORGE WATERWAY**, an inlet off the Inner Harbour: you can rent a kayak at the **GORGE KAYAKING CENTRE** (2940 Jutland Rd; 250/380-4668 or 877/380-4668); **OCEAN RIVER SPORTS** (1437 Store St; 250/381-4233) rents kayaks and canoes.

RESTAURANTS

Cafe Brio / ★★★

 944 FORT ST, VICTORIA; 250/383-0009 Owners Greg Hays and Silvia Marcolini run this lively Antique Row restaurant, serving Pacific Northwest cuisine with Italian leanings. The menu changes daily based, in part, on what's in season at local organic farms. Appetizers might include seared Alaskan scallops or crispy quail. Entrees range from red wine–braised beef short ribs to delightful and affordable dinner selections like linguine with chanterelles, pancetta, cream, and fresh herbs. The wine list is well chosen, with a good selection of West Coast wines and minimal markups. *$$–$$$; AE, MC, V; no checks; lunch Mon–Fri May–Sept, dinner every day; full bar; reservations recommended; www.cafe-brio.com; downtown.* &

Herald Street Caffe / ★★★

546 HERALD ST, VICTORIA; 250/381-1441 This lively Old Town restaurant has served fine, innovative West Coast cuisine for more than 20 years. The interior is filled with grand floral arrangements and eclectic local art. Appetizers such as Dungeness crab cakes with cilantro-lime pesto and tomato salsa, and alder-smoked salmon on a potato tart, are delicious. Longtime favorites on the menu include a signature bouillabaisse, slow-roasted duckling with orange-vanilla sauce, and loin of lamb with mint and whole-grain mustard. Desserts change frequently, but crumbles, homemade ice creams, and sorbets are always available. An excellent wine list is combined with knowledgeable, courteous service. This is an ideal post-theater venue—open till 11pm Fri and Sat. *$$$; AE, DC, MC, V; no checks; lunch Wed–Sun, dinner every day; full bar; reservations recommended; heraldstcaffe@ shaw.ca; www.cafe-brio.com/dining/HeraldStreetCaffe.htm; at Government St.* &

Il Terrazzo Ristorante / ★★☆

555 JOHNSON ST, VICTORIA; 250/361-0028 You'll find a true taste of Italy in this beautiful restaurant tucked away on Waddington Alley. Surrounded by six outdoor fireplaces and an abundance of plants and flowers, Il Terrazzo offers a haven of privacy in busy Old Town. Alfresco dining on the covered, heated terrace is possible nearly year-round. Passionate chefs create northern Italian cuisine bursting with flavor. Classic minestrone, char-grilled baby squid, wood-oven pizzas, pastas, and entrees such as osso buco attest to the menu's diversity. An extensive wine list showcases a range of fine Italian and New World wines. *$$$; AE, DC, MC, V; no checks; lunch Mon–Sat, dinner every day (no lunch Sat in winter); full bar; reservations recommended; terrazzo@pacificcoast.net; www.ilterrazzo.com; off Waddington Alley, near Market Square.* &

J & J Wonton Noodle House / ★★

1012 FORT ST, VICTORIA; 250/383-0680 You might bypass the unassuming facade on this popular Chinese restaurant. But when the door opens and you catch the tantalizing aroma of ginger, garlic, and black beans, you won't. This busy, modest, spotlessly clean restaurant treats you to the flavors of Hong Kong, Singapore, Sichuan, and northern China. A large kitchen window lets you watch chefs prepare wonton soup, imperial prawn with spicy garlic wine sauce, spicy ginger-fried chicken, or Sichuan braised beef hot pot. Noodles are made fresh daily. Service is friendly, efficient, and knowledgeable. *$; MC, V; no checks; lunch, dinner Tues–Sat; beer and wine; reservations recommended for 4 or more; www.jjnoodlehouse.com; between Vancouver and Cook Sts.* &

Kaz Japanese

1619 STORE ST, VICTORIA; 250/386-9121 The center of attention in this small, understated restaurant is its soft-spoken, humble owner, Kaz Motohashi. A traditionalist, Motohashi has nonetheless adapted his menu to western tastes. Along with fine nigiri-sushi such as *sake* (salmon), *tako* (octopus), and ahi (Hawaiian tuna), you'll find a range of North American–style rolls, such as prawn tempura roll and California roll (with real crab). The menu offers other delicacies, such as noodle soup, curry rice, and teriyaki. Start with the addictive chicken *karaage* (deep-fried marinated chicken wings) or the light and crispy tempura. Locals come for the food, not the atmosphere: the bright lights and pop music aren't for everyone. *$–$$; AE, DC, MC, V; no checks; lunch, dinner Mon–Sat; beer and wine; reservations not necessary; at Fisgard St.* &

Re-Bar Modern Food / ★★

50 BASTION SQUARE, VICTORIA; 250/361-9223 Victoria's original vegetarian health-food restaurant is packed at lunch and dinner. Sip one of the refreshing fresh fruit drinks, such as the Atomic Glow (apple, strawberry, and ginger juices) or the Soul Charge (carrot, apple, celery, ginger, and Siberian ginseng) while perusing the menu. Delicious enchiladas, curries, and almond burgers are specialties, along with pastas and salads. Breads are all home-made. Honey-ginger dressing and basil vinaigrette are delicious salad-toppers. Friendly, helpful service exemplifies the Re-Bar's philosophy. *$–$$; AE, DC, MC, V; no checks; breakfast Mon–Fri, lunch every day, dinner Mon–Sat (dinner Tues–Sat in winter), brunch Sat–Sun; beer and wine; reservations recommended (not accepted for weekend brunch); at Langley St.*

Sam's Deli / ★

805 GOVERNMENT ST, VICTORIA; 250/382-8424 As many downtown office workers can attest, this 20-year-old restaurant offers the most bang for your buck. Located a stone's throw from the Empress Hotel and the Inner Harbour, this busy deli offers cafeteria-style service. The shrimp-and-avocado sandwich is a favorite, as are large tureens of the day's soup. The ploughman's lunch—a selection of pâté, cheese, kosher dill pickles, fresh fruit, and sourdough—is also popular. Salads, pastrami or roast beef on rye, and a range of local draft beers and natural fruit juices are also available. Large windows and a sizable patio provide great people watching, or get takeout and picnic at the Inner Harbour. *$; MC, V; no checks; lunch, dinner every day; beer and wine; reservations not accepted; www. samsdeli.com; at Humboldt St.* &

Spice Jammer Restaurant / ★★

852 FORT ST, VICTORIA; 250/480-1055 This pretty little Indian restaurant, with western decor, is overseen with effervescent charm and good humor by manager Amin Essa. His wife, Billie, is the chef who makes excellent curries. A window onto the kitchen offers a glimpse of cooks preparing East Indian and East African dishes, with an emphasis on tandoori-style cooking (naan, chicken tikka, spicy prawns). Appetizers range from vegetable, chicken, or beef samosas to fried *mogos* (an East African dish of fried cassava-root wedges served with tamarind chutney). The curries come mild, medium, hot, or—if you dare—extra hot. Wake up your senses with vindaloos and masalas, as well as bhuna beef, *palak* lamb, *aloo gobi,* and rice pilaf, cooked with cardamom, cumin, saffron, and cinnamon. Token alternatives to curries are offered, but don't give them a second glance. *$–$$; AE, MC, V; no checks; lunch Tues–Sat, dinner Tues–Sun; full bar; reservations recommended; spicejammer@aol. com; downtown.* &

Spinnakers / ★

308 CATHERINE ST, VICTORIA; 250/386-2739 One of the first brewpubs in Canada, Spinnakers has been around since 1984. On the waterfront west of the Inner Harbour, it has one of the best views of any pub in Victoria. In the Taproom upstairs, traditional pub fare—fish-and-chips (lingcod, wild salmon, or Pacific halibut), burgers, pastas, and curries—is the order of the day. Noggins chowder is fresh and consistently tasty; or try one of the dinner specials such as braised rockfish or ale-braised lamb shanks. (You'll also find pub games here.) Downstairs in the all-ages dining room, you'll find a similar menu. Both levels serve beers brewed on-site, including Tsarist stout and Jameson's Scottish ale. A gift/bake shop at the entrance sells house-baked goods, Spinnaker's malt vinegar, and pub memorabilia. *$; AE, DC, MC, V; no checks; breakfast, lunch, dinner every day; full bar; reservations recommended (dining room), not accepted (Taproom); spinnakers@spinnakers.com; www.spinnakers.com; across Johnson St Bridge from downtown.*

Victorian Restaurant / ★★★

45 SONGHEES RD, VICTORIA; 250/360-5800 Here's an elegant space with an unsurpassed Inner Harbour view, in one of Victoria's finest hotels, the Delta Victoria Ocean Pointe Resort and Spa (see review). Unquestionably one of the best chefs in Victoria, Craig Stoneman has created a superb menu, from sautéed pheasant, wild mushroom, and sundried cranberry ragout, to tandoori-spiced venison loin. Or opt for the creative three-, four-, or five-course table d'hôte menu. The maître d' does a remarkable job of pairing food and wine, and his servers are among the most polished in town. *$$$$; AE, DC, JCB, MC, V; no checks; dinner every day May–Sept (closed Jan, some weeknight closures in off-season); full bar; reservations recommended; www.deltahotels.com; across Johnson St Bridge from downtown.*

LODGINGS

Abigail's Hotel / ★★★

906 MCCLURE ST, VICTORIA; 250/388-5363 OR 800/561-6565 This elegant 22-room heritage manor overlooking Quadra Street was joined in recent years by a coach house with additional suites. The substantial, four-story Tudor facade promises grandeur and the standard rooms, thoroughly modernized and furnished with a mix of new and antique furniture, are all in good taste. Third-floor Celebration Suites display more elaborate furnishings and fixtures, such as a wrought-iron bedstead nestled in a canopied niche, marble bathrooms, and double Jacuzzi tubs. Some top-floor rooms feature luxurious double-sided wood-burning fireplaces, facing both bedroom and deep tub. Rooms in the Coach House have an equally antique feel, and come at the top end of the hotel's price range. Down duvets promise cozy nights, and mornings bring a three-course breakfast in the country-style dining room. No children under 10. *$$$–$$$$; AE, MC, V; no checks; www.abigailshotel.com; at Quadra St.*

Andersen House Bed & Breakfast / ★★

301 KINGSTON ST, VICTORIA; 250/388-4565 OR 877/264-9988 An exceptionally ornate and well-preserved home built in 1891 for a prosperous sea captain, Andersen House has four pleasing rooms. Inside the Queen Anne–style structure, furnishings are a mix of antiques, Persian rugs, and contemporary art. The spacious Captain's Apartment has a colorful art deco–inspired stained-glass window beside the tub, views of the Parliament Buildings, and a separate sitting room. The Casablanca Room has a private balcony with steps to the lush garden, whose fruit harvests go into jams served at breakfast. Downstairs, the Garden Suite has a private entrance. Three rooms feature jetted tubs for two, and all offer romantic touches such as champagne goblets and CD players. The dining room's 12-foot ceilings and dramatic antique chandelier are rendered homey by a communal breakfast table. *$$$$; MC, V; checks OK; hosts@andersenhouse.com; www.andersenhouse.com; at Pendray St.*

Beaconsfield Inn / ★★★

998 HUMBOLDT ST, VICTORIA; 250/384-4044 This nine-room Edwardian manor, built by businessman R. P. Rithet as a wedding gift for his daughter, is tastefully furnished in Edwardian antiques. In downstairs rooms, swirling art nouveau designs glimmer in rows of stained-glass windows. The Emily Carr and Duchess suites display understated, jewel-toned elegance. Others are bright, airy retreats with flowered bedspreads. Most rooms have fireplaces and many have whirlpool tubs for two. Common rooms are the true wonders: the library, where full afternoon tea and sherry are served, harkens back to the days of smoking jackets, with wood paneling and dark leather couches. Complimentary full breakfast is served at intimate dining room tables, or by the fountain in the adjacent conservatory. *$$$$; MC, V; no checks; beaconsfield@islandnet.com; www.beaconsfieldinn. com; at Vancouver St.*

Delta Victoria Ocean Pointe Resort and Spa / ★★★

45 SONGHEES RD, VICTORIA; 250/360-2999 OR 800/667-4677 Dominating the Inner Harbour along with the great monuments of the Empress and the Parliament Buildings, the Ocean Pointe's exterior doesn't share their built-for-the-ages demeanor. Its interior, however, is luxurious, with sweeping views from the spacious lobby on up. Standard rooms, while well kept, are fairly standard: one pays for what is outside the window. For luxury, splurge on a Specialty Suite—bedroom, two bathrooms, living and dining area, small kitchen, and miles of window views. The Ocean Pointe is making a name for itself with its full-service spa and Victorian Restaurant (see review). *$$$$; AE, DC, JCB, MC, V; no checks; deltanet@deltahotels.com; www.deltahotels.com; across Johnson St Bridge.* &

Fairmont Empress Hotel / ★★★

721 GOVERNMENT ST, VICTORIA; 250/384-8111 OR 800/441-1414 This ivy-draped complex, built in 1908 in the style of a French chateau, remains one of Victoria's key landmarks. The main-floor lobby is a public gallery, with tourists gathering to admire the historic photos and antique chandeliers, and to sip afternoon tea. Standard rooms are small and expensive for what you get (the privilege of the Empress name); a newer 21-room Entrée Gold section has its own check-in area and gilded Victorian salon. Satisfyingly luxurious rooms can be had, with stellar views to match. A new spa, opened in January 2002, offers a range of conventional and alternative treatments, including aromatherapy, Shiatsu, and Kur treatments, which use algae, mud, and thermal water. The Empress Room is the most visually impressive dining room in Victoria. The grand space retains the original carved beams in the ceiling, tapestried walls, and spacious tables. Entrees such as citrus-dusted sable fish with ginger smashed plantain, and macadamia nut–crusted rack of lamb with roasted barley risotto are original and well executed. *$$$$; AE, DC, DIS, JCB, MC, V; no checks; www.fairmont.com; between Humboldt and Belleville Sts.* ♿

A Haterleigh Heritage Inn / ★★

243 KINGSTON ST, VICTORIA; 250/384-9995 OR 866/234-2244 This turn-of-the-century heritage home, which popular upper-crust architect Thomas Hooper built for himself in 1901, bills itself as "Victoria's most romantic inn." The Day Dreams suite is a floral confection with a wedding cake–style archway between rooms and a Jacuzzi tub. Stained-glass windows are large and exceptional, particularly the curved set in the period Morning Parlor. At the back, the Secret Garden Room has a view of the Olympic Mountains. Everything antique in the eight-room inn is in mint condition. Proprietors Paul and Elizabeth Kelly treat guests to three-course breakfasts, and sherry and chocolates on arrival. *$$$$; MC, V; no checks; paulk@haterleigh.com; www.haterleigh.com; at Pendray St.*

Joan Brown's Bed & Breakfast / ★★

729 PEMBERTON RD, VICTORIA; 250/592-5929 Joan Brown is a gregarious B&B proprietor, and she'll welcome you warmly into her 1883 mansion built for a former provincial lieutenant governor. Although the Rocklands neighborhood home has long lost its wood siding for stucco, all the ornate wooden fretwork and classical columns are in place. Stained glass and chandeliers are fit for a king's representative, and the sitting room is over-the-top Victorian—all floral swags and bric-a-brac. Upstairs rooms, some with garden views, are decorated with Laura Ashley prints; furnishings are a homey mix of antique and modern. Walk a block to the groomed gardens of the present lieutenant governor's mansion, or three blocks to the grandiose halls of Craigdarroch Castle (see Major Attractions in this chapter). The well-stocked library will keep you occupied on a rainy afternoon. *$$–$$$; no credit cards; checks OK; off Fort St.*

Laurel Point Inn / ★★★

680 MONTREAL ST, VICTORIA; 250/386-8721 OR 800/663-7667 With its lush garden setting on an oceanfront peninsula with sweeping views, the modern Laurel Point Inn is popular with chic wedding parties. For guests, the angular, set-back design means all of the 200 rooms have ocean views. Art is a hallmark here: hallways and best rooms feature fine Asian and indigenous pieces. The nicest rooms are in the newer South Wing, and junior suites offer the most bang for the buck—sliding tatami-style doors lead into vast bathrooms with deep soaker tubs—while the moderate-sized rooms feel spacious with pale wood paneling and cream-colored bedspreads. *$$$$; AE, DC, JCB, MC, V; no checks; reservations@laurelpoint.com; www.laurelpoint.com; follow Douglas St south, turn west on Belleville St.* ♿

Magnolia Hotel & Spa / ★★

623 COURTNEY ST, VICTORIA; 250/381-0999 OR 877/624-6654 The 64-room Magnolia styles itself after European boutique hotels, with attentive service, tastefully luxurious rooms and suites, and a full-service spa to complete the pampering.

First impressions count: the lobby is paneled in rich mahogany, and underfoot are limestone tiles. Many rooms have gas fireplaces, such as our favored seventh-floor "diamond level" corner suite, with reasonably good harbor views. Sumptuous bathrooms have marble counters and deep soaker baths; robes and even umbrellas are thoughtfully provided. For business travelers, rooms have desks with data ports and multiline speaker phones; a conference room is available. Downstairs, Hugo's Grill and Brew Pub is all dark wood and artful metal trellising. The Magnolia is just off Government Street's shopping attractions and a block from the Empress. *$$$$; AE, DC, DIS, E, JCB, MC, V; no checks; sales@magnoliahotel.com; www.magnolia hotel.com; at Gordon St.*

Prior House Bed & Breakfast Inn / ★★★

🌲 **620 ST. CHARLES ST, VICTORIA; 250/592-8847 OR 877/924-3300** Truly a queen among B&Bs, this large 1912 manor is sure to impress with its dramatic stonework lower levels and Tudor styling above. Gardens are splendid, and visible from numerous rooms, some with balconies. Most luxurious is the Lieutenant Governor's Suite: the bath is glamorous with mirrored walls and ceilings, green marble whirlpool tub and long vanity counter, gold swan fixtures, and crystal chandeliers. The bedroom has a more traditional antique feel. The third-floor Windsor Suite has French doors leading to a private balcony with a sweeping view; a whirlpool tub sits under a skylight. More private, ground-level garden suites have separate entrances, patio space, and one or two bedrooms, but lack the aged patina of upstairs rooms. *$$$$; MC, V; checks OK; innkeeper@priorhouse.com; www.priorhouse. com; in the Rockland residential neighborhood.*

Sooke to Port Renfrew

Forty minutes west of Victoria on Highway 14, Sooke is a quiet town worth visiting; residents are committed to retaining the natural beauty and rural character of the area, dotted with old farmsteads, beaches, and contemplative forests and park reserves. Beyond Sooke, the road continues past stellar beaches to Port Renfrew.

ROYAL ROADS UNIVERSITY (2005 Sooke Rd, Victoria; 250/391-2511 or 250/391-2600, ext. 4456), on the road to Sooke, is a grand former Dunsmuir family castle in medieval style; the beautiful grounds are open daily, dawn to dusk. Castle tours are also available. Also on the way to Sooke is the old farmstead town of **METCHOSIN;** a drive along back ways like Happy Valley Road is a pastoral pleasure, with small farms set in rolling valleys and hills. In this area, the shallow, relatively warm waters of **WITTY'S LAGOON REGIONAL PARK** (west of Victoria via Hwy 14 and Metchosin Rd) are popular with local families.

Locals pack the booths at the '50s-era **MOM'S CAFE** (2036 Shields Rd; 250/642-3314) for hearty diner fare. For local crafts, organic vegetables, and children's activities, stop by the **SOOKE COUNTRY MARKET** (at Otter Point Rd and West Coast Rd; 250/642-7528; Sat May–Sept). The entire coast between Sooke and Port Renfrew has excellent parks with trails down to ocean beaches; **CHINA BEACH** (23 miles/37 km west of Sooke) is the start of the accessible but rigorous **JUAN DE FUCA MARINE TRAIL** (250/391-2300). **SOMBRIO BEACH** (34 miles/57 km west of Sooke) is popular with local surfers. **BOTANICAL BEACH** (follow signs at end of paved road

VANCOUVER ISLAND THREE-DAY TOUR

DAY ONE: From Victoria, get a charging start with a healthful breakfast at **RE-BAR MODERN FOODS;** then head north and hop aboard one of the many Swartz Bay ferries plying the island-bejeweled waters, to **SALT SPRING ISLAND.** Browse the crafts and organic produce of the popular **SATURDAY MARKET** in the heart of Ganges, the largest village in the Gulf Islands. Have a casual lunch at **MOBY'S MARINE PUB,** and drive up Cranberry Road to the top of **MOUNT MAXWELL** for a panorama of the archipelago, from Salt Spring to the U.S. mainland. Check into a room at the splendid **HASTINGS HOUSE.** Have dinner by the fireplace in the highly rated dining room.

    DAY TWO: After a delicious full breakfast at Hastings House, zip out to **VESUVIUS BAY** on the island's western side and catch the ferry to Crofton on Vancouver Island just south of Chemainus. From there, drive north on the Trans-Canada Highway (Hwy 1). Just past Ladysmith, take a side-trip to Yellow Point to lunch at the **CROW AND GATE NEIGHBOURHOOD PUB.** At Nanaimo, continue north on the faster inland Highway 19 to **PARKSVILLE,** then take Highway 4A west to visit the whimsical village of **COOMBS;** ponder the goats grazing on the grass roof of the **OLD COUNTRY MARKET** and browse some shops. Continue west, joining Highway 4, and pause on the road to Port Alberni to admire the towering old-growth trees of Cathedral Grove in **MACMILLAN PROVINCIAL PARK.** The long drive across the island takes you past lakes and along rivers to the Pacific, where you turn north toward Tofino. Check into a waterfront room at the **WICKANINNISH INN** just outside of Tofino, and dine in the exquisite **POINTE RESTAURANT** there.

    DAY THREE: Grab an organic coffee and muffin at the earthy **COMMON LOAF BAKE SHOP** in Tofino. Wander the small downtown strip, poking around in the shops there for First Nations art and hemp clothing and body products. Lunch at the casual **SCHOONER ON SECOND,** driving to the inimitable **LONG BEACH** to soak in the natural splendor. Pack your memories into the car and head back the way you came, pausing to dine at **MAHLE HOUSE** in Nanaimo, and stay over at the **DREAM WEAVER B&B** in Cowichan Bay.

just west of Port Renfrew) has exceptionally low tides that expose miles of sea life in sheltering pools.

RESTAURANTS

Country Cupboard Cafe

402 SHERINGHAM POINT RD, SOOKE; 250/646-2323 Proprietor Jennie Vivian knows three words to keep them coming: mile-high cheesecakes. Regulars include chocolate amaretto and caramel pecan, while vanilla white chocolate makes an occasional appearance. Pies, too, are fantastic creations: perhaps coconut raisin? Hearty main-course standards include pork baby back ribs and grilled spring salmon. Huge burgers, oyster burgers, steamed Sooke clams, and smoked salmon satisfy local loggers and those fresh off nearby French Beach. A small wine list features BC vintages. Patio dining makes room for summer crowds. *$–$$; MC, V; no checks; lunch, dinner every day; beer and wine; reservations recommended; at West Coast Rd, 15 minutes west of Sooke.*

Sooke Harbour House / ★★★★

1528 WHIFFEN SPIT RD, SOOKE; 250/642-3421 OR 800/889-9688 Owners Frederique and Sinclair Philip, and their team of chefs, have garnered international attention for their rare dedication to the freshest local ingredients blended with a good deal of energy and flashes of innovation. Organically grown edible plants from the inn's own gardens complement what dedicated island farmers, fishermen, and the wilderness provide. The menu changes daily, but sample entrees range from silver gray rockfish with caramelized apple juice, lemongrass, ginger and tamari sauce, to seared squab and fois gras medallion with a preserved berry, sage, and squab stock reduction. Sooke Harbour House's award-winning wine list features excellent French vintages and an impressive array from BC. You'll pay dearly for all this attention to detail, but the commitment to flavors may make you forget the high tariff. *$$$$; DC, E, JCB, MC, V; checks OK; dinner every day; full bar; reservations required; info@sookeharbourhouse.com; www.sookeharbourhouse.com; end of Whiffen Spit Rd, off Hwy 14.* ♿

LODGINGS

Fossil Bay Resort / ★★

1603 WEST COAST RD, SOOKE; 250/646-2073 This one wins raves from even fussy, seasoned travelers; private hot tubs with views of the Strait of Juan de Fuca and the Olympic Mountains linger foremost in their minds. Cliffside cottages, featuring simple basics and full kitchens plus cozy fires, are islands of solitude. The modern design is reminiscent of a subdivision, but the joy of doing nothing is delightfully old-fashioned. Pets are accepted in two of six cottages. *$$$–$$$$; MC, V; checks OK; 2-night min, 3-night min on holiday weekends; wild@fossilbay.com; www.fossilbay.com; 15 miles (25 km) west of Sooke.*

Hartmann House / ★★★

5262 SOOKE RD, SOOKE; 250/642-3761 This exquisite three-room B&B exudes Northwest charm. Outside and in, the handcrafted, cedar-sided home is alive with blossoms: the bay-windowed exterior is draped with pink flowers in season; an old-fashioned porch with white wicker chairs overlooks well-groomed gardens. The Honeymoon Suite is the largest and most luxurious, with a four-poster canopy bed, whirlpool tub, fireplace, kitchenette, and hardwood floors; French doors lead to the garden. Expect to see garden herbs, fruits, and flowers gracing the well-supplied breakfast table. *$$$–$$$$; V; no checks; 2-night min for Honeymoon Suite; info@hartmannhouse.bc.ca; www.hartmannhouse.bc.ca; 3½ miles (6 km) east of Sooke.*

Markham House / ★★★

1853 CONNIE RD, SOOKE; 250/642-7542 OR 888/256-6888 For an English country-garden setting, book into the Tudor-style Markham House. Virgil the chocolate Lab is as welcoming as innkeepers Lyall and Sally Markham, who know when to leave you alone and when to invite you to chat on the veranda. People choose Markham House for gentle pleasures: fireside port before turning in, feather beds, and country hospitality. Immaculately groomed grounds include a small river, a trout pond, a putting green, and iris gardens with more than 100 species. The two bedrooms have private baths; one has a double Jacuzzi overlooking the pond. The self-contained Honeysuckle Cottage is spotlessly clean and filled with antiques. *$$–$$$; AE, DC, DIS, E, JCB, MC, V; checks OK; mail@markham house.com; www.markhamhouse.com; turn south off Hwy 14 east of Sooke.*

Ocean Wilderness Inn & Spa / ★

109 WEST COAST RD, SOOKE; 250/646-2116 OR 800/323-2116 A groomed English garden, popular with wedding parties, surrounds this wood-sided inn, set in 5 acres of old-growth rain forest. Nine rooms—some with ocean views—are done in antique style, featuring fanciful, fabric-canopied beds. A log-constructed living room has a natural stone fireplace; in the dining room, country breakfasts are made with farm-fresh produce. Reserve a soak in the hot tub, enclosed in a Japanese gazebo for privacy. A range of spa services, including mud and seaweed treatments, hot stone treatments, body wraps, and massages are available at the Rainforest Rejuvenation Spa. Pets and children welcome. *$$–$$$; AE, MC, V; checks OK; ocean@sookenet.com; www.sookenet.com/ocean; 10 minutes west of Sooke.* &

Point No Point Resort / ★

1505 WEST COAST RD, SOOKE; 250/646-2020 The Soderberg family owns a mile of beach and 40 acres of undeveloped coastline facing the Strait of Juan de Fuca and the Pacific. They rent 24 reasonably rustic cabins among the trees near the cliff, catering to those who eschew TV and phones in favor of remote beauty. Some cabins allow pets; nine newer, pricier cabins have hot tubs. The only distractions are the crash of rolling swells, and the crackle of the fire. Wood is supplied, but bring your own food, though the dining room serves highly rated lunch, afternoon tea, and dinner (dinner Wed–Sun only; restaurant closed Jan). *$$$–$$$$; AE, MC, V; checks OK; 2-night min on weekends, 3-night min on long weekends. Hwy 14, 15 miles (24 km) west of Sooke.* &

Sooke Harbour House / ★★★★

1528 WHIFFEN SPIT RD, SOOKE; 250/642-3421 OR 800/889-9688 This bucolic establishment is widely considered one of British Columbia's finest inns, located at water's edge, on the end of a quiet neighborhood road. A sensitive addition to the original 1929 white clapboard house accommodates the inn's popularity. All rooms but one have views of the Strait of Juan de Fuca and the Olympic Mountains, as well as decks and fireplaces. Distinctive theme rooms delight the curious and the refined: the Mermaid Room is lavished with suitably fabled art, and the Ichthyologist's Study features a stunning salmon carving and line drawings of fish. The Victor Newman Longhouse Room features museum-quality First Nations art. Expect extras such as fresh-cut flowers, robes, and a decanter of fine port. The lavish complimentary breakfast—hazelnut-maple syrup waffles with loganberry purée, or fresh garden vegetable quiche with scones and preserves, for example—is delivered to your room. Also included is a light lunch in season (lower off-season rates include a continental breakfast). An in-house masseuse and reflexologist are on call; should you wish to venture out, perhaps to the acclaimed Sooke Harbour House restaurant (see review), a beauty consultant is available. A conference facility was added in 1999. *$$$$; DC, E, JCB, MC, V; checks OK; info@sookeharbourhouse.com; www.sookeharbourhouse.com; end of Whiffen Spit Rd, off Hwy 14.* &

Sidney and the Saanich Peninsula

This pretty, rural area, although increasingly encroached on by development, holds some bucolic corners, particularly off W Saanich Road. While waiting in the ferry lineup to Vancouver, duck into the nearby **STONEHOUSE PUB** (2215 Canoe Cove Rd, Sidney; 250/656-3498) for a snack or a beer.

RESTAURANTS

Carden Street West / ★★★

1164 STELLY'S CROSS RD, BRENTWOOD BAY; 250/544-1475 The name of this rural restaurant doesn't relate to its current address, but to its original site, the still-popular Carden Street Cafe in Guelph, Ontario. When the owners moved to Vancouver Island, they brought with them philosophies that made their first effort so successful: personalized service and delicious food. Area residents are frequent visitors to this charming cedar building (formerly a fruit and vegetable market). The 40-seat dining room is gardenlike and full of rich, tropical colors. Connie O'Brien's main menu is "spicy international"—inspired by the owners' many travels—and includes outstanding West African and Southeast Asian–style curries. Specials offer a range of less spicy, but full-flavored tastes. The wine list is short but interesting, and a good choice of beer and fruity drinks goes well with spicier flavors. Desserts include homemade cheesecake, chocolate mousse, and light-as-air pavlovas. *$$$; AE, MC, V; local checks only; dinner Tues–Sat (closed Jan); full bar; reservations recommended; at W Saanich Rd.* &

Deep Cove Chalet / ★★★

11190 CHALET RD, SIDNEY; 250/656-3541 Chef-owner Pierre Koffel brings European opulence to this stunning, rural seaside setting in Sidney. The large windows of this 1913 wooden lodge overlook meticulously kept lawns and a splendid view of Saanich Inlet. Guests can stroll the manicured lawns between courses, wine glasses in hand. Lobster bisque, cheese soufflé, scrambled eggs and caviar, sautéed oysters with béarnaise sauce, and beef Wellington are classics. The extensive wine list offers fine vintages from Burgundy, Bordeaux, and California. Groups can book a private dining suite upstairs. *$$$$; AE, MC, V; local checks only; lunch Wed–Sun, dinner Tues–Sun; full bar; reservations recom-*

mended; deepcovechalet@shaw.ca; www.deepcovechalet.com; northwest of Sidney, call for directions. &

The Latch Dining Room / ★★

2328 HARBOUR RD, SIDNEY; 250/656-6622 Set in a 1925 heritage home designed by noted Victoria architect Samuel Maclure for the lieutenant governor of British Columbia, this casual-elegant restaurant focuses on fresh Pacific Northwest flavors in European-style cooking. The daily changing menu might feature appetizers such as steamed Salt Spring Island mussels, or an avocado, prawn, and ahi tuna salad. Entrees range from rack of lamb to New York steak with roasted-garlic mashed potatoes, or a vegetarian baked pumpkin and goat cheese gâteau. Desserts tantalize: perhaps Kahlúa crème caramel and tiramisu. Five guest suites take advantage of antique rich wood paneling hewn from local Douglas fir. A new 20-suite country-style hotel on the property, the Shoal Harbour Inn, features water and garden vistas, fireplaces, and high-speed Internet access. *$$–$$$$; AE, MC, V; no checks; dinner every day (Thurs–Sun in winter); full bar; reservations recommended; latch@latch inn.com; www.shoalharbourinn.com; ½ mile (1 km) north of Sidney.*

Malahat

The Malahat is a talismanic word among local drivers: it signals steep roads with few passing lanes, and obscuring winter fogs. But for leisurely drives, the Malahat (Trans-Canada Hwy/Hwy 1, from Victoria to Mill Bay) is one of the prettiest drives on the island. Lush Douglas fir forests hug the narrow-laned highway, past beloved **GOLDSTREAM PROVINCIAL PARK** (3400 Trans-Canada Hwy/Hwy 1; 250/391-2300 or 250/478-9414)—where you can view the salmon run between mid-October and early December—and at the summit, northbound pullouts offer breathtaking views over Saanich Inlet and the surrounding undeveloped hills.

RESTAURANTS

The Dining Room at the Aerie Resort / ★★★★

600 EBEDORA LN, MALAHAT; 250/743-7115 OR 800/518-1933 Perched high on Malahat Mountain, the Aerie Resort's (see review) dining room is as spectacular and inspiring as its view. Chef Christophe Letard incorporates local wild mushrooms and other forest edibles into his seasonally changing menu, creating imaginative regional cuisine. Entrees might include free-range chicken en croûte with foie gras and an herb and forest mushroom fricassee; or beef tenderloin wrapped in applewood-smoked bacon, served with blue cheese and basil ravioli. Multicourse tasting menus (including a vegetarian option) are a good way to sample what the kitchen offers. Don't pass up a dessert of warm Callebaut chocolate fondant. Service is top-notch, and the superb wine list has plenty of notable BC wines. *$$$$; AE, DC, MC, V; no checks; lunch, dinner every day; full bar; reservations recommended; aerie@relaischateaux.com; www.aerie.bc.ca; 30 minutes from downtown Victoria, take Spectacle Lake turnoff from Trans-Canada Hwy.* &

Malahat Mountain Inn / ★★

265 TRANS-CANADA HWY, MALAHAT; 250/478-1944 Funky, casual, and imaginative best describe the cuisine at this view-blessed restaurant on the Malahat drive (Hwy 1). Large wrought-iron candlesticks and greenery punctuate the dramatic color scheme, booths offer cozy intimacy, and a Saturday night jazz quartet adds to the appeal. The menu is big on seafood and pastas; produce is organic, and meat is free-range. Soup specials change daily—perhaps tasty beef barley with caramelized onion. At dinner, vegetarians dig into the lemon-spinach primavera linguini; meatier fare includes a pan-roasted lamb sirloin, and a lamb osso buco. Finish with a creamy lemon pie. *$$–$$$; AE, MC, V; no checks; lunch, dinner every day; full bar; reservations recommended; hospitality@telus.net; at top of the Malahat drive (Hwy 1).*

LODGINGS

The Aerie Resort / ★★★★

600 EBEDORA LN, MALAHAT; 250/743-7115 OR 800/518-1933 Celebrities in search of discreet luxury seek out the Aerie Resort, which regular folk prefer for festive grandeur. The Aerie has hosted more than 600 weddings since it opened in 1991. Accolades are invariably heaped upon this modern view resort in the lush hillsides of the Malahat region, a half-hour's drive from downtown Victoria. Gleaming white, terraced units were designed as a modern take on Mediterranean villages. Set in 85 acres of meticulously kept gardens, it achieves an idyllic Isle-of-Capri mood. Most rooms feature whirlpool tubs, fireplaces, private decks, Persian and Chinese silk carpets, and plush modern furnishings. Resort amenities such as an indoor pool, indoor and outdoor hot tubs, a tennis court, and a spa offering massage, aromatherapy, and other services, ensure a relaxing stay. Rates include full breakfast in the spectacular Dining Room (see review). *$$$$; AE, DC, MC, V; no checks; aerie@relaischateaux.com; www.aerie. bc.ca; 30 minutes from downtown Victoria, take Spectacle Lake turnoff from Trans-Canada Hwy.* &

The Gulf Islands

Stretching for 149 miles (240 km) up the broad expanse of the Strait of Georgia are clusters of lushly forested islands, Canada's version of the U.S. San Juans. From the air or by boat, these islands appear positively Edenic. Well-stocked stores, bank machines, and even restaurants are scarce to nonexistent on many of the islands, so plan accordingly. But natural beauty and recreational opportunities abound—all in the rain shadow of Vancouver Island's mountains. Like Victoria, the Gulf Islands are considerably less rainy than Vancouver—but bring rain gear in winter. The islands are harmoniously inhabited by artisans and small-scale organic farmers.

The Gulf Islands fall into three groups. The best known and most populous are the **SOUTHERN ISLANDS**: of these, Salt Spring, Galiano, Mayne, Saturna, and Pender are accessible via the ferry terminal at Swartz Bay outside Victoria (or from Tsawwassen outside Vancouver), while Gabriola is reached from Nanaimo. Visited several times a day by ferry, the Southern Gulf Islands—particularly Salt Spring and Galiano—offer the widest selection of inns, eateries, shopping, and services. Farther north, laid-back **DENMAN AND HORNBY ISLANDS**, with trails beloved by mountain bikers, are a short hop from Buckley Bay, 12 miles (20 km) south of Courtenay. Quadra, Cortes, and Sonora make up the closely linked **DISCOVERY ISLANDS**— fishing and boating meccas east of Campbell River. If you're visiting in summer, reserve accommodations before venturing onto the ferry.

ACCESS AND INFORMATION

BC FERRIES (250/386-3431 or 888/223-3779; www.bcferries.bc.ca) offer many trips daily, but plan ahead in summer for car traffic; popular runs fill fast. Island hopping is possible, but schedules are complex and times do not always mesh; see specific islands below for details. Advance reservations are possible between the BC mainland and the Southern Gulf Islands at no extra charge. Less stressful—and less expensive—is leaving the car at home; most inns and B&Bs offer ferry pickup. Bring your own bike or rent one; the islands (with the exception of busy Salt Spring) are wonderful (if hilly) for cycling. **TOURISM VANCOUVER ISLAND** (335 Wesley St, Ste 203, Nanaimo; 250/754-3500; www.islands.bc.ca) has information on touring the Gulf Islands.

Salt Spring Island

Salt Spring is the largest and most populous of the Southern Gulf Islands (with 10,000 residents), and is packed densely with artisans' studios and pastoral farms. Non-native settlement here dates back to the mid-19th century, and early settlers included African-Americans from San Francisco in the decades after the Civil War. The *Kanakas,* as the indigenous people of Hawaii were then called, also played an important role.

Today, the pioneer landscape has left an imprint of postcard farms and two sweet stone-and-wood churches on the Fulford-Ganges Road. Ancient Douglas fir forests cloak small mountains, interspersed with sparkling lakes. **MOUNT MAXWELL PROVINCIAL PARK** (7 miles/11 km southwest of Ganges via the Fulford-Ganges Rd and Cranberry Rd), on the west side of the island 2,000 feet above sea level, has a rewarding view. For camping, the beach at **RUCKLE PROVINCIAL PARK** (10 minutes from Fulford Harbour ferry dock, take right onto Beaver Rd; 250/391-2300) on the island's east side is good, and fishing enthusiasts head to **ST. MARY LAKE** (north of Ganges on North End Rd) seeking bass and trout. Warm ocean currents allow pleasant summer swimming in the clear ocean waters.

The big draw for locals and tourists is the **SALT SPRING ISLAND SATURDAY MARKET** (Centennial Park, Ganges; 250/537-4448; www.saltspringmarket.com; Apr–Oct): local goat cheeses pressed with violets, organic produce, pottery, hand-smoothed wooden bowls, and more. Similarly fine wares can be found at the much-praised **ARTCRAFT** (250/537-0899) sale in Ganges's Mahon Hall, daily June through mid-September. The annual (since 1896) September **SALT SPRING FALL FAIR** (Farmer's Institute, 351 Rainbow Rd) is a family favorite, with sheep shearing, crafts, animals, games for kids, baked goods, and more. Enjoy a snack and organic coffee at the vegetarian bakery and cafe, **BARB'S BUNS** (1-121 McPhillips Ave, Ganges; 250/537-4491); views, hearty meals, and microbrews at **MOBY'S MARINE PUB** (124

Upper Ganges Rd, Ganges; 250/537-5559); and wood-fired pizzas at the **RAVEN STREET MARKET-CAFÉ** (321 Fernwood Rd, north end of island; 250/537-2273).

Three BC Ferries routes serve Salt Spring. From Victoria, ferries leave Swartz Bay, and land 35 minutes later at Salt Spring's **FULFORD HARBOUR,** a small artists' village at the island's south end. Ferries leave less frequently from Tsawwassen on the mainland for the three-hour trip to **LONG HARBOUR** on the island's northeast shore. A short hop from the Vancouver Island mill town of Crofton takes you to Salt Spring's **VESUVIUS BAY,** on the island's northwest side, notable for the congenial waterfront pub at the **VESUVIUS INN** (805 Vesuvius Bay Rd, northwest of Ganges; 250/537-2312). **SALT SPRING'S VISITOR INFORMATION CENTRE** (250/537-5252 or 866/216-2936; 121 Lower Ganges Rd, Ganges; www.saltspringtoday.com) has more information.

RESTAURANTS

Calvin's Bistro

133 LOWER GANGES RD, GANGES; 250/538-5551 Casual restaurants come and go in Ganges, but Calvin's, with its harbor-view patio, fresh seafood, and local popularity, should stand the test of time. The lunch menu features sandwiches, fish-and-chips, and a host of burgers: chicken, lamb, salmon, veggie, and—in a nod to the owners' European roots—schnitzel. At dinner, fresh seafood, including local mussels, salmon with a leek and pine nut sauce, and halibut in white-wine cream, shares the menu with such Swiss specialties as chicken Zürigois (sliced chicken in a mushroom and white-wine sauce), and a daily lamb special. Booth seating, casual ambience, and a kids' menu make this one of the island's better family options, especially at lunch. *$$–$$$; AE, MC, V; local checks only; full bar; breakfast, lunch Mon–Sat, dinner every day, brunch Sun (dinner Tues–Sat Oct–Mar); reservations recommended; www.calvinsbistro.com; on the waterfront in Ganges.*

Hastings House / ★★★

160 UPPER GANGES RD, GANGES; 250/537-2362 OR 800/661-9255 The English country-house ambience of this well-known inn (see review) extends to its atmospheric dining room, where an enormous Inglenook fireplace warms the foyer, and upholstered chairs, candlelight, and white linens provide understated luxury. The five-course prix-fixe menu changes daily, relying on fresh local ingredients (many from the inn's gardens) and offering such appetizers as celeriac and prosciutto bisque with chive cream or seared spring salmon with pattypan squash and nasturtium jus. Entrees run from peppered pheasant breast with orchard pears to saffron-steamed halibut with rosemary ratatouille. Salt Spring Island lamb is almost always available, but sells out quickly each evening. The same menu is served on the covered veranda and in the snug, a tiny 12-seat room next to the wine cellar; alternatively, you can book the one table in the kitchen and watch chef Marcel Kauer in action. Gentlemen: jackets are required in the dining room. *$$$$; AE, MC, V; no checks; dinner every day (closed mid-Nov–mid-Mar); full bar; reservations required; hasthouse@saltspring.com; www.hastingshouse.com; just north of Ganges.*

Restaurant House Piccolo / ★★★★

108 HEREFORD AVE, GANGES; 250/537-1844 Chef Piccolo Lyytikainen, a member of the prestigious Chaîne des Rôtisseurs, brings upscale European cuisine to this intimate Ganges restaurant, widely regarded as among the finest in the region. Set in a tiny heritage house, House Piccolo's candlelit ambience achieves romance without formality. Starters include herb-crusted beef carpaccio and a delicious grilled prawn and scallop brochette. Main dishes range from charbroiled fillet steak with Gorgonzola sauce to pan-roasted Muscovy duck breast, and local Salt Spring Island lamb. Vegetarians enjoy black truffle risotto; chocolate lovers the decadent, baked-to-order warm chocolate cake. The excellent wine list includes an extensive selection of European wines and some Vancouver Island varieties. *$$$$; MC, V; local checks only; dinner every day; full bar; reservations recommended; www.housepiccolo.com; downtown Ganges.*

LODGINGS

Anne's Oceanfront Hideaway / ★★

168 SIMSON RD, SALT SPRING ISLAND; 250/537-0851 OR 888/474-2663 In this immaculate home with views of Stuart Channel and Vancouver Island, sign in to the Garry Oak Room and rest placidly on the four-poster bed. On quiet island evenings, contemplate the sunset from the wraparound veranda, and anticipate the smell of morning baking. The inn's four rooms are decorated in country floral style. Wheelchair users praise accessibility here, and others applaud the hospitality of proprietors Rick and Ruth-Anne Broad. A four-course breakfast might include eggs in phyllo pastry with lamb patties and chutney. Take advantage of the hot tub, aromatherapy massage services, canoes, and bikes. *$$$–$$$$; AE, MC, V; no checks; annes@saltspring.com; www.annesoceanfront.com; north of Vesuvius ferry terminal.* &

Beddis House Bed and Breakfast / ★★

131 MILES AVE, SALT SPRING ISLAND; 250/537-1028 Charming Beddis House, a white clapboard farmhouse built in 1900, is on a private beach on Ganges Harbour. Hidden at the end of a country road, it's far enough from town that you can see the stars at night and the seals and otters during the day. Guests make themselves at home in the modern coach house. It contains three very private rooms with clawfooted tubs, country-style furniture, woodstoves, and decks or balconies that look toward the water. Breakfast and afternoon tea are served in the old house and its guest lounge. *$$$; MC, V; no checks; closed mid-Dec–late Jan; beddis@salt spring.com; www.saltspring.com/beddishouse; follow Beddis Rd from Fulford-Ganges Rd, turn left onto Miles Ave.*

Bold Bluff Retreat / ★★

1 BOLD BLUFF, SALT SPRING ISLAND; 250/653-4377 Families love this secluded, eco-friendly, no-smoking retreat, accessible only by boat and bordering 5,000 acres of protected land. Salty's Cabin sits on a rocky outcropping where the tide rushes in and out right under the deck. Solar power, a composting toilet, and a propane stove ensure a self-sufficient holiday. Guests also enjoy the private dock and hot outdoor shower. The Garden Cottage, which sleeps up to six, is nestled in an old orchard, accented by a luxuriant rose arbor. Antique furnishings and a piano lend a warm glow inside the rustic shingled cottage. Amenities include a full kitchen and bath. A French door leads onto a porch with Adirondack chairs; a trampoline, swing, private wharf and beach make this an excellent family spot. Singles and couples will enjoy the single water-view B&B room in the main house, a 1940 cedar lodge. Owner Tamar Griggs will gladly pick up guests for the 5-minute boat ride from Burgoyne Bay or the 10-minute jaunt from Maple Bay on Vancouver Island. Pets are welcome, but in Salty's Cabin kids must be over 6 for safety reasons. *$$$; no credit cards; checks OK; 1-week min in cabins Jul–Aug; Salty's Cabin and B&B closed Nov–Mar; boldbluff@saltspring.com; www.boldbluff.com; accessible only by boat, from Burgoyne Bay, 10 minutes northwest of Fulford Harbour, and from Maple Bay on Vancouver Island.*

Hastings House / ★★★

160 UPPER GANGES RD, GANGES; 250/537-2362 OR 800/661-9255 This 25-acre seaside estate is one of the best-known getaways on the Southern Gulf Islands. Pass the bucolic pasture of frolicking lambs and, as the weathered barn and old farmhouse come into view, it feels as stately as England, circa 1820. Varied accommodations (18 units in all) are individually decorated with Persian rugs, antiques, and modern country plaids and florals. The Farmhouse has two two-level suites overlooking the water. In the Manor House, two upstairs suites feature the same lovely views from casement windows, warmed by stone fireplaces. The Post is a secluded, compact cabin popular with honeymooners. The current refined decor belies its history as a Hudson's Bay Company trading post. The wood-sided barn is richly weathered and divided into smaller suites overlooking the garden and pasture. Fireplaces or woodstoves are a given throughout; double whirlpool tubs are in select rooms. Seven new Hillside Suites offer ocean views in a modern West Coast–style wood building (but also overlook the patio of the pub next door). The formal dining room offers refined cuisine (see review). *$$$$; AE, MC, V; no checks; 2-night min on weekends and holidays; closed mid-Nov–mid-Mar; hasthouse@saltspring.com; www.hastingshouse.com; just north of Ganges.*

The Old Farmhouse Bed & Breakfast / ★★★★

1077 N END RD, SALT SPRING ISLAND; 250/537-4113 On this island boasting almost 100 B&Bs, the Old Farmhouse stands out. Hosts Gerti and Karl Fuss transformed their two-story white clapboard heritage home into a picture-perfect inn. Four guest rooms, each with private bath and patio or balcony, are charmingly decorated: brilliant white wainscoting, floral wallpaper, French doors, polished pine floors, sparkling stained-glass windows, feather beds and starched duvets, fresh flowers. The professional hosts know everything about the island, down to ferry times. A gazebo, hammock, and two swings on the three-acre property assist in relaxation. Morning coffee is delivered to your room, followed by an elegant and copious breakfast at the country dining room table. *$$$; V; checks OK; closed Oct–Easter; farmhouse@saltspring.com; bbcanada.com/old farmhouse/; 2½ miles (4 km) north of Ganges.*

North and South Pender Islands

Much of these two islands, united by a small bridge, is green and rural, but a massive subdivision on North Pender was one of the catalysts for the creation of the watchdog Islands Trust in the 1970s. Thank this group for helping the Penders, along with other Southern Gulf Islands, retain their charm. The population here is decidedly residential, so don't expect many restaurants, lodgings, or shops. Beaches, however, abound: **MORTIMER SPIT** (at the western tip of South Pender) and **GOWLAND POINT BEACH** (at end of Gowland Point Rd on South Pender) are among 20 public ocean-access points. Maps are available at the **PENDER ISLAND VISITOR INFORMATION CENTRE** (2332 Otter Bay Rd; 250/629-6541; open mid-May–Labor Day).

To take advantage of the fabled Gulf Island viewscape, **MOUNT ELIZABETH** (off Clam Bay Rd on North Pender) and **MOUNT NORMAN** (accessible from Ainslie Rd or Canal Rd on South Pender) have established trail systems. The gentle terrain of South Pender is particularly appealing for cyclists; rent bikes at **OTTER BAY MARINA** (2311 MacKinnon Rd; 250/629-3579) on North Pender. While waiting for the ferry at Otter Bay on North Pender, grab an excellent burger (try a venison or oyster variation) at the humble trailer **THE STAND** (Otter Bay Ferry Terminal; 250/629-3292).

LODGINGS

Poets Cove Seaside Resort at Bedwell Harbour / UNRATED

👫 **9801 SPALDING RD, SOUTH PENDER ISLAND; 250/629-3212 OR 888/512-7638** The name has changed and a massive face-lift is in the works, but this sprawling complex, known for decades as Bedwell Harbour Resort, retains its idyllic location: a sheltered cove and marina, backed by a gentle, wooded hillside, with stunning sunset views. Facilities include a marina, cabins, villas, hotel rooms, a pub, restaurant, general store, pool—you name it. Newer, more luxurious condominium accommodations are available—two-bedroom villas done in broad pine, with kitchens, fireplaces, and decks. By May 2003 several new cabins, a spa and fitness center, and a new pool will be open. $$$; AE, MC, V; no checks; closed mid-Sep–Mar; poetscove@bedwell-harbour.com; www.poetscove.com; follow Canal Rd from bridge to Spalding Rd, Spalding to Bedwell Harbour.

Saturna Island

The second-largest of the Southern Gulf Islands, Saturna has a scant 350 residents: no traffic jams, no village center, but two general stores, a bakery, and a pub overlooking the **LYALL HARBOUR** ferry stop. No camping is available on the island, but hiking abounds: climb **MOUNT WARBURTON**, the second-highest peak in the Southern Gulf Islands. **WINTER COVE MARINE PROVINCIAL PARK** (1 mile/1.6 km from ferry dock, at Saturna Point) is an inviting place to beachcomb or picnic above the Strait of Georgia, or drive to the tidal pools and sculpted sandstone of remote **EAST POINT. SATURNA VINEYARD** (8 Quarry Trail, 250/539-5139 or 877/918-3388), attached to its namesake lodge and restaurant (see review), is planted with pinot noir, merlot, chardonnay, and gewürztraminer. Tastings and tours are available year-round.

LODGINGS

Saturna Lodge and Restaurant / ★

130 PAYNE RD, SATURNA ISLAND; 250/539-2254 OR 888/539-8800 This lovely frame lodge sits high on a hill overlooking Boot Cove. Windows wrap around the dining room, where a crackling fire beckons on cool evenings. Seven bright and sunny rooms upstairs are individually decorated and contemporary in feel, with pleasant sitting areas and ocean or garden views. All have private baths; the honeymoon suite has a soaker tub and private balcony. A hot tub is in the garden. Guests are picked up from the Saturna ferry dock and boaters are welcome to use the lodge moorage. The menu at the restaurant (serving breakfast to guests, dinner to the public) features Saturna-raised lamb, local seafood, and organic produce; the wine cellar features Northwest vintages, including Saturna's own. *$$$; MC, V; checks OK; closed mid-Oct–mid-May; satlodge@gulfislands.com; www.saturna-island.bc. ca; follow signs from ferry.*

Mayne Island

During the Cariboo Gold Rush of the mid-1800s, Mayne was the Southern Gulf Islands's commercial and social hub, a way station between Victoria and Vancouver. Today, the pace of life is more serene. Rolling orchards and warm rock-strewn beaches dominate this pocket-sized island of 5 square miles (13 square km). Hike up **MOUNT PARKE** to reach Mayne's highest point, with a view of ferries plying Active Pass between the islands and mainland. A complete bicycle tour of the island takes five hours—longer if you stop for a pint at the well-worn **SPRINGWATER LODGE** (400 Fernhill Dr; 250/539-5521).

RESTAURANTS

Oceanwood Country Inn / ★★★

630 DINNER BAY RD, MAYNE ISLAND; 250/539-5074 Four-course dinners in the dining room overlooking Navy Channel are exquisitely prepared and feature entree choices such as nettle and almond–stuffed sole or boneless quail stuffed with mushrooms and hazelnuts. Appetizers are strikingly unique: smoked sable fish and beet terrine with stinging nettle juice, for example. At dessert, a goat cheese cake with walnut sabayon and rosemary caramel roasted apples might make an appearance. The careful wine list features Pacific Northwest wines. *$$$$; MC, V; Canadian checks only; dinner every day (closed Dec–Feb); full bar; reservations required; oceanwood@gulfislands.com; www.oceanwood.com; right on Dalton Dr, right on Mariners, immediate left onto Dinner Bay Rd, look for signs.*

LODGINGS

A Coachhouse on Oyster Bay / ★★

511 BAYVIEW DR, MAYNE ISLAND; 250/539-3368 OR 888/629-6322 Snuggle by the fire in one of three spacious rooms, or sit a while by your window gazing at the expansive view over the Strait of Georgia to the mainland's monumental Coast Mountains. All rooms have four-poster beds; one has an oceanview deck with a private hot tub. Get closer to the view in the outdoor hot tub, just inches from the high tide line. The stone-paved drive lends a touch of elegance, as does the garden gazebo. The satisfying four-course breakfast often includes cereal, blueberry muffins, fresh fruit, and hot peach crepes. Avid scuba divers, hosts Heather and Brian Johnston can recommend the best dive sites around the island; they also arrange kayak rentals. *$$$; MC, V; bhjohnston@gulfislands.com; www. acoachhouse.com; just east of Georgina Point Lighthouse.*

Oceanwood Country Inn / ★★★

630 DINNER BAY RD, MAYNE ISLAND; 250/539-5074 The split-level, high-ceilinged Wisteria Room is the largest of the 12 rooms at the Oceanwood Country Inn, and features a country gingham theme and a view over Navy Channel from the deck hot tub. Fireplaces and deep soaker tubs are features of many rooms. Some, like the Lilac Room, are done in a floral theme with hand-stenciling; others, like the blue-hued Heron Room, come in more soothing masculine tones. Rooms overlook either ocean or garden, replete with roses, daffodils, tulips, dahlias, and lavender. Mingle with other guests in the games room or library; walk down the path to the rocky beach after dinner. Look for fresh-squeezed fruit and vegetable juices, croissants or coffee cake, and hearty hot country-style entrees at breakfast. After a day of kayaking or bird-watching, settle into a meal at the excellent dining room (see review). *$$$–$$$$; MC, V; Canadian checks only; closed Dec–Feb; oceanwood@gulfislands.com; www.oceanwood.com; right on Dalton Dr, right on Mariners, immediate left onto Dinner Bay Rd, look for signs.*

Galiano Island

Residents here dismiss bustling Salt Spring as "towny," as well they might on their undeveloped, secluded island. Dedicated locals work hard to protect the natural features along the island's narrow 19 miles (30 km): densely forested cliffs, towering bluffs, wildflower meadows, and sheltered harbors.

On **BODEGA RIDGE,** trails wind through old-growth forests and skirt flower-studded fields; views stretch to Washington State's Olympic Mountains. From **BLUFFS PARK** and **MOUNT GALIANO,** you can watch eagles, ferries, and sweeping tides on Active Pass. Most Galiano roads—especially the partially paved eastern route—accommodate bicycles untroubled by traffic, but there's some steep going. **GULF ISLANDS KAYAKING** (250/539-2442) lets you see the islands by water. **MONTAGUE HARBOUR** (5 miles/8 km west of ferry dock at Sturdies Bay; 800/689-9025 for camping reservations), on the island's west side, is a lovely, sheltered bay with beaches, picnic and camping areas, boat launch, and stunning sunset views.

Despite being the closest of the Southern Gulf Islands from the Tsawwassen ferry (one hour), Galiano has a sparse 1,200 residents and only a few services and shops, clustered at the south end. Eateries are scarce, though you'll find hearty pub food and local color at the **HUMMINGBIRD INN** (Sturdies Bay and Georgeson Rds; 250/539-5472). Have lunch in the vegetarian-friendly, **DAYSTAR MARKET CAFÉ** (on Georgeson Bay Rd; 250/539-2800; open May–Oct). While away time in the Sturdies Bay ferry lineup at Village Bay at **TRINCOMALI BAKERY AND DELI** (2540 Sturdies Bay Rd; 250/539-2004).

RESTAURANTS

Woodstone Country Inn / ★★★

743 GEORGESON BAY RD, GALIANO ISLAND; 250/539-2022 OR 888/339-2022 The dining room at this inn (see review) ranks high: co-innkeeper/chef Gail Nielsen-Pich serves a fine four-course table d'hôte dinner that might include cioppino of fresh mussels, shrimp, and seafood in spicy tomato ragout, maple baked salmon, or vegetarian spinach and ricotta pie with roasted-garlic and tomato sauce. Desserts are outstanding; Galiano residents are fiercely loyal to the bread pudding with rum sauce. Enjoy the feast in a neoclassical room (think Italianate columns) overlooking serene fields. *$$$$; AE, MC, V; checks OK; dinner every day (closed Dec–Jan); full bar; reservations required; woodstone@gulfislands.com; www.gulfislands.com/woodstone; bear left off Sturdies Bay Rd, and follow signs.* &

LODGINGS

THE BELLHOUSE INN / ★★★

29 FARMHOUSE RD, GALIANO ISLAND; 250/539-5667 OR 800/970-7464 Andrea Porter and David Birchall are consummate gentlefolk farmers, conversing with guests and feeding sheep with equal aplomb. This historic wood-shingled farmhouse, painted soothing barn red, contains three lovely upstairs guest rooms; two of which have balconies. One boasts picture windows, allowing an expansive view of Bellhouse Bay from bed, and a Jacuzzi. Guests can play croquet, or laze in a hammock. A popular wedding location, the Bellhouse is our favorite Galiano spot. Heritage touches include antique opera glasses; the comfortable guest lounge is lined with books. Large breakfasts consist of fruit, granola, and hearty egg dishes such as seafood eggs Benedict. Meander the inn's 6 pleasant acres and into nearby Bellhouse Park, make your way to the sandy beach (a rare treat on Galiano), or join David for a sailboat tour. Larger groups can spread out in the duplex cabin; each side has two bedrooms, a kitchen, and private patio. *$$$; MC, V; Canadian checks only; info@bellhouse.com; www.bellhouseinn.com; uphill from ferry terminal, left on Burrill, left on Jack, right on Farmhouse.*

Woodstone Country Inn / ★★★

743 GEORGESON BAY RD, GALIANO ISLAND; 250/539-2022 OR 888/339-2022 This modern, executive-style manor house overlooks field and forest, and is a choice stopover for large cycling tours and business retreats. The best of the 12 rooms are on the lower level and feature private patios. The tone of the refined decor is set by classic English-print fabrics in florals and stripes; Persian rugs warm the floors in some rooms and antiques add country charm, as does hand stenciling on the walls. All but two rooms have fireplaces, while one upper-end room has a double Jacuzzi. Breakfast and afternoon tea are included. Locals recommend the upscale dining room (see review). *$$–$$$; AE, MC, V; checks OK; closed Dec–Jan; woodstone@gulfislands.com; www.gulfislands.com/woodstone; bear left off Sturdies Bay Rd, and follow signs.* &

Gabriola Island

Although this most accessible island has become a bedroom community for nearby Nanaimo (20 minutes by ferry), it remains fairly rustic. The highlight of the fine seaside walks along the west shore are the **MALASPINA GALLERIES** (take Taylor Bay Rd to Malaspina Dr and park at road's end), fanciful rock formations, and caves carved by the sea. (Bring good shoes; it's rocky.) You'll have to look elsewhere, however, for recommended accommodations.

Denman and Hornby Islands

Tranquil and bucolic, the sister islands of Denman and Hornby sit just off the east coast of central Vancouver Island. The larger, Denman—10 minutes by ferry from Buckley Bay, 12 miles (20 km) south of Courtenay—is known for pastoral farmlands and talented artisans. The relatively flat landscape and untraveled byways make it a natural for cyclists. Work up an appetite and stop for pizza and locally roasted organic coffee at the **DENMAN BAKERY AND PIZZERIA** (3646 Denman Rd, Denman Island; 250/335-1310).

Ten minutes from Denman by ferry, Hornby is a dream for mountain bikers seeking idyllic—or hair-raising—forest trails. Locals favor the burgers and Caesar salads of the **THATCH PUB** (4305 Shingle Spit Rd, Hornby Island; 250/335-2833). Hornby's **HELLIWELL PROVINCIAL PARK** (far northern tip of island) impresses with dramatic seaside cliffs and lush forest, while beach lovers seek out **TRIBUNE BAY PROVINCIAL PARK** (east shore of northern isthmus).

LODGINGS

Sea Breeze Lodge

5205 FOWLER RD, HORNBY ISLAND; 250/335-2321 OR 888/516-2321
Owned for decades by the Bishop family, Sea Breeze has evolved into a comfortable family retreat with a loyal following. Most of the 14 rustic cottages are on the waterfront; some have fireplaces. Best is the view; enjoy it from the hot tub. Cabin rates include three home-cooked meals, June through September; expect comfort foods such as wholesome soups from the lodge's own cookbook. The Bishops happily accommodate dietary needs, from vegetarian to vegan. The dining room is open weekends only in fall, and is closed in winter; cabins with kitchens are available year-round. *$$$$; MC, V; checks OK; 2-night min in summer; info@sea breezlodge.com; www.seabreezelodge.com; on Tralee Point.*

Discovery Islands

The closely linked Discovery Islands—fishing and boating meccas east of Campbell River—include **QUADRA, CORTES,** and **SONORA.** To visit the most accessible Discovery Islands (Quadra and Cortes), take the 10-minute ferry ride from Campbell River to Quadra's Heriot Bay dock; from there, another 45-minute ferry takes you to Cortes. To reach Sonora Island, take a private boat or regularly scheduled floatplane service from Campbell River through **CORIL AIR** (3050 Spit Rd, Campbell River; 250/287-8371). The **KWAGIULTH MUSEUM AND CULTURAL CENTRE** (in

Cape Mudge Village, near Quathiaski Cove, Quadra Island; 250/285-3733) exhibits a fascinating array of First Nations ceremonial regalia.

LODGINGS

April Point Lodge / ★★★

900 APRIL POINT RD, QUADRA ISLAND; 250/285-2222 OR 800/663-7090
This island getaway, centered around a cedar lodge built on pilings over the water, draws serious fisher folk from all over the world. Though guided fishing is the major activity here (fishing packages are mandatory in July and August), April Point also offers family-oriented activities such as bicycle, scooter, and kayak rentals, helicopter tours, and ocean-going whale- and bear-watching trips. The resort's spacious and freshly decorated accommodations range from large guest houses to lodge rooms and comfortable cabins; some have fireplaces, Jacuzzis, living rooms, kitchens, and sundecks, and all have water views. The main lodge is sunny and cheerful, and food (including fresh sushi) at the restaurant is very good—seafood is the focus and wraparound windows offer dramatic water views. Guests at April Point have access to the pool, hot tubs, tennis courts, and other facilities at Painter's Lodge (see review in Campbell River section), April Point's sister resort in nearby Campbell River. *$$$; AE, DC, DIS, E, MC, V; no checks; info@obmg.com; www.obmg.com; 10 minutes north of ferry dock or accessible by free water taxi from Painter's Lodge.*

Sonora Resort and Conference Centre / ★★

SONORA ISLAND; 604/233-0460 OR 888/576-6672 Sonora Resort is big and posh—a multimillion-dollar resort for those who want to fish from the lap of luxury. You'll pay about $1,000 (Canadian) per night, but everything (except professional massage) is included: airfare from Vancouver, guided fishing, rods and tackle, rain gear, gourmet meals, drinks, and more. Luxurious suites with Jacuzzis are grouped in six lodges; each has a common room with hot tub, steam bath, and complimentary bar. Other amenities include billiards tables, a small convention center, fitness room, lap pool, and tennis courts. The competent kitchen serves a well-selected variety of fresh seafood. At lunch, the chef boats out to barbecue the catch; dinners may be prepared on a Japanese teppanyaki grill outdoors. *$$$$; AE, MC, V; checks OK; 2-night min; open June–Sept; www.sonoraresort.com; 30 miles (48 km) north of Campbell River, accessible only by private boat or regular floatplane service.*

Tsa-Kwa-Luten Lodge / ★★

I LIGHTHOUSE RD, QUADRA ISLAND; 250/285-2042 OR 800/665-7745 Built on an 1,100-acre forest by the Laichwiltach First Nation, this oceanview lodge was inspired by traditional longhouse design. Native art is featured throughout the lodge and its 34 units, which include four self-contained cottages. The star attraction here, as elsewhere in the salmon-rich Campbell River area, is fishing; guided packages are available. Costars include the great outdoors and good views, mountain biking (rent at lodge), or the outstanding Kwagiulth Museum (a 45-minute forest walk away). Alternately, stroll beaches to ponder ancient Native petroglyphs, or walk to nearby Cape Mudge Lighthouse. Lodge staff can arrange eco-adventure tours, heli-hiking, scuba diving, or kayaking; or guests can opt for a relaxing massage or a First Nations cultural package. The lodge hosts Kwagiulth storytelling and salmon barbecues monthly in summer. The Hamaelas dining room serves three meals every day—New York steak, vegetarian pasta, cedar-baked salmon, clams, and other fresh seafood; seasonal pies—try blackberry or sour cream and peach—make welcome appearances. *$$$; AE, DC, E, MC, V; no checks; open May–Sept; tkllodge@connected. bc.ca; www.capemudgeresort.bc.ca; 10 minutes south of ferry dock.*

The Cowichan Valley and Southeast Shore

The Cowichan Valley is a gentle stretch of farmland and forest from the town of Shawnigan Lake north to Chemainus; the microclimate of this pleasant area lends itself to grape growing, making it the island's only vineyard region. Try a pinot noir at **BLUE GROUSE VINEYARDS** (Blue Grouse Rd, off Lakeside Rd, Duncan; 250/743-3834); also visit **CHERRY POINT VINEYARDS** (840 Cherry Point Rd, Cobble Hill; 250/743-1272) and **VIGNETI ZANATTA** (5039 Marshall Rd, Duncan; 250/748-2338), which has an on-site restaurant (lunch and dinner). At **MERRIDALE CIDER WORKS** (1230 Merridale Rd, Cobble Hill; 250/743-4293), cider is made in the English tradition; the best time to visit is mid-September to mid-October, when local apples are run through the presses. The rolling, pastoral landscape continues through the Chemainus Valley north to the hub towns of Nanaimo and Parksville.

Cowichan Bay

This sweet little seaside town off Highway 1 has a few restaurants, craft stores, and marinas. The Wooden Boat Society displays and Native artisan's studio at the **COWICHAN BAY MARITIME CENTRE AND MUSEUM** (1761 Cowichan Bay Rd; 250/746-4955; www.classicboats.org) are worth a visit.

LODGINGS

Dream Weaver Bed & Breakfast / ★★

1682 BOTWOOD LN, COWICHAN BAY; 250/748-7688 OR 888/748-7689
This modern wood-shake home has plenty of character, modeled on gabled, multistoried, Victorian-era construction. Rooms range from feminine florals to gentlemanly and distinguished. The large Magnolia Suite, nestled in the top-floor gables, is done in traditional white cottons and flower prints, with a double Jacuzzi tub opposite the gas fireplace. A small balcony offers views of picturesque Cowichan Bay. The Primrose Suite evokes the mood of an old-style smoking room, with deep hues and salon armchairs, but features contemporary clean lines; fully modern amenities include Jacuzzi, gas fireplace, TV, VCR, and CD player. Hosts Cathy and Ken McAllister serve guests a full breakfast. *$$–$$$; MC, V; no checks; dreamwvr@islandnet.com; www.vancouverisland-bc.com/ dreamweaver; in village center.*

Duncan

Forty-five minutes north of Victoria on the Trans-Canada Highway (Hwy 1), the City of Totems is designated by little totem poles sprinkled along the roadside—

some more artistic than others. Another claim to fame is the world's largest hockey stick, notably affixed to a community arena on the west side of the highway. In the old downtown, a good lunch can be had at the popular **ISLAND BAGEL COMPANY** (48 Station St; 250/748-1988). **THE QUW'UTSUN' CULTURAL AND CONFERENCE CENTRE** (200 Cowichan Wy; 250/746-8119 or 877/746-8119) on Duncan's southern edge is a must-see for admirers of First Nations arts and crafts. In summer, watch as the region's renowned Cowichan sweaters—handmade of thick wool with indigenous designs in cream and browns or grays—are knit. The center also features an open-air carving shed, where carvers craft 12- to 20-foot totem poles. The gallery and gift shop is excellent.

RESTAURANTS

The Quamichan Inn / ★★

1478 MAPLE BAY RD, DUNCAN; 250/746-7028 Chef Steve Muggeridge turns out fresh seafood dishes and steak favorites to satisfied diners at this dependable establishment, owned by Pam and Clive Cunningham for the past 20 years. Look for homemade ice cream in summer. Take your after-dinner coffee in the garden of this restored turn-of-the-20th-century home, profuse with fragrant wisteria, blooming fuchsias, and colorful dahlias. The proprietors gladly pick up yachties and drop them off after dinner. Accommodations consist of three guest rooms; rates include an English hunt breakfast: eggs, bacon, sausage, and fried tomato. *$$$; AE, MC, V; checks OK; dinner Wed–Sun; full bar; reservations recommended; quamichaninn@home. com; www.quamichaninn.com; just east of Duncan, take exit off Hwy 1 at Duncan, turn right at Chevron, left onto Maple Bay Rd.* &

LODGINGS

Fairburn Farm Country Manor / ★★

3310 JACKSON RD, DUNCAN; 250/746-4637 This lovingly restored 1884 manor house is at the heart of a 130-acre farm, where part of the charm—especially for animal-loving kids—is the chance to pitch in with chores. Always innovative, hosts Anthea and Darrel Archer recently shifted from sheep farming to operating North America's first water buffalo dairy (and are accomplished B&B hosts). Breakfasts include farm-raised products such as freshly churned butter, homemade bread, local preserves, and frittatas of free-range eggs and organic yellow tomatoes. Spotlessly clean rooms are simply decorated with cozy furniture, local art, and historical photos; tall windows offer views across the gardens, fields, and surrounding forest. Some of the six large rooms have fireplaces and whirlpool tubs and all are phone- and TV-free. Three rooms have en suite baths; the others have private baths. A self-contained two-bedroom cottage overlooks the fields. Trails in the woods and boats on the creek beckon. *$$–$$$; MC, V; checks OK; 3-day min in cottage; open Apr–mid-Oct; info@fairburnfarm.bc.ca; www.fairburnfarm.bc.ca; 7 miles (11 km) south of Duncan.*

Chemainus

Heralded as "the little town that did," seaside Chemainus bounced back from the closure of its logging mill and turned to tourism with flair. Buildings are painted with **MURALS** depicting the town's colorful history, making Chemainus a noted tourist attraction on Highway 1A. The whole town has a theatrical feel, underlined by dinner theater productions at the popular **CHEMAINUS THEATRE** (9737 Chemainus Rd; 250/246-9820 or 800/565-7738).

RESTAURANTS

The Waterford Restaurant / ★★

9875 MAPLE ST, CHEMAINUS; 250/246-1046 The Waterford, ensconced in a heritage building in the old town, features Victorian-inspired, floral-swag decor that speaks to the heart of an older clientele. Lunch prices are reasonable for upscale cuisine offered by chef Dwayne Maslen: sole amandine, mushroom or seafood crepes, or prawns. Dinner is slightly pricier: choices can include rack of lamb Dijon, chicken Monte Cristo with ham, fresh tomatoes, and *emmantal,* or various treatments of venison, rabbit, or duck. *$$; AE, MC, V; no checks; lunch, dinner Tues–Sun (winter hours vary; closed Jan); full bar; reservations recommended; waterfordrestaurant@shaw.ca; a few blocks from downtown.* &

LODGINGS

Bird Song Cottage / ★★
Castlebury Cottage / ★★

9909 MAPLE ST, CHEMAINUS; 250/246-9910 / 9910 CROFT ST, CHEMAINUS; 250/246-9228 Bird Song Cottage is a bacchanal of imaginative Victoriana. The exterior of this lavender-and-white gingerbread cottage delights period purists. Inside, oil portraits, a grand piano, and a Celtic harp compete with an extensive fancy hat collection. Songs of (caged) birds are also present. Hosts Larry and Virginia Blatchford keep costumes on hand, ready to provide larger groups with a dress-up Serendipity Tea. Three guest rooms feature private baths, duvets, fresh-cut flowers, and line-dried linens. The Bluebird and Hummingbird overflow with lace and florals, while the Nightingale is more sedate in rich green and gold stripes. Paintings are by Virginia's sister, a Chemainus mural artist. Friday and Saturday mornings, when the host is home, breakfast is accompanied by piano music. Ask about romance packages, with theater tickets, a carriage ride, and an in-suite catered five-course dinner with live harpist.

Equally theatrical is the Blatchfords' medieval-themed, one-suite Castlebury Cottage, where you sleep beneath purple velvet bed curtains, soak in the big marble tub, or do the Juliet thing from either of the two balconies. Though dramatically medieval right down to the resident suit of armor, the cottage features a modern kitchenette, TV, VCR, and CD player. A second suite downstairs (called the Dungeon) can be booked only as part of the whole cottage. *$$ (Bird Song), $$$$ (Castlebury); AE, MC, V; no checks; 2-night min (Castlebury); info@castleburycottage. com; birdsong@islandnet.com; www.romanticbb.com (Bird Song); www.castleburycottage.com; downtown.*

Ladysmith

RESTAURANTS

Crow and Gate Neighbourhood Pub / ★★

2313 YELLOW POINT RD, LADYSMITH; 250/722-3731 The Crow and Gate was one of the first neighborhood pubs in BC, and retains pride of place as the nicest pub we have seen in this region. English fowl stroll the pastoral grounds, and quaint buildings give the feel of a gentleman's farm. Inside this popular watering hole, light from the flames of two substantial fires glint off diamond-pane windows; long plank tables invite conversation. Traditional English pub fare includes highly praised steak-and-kidney pie, ploughman's lunch, beef dip, and—in a nod to local conditions—panfried oysters. *$; MC, V; no checks; lunch, dinner every day; full bar; reservations not accepted; 8 miles (13 km) south of Nanaimo.*

LODGINGS

Yellow Point Lodge / ★★

3700 YELLOW POINT RD, LADYSMITH; 250/245-7422 This well-loved oceanfront lodge draws guests back every year, from honeymoon to anniversary—even in winter (weekends are often booked months in advance). The log-and-timber lodge has rooms within hearing range of the crashing surf. Cabins around the property range from very rustic, summer-only cabins to cozy one-bedroom cottages. The one-room White Beach cabins are closest to the water; each features a log-constructed bed with a view, and a wood stove nestled in a rustic beamed interior. Water along the private 1½ miles (2.4 km) of coastline is exceptionally clear. Daily rates include most activities and three meals served at group tables in the lodge: comfort foods like beef and mashed potatoes, or classic BC salmon. Recreational facilities include tennis courts, kayaks, mountains bikes, jogging trails, an outdoor saltwater pool, and a sauna and hot tub in a wooded copse. *$$$; AE, MC, V; checks OK; 2-night min on weekends, 3-night min on holidays; www.yellowpointlodge.com; 9 miles (14.5) km east of Ladysmith.*

Nanaimo

Nanaimo is more than the strip mall it appears to be from the highway (19 and 19A join in Nanaimo). The early island settlement of Nanaimo began as a coal mining hub. The **HUDSON'S BAY COMPANY BASTION** (at Bastion and Front Sts; summer only), built in 1853, is one of few forts of this type left standing in North America. It's part of the **NANAIMO DISTRICT MUSEUM** (100 Cameron Rd; 250/753-1821), which also has a replica of a Chinatown street.

In Nanaimo's **OLD TOWN,** near the old train station, cafes mix with vintage shops and houseware boutiques. Lunch at **DELICADO'S** (358 Wesley St; 250/753-6524) on wraps fired with chipotle sauce and black-bean-and-corn salsa, or at **GINA'S** (47 Skinner St; 250/753-5411), an ever-popular Mexican restaurant.

Not only is Nanaimo a transportation hub, with frequent ferries to Vancouver, it's also a good place to launch a **SCUBA DIVING** holiday. Numerous companies offer equipment rentals and guided tours. Thrill seekers head for the **BUNGY ZONE** (15

MILE ZERO

Along waterfront Dallas Road in Victoria, tour buses flock to the simple wooden sign put up by the Canadian Automobile Association in the 1950s to mark the beginning, or end, of the Trans-Canada Highway. (Overlook the fact that you must complete the last stretch of highway by getting on a ferry and crossing the Strait of Georgia.) It's symbolic of the great 19th-century dreams Victoria once had to be the jumping-off point for the wealth of the Canadian nation.

The highway marker provides a link to a time when Victoria was a busier port than Vancouver. When the politicians of Victoria voted to join the Canadian confederation in 1871, it was only on the promise of a railway link extending to the capital. When Ottawa was slow to complete even the mainland route, politicians in Victoria began to threaten separation. But local citizens didn't sit back and wait. The promise of black gold—in those days, coal—became the impetus for a privately developed rail line from Victoria to Nanaimo, finished in 1886, at great personal gain to coal magnate Robert Dunsmuir. The government not only gave him an efficient means to ship his coal to port, it compensated his work with 2 million acres of prime Vancouver Island land and $750,000 in cold cash. Dunsmuir's empire was assured. See the more visible signs of his wealth in his two Victoria-area mansions, Craigdarroch Castle, now a museum, and Hatley Park, now Royal Roads University.

While Dunsmuir's wealth flourished, the fortunes of Victoria were on the wane: the large port of Vancouver was far outstripping the business and population of colonial Victoria. But big dreams die hard. By the 1950s, age of the automobile, Victoria clung to its right as Mile Zero of any transcontinental project. When, in 1954, the BC government made a go of reviving its lagging section of the Trans-Canada Highway, Victoria made sure it was at the front of the line.   —*Alisa Smith*

minutes south of Nanaimo; 250/753-5867 or 800/668-7771) to experience North America's only legal bungy jumping bridge, over the Nanaimo River. Check out the **BATHTUB RACE** on the third weekend of July, a tradition since 1967. **BIKE TRAILS**— meandering lanes and wilderness single-tracks—snake around the city's edge.

The spit at **PIPER'S LAGOON** (northeast of downtown) extends into the Strait of Georgia, backed by sheer bluffs, great for bird-watching. **NEWCASTLE ISLAND PROVINCIAL MARINE PARK** is an auto-free wilderness reached by a summer foot-passenger ferry from Nanaimo's inner harbor.

Golf courses with views proliferate from Nanaimo northward. Most noteworthy is the **NANAIMO GOLF CLUB** (2800 Highland Blvd; 250/758-6332), a demanding 18-hole course 3 miles (5 km) north of the city. Others include **PRYDE VISTA GOLF CLUB** (155 Pryde Ave; 250/753-6188), 2 miles (3 km) north of Nanaimo, and **FAIR-**

WINDS (3730 Fairwinds Dr; 250/468-7666 or 888/781-2777), at Nanoose Bay. **TOURISM NANAIMO** (250/756-0106) has more information.

RESTAURANTS

The Mahle House / ★★★

2104 HEMER RD, CEDAR; 250/722-3621 Find this cozy 1904 home-turned-restaurant in Cedar, just minutes southeast of Nanaimo, and sample the inventive cuisine of chef/co-owner Maureen Loucks. Begin with "porcupine" prawns, quickly deep-fried in shredded phyllo; then taste chicken stuffed with crab and drizzled with saffron sauce. The vegetarian platter includes roasted-garlic-and-goat-cheese mashed potatoes. The mixed grill is for adventurous meat eaters, highlighting Jamaican jerk pork and local Selby Street sausage. Vegetables and herbs come from the house garden; the rabbit comes from down the road, the salmon from Yellow Island, and the scallops from Qualicum Beach. Desserts are exquisite: Harlequin Mousse with white and dark chocolate sauce and a swirl of chocolate and caramel, crème brûlée Napoleon, and peanut butter pie. Co-owner Delbert Horrocks takes justifiable pride in his extensive, award-winning wine list. *$$$; AE, MC, V; no checks; dinner Wed–Sun; full bar; reservations recommended; www.mahlehouse.com; at Cedar.* &

Parksville

Parksville and the surrounding area are renowned for sandy beaches, especially in lovely **RATHTREVOR BEACH PROVINCIAL PARK** (off Hwy 19A, 1 mile/2 km south of Parksville; 250/954-4600). Families love its lengthy shallows and relatively warm water temperatures, camping, and August's annual sand-castle competition. **MORNINGSTAR** (525 Lowry's Rd; 250/248-2244) offers golfing.

A little farther afield, picnic at thunderous **ENGLISHMAN RIVER FALLS PROVINCIAL PARK** (8 miles/12.8 km southwest of town; 250/954-4600), and mosey along to **COOMBS,** a tiny town on Highway 4A that hovers between cute and kitsch with its overblown pioneer theme, based on a small core of true old-time buildings. Shop for produce and gifts at the popular **OLD COUNTRY MARKET** (mid-Mar–Nov), where goats graze on the grassy roof. **MACMILLAN PROVINCIAL PARK** (20 miles/32 km west of Parksville on Hwy 4; 250/954-4600) contains **CATHEDRAL GROVE,** a sky-high old-growth forest of Douglas firs and cedars up to 800 years old.

RESTAURANTS

Red Pepper Grill / ★

193 MEMORIAL AVE, PARKSVILLE; 250/248-2364 This turn-of-the-20th-century home set in an established garden has a cheery yellow exterior, and a cozy, intimate interior layout. Chef Allan Virs's Italian and California-style cuisine is designed to please, not surprise; his menu features seafood, pasta, ribs, and highly praised steak and prawns. Finish with a "tuxedo" brownie, layered with dark and light chocolate, and a raspberry filling. *$$; AE, MC, V; no checks; lunch Mon–Fri, dinner every day (closed Mon in winter); full bar; reservations recommended; www.redpeppergrill. com; at McMillan St.*

LODGINGS

Tigh-Na-Mara Resort Hotel / ★★

1095 E ISLAND HWY, PARKSVILLE; 250/248-2072 OR 800/663-7373 Of the resorts that sprawl the length of Rathtrevor Beach, Tigh-Na-Mara stands out. The minivillage of log cottages are spread throughout 22 acres of wooded grounds. Cottages offer privacy, kitchens, porches, and barbecues, as well as fireplaces (standard in all rooms). Oceanfront condominium accommodations are newer and spiffier, with log-beam details; some have jetted tubs and kitchens. The new Forest Studios and Woodland Suites are most upscale; they surround a new spa facility. Guests can use an exercise room, indoor pool and hot tub, steam room, or tennis courts—and 500 feet of beachfront. The on-site restaurant is popular. Kids like the long sandy beach, playgrounds, and activities run by resort staff. Pets OK in some cottages during off-season. $$–$$$; AE, DC, MC, V; local checks only; 3- to 7-night min in summer, 2-night min on winter weekends; info@tigh-na-mara.com; www.tigh-na-mara.com; 1¼ miles (2 km) south of Parksville on Hwy 19A.

Qualicum Beach

This little town 20 minutes north of Parksville on Highway 19A has a pleasant beachfront promenade and a growing downtown shopping district. For its size, it has a good selection of cafes—a favorite is the earthy lunch spot HARVEST MOON CAFÉ (133 2nd Ave; 250/752-2068). For more retro character, drive 10 minutes north for coffee at the COLA DINER (6060 W Island Hwy; 250/757-2029), a joyful ode to a 1950s burger joint in sparkly red vinyl and chrome. Then get some exercise golfing at EAGLECREST (2035 W Island Hwy; 250/752-9744).

RESTAURANTS

Lefty's / ★

710 MEMORIAL AVE, QUALICUM BEACH; 250/752-7530 / 101-280 E ISLAND HWY, PARKSVILLE; 250/954-3886 The bright, funky ambience and art-filled walls here rival casual cafe experiences of Vancouver or Victoria, and food is priced accordingly. Baked-on-the-premises coconut cream pie is superior. Specialties include wraps stuffed with fresh West Coast fusions like Cajun chicken; flavorful chorizo sausage pizza; or cheddar corn pie, a quiche-like creation. At dinner, Lefty's transitions to pastas, stir-fries, and steak and prawns. Organic coffees are a bonus. A new Parksville location offering the same menu opened in 2000. $$; MC, V; no checks; breakfast, lunch, dinner every day; full bar; reservations recommended; leftysff@nanaimo. ark.com; www.leftys.tv; at Fern in Qualicum Beach, and in Parksville's Thrifty Foods Centre on the Island Hwy.

Old Dutch Inn / ★

2690 E ISLAND HWY, QUALICUM BEACH; 250/752-6914 This place has dreamy breakfasts—and waitresses in triple-peaked, starched lace caps. The Dutch theme is taken seriously, with turned oak chairs and Delft tiles. The Dutchie is a delicious sort of French toast sandwich filled with homemade blueberry preserves. Also try classic pannekoeken or Eggs Benedict Old Dutch with fine smoked salmon. Join retirees and travelers at lunch for a *uitsmijter,* an open-faced sandwich with Dutch smoked ham and cheese, or Indonesian-inspired *loempia,* a 10-spice spring roll with pork and roast peanuts. (Vegetarians are happiest here at breakfast.) Expansive windows look out on Qualicum Bay. *$; MC, V; no checks; breakfast, lunch, dinner every day; full bar; reservations recommended; info@olddutchinn.com; www.olddutchinn. com; on Highway 19A.*

LODGINGS

Bahari Bed & Breakfast / ★★

5101 W ISLAND HWY, QUALICUM BEACH; 250/752-9278 OR 877/752-9278 Enter through the modern gray-toned exterior via double carved doors dominated by a large seashell handle. Inside, glimmering hammered copper contributes to an Asian-inspired tree design. The look here is modern and adventurous—the epitome of Pacific Rim style. The two-story foyer, hung with a dramatic Japanese kimono, feels like a modern museum. First-class art and materials include a vivid green raw-silk bedspread in the garden-view room. All four rooms have fireplaces, and three have ocean views. A private hot tub in the woods overlooks Georgia Strait and the Northern Gulf Islands. Children are welcome in the two-bedroom, 1,200-square-foot suite with a kitchen. *$$$–$$$$; AE, MC, V; no checks; 2-night min for suite; closed Dec–Jan; relax@baharibandb.com; www.baharibandb.com; 10 minutes north of town on Hwy 19A.*

Hollyford Bed & Breakfast / ★★

106 HOYLAKE RD E, QUALICUM BEACH; 250/752-8101 OR 877/224-6559 This 1920s cottage surrounded by holly hedges and laurels has been thoughtfully reno-vated to add three guest rooms in a private wing. The antique ambience is made more unique with the addition of host Jim Ford's collection of western and Royal Canadian Mounted Police memorabilia. Breakfast, served on sterling silver and Waterford crystal in the dining room, often features gourmet takes on Irish cuisine: home-baked scones, followed by Irish tortière with Dubliner cheese, for example. Lazy afternoons call for tea on the little deck surveying the snug garden. The hosts like to pamper guests, delivering wake-up trays of OJ and coffee to rooms before breakfast, and evening tuck-in trays of sherry, Perrier, and homemade truffles. Sodas, popcorn, coffee, and tea are available with the in-room VCRs and videos. *$$$; MC, V; no checks; mail@hollyford.ca; www.hollyford.ca; off Hwy 4 (Memorial Ave).*

Barkley Sound and Tofino

Most visitors pass through Port Alberni on the way to Tofino via Highway 4, or wait to take the scenic boat trip on the **LADY ROSE** or **FRANCES BARKLEY** (250/723-8313 or 800/663-7192) to Barkley Sound and Bamfield, Ucluelet, or the Broken Group Islands. Boats offer passenger day trips as well as freight service.

Port Alberni

Shops, galleries, and restaurants cluster at the Harbour Quay, where boats to Barkley Sound dock in this industrial logging and fishing town. A favored nosh stop is the **CLAM BUCKET** (4479 Victoria Quay; 250/723-1315).

LODGINGS

Eagle Nook Wilderness Resort / ★★

 BARKLEY SOUND; 250/723-1000 OR 800/760-2777 No roads lead to the wilderness oasis of Eagle Nook, and that's what makes it special. It caters to the outdoors lover who revels in luxury at the end of a rugged day of kayaking, fishing, or helicopter tours (dubbed heli-venture trips). Guests enjoy hiking the trails interlacing the resort's 70 forested acres or joining daylong nature cruises to see harbor seals, cormorants, and bald eagles in the Broken Group Islands, part of Pacific Rim National Park Reserve. Back at the resort, guests feast on satisfying West Coast or continental meals from comfortable window seats before a roaring fire. All 23 rooms have ocean views; two one-bedroom cabins have water views and sitting areas, fireplaces, and kitchenettes. The resort's oceanside deck features a hot tub and adjacent cedar-hut sauna. Most visitors arrive via the resort water-taxi service from Port Alberni's Harbour Quay; local floatplane operators offer direct flights to and from Seattle. Rates include all meals and water taxi from Port Alberni. *$$$$; AE, MC, V; no checks; 2-night min; open June–Sept; www.wildernessgetaway.com; accessible by boat or floatplane only.*

Bamfield

This tiny fishing village of 500, home to a marine biology research station, is reached by boat (see introduction to this section), or via logging road from Port Alberni or Lake Cowichan. Bamfield bustles when the **WEST COAST TRAIL** summer season hits—it's the end of the line for the world-famous, five-to-seven-day, mettle-testing wilderness trail that's so popular hikers have to make reservations. For reservations and information on this spectacular, coast-hugging trek, contact **TOURISM BC** (250/387-1642 or 800/435-5622). To get a taste, do a day hike within earshot of the pounding surf of Bamfield. The **BAMFIELD CHAMBER OF COMMERCE** (250/728-3006; bamcham@cedar.alberni.net) has information.

LODGINGS

Wood's End Landing Cottages / ★

380 LOMBARD ST, BAMFIELD; 250/728-3383 OR 877/828-3383 The four cute cedar-shake-and-driftwood cabins here have a craftsman's touch. Proprietor Terry Giddens built them out of materials he beachcombed and recycled from tumbledown Bamfield buildings. The cabins and two additional suites, set among 50-year-old perennial gardens, overlook Bamfield Inlet. The hilltop Woodsman cabin and Angler suite have the best views. Cabins have two loft bedrooms and cooking facilities. It's a remote area, so bring your food (town cafes offer meals in season) and toys. A rowboat is available for guest use, and Giddens runs nature tours and fishing trips. *$$–$$$$; MC, V; no checks; woodsend@island.net; www.woodsend.travel.bc. ca; across inlet from government docks.*

Ucluelet

"Ukie" is still a little rough around the edges, as the economic staples of fishing and logging only recently began to wane. This ugly duckling is making a go at becoming a tourism swan like sister town Tofino. With the development of view-rich **AMPHITRITE POINT,** including Roots Lodge at Reef Point (see review), it's making a good start.

Budget B&B accommodations line the road into town, and offer easy access to **PACIFIC RIM NATIONAL PARK RESERVE** (250/726-4212); stop by the visitor center just inside the park entrance, off Highway 4. Three separate areas of the park allow visitors to appreciate the abundant wildlife and grand vistas of the Pacific Ocean. For hikers, the **WEST COAST TRAIL** reigns supreme (see Bamfield section). The **BROKEN GROUP ISLANDS,** accessible only by boat, attract intrepid kayakers and scuba divers. Visitors to Ucluelet have come to enjoy the expanse of awe-inspiring **LONG BEACH**. The park's lone campground, **GREEN POINT** (at the park's midway point, well marked by signs; 800/689-9025), is often full during peak times and is closed in winter.

Six miles (10 km) north of Ucluelet, the **WICKANINNISH INTERPRETIVE CENTRE** (1 Wickaninnish Rd; 250/726-4701; open daily in summer) has oceanic exhibits and an expansive view, shared by the on-site Wickaninnish Restaurant (not to be confused with the Wickaninnish Inn; see review in Tofino section).

During March and April, 20,000 gray whales migrate past the West Coast on their way to the Bering Sea, and can often be seen from shore; orcas and humpbacks cruise the waters much of the year. For close-up views, **WHALE-WATCHING TOURS** leave from both Ucluelet and Tofino; tours are easy to arrange once you arrive. The **PACIFIC RIM WHALE FESTIVAL** (250/726-4641; mid-Mar–early Apr) hosts events here and in Tofino.

RESTAURANTS

Matterson House / ★

1682 PENINSULA RD, UCLUELET; 250/726-2200 Tofino residents happily make the half-hour drive to Ucluelet for a filling, satisfying breakfast or dinner (generous helpings at reasonable prices) at casual Matterson House. Breakfast standards such as eggs Benedict and huevos rancheros make way for lunch's Matterson Monster Burger, fully loaded with bacon, cheese, mushrooms, and more. Look for Caesar salads, chicken burgers, and homemade bread—and nothing deep-fried. Dinner sees hungry hikers and residents dig into prime rib, a mixed seafood platter, or veggie lasagne. Desserts feature fruit crumbles and cheesecakes such as Kahlúa espresso. *$$; MC, V; local checks only; breakfast, lunch, dinner every day; full bar; reservations recommended; on Hwy 4 on the way into town.*

LODGINGS

Roots Lodge at Reef Point / ★

310 SEABRIDGE WY, UCLUELET; 250/726-2700 OR 888/594-7333 The Roots Lodge complex—owned by and named for the Canadian retailer—aims to be a player in the Long Beach area's highly competitive luxury class—but is not yet complete. Part of an ambitious development plan for pretty Amphitrite Point, the lodge will eventually adjoin condominiums and restaurants, connected by boardwalks. The 12-suite lodge, with a dining room where guests eat family style, has a nouveau cannery

SURF'S UP, EH?

Ever thought to hang ten in the Great White North? Canadian and California surfers alike get hyped on the excellent breaks and pristine beaches around Tofino. Legendary **LONG BEACH,** an 11-mile (17 km) crescent backed by Douglas fir forests, was first surfed by American draft dodgers who came to live rent-free on the then-isolated beach. In Canada, surfing is a winter sport: that's when tsunamis off Japan bring the year's best waves. As other tourists cuddle up to cozy fires to watch the storms, committed surfers hit the beach in thick hooded wet suits. With proper gear, the cold is kept at bay.

Winter waves are a little too wild for beginners, but sunny days after May 1 bring throngs of boys and girls of summer with their flowered shorts and surfboards to catch more mellow waves. A number of options exist for seasoned surfers or newbies wanting to give it a try:

SURF SISTER (250/725-4456 or 877/724-7873) offers supportive women-only weekend clinics or individual lessons and surf camps for men and women. "A girl's thing is where it's at," enthuses Jenny Hudnall, the school's bubbly founder. Take her word for it: she's among the best surfers, male or female, in Tofino. Taking a clinic gives newbies the pointers they need to get up on the board and stay safe in the water.

LIVE TO SURF (1180 Pacific Rim Hwy; 250/725-4464), run by longtime local surfer gal Liz Zed, offers lessons to men and women, and rents wet suits and boards.

INNER RHYTHM SURF CAMPS (250/726-2211) organizes surfing safaris: let them pack the gear, and all you have to do is hop in the van and chat with the wave-loving wahine beside you.

For those not venturing as far as Tofino, good winter surfing can also be had at **JORDAN RIVER** and **SOMBRIO BEACH,** on the West Coast Highway a couple of hours from Victoria; rent gear in town before heading out in the obligatory VW van.

—Alisa Smith

look: natural wood and chic corrugated aluminum. Twenty cabins along the beach and in the woods feature kitchenettes, loft bedrooms, custom Roots home furnishings and, in some, private hot tubs. Adventure packages include guided kayaking, surfing lessons, mountain biking, and whale-watching; but relaxing is also popular. *$$$–$$$$; AE, MC, V; no checks; rootslodge@telus.net; www.livehotels.net; follow highway through town toward lighthouse.*

A Snug Harbour Inn / ★★

460 MARINE DR, UCLUELET; 250/726-2686 OR 888/936-5222 The million-dollar view here encompasses the rugged coast and islands where harbor seals and orcas play. Through powerful binoculars in the sitting room, guests can feel they've already taken a whale-watching tour. Expect luxury: room decor is modern and original, especially in the dramatic black-carpeted Atlantis Room—popular with honeymooners—featuring a black whirlpool tub. Others favor the split-level Lighthouse Room, with the best view, round brass ships' portholes, and picture windows. Two new rooms in a separate building feature one wheelchair-accessible unit. *$$$$; MC, V; no checks; 2-night min; info@awesomeview.com; www.awesomeview.com; through village and right on Marine Dr.*

Tauca Lea by the Sea / ★★

1971 HARBOUR CRES, UCLUELET; 250/726-4625 OR 800/979-9303 Kayak from the door of this resort complex set on a peninsula on the edge of Ucluelet. Each of the one- and two-bedroom apartment-sized suites has a full kitchen and private balcony, gas fireplace, and Barkley Sound views. Spacious, light-filled suites are decorated with leather armchairs and handcrafted furniture; a few higher-end units have hot tubs. Tauca Lea is operated by the highly regarded Coast hotel chain. At press time, plans were in place to open a spa and art gallery. The Boat Basin Restaurant, with patio dining, stunning marina views, and Pacific Northwest menu, is already getting rave reviews from locals. Pets welcome. *$$$$; AE, MC, V; no checks; info@coasthotels.com; www.coasthotels.com; from Hwy 4 turn left onto Seaplane Base Rd.*

Tofino

At the end of Highway 4 is the wild West Coast, drawing surfers, kayakers, and nature lovers from all over the world. Tofino has been called "the next Whistler," as condo and hotel developments burgeon between town and Pacific Rim National Park Preserve: we only hope careful planning keeps the spirit of this special place intact. A large number of international visitors has resulted in more excellent hotels, B&Bs, and restaurants than one would expect from a town of fewer than 2,000.

People arrive at Tofino primarily by car, via the winding mountainous route of **HIGHWAY 4** (5 hours from Victoria). **NORTH VANCOUVER AIR** (604/278-1608 or 800/228-6608) flies from Seattle and Vancouver—but you'll want a car here (try Budget for rentals; 250/725-2060).

You can explore the coast with one of numerous water-taxi or whale-watching companies, by floatplane, or by kayak. **TOFINO SEA KAYAKING COMPANY** (320 Main; 250/725-4222 or 800/863-4664) offers kayak rentals, or guided tours with experienced boaters and naturalists. **REMOTE PASSAGES** (71 Wharf St; 250/725-3330 or 800/666-9833) offers guided kayak and Zodiac tours. The floatplanes of **TOFINO AIR LINES** (50 1st St; 250/725-4454 or 866/486-3247) take guests to remote sea lion caves and beaches. The Pacific Rim Whale Festival (mid-Mar–early Apr) hosts events here and in Ucluelet; contact the **TOFINO VISITORS' CENTRE** (250/725-3414; www.tofinobc.org).

A number of boat and floatplane companies offer day trips to the calming pools of **HOT SPRINGS COVE;** overnight at the six-room **HOT SPRINGS COVE LODGE** (250/670-1106 or 888/871-9977). The 12-acre **TOFINO BOTANICAL GARDENS** (1084 Pacific Rim Hwy; 250/725-1220) features displays of indigenous plant life in a scenic waterfront setting. Locals recommend the Pacific Northwest cuisine at the on-site **CAFE PAMPLONA** (250/725-1273).

Gift shops and galleries are sprinkled throughout town. The longhouse of the **EAGLE AERIE GALLERY** (350 Campbell St; 250/725-3235 or 800/663-0669) sells art by Tsimshian Roy Henry Vickers. **HOUSE OF HIMWITSA** (300 Main St; 250/725-2017 or 800/899-1947) features First Nations masks, jewelry, and gifts. **FIBER OPTIONS** (120 4th St, Ste 5; 250/725-2192) displays hemp and organic cotton products—from linenlike dresses to natural soaps. Get organic coffee and baked treats at the **COMMON LOAF BAKE SHOP** (180 1st St; 250/725-3915).

RESTAURANTS

The Pointe Restaurant / ★★★★

OSPREY LN AT CHESTERMAN BEACH (WICKANINNISH INN), TOFINO; 250/725-3100 OR 800/333-4604 In this truly outstanding environment, natural cedar posts and beams soar to a 20-foot ceiling, centered around a circular wood-burning stove with a hammered-copper hood and chimney. The restaurant is perched over a rocky headland; waves crash just outside the 240-degree panoramic windows, adding drama to your meal. Chef Jim Garraway's distinctively West Coast Canadian menu focuses on fresh, local seafood (including oysters) and produce, much of it organic. The wine list features many deserving BC vintages. An à la carte menu features Long Beach Dungeness crab, grilled wild salmon, and good vegetarian selections, but many diners opt for one of the multicourse tasting menus. All is artfully presented. *$$$$; AE, DC, MC, V; no checks; breakfast, lunch, dinner every day; full bar; reservations recommended; info@wickinn.com; www.wickinn. com; off Hwy 4, 2½ miles (4 km) south of Tofino.* &

RainCoast Café / ★★

120 4TH ST, TOFINO; 250/725-2215 Husband-and-wife team Lisa Henderson and Larry Nickolay operate one of the best restaurants in Tofino. The decor of their intimate nine-table room is sleek and modern—as is the menu, which focuses on seafood, often with an Asian twist. The fish bowl features prawns, clams, mussels, halibut, shrimp, and more in a mango and jalapeño-scented coconut broth. Also popular are halibut in Thai red curry sauce, and salmon in a spring roll wrapper. Vegetarians are well catered to: look for wild rice cakes with cashew-ginger sauce or Thai-seared tofu over buckwheat soba noodles. For dessert, try chocolate peanut butter pie. *$$$; AE, MC, V; local checks only; dinner every day; beer and wine; reservations recommended; near First Street Wharf.* &

The Schooner on Second / ★

331 CAMPBELL ST, TOFINO; 250/725-3444 This historic central Tofino restaurant—part red clapboard building, part old schooner—has been satisfying hungry locals for a quarter of a century, in various incarnations. These days, the menu features fresh local seafood, island-grown produce, and plenty of hearty meat dishes. Try the Catface Bouillabaisse, a medley of finfish and shellfish in tomato-scented saffron broth. Breakfasts of huevos rancheros, smoked-salmon bagels, and eggs Benny with homemade hollandaise are popular; you can even order a whole Dungeness crab, fresh off the boat. *$$$; AE, MC, V; no checks; breakfast, lunch,*

*dinner every day; full bar; reservations recommended; vicsdine@island.net; www.
schoonerestaurant.com; downtown, at corner of 2nd St.*

LODGINGS

Cable Cove Inn / ★

201 MAIN ST, TOFINO; 250/725-4236 OR 800/663-6449 Tucked at the edge of
Tofino's town center, Cable Cove Inn looks past the wharves to Meares Island, and
out to the open sea. Seven rooms exude a distinguished air, with mahogany-toned
furniture and green marble whirlpool tubs or private outdoor hot tubs. All rooms
have fireplaces and private, ocean-facing decks; one corner unit has a wraparound
balcony. Steps lead to the sheltered cove below the inn. A cozy wood-burning stove
in the upstairs lounge is surrounded by cushy leather couches; continental breakfast
is served, and a full kitchen is available for guests. Northwest Coast Native prints
grace the walls. The inn is adults-only, but a townhouse a few yards from the beach
welcomes families. *$$$; AE, MC, V; local checks only; 2-night min in summer (inn),
1-week min (townhouse); cablecin@island.net; www.cablecoveinn.com; west end of
Main St.*

Clayoquot Wilderness Resorts / ★★★

QUAIT BAY; 250/726-8235 OR 888/333-5405 This two-part resort offers
among the most luxurious wilderness adventures on the West Coast. Choose
from a room at the main lodge, which floats on a barge on the edge of Clay-
oquot Sound, or camp out at the inn's Wilderness Outpost on the banks of the Bed-
well River. The lodge, 30 minutes by water taxi from Tofino, is moored next to a
large tract of private wilderness with plenty of room to ride, hike, kayak, fish, or
take a whale-watching tour. Come evening, guests dine on fine Pacific Northwest
cuisine at a long table by the fire or at intimate tables for two. A full-service spa and
exercise room add to the pampering. Accommodations at the Wilderness Outpost
put a whole new spin on camping: guests sleep in roomy safari-style tents outfitted
with Oriental rugs, propane heaters, handmade furniture, and private decks, and
dine on fresh seafood and fine wine on china and crystal. By day, explore the wilder-
ness by horse (each guest is assigned a mount for the duration of their stay), moun-
tain bike, canoe, or kayak; then relax in the wood-fired hot tub or sauna and enjoy
the deep silence. Rates at both locations include all meals and transportation from
Tofino. *$$$$; AE, MC, V; no checks; 2-night min; closed Nov–Apr; info@wild
retreat.com; www.wildretreat.com; accessible only by boat or floatplane.*

InnChanter / ★★★

HOTSPRINGS COVE; 250/670-1149 Locals recommend this unique,
luxuriously refitted 1920s boat moored in Hotsprings Cove. The ele-
gant floating B&B done in velvet and candelabras features five state-
rooms, a salon with wood-burning fireplace, and a 700-square-foot sundeck. Host
Shaun Shelongosky is a brilliant and quirky conversationalist, and an excellent chef
who attends to all guest meals (included). He specializes in sumptuous vegetarian
fare, but uses a lot of fresh seafood—look for a salmon barbecue on deck—and for
meat eaters prepares such dishes as whiskey-stuffed chicken marinated in honey and

garlic. Best, when the hot springs day tours leave, you can row ashore and have them to yourself. Reach the *InnChanter* by floatplane or water taxi, booked at the government dock in Tofino. *$$$; no credit cards; checks ok; www.innchanter.com; take floatplane or water taxi to Hotsprings Cove.*

Middle Beach Lodge / ★★★

400 MACKENZIE BEACH RD, TOFINO; 250/725-2900 The wonderful rooms at this oceanfront complex are spacious, and decor is tasteful and homey: wicker chairs, crisp natural-toned bedding and curtains, cheery colors. Each of the two main lodges has a large lobby graced with weathered antiques and a massive stone fireplace. The Lodge at the Beach is kept romantic and quiet with an adults-only policy; the rates are refreshingly low. The newer, pricier, Lodge at the Headlands welcomes kids over 12 and includes some suites with full kitchens. Palatial, two-level oceanfront cabins have large waterside patios, but are kept down-to-earth with plank flooring recovered from historic Victoria warehouses. Immense windows let in light, and kitchenettes allow independence. The lodges serve a continental breakfast of home-baked goods and jams, and high season brings fresh-fish barbecues and nightly dinners in the restaurant. *$$–$$$$; AE, MC, V; no checks; 2-night min Jul–Aug; lodge@middlebeach.com; www.middlebeach.com; south of Tofino off Hwy 4.*

Paddlers' Inn Bed and Breakfast

320 MAIN ST, TOFINO; 250/725-4222 This simple, white, wood-sided establishment—Tofino's original hotel—has been brightened with red-and-blue window boxes and trim, and turned into a kayaking mecca. The on-site headquarters of the Tofino Sea Kayaking Company allows guests to arrange guided tours landing at the Vargas Island Inn (see review) and other coastal pit stops. In the convivial bookstore and coffee bar, owner Dorothy Baertt dispenses useful information along with espresso. Upstairs, five simple rooms (sharing two baths) are appointed with Scandinavian-style furniture. Some overlook the waterfront. Guests serve themselves from the kitchen continental breakfast bar. *$; MC, V; checks OK; closed Nov–Feb; paddlers@island.net; www.tofino-kayaking.com; just above 1st St dock.*

Vargas Island Inn

VARGAS ISLAND; 250/725-3309 Kayakers are keen on the Vargas Island Inn: after a couple of hours' paddling from Tofino, twin gables on a venerable Tudor-style home prompt cries of "Land ho!" Accommodation choices are rooms in the inn, three cabins, or camping in the cedar woods above the beach. It's best described as rustic, with no phones, and propane or solar-generated power. Take the 2-mile (3 km) hike to the pretty beach at Ahous Bay, a provincial park; then return for a soothing wood-fired sauna on the beach. The hosts have a long history here: Neil Buckle's grandfather was a lighthouse keeper on a nearby island at the beginning of the 20th century, and settled here in 1910. Bring your own food: the cabins have cooking facilities, and a there's a communal kitchen in the lodge. The hosts also sell some supplies. *$; V; checks OK; accessible by water taxi or private boat from Tofino.*

Wickaninnish Inn / ★★★★

 OSPREY LN AT CHESTERMAN BEACH, TOFINO; 250/725-3100 OR 800/333-4604 Set dramatically on the edge of the crashing surf, the Wickaninnish is known for pioneering the concept of winter storm-watching, and has been touted from the time it opened in 1996: it is one of few places on Vancouver Island booked full year-round. Service is impeccable, and the artful environment includes architectural details by master carver Henry Nolla, handmade driftwood chairs, and furniture custom-crafted from recycled old-growth fir. All rooms feature ocean views, fireplaces, private balconies, and double soaker tubs set before ocean-view windows. The soothing, full-service Ancient Cedars Spa downstairs offers aromatherapy, hydrotherapy, massage, facials, and other pamperings. The crowning glory is The Pointe Restaurant (see review). Some rooms allow pets. *$$$$; AE, DC, MC, V; no checks; info@wickinn.com; www.wickinn.com; off Hwy 4, 3 miles (5 km) south of Tofino.* &

The Comox Valley

The Comox Valley, on the island's middle east coast, has skiing in winter, water sports in summer, a quaint shopping district in the town of Courtenay on Highway 19A, and scenic access to Powell River on Highway 101 on the mainland Sunshine Coast via BC Ferries (250/386-3431 or 888/223-3779 in BC only; www.bcferries.bc.ca). Skiers flock to **MOUNT WASHINGTON** (250/338-1386), where five chairlifts operate for more than 140 days of the year, and cross-country skiers enjoy 25 miles (40 km) of track.

Fanny Bay

Blink and you'll miss this tiny hamlet. For a true roadhouse experience, stop at the **FANNY BAY INN** (7480 W Island Hwy; 250/335/2323)—or the FBI, as it is more familiarly known. The mostly standard pub fare menu features Fanny Bay Oysters, panfried or in burgers.

Courtenay and Comox

These adjacent towns are the hub of the valley. Courtenay's in-town browsing ranges from antique, kitchenware, and retro clothing shops to the thought-of-everything **TRAVELLER'S TALE SHOP** (526 Cliffe Ave, Courtenay; 250/703-0168). Break for a delectable treat at **HOT CHOCOLATES** (238 5th St, Courtenay; 250/338-8211). Locals recommend the eclectic eats at **ATLAS CAFE** (250 6th St, Courtenay; 250/338-9838). Dinosaur fossils found in the Comox Valley are on display at the **COURTENAY AND DISTRICT MUSEUM AND PALAEONTOLOGY CENTRE** (207 4th St, Courtenay; 250/334-0686). The ferry to Denman Island leaves from Buckley Bay, about 10 minutes south of Courtenay.

RESTAURANTS

The Old House Restaurant / ★★

1760 RIVERSIDE LN, COURTENAY; 250/338-5406 This carefully restored, rambling pioneer home rests amid colorful flower gardens and verdant trees. Across the river, a working sawmill sets the tone of old Courtenay. Inside, four roaring stone fireplaces beckon on cool days, while exposed beams and garden views create a charming ambience. Start dinner at this white-tablecloth establishment with mushrooms stuffed with shrimp, crab, spinach, and cream cheese. Next, opt for a fresh BC salmon fillet baked on a cedar plank and sparked with homemade fruit salsa, or panfried maple rye pork medallions. The chocolate kilo cake is rich white chocolate sponge and mocha mousse; also good is butter pecan bread pudding with warm caramel rum sauce. *$$–$$$; AE, DC, MC, V; no checks; lunch, dinner every day; full bar; reservations recommended; just before 17th St Bridge to Comox.* &

LODGINGS

Greystone Manor / ★

4014 HAAS RD, COURTENAY; 250/338-1422 Extensive English flower gardens are the jewel of this establishment; enjoy the vibrant colors out your window and contemplate views of the Strait of Georgia and the Coast Mountains beyond. Greystone Manor is a welcome alternative to a night in a featureless highway hotel. Three guest rooms with private baths (one is across the hall) give you all the basics—though ours was fairly small. Decor of this 1918 home is highlighted with antiques; the common parlor has a cozy woodstove and original hardwood floors. *$$; MC, V; no checks; greyston@island.net; www.bbcanada.com/1334.html; 2 miles (3 km) south of Courtenay off Hwy 19A.*

Kingfisher Oceanside Resort and Spa / ★

4330 S ISLAND HWY, ROYSTON; 250/338-1323 OR 800/663-7929 Kingfisher's spa, where massages and facials start at $80 (Canadian), features ocean-themed treatments such as seaweed body wraps and sea body polishing. Therapists offer massages in one of 15 treatment rooms or on the beach. Outdoor adventure trips and fitness/stretch classes are also available, though the best features here are the whimsical ones: the Pacific Mist Steam Room (women only) looks like a mermaid's cave; the outdoor swimming pool has a miniwaterfall for massaging your neck and shoulders. The new beachfront suites, with sea-themed decor, ocean views, beach-rock fireplaces, and kitchens, are the nicest accommodations. Oceanview rooms, set back from the sea, are blander but good value. The restaurant offers seafood standards, vegetarian choices, and some spa cuisine. *$$$–$$$$; AE, DC, DIS, MC, V; no checks; 2-night min on weekends in suites; info@kingfisherspa.com; www.spa2001.com; in Royston, 5 miles (8 km) south of Courtenay off Hwy 19A.*

Campbell River and North Vancouver Island

The north end of Vancouver Island sees raw industrial towns abutting unpopulated wilderness featuring plenty of outdoor pursuits, from Hemingway-worthy fishing expeditions to spectacular hiking.

Campbell River

If you're here, you're probably fishing: Campbell River is known as the "salmon capital of the world." Bag your limit of Tyee, chinook, pink, or chum salmon pretty much year-round on one of many **FISHING CHARTERS** located on the waterfront.

Fly-fishing the river for pinks is gaining popularity. Seattle's **KENMORE AIR** (800/543-9595) flies directly to local fishing lodges. From Vancouver, **AIR CANADA** (888/247-2262) and **PACIFIC COASTAL AIR** (800/663-2872) serve Campbell River's airport.

The **MUSEUM AT CAMPBELL RIVER** (470 Island Hwy; 250/287-3103) is one of the island's best small museums, featuring intriguing displays of First Nations art and artifacts. The museum gift shop is a good place to pick up First Nations art and jewelry. For more art, and traditional dance performances in summer, check out the **WEI WAI KUM HOUSE OF TREASURES** (1370 Island Hwy; 250/286-1440). It's set in a beautiful longhouse building, incongruously tucked behind a shopping mall. Locals like the fresh pastas at **FUSILLI GRILL** (220 Dogwood St; 250/830-0090).

During August's **SALMON FESTIVAL**, this mall-rich town of 30,000 is abuzz with famous and ordinary fisherfolk. The **VISITOR INFO CENTRE** (1235 Shoppers Row; 250/287-4636) can provide info on the festival, as well as on the region's trails and dive sites.

STRATHCONA PROVINCIAL PARK (about 30 miles/48 km west of town on Hwy 28; 250/954-4600) is a place of superlatives. It contains Canada's highest waterfall as well as Vancouver Island's tallest mountain, and offers a wide range of landscapes, including a glacier, alpine meadows and lakes, and large stands of virgin cedar and Douglas fir. Mountaineers and rock climbers get their thrills here. Easily accessible by road, the park has campgrounds and boat-launching facilities at Buttle Lake. The park also has fine trout lakes and an extensive trail system for backpacking. An information kiosk is open in summer.

RESTAURANTS

Koto Japanese Restaurant / ★★

80 10TH AVE, CAMPBELL RIVER; 250/286-1422 It makes sense: a very fresh sushi bar in the middle of fishing country. Chef Takeo (Tony) Maeda has single-handedly developed the locals' taste for nigiri. Teriyaki is a big seller too—beef, chicken, or salmon—but look for more exotic food from the deep, such as freshwater eel, flying-fish roe, and octopus. It's a nice meal, especially if you pull into town late. *$$; AE, MC, V; no checks; lunch Tues–Fri, dinner Tues–Sat; full bar; reservations recommended; behind HSBC Bank building.*

LODGINGS

Painter's Lodge / ★★

1625 MCDONALD RD, CAMPBELL RIVER; 250/286-1102 OR 800/663-7090 Fishing is the raison d'être of this lodge run by the reputable Oak Bay Marine Group of Victoria, but whale- and bear-watching tours, a pool, a hot tub, and tennis courts appeal to nonanglers, and you couldn't ask for a prettier location. Prime suites in the main lodge overlook Discovery Passage and Quadra Island. At 5am, the hotel is abustle with eager fishers, and the sounds of Boston whalers can be heard. Strive to catch the big one here, and maybe your photo will join the historic row in the plush lobby. Relax in the Fireside Lounge or pub to hear stories of ones that got away. Fare in the Legends dining room is not especially inspired, but fresh-caught fish and seafood staples help compensate. Ask about fishing packages. A free 10-minute water taxi runs to April Point Lodge, Painter's sister resort on Quadra Island (see review in Discovery Islands section). *$$$–$$$$; AE, DC, MC, V; no checks; only fishing packages Jul–Aug; open Apr–Oct; obmg@pinc.com; www.obmg.com; 2½ miles (4 km) north of Campbell River.*

Strathcona Park Lodge / ★

EDGE OF STRATHCONA PARK, CAMPBELL RIVER; 250/286-3122 This lakeside lodge is a mecca for those who enjoy healthful, active living. The instructors here know their stuff and gently guide even the most timid of city slickers through such outward-boundish pursuits as hiking, kayaking, rock climbing, outdoor survival skills, and orienteering. The ropes course is a hit with kids, and isn't as scary as it looks. Accommodations in the log-and-timber lodge and self-contained lakefront cabins with kitchens are modest but attractive, and everywhere on-site are jaw-dropping views of Upper Campbell Lake and surrounding peaks. Meals are hearty, healthy, and served buffet style at long tables in the Whale Room. Ask about family, youth, elder, and wellness packages. *$$; MC, V; checks OK; limited facilities Dec–Feb; info@strathcona.bc.ca; www.strathcona.bc.ca; 28 miles (45 km) west of Campbell River.*

Gold River

With the recent closure of the mill in this pretty town, many inhabitants are moving on—though retirees are moving in. From here, the utilitarian MV *Uchuck III* (on Government Dock, 7 miles/12 km past the village at the end of Hwy 28; 250/283-2325; reservations required) embarks on one- and two-day cruises along the largely uninhabited western coast of Vancouver Island, a breathtaking stretch of rugged inlets and islands. On the way to the remote settlements of **KYUQUOT** or **ZEBALLOS** the boat stops at logging camps, fish farms, and settlers' cabins; you spend the night in a bed-and-breakfast and return the next day.

Port McNeill and Telegraph Cove

The major asset of this remote area is its proximity to all things wild and wonderful—boating, diving, whale-watching, salmon fishing, and tide pooling. The inspiring **U'MISTA CULTURAL CENTRE** (Front St; 250/974-5403) in the nearby town of Alert Bay is only a short ferry ride from the Port McNeill waterfront (schedules are available there); learn about potlatch traditions of the local Kwakwaka'wakw people. Whale-watching (June–Oct) is superior from the town of **TELEGRAPH COVE**, a village built on stilts 13 miles (21 km) south of Port McNeill. **STUBBS ISLAND CHARTERS** (24 Boardwalk; 250/928-3185 or 800/665-3066) offers cruises to view orcas in Johnstone Strait. Old homes in Telegraph Cove have been gaily painted and revived as overnight lodgings. Contact **TELEGRAPH COVE RESORT** (250/928-3131 or 800/200-4665) for reservations. Kayaking and bear-watching tours are also available.

LODGINGS

Hidden Cove Lodge / ★★

TELEGRAPH COVE; 250/956-3916 Sandra and Dan Kirby's waterfront retreat on 8-½ acres is interspersed with walking trails and offers back-to-basics relaxation. Eight rooms with private baths are furnished in pine, and rates include home-cooked breakfasts such as eggs Benedict or pancakes. In summer (mid-May–mid-Oct) Sandra and the lodge staff cook dinners of Dungeness crab, baby back spareribs, salmon, halibut, or other hearty favorites. Two two-bedroom waterfront cottages with fireplaces and full kitchens allow families to cook on their own. A five-bedroom, two-bathroom guest house is the newest addition. The Kirbys can sign you up with local companies for kayaking, whale-watching, heli-fishing, or grizzly viewing; two outdoor hot tubs await your return. A wraparound, window-lined lounge allows for quiet contemplation of herons, eagles, and whales, or a chance to mix with other guests. *$$$; MC, V; no checks; hidcl@island.net; www.hiddencovelodge.com; 20 minutes south of Port McNeill; take Beaver Cove/Telegraph Cove cutoff from Hwy 19.*

Port Hardy

A harborfront promenade sweetens the stay in this gritty town at the end of Highway 19. Logging, fishing, and mining have long provided most of the employment here, though these industries are fading. Travelers stop to catch the acclaimed 15-hour **BC FERRIES CRUISE** north to Prince Rupert on the mainland or to Bella Coola and Bella Bella on the midcoast (reservations required: 250/949-6722 or 888/223-3779). Book summer accommodations well in advance: ferry passengers tend to fill the hotels.

The famous Edward S. Curtis silent film *In the Land of the War Canoes*—part anthropology, part fanciful potboiler—was filmed in nearby **FORT RUPERT** (off Hwy 19, 3 miles south of Port Hardy; 250/949-6012), a good place to purchase authentic First Nations art.

Some well-traveled islanders call **CAPE SCOTT PROVINCIAL PARK** (37 miles/63 km west of Port Hardy; 250/954-4600) the most beautiful place on earth. A 1½-hour drive over gravel roads west of Port Hardy, and a 45-minute walk take you to spectacular San Josef Bay; camping is permitted. A longer, more challenging hike leads to the island's northern tip; the **PORT HARDY VISITOR INFO CENTRE** (7250 Market St; 250/949-7622) provides information.

LODGINGS

Oceanview Bed & Breakfast / ★

7735 CEDAR PL, PORT HARDY; 250/949-8302 Locals judge this well-appointed executive-style home to be one of the best B&Bs in the area. One of the large rooms has a sweeping ocean view; another has two beds, a reading nook with an ocean view, and an en suite bathroom (the other two share a bath). All three feature homey touches such as substantial bedsteads in brass or wrought iron, pine armoires, down duvets and wall stenciling, as well as TVs (but no phones). The shore is a 10-minute walk, and hosts Bob and Chantal Charlie serve a hearty breakfast of home-baked bread, muffins, cold meats and cheeses, fruit, yogurt, and more. *$$; cash only; oceanvue@island.net; www.island.net/~oceanvue; follow Hwy 19 through town, left on Market St, left on Cedar Pl.*

SOUTHERN INTERIOR
AND THE KOOTENAYS

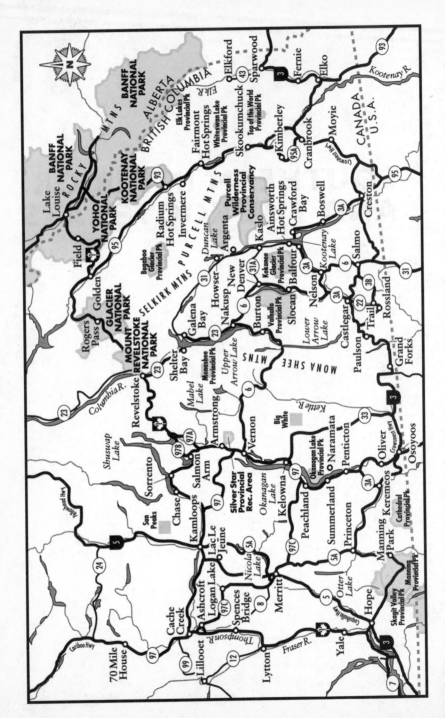

SOUTHERN INTERIOR AND THE KOOTENAYS

This corner of Canada is vertically defined. Draw away from the West Coast's ocean beaches, and you run smack up against range upon range of mountains: the Coast Mountains, the Cascades, the Monashees, the Selkirks, the Purcells, and the Rockies.

Which isn't to say there aren't open spaces among the peaks. In the Okanagan region, for example, gently undulating benchland is intensely planted with vineyards above broad, blue lakes. Wilder corners of the Okanagan's semidesert burn with yellow sagebrush blossoms.

Traversing the Kootenays—that land where the peace-and-love generation abides—the going gets extreme. Many valleys in this cedar-and-pine-carpeted wilderness receive only a shaft or two of sunlight in winter months—too many pinnacles get in the way. To make sense of the Kootenays, imagine four mountain ranges puckered together like an accordion's bellows. No wonder roads in this part of BC scatter off in more directions than windblown fireweed seeds. When the Rockies finally present themselves, they project a stateliness that makes the rest of the pack look like peaks in training.

ACCESS AND INFORMATION

Almost every main road or highway in BC intersects with the **TRANS-CANADA HIGHWAY** (Hwy 1) at some point. In this region, **HIGHWAY 1** covers 372 miles (600 km) between Hope and the BC-Alberta border. Other major highways here include **HIGHWAY 5** (Coquihalla Hwy), the most direct route between Hope and Kamloops; **HIGHWAY 97C**, linking Highway 1 to the Okanagan; **HIGHWAY 97** through the Okanagan; and **HIGHWAY 3** (Crowsnest Highway), which skirts the U.S. border.

Kamloops is served by **AIR CANADA JAZZ** (888/247-2262; www.flyjazz.ca) and **VIA RAIL** (800/561-8630 or 888/VIA-RAIL; www.viarail.ca). **GREYHOUND CANADA** (800/231-2222; www.greyhound.ca) offers daily service along the Trans-Canada Highway and through the Okanagan. **KELOWNA INTERNATIONAL AIRPORT** (250/765-5125) is served by **AIR CANADA JAZZ, HORIZON AIR** (800/547-9308; www.horizonair.com), and **WESTJET** (800/538-5696; www.westjet.com).

Kamloops and the Thompson River

As the Coquihalla Highway (Hwy 5) winds north from Hope to Kamloops, it passes through semiarid desert and gently rolling highlands, paralleling the Fraser and Thomson Rivers. Wide-open views of sagebrush-covered mountainsides shaped by eons of weathering and lonesome beauty prevail here, as do famous fly-fishing waters.

Merritt

The waters around Merritt (population 7,200) are famous for producing fighting rainbow trout. **FLY-FISHING** is the style of choice, and "A lake a day as long as you stay" is no idle boast for the Nicola Valley. Close to 50 percent of BC's total freshwater sportfishing occurs in the Thompson-Nicola region: the Thompson and Nicola Rivers are historic salmon-spawning tributaries of the Fraser River, and the smaller tributary streams are where rainbow trout, Dolly Varden, and kokanee lay their eggs.

It's the lakes, however, that attract anglers. Chapperon, Douglas, and Nicola Lakes have long been noted for ample fish stocks. **NICOLA LAKE**, renowned for its depth, is said to harbor more than 20 varieties of fish, some weighing up to 20 pounds. The easiest to reach, it's located about 4 miles (7 km) east of Merritt on Highway 5A. Use the boat launch at **MONCK PROVINCIAL PARK** (off Hwy 5A, 13½ miles / 22 km north of Merritt; 250/851-3000) for access. Licenses, tackle, and sound advice are available at **MCLEOD'S DEPARTMENT STORE** (2088 Quilchena Ave; 250/378-5191).

LODGINGS

Sundance Ranch / ★★

KIRKLAND RANCH RD, ASHCROFT; 250/453-2422 At this dude ranch set in high plateau country, east of the Thompson River, low ranch buildings of dark-stained wood contain handsome pine-paneled rooms. The outdoor pool is grand, and there's a tennis court, but the real attraction is the corral. A large herd of horses is available for two daily rides—morning and late afternoon—with groups split by experience. Excellent evening meals are often served on the patio; Saturday nights there's a dance. Rustic public rooms set the scene for drinks, parties, and games. You'll sleep well, breathing the cool, sage-scented air. Sundance operates on the American Plan, with everything included: accommodations, meals, and use of all facilities. Children can stay in their own "Kids Wing" or with their parents. Weekends, May through September, the ranch is booked months in advance. *$$; MC, V; no checks; open mid-Mar–Oct; sundance@wkpowerlink.com; www.sundance-ranch.com; 5 miles (8 km) south of Ashcroft.* &

Kamloops

Kamloops (population 80,000) is the largest urban area along the Trans-Canada Highway between Vancouver and Calgary. It sprawls across the weathered slopes of the Thompson Plateau through which runs the mighty Thompson River, whose north and south arms converge here. With the forest industry waning, Kamloops (a Shuswap First Nations term for "meeting of the waters") is turning its attention to tourism. Fly-in fishing lodges are located on many of the 700 lakes in the region, where anglers cast for trophy-sized **KAMLOOPS TROUT**, a unique strain that puts on an eye-popping, acrobatic performance when hooked. The **KAMLOOPS VISITOR INFO CENTRE** (1290 W Trans-Canada Hwy; 250/372-7722 or 800/662-1994; www.venturekamloops.com) can provide a list of lodges.

SOUTHERN INTERIOR THREE-DAY TOUR

DAY ONE: Rise early for a walk along Kelowna's lakefront promenade, stopping to enjoy breakfast al fresco at **THE GRAND OKANAGAN.** Drive over a unique floating bridge to **MISSION HILL FAMILY ESTATE** for a winery tour. Continue south along Lake Okanagan to **OSOYOOS,** stopping at one of the many roadside stalls to enjoy a picnic of your favorite variety of fruits and freshly squeezed juices. Walk off lunch along the interpretive boardwalk at the **DESERT CENTRE,** protecting Canada's only true desert. It's a three-hour drive through the wilderness of the Monashee Mountains to Rossland. Check in to your room at the **RAM'S HEAD INN** before descending to town, where you'll enjoy a casual dinner at the always-popular **SUNSHINE CAFE.** Spend the rest of the evening curled up in front of a log fire with a good book at the inn.

DAY TWO: After breakfast at the Ram's Head, drive to Nelson for a self-guided walking tour of the historic downtown precinct. Grab lunch at the **RICE BOWL RESTAURANT** (301 Baker St; 250/354-4129). After lunch, drive north on Highways 3A and 31 to **AINSWORTH HOT SPRINGS.** Trade your clothes for a bathing suit and relax in the resort's public soaking pools. Drive the short distance along Kootenay Lake to **KASLO.** Find a table on the patio at the **ROSEWOOD CAFE** for an early dinner, and revel in your newfound sense of well-being. Enjoy the scenic evening drive on Highway 31A between Kaslo and New Denver, and let your eyes do the work as you sightsee along Slocan and Upper Arrow Lakes. Catch the ferry across Upper Arrow Lake from Galena Bay to Shelter Bay. It's only a short drive from Shelter Bay to **MULVEHILL CREEK WILDERNESS INN** south of Revelstoke. Walk through the surrounding forest to enjoy the extraordinary stillness.

DAY THREE: After a leisurely breakfast in the dining room, head for the inn's beach on **UPPER ARROW LAKE.** When you're ready, drive into **REVELSTOKE** and stop at **THE 112** for a weekday lunch. Point your car's nose up the **MEADOWS IN THE SKY PARKWAY** in nearby **MOUNT REVELSTOKE NATIONAL PARK.** Have plenty of film ready to record the profusion of wildflowers. Look east toward Rogers Pass and the massive Illecillewaet Glacier. That's where you're headed once you return to the Trans-Canada Highway (Hwy 1). Pull over at the top of the pass for a visit to the uniquely shaped information center. Primed by a crash course here in the century of mountaineering tradition in **GLACIER NATIONAL PARK,** enjoy the drive past the peaks to **GOLDEN.** Drive on to **EMERALD LAKE LODGE** in **YOHO NATIONAL PARK** for dinner and the night.

RESTAURANTS

Peter's Pasta / ★

149 VICTORIA ST, KAMLOOPS; 250/372-8514 What Peter's Pasta lacks in ambience, it makes up for in sauces. It's easy to overlook this narrow cafe in downtown Kamloops, but the locals rave about the homemade pasta that Peter puts on your plate. Given that its popularity outweighs its modest size, you may encounter a short wait. Diners choose from four pastas and a generous range of sauces, including clam, tomato, and alfredo. Small or large portions come with tasty garlic bread. Salads are extra, but you may not need one. The dessert menu includes several Italian ices and chocolate mousse. *$; MC, V; no checks; lunch Tues–Fri, dinner Tues–Sat; beer and wine; reservations recommended; downtown.*

LODGINGS

Riverland Motel / ★

1530 RIVER ST, KAMLOOPS; 250/374-1530 OR 800/663-1530 When visiting Kamloops, you'll want to stay beside the banks of the South Thompson River. Not just because rivers have a soothing quality to them, but also because the centrally located Riverland Motel is a traveler's dream. It offers quick access to major highways and is within walking distance of dining, shopping, and scenic attractions. Request a riverside room for a view of the weathered palisades that rise above the South Thompson's north shore. Opened in 1991, the motel's 58 standard rooms are clean and pleasantly furnished, with refrigerators in all rooms. Other soothing amenities include an indoor pool and whirlpool, laundry facilities, and complimentary continental breakfast. For a few dollars more, choose a kitchen unit or an executive suite, complete with Jacuzzi. Let the kids loose on the broad lawn between the hotel and the river. The adjacent Storms Restaurant features a full lunch and dinner menu of creative pastas, seafood, ribs, and racks, best enjoyed on the sheltered patio overlooking the river. *$–$$; AE, MC, V; no checks; riverlandmotel@kamloops.com; www.riverlandmotel.kamloops.com; from Hwy 1, take exit 374 toward Jasper, then the first left.* &

Sun Peaks Resort

Sun Peaks truly arrived as a four-season mountain resort when Canada Post officially awarded it with a postal code of its own in 1998. Now that's recognition. (Originally known as Tod Mountain, major investor Nippon Cable chose the name to reflect a change in image, from regional ski hill to international year-round recreation destination.) The finishing touches have since been put on five artfully configured slopeside hotels that anchor the village. Decidedly European, the atmosphere feels like a neighborhood, and nothing seems out of place. From November to April, Sun Peaks hosts skiers and snowboarders who come for the crisp, dry powder snow on **MOUNT TOD**. It features 2,890 feet of vertical drop, 1,000 acres of marked skiable terrain (and 10,227 skiable acres total), and nine lifts. Another part of the draw is the wide variety of other winter activities, including snow-cat skiing, sleigh rides, dogsledding, and snowshoeing. In summer, the ski lifts transport hikers and cyclists to high alpine meadows, while golfers stride the fairways of the resort's golf course.

SKIING THE SOUTHERN INTERIOR

An influx of European miners in the late 1890s was responsible for introducing skiing to British Columbia. Olaus Jeldness, a legendary Norwegian who had prospected all over the West, organized a ski race on **RED MOUNTAIN,** despite claiming it was "far too steep and the snow conditions too extreme" for a proper race. After hiking to the summit, Jeldness gave the starting signal before strapping on his own skis and schussing off after the rest of the field. Despite their head start, Jeldness easily passed the other racers to become Canada's first national champion.

Over the ensuing century, skiing grew in popularity with the locals as lifts were strung up over 30 mountains through the region. In the late 1980s and early 1990s, many of these community-owned ski hills were sold to out-of-town developers, armed with grand expansion plans that inevitably included bigger and faster lifts, accommodations, residential subdivisions, and golf courses. **SUN PEAKS,** north of Kamloops, was typical. "In the past," resident Olympic gold medalist Nancy Greene Raine recalls, "this was perceived as a place where a small group of rugged, wild, and woolly skiers went to enjoy some of the best powder skiing in the province." Mirroring other resorts throughout the interior, expansion at Sun Peaks has changed attitudes. "We see ourselves as the second step on a two-step holiday—mega and mellow," Greene Raine explains. "More visitors are coming to Canada on a two-week ski holiday. They take a week at Whistler-Blackcomb for the big hit, then they want to come to a resort where they can get the feeling for small-town Canada. We're a small resort where you actually meet people."

Mirroring the evolution of Sun Peaks as a world-class, four-season resort are the three major Okanagan resorts, **SILVER STAR, BIG WHITE,** and **APEX MOUNTAIN,** as well as **PANORAMA,** in the Purcell Mountains. Transformations are continuing unabated: **FERNIE ALPINE RESORT**—legendary as a laidback, powder-filled hideaway—doubled its size in 1999; **KICKING HORSE MOUNTAIN RESORT** replaced Golden's small local hill in 2000–01; while future plans at **POWDER SPRINGS**—known for decades as Mount Mackenzie Ski Hill to the locals—include linking an expanded resort to nearby Revelstoke by gondola.

Some things will never change, though. Whether you choose to vacation in a luxurious Sun Peaks slopeside condo or make the trek up a gravel road to lost-in-time **WHITEWATER** from Nelson, you are guaranteed a bigger bang for your buck than at better-known Whistler and Banff and, more important, some of the world's best lift-served powder skiing.

—Andrew Hempstead

Thirty miles (50 km) northeast of Kamloops on Highway 5 and Tod Mountain Road, Sun Peaks takes about 45 minutes to reach from Highway 1, but it's a pleasant drive along the North Thompson River. The resort, operated by the **SUN PEAKS RESORT CORPORATION** (3150 Creekside Wy, Ste 50; 250/578-7842 or 800/807-3257; info@sunpeaksresort.com; www.sunpeaksresort.com) is self-contained, so you won't need your car once you're here.

LODGINGS

Father's Country Inn / ★★

TOD MOUNTAIN RD, HEFFLEY CREEK; 250/578-7308 A stay at Father's Country Inn, a bed-and-breakfast hideaway 4 miles (7 km) west of Sun Peaks Resort, confirms that no matter how far you roam, you'll still find surprises. Proprietor David Conover Jr. comes by his profession honestly. For decades, his parents ran a popular resort on one of BC's Southern Gulf Islands. There, Conover learned the art of making serious coffee and killer pancakes (by prior arrangement, he also prepares dinners). Conover fills plates and cups to the brim for guests who anticipate long days in the outdoors. Chances are, the conversation may turn to the photographic print business he runs from his rambling six-room inn. Conover markets not only his resort legacy but the images his father took of Marilyn Monroe, whom Conover Sr. befriended while on a photo shoot for the U.S. Army in Los Angeles during World War II. Her young face is displayed throughout the inn. Father's Country Inn's plain exterior masks the richness of its interior, which includes a swimming pool. Guest rooms, each named for a season and decorated accordingly, are equipped with fireplaces and sumptuous tubs. Snow trekkers appreciate the inn's fully equipped ski room complete with drying racks, lockers, and a waxing bench. *$; MC, V; checks OK; mmfathers@telus.net; www.dconover.com; from Hwy 5, follow Tod Mountain Rd 14 miles (23 km) toward Sun Peaks Resort.* &

Nancy Greene's Cahilty Lodge / ★

3220 VILLAGE WY, SUN PEAKS RESORT; 250/578-7454 OR 800/244-8424 Having perfected their hostelry skills at Whistler in the 1980s, Nancy Greene Raine and her husband, Al, migrated east across the Coast Mountains to Sun Peaks and opened the Cahilty Lodge, named for a pioneer ranching family. It's a condominium hotel, and room amenities range from those with modest cooking facilities (coffeemaker and microwave) to fully equipped suites that sleep eight. A hot tub and an exercise room are downstairs, plus a ski and mountain-bike room. Also downstairs is Macker's Bistro, arguably the most consistent restaurant at Sun Peaks. Laidback and mellow in tone, the menu is imaginative, if limited, and skewed toward families and fun. Adjacent to the lodge is the resort's sports center with swimming pool and weight room, outdoor skating rink, and tennis courts. The lodge's centerpiece is Greene Raine's trophy cabinet in the entranceway. If the sociable hostess takes a shine to you, she might let you try on her Olympic gold medal. *$$–$$$; AE, DC, JTB, MC, V; no checks; info@cahiltylodge.com; www.cahilty lodge.com; east on Creekside Wy to Village Wy.* &

Sun Peaks Lodge / ★★

3185 CREEKSIDE WY, SUN PEAKS RESORT; 250/578-7878 OR 800/333-9112 Some lodgings are so special that, once in your room, you simply want to throw yourself into a comfy chair and revel in your good fortune. Such is the ambience at Sun Peaks Lodge. Built by Germany's Stumbock Club, the trappings are worthy of those in a quality European hotel, from harmonious decor to comfy terry-cloth robes. Wrap yourself in one and head for the sauna, steam room, and hot tub. Many of the 44 rooms feature windowed breakfast nooks. Step from the lodge to the high-speed quad chairlifts that—winter and summer—ascend Mount Tod. Also here is the Val Senales fine dining room, where a buffet breakfast (included in winter) and multicourse dinners are prepared. Tucked into the ground floor is the resort's best-kept secret: the Stube, a traditional European wine cellar where lunch, après-ski, and late-evening fare is served amid cozy wood paneling. *$$–$$$; MC, V; no checks; info@sunpeakslodge.com; www.sunpeakslodge.com; in the heart of Sun Peaks Resort.* &

The Okanagan Valley

Beloved for a mild climate and an unparalleled variety of landscape that ranges from desert to snowcapped peaks, the Okanagan has something for everyone: swimming, boating, golfing, hiking, skiing and snowboarding, orchards, and vineyards.

From Highway 1 east of Kamloops, at Monte Creek, Highway 97 runs south to the head of Lake Okanagan at Vernon. As you head down the valley, you'll encounter orchards and vineyards, testimony to the presence of some of the best fruit- and vegetable-growing land in the world, while dozens of parks surround 79-mile (128 km) Lake Okanagan. As you pass through the lush Oliver and Osoyoos regions, near the Canadian-U.S. border, you'll find spectacular backcountry, with the remains of old mining settlements dotting the highway.

Vernon and Silver Star

For decades, Vernon (population 35,500) was one of the largest fruit-producing towns in the British Empire, thanks to the abundance of freshwater for irrigation—also great for swimming on those hot days. One of many farms surrounding the city, **DAVISON ORCHARDS** (Bella Vista Rd; 250/549-3266) encourages visitors with a self-guided walk, wagon tours, a petting zoo, a cafe, and, of course, bountiful fresh produce for sale. High above Vernon, **SILVER STAR MOUNTAIN RESORT** (Silver Star Rd, east of Hwy 97; 250/542-0224 or 800/663-4431; info@skisilverstar.com; www.silverstarmtn.com) is the main draw for winter recreation in the north Okanagan, offering 2,500 feet of vertical drop, 2,725 acres of skiable terrain, and 10 lifts. Cross-country skiers and snowshoers head out along 50 miles (80 km) of forested trails. In the 1990s, the establishment of the National Altitude Training Centre added status to the resort. With its Victorian-style mining-town atmosphere and an extensive schedule of summer activities, Silver Star has cemented Vernon's reputation as a four-season destination. For local information, contact **VERNON TOURISM** (Hwy 97 S; 250/542-3256 or 800/665-0795; info@vernontourism.com; www.vernontourism.com).

RESTAURANTS

Eclectic Med Restaurant / ★

3117 32ND ST, VERNON; 250/558-4646 Since May 1996, British-import Andrew Fradley's Eclectic Med Restaurant has been winning the hearts (and palates) of epicureans in Vernon. Mediterranean as much in style and attitude as menu influence, EM was voted "best romantic dinner" in the north Okanagan in 1999. Small wonder. One look at its Mexican clay tile flooring, butter-colored walls, wooden shutters, heavy jute sailcloth curtains, wovenback beech-wood chairs, and birch tables, and you know you've entered another realm. Be transported by Caribbean, Thai, East Indian, and other cross-pollinating influences. Chilean sea bass, Moroccan lamb, salmon Tropicana, and Calypso pork top the extensive menu. Combinations harken back to North African–born Fradley's dozen years in Portugal before arriving in Canada. Cocktails are served casually in heavy-based tumblers, as are hefty 7-ounce portions of wine. Try the hand-mixed sangria, fresh-squeezed margaritas, or traditional martinis. The wine list is notable for a selection of reserve wines from Okanagan estate wineries. *$$; AE, MC, V; no checks; lunch Mon–Fri, dinner every day; full bar; reservations recommended; at 32nd Ave in central Vernon.* &

LODGINGS

Pinnacles Suite Hotel / ★★

SILVER STAR MOUNTAIN RESORT; 250/542-4548 OR 800/551-7466 The Pinnacles Suite Hotel, poised on the open slopes above Silver Star's mountain village, has the best seat in town. Guests ski, snowboard, mountain bike, or walk from their door onto the slopes. Come and go as you please: each suite has its own private entrance, a spacious living area, full bath, and kitchen, plus an outside ski locker. Rooftop hot tubs are the perfect place to relax after a day on the slopes. Sharing the facilities is the adjacent Kickwillie Inn (same contact information), Silver Star's original day lodge renovated to hold seven self-contained suites. Suites 1 and 2 enjoy mountain views and, along with Suite 3, boast fireplaces. In this sublime setting, the absence of television is a blessing, particularly for those who treasure time together. If you really can't unplug, a TV room is located beside the ski waxing room. *$$; AE, MC, V; checks OK; reserve@pinnacles.com; www.silverstarmtn.com; 14 miles (22 km) northeast of Vernon.*

Kelowna

Sprawled on the sides of Lake Okanagan's hourglass waist, Kelowna ("grizzly bear" in the native Okanagan dialect) is the largest (population 100,000)—and liveliest—city in the valley. Wineries dominate this area, with more than 40 open for tours and tastings. Right downtown, the Okanagan's oldest winery, **CALONA WINES** (1125 Richter St; 250/762-3332), is a good starting point for a wine-country tour. South of downtown, **MISSION HILL FAMILY ESTATE** (1730 Mission Hill Rd, Westbank; 250/768-7611) was voted Winery of the Year at the 2001 Canadian Wine Awards. Perched high atop a ridge, a massive expansion program completed in 2001 included a Wine and Food Interpretation Centre.

Kelowna is a jumping-off point for outdoor fun, whether at the lakeside beach or exploring the nearby **MONASHEE MOUNTAINS**. The area also boasts 16 of the 39 **GOLF COURSES** between Vernon and Osoyoos. Most open in March, and some years golfers play into November. Kelowna even has its own version of the Loch Ness monster: Ogopogo. No one claimed a $2 million reward offered through 2001 for providing proof of his existence, but enough sightings over the past 100 years have kept cryptologists searching and locals selling T-shirts. For more information on wineries and other activities, contact the **KELOWNA VISITOR INFO CENTRE** (544 Harvey Ave; 250/861-1515 or 800/663-4345; kvb@kelownachamber.org; www.kelownachamber.org).

RESTAURANTS

de Montreuil Restaurant / ★★★

368 BERNARD AVE, KELOWNA; 250/860-5508 Okanagan-born Grant de Montreuil introduced more than just original cooking to Kelowna's restaurant scene; his elegant downtown dining room offers a fixed-price menu of "Cascadian cuisine" with a twist. Guests can choose two to four courses from appetizers (perhaps wild boar pâté with plum chutney), salads (sautéed hot and cold spinach with chorizo), soups (halibut broth with wild mushrooms), and entrees (wild sockeye glazed with lavender jelly, or roasted free-range chicken infused with tarragon and lime on a bed of potatoes, carrots, and snow peas). The kitchen favors locally grown organic ingredients. Everything on the menu (which can change overnight) bursts with flavors and seasonings. Never expect the same thing twice at this 80-seat gallery restaurant. Diners can order à la carte, but shouldn't. Lunch is more casual: sandwiches, burgers, and pizzas. Bottled microbrews only, and a wide representation of local estate, cottage, and farmgate wines. *$$–$$$; AE, MC, V; no checks; lunch Mon–Fri, dinner every day; full bar; reservations recommended; demontreuil@shaw.ca; corner of Pandosy St.* &

Doc Willoughby's Downtown Grill

353 BERNARD AVE, KELOWNA; 250/868-8288 Doc Willoughby's has a pub atmosphere, but it isn't a pub. Darren Nicoll and Dave Willoughby (the restaurant is named for his grandfather) stripped this 1908 landmark in downtown Kelowna to the walls, then rebuilt it with wood salvaged from a century-old site in Vancouver's Gastown. Hardwood floors, solid maple tables, and a prominent bar (featuring six custom-brewed draft beers) provide the atmosphere; upscale pub fare and regular live music define the flavor. Traditional dishes such as shepherd's pie share the billing with Arizona egg rolls. Cedar plank salmon is the priciest item on an affordable menu. Pizza, pasta, stir-fry, and hot-baked chocolate chip cookies with two scoops of vanilla ice cream and fudge sauce are other highlights. The wine bar features more than a dozen BC's Vintners Quality Alliance (VQA) wines. Triple your fun with a flight of three 2-ounce samples. *$–$$; AE, MC, V; no checks; lunch Mon–Sat, dinner every day; full bar; reservations not necessary; docwilloughby@shaw.ca; near Pandosy St.* &

Fresco / ★★★

1560 WATER ST, KELOWNA; 250/868-8805 Renowned chef Rod Butters arrived in the Okanagan via the Chateau Whistler and Vancouver's Pacific Palisades in the summer of 2001 to open the latest addition to Kelowna's fine-dining scene. With his wife, Audrey Surrao, at his side and the shell of a downtown heritage building to work with, he has created a wonderfully understated atmosphere to enjoy some of the valley's finest culinary creations. The menu is typically West Coast, but more adventurous than you'd expect this far from Vancouver, combining lots of organically grown produce with Asian flavors and a European flair for presentation. The four-course, fixed-price Signature Collection showcases the best of Butters's cooking, with a short but varied choice of entrees that changes with the seasons. For dessert, try the chocolate mashed potato brioche with burnt almond caramel sauce and raspberry compote. *$$; AE, DC, MC, V; no checks; dinner Tues–Sun; full bar; reservations recommended; 2 blocks from Harvey Ave.* &

LODGINGS

The Grand Okanagan / ★★★★

1310 WATER ST, KELOWNA; 250/763-4500 OR 800/465-4651 "The Grand," as the staff of the red-roofed resort refer to it, could as easily be in San Diego as on the east side of Lake Okanagan. Its modernist design presents a dignified profile that harkens back to Kelowna's Mission past and proclaims the city's triumphant emergence as an international destination. Rooms in the 10-story main tower have panoramic views—all are decorated in soft pastel shades. Suites on the 9th (smoking) and 10th (nonsmoking) floors enjoy their own lounge, where complimentary continental breakfast is served. Robes, newspapers delivered to the door, and underground parking are other perks. Even the standard rooms are superior to anything else in the valley: floor-to-ceiling windows open onto small balconies, and coziness abides. Plan excursions to the nearby wine country, alpine resorts, bike trails, or golf courses. Or use the resort's fitness facility: spa, hot tubs, saunas, and indoor/outdoor pool. Two restaurants, two lounges, and an Internet cafe complement the adjacent Lake City Casino. Beware the masked one-arm bandits. *$$$$; AE, DC, DIS, MC, V; business checks OK; reserve@grandokanagan. com; www.grandokanagan.com; 5 blocks north of Hwy 97.* &

Hotel Eldorado / ★★★

500 COOK RD, KELOWNA; 250/763-7500 Built further south along the lake for an émigré Austrian countess in 1926, the Eldorado was barged to its present location in 1989, but burnt to the ground the following year. Owner Jim Nixon meticulously restored the grand dame with hardwood floors, a stone fireplace, antique furnishings, and a great collection of Okanagan memorabilia. Each of the 20 rooms features elegant touches such as antique armoires; most have private balconies with water views, some even sport Jacuzzis. Make summer reservations at least three months in advance; the Eldorado's waterfront location and private marina are extremely popular. Winter packages include breakfast and lift tickets to nearby Big White Ski Resort (see below). The hotel's restaurant fare is consistently excellent. Breakfast in its sunroom is an extremely pleasant way to wake up, particularly when a soft breeze wafts in off the lake. The local vineyards are well represented on the Eldorado's dining and bar menus. *$$–$$$; AE, DC, MC, V; no checks; info@el doradokelowna.com; www.eldoradokelowna.com; 4 miles (6.5 km) south of down-town on Pandosy St.* &

Lake Okanagan Resort / ★

2751 WESTSIDE RD, KELOWNA; 250/769-3511 OR 800/663-3273 When Lake Okanagan Resort appeared on the scene in the 1980s, it had a dynamic impact on valley standards, with its lakefront location and wide-ranging facilities. For many years—and for many families—this was the place to stay, particularly in summer. All accommodations include kitchen facilities, and most sought-after are the Jacuzzi suites—each of which includes a living room, entertainment center, kitch-enette, dining area, full bath with separate bedroom and king-sized bed, Jacuzzi, and private balcony. At the north end of the property, 13 three-bedroom condos and chalets have a parklike setting. Getting around the 300-acre property can be a chal-lenge; the hillside rises steeply above the private beach and though chalets and condos have a gentler incline, they're farther from the beach. The Kingfisher Building, the resort's central facility, holds numerous eateries, including the Chateau Dining Room. The resort also boasts a marina, tennis courts, a nine-hole, par-3 golf course, and horseback riding. This is the perfect place to let everyone in the family do their own thing. *$$$; AE, MC, V; checks OK; info@okanaganresort.com; www. lakeokanagan.com; 14 miles (22 km) northwest of Kelowna.* &

Big White

BIG WHITE SKI RESORT (Big White Rd, 14 miles/23 km east of Hwy 33; 250/765-3101; bigwhite@bigwhite.com; www.bigwhite.com) is less than an hour's drive southeast of Kelowna on the western perimeter of the Monashees. This mountain village boasts the highest elevation of any winter resort in BC (5,760 feet/1,755 m), offering 2,700 feet of vertical drop, 2,565 acres of patrolled terrain, and 13 lifts, including a high-speed gondola. In winter, you can ski from the door of your con-dominium, lodge, or vehicle. But once you arrive at Big White, you have to leave your wheels behind. As the horse-drawn wagon that serves as local transportation trots by, hop on; park yourself on a hay bale and let the team of vapor-snorting Percherons do the rest.

The base area has expanded greatly in the past five years. It now offers accom-modations for up to 10,000 guests at any one time; book through **BIG WHITE CEN-TRAL RESERVATIONS** (800/663-2772; cenres@bigwhite.com; www.bigwhite.com). More than a dozen restaurants—**RAAKEL'S** and the **KETTLE VALLEY STEAKHOUSE** are best bets—dot the village, as do bars, boutiques, and rental shops.

LODGINGS

White Crystal Inn / ★★

BIG WHITE RD, KELOWNA; 800/663-2772 One of the best small resort hotels in Canada, this classic four-story chalet has grown. The addition of a new wing took it from 20 rooms to 50. So successful was the original design that Big White Resort copied it for the new Chateau Big White nearby. But they couldn't replicate the

White Crystal's impeccable location adjacent to the resort's main gondola. The White Crystal retains its intimacy. All rooms are outfitted in cedar and slate; each comes with a fireplace, two queen-sized beds, and a small kitchen. For larger groups, some rooms feature lofts with three single beds. Downstairs you'll find a sauna, ski and snowboard lockers, plus heated parking. On the lodge's main floor is a restaurant overseen by Grant de Montreuil, of Kelowna fame (see de Montreuil Restaurant above) and a more casual bistro. A generous buffet breakfast is included, served in the brightly lit bistro with woody Canadiana accents. Room service is also available. *$$; AE, MC, V; checks OK; cenres@bigwhite.com; www.bigwhite.com; on right as you enter resort.*

Penticton

Penticton, the "Peach City" (population 34,000), might just as easily be called Festival City. It always has some serious fun going on, including the rockin'-good-time August **PEACH FESTIVAL** (250/493-4055 or 800/663-5052), now in its sixth decade; weeklong wine festivals in late April and October (250/861-6654; www.owfs.com); the May **MEADOWLARK FESTIVAL** (250/492-5275), a nature festival in Penticton and nearby Okanagan Mountain Provincial Park celebrating the return of the meadowlark, a barometer species; and a jazz festival in September. The **PENTICTON VISITOR INFO CENTRE** (185 Lakeshore Dr; 250/493-4055 or 800/663-5052; penchamber@img.net; www.penticton.org) has more information on all festivals.

Oenophiles who want to plot a **WINE TOUR** itinerary (and those who simply aspire to informed conversation on the 300-plus varieties of wine produced in the region) should visit the **BC WINE INFORMATION CENTRE** (888 Westminster Ave W; 250/490-2006; www.bcwineinfo.com).

APEX MOUNTAIN RESORT is 21 miles (33 km) west of town (on Green Mountain Rd; 250/292-8222 or 877/777-2739; info@apexresort.com; www.apexresort. com). With 67 named runs, including a series of black-diamond powder chutes on the slopes below Beaconsfield Mountain (elevation 7,187 feet/2,178 m), Apex more than holds its own. It has 2,000 feet of vertical drop, 1,112 acres of skiable terrain, and five lifts.

RESTAURANTS

Granny Bogner's Restaurant / ★★★

302 ECKHARDT AVE, PENTICTON; 250/493-2711 One of the Okanagan's best restaurants is also one of the most consistent: great food, great location, great building, and desserts that alone make the trip worthwhile. Diners relax in front of the fireplace in the rambling Arts and Crafts–style house with a glass of wine or after-dinner coffee. The menu covers a broad spectrum, but it's presentation that sets Granny Bogner's apart. Entrees arrive garnished with an eye for color and shape; vegetables are artfully arranged. Chef Peter Hebel loves to play with shrimp, crab, or smoked salmon. Start with the baked oysters casino, or perhaps the bouillabaisse (a real bargain). Fillets of halibut, red snapper, or salmon Courtenay poached in white wine and glazed with hollandaise sauce comes next. Hebel's Swiss background shines in beef rouladen with red cabbage and spaetzle; also good is the chateaubriand bouquetière in béarnaise sauce. Dessert specials often use fresh local fruit. The wine list represents the best local wineries and includes a selection of Okanagan ice wines. *$$; AE, MC, V; no checks; dinner Tues–Sat; full bar; reservations recommended; 2 blocks south of Main St.* &

LODGINGS

God's Mountain Crest Chalet / ★★

4898 LAKESIDE RD, PENTICTON; 250/490-4800 At God's Mountain Crest Chalet, Martha Stewart might meet her match in owner Ulric Lejeune. Interior-designer Lejeune and his wife, Ghitta, have created the Club Med of B&Bs. The rambling Mediterranean-style mansion overlooks broad Skaha Lake and the rolling hills beyond. Inside is an eclectic blend of curios, antiques, and subtle religious iconography. Scarves drape the length of the 60-foot-long grand salon. Quiet pervades, even at breakfast, when guests gather for sumptuous epicurean buffets. Sit in the shrouded intimacy of an opium bed or at the glass-topped table where conversation swirls around Lejeune's Teutonic presence. (On request, breakfasts are served to guest rooms on silver trays.) Nine guest rooms and suites are spread over three floors. Request Suite 5: tastefully appointed, it features a raised tub with lake views. All suites open onto verandas or private balconies and are fitted with reflective glass for privacy and temperature control. A large swimming pool and hot tub (for late-night stargazing) are surrounded by gardens and orderly rows of grapevines. *$$; MC, V; checks OK; godsmountain@vacationmail.com; www.gods mountain.com; 3 miles (5 km) south of Penticton.*

Naramata

North of Penticton, the picturesque village of Naramata (population 1,000) is surrounded by vineyards and orchards. Continuing north, rugged Naramata Road ends at **OKANAGAN MOUNTAIN PROVINCIAL PARK** (east side of Lake Okanagan, 13 miles/21 km north of Penticton; 250/494-6500) with dramatic prospects. Sage-covered slopes and bleached headlands jut out into the broad lake.

RESTAURANTS

Country Squire / ★★

3950 1ST ST, NARAMATA; 250/496-5416 After 20 years at the helm of the Country Squire, chef Patt Dyck and her husband (and maître d' at the restaurant), Ron, show no sign of flagging. They've found a winning—and unique—formula. Be prepared to order your entree when you make a reservation at this small, relaxed restaurant. From there, Patt designs a five-course meal to complement your selection. Choices include beef tenderloin robed in pâté de foie gras and mushroom duxelle, then wrapped in puff pastry and served with brown and béarnaise sauces. The dish is "celebrated" tableside—a German term for carved and flambéed. Other options are Madagascar-style pork tenderloin, grain-fed Alberta beef, rack of lamb smothered in a rosemary sauce, boneless breast of French guinea fowl, Pacific prawns shelled and broiled in seasoned butter and fresh shallot sauce, and fillet of sea bass baked with basil, oregano, and artichoke hearts in edible parchment paper. An outstanding tenderloin of locally raised venison is marinated in red wine, fresh herbs, and juniper berries, then roasted and served with a black Muscat, red currant, and black currant sauce. The wine list is as deep as Lake Okanagan. *$$; MC, V; local checks only; dinner Wed–Sun; full bar; reservations required; csquire@vip.net; www.country-squire.com; follow 1st St north along lake.* &

LODGINGS

Sandy Beach Lodge & Resort / ★★

4275 MILL RD, NARAMATA; 250/496-5765 The resort's log cabins are completely booked two years in advance for July and August (priority is given to returning guests). That said, six B&B rooms in the main lodge are still up for grabs—and are a real bargain at this retreat on Lake Okanagan. Each has its own private, covered veranda overlooking the lake. Lighted tennis courts, a swimming pool, and hot tub bookend the lodge, which also houses a restaurant and a bright sitting room dominated by a fieldstone hearth. Thirteen two-bedroom cabins are scattered throughout the property, some on a swath of private beach. Each features a kitchen, comfortable living area, and a deck equipped with a barbecue. Green lawns between them are perfect for croquet. Everything is immaculate and looks as if it just opened yesterday. May and September are pleasant months to visit, when competition for the resort's rowboats and canoes is less fierce. Rates are reduced outside the busy summer months. *$$–$$$; MC, V; no checks; sandybeachresort@home. com; www.sandybeachresort.com; end of Mill Rd off Robson.* &

Oliver and Osoyoos

The 12-mile (20 km) stretch of Highway 97 between Oliver (population 5,000) and Osoyoos (population 4,800) boasts the most vibrant agricultural land in the valley. Over the past decade, this has become the preferred grape-growing region for classic European varietals like pinot noir, merlot, and cabernet franc, all of which thrive in the warm climate. The **DESERT CENTRE** (west on 146th Ave off Highway 97; 250/495-2420; www.desert.org) protects a "pocket desert," where less than 12 inches of precipitation falls annually. It is desert in the truest sense, with cacti, prickly pear, sagebrush, and rattlesnakes surviving in the dry, sandy environment. **OSOYOOS VISITOR INFO CENTRE** (Hwys 3 and 97; 250/495-7142 or 888/676-9667; tourism@osoyooschamber.ca) has regional information.

RESTAURANTS

Jacques' Wine Country Inn / ★★

34646 HWY 97, OLIVER; 250/498-4418 Jacques' Wine Country Inn is the place to taste the region's natural abundance. Chef Jacques Guerin and his wife (and manager of the inn), Suzi, have been serving it right since 1977. Seasonal vegetables grace dishes such as roast garlic and potato soup; fresh salads include sautéed apple wrapped in phyllo with goat cheese on mixed greens with balsamic vinaigrette and roasted walnuts. Inspired entrees tempt the palate: medallions of pork slowly grilled with maple syrup and garnished with gingered pear compote and port demi-glace.

Chicken and seafood are other routes to follow. *Specialite de la maison* is Jacques' pepper steak, pan seared in brandy and topped with a chardonnay-based cream sauce. Guerin's classical touch betrays his Parisian roots. The wine-cellar atmosphere is completed by a wood-beamed ceiling, built by legendary Okanagan wine pioneer Joe Busnardo. Jacques' features an extensive list of local wines. For privacy, request seating in Jacques' intimate grotto. *$$; AE, MC, V; no checks; dinner Tues–Sun (closed Oct and Jan); full bar; reservations recommended; downtown at 346th St.*

LODGINGS

Vaseux Lake Lodge / ★

9710 SUNDIAL RD, OLIVER; 250/498-0516 Billed as the smallest resort in the Okanagan, Vaseux Lake Lodge consists of four townhomes. Built in 1995, the two-story lodge's hidden beauty is revealed once you step inside and view the lake. Sunlight floods through skylights in the vaulted ceiling, as well as through floor-to-ceiling windows on the main floor. Scandinavian furnishings and down duvets provide understated warmth. The one-bedroom, one-bath townhomes are self-contained and completely outfitted, including full kitchens (groceries are available in nearby Oliver) and barbecues, but guests should arrange their own boats and beach toys. Each unit has its own library with books on the region's natural history; since 1922, Vaseux Lake has been a designated wildlife sanctuary. Each season has its own attractions. In spring and fall, bird-watchers flock here. No powerboats are allowed on the shallow 2½-mile (4 km) lake. Paddle with turtles and beavers, and watch as eagles and osprey practice fishing skills while bighorn sheep frolic on the slopes of McIntyre Bluff (bring your binoculars). *$$; MC, V; checks OK; info@vaseuxlakelodge.com; www.vaseuxlakelodge.com; south end of Vaseux Lake, one block west of Hwy 97.*

Keremeos

LODGINGS

Cathedral Lakes Lodge / ★★

CATHEDRAL PROVINCIAL PARK; 250/226-7560 (SEASONAL) OR 888/255-4453 Cathedral Lakes Resort is tucked deep in the heart of the Cascades, so getting here is half the adventure. Set below a stunning catalog of peaks, the rustic lodge may inspire you to try backcountry camping here on the Canadian-U.S. border. They do the driving on the 13-mile (21 km) restricted-access fire road that leads from Highway 3 to the lodge, 6,800 feet (2,072 m) above sea level. Hiking trails from the lodge access even higher elevations, including a 8,200-foot (2,500 m) ridge, from which you'll get views of the Cascade range's Mount Baker and Mount Rainier. Or launch a canoe on Lake Quiniscoe, one of four trout-stocked lakes close to the lodge. If you're a duo, reserve Herb Clark's circa 1930s cabin; *amore rustica* never looked so good. Ten other cabins offer a variety of room configurations, some with bunk beds and all with shared bathrooms. In the main lodge, guests enjoy more spacious, modern surroundings, but bathrooms are still shared. The lodge's all-inclu-

sive American Plan comes with pack lunches for summiteers. Book well ahead. *$$;
no credit cards; checks OK; 2-night min; open Jun–Oct; info@cathedral-lakes-
lodge.com; www.cathedral-lakes-lodge.com; turn south on Ashnola River Rd, 3
miles (5 km) west of Keremeos, then 13 miles (21 km) to lodge base camp.*

The Kootenays

The Kootenays, east of the Okanagan on Highway 3, are a world of two minds.
Yahk, a small town on Highway 3 between Creston and Cranbrook, marks the great
divide between the western and eastern hemispheres of this cranial conundrum. It's
hard to finger what exactly characterizes the difference between the west and east
Kootenays. Winter sunlight barely brushes the steep-sided valleys of the west Koote-
nays, but residents can escape cabin fever in several lively towns, such as Castlegar,
Nelson, or Trail. In contrast, a brilliant winter sun splashes cheerily down on the
broad slopes of the Columbia and Elk Valleys in the east Kootenays. Out here there
are far fewer signs of human habitation. Open grasslands stretch out on all sides
while the Rockies preside sedately above. Yet those who know this region well refer
to all of it simply as "deep country."

Throughout both the east and west Kootenay regions winds the majestic
COLUMBIA RIVER, with its source in Columbia Lake. The river flows north for
more than 186 miles (300 km) before hooking west and south to begin its long
journey—more than 250 miles (400 km)—to the U.S. border. For nearly half this
length, it widens to form **UPPER AND LOWER ARROW LAKES,** vast reservoirs of
water that moderate winter temperatures and help retain moisture in the local
atmosphere, thus greatly influencing the types of vegetation found there.

Rossland

At 3,356 feet (1,023 m) elevation, Rossland (population 4,000) is snugly perched
close to **RED MOUNTAIN SKI AREA** (3 miles/5 km northwest of Rossland on Hwy
3B; 250/362-7700, 250/362-7384, or 800/663-0105; redmtn@ski-red.com; www.
ski-red.com), legendary throughout North America for its skiing and snowboarding.
In the 1890s, when Rossland was at the peak of its gold mining boom, Red Moun-
tain hosted the first Canadian Ski Racing Championships. The mountain has since
produced two of the best women skiers to ever represent Canada, Olympic gold
medal winners Nancy Greene Raine and Kerrin Lee-Gartner. Today the resort offers
2,900 feet of vertical drop, 1,200 acres of skiable terrain, six lifts, and some of the
country's best off-piste skiing and boarding. The **BLACK JACK CROSS-COUNTRY
SKI CLUB** (Hwy 3B; 250/362-5811; www.rossland.com/blackjack) lies at the base
of Red Mountain. More than 19 miles (30 km) of tracked trails lead from a new
trailhead chalet through evergreen forests, across frozen lakes, and past abandoned
homesteads.

Stroll Rossland's steep streets to admire the solid construction of the **MINERS'
UNION HALL** (1895) on Columbia Avenue, the **FLYING STEAMSHOVEL INN**
(1898) and the **ROSSLAND LIGHT OPERA BUILDING** (1911) on Washington Street,
and **ST. ANDREW'S UNITED CHURCH** (1898) on Queen Street. The scale of the her-
itage buildings that line many of Rossland's streets reflect the boom times and glory

years of a century ago. Based at the **LE ROI GOLD MINE** (open for tours), the **ROSS-LAND VISITOR INFO CENTRE** (Columbia Ave and Hwy 3B; 250/362-7722 or 877/969-7669; chamber@rossland.com; www.rossland.com) has information.

RESTAURANTS

Sunshine Cafe / ★

2116 COLUMBIA AVE, ROSSLAND; 250/362-5070 Virtually anyone feels a bit of sunshine in Rossland's favorite little cafe, which features a range of internationally inspired foods. The food doesn't try to be fancy, just good, and there's lots of it. Start with the Malaysian egg rolls (ground beef, coconut, and spices) dipped in a plum sauce, then go on to one of the Mexican dishes, the Budgie Burger (boneless chicken breast with ham or Swiss), or curried chicken. Huevos rancheros are a breakfast favorite. Mealtimes are crowded, especially during ski season. *$; MC, V; local checks only; breakfast, lunch, dinner every day; beer and wine; reservations not necessary; mgypsy@direct.ca; just east of Queen St.*

LODGINGS

Ram's Head Inn / ★★★

RED MOUNTAIN RD, ROSSLAND; 250/362-9577 OR 877/267-4323 The Ram's Head Inn has been singled out by more than one travel guide as the place to stay in the Kootenays, despite the competition for that honor. What sets the Ram's Head apart is its cozy size—34 guests maximum—and little touches, such as a pair of slippers waiting for you at the door. The inn's slope-side setting also works in its favor. Conversation comes easily among guests as they gather for an early morning breakfast or relax on an overstuffed couch beside the towering granite fireplace after a day exploring nearby ski trails. Guests have a choice of 14 rooms with private baths; the larger ones have balconies. All are elegantly furnished with hand-hewn timber beds, maple armoires, eiderdown comforters, TVs, and telephones. The ground floor (hidden from view by snowbanks in winter) is taken up with ski lockers, a waxing room, a game room with pool table, and a sauna. A barrel-shaped hot tub steams outside. *$$–$$$; AE, DC, DIS, MC, V; checks OK; theinn@ramshead.bc.ca; www.ramshead.bc.ca; off Hwy 3B at Red Mountain Rd.*

Slocan Lake

A century ago, **NEW DENVER** (population 650) was a mining town; today it's the modest commercial hub of the Slocan Valley. Visit the town's **SILVERY SLOCAN MUSEUM** (202 6th Ave, New Denver; 250/358-2201) to get the complete picture on its pioneer past. During World War II, an internment camp at New Denver housed some 2,000 Japanese Canadians displaced from their West Coast homes.

VALHALLA PROVINCIAL PARK (west side of Slocan Lake; 250/442-4200) is a magnificent world-class wilderness area including nearly 20 miles (30 km) of the pristine wilderness shoreline of Slocan Lake. According to Norse mythology, Valhalla was a palace roofed with shields wherein lived the bravest of the slain Norse warriors. There, under the god Odin, they lived a happy life waiting for the day they would march out of the palace and do battle with the giants. The spirit of Valhalla lives on in the splendor of this portion of southeastern BC, where great palaces of rock call forth majestic images with names such as Asgard, Gimli, and Thor. The Valhalla Range is a dramatically diverse area in the Selkirks. Deep river valleys, large subalpine lakes, and magnificent granite peaks to 9,275 feet (2,827 m) grace this park. In the northwest, New Denver Glacier (9,049 feet/2,758 m) dominates the landscape. The **NEW DENVER VISITOR INFO CENTRE** (101 Eldorado St; 250/358-2719) holds a list of boat operators who transport visitors across to the park.

LODGINGS

Silverton Resort / ★

LAKE AVE, SILVERTON; 250/358-7157 You'll be pleased with this little resort in the heart of Hidden Valley. Bill Lander's cabins on the shores of Slocan Lake are a great place for water play; bring your canoe, kayak, or rowboat, or rent one. Mountain bikes are available too. This is also a great place to do nothing—just sit on the sundeck and enjoy the view. The lake is so large it remains ice-free year-round. Guest stay in one of six hemlock-log cabins—all spotlessly clean and named after mythological heroes. Four have sleeping lofts; all have kitchens and south-facing decks and are at the water's edge (though not far from the road). In winter, the fireplace in cabin 4 (Thor) adds a special touch to its charm. Also available is the 1,500-square-foot main lodge, with a washer and dryer, large country-style kitchen, living/dining area on the main floor, and two large bedrooms upstairs. It accommodates up to eight. The lakefront resort overlooking Valhalla Provincial Park is pure heaven—but plenty of others feel the same, so make July and August reservations no later than March. *$$; MC, V; checks OK; www.silvertonresort.com; on lakeshore beside Hwy 6.* &

Nakusp

Nakusp (population 1,850) occupies a crook in the arm of Upper Arrow Lake and is set squarely between the Monashee and Selkirk Mountains. This is hot spring country. Along Highway 23 between Nakusp and Galena Bay at the northern end of Upper Arrow Lake are two commercial and four wilderness springs. You can't drive to the wilderness springs in winter (backroads aren't plowed), although you can reach them on snowshoes or skis.

LODGINGS

Halcyon Hot Springs Resort

HWY 23, NAKUSP; 250/265-3554 OR 888/689-4699 In 1999, like the proverbial phoenix, Halcyon Hot Springs Resort rose from the ashes of its long-defunct predecessor, which operated here between the 1890s and 1950s. One- and two-bedroom chalets sleep up to six and are equipped with en suite bathrooms, kitchenettes, TVs, phones, and sundecks. Nearby, in the sheltering forest, are four cabins that each sleep six on twin bunks and a double futon. Cabin guests share a communal bathroom. A licensed restaurant is located in the main building. Halcyon in Greek means "calm, serene," and that's how one feels after bathing in the two hottest pools, kept at 95°F (35°C) and 107°F (42°C). The cold plunge pool is a bracing 55°F (13°C). An outdoor swimming pool (83°F/28°C) is open in summer. Mineral analysis of the water reveals a higher quantity of lithia, a natural relaxant, than any spring in this thermally active region. *$$; AE, MC, V; no checks; info@ halcyon-hotsprings.com; www.halcyon-hotsprings.com; 20 miles (32 km) north of Nakusp.* &

Kaslo

New Denver anchors scenic Highway 31A as it snakes east for 29 miles (47 km) over the Selkirk range to Kaslo (population 1,100). Along the way, it follows the railbed of the Kaslo & Slocan Railway, and passes a turn-off to the ghost town of **SANDON**, once home to 5,000 miners who worked a rich silver deposit on the lower slopes of Idaho Peak in the 1890s.

Much like the beached stern-wheeler SS *Moyie* (324 Front St; 250/353-2525; open daily, 9:30am–4:30pm mid-May–mid-Sept), this former mining hub on **KOOTENAY LAKE** (among BC's largest freshwater lakes) retains the flavor of its glory years. The steamer was affectionately known as "the sweetheart of the lake" in her heyday.

RESTAURANTS

Rosewood Cafe / ★★

1435 FRONT ST, KASLO; 250/353-7673 The Rosewood has a loyal clientele of grown-ups (and kids) who visit from as far afield as Spokane, Washington. Reservations are a must in summer, when tourists flock to Kaslo. The fact that chef Grant Mackenzie does much of his cooking outdoors on an 8-foot barbecue helps. You'll smell the Rosewood long before you reach its white picket fence. Since it opened in 1994, the capacity has expanded to 125 seats, 55 of which are on a spacious patio overlooking Kootenay Lake. Each year the menu is completely revised. Many dishes are available in both half and full size, because portions are typically large. Everything is made fresh daily and tastes like it, from mayonnaise to bread to sauces. Alberta prime rib, local venison, blackened BC red snapper, and jambalaya are specialties. Vegetarian selections, such as tortellini with curried tomato sauce, reflect chef Mackenzie's multicultural influences. A fresh sheet has 8 to 10 daily specials. The Rosewood prides itself on the depth (and breadth) of its wine and cocktail menu. *$$; MC, V; local checks only; lunch, dinner every day, brunch Sun (closed Jan); full bar; reservations recommended; rosewood@netidea.com; at east end of Front St.* &

Ainsworth Hot Springs

Ainsworth Hot Springs is a sleepy spot on Highway 31, about 12 miles (19 km) south of Kaslo and 30 miles (50 km) north of Nelson. It was a boomtown during the heyday of silver, zinc, and lead mining in the Kootenays in the 1890s. Today, if it weren't for the hot springs, it's likely that few travelers would slow down through the small community perched above **KOOTENAY LAKE**, which at almost 99 miles (160 km) long is one of BC's largest freshwater lakes.

AINSWORTH HOT SPRINGS RESORT (10 miles/16 km north of Balfour on Hwy 31; 250/229-4212 or 800/668-1171; reserve@hotnaturally.com; www.hotnaturally. com) boasts a most unusual setting: a former mine shaft entrance into which several steamy springs vent. Hot water drips from the rough-hewn granite ceiling and flows waist-deep through a narrow, horseshoe-shaped tunnel into the resort's large outdoor pool. Mist trapped in the tunnel thickens the air, further augmenting the subterranean experience. Mineral deposits left by hot springs that seep down the sides of the tunnel have coated the walls with a smooth, ceramic-like glaze in shades of white, red, and green. The overall effect is mind bending. Water inside the caves reaches 111°F (44°C) or hotter; in the nearby glacier-fed plunge pool it's a frigid 39°F (4°C). Water in the swimming pool is a calming 95°F (35°C). Lodgings and a restaurant are available.

Crawford Bay

The tiny community of Crawford Bay (population 200), accessible from Balfour on Highway 3A via the world's longest free ferry ride, is home to many artisans, including Canada's only manufacturer of traditional straw brooms. Crawford Bay is popular with golfers for the picturesque and challenging **KOKANEE SPRINGS GOLF COURSE** (16082 Woolgar Rd; 250/227-9226; info@kokaneesprings.com; www.kokaneesprings.com).

LODGINGS

Wedgwood Manor / ★★

16002 CRAWFORD CREEK RD, CRAWFORD BAY; 250/227-9233 OR 800/862-0022 On 50 acres that tilt west toward the Selkirks, this lovely 1910 board-and-batten house is one of the finest lodgings in southeastern British Columbia. Downstairs are a dining room and a parlor with a fireplace (where afternoon tea is served). All six guest rooms have private baths. The four spacious upstairs rooms open onto a quiet, comfortable reading room; the Charles Darwin Room and the Commander's Room get most afternoon sun. The room off the parlor is tiny, but has a garden view from the double bed. In summer, the large front porch is a pleasant spot from which to gaze out over the lawn and flower gardens to Kokanee Glacier across the lake. The owners have taken over the former servants' quarters next door. $$; MC, V; checks OK; open Apr–mid-Oct; wedgwood@ netidea.com; www.bctravel.net/wedgwood; east of Nelson on Hwy 3A, take Balfour ferry to Kootenay Bay. &

Nelson

Nestled in a valley on the shore of **KOOTENAY LAKE** south of Balfour, Nelson (population 9,700) sprang up with the silver and gold mining boom in the late 1890s and has retained its Victorian character. Its main streets have changed little in over a century; more than 350 heritage homes and commercial buildings are listed in this picturesque city. Pick up a map (or join a free guided tour in summer) at the **NELSON VISITOR INFO CENTRE** (225 Hall St; 250/352-3433; www.discovernelson.com). Built on a hillside above the Kootenay River, Nelson's steep streets are best scaled in sturdy shoes. For the grandest overall view of Nelson, stroll to the vista point in **GYRO PARK** (corner of Park and Morgan Sts), on a hillside just east of the town center. The park has picturesque gardens and a wading pool. The lookout has a panoramic vista of the town, Kootenay Lake, and the rock and ice formations that rise above.

An interesting pictorial exhibit of the region's history is at the **NELSON MUSEUM** (402 Anderson St; 250/352-9813; open year-round). The entire town turns into an art gallery, with the work of around 100 local artists exhibited in shops, restaurants, and galleries during the **NELSON ARTWALK** (250/352-2402; June–Aug); pick up a map at the Visitor Info Centre. Nelson has raised afternoon browsing to a fine art. In addition to the many galleries, downtown offers a plethora of other interesting shops. Outdoor enthusiasts stop at Canada's only **PATAGONIA** factory outlet (333 Baker St; 250/352-6411). For art and crafts by regional artists, visit the **CRAFT CONNECTION** (441 Baker St; 250/352-3006). The **KOOTENAY BAKER** (295 Baker St; 250/352-2274) boasts one of the best selections of health foods in the region, including organic baked goods.

The mountains surrounding Nelson are a mecca for hikers, backcountry skiers, and sightseers; a popular destination is **KOKANEE GLACIER PROVINCIAL PARK** (18 miles/29 km northeast of Nelson off Hwy 3A; 250/825-4421). Your initial reaction to **WHITEWATER SKI & WINTER RESORT** (12 miles/19 km south of Nelson on Hwy 6; 250/352-4944 or 800/666-9420, 250/352-7669 snow report; info@skiwhitewater.com; www.skiwhitewater.com) in the Selkirk Mountains ultimately depends on what's important to you in a downhill skiing/snowboarding vacation. In an age of on-slope sushi bars and handcrafted microbreweries at the base of the lifts, Whitewater represents a Zen approach to ski development; it's basically four ski lifts strung up in the wilderness. Or you might see it as big peaks; a ton of light, dry powder; and some rudimentary, no-nonsense lifts to get you to the top. Whitewater's high base elevation of 5,400 feet (1,640 m) ensures plentiful snow (40 feet/13 m annual average), few midseason thaws, 1,300 feet of vertical drop, and 2,000 acres of skiable terrain. The resort is also home to the **WHITEWATER NORDIC CENTRE** and 11 miles (18 km) of groomed cross-country skiing trails.

RESTAURANTS

All Seasons Cafe / ★★

620 HERRIDGE LN, NELSON; 250/352-0101 In business since 1995, All Seasons Cafe is downtown, but on a narrow lane that takes a while to find. A storybook ambience envelops those who finally reach its doors. For a quick meal, ask for a seat near the bar. Sip a microbrew while you marvel at the smooth texture of the gravlax appetizer. Otherwise, ask for a table in the garden; overhead heaters ensure warmth even on cool spring or fall evenings. Art in the main dining room prompts an opinion should conversation lag. All Seasons's professed style of "Left Coast Inland Cuisine" leads to seriously scented dishes, such as maple-infused Pacific salmon served on risotto and smothered in a fresh basil vinaigrette. A steady stream of fresh sage-and-oregano bread arrives by the basket (ask to take a loaf home). Finish with a green tea brûlée with hazelnut biscotti. Sunday brunch features delicacies such as an asparagus and Brie flan with Italian figs and warm honey. *$$; MC, V; local checks* *only; dinner every day, brunch Sun; full bar; reservations recommended; allseas@ netidea.com; www.allseasonscafe.com; between Hall and Josephine Sts.* &

Fiddler's Green / ★

2710 LOWER SIX MILE RD, NELSON; 250/825-4466 Summer dining is best, but regardless of the season, this is Nelson's favorite spot for a special-occasion dinner. Locals may quibble over whether the food is the best in town, but they agree unanimously that this old estate house has the best atmosphere and garden dining. Choose from three intimate dining rooms and one larger area (if the season calls for inside dining, ask to sit next to the fireplace). As the seasons change, chef Mark Giffin ushers in new menu offerings such as a warm roasted winter vegetable and goat cheese tart. Though it serves many reliable chicken, beef, pork, and lamb entrees, Fiddler's Green caters to a growing local fondness for vegetarian and seafood dishes. Try crisp artichoke and chickpea falafel on a bed of steamed spinach with quinoa tabbouleh and lemon parsley yogurt. The delicious house salad is a blend of locally grown mixed greens tossed with pumpkin seeds and slices of poached pear, drizzled with a Gorgonzola and cranberry vinaigrette. After savoring the salmon and prawn cakes accompanied by watercress mayo and crispy leeks, who needs dessert? As overseen by hosts Harald and Lynda Manson, service here is understated and cheerily attentive. *$$; MC, V; checks only; dinner Wed–Sun, brunch Sun; full bar; reservations recommended; mail@fiddlersgreen.ca; www.fiddlers green.ca; north on Hwy 3A.*

LODGINGS

Inn the Garden

408 VICTORIA ST, NELSON; 250/352-3226 OR 800/596-2337 This B&B is where many Nelson residents book their out-of-town guests: high praise indeed. Toronto ex-pats Lynda Stevens and Jerry Van Veen bought this Victorian home, only a block from Main Street, and decorated it in a garden theme. Each room is named for a tree. Fir is the smallest and the only one with a private bath (the downside is that it adjoins the noisy bathroom shared by the other four rooms on the second floor). North-facing rooms enjoy views of Nelson's waterfront. Upstairs, the Tamarack Suite occupies the third floor. Complete with a small kitchen, sitting room, and bath, it's roomy enough for two couples to share. The best deal is the adjacent three-bedroom bungalow. Although the terraced grounds are landscaped, the bungalow's flower-festooned backyard is tops. Stevens stocks the bungalow kitchen for breakfasts but leaves the rest of the meals for guests to arrange. If you run low on Stevens's homemade granola or fresh-baked muffins, hop next door to the main house to replenish the larder. Ask about special rates on Whitewater lift tickets. *$$; AE, MC, V; checks OK; innthegarden@subpub.net; www.innthegarden.com; 1 block south of Baker St.*

Willow Point Lodge

2211 TAYLOR DR, NELSON; 250/825-9411 OR 800/949-2211 You'll feel quite welcome in Anni Mühlegg's rambling, three-story 1920 Edwardian home perched on a hill amid 3½ spacious acres. The living room features a large stone fireplace; breakfast is served in the sumptuous dining room or on the open deck in summer. Of the five guest rooms, the spacious Green Room is tops: it sports a large, private, covered balcony looking out toward the Selkirk Mountains and Kootenay Lake. All rooms feature private baths. Over the past several years the already parklike setting has been further enhanced with the planting of hundreds of perennials. Enjoy the garden from the cool of a peaceful gazebo. A walking trail leads from the house to three nearby waterfalls, the farthest being a pleasant 30-minute stroll. In winter, Whitewater ski packages are available. After a day in the powder, a soak in Willow Point's large outdoor spa is guaranteed to soothe aches and pains. Note: The lodge fills quickly in summer; reserve well in advance. *$$; MC, V; local checks only; willowpl@uniserve.com; www.pixsell.bc.ca/bcbbd/4/4000193.htm; 2½ miles (4 km) north of Nelson.* &

Kimberley

Like many foundering mining towns in the 1970s, Kimberley (population 7,000), on the west side of the broad Columbia Valley, looked to tourism and—like Leavenworth, Washington—chose a Bavarian theme to bolster its economy. Since the 2001 closure of the Cominco zinc mine, Kimberley's largest employer, tourism is more important than ever to the local economy. Accordion music is played on loudspeakers at the center of the **BAVARIAN PLATZL** (the town's three-block walking street). For a quarter, a yodeling puppet pops out of the upper window of Canada's largest cuckoo clock. With so many Bavarian-themed restaurants in one place, competition among chefs is of Wagnerian proportions. If you're shopping for some goodies for your picnic lunch (or dinner at your condo), head for **KIMBERLEY SAUSAGE AND MEATS** (360 Wallinger Ave; 250/427-7766).

At 3,650 feet (1,113 m), Kimberley is the highest incorporated city in Canada. From this height, views of the snowcapped Rockies are stunning. The **HERITAGE MUSEUM** (105 Spokane St; 250/427-7510) has an excellent display of the town's mining history and memorabilia. Gardeners shouldn't miss the teahouse, greenhouse, and immaculately kept **COMINCO GARDENS** (306 3rd Ave; 250/427-2293), once maintained by Cominco and now by the city, on the grounds of the Kimberley District Hospital. A footpath leads from the Platzl to the gardens.

KIMBERLEY ALPINE RESORT (Gerry Sorenson Wy; 250/427-4881 or 800/258-7669; info@skikimberley.com; www.skikimberley.com) west of town has more than 50 downhill runs, 2,465 feet of vertical drop, 1,800 acres of patrolled terrain, nine lifts, and some of the longest night-lit runs in North America. There are 18 miles (30 km) of Nordic trails, most of which are groomed daily. A frenzy of nonstop construction currently characterizes the resort, where a slopeside Marriott hotel anchors the base village.

RESTAURANTS

Old Bauern Haus / ★

280 NORTON AVE, KIMBERLEY; 250/427-5133 Tony and Ingrid Schwarzenberger, who built the House Alpenglow (see review), brought a 360-year-old Bavarian farmhouse to Kimberley and reassembled it. As in the Alpenglow, wood is everywhere. In a town where Bavarian flavor is as heavy as Sacher torte, this is the genuine article.

You'll feel as if you've stepped through a time warp. Heidi and her grandfather might just as easily be sitting at one of the hand-carved tables. The menu beautifully reflects Kimberley's Bavarian feel: goulash soups, Wiener schnitzel, raclette, *maultaschen* (ravioli stuffed with spinach and ricotta), spicy Debrecziner sausage, apfelstrudel, and homemade ice cream. In winter, the rough-hewn but artfully arranged wood-plank walls ooze warmth. In summer, mountain breezes whisper among the tall sunflowers in the brightly hued garden, where patio tables are set. *$$; MC, V; local checks only; dinner every day (closed 2 weeks each Nov and Apr); full bar; reservations recommended; luis@cyberlink.bc.ca; left off Gerry Sorenson Wy.* &

LODGINGS

House Alpenglow / ★★

3 ALPENGLOW CT, KIMBERLEY; 250/427-0273 OR 877/257-3645 The three guest rooms at this B&B are spacious, quiet, and lovingly furnished. The wooden ambience is everywhere, even the ceilings. All rooms feature king-sized beds; two have en suite baths. Room 3 has a private entrance to the outdoor hot tub and yard. (In this forested setting, guests are apt to find themselves sharing the yard with foraging wildlife, such as deer or bears.) Breakfast shows that Merna Abel loves to cook. Smells of fresh croissants and muffins fill the morning air, enticing guests. Abel's jams and jellies sweeten the feast. After a plateful of bratwurst and cheese on homemade pumpernickel or rye bread, you may not need to eat again until supper. Halfway between downtown Kimberley and Kimberley Alpine Resort, Alpenglow is several minutes downhill from the ski and hiking trails. If you're not inclined to drive to town for dinner, the Old Bauern Haus (see review) is across the street. *$; MC, V; checks OK; alpenglo@rockies.net; www.kimberleybc.net/alpen glow; west side of Gerry Sorenson Wy, near Trickle Creek Golf Resort.*

Inn West/Kirkwood Inn / ★

840 NORTH STAR DR, KIMBERLEY; 250/427-7616 OR 800/663-4755 Three miles (5 km) uphill from Kimberley, adjacent to Trickle Creek Golf Resort and Kimberley Alpine Resort, is the Inn West/Kirkwood Inn. Guests can choose one- or two-bedroom hotel rooms (Inn West) or condominium suites (Kirkwood Inn). The fully equipped condos have full kitchens, gas fireplaces, and Jacuzzis, as well as access to laundry facilities and a sauna, hot tub, and heated swimming pool (seasonal). Each condo has a balcony with barbecue, and skylights ensure that these high-ceilinged units are brightly lit. Hotel rooms are smaller versions of the condos and include similar amenities, such as gas fireplaces, balconies, and barbecues. The newly renovated facility is clean and quiet. In winter, guests can step out of their rooms onto the Kimberley Nordic Club trails, or take the short walk to ski lifts; ski packages are available. Reserve well in advance for mid-July, when the annual International Old-Time Accordion Championship is in full swing. *$$; AE, MC, V; no checks; reservations@innwestkirkwood.ca; www.innwestkirkwood.com; adjacent to Kimberley Alpine Resort.* &

Fernie

The craggy cleft of the Lizard Range above **FERNIE ALPINE RESORT** (5339 Ski Area Rd; 250/423-4655 or 800/258-7669, 250/423-3555 snow report; info@skifernie. com; www.skifernie.com) is often likened to an open catcher's mitt. Sheer limestone faces tower above the resort, trapping snow-laden storms and making Fernie, along with Whitewater and Red Mountain, a must-ski on BC's powder circuit. The ski area rises visibly about 3 miles (5 km) from Main Street, from which you can see the massive bowls. Trails on the lower mountain cut through dense forest.

In the late 1990s, the resort underwent the largest expansion of any winter resort in North America. It doubled the size of its terrain with the addition of three new lifts for a total of nine and, in 1999, the finishing touches were put on seven new lodges. It has 2,811 feet of vertical drop and 2,500 acres of skiable terrain. Then again, prime parking at the bottom of the slopes is reserved for people who arrive in RVs from small towns across the prairies, the backbone of the resort's clientele. With them in mind, Fernie provides a spiffy changing room, complete with showers. Like so many of BC's small-town winter resorts, Fernie has diversified in recent years, offering guests sleigh rides, snowmobile tours, dogsledding, snowshoeing, as well as the opportunity to take part in a twice-weekly torchlight ski run.

An elegant stone courthouse presides over the major changes occurring in downtown Fernie (population 5,500), which has traditionally been more a rough-and-tumble mining and logging town than an alpine resort. Après-ski action gets pretty wild at the many downtown drinking holes as well as up at the resort. The 1992 Olympic gold medalist Kerrin Lee-Gartner brings respectability to Fernie, where she relocated in 1999 from Calgary to construct Snow Creek Lodge. Visitors are as likely to cross paths with the downhiller and her young family at local restaurants—such as the funky **BLUE TOQUE DINER** (561 Hwy 3; 250/423-4637)—as they are on the slopes.

LODGINGS

Griz Inn Sport Hotel / ★

5369 SKI AREA RD, FERNIE; 250/423-9221 OR 800/661-0118 When the Griz Inn opened in 1983, it signaled the beginning of a new era in tourism at Fernie Alpine Resort, which had been primarily the preserve of locals. For the next 15 years, the Griz and the lodge across the way, the Wolf Den, provided the only overnight accommodations at the base of the lifts. Beginning in 2000, visitors can consider a sweeping list of new lodges and condos, though none outperforms the Griz's prime location. Guests enjoy second-to-none views of the mountains and trails from private balconies. Built with families in mind, the largest suites sleep 12–16 in a combination of bedrooms, lofts, and pullout couches. All suites have full kitchens and are clean and bright. The Griz features a large indoor pool, two outdoor hot tubs, and a sauna. The inn's Powderhorn Restaurant serves early-morning breakfasts through late-night snacks. *$$; AE, MC, V; checks OK; closed briefly in late spring, early fall; reservations@grizinn.com; www.grizinn. com; off Hwy 3 west of Fernie.* &

Fairmont Hot Springs

North of Fernie and Kimberley on Highway 95, Fairmont Hot Springs Resort has quietly accommodated both soakers and skiers since the 1920s with the biggest out-door thermal pool and the only private (guests only) ski resort in western Canada. Don't miss the view from the switchback road above the resort of the Columbia Valley to the Selkirk and Bugaboo Mountains, including the beginning of the 1,200-mile (2,000 km) Columbia River. Viewpoints in the east Kootenays don't come any better than this.

LODGINGS

Fairmont Hot Springs Resort / ★★

FAIRMONT HOT SPRINGS; 250/345-6311 OR 800/663-4979 Even with the hot springs, Fairmont Hot Springs Resort smells like a rose; in contrast to many other thermal springs, Fairmont's are odorless and sulfur-free. In summer, wild perfumes from the pine forest intermingle with those from beds of marigolds and petunias lining the walkways. Attention to detail is astonishing; all appointments have been thoughtfully chosen and blended to harmonious perfection. Archival photographs adorn the walls, reminding guests that they are partaking in a centuries-old tradition; it just wasn't as comfortable back then. Many of the 140 guest units come with kitchens that can be hidden from view by folding wooden doors. A dining area adjoins two queen-sized beds. Each room has a private balcony or patio with lounge chairs, perfect for relaxing after a long soak. The Olympic-sized hot-spring pool lies below. Rooms 492, 494, and 496 are the most private of the ground-floor rooms. The resort has a full-service dining room, coffee shop, and lounge. *$$$; AE, DC, DIS, MC, V; no checks; info@fairmonthotsprings.com; www. fairmonthotsprings.com; turn east off Hwy 93/95.* &

Radium Hot Springs

Near the town of the same name, **RADIUM HOT SPRINGS** (Hwy 93, 2 miles/3 km from the junction of Hwy 95; 250/347-9485) makes an ideal soaking stop at the base of the Kootenay Range. The hot springs, open to the public year-round, are equipped with two pools: one heated, the other cooler for swimming. Like Fairmont's hot springs, these waters are free of odorous sulfur. Water temperatures vary with the seasons; in spring the snowmelt cools the thermal springs.

For an added experience, continue northeast from the hot springs through **KOOTENAY NATIONAL PARK** (250/347-9615; www.parkscanada.gc.ca/kootenay). Some of the best viewpoints in the east Kootenays are dotted along this stretch of Highway 93. Standouts include Kootenay Valley Viewpoint, about 9 miles (15 km) east of Radium Hot Springs; Hector Gorge Viewpoint, at 29 miles (46 km); and the Continental Divide, about 60 miles (95 km) away at the Alberta border. Those vis-iting the hot springs or continuing further into Kootenay National Park must stop at the park entrance and pay a fee.

The busiest time of year at **PANORAMA MOUNTAIN VILLAGE** (250/342-6941 or 800/663-2929; paninfo@intrawest.com; www.panoramaresort.com), west of Inver-mere, is winter. Skiers and snowboarders take advantage of the resort's impressive

4,000 feet of vertical drop and 2,847 acres of terrain, which expanded for the 2001–02 season to include the experts-only Taynton Bowl. Golfing at the Greywolf golf course is summer's main attraction.

LODGINGS

Radium Resort / ★★

8100 GOLF COURSE RD, RADIUM HOT SPRINGS; 250/347-9311 OR 800/667-6444 Golf is the show at this resort: nearly all rooms look onto fairways or greens of an 18-hole course. Nongolfers can play tennis, squash, or racquetball—or relax on balconies or the patio outside the indoor swimming pool. Some of the 118 guest rooms are two-bedroom condominiums. Standard rooms are in separate buildings connected by covered walkways. The best lodgings of the lot—condos or "villas"—are a vigorous walk from the full-service dining room; the resort also offers a B&B package in winter, when many restaurants in nearby Radium are closed. Golf and ski packages are also available. *$$–$$$; AE, DC, JCB, MC, V; checks OK; reservations@radiumresort.com; www.radiumresort.com; south of Radium Hot Springs on Hwy 93.* &

Trans-Canada Highway and the National Parks

Field

You can't go much farther east than Field and still be in British Columbia. Field (population 300) is the modest commercial hub, as it were, of **YOHO NATIONAL PARK**. With adjacent **BANFF, JASPER,** and **KOOTENAY NATIONAL PARKS,** Yoho is part of a vast Rocky Mountain wilderness protected by UNESCO as a World Heritage Site. The Trans-Canada Highway (Hwy 1) parallels the Kicking Horse River as it winds through a beautiful, broad valley, but by the time it reaches the park's headquarters in Field, about 18.5 miles (30 km) from its west gate, the tone of the landscape shifts to one of glaciated peaks.

Extensive hiking is found along 190 miles (300 km) of trails in Yoho, a park characterized by rock walls and waterfalls. A highlight for many visitors is the strenuous hike to the **BURGESS SHALE,** famous around the world for unraveling the mysteries of a major stage of evolution. Access to the site is permitted only with a registered guide from the Yoho-Burgess Shale Foundation (800/343-3006; burgshal@rockies. net; www.burgess-shale.bc.ca).

For more information, call the **FIELD VISITOR CENTRE** (250/343-6783; www.parkscanada.gc.ca/yoho). A park pass is required for all visitors to national parks, and is available at the visitor center. Permits are good in national parks throughout Canada.

LODGINGS

Emerald Lake Lodge / ★★★★

YOHO NATIONAL PARK; 250/343-6321 OR 800/663-6336 Emerald Lake Lodge was one of a string of hotels built by the Canadian Pacific Railway 100 years ago. When it opened in 1902, it was considered the

CPR's crowning jewel. After falling on hard times, the lodge was restored to elegance in 1986 by the owners of Deer Lodge in Lake Louise, Alberta, and Buffalo Mountain Lodge in Banff, Alberta. On a 13-acre peninsula that overlooks aptly named Emerald Lake, the lodge features 85 spacious rooms spread among 24 chalet-style buildings. Rooms feature twig chairs and duvet-covered beds in front of fieldstone fireplaces. Private decks open onto the lake and Presidential Range peaks. (Note: Some cabins are less than soundproof.) Built of massive hand-hewn timbers, the main lodge houses a grand salon with two towering fireplaces, a formal glassed-off dining room, and the Kicking Horse Bar, furnished with 1890 oak saloon fixtures brought from Canada's Yukon Territory. Upstairs, a majestic, green-felt billiards table occupies center stage in the games room. Formal meals are served year-round in the Mount Burgess dining room. In summer, casual fare is served at Cilantro on the Lake, an airy bistro adjacent to the boathouse. Stop for afternoon tea on the main lodge's veranda. *$$$$; AE, DC, MC, V; no checks; manager@emeraldlake lodge.com; www.crmr.com; 6 miles (10 km) south of Hwy 1.* &

Golden

LODGINGS

Hillside Lodge / ★

1740 SEWARD FRONTAGE RD, GOLDEN; 250/344-7281 A century ago, the Canadian Pacific Railway constructed several Alps-style chalets in Golden to house Swiss mountain guides, who escorted CPR lodge guests into Glacier National Park. More recently, Hubert and Sonja Baier built similar cabins for guests in search of a tranquil Rocky Mountain retreat. Five cabins (a two-bedroom and four one-bedrooms) and a main lodge with four en suite rooms are nestled beside the Blaeberry River on a benchland above the Columbia River Valley. Each brightly lit, fresh-smelling cabin is furnished with a wood-burning fireplace and handcrafted Bavarian furniture. Views stretch out on all sides. Guests share the 60-acre property with wildlife and the docile llamas that the Baiers raise. Breakfast (included) is served in the main lodge beside a cheery hearth in winter, and on the porch in summer. Fresh-baked goodies with homemade jams, muesli (Alpine granola), cold cuts, and cheese fortify guests for exploring. Dinner is available by prior arrangement. The charming Baiers are willing to make arrangements for white-water rafting, horseback riding, snowshoeing, tobogganing, or cross-country skiing. *$$; MC, V; no checks; hillside@ rockies.net; www.mistaya.com/hillside; 8 miles (13 km) west of Golden.*

Revelstoke

Revelstoke (population 8,600), 350 miles (565 km) east of Vancouver and nestled beside **MOUNT REVELSTOKE NATIONAL PARK** (250/837-7500; www.parks canada.gc.ca/revelstoke), is a railway town with a blend of Anglo, Italian, and Dutch residents. Scenically located beside the Columbia River, it's a great place to unwind; or make it your base for exploring Mount Revelstoke, Glacier, and Yoho National Parks to the east. The town is also just the right size for a stroll through well-tended neighborhood streets; pick up a self-guided heritage walking-and-driving tour brochure from the **REVELSTOKE VISITOR INFO CENTRE** (204 Campbell Ave;

250/837-5345 or 800/487-1493; www.revelstokecc.bc.ca). Steep-pitched metal roofs confirm the area's heavy snowfall, as does the **CANADIAN AVALANCHE CENTRE** (300 1st St W; 250/837-2435 or 800/667-1105; canav@avalanche.ca; www.avalanche.ca) downtown, a font of information and a must-see for backcountry snow trekkers.

In summer, drive the 15½-mile (25 km) **MEADOW IN THE SKY PARKWAY** to the highest elevation of any public road in Canada and a view of surrounding icefields: nothing beats the scenic drive from Revelstoke east to **ROGERS PASS** in **GLACIER NATIONAL PARK**. As the road climbs toward the pass, a series of roadside pullouts lead to viewpoints. Short interpretive trails, such as the Skunk Cabbage and the Giant Cedars, are sheltered by thick forest. A constant roar rises from the Illecillewaet River. Designed to resemble one of the snowsheds that protects the railroad from avalanches, **ROGERS PASS INFORMATION CENTRE** (250/837-7500; www.parkscanada.gc.ca/glacier) features a fascinating display that documents the park's natural and human history. Tucked between the Monashee and Selkirk Mountains, this is one of the most scenic locales in the province.

RESTAURANTS

The 112 / ★

112 1ST ST E, REVELSTOKE; 250/837-2107 OR 888/245-5523 Located in historic downtown Revelstoke's Regent Inn, built in 1931, The 112 is a unanimous favorite among locals. The dining room's cedar-paneled interior and historic ambience would be the pride of any town, but the great food is its biggest draw. Chef Peter Mueller specializes in veal dishes; the clams béarnaise, lasagne Florentine with Dungeness crab, seafood cioppino, lamb Provençal, or veal Oscar are all highly recommended. The wine list includes French and Australian labels but emphasizes BC vintners. On Sundays, when The 112 is closed, the Regent Inn's pub menu proffers a mild sampling of The 112's delights. It's solid pub fare—zesty Caesar salads, zingy wings, burgers, and a trendy selection of wraps—with a neighborhood flavor. *$$; AE, MC, V; local checks only; lunch Mon–Fri, dinner Mon–Sat; full bar; reservations recommended; regent@regentinn.com; www.regentinn.com; beside Grizzly Plaza.* ₠

LODGINGS

Mulvehill Creek Wilderness Inn / ★★

4200 HWY 23 S, REVELSTOKE; 250/837-8649 OR 877/837-8649 Revelstoke has dubbed Cornelia and René Hueppi "the happy Hueppis." This dynamic Swiss couple have created a remarkable wilderness inn, 20 minutes south of Revelstoke. The inn, with board-and-batten construction and a small tower room, is nestled in a tranquil, brightly lit clearing. The rambling ranch house structure holds eight suites (a half suite is available for children), each furnished with original wildlife artwork and painted in soft shades. The Otter's Burrow is the largest, with private deck and Jacuzzi, perfect for honeymooners. An extensively planted garden contains a large heated outdoor pool and hot tub. A buffet breakfast offers homemade jams and jellies, fresh bread and muffins, fruit salad, egg dishes courtesy of the inn's chickens, and fresh cheese and produce from local suppliers. In winter, guests can snowshoe, toboggan, or cross-country ski an extensive trail network on nearby Mount McPherson. In summer, guests can canoe, or make an enjoyable trek to a nearby fish-filled lake. By arrangement, Cornelia will prepare your catch. Otherwise, dinner in the inn's spacious dining room includes raclette, fondue, and other Swiss specialties. (Breakfast is included, but dinner is extra and requires a day's notice.) Reservations are a must June through August. *$$; AE, MC, V; checks OK; info@mulvehillcreek.com; www.mulvehillcreek.com; 12 miles (19 km) south of Revelstoke.*

NORTHERN MAINLAND BRITISH COLUMBIA

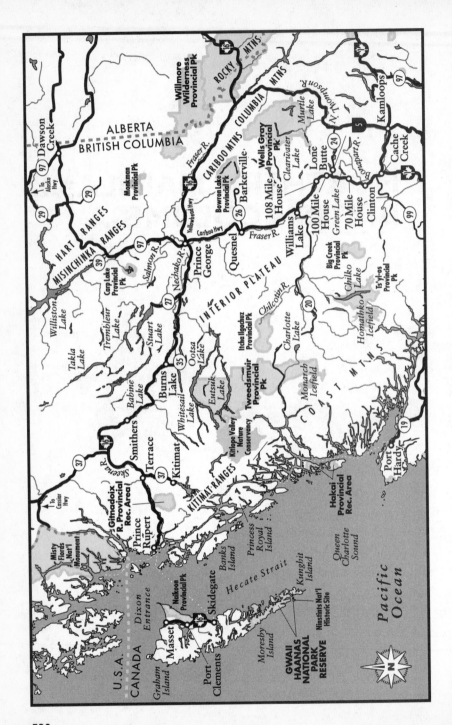

NORTHERN MAINLAND BRITISH COLUMBIA

From the rain-forested Central Coast to the northeastern Rockies, northern British Columbia is a vast, underpopulated wilderness, steeped in history. Legendary explorer Alexander Mackenzie walked this way in 1793, becoming the first European to cross North America by land. Routes through the region follow centuries-old Native trading trails, or those of the more recent Gold Rush and Telegraph Trails. Evidence from the days of the stampeders persists in places such as the roadhouses at Hat Creek, 108 Mile House, and Cottonwood Creek.

The heart of central BC is the vast Interior Plateau, a land of lakes of all sizes. This is fishing country, but also a land of long, cold winters and short, hot summers. In winter, the temperature can drop below minus 20°F (-30°C) for weeks on end. In summer, clouds of insects swarm in early evening. If you plan to travel in this area, know your enemies and come prepared.

Finding the best restaurant or lodging in the most northerly parts of BC is a simple task: if they're open, they must be doing something right. This is particularly true along the Alaska Highway (Hwy 97) and the Stewart-Cassiar Highway (Hwy 37).

ACCESS AND INFORMATION

HIGHWAYS 16, 37, and **97** run through northern BC. The latter is the main access road to the region from southern BC. Many towns along Highway 97—otherwise known as the Cariboo Highway—are helpfully referred to by distance from Lillooet (mile 0) north along the Gold Rush Trail, which preceded construction of the Cariboo Highway. Thus, 70-Mile House, marks the distance between Lillooet and this point, the original site of a pioneer roadhouse. (Note: Lillooet itself lies west of Highway 97 on Highway 99. See Lower Mainland section.) From Dawson Creek—actual mile 0 on the Alaska Highway—Highway 97 winds north and northwest to Watson Lake on the BC-Yukon border, via Fort St. John and Fort Nelson (just over 700 miles/1,140 km).

PRINCE GEORGE AIRPORT (4141 Airport Rd, Prince George; 250/963-2400) is home base to **NT AIR** (800/963-9611), **WESTJET** (800/538-5696), **CENTRAL MOUNTAIN AIR** (800/663-3721), and **AIR CANADA JAZZ** (250/561-2905 or 888/247-2262; www.flyjazz.ca). Air Canada Jazz also takes passengers from Vancouver to Sandspit on Moresby Island in the Queen Charlottes. **MONTAIR AVIATION** (604/946-6688) connects Vancouver with Massett. **HARBOUR AIR SEAPLANES** (800/689-4234) flies from Prince Rupert to Sandspit, Queen Charlotte City, and Massett. Air BC/AirCanada and Central Mountain Air link southern BC with Terrace and Smithers, on Highway 16 near Kitwanga.

BC RAIL's (604/984-5246 or 800/984-5246; www.bcrail.com) Cariboo Prospector makes three north-south runs weekly between North Vancouver and Prince George. **VIA RAIL**'s (800/561-8630 or 888/VIA-RAIL; www.viarail.ca) Skeena provides east-west service from Jasper, Alberta, to Smithers and Prince Rupert.

BC FERRIES (250/669-1211; www.bcferries.bc.ca) takes travelers from Prince Rupert to Skidegate Landing on Graham Island in the Queen Charlotte Islands and to Port Hardy on Vancouver Island to the south. The **ALASKA MARINE HIGHWAY** (800/642-0066) links Prince Rupert with Skagway in Alaska to the north and Bellingham, Washington, to the south.

The Cariboo Highway

Clinton

Clinton (population 900) anchors the exotically colored Bonaparte River valley at mile 47 on the historic Gold Rush Trail, 270 miles (450 km) north of Vancouver. From here north, the route leads out of the Coast Mountains and onto the open Fraser Plateau. History is the frontier trading post's strong suit. Framed by wrought iron and pine, the **PIONEER MEMORIAL CEMETERY** (east side of Hwy 97) at the north end of town presents an apt gateway to northern BC. Times were a lot rougher in years past, as a quick scan of old photos mounted in the **CARIBOO LODGE RESORT** (Clinton; 250/459-7992) attests.

At the town's annual **MAY BALL RODEO** (250/459-2261), raffia-festooned horses and floats parade along the Cariboo Highway (Hwy 97) to the Clinton fairground, where chuckwagon drivers and saddle bronc riders hold sway. Rodeo time kicks off with the Ball and Tea, the longest continually held event in British Columbia (more than 130 years). For more information on Clinton, the self-styled "guest ranch capital of BC," contact the mayor's office (306 Lebourdais Ave; 250/459-2261).

LODGINGS

Echo Valley Ranch Resort / ★★★★

 BOX 16, JESMOND; 250/459-2386 OR 800/253-8831 Falcons and eagles soar at Echo Valley, the Cariboo's premier guest ranch. In 2001, construction of a new east-meets-west Baan Thai wellness center completed a complex of six imposing peeled-log cabins and lodges artfully positioned on an open shoulder of land above Cripple Creek. Guests stay in the central six-bedroom Dove Lodge (named for owners Nan and Norm Dove), the nine-bedroom Lookout Lodge, two private cabins (with private bedrooms, bathrooms, sitting areas, fireplaces, lofts, and private decks), or one special cabin set aside in a refuge of its own with a four-poster bed, fireplace, romantically furnished sitting area, and private deck with outdoor Jacuzzi. One caveat: in winter, light sleepers should request rooms elsewhere than Dove Lodge's main floor, where a heating system proves bothersomely loud. Otherwise, it's all here: welcoming ambience, pampering amenities (including full spa and swimming pool), and warm family atmosphere—as well as sumptuous gourmet meals. Norm or one of his pilots can fly guests in from Kamloops or pick them up at the BC Rail stop at nearby Kelly Lake. $$$$; MC, V; *no checks; 3-night min; Wed or Sat arrival dates May–Sept, Mon–Sun winter; evranch@uniserve.com; www.evranch.com; on unpaved Big Bar Rd 30 miles (50 km) west of Clinton on Hwy 97.* &

NORTHERN MAINLAND BRITISH COLUMBIA
THREE-DAY TOUR

DAY ONE: Start your day in Prince Rupert with a walk through downtown. Begin at the **VISITOR INFORMATION CENTRE,** where a ceremonial pole featuring an eagle sets the tone. At the **MUSEUM OF NORTHERN BRITISH COLUMBIA,** learn about interpretations of carving styles throughout the Northwest Coast, and then visit the **KWINITSA STATION RAILWAY MUSEUM.** Have lunch at the **COW BAY CAFÉ;** then tour the harbor and nearby **DODGE COVE** with the Prince Rupert Water Taxi, or rent a kayak or canoe at Sea Sport or Ecotrek Kayaks and go for a paddle. Don't miss the **NORTH PACIFIC CANNERY VILLAGE NATIONAL HISTORIC SITE** in nearby Port Edward. In the afternoon, check into **EAGLE BLUFF BED & BREAKFAST** and relax to the sound of the ocean lapping against the wharf. Then it's off to dinner at nearby **SMILE'S SEAFOOD CAFÉ.**

DAY TWO: After breakfast at Eagle Bluff, head for the BC Ferry terminal for the 8-hour crossing to the **QUEEN CHARLOTTE ISLANDS** (Haida Gwaii). Lunch on the ferry, then at Skidegate stop at the **HAIDA GWAII MUSEUM** and look for whales. Head north to Massett where, by prior arrangement, dinner is waiting at **COPPER BEECH HOUSE.**

DAY THREE: Breakfast at the Copper Beech House fortifies you for the trip out to nearby Rose Spit in **NAIKOON PARK.** Spend the morning exploring its beach and digging for razor clams. After a picnic lunch, drive south to Tlell. Spend the afternoon beachcombing before heading to Queen Charlotte City for dinner, where you'll have to choose between **HOWLER'S BISTRO** or **OCEANA.** Afterward, stroll the town's waterfront. Then it's off to Skidegate to catch the overnight ferry sailing back to the mainland at Prince Rupert.

Interlakes District

Detour east off Highway 97 at either 70 Mile or 93 Mile House and you'll be in the Interlakes microregion. **GREEN LAKE** is the first of hundreds of lakes, large and larger, strung between here and the North Thompson River. For a quick sample, drive the Green Lake scenic loop north from Green Lake to Lone Butte on Highway 24. Each lake boasts at least one guest ranch or fishing camp.

LODGINGS

Crystal Waters Guest Ranch / ★★

HWY 24, BRIDGE LAKE; 250/593-4252 OR 800/593-2252 Saddle up with rodeo man Gary Cleveland and spend a day roaming Crystal Waters's 640 acres. Chow down on hearty ranch-raised repast. Soak in the unique wood-fired, lakeside hot tub. Cleveland and his wife, Marisa Peters, perfected the art of guest ranching while working at several nearby spreads, including Cleveland's father's fishing camp. Here at Crystal Waters, they've distilled the appealing essence of a small guest-ranch experience: intimacy and spontaneity. Demonstrate that you can handle a horse, and you're free to roam. (Few guest ranches in the Cariboo offer this alternative to guided rides.) Canoes are available to explore Crystal Lake. Five quiet, honey-hued log cabins, two at lakeside, accommodate two to eight guests each. Sweet, homey touches abound, such as the omnipresent use of horseshoes for door handles and coat hangers, and towel racks shaped from polished tree roots. A firelit guest lodge rebuilt from the old homestead and relocated near lakeside provides a quiet retreat. *$$–$$$; MC, V; checks OK; open Dec–Oct; holiday@crystalwatersranch.com; www.crystalwatersranch.com; 3 miles (5 km) southwest of Hwy 24 at Bridge Lake on North Bonaparte Rd.* &

100 Mile House

Arguably the best track-set, cross-country skiing in BC is found on the 120 miles (200 km) of community trails that loop between 100 Mile House (population 1,900) and 108 Mile Ranch (population 2,038). For information on cross-country skiing in the Cariboo, contact **GUNNER'S CYCLE & SKI SHOP** (250/791-6212) next to the Best Western in 108 Mile Ranch.

RESTAURANTS

Trails End Restaurant / ★★
1871 Lodge / ★★

HWY 97 (THE HILLS HEALTH AND GUEST RANCH), 108 MILE HOUSE; 250/791-5225 You don't have to stay at The Hills (see review) to enjoy its two dining facilities. Trails End is located in the main lodge; a more informal dinner is served on weekends in the ranch's newer 1871 Lodge. Both dining rooms feature cozy corners with fireplaces. In keeping with the ranch's healthful theme, the Trails End menu includes both generous Cariboo country selections and lighter spa fare, with the emphasis on seafood, meat, and vegetarian dishes, prepared with a sure and understated hand. A Swiss-inspired dinner menu in the 1871 Lodge includes all-you-can-eat fondue, hot-rock steaks cooked at your table, or a nightly chef's special. BC microbrews and wines are highlighted. *$$–$$$; AE, MC, V; checks OK; breakfast, lunch, dinner Mon–Sun, brunch Sun; full bar; reservations required; info@thehillsbc.com; www.thehillsbc.com; east side of Hwy 97 just north of main intersection.* &

LODGINGS

The Hills Health and Guest Ranch / ★★★

HWY 97, 108 MILE HOUSE; 250/791-5225 Since 1985, Pat and Juanita Corbett's Hills Health and Guest Ranch has epitomized the essence of the Cariboo region: hardworking, free spirited, family centered, health oriented. Recipients of three International Specialty Spa of the Year awards, the Hills shows the Corbetts' personal touch everywhere. Guests can choose hotel-style rooms in either the Ranch House or Manor House Lodge (breakfast included), or private self-contained chalets that sleep six. Lodge rooms are outfitted with twin beds, rocking chairs, and floral touches. Best views are from Manor House rooms (odd-numbered 31–47) that overlook the ranch's private ski and snowboard hill. Chalets 1–4 also overlook the hill with ski-in/ski-out potential. The faux-log chalets are more simply furnished than lodge rooms, have complete kitchens and large decks with gas barbecues, and are pet friendly. Main attractions are the large spa and fitness center, including heated swimming pool, saunas, and hydrotherapy pools. Hundreds of kilometers of cross-country ski trails lace the woods. Tie on your skates on the pond beside Willy's Wigwam, a cozy environment for warming hands and feet. In summer, twice-daily guided hikes are offered, and a rack of mountain bikes is at guests' disposal, as is a corral of patient horses. *$$–$$$; AE, MC, V; checks OK; info@thehillsbc.com; www.thehillsbc.com; east side of Hwy 97 just north of main intersection.* &

The Wolf Den Country Inn / ★

CANIM LAKE RD, FOREST GROVE; 250/397-2108 OR 877/397-2108 Chantelle and Jamie Ross retreated to Forest Grove in 1992 to establish a country inn and outdoor adventure center. Their rambling log rancher on 160 acres has four guest rooms, each with its own floor-to-ceiling window that overlooks Bridge Creek. Snuggle on the Pendleton blanket–draped couches; a stone fireplace blazes in the private guest living room. An outdoor hot tub on the broad deck is open to the stars. Purebred Siberian huskies sit kenneled in the 20-acre pasture below the inn. Exceptionally quiet, the dogs are clean and great with children. The Rosses offer intimate (six-person max) dogsledding adventures in winter, or guided horseback and canoe outings in summer. The Wolf Den specializes in women's and kids' groups. Stay the night just to wake up to one of Chantelle's farm-fresh breakfasts. She also takes requests for gourmet lunches or dinners. *$–$$; MC, V; checks OK; info@wolfden-adventures.com; www.wolfden-adventures.com; 19 miles (30 km) east of Hwy 97 at 100 Mile House.*

Barkerville Historic Town

Historic Barkerville is a blend of authentic, well-preserved heritage storefronts and restored homes in a wilderness setting tucked in the Cariboo Mountains. At the height of the Cariboo gold rush, it was the largest city west of Chicago and north of San Francisco. As testament to this, nearly 100 of the homes, stores, and workshops that remain are open for viewing—14 of them, such as the post office, are still operational. More than 40 pre-1900 buildings line the streets, most mounted on raised foundations to dodge the annual spring flooding of nearby Williams Creek.

Barkerville is located east of Quesnel and Highway 97 at the northern terminus of the Gold Rush Trail. Highway 26 winds and climbs past viewpoints with historical connections to the gold rush of the 1860s. The **QUESNEL VISITOR INFO CENTRE** (Le Bourdais Park, 705 Carson Ave, Quesnel; 250/992-8716 or 800/992-4922) stocks brochures on various points of interest.

Prince George

The largest city in the BC interior, Prince George (population 78,000), "City of Bridges," is the crossroad of rivers, railroads, and highways. The mighty Fraser and Nechako Rivers blend near old **FORT GEORGE** (south end of 20th Ave), now a municipal park; get information from **FRASER–FORT GEORGE REGIONAL MUSEUM** (333 Gorse St; 250/562-1612). Walk or bike the park's riverside pathways to sense the site's importance in the destiny of the region. Highway 16 leads east to the Rockies and west to Prince Rupert; Highway 97 leads north to Dawson Creek and the Alaska Highway. Whichever direction you're headed, there's not much to keep you in this mill town: a municipal pool, art gallery, and park are downtown. **COAST INN OF THE NORTH** (770 Brunswick St, Prince George; 250/563-0121 or 800/663-1144; infonorth@coasthotels.com; www.coasthotels.com), with its 150 quaint, well-appointed rooms, is the best bet if you're overnighting.

The Northwest Coast

Prince Rupert

Rainy days outnumber sunny ones by a wide margin in Prince Rupert (population 17,681), BC's northernmost port. On the upside, there are lots of interesting things to do indoors here. Don't miss the **MUSEUM OF NORTHERN BRITISH COLUMBIA** (1st Ave E and McBride St; 250/624-3207). Under its cedar-shaked, copper-flashed roof sits one of the province's finest collections of Native art. A local artist may be creating a piece while you're here, such as a ceremonial apron woven from mountain-goat hair. From the museum, an elevated walkway leads to the waterfront and the **KWINITSA STATION RAILWAY MUSEUM** (north end of Bill Murray Dr in Waterfront Park; 250/627-0938).

Prince Rupert is home to one of the best collections of **CEREMONIAL (TOTEM) POLES** on the West Coast. Begin at the Visitor Info Centre (100 1st Ave W; 250/624-5637 or 800/667-1994; prtravel@citytel.net). You'll find more of the traditionally carved poles (in Tsimshian or Haida style) at City Hall (424 3rd Ave W), the Civic Centre (1000 McBride St), Moose Tot Park (6th Ave and McBride St), and Totem Park (Summit Ave). If it's not raining, walk up to Roosevelt Park (Summit Ave) for a view of downtown and the inner harbor. You can tour the harbor and nearby **DODGE COVE** with the **PRINCE RUPERT WATER TAXI** (Cow Bay; 250/624-3337), or rent a kayak or canoe at **SEA SPORT** (295 1st Ave E; 250/624-5337) or **ECOTREK KAYAKS** (203 Cow Bay Rd; 250/624-8311), in a boathouse on the wharf. A good spot to warm up afterward is the **COW BAY CAFÉ** (205 Cow Bay Rd; 250/624-1212).

Just south of town in Port Edward is the **NORTH PACIFIC CANNERY VILLAGE NATIONAL HISTORIC SITE** (1889 Skeena Dr, 7 miles/11 km southwest of Hwy 16; 250/628-3538; open May 15–Sept 15). Until the 1970s, it employed as many as 1,500 workers. Boardwalks link offices, stores, cafes, and homes with the West Coast's oldest standing cannery, perched on the banks at the mouth of the Skeena River.

Index

We Stand By Our Reviews

Sasquatch Books is proud of *Best Places Northwest*. Our editors and contributors go to great lengths and expense to see that all of the restaurant and lodging reviews are as accurate, up-to-date, and honest as possible. If we have disappointed you, please accept our apologies; however, if a recommendation in this 14th edition of *Best Places Northwest* has seriously misled you, Sasquatch Books would like to refund your purchase price. To receive your refund:

1. Tell us where and when you purchased your book and return the book and the book-purchase receipt to the address below.
2. Enclose the original restaurant or lodging receipt from the establishment in question, including date of visit.
3. Write a full explanation of your stay or meal and how *Best Places Northwest* misled you.
4. Include your name, address, and phone number.

Refund is valid only while this 14th edition of *Best Places Northwest* is in print. If the ownership, management, or chef has changed since publication, Sasquatch Books cannot be held responsible. Tax and postage on the returned book is your responsibility. Please allow six to eight weeks for processing.

Please address to Satisfaction Guaranteed, *Best Places Northwest*, and send to:
Sasquatch Books
615 Second Avenue, Suite 260
Seattle, WA 98104

Best Places Northwest Report Form

Based on my personal experience, I wish to nominate the following restaurant, place of lodging, shop, nightclub, sight, or other as a "Best Place"; or confirm/correct/disagree with the current review.

_____

_____

_____

_____

(Please include address and telephone number of establishment, if convenient.)

REPORT

Please describe food, service, style, comfort, value, date of visit, and other aspects of your experience; continue on another piece of paper if necessary.

_____

_____

_____

_____

_____

_____

_____

I am not concerned, directly or indirectly, with the management or ownership of this establishment.

SIGNED _____

ADDRESS _____

_____

PHONE _____ **DATE** _____

Please address to *Best Places Northwest* and send to:
SASQUATCH BOOKS
615 SECOND AVENUE, SUITE 260
SEATTLE, WA 98104
Feel free to email feedback as well: **BESTPLACES@SASQUATCHBOOKS.COM**